THE LOEB CLASSICAL LIBRARY
FOUNDED BY JAMES LOEB 1911

EDITED BY
JEFFREY HENDERSON

EDITOR EMERITUS
G. P. GOOLD

PLATO

III

LCL 166

PLATO

LYSIS · SYMPOSIUM · GORGIAS

WITH AN ENGLISH TRANSLATION BY

W. R. M. LAMB

HARVARD UNIVERSITY PRESS
CAMBRIDGE, MASSACHUSETTS
LONDON, ENGLAND

First published 1925
Reprinted 1932, 1939, 1946, 1953, 1961, 1967,
1975, 1983, 1991, 1996, 2001

LOEB CLASSICAL LIBRARY® is a registered trademark
of the President and Fellows of Harvard College

ISBN 0-674-99184-2

*Printed in Great Britain by St Edmundsbury Press Ltd,
Bury St Edmunds, Suffolk, on acid-free paper.
Bound by Hunter & Foulis Ltd, Edinburgh, Scotland.*

CONTENTS

PREFACE	vii
GENERAL INTRODUCTION	ix
LIST OF PLATO'S WORKS	xxi
LYSIS	1
SYMPOSIUM	73
GORGIAS	247
INDEX	534

PREFACE

THE Greek text in this volume is based on the recension of Schanz; a certain number of emendations by other scholars have been adopted, and those of any importance are noted as they occur.

The special introductions are intended merely to prepare the reader for the general character and purpose of each dialogue.

W. R. M. LAMB.

GENERAL INTRODUCTION

PLATO was born in 427 B.C. of Athenian parents who could provide him with the best education of the day, and ample means and leisure throughout his life. He came to manhood in the dismal close of the Peloponnesian War, when Aristophanes was at the height of his success, and Sophocles and Euripides had produced their last plays. As a boy he doubtless heard the lectures of Gorgias, Protagoras, and other sophists, and his early bent seems to have been towards poetry. But his intelligence was too progressive to rest in the agnostic position on which the sophistic culture was based. A century before, Heracleitus had declared knowledge to be impossible, because the objects of sense are continually changing; yet now a certain Cratylus was trying to build a theory of knowledge over the assertion of flux, by developing some hints let fall by its oracular author about the truth contained in names. From this influence Plato passed into contact with Socrates, whose character and gifts have left a singular impress on the thought of mankind. This effect is almost wholly due to Plato's applications and extensions of

his master's thought; since, fortunately for us, the pupil not only became a teacher in his turn, but brought his artistic genius into play, and composed the memorials of philosophic talk which we know as the Dialogues. Xenophon, Antisthenes, and Aeschines were other disciples of Socrates who drew similar sketches of his teaching: the suggestion came from the " mimes " of the Syracusan Sophron, —realistic studies of conversation between ordinary types of character. As Plato became more engrossed in the Socratic speculations, this artistic impulse was strengthened by the desire of recording each definite stage of thought as a basis for new discussion and advance.

When Plato was twenty years old, Socrates was over sixty, and had long been notorious in Athens for his peculiar kind of sophistry. In the *Phaedo* he tells how he tried, in his youth, the current scientific explanations of the universe, and found them full of puzzles. He then met with the theory of Anaxagoras,—that the cause of everything is " mind." This was more promising: but it led nowhere after all, since it failed to rise above the conception of physical energy; this " mind " showed no intelligent aim. Disappointed of an assurance that the universe works for the best, Socrates betook himself to the plan of making *definitions* of " beautiful," " good," " large," and so on, as qualities observed in the several classes of beautiful, good and large material things, and then employing these propositions, if they

GENERAL INTRODUCTION

appeared to be sound, for the erection of higher hypotheses. The point is that he made a new science out of a recognized theory of "ideas" or "forms," which had come of reflecting on the quality predicated when we say "this man is good," and which postulates some sure reality behind the fleeting objects of sense. His "hypothetical" method, familiar to mathematicians, attains its full reach and significance in the *Republic*.

The Pythagoreans who appear in the intimate scene of the *Phaedo* were accustomed to the theory of ideas, and were a fit audience for the highest reasonings of Socrates on the true nature of life and the soul. For some years before the master's death (399 B.C.) Plato, if not a member of their circle, was often a spell-bound hearer of the "satyr." But ordinary Athenians had other views of Socrates, which varied according to their age and the extent of their acquaintance with him. Aristophanes' burlesque in the *Clouds* (423 B.C.) had left a common impression not unlike what we have of the King of Laputa. Yet the young men who had any frequent speech with him in his later years, while they felt there was something uncanny about him, found an irresistible attraction in his simple manner, his humorous insight into their ways and thoughts, and his fervent eloquence on the principles of their actions and careers. He kept no school, and took no fees; he distrusted the pretensions of the regular sophists, with whom he was carelessly confounded; moreover, he professed

GENERAL INTRODUCTION

to have no knowledge himself, except so far as to know that he was ignorant. The earliest Dialogues, such as the *Apology*, *Crito*, *Euthyphro*, *Charmides*, *Laches*, and *Lysis*, show the manner in which he performed his ministry. In rousing men, especially those whose minds were fresh, to the need of knowing themselves, he promoted the authority of the intellect, the law of definite individual knowledge, above all reason of state or tie of party; and it is not surprising that his city, in the effort of recovering her political strength, decided to hush such an inconvenient voice. He must have foreseen his fate, but he continued his work undeterred.

Though he seems, in his usual talk, to have professed no positive doctrine, there were one or two beliefs which he frequently declared. Virtue, he said, is knowledge; for each man's good is his happiness, and once he knows it clearly, he needs must choose to ensue it. Further, this knowledge is innate in our minds, and we only need to have it awakened and exercised by "dialectic," or a systematic course of question and answer. He also believed his mission to be divinely ordained, and asserted that his own actions were guided at times by the prohibitions of a "spiritual sign." He was capable, as we find in the *Symposium*, of standing in rapt meditation at any moment for some time, and once for as long as twenty-four hours.

It is clear that, if he claimed no comprehensive theory of existence, and although his ethical reliance

GENERAL INTRODUCTION

on knowledge, if he never analysed it, leaves him in a very crude stage of psychology, his logical and mystical suggestions must have led his favourite pupils a good way towards a new system of metaphysics. These intimates learnt, as they steeped their minds in his, and felt the growth of a unique affection amid the glow of enlightenment, that happiness may be elsewhere than in our dealings with the material world, and that the mind has prerogatives and duties far above the sphere of civic life.

After the death of Socrates in 399, Plato spent some twelve years in study and travel. For the first part of this time he was perhaps at Megara, where Eucleides, his fellow-student and friend, was forming a school of dialectic. Here he may have composed some of the six Dialogues already mentioned as recording Socrates' activity in Athens. Towards and probably beyond the end of this period, in order to present the Socratic method in bolder conflict with sophistic education, he wrote the *Protagoras*, *Meno*, *Euthydemus*, and *Gorgias*. These works show a much greater command of dramatic and literary art, and a deeper interest in logic. The last of them may well be later than 387, the year in which, after an all but disastrous attempt to better the mind of Dionysius of Syracuse, he returned to Athens, and, now forty years of age, founded the Academy; where the memory of his master was to be perpetuated by continuing and expanding the

GENERAL INTRODUCTION

Socratic discussions among the elect of the new generation. The rivalry of this private college with the professional school of Isocrates is discernible in the subject and tone of the *Gorgias*. Plato carried on the direction of the Academy till his death, at eighty-one, in 346; save that half-way through this period (367) he accepted the invitation of his friend Dion to undertake the instruction of the younger Dionysius at Syracuse. The elder tyrant had been annoyed by the Socratic freedom of Plato's talk: now it was a wayward youth who refused the yoke of a systematic training. What that training was like we see in the *Republic*, where true political wisdom is approached by an arduous ascent through mathematics, logic, and metaphysics. Plato returned, with less hopes of obtaining the ideal ruler, to make wonderful conquests in the realm of thought.

The *Meno* and *Gorgias* set forth the doctrine that knowledge of right is latent in our minds: dialectic, not the rhetoric of the schools, is the means of eliciting it. The method, as Plato soon perceived, must be long and difficult: but he felt a mystical rapture over its certainty, which led him to picture the immutable "forms" as existing in a world of their own. This feeling, and the conviction whence it springs—that knowledge is somehow possible, had come to the front of his mind when he began to know Socrates. Two brilliant compositions, the *Cratylus* and *Symposium*, display the strength of the conviction, and then, the noble fervour of the

GENERAL INTRODUCTION

feeling. In the latter of these works, the highest powers of imaginative sympathy and eloquence are summoned to unveil the sacred vision of absolute beauty. The *Phaedo* turns the logical theory upon the soul, which is seen to enjoy, when freed from the body, familiar cognition of the eternal types of being. Here Orphic dogma lends its aid to the Socratic search for knowledge, while we behold an inspiring picture of the philosopher in his hour of death.

With increasing confidence in himself as the successor of Socrates, Plato next undertook, in the *Republic*, to show the master meeting his own unsatisfied queries on education and politics. We read now of a " form " of good to which all thought and action aspire, and which, contemplated in itself, will explain not merely why justice is better than injustice, but the meaning and aim of everything. In order that man may be fully understood, we are to view him " writ large " in the organization of an ideal state. The scheme of description opens out into many subsidiary topics, including three great proposals already known to Greece,—the abolition of private property, the community of women and children, and the civic equality of the sexes. But the central subject is the preparation of the philosopher, through a series of ancillary sciences, for dialectic ; so that, once possessed of the supreme truth, he may have light for directing his fellow-men. As in the *Phaedo*, the spell of mythical revelation is

GENERAL INTRODUCTION

brought to enhance the discourse of reason. The *Phaedrus* takes up the subject of rhetoric, to lead us allegorically into the realm of "ideas," and thence to point out a new rhetoric, worthy of the well-trained dialectician. We get also a glimpse of the philosopher's duty of investigating the mutual relations of the "forms" to which his study of particular things has led him.

A closer interest in logical method, appearing through his delight in imaginative construction, is one distinctive mark of this middle stage in Plato's teaching. As he passes to the next two Dialogues, the *Theaetetus* and *Parmenides*, he puts off the aesthetic rapture, and considers the ideas as categories of thought which require co-ordination. The discussion of knowledge in the former makes it evident that the Academy was now the meeting-place of vigorous minds, some of which were eager to urge or hear refuted the doctrines they had learnt from other schools of thought; while the arguments are conducted with a critical caution very different from the brilliant and often hasty zeal of Socrates. The *Parmenides* corrects an actual or possible misconception of the theory of ideas in the domain of logic, showing perhaps how Aristotle, now a youthful disciple of Plato, found fault with the theory as he understood it. The forms are viewed in the light of the necessities of thought: knowledge is to be attained by a careful practice which will raise our minds to the vision of all parti-

GENERAL INTRODUCTION

culars in their rightly distinguished and connected classes.

Plato is here at work on his own great problem :—If what we know is a single permanent law under which a multitude of things are ranged, what is the link between the one and the many? The *Sophist* contains some of his ripest thought on this increasingly urgent question: his confident advance beyond Socratic teaching is indicated by the literary form, which hardly disguises the continuous exposition of a lecture. We observe an attention to physical science, the association of soul, motion, and existence, and the comparative study of being and not-being. The *Politicus* returns to the topic of state-government, and carries on the process of acquiring perfect notions of reality by the classification of things. Perhaps we should see in the absolute "mean" which is posited as the standard of all arts, business, and conduct, a contribution from Aristotle. The *Philebus*, in dealing with pleasure and knowledge, dwells further on the correct division and classification required if our reason, as it surely must, is to apprehend truth. The method is becoming more thorough and more complex, and Plato's hope of bringing it to completion is more remote. But he is gaining a clearer insight into the problem of unity and plurality.

The magnificent myth of the *Timaeus*, related by a Pythagorean, describes the structure of the universe, so as to show how the One manifests

GENERAL INTRODUCTION

itself as the Many. We have here the latest reflections of Plato on space, time, soul, and many physical matters. In the lengthy treatise of the *Laws*, he addresses himself to the final duty of the philosopher as announced in the *Republic*: a long habituation to abstract thought will qualify rather than disqualify him for the practical regulation of public and private affairs. Attention is fixed once more on soul, as the energy of the world and the vehicle of our sovereign reason.

Thus Plato maintains the fixity of the objects of knowledge in a great variety of studies, which enlarge the compass of Socrates' teaching till it embraces enough material for complete systems of logic and metaphysics. How far these systems were actually worked out in the discussions of the Academy we can only surmise from the Dialogues themselves and a careful comparison of Aristotle; whose writings, however, have come down to us in a much less perfect state. But it seems probable that, to the end, Plato was too fertile in thought to rest content with one authoritative body of doctrine. We may be able to detect in the *Timaeus* a tendency to view numbers as the real principles of things; and we may conjecture a late-found interest in the physical complexion of the world. As a true artist, with a keen sense of the beauty and stir of life, Plato had this interest, in a notable degree, throughout: but in speaking of his enthusiasm for science we must regard him rather as a great inventor of

GENERAL INTRODUCTION

sciences than as what we should now call a scientist. This is giving him a splendid name, which few men have earned. Some of his inventions may be unrealizable, but it is hard to find one that is certainly futile. There are flaws in his arguments: to state them clearly and fairly is to win the privilege of taking part in a discussion at the Academy.

W. R. M. LAMB.

[NOTE.—*Each of the Dialogues is a self-contained whole. The order in which they have been mentioned in this Introduction is that which agrees best in the main with modern views of Plato's mental progress, though the succession in some instances is uncertain.*]

BIBLIOGRAPHICAL ADDENDUM (1983)

General:

W. K. C. Guthrie, *A History of Greek Philosophy*, 6 vols, Cambridge 1962–1981 (in particular: Vol. 4 1975 pp. 134–154, *Lysis*; pp. 284–312, *Gorgias*; pp. 365–396, *Symposium*; pp. 562–581, Bibliography)

Symposium:

Edited by K. J. Dover (Introduction, Text, Commentary), Cambridge 1980

Gorgias:

Edited by E. R. Dodds (Introduction, Text, Commentary), Oxford 1959

BIBLIOGRAPHY

The following give useful accounts of Socratic and Platonic thought:—

T. Gomperz: *The Greek Thinkers*, vols. ii. and iii. Murray, 1901–5.

W. Lutoslawski: *The Origin and Growth of Plato's Logic.* Longmans, 1897.

R. L. Nettleship: *Philosophic Lectures and Remains.* 2 vols. Macmillan, 2nd ed., 1901.

D. G. Ritchie: *Plato.* T. and T. Clark, 1902.

J. A. Stewart: *The Myths of Plato.* Macmillan, 1905.

" " *Plato's Doctrine of Ideas.* Clarendon Press, 1909.

A. E. Taylor: *Plato.* Constable, 1911.

A. M. Adam: *Plato: Moral and Political Ideals.* Camb. Univ. Press, 1913.

H. Jackson: *Presocratics, Socrates and the Minor Socratics, Plato and the Old Academy* (Cambridge Companion to Greek Studies). Camb. Univ. Press, 1905.

J. Burnet: *Greek Philosophy : Thales to Plato.* Macmillan, 1914.

F. M. Cornford: *Before and after Socrates.* Camb. Univ. Press, 1932.

The following are important editions:—

J. Adam: *The Republic.* 2 vols. Camb. Univ. Press, 1902.
W. H. Thompson: *The Phaedrus.* Bell, 1868.
" " *The Gorgias.* Bell, 1871.
R. D. Archer-Hind: *The Phaedo.* Macmillan, 2nd ed., 1894.
" " *The Timaeus.* Macmillan, 1888.
J. Burnet. *The Phaedo.* Clarendon Press, 1911.
L. Campbell: *The Theaetetus.* Clarendon Press, 1883.
" " *The Sophistes and Politicus.* Clarendon Press, 1867.
E. S. Thompson: *The Meno.* Macmillan, 1901.
E. B. England: *The Laws.* 2 vols. Manch. Univ. Press, 1921.

LIST OF PLATO'S WORKS showing their division into volumes in this edition and their place in the edition of H. Stephanus (vols. I–III, Paris, 1578).

VOLUME		PAGES
I. Euthyphro		I. 2A–16
Apology		I. 17A–42
Crito		I. 43A–54E
Phaedo		I. 57A–118
Phaedrus		III. 227A–279C
II. Laches		II 178A–201C
Protagoras		I. 309A–362
Meno		II. 70A–100B
Euthydemus		I. 271A–307C
III. Lysis		II. 203A–223B
Symposium		III. 172A–223D
Gorgias		I. 447A–527E
IV. Cratylus		I. 383A–440E
Parmenides		III. 126A–166C
Greater Hippias		III. 281A–304E
Lesser Hippias		I. 363A–376C
V. Republic I : Books I–V		II. 327A–480
VI. Republic II : Books VI–X		II. 484A–621D

xxi

LIST OF PLATO'S WORKS

VOLUME		PAGES
VII.	Theaetetus	I. 142A–210D
	Sophist	I. 216A–268B
VIII.	The Statesman	II. 257A–311C
	Philebus	II. 11A–67B
	Ion	I. 530A–542B
IX.	Timaeus	III. 17A–92C
	Critias	III. 106A–121C
	Cleitophon	III. 406A–410E
	Menexenus	II. 234A–249E
	Epistles	III. 309A–363C
X.	The Laws I: Books I-VI	II. 624A–785B
XI.	The Laws II: Books VII-XII	II. 788A–969D
XII.	Charmides	II. 153A–176D
	Alcibiades I and II	II. 103A–151C
	Hipparchus	II. 225A–232C
	The Lovers	I. 132A–139
	Theages	I. 121A–131
	Minos	II. 313A–321D
	Epinomis	II. 973A–992E

LYSIS

INTRODUCTION TO THE *LYSIS*

In the *Lysis* Socrates relates how he was taken by some young friends into a wrestling-school, where he finds a large and well-dressed company of youths and boys assembled for a sacrificial ceremony in honour of Hermes. He proceeds to a narrative of two conversations which he had with a handsome boy, Lysis, and his friend Menexenus : the first one (207-210) is a simple, introductory talk on the motives of personal affection, which are surmised to depend on a sense of utility, and therefore on knowledge. The second and main discussion (211-223) deals with the nature of friendship ; and although this relation is in the end left unexplained, we are conducted through a number of speculations whose method and incidental suggestions are of deep interest to the student of morals. Menexenus is a keen disputant, and it seems as if Socrates, bent merely on a rapid review of the difficulties of the subject, were anxious to ply his questions in a swift and summary fashion which would allow the quick-witted boy to follow his thought, but not to challenge or correct it. For the moment, at any rate, he is content to lead his young friend into a maze of analogical reasoning, from which neither of them can find any certain egress. The following is an outline of the discussion :—

INTRODUCTION TO THE *LYSIS*

213. Instances are given which show that neither the loving nor the loved person is necessarily a "friend."

214-215. We try the relation of likeness, as suggested by the poets, and find (1) that only when persons are alike in goodness are they friends; and yet (2) that the good have no need of friends.

216. Again, unlikeness seems to lead to friendship; but this explanation is also found to be quite inadequate.

217-218. Perhaps we may say, on the analogy of medicine, that a thing—like the human body—which is neither good nor evil in itself, has need of good through the presence of evil, which requires a remedy; friendship may be this sort of craving for good.

219-221. But we must distinguish between that which we desire and that for the sake of which we desire it; between the end in view and the reason for pursuing it. We must find some meaning for friendship which is higher than the notion of a thing desired because of something else (*e.g.* evil).

222. Again, is friendship a desire of something that belongs to one by a natural affinity? But this only brings us back to the difficulties about likeness and the good, and we attain no solution of the main question.

The result is not positively instructive or helpful, except that we learn how large and morally important is the question that we have been discussing, and are so far prepared for the splendid revelations of the *Phaedrus* and *Symposium*, and for the careful reasoning of Aristotle's *Ethics*. It is characteristic of Socrates that he takes the prevalent and accepted

INTRODUCTION TO THE *LYSIS*

vogue of strong attachments between young Athenians of his later days as a means of arousing interest in moral speculation; and although here and there, as we shall observe, he hastens on to this main object with insufficient attention to strict logic, his educational method is brilliantly illustrated and recommended by the art of Plato. Indeed one might say that, in one aspect of the dialogue, the mere tone of Socrates towards the boys is itself a lesson in friendship.

ΛΥΣΙΣ

[Η ΠΕΡΙ ΦΙΛΙΑΣ· ΜΑΙΕΥΤΙΚΟΣ]

ΤΑ ΤΟΥ ΔΙΑΛΟΓΟΥ ΠΡΟΣΩΠΑ

ΣΩΚΡΑΤΗΣ, ΙΠΠΟΘΑΛΗΣ, ΚΤΗΣΙΠΠΟΣ, ΜΕΝΕΞΕΝΟΣ, ΛΥΣΙΣ

Ἐπορευόμην μὲν ἐξ Ἀκαδημείας εὐθὺ Λυκείου τὴν ἔξω τείχους ὑπ᾽ αὐτὸ τὸ τεῖχος· ἐπειδὴ δ᾽ ἐγενόμην κατὰ τὴν πυλίδα ᾗ ἡ Πάνοπος κρήνη, ἐνταῦθα συνέτυχον Ἱπποθάλει τε τῷ Ἱερωνύμου καὶ Κτησίππῳ τῷ Παιανιεῖ καὶ ἄλλοις μετὰ τούτων νεανίσκοις ἀθρόοις συνεστῶσι. καί με προσιόντα ὁ Ἱπποθάλης ἰδών, Ὦ Σώκρατες, ἔφη, ποῖ δὴ πορεύῃ καὶ πόθεν;

Ἐξ Ἀκαδημείας, ἦν δ᾽ ἐγώ, πορεύομαι εὐθὺ Λυκείου.

Δεῦρο δή, ἦ δ᾽ ὅς, εὐθὺ ἡμῶν. οὐ παραβάλλεις; ἄξιον μέντοι.

Ποῖ, ἔφην ἐγώ, λέγεις, καὶ παρὰ τίνας τοὺς ὑμᾶς;

Δεῦρο, ἔφη, δείξας μοι ἐν τῷ καταντικρὺ τοῦ τείχους περίβολόν τέ τινα καὶ θύραν ἀνεῳγμένην.

LYSIS

[or ON FRIENDSHIP: "OBSTETRIC"[1]]

CHARACTERS

SOCRATES, HIPPOTHALES, CTESIPPUS, MENEXENUS, LYSIS

(Socrates relates a conversation that he had in a wrestling-school)

I WAS making my way from the Academy straight to the Lyceum, by the road outside the town wall, —just under the wall; and when I reached the little gate that leads to the spring of Panops,[2] I chanced there upon Hippothales, son of Hieronymus, and Ctesippus of Paeania, and some other youths with them, standing in a group together. Then Hippothales, as he saw me approaching, said: Socrates, whither away, and whence?

From the Academy, I replied, on my way straight to the Lyceum.

Come over here, he said, straight to us. You will not put in here? But you may as well.

Where do you mean? I asked; and what is your company?

Here, he said, showing me there, just opposite the wall, a sort of enclosure and a door standing

[1] *i.e.* facilitating the birth of correct notions, as Socrates humorously claimed to do.
[2] *i.e.* of Hermes, the "all-seeing."

PLATO

διατρίβομεν δέ, ἦ δ' ὅς, αὐτόθι ἡμεῖς τε αὐτοὶ καὶ ἄλλοι πάνυ πολλοὶ καὶ καλοί.

Ἔστι δὲ δὴ τί τοῦτο, καὶ τίς ἡ διατριβή;

Παλαίστρα, ἔφη, νεωστὶ ᾠκοδομημένη· ἡ δὲ διατριβὴ τὰ πολλὰ ἐν λόγοις, ὧν ἡδέως ἄν σοι μεταδιδοῖμεν.

Καλῶς γε, ἦν δ' ἐγώ, ποιοῦντες· διδάσκει δὲ τίς αὐτόθι;

Σὸς ἑταῖρός γε, ἦ δ' ὅς, καὶ ἐπαινέτης, Μίκκος.

Μὰ Δία, ἦν δ' ἐγώ, οὐ φαῦλός γε ἀνήρ, ἀλλ' ἱκανὸς σοφιστής.

Βούλει οὖν ἕπεσθαι, ἔφη, ἵνα καὶ ἴδῃς τοὺς ὄντας αὐτόθι;

Πρῶτον[1] ἡδέως ἀκούσαιμ' ἂν ἐπὶ τῷ καὶ εἴσειμι καὶ τίς ὁ καλός.

Ἄλλος, ἔφη, ἄλλῳ ἡμῶν δοκεῖ, ὦ Σώκρατες.

Σοὶ δὲ δὴ τίς, ὦ Ἱππόθαλες; τοῦτό μοι εἰπέ

Καὶ ὃς ἐρωτηθεὶς ἠρυθρίασεν. καὶ ἐγὼ εἶπον· Ὦ παῖ Ἱερωνύμου Ἱππόθαλες, τοῦτο μὲν μηκέτι εἴπῃς, εἴτε ἐρᾷς του εἴτε μή· οἶδα γὰρ ὅτι οὐ μόνον ἐρᾷς, ἀλλὰ καὶ πόρρω ἤδη εἶ πορευόμενος τοῦ ἔρωτος. εἰμὶ δ' ἐγὼ τὰ μὲν ἄλλα φαῦλος καὶ ἄχρηστος, τοῦτο δέ μοί πως ἐκ θεοῦ δέδοται, ταχὺ οἵῳ τ' εἶναι γνῶναι ἐρῶντά τε καὶ ἐρώμενον.

Καὶ ὃς ἀκούσας πολὺ ἔτι μᾶλλον ἠρυθρίασεν. ὁ οὖν Κτήσιππος, Ἀστεῖόν γε, ἦ δ' ὅς, ὅτι ἐρυθριᾷς, ὦ Ἱππόθαλες, καὶ ὀκνεῖς εἰπεῖν Σωκράτει τοὔνομα·

[1] αὐτοῦ ante πρῶτον secl. Burnet.

LYSIS

open. We pass our time there, he went on; not only we ourselves, but others besides,—a great many, and handsome.

And what, pray, is this place, and what your pastime?

A wrestling-school, he said, of recent construction; and our pastime chiefly consists of discussions, in which we should be happy to let you have a share.

That is very good of you, I said; and who does the teaching in there?

Your own comrade, he replied, and supporter, Miccus.

Upon my word, I said, he is no slight person, but a qualified professor.

Then will you please come in with us, he said, so as to see for yourself the company we have in there?

I should be glad to hear first on what terms I am to enter, and who is the handsome one.

Each of us, he replied, has a different fancy, Socrates.

Well, and who is yours, Hippothales? Tell me that.

At this question he blushed; so I said: Ah, Hippothales, son of Hieronymus, you need not trouble to tell me whether you are in love with somebody or not: for I know you are not only in love, but also far advanced already in your passion. In everything else I may be a poor useless creature, but there is one gift that I have somehow from heaven,—to be able to recognize quickly a lover or a beloved.

When he heard this, he blushed much more than ever. Then Ctesippus remarked: Quite charming, the way you blush, Hippothales, and shrink from

PLATO

ἐὰν δ' οὗτος καὶ σμικρὸν χρόνον συνδιατρίψῃ σοι, παραταθήσεται ὑπὸ σοῦ ἀκούων θαμὰ λέγοντος. ἡμῶν γοῦν, ὦ Σώκρατες, ἐκκεκώφωκε τὰ ὦτα καὶ ἐμπέπληκε Λύσιδος· ἂν μὲν δὴ καὶ ὑποπίῃ, εὐμαρία ἡμῖν ἐστὶ καὶ ἐξ ὕπνου ἐγρομένοις Λύσιδος οἴεσθαι τοὔνομα ἀκούειν. καὶ ἃ μὲν καταλογάδην διηγεῖται, δεινὰ ὄντα, οὐ πάνυ τι δεινά ἐστιν, ἀλλ' ἐπειδὰν τὰ ποιήματα ἡμῶν ἐπιχειρήσῃ καταντλεῖν καὶ συγγράμματα. καὶ ὅ ἐστι τούτων δεινότερον, ὅτι καὶ ᾄδει εἰς τὰ παιδικὰ φωνῇ θαυμασίᾳ, ἣν ἡμᾶς δεῖ ἀκούοντας ἀνέχεσθαι. νῦν δὲ ἐρωτώμενος ὑπὸ σοῦ ἐρυθριᾷ.

Ἔστι δέ, ἦν δ' ἐγώ, ὁ Λύσις νέος τις, ὡς ἔοικε· τεκμαίρομαι δέ, ὅτι ἀκούσας τοὔνομα οὐκ ἔγνων.

Οὐ γὰρ πάνυ, ἔφη, τὶ αὐτοῦ τοὔνομα λέγουσιν, ἀλλ' ἔτι πατρόθεν ἐπονομάζεται διὰ τὸ σφόδρα τὸν πατέρα γιγνώσκεσθαι αὐτοῦ. ἐπεὶ εὖ οἶδ' ὅτι πολλοῦ δεῖς τὸ εἶδος ἀγνοεῖν τοῦ παιδός· ἱκανὸς γὰρ καὶ ἀπὸ μόνου τούτου γιγνώσκεσθαι.

Λεγέσθω, ἦν δ' ἐγώ, οὗτινος ἔστιν.

Δημοκράτους, ἔφη, τοῦ Αἰξωνέως ὁ πρεσβύτατος υἱός.

Εἶεν, ἦν δ' ἐγώ, ὦ Ἱππόθαλες, ὡς γενναῖον καὶ νεανικὸν τοῦτον τὸν ἔρωτα πανταχῇ ἀνηῦρες· καί μοι ἴθι ἐπίδειξαι ἃ καὶ τοῖσδε ἐπιδείκνυσαι, ἵνα εἰδῶ εἰ ἐπίστασαι ἃ χρὴ ἐραστὴν περὶ παιδικῶν πρὸς αὐτὸν ἢ πρὸς ἄλλους λέγειν.

Τούτων δέ τι, ἔφη, σταθμᾷ, ὦ Σώκρατες, ὧν ὅδε λέγει;

---

[1] *i.e.* "son of Democrates" (see below).

LYSIS

telling Socrates the name; yet, if he spends but a little time with you, he will find you a regular torment, as he hears you repeat it again and again. He has deafened our ears, I can tell you, Socrates, by cramming them with "Lysis": let him be a trifle in liquor, and as likely as not we start out of our sleep fancying we hear the name of Lysis. The descriptions he gives us in conversation, though dreadful enough, are not so very bad: it is when he sets about inundating us with his poems and prose compositions. More dreadful than all, he actually sings about his favourite in an extraordinary voice, which we have the trial of hearing. And now, at a question from you, he blushes!

Lysis apparently, I said, is somebody quite young: this I infer from the fact that I did not recognize the name when I heard it.

That is because they do not usually call him by his name, he replied; he still goes by his paternal title,[1] as his father is so very well known. You must, I am sure, be anything but ignorant of the boy's appearance: that alone would be enough to know him by.

Let me hear, I said, whose son he is.

The eldest son, he replied, of Democrates of Aexone.

Ah well, I said, Hippothales, what an altogether noble and gallant love you have discovered there! Now please go on and give me a performance like those that you give your friends here, so that I may know whether you understand what a lover ought to say of his favourite to his face or to others.

Do you attach any weight, Socrates, he asked, to anything you have heard this fellow say?

PLATO

Πότερον, ἦν δ' ἐγώ, καὶ τὸ ἐρᾶν ἔξαρνος εἶ οὗ λέγει ὅδε;

Οὐκ ἔγωγε, ἔφη, ἀλλὰ μὴ ποιεῖν εἰς τὰ παιδικὰ μηδὲ συγγράφειν.

Οὐχ ὑγιαίνει, ἔφη ὁ Κτήσιππος, ἀλλὰ ληρεῖ τε καὶ μαίνεται.

Καὶ ἐγὼ εἶπον· Ὦ Ἱππόθαλες, οὔ τι τῶν μέτρων δέομαι ἀκοῦσαι οὐδὲ μέλος εἴ τι πεποίηκας εἰς τὸν νεανίσκον, ἀλλὰ τῆς διανοίας, ἵνα εἰδῶ τίνα τρόπον προσφέρῃ πρὸς τὰ παιδικά.

Ὅδε δήπου σοι, ἔφη, ἐρεῖ· ἀκριβῶς γὰρ ἐπίσταται καὶ μέμνηται, εἴπερ, ὡς λέγει, ὑπ' ἐμοῦ ἀεὶ ἀκούων διατεθρύληται.

Νὴ τοὺς θεούς, ἔφη ὁ Κτήσιππος, πάνυ γε. καὶ γάρ ἐστι καταγέλαστα, ὦ Σώκρατες. τὸ γὰρ ἐραστὴν ὄντα καὶ διαφερόντως τῶν ἄλλων τὸν νοῦν προσέχοντα τῷ παιδὶ ἴδιον μὲν μηδὲν ἔχειν λέγειν, ὃ οὐχὶ κἂν παῖς εἴποι, πῶς οὐχὶ καταγέλαστον; ἃ δὲ ἡ πόλις ὅλη ᾄδει περὶ Δημοκράτους καὶ Λύσιδος τοῦ πάππου τοῦ παιδὸς καὶ πάντων πέρι τῶν προγόνων, πλούτους τε καὶ ἱπποτροφίας καὶ νίκας Πυθοῖ καὶ Ἰσθμοῖ καὶ Νεμέᾳ τεθρίπποις τε καὶ κέλησι, ταῦτα ποιεῖ τε καὶ λέγει, πρὸς δὲ τούτοις ἔτι τούτων κρονικώτερα. τὸν γὰρ τοῦ Ἡρακλέους ξενισμὸν πρῴην ἡμῖν ἐν ποιήματί τινι διῄει, ὡς διὰ τὴν τοῦ Ἡρακλέους συγγένειαν ὁ πρόγονος αὐτῶν ὑποδέξαιτο τὸν Ἡρακλέα, γεγονὼς αὐτὸς ἐκ Διός τε καὶ τῆς τοῦ δήμου ἀρχηγέτου θυγατρός, ἅπερ αἱ γραῖαι

---

[1] The Pythian Games were held at Delphi, the Isthmian

LYSIS

Tell me, I said; do you deny being in love with the person he mentions?

Not I, he replied; but I do deny that I make poems and compositions on my favourite.

He is in a bad way, said Ctesippus; why, he raves like a madman!

Then I remarked: Hippothales, I do not want to hear your verses, or any ode that you may have indited to the youth; I only ask for their purport, that I may know your manner of dealing with your favourite.

I expect this fellow will tell you, he replied: he has an accurate knowledge and recollection of them, if there is any truth in what he says of my having dinned them so constantly in his ears.

Quite so, on my soul, said Ctesippus; and a ridiculous story it is too, Socrates. To be a lover, and to be singularly intent on one's boy, yet to have nothing particular to tell him that a mere boy could not say, is surely ridiculous: but he only writes and relates things that the whole city sings of, recalling Democrates and the boy's grandfather Lysis and all his ancestors, with their wealth and the horses they kept, and their victories at Delphi, the Isthmus, and Nemea,[1] with chariot-teams and coursers, and, in addition, even hoarier antiquities than these. Only two days ago he was recounting to us in some poem of his the entertainment of Hercules,—how on account of his kinship with Hercules their forefather welcomed the hero, being himself the offspring of Zeus and of the daughter of their deme's founder; such old wives' tales, and

near Corinth, and the Nemean at Nemea, between Corinth and Argos.

PLATO

ᾄδουσι, καὶ ἄλλα πολλὰ τοιαῦτα, ὦ Σώκρατες· ταῦτ' ἐστὶν ἃ οὗτος λέγων τε καὶ ᾄδων ἀναγκάζει καὶ ἡμᾶς ἀκροᾶσθαι.

Καὶ ἐγὼ ἀκούσας εἶπον· Ὦ καταγέλαστε Ἱππόθαλες, πρὶν νενικηκέναι ποιεῖς τε καὶ ᾄδεις εἰς σαυτὸν ἐγκώμιον;

Ἀλλ' οὐκ εἰς ἐμαυτόν, ἔφη, ὦ Σώκρατες, οὔτε ποιῶ οὔτε ᾄδω.

Οὐκ οἴει γε, ἦν δ' ἐγώ.

Τὸ δὲ πῶς ἔχει; ἔφη.

Πάντων μάλιστα, εἶπον, εἰς σὲ τείνουσιν αὗται αἱ ᾠδαί. ἐὰν μὲν γὰρ ἕλῃς τὰ παιδικὰ τοιαῦτα ὄντα, κόσμος σοι ἔσται τὰ λεχθέντα καὶ ᾀσθέντα καὶ τῷ ὄντι ἐγκώμια ὥσπερ νενικηκότι, ὅτι τοιούτων παιδικῶν ἔτυχες· ἐὰν δέ σε διαφύγῃ, ὅσῳ ἂν μείζω σοι εἰρημένα ᾖ ἐγκώμια περὶ τῶν παιδικῶν, τοσούτῳ μειζόνων δόξεις καλῶν τε καὶ ἀγαθῶν ἐστερημένος καταγέλαστος εἶναι. ὅστις οὖν τὰ ἐρωτικά, ὦ φίλε, σοφός, οὐκ ἐπαινεῖ τὸν ἐρώμενον πρὶν ἂν ἕλῃ, δεδιὼς τὸ μέλλον ὅπῃ ἀποβήσεται. καὶ ἅμα οἱ καλοί, ἐπειδάν τις αὐτοὺς ἐπαινῇ καὶ αὔξῃ, φρονήματος ἐμπίπλανται καὶ μεγαλαυχίας· ἢ οὐκ οἴει;

Ἔγωγε, ἔφη.

Οὐκοῦν ὅσῳ ἂν μεγαλαυχότεροι ὦσι, δυσαλωτότεροι γίγνονται;

Εἰκός γε.

Ποῖός τις οὖν ἄν σοι δοκεῖ θηρευτὴς εἶναι, εἰ ἀνασοβοῖ θηρεύων καὶ δυσαλωτοτέραν τὴν ἄγραν ποιοῖ;

Δῆλον ὅτι φαῦλος.

LYSIS

many more of the sort, Socrates,—these are the things he tells and trolls, while compelling us to be his audience.

When I heard this I said: Oh, you ridiculous Hippothales, do you compose and chant a triumph-song on yourself, before you have won your victory?

It is not on myself, Socrates, he replied, that I either compose or chant it.

You think not, I said.

Then what is the truth of it? he asked.

Most certainly, I replied, it is you to whom these songs refer. For if you prevail on your favourite, and he is such as you describe, all that you have spoken and sung will be so much glory to you, and a veritable eulogy upon your triumph in having secured such a favourite as that: whereas if he eludes your grasp, the higher the terms of your eulogy of your favourite, the greater will seem to be the charms and virtues you have lost, and you will be ridiculed accordingly. Hence anyone who deals wisely in love-matters, my friend, does not praise his beloved until he prevails, for fear of what the future may have in store for him. And besides, these handsome boys, when so praised and extolled, become full of pride and haughtiness: do you not think so?

I do, he said.

And then, the haughtier they are, the harder grows the task of capturing them?

Yes, apparently.

And what do you think of a hunter who should scare away his quarry in hunting and make it harder to catch?

Clearly he would be a poor one.

B Καὶ μὲν δὴ λόγοις τε καὶ ᾠδαῖς μὴ κηλεῖν ἀλλ' ἐξαγριαίνειν πολλὴ ἀμουσία· ἢ γάρ;

Δοκεῖ μοι.

Σκόπει δή, ὦ Ἱππόθαλες, ὅπως μὴ πᾶσι τούτοις ἔνοχον σαυτὸν ποιήσεις διὰ τὴν ποίησιν· καίτοι οἶμαι ἐγὼ ἄνδρα ποιήσει βλάπτοντα ἑαυτὸν οὐκ ἄν σε ἐθέλειν ὁμολογῆσαι ὡς ἀγαθός ποτ' ἐστὶ ποιητής, βλαβερὸς ὢν ἑαυτῷ.

Οὐ μὰ τὸν Δία, ἔφη· πολλὴ γὰρ ἂν ἀλογία εἴη· ἀλλὰ διὰ ταῦτα δή σοι, ὦ Σώκρατες, ἀνακοινοῦμαι,
C καὶ εἴ τι ἄλλο ἔχεις, συμβούλευε τίνα ἄν τις λόγον διαλεγόμενος ἢ τί πράττων προσφιλὴς παιδικοῖς γένοιτο.

Οὐ ῥᾴδιον, ἦν δ' ἐγώ, εἰπεῖν· ἀλλ' εἴ μοι ἐθελήσαις αὐτὸν ποιῆσαι εἰς λόγους ἐλθεῖν, ἴσως ἂν δυναίμην σοι ἐπιδεῖξαι, ἃ χρὴ αὐτῷ διαλέγεσθαι ἀντὶ τούτων ὧν οὗτοι λέγειν τε καὶ ᾄδειν φασί σε.

Ἀλλ' οὐδέν, ἔφη, χαλεπόν. ἂν γὰρ εἰσέλθῃς μετὰ Κτησίππου τοῦδε καὶ καθεζόμενος διαλέγῃ, οἶμαι μὲν καὶ αὐτός σοι πρόσεισι· φιλήκοος γάρ,
D ὦ Σώκρατες, διαφερόντως ἐστί, καὶ ἅμα, ὡς Ἑρμαῖα ἄγουσιν, ἀναμεμειγμένοι ἐν ταὐτῷ εἰσιν οἵ τε νεανίσκοι καὶ οἱ παῖδες· πρόσεισιν οὖν σοι· εἰ δὲ μή, Κτησίππῳ συνήθης ἐστὶ διὰ τὸν τούτου ἀνεψιὸν Μενέξενον· Μενεξένῳ μὲν γὰρ δὴ πάντων μάλιστα ἑταῖρος ὢν τυγχάνει. καλεσάτω οὖν οὗτος αὐτόν, ἐὰν ἄρα μὴ προσίῃ αὐτός.

Ταῦτα, ἦν δ' ἐγώ, χρὴ ποιεῖν. καὶ ἅμα λαβὼν

LYSIS

And hence to use speech and song, not for charming but for driving wild, would be gross fatuity, would it not?

I think so.

Then take care, Hippothales, not to make yourself guilty of all these things by your verse-making; indeed I fancy you will not like to allow that a man who damages himself by poetry can be a good poet, so long as he is damaging to himself.

On my soul, no, he said; of course it would be most absurd. But this is the very reason, Socrates, why I impart my feelings to you, and ask you for any useful advice you can give as to what conversation or conduct will help to endear one to one's favourite.

That is not an easy thing to tell, I replied; but if you will agree to get him to have a talk with me, I daresay I could show you an example of the conversation you should hold with him, instead of those things that your friends say you speak and sing.

There is no difficulty about that, he said. If you will go in with Ctesippus here, and take a seat and talk, I think he will come to you of his own accord; he is singularly fond of listening, Socrates, and besides, they are keeping the Hermaea,[1] so that the youths and boys are all mingled together. So he will come to you: but if he does not, Ctesippus is intimate with him, as being a cousin of Menexenus; for Lysis has chosen Menexenus for his particular friend. So let Ctesippus call him if you find that he does not come of himself.

That is what I must do, I said. Whereupon I took

[1] The festival of Hermes, who was specially honoured in wrestling-schools.

τὸν Κτήσιππον προσῇα εἰς τὴν παλαίστραν· οἱ δ᾽ ἄλλοι ὕστεροι ἡμῶν ἦσαν. εἰσελθόντες δὲ κατελάβομεν αὐτόθι τεθυκότας τε τοὺς παῖδας καὶ τὰ περὶ τὰ ἱερεῖα σχεδόν τι ἤδη πεποιημένα, ἀστραγαλίζοντάς τε δὴ καὶ κεκοσμημένους ἅπαντας. οἱ μὲν οὖν πολλοὶ ἐν τῇ αὐλῇ ἔπαιζον ἔξω, οἱ δέ τινες τοῦ ἀποδυτηρίου ἐν γωνίᾳ ἠρτίαζον ἀστραγάλοις παμπόλλοις, ἐκ φορμίσκων τινῶν προαιρούμενοι· τούτους δὲ περιέστασαν ἄλλοι θεωροῦντες. ὧν δὴ καὶ ὁ Λύσις ἦν, καὶ εἱστήκει ἐν τοῖς παισί τε καὶ νεανίσκοις ἐστεφανωμένος καὶ τὴν ὄψιν διαφέρων, οὐ τὸ καλὸς εἶναι μόνον ἄξιος ἀκοῦσαι, ἀλλ᾽ ὅτι καλός τε κἀγαθός. καὶ ἡμεῖς εἰς τὸ καταντικρὺ ἀποχωρήσαντες ἐκαθεζόμεθα—ἦν γὰρ αὐτόθι ἡσυχία—καί τι ἀλλήλοις διελεγόμεθα. περιστρεφόμενος οὖν ὁ Λύσις θαμὰ ἐπεσκοπεῖτο ἡμᾶς, καὶ δῆλος ἦν ἐπιθυμῶν προσελθεῖν. τέως μὲν οὖν ἠπόρει τε καὶ ὤκνει μόνος προσιέναι· ἔπειτα ὁ Μενέξενος ἐκ τῆς αὐλῆς μεταξὺ παίζων εἰσέρχεται, καὶ ὡς εἶδεν ἐμέ τε καὶ τὸν Κτήσιππον, ᾔει παρακαθιζησόμενος· ἰδὼν οὖν αὐτὸν ὁ Λύσις ἕσπετο καὶ συμπαρεκαθέζετο μετὰ τοῦ Μενεξένου. προσῆλθον δὴ καὶ οἱ ἄλλοι, καὶ δὴ καὶ ὁ Ἱπποθάλης, ἐπειδὴ πλείους ἑώρα ἐφισταμένους, τούτους ἐπηλυγισάμενος προσέστη ᾗ μὴ ᾤετο κατόψεσθαι τὸν Λύσιν, δεδιὼς μὴ αὐτῷ ἀπεχθάνοιτο· καὶ οὕτω προσεστὼς ἠκροᾶτο.

Καὶ ἐγὼ πρὸς τὸν Μενέξενον ἀποβλέψας, Ὦ παῖ Δημοφῶντος, ἦν δ᾽ ἐγώ, πότερος ὑμῶν πρεσβύτερος;

LYSIS

Ctesippus with me into the wrestling-school, and the others came after us. When we got inside, we found that the boys had performed the sacrifice in the place and, as the ceremonial business was now almost over, they were all playing at knuckle-bones and wearing their finest attire. Most of them were playing in the court out-of-doors; but some were at a game of odd-and-even in a corner of the undressing-room, with a great lot of knuckle-bones which they drew from little baskets; and there were others standing about them and looking on. Among these was Lysis: he stood among the boys and youths with a garland on his head, a distinguished figure, deserving not merely the name of well-favoured, but also of well-made and well-bred. As for us, we went and sat apart on the opposite side—for it was quiet there—and started some talk amongst ourselves. The result was that Lysis ever and anon turned round to observe us, and was obviously eager to join us. For a while, however, he hesitated, being too shy to approach us alone; till Menexenus stepped in for a moment from his game in the court and, on seeing me and Ctesippus, came to take a seat beside us. When Lysis saw him, he came along too and sat down with Menexenus. Then all the others came to us also; and I must add that Hippothales, when he saw a good many of them standing there, stood so as to be screened by them, in a position where he thought Lysis would not catch sight of him, as he feared that he might irritate him; in this way he stood by and listened.

Then I, looking at Menexenus, asked him: Son of Demophon, which is the elder of you two?

Ἀμφισβητοῦμεν, ἔφη.

Οὐκοῦν καὶ ὁπότερος γενναιότερος, ἐρίζοιτ' ἄν, ἦν δ' ἐγώ.

Πάνυ γε, ἔφη.

Καὶ μὴν ὁπότερός γε καλλίων, ὡσαύτως.

Ἐγελασάτην οὖν ἄμφω.

Οὐ μὴν ὁπότερός γε, ἔφην, πλουσιώτερος ὑμῶν, οὐκ ἐρήσομαι· φίλω γάρ ἐστον. ἢ γάρ;

Πάνυ γ', ἐφάτην.

Οὐκοῦν κοινὰ τά γε φίλων λέγεται, ὥστε τούτω γε οὐδὲν διοίσετον, εἴπερ ἀληθῆ περὶ τῆς φιλίας λέγετον.

Συνεφάτην.

Ἐπεχείρουν δὴ μετὰ τοῦτο ἐρωτᾶν ὁπότερος δικαιότερος καὶ σοφώτερος αὐτῶν εἴη. μεταξὺ οὖν τις προσελθὼν ἀνέστησε τὸν Μενέξενον, φάσκων καλεῖν τὸν παιδοτρίβην· ἐδόκει γάρ μοι ἱεροποιῶν τυγχάνειν. ἐκεῖνος μὲν οὖν ᾤχετο· ἐγὼ δὲ τὸν Λύσιν ἠρόμην, Ἦ που, ἦν δ' ἐγώ, ὦ Λύσι, σφόδρα φιλεῖ σε ὁ πατὴρ καὶ ἡ μήτηρ; Πάνυ γε, ἦ δ' ὅς. Οὐκοῦν βούλοιντο ἄν σε ὡς εὐδαιμονέστατον εἶναι; Πῶς γὰρ οὔ; Δοκεῖ δέ σοι εὐδαίμων εἶναι ἄνθρωπος δουλεύων τε καὶ ᾧ μηδὲν ἐξείη ποιεῖν ὧν ἐπιθυμοῖ; Μὰ Δί' οὐκ ἔμοιγε, ἔφη. Οὐκοῦν εἴ σε φιλεῖ ὁ πατὴρ καὶ ἡ μήτηρ καὶ εὐδαίμονά σε ἐπιθυμοῦσι γενέσθαι, τοῦτο παντὶ τρόπῳ δῆλον ὅτι προθυμοῦνται ὅπως ἂν εὐδαιμονοίης. Πῶς γὰρ οὐχί; ἔφη. Ἐῶσιν ἄρα σε ἃ βούλει ποιεῖν, καὶ οὐδὲν ἐπιπλήττουσιν οὐδὲ διακωλύουσι ποιεῖν ὧν ἂν ἐπιθυμῇς; Ναὶ μὰ Δί' ἐμέ γε, ὦ Σώκρατες, καὶ μάλα γε πολλὰ

LYSIS

It is a point in dispute between us, he replied.

Then you must also be at variance, I said, as to which is the nobler.

Yes, to be sure, he said.

And moreover, which is the more beautiful, likewise.

This made them both laugh.

But of course I shall not ask, I said, which of you is the wealthier; for you are friends, are you not?

Certainly we are, they replied.

And, you know, friends are said to have everything in common, so that here at least there will be no difference between you, if what you say of your friendship is true.

They agreed.

After that I was proceeding to ask them which was the juster and wiser of the two, when I was interrupted by somebody who came and fetched away Menexenus, saying that the wrestling-master was calling him: I understood that he was taking some part in the rites. So he went off; and then I asked Lysis: I suppose, Lysis, your father and mother are exceedingly fond of you? Yes, to be sure, he replied. Then they would like you to be as happy as possible? Yes, of course. Do you consider that a man is happy when enslaved and restricted from doing everything he desires? Not I, on my word, he said. Then if your father and mother are fond of you, and desire to see you happy, it is perfectly plain that they are anxious to secure your happiness. They must be, of course, he said. Hence they allow you to do what you like, and never scold you, or hinder you from doing what you desire? Yes, they do, Socrates, I assure you:

κωλύουσιν. Πῶς λέγεις; ἦν δ' ἐγώ. βουλόμενοί σε μακάριον εἶναι διακωλύουσι τοῦτο ποιεῖν ὃ ἂν βούλῃ; ὧδε δέ μοι λέγε. ἢν ἐπιθυμήσῃς ἐπί τινος τῶν τοῦ πατρὸς ἁρμάτων ὀχεῖσθαι λαβὼν τὰς ἡνίας, ὅταν ἁμιλλᾶται, οὐκ ἂν ἐῷέν σε ἀλλὰ διακωλύοιεν; Μὰ Δί' οὐ μέντοι ἄν, ἔφη, ἐῷεν. Ἀλλὰ τίνα μήν; Ἔστι τις ἡνίοχος παρὰ τοῦ πατρὸς μισθὸν φέρων. Πῶς λέγεις; μισθωτῷ μᾶλλον ἐπιτρέπουσιν ἢ σοὶ ποιεῖν ὅ τι ἂν βούληται περὶ τοὺς ἵππους, καὶ προσέτι αὐτοῦ τούτου
B ἀργύριον τελοῦσιν; Ἀλλὰ τί μήν; ἔφη. Ἀλλὰ τοῦ ὀρικοῦ ζεύγους, οἶμαι, ἐπιτρέπουσί σοι ἄρχειν, κἂν εἰ βούλοιο λαβὼν τὴν μάστιγα τύπτειν, ἐῷεν ἄν. Πόθεν, ἦ δ' ὅς, ἐῷεν; Τί δέ; ἦν δ' ἐγώ· οὐδενὶ ἔξεστιν αὐτοὺς τύπτειν; Καὶ μάλα, ἔφη, τῷ ὀρεοκόμῳ. Δούλῳ ὄντι ἢ ἐλευθέρῳ; Δούλῳ, ἔφη. Καὶ δοῦλον, ὡς ἔοικεν, ἡγοῦνται περὶ πλείονος ἢ σὲ τὸν υἱόν, καὶ ἐπιτρέπουσι τὰ ἑαυτῶν
C μᾶλλον ἢ σοί, καὶ ἐῶσι ποιεῖν ὅ τι βούλεται, σὲ δὲ διακωλύουσι; καί μοι ἔτι τόδε εἰπέ. σὲ αὐτὸν ἐῶσιν ἄρχειν σεαυτοῦ, ἢ οὐδὲ τοῦτο ἐπιτρέπουσί σοι; Πῶς γάρ, ἔφη, ἐπιτρέπουσιν; Ἀλλ' ἄρχει τίς σου; Ὅδε, παιδαγωγός, ἔφη. Μῶν δοῦλος ὤν; Ἀλλὰ τί μήν; ἡμέτερός γε, ἔφη. Ἦ δεινόν, ἦν δ' ἐγώ, ἐλεύθερον ὄντα ὑπὸ δούλου ἄρχεσθαι. τί δὲ ποιῶν αὖ οὗτος ὁ παιδαγωγός σου ἄρχει; Ἄγων δήπου, ἔφη, εἰς διδασκάλου. Μῶν μὴ καὶ οὗτοί σου ἄρχουσιν, οἱ διδάσκαλοι;
D Πάντως δήπου. Παμπόλλους ἄρα σοι δεσπότας

---

[1] The παιδαγωγός was a trusted slave who was appointed to attend on a boy out of school hours and to have a general control over his conduct and industry.

LYSIS

they stop me from doing a great many things. How do you mean? I said: they wish you to be happy, and yet hinder you from doing what you like? But answer me this: suppose you desire to ride in one of your father's chariots and hold the reins in some race; they will not allow you, but will prevent you? That is so, to be sure, he said; they will not allow me. But whom would they allow? There is a driver, in my father's pay. What do you say? A hireling, whom they trust rather than you, so that he can do whatever he pleases with the horses; and they pay him besides a salary for doing that! Why, of course, he said. Well, but they trust you with the control of the mule-cart, and if you wanted to take the whip and lash the team, they would let you? Nothing of the sort, he said. Why, I asked, is nobody allowed to lash them? Oh yes, he said, the muleteer. Is he a slave, or free? A slave, he replied. So it seems that they value a slave more highly than you, their son, and entrust him rather than you with their property, and allow him to do what he likes, while preventing you? And now there is one thing more you must tell me. Do they let you control your own self, or will they not trust you in that either? Of course they do not, he replied. But some one controls you? Yes, he said, my tutor[1] here. Is he a slave? Why, certainly; he belongs to us, he said. What a strange thing, I exclaimed; a free person controlled by a slave! But how does this tutor actually exert his control over you? By taking me to school, I suppose, he replied. And your schoolmasters, can it be that they also control you? I should think they do! Then quite a large number of masters

23

καὶ ἄρχοντας ἑκὼν ὁ πατὴρ ἐφίστησιν. ἀλλ᾽
ἆρα ἐπειδὰν οἴκαδε ἔλθῃς παρὰ τὴν μητέρα, ἐκείνη
σε ἐᾷ ποιεῖν ὅ τι ἂν βούλῃ, ἵν᾽ αὐτῇ μακάριος
ᾖς, ἢ περὶ τὰ ἔρια ἢ περὶ τὸν ἱστόν, ὅταν ὑφαίνῃ;
οὔ τι γάρ που διακωλύει σε ἢ τῆς σπάθης ἢ τῆς
κερκίδος ἢ ἄλλου του τῶν περὶ ταλασιουργίαν
ὀργάνων ἅπτεσθαι. Καὶ ὃς γελάσας, Μὰ Δία,
ἔφη, ὦ Σώκρατες, οὐ μόνον γε διακωλύει, ἀλλὰ
E καὶ τυπτοίμην ἂν εἰ ἁπτοίμην. Ἡράκλεις, ἦν
δ᾽ ἐγώ, μῶν μή τι ἠδίκηκας τὸν πατέρα ἢ τὴν
μητέρα; Μὰ Δί᾽ οὐκ ἔγωγε, ἔφη.

Ἀλλ᾽ ἀντὶ τίνος μὴν οὕτω σε δεινῶς διακωλύουσιν εὐδαίμονα εἶναι καὶ ποιεῖν ὅ τι ἂν βούλῃ, καὶ
δι᾽ ἡμέρας ὅλης τρέφουσί σε ἀεί τῳ δουλεύοντα
καὶ ἑνὶ λόγῳ ὀλίγου ὧν ἐπιθυμεῖς οὐδὲν ποιοῦντα;
ὥστε σοι, ὡς ἔοικεν, οὔτε τῶν χρημάτων τοσούτων
209 ὄντων οὐδὲν ὄφελος, ἀλλὰ πάντες αὐτῶν μᾶλλον
ἄρχουσιν ἢ σύ, οὔτε τοῦ σώματος οὕτω γενναίου
ὄντος, ἀλλὰ καὶ τοῦτο ἄλλος ποιμαίνει καὶ θερα-
πεύει· σὺ δὲ ἄρχεις οὐδενός, ὦ Λύσι, οὐδὲ ποιεῖς
οὐδὲν ὧν ἐπιθυμεῖς. Οὐ γάρ πω, ἔφη, ἡλικίαν
ἔχω, ὦ Σώκρατες. Μὴ οὐ τοῦτό σε, ὦ παῖ
Δημοκράτους, κωλύῃ, ἐπεὶ τό γε τοσόνδε, ὡς
ἐγᾦμαι, καὶ ὁ πατὴρ καὶ ἡ μήτηρ σοι ἐπιτρέπουσι,
καὶ οὐκ ἀναμένουσιν ἕως ἂν ἡλικίαν ἔχῃς. ὅταν
γὰρ βούλωνται αὐτοῖς τινα ἀναγνωσθῆναι ἢ γρα-
B φῆναι, σέ, ὡς ἐγᾦμαι, πρῶτον τῶν ἐν τῇ οἰκίᾳ
ἐπὶ τοῦτο τάττουσιν. ἦ γάρ; Πάνυ γ᾽, ἔφη.
Οὐκοῦν ἔξεστί σοι ἐνταῦθ᾽ ὅ τι ἂν βούλῃ πρῶτον
τῶν γραμμάτων γράφειν καὶ ὅ τι ἂν δεύτερον· καὶ

LYSIS

and controllers are deliberately set over you by your father. But when you come home to your mother, she surely lets you do what you like, that she may make you happy, either with her wool or her loom, when she is weaving? I take it she does not prevent you from handling her batten, or her comb, or any other of her wool-work implements. At this he laughed and said: I promise you, Socrates, not only does she prevent me, but I should get a beating as well, if I laid hands on them. Good heavens! I said: can it be that you have done your father or mother some wrong? On my word, no, he replied.

Well, what reason can they have for so strangely preventing you from being happy and doing what you like? Why do they maintain you all day long in constant servitude to somebody, so that, in a word, you do hardly a single thing that you desire? And thus, it would seem, you get no advantage from all your great possessions—nay, anyone else controls them rather than you—nor from your own person, though so well-born, which is also shepherded and managed by another; while you, Lysis, control nobody, and do nothing that you desire. It is because I am not yet of age, Socrates, he said. That can hardly be the hindrance, son of Democrates, since there is a certain amount, I imagine, that your father and mother entrust to you without waiting until you come of age. For when they want some reading or writing done for them, it is you, I conceive, whom they appoint to do it before any others of the household. Is it not so? Quite so, he replied. And you are free there to choose which letter you shall write first and which second,

ἀναγιγνώσκειν ὡσαύτως ἔξεστι. καὶ ἐπειδάν, ὡς ἐγᾦμαι, τὴν λύραν λάβῃς, οὐ διακωλύουσί σε οὔθ' ὁ πατὴρ οὔθ' ἡ μήτηρ ἐπιτεῖναί τε καὶ ἀνεῖναι ἣν ἂν βούλῃ τῶν χορδῶν, καὶ ψῆλαι καὶ κρούειν τῷ πλήκτρῳ. ἢ διακωλύουσιν; Οὐ δῆτα. Τί ποτ' ἂν οὖν εἴη, ὦ Λύσι, τὸ αἴτιον ὅτι ἐνταῦθα μὲν οὐ
C διακωλύουσιν, ἐν οἷς δὲ ἄρτι ἐλέγομεν κωλύουσιν; Ὅτι, οἶμαι, ἔφη, ταῦτα μὲν ἐπίσταμαι, ἐκεῖνα δ' οὔ. Εἶεν, ἦν δ' ἐγώ, ὦ ἄριστε· οὐκ ἄρα τὴν ἡλικίαν σου περιμένει ὁ πατὴρ ἐπιτρέπειν πάντα, ἀλλ' ᾗ ἂν ἡμέρᾳ ἡγήσηταί σε βέλτιον αὑτοῦ φρονεῖν, ταύτῃ ἐπιτρέψει σοι καὶ αὑτὸν καὶ τὰ αὑτοῦ. Οἶμαι ἔγωγε, ἔφη. Εἶεν, ἦν δ' ἐγώ· τί δέ; τῷ γείτονι ἆρ' οὐχ ὁ αὐτὸς ὅρος ὥσπερ τῷ πατρὶ περὶ σοῦ; πότερον οἴει αὐτὸν ἐπιτρέψειν σοι τὴν αὑτοῦ οἰκίαν οἰκονομεῖν, ὅταν σε ἡγήσηται βέλτιον
D περὶ οἰκονομίας ἑαυτοῦ φρονεῖν, ἢ αὐτὸν ἐπιστατήσειν; Ἐμοὶ ἐπιτρέψειν οἶμαι. Τί δ'; Ἀθηναίους οἴει σοι οὐκ ἐπιτρέψειν τὰ αὑτῶν, ὅταν αἰσθάνωνται ὅτι ἱκανῶς φρονεῖς; Ἔγωγε. Πρὸς Διός, ἦν δ' ἐγώ, τί ἄρα ὁ μέγας βασιλεύς; πότερον τῷ πρεσβυτάτῳ υἱεῖ, οὗ ἡ τῆς Ἀσίας ἀρχὴ γίγνεται, μᾶλλον ἂν ἐπιτρέψειεν ἑψομένων κρεῶν [ἐμβάλλειν]¹ ὅ τι ἂν βούληται ἐμβαλεῖν εἰς τὸν
E ζωμόν, ἢ ἡμῖν, εἰ ἀφικόμενοι παρ' ἐκεῖνον ἐνδειξαίμεθα αὐτῷ, ὅτι ἡμεῖς κάλλιον φρονοῦμεν ἢ ὁ υἱὸς αὐτοῦ περὶ ὄψου σκευασίας; Ἡμῖν δῆλον ὅτι, ἔφη. Καὶ τὸν μέν γε οὐδ' ἂν σμικρὸν ἐάσειεν

¹ ἐμβάλλειν secl. Heindorf.

26

LYSIS

and you have a like choice in reading. And, I suppose, when you take your lyre, neither your father nor your mother prevents you from tightening or slackening what string you please, or from using your finger or your plectrum at will: or do they prevent you? Oh, no. Then whatever can be the reason, Lysis, why they do not prevent you here, while in the matters we were just mentioning they do? I suppose, he said, because I understand these things, but not those others. Very well, I said, my excellent friend: so it is not your coming of age that your father is waiting for, as the time for entrusting you with everything; but on the day when he considers you to have a better intelligence than himself, he will entrust you with himself and all that is his. Yes, I think so, he said. Very well, I went on, but tell me, does not your neighbour observe the same rule as your father towards you? Do you think he will entrust you with the management of his house, as soon as he considers you to have a better idea of its management than himself, or will he direct it himself? I should say he would entrust it to me. Well then, do you not think that the Athenians will entrust you with their affairs, when they perceive that you have sufficient intelligence? I do. Ah, do let me ask this, I went on: what, pray, of the Great King? Would he allow his eldest son, heir-apparent to the throne of Asia, to put what he chose into the royal stew, or would he prefer us to do it, supposing we came before him and convinced him that we had a better notion than his son of preparing a tasty dish? Clearly he would prefer us, he said. And he would not allow the prince to put in the smallest bit,

27

ἐμβαλεῖν· ἡμᾶς δέ, κἂν εἰ βουλοίμεθα δραξάμενοι τῶν ἁλῶν ἐῴη ἂν ἐμβαλεῖν. Πῶς γὰρ οὔ; Τί δ' εἰ τοὺς ὀφθαλμοὺς ὁ υἱὸς αὐτοῦ ἀσθενοῖ, ἆρα ἐῴη ἂν αὐτὸν ἅπτεσθαι τῶν ἑαυτοῦ ὀφθαλμῶν, μὴ ἰατρὸν ἡγούμενος, ἢ κωλύοι ἄν; Κωλύοι ἄν. Ἡμᾶς δέ γε εἰ ὑπολαμβάνοι ἰατρικοὺς εἶναι, κἂν εἰ βουλοίμεθα διανοίγοντες τοὺς ὀφθαλμοὺς ἐμπάσαι τῆς τέφρας, οἶμαι, οὐκ ἂν κωλύσειεν, ἡγούμενος ὀρθῶς φρονεῖν. Ἀληθῆ λέγεις. Ἆρ' οὖν καὶ τἆλλα πάντα ἡμῖν ἐπιτρέποι ἂν μᾶλλον ἢ ἑαυτῷ καὶ τῷ υἱεῖ, περὶ ὅσων ἂν δόξωμεν αὐτῷ σοφώτεροι ἐκείνων εἶναι; Ἀνάγκη, ἔφη, ὦ Σώκρατες.

Οὕτως ἄρα ἔχει, ἦν δ' ἐγώ, ὦ φίλε Λύσι· εἰς μὲν ταῦτα, ἃ ἂν φρόνιμοι γενώμεθα, ἅπαντες ἡμῖν ἐπιτρέψουσιν, Ἕλληνές τε καὶ βάρβαροι καὶ ἄνδρες καὶ γυναῖκες, ποιήσομέν τε ἐν τούτοις ὅ τι ἂν βουλώμεθα, καὶ οὐδεὶς ἡμᾶς ἑκὼν εἶναι ἐμποδιεῖ, ἀλλ' αὐτοί τε ἐλεύθεροι ἐσόμεθα ἐν αὐτοῖς καὶ ἄλλων ἄρχοντες, ἡμέτερά τε ταῦτα ἔσται· ὀνησόμεθα γὰρ ἀπ' αὐτῶν· εἰς ἃ δ' ἂν νοῦν μὴ κτησώμεθα, οὔτε τις ἡμῖν ἐπιτρέψει περὶ αὐτὰ ποιεῖν τὰ ἡμῖν δοκοῦντα, ἀλλ' ἐμποδιοῦσι πάντες καθ' ὅ τι ἂν δύνωνται, οὐ μόνον οἱ ἀλλότριοι, ἀλλὰ καὶ ὁ πατὴρ καὶ ἡ μήτηρ καὶ εἴ τι τούτων οἰκειότερόν ἐστιν, αὐτοί τε ἐν αὐτοῖς ἐσόμεθα ἄλλων ὑπήκοοι, καὶ ἡμῖν ἔσται ἀλλότρια· οὐδὲν γὰρ ἀπ' αὐτῶν ὀνησόμεθα. συγχωρεῖς οὕτως ἔχειν; Συγχωρῶ. Ἆρ' οὖν τῳ φίλοι ἐσόμεθα καί τις ἡμᾶς φιλήσει ἐν τούτοις, ἐν οἷς ἂν ὦμεν ἀνωφελεῖς; Οὐ δῆτα,

LYSIS

whereas he would let us have our way even if we wanted to put in salt by the handful. Why, of course. Again, if his son had something the matter with his eyes, would he let him meddle with them himself, if he considered him to be no doctor, or would he prevent him? He would prevent him. But if he supposed us to have medical skill, he would not prevent us, I imagine, even though we wanted to pull the eyes open and sprinkle them with ashes, so long as he believed our judgement to be sound. That is true. So he would entrust us, rather than himself or his son, with all his other affairs besides, wherever he may feel we are more skilled than they? Necessarily, he said, Socrates.

The case then, my dear Lysis, I said, stands thus: with regard to matters in which we become intelligent, every one will entrust us with them, whether Greeks or foreigners, men or women; and in such matters we shall do as we please, and nobody will care to obstruct us. Nay, not only shall we ourselves be free and have control of others in these affairs, but they will also belong to us, since we shall derive advantage from them; whereas in all those for which we have failed to acquire intelligence, so far will anyone be from permitting us to deal with them as we think fit, that everybody will do his utmost to obstruct us—not merely strangers, but father and mother and any more intimate person than they; and we on our part shall be subject to others in such matters, which will be no concern of ours, since we shall draw no advantage from them. Do you agree to this account of the case? I agree. Then will anyone count us his friends or have any affection for us in those matters for which we are

ἔφη. Νῦν ἄρα οὐδὲ σὲ ὁ πατὴρ οὐδὲ ἄλλος ἄλλον οὐδένα φιλεῖ, καθ' ὅσον ἂν ᾖ ἄχρηστος. Οὐκ ἔοικεν, ἔφη. Ἐὰν μὲν ἄρα σοφὸς γένῃ, ὦ παῖ, D πάντες σοι φίλοι καὶ πάντες σοι οἰκεῖοι ἔσονται· χρήσιμος γὰρ καὶ ἀγαθὸς ἔσῃ· εἰ δὲ μή, σοὶ οὔτε ἄλλος οὐδεὶς οὔτε ὁ πατὴρ φίλος ἔσται οὔτε ἡ μήτηρ οὔτε οἱ οἰκεῖοι. οἷόν τε οὖν ἐπὶ τούτοις, ὦ Λύσι, μέγα φρονεῖν, ἐν οἷς τις μήπω φρονεῖ; Καὶ πῶς ἄν; ἔφη. Εἰ δ' ἄρα σὺ διδασκάλου δέῃ, οὔπω φρονεῖς. Ἀληθῆ. Οὐδ' ἄρα μεγαλόφρων εἶ, εἴπερ ἄφρων ἔτι. Μὰ Δία, ἔφη, ὦ Σώκρατες, οὔ μοι δοκεῖ.

E Καὶ ἐγὼ ἀκούσας αὐτοῦ ἀπέβλεψα πρὸς τὸν Ἱπποθάλη, καὶ ὀλίγου ἐξήμαρτον· ἐπῆλθε γάρ μοι εἰπεῖν ὅτι Οὕτω χρή, ὦ Ἱππόθαλες, τοῖς παιδικοῖς διαλέγεσθαι, ταπεινοῦντα καὶ συστέλλοντα, ἀλλὰ μὴ ὥσπερ σὺ χαυνοῦντα καὶ διαθρύπτοντα. κατιδὼν οὖν αὐτὸν ἀγωνιῶντα καὶ τεθορυβημένον ὑπὸ τῶν λεγομένων, ἀνεμνήσθην ὅτι καὶ προσεστὼς λανθάνειν τὸν Λύσιν ἐβούλετο· ἀνέλαβον οὖν ἐμαυτὸν καὶ ἐπέσχον τοῦ λόγου. καὶ ἐν τούτῳ ὁ Μενέξενος πάλιν ἧκε, καὶ ἐκαθέζετο παρὰ τὸν Λύσιν, ὅθεν καὶ ἐξανέστη. ὁ οὖν Λύσις μάλα παιδικῶς καὶ φιλικῶς, λάθρᾳ τοῦ Μενεξένου, σμικρὸν πρός με λέγων ἔφη· Ὦ Σώκρατες, ἅπερ καὶ ἐμοὶ λέγεις, εἰπὲ καὶ Μενεξένῳ.

Καὶ ἐγὼ εἶπον, Ταῦτα μὲν σὺ αὐτῷ ἐρεῖς, ὦ Λύσι· πάντως γὰρ προσεῖχες τὸν νοῦν.

Πάνυ μὲν οὖν, ἔφη.

LYSIS

useless? Surely not, he said. So now, you see, your father does not love you, nor does anyone love anyone else, so far as one is useless. Apparently not, he said. Then if you can become wise, my boy, everybody will be your friend, every one will be intimate with you, since you will be useful and good; otherwise, no one at all, not your father, nor your mother, nor your intimate connexions, will be your friends. Now is it possible, Lysis, to have a high notion of yourself in matters of which you have as yet no notion? Why, how can I? he said. Then if you are in need of a teacher, you have as yet no notion of things? True. Nor can you have a great notion of yourself, if you are still notionless. Upon my word, Socrates, he said, I do not see how I can.

On hearing him answer this, I glanced at Hippothales, and nearly made a blunder, for it came into my mind to say: This is the way, Hippothales, in which you should talk to your favourite, humbling and reducing him, instead of puffing him up and spoiling him, as you do now. Well, I noticed that he was in an agony of embarrassment at what we had been saying, and I remembered how, in standing near, he wished to hide himself from Lysis. So I checked myself and withheld my speech. In the meantime, Menexenus came back, and sat down by Lysis in the place he had left on going out. Then Lysis, in a most playful, affectionate manner, unobserved by Menexenus, said softly to me: Socrates, tell Menexenus what you have been saying to me.

To which I replied: You shall tell it him yourself, Lysis; for you gave it your closest attention.

I did, indeed, he said.

211

Πειρῶ τοίνυν, ἦν δ' ἐγώ, ἀπομνημονεῦσαι αὐτὰ
B ὅτι μάλιστα, ἵνα τούτῳ σαφῶς πάντα εἴπῃς· ἐὰν
δέ τι αὐτῶν ἐπιλάθῃ, αὖθίς με ἀνερέσθαι ὅταν
ἐντύχῃς πρῶτον.

Ἀλλὰ ποιήσω, ἔφη, ταῦτα, ὦ Σώκρατες, πάνυ
σφόδρα, εὖ ἴσθι. ἀλλά τι ἄλλο αὐτῷ λέγε,
ἵνα καὶ ἐγὼ ἀκούω, ἕως ἂν οἴκαδε ὥρα ᾖ
ἀπιέναι.

Ἀλλὰ χρὴ ποιεῖν ταῦτα, ἦν δ' ἐγώ, ἐπειδή γε
καὶ σὺ κελεύεις. ἀλλὰ ὅρα ὅπως ἐπικουρήσεις
μοι, ἐάν με ἐλέγχειν ἐπιχειρῇ ὁ Μενέξενος· ἢ οὐκ
οἶσθα ὅτι ἐριστικός ἐστιν;

Ναὶ μὰ Δία, ἔφη, σφόδρα γε· διὰ ταῦτά τοι
καὶ βούλομαί σε αὐτῷ διαλέγεσθαι.

C Ἵνα, ἦν δ' ἐγώ, καταγέλαστος γένωμαι;

Οὐ μὰ Δία, ἔφη, ἀλλ' ἵνα αὐτὸν κολάσῃς.

Πόθεν; ἦν δ' ἐγώ· οὐ ῥᾴδιον· δεινὸς γὰρ ὁ
ἄνθρωπος, Κτησίππου μαθητής. πάρεστι δέ τοι
αὐτός—οὐχ ὁρᾷς;—Κτήσιππος.

Μηδενός σοι, ἔφη, μελέτω, ὦ Σώκρατες, ἀλλ'
ἴθι διαλέγου αὐτῷ.

Διαλεκτέον, ἦν δ' ἐγώ.

Ταῦτα οὖν ἡμῶν λεγόντων πρὸς ἡμᾶς αὐτούς,
Τί ὑμεῖς, ἔφη ὁ Κτήσιππος, αὐτὼ μόνω ἑστιᾶ-
σθον, ἡμῖν δὲ οὐ μεταδίδοτον τῶν λόγων;

D Ἀλλὰ μήν, ἦν δ' ἐγώ, μεταδοτέον. ὅδε γὰρ
τι ὧν λέγω οὐ μανθάνει, ἀλλά φησιν οἴεσθαι
Μενέξενον εἰδέναι, καὶ κελεύει τοῦτον ἐρωτᾶν.

Τί οὖν, ἦ δ' ὅς, οὐκ ἐρωτᾷς;

Ἀλλ' ἐρήσομαι, ἦν δ' ἐγώ. καί μοι εἰπέ, ὦ
Μενέξενε, ὃ ἄν σε ἔρωμαι. τυγχάνω γὰρ ἐκ
παιδὸς ἐπιθυμῶν κτήματός του, ὥσπερ ἄλλος

32

LYSIS

Then try, I went on, to recollect it as well as you can, so that you tell him the whole of it clearly: but if you forget any of it, mind that you ask me for it again when next you meet me.

I will do so, Socrates, he said, by all means, I assure you. But tell him something else, that I may hear it too, until it is time to go home.

Well, I must do so, I said, since it is you who bid me. But be ready to come to my support, in case Menexenus attempts to refute me. You know what a keen disputant he is.

Yes, on my word, very keen; that is why I want you to have a talk with him.

So that I may make myself ridiculous? I said.

No, no, indeed, he replied; I want you to trounce him.

How can I? I asked. It is not easy, when the fellow is so formidable—a pupil of Ctesippus. And here—do you not see?—is Ctesippus himself.

Take no heed of anyone, Socrates, he said; just go on and have a talk with him.

I must comply, I said.

Now, as these words passed between us,—What is this feast, said Ctesippus, that you two are having by yourselves, without allowing us a share in your talk?

Well, well, I replied, we must give you a share. My friend here fails to understand something that I have been saying, but tells me he thinks Menexenus knows, and he urges me to question him.

Why not ask him then? said he.

But I am going to, I replied. Now please answer, Menexenus, whatever question I may ask you. There is a certain possession that I have desired

PLATO

211

ἄλλου. ὁ μὲν γάρ τις ἵππους ἐπιθυμεῖ κτᾶσθαι,
E ὁ δὲ κύνας, ὁ δὲ χρυσίον, ὁ δὲ τιμάς· ἐγὼ δὲ πρὸς
μὲν ταῦτα πρᾴως ἔχω, πρὸς δὲ τὴν τῶν φίλων
κτῆσιν πάνυ ἐρωτικῶς, καὶ βουλοίμην ἄν μοι
φίλον ἀγαθὸν γενέσθαι μᾶλλον ἢ τὸν ἄριστον ἐν
ἀνθρώποις ὄρτυγα ἢ ἀλεκτρυόνα, καὶ ναὶ μὰ Δία
ἔγωγε μᾶλλον ἢ ἵππον τε καὶ κύνα· οἶμαι δὲ,
νὴ τὸν κύνα, μᾶλλον ἢ τὸ Δαρείου χρυσίον κτή-
σασθαι δεξαίμην πολὺ πρότερον ἑταῖρον, μᾶλλον ἢ
αὐτὸν Δαρεῖον· οὕτως ἐγὼ φιλέταιρός τίς εἰμι.
212 ὑμᾶς οὖν ὁρῶν, σέ τε καὶ Λύσιν, ἐκπέπληγμαι καὶ
εὐδαιμονίζω, ὅτι οὕτω νέοι ὄντες οἷοι τ' ἐστὸν
τοῦτο τὸ κτῆμα ταχὺ καὶ ῥᾳδίως κτᾶσθαι, καὶ σύ
τε τοῦτον οὕτω φίλον ἐκτήσω ταχύ τε καὶ σφόδρα, καὶ αὖ οὗτος σέ· ἐγὼ δὲ οὕτω πόρρω εἰμὶ τοῦ
κτήματος, ὥστε οὐδ' ὅντινα τρόπον γίγνεται φίλος
ἕτερος ἑτέρου οἶδα, ἀλλὰ ταῦτα δὴ αὐτά σε βούλομαι ἐρέσθαι ἅτε ἔμπειρον.

Καί μοι εἰπέ· ἐπειδάν τίς τινα φιλῇ, πότερος
B ποτέρου φίλος γίγνεται, ὁ φιλῶν τοῦ φιλουμένου
ἢ ὁ φιλούμενος τοῦ φιλοῦντος· ἢ οὐδὲν διαφέρει;
Οὐδέν, ἔφη, ἔμοιγε δοκεῖ διαφέρειν. Πῶς λέγεις;
ἦν δ' ἐγώ· ἀμφότεροι ἄρα ἀλλήλων φίλοι γίγνονται,
ἐὰν μόνος ὁ ἕτερος τὸν ἕτερον φιλῇ; Ἔμοιγε, ἔφη,
δοκεῖ. Τί δέ; οὐκ ἔστι φιλοῦντα μὴ ἀντιφιλεῖσθαι ὑπὸ τούτου ὃν ἂν φιλῇ; Ἔστιν. Τί δέ; ἆρα
ἔστι καὶ μισεῖσθαι φιλοῦντα; οἷόν που ἐνίοτε δοκοῦσι καὶ οἱ ἐρασταὶ πάσχειν πρὸς τὰ παιδικά·

LYSIS

from my childhood, as every one does in his own way. One person wants to get possession of horses, another dogs, another money, and another distinctions : of these things I reck little, but for the possession of friends I have quite a passionate longing, and would rather obtain a good friend than the best quail or cock in the world ; yes, and rather, I swear, than any horse or dog. I believe, indeed, by the Dog, that rather than all Darius's gold I would choose to gain a dear comrade—far sooner than I would Darius himself, so fond I am of my comrades. Accordingly, when I see you and Lysis together, I am quite beside myself, and congratulate you on being able, at such an early age, to gain this possession so quickly and easily ; since you, Menexenus, have so quickly and surely acquired his friendship, and he likewise yours : whereas I am so far from acquiring such a thing, that I do not even know in what way one person becomes a friend of another, and am constrained to ask you about this very point, in view of your experience.

Now tell me : when one person loves another, which of the two becomes friend of the other— the loving of the loved, or the loved of the loving ? Or is there no difference ? There is none, he replied, in my opinion. How is that ? I said ; do you mean that both become friends mutually, when there is only one loving the other ? Yes, I think so, he replied. But I ask you, is it not possible for one loving not to be loved in return by him whom he loves ? It is. But again, may he not be even hated while loving ? This, I imagine, is the sort of thing that lovers do sometimes seem to incur with their

C φιλοῦντες γὰρ ὡς οἷόν τε μάλιστα οἱ μὲν[1] οἴονται οὐκ ἀντιφιλεῖσθαι, οἱ δὲ καὶ μισεῖσθαι· ἢ οὐκ ἀληθὲς δοκεῖ σοι τοῦτο; Σφόδρα γε, ἔφη, ἀληθές. Οὐκοῦν ἐν τῷ τοιούτῳ, ἦν δ' ἐγώ, ὁ μὲν φιλεῖ, ὁ δὲ φιλεῖται; Ναί. Πότερος οὖν αὐτῶν ποτέρου φίλος ἐστίν; ὁ φιλῶν τοῦ φιλουμένου, ἐάν τε καὶ ἀντιφιλῆται ἐάν τε καὶ μισῆται, ἢ ὁ φιλούμενος τοῦ φιλοῦντος; ἢ οὐδέτερος αὖ ἐν τῷ τοιούτῳ οὐδετέρου φίλος ἐστίν, ἂν μὴ ἀμφότεροι ἀλλήλους
D φιλῶσιν; Ἔοικε γοῦν οὕτως ἔχειν. Ἀλλοίως ἄρα νῦν ἡμῖν δοκεῖ ἢ πρότερον ἔδοξεν. τότε μὲν γάρ, εἰ ὁ ἕτερος φιλοῖ, φίλω εἶναι ἄμφω· νῦν δέ, ἂν μὴ ἀμφότεροι φιλῶσιν, οὐδέτερος φίλος. Κινδυνεύει, ἔφη. Οὐκ ἄρα ἐστὶ φίλον τῷ φιλοῦντι οὐδὲν μὴ οὐκ ἀντιφιλοῦν. Οὐκ ἔοικεν. Οὐδ' ἄρα φίλιπποί εἰσιν οὓς ἂν οἱ ἵπποι μὴ ἀντιφιλῶσιν, οὐδὲ φιλόρτυγες, οὐδ' αὖ φιλόκυνές γε καὶ φίλοινοι καὶ φιλογυμνασταὶ καὶ φιλόσοφοι, ἂν μὴ ἡ σοφία αὐτοὺς ἀντιφιλῇ. ἢ φιλοῦσι μὲν ταῦτα ἕκαστοι,
E οὐ μέντοι φίλα ὄντα, ἀλλὰ ψεύδεθ' ὁ ποιητής, ὃς ἔφη—

ὄλβιος, ᾧ παῖδές τε φίλοι καὶ μώνυχες ἵπποι
καὶ κύνες ἀγρευταὶ καὶ ξένος ἀλλοδαπός;

Οὐκ ἔμοιγε δοκεῖ, ἦ δ' ὅς. Ἀλλ' ἀληθῆ δοκεῖ λέγειν σοι; Ναί. Τὸ φιλούμενον ἄρα τῷ φιλοῦντι φίλον ἐστίν, ὡς ἔοικεν, ὦ Μενέξενε, ἐάν τε φιλῇ ἐάν τε καὶ μισῇ· οἷον καὶ τὰ νεωστὶ γεγονότα
παιδία, τὰ μὲν οὐδέπω φιλοῦντα, τὰ δὲ καὶ μι-

---

[1] οἱ μὲν Heindorf : οἰόμενοι MSS.

LYSIS

favourites: they love them with all their might, yet they feel either that they are not loved in return, or that they are actually hated. Or do you not think this is true? Very true, he replied. Now in such a case, I went on, the one loves and the other is loved? Yes. Which of the two, then, is a friend of the other? Is the loving a friend of the loved, whether in fact he is loved in return or is even hated, or is the loved a friend of the loving? Or again, is neither of them in such a case friend of the other, if both do not love mutually? At any rate, he said, it looks as if this were so. So you see, we now hold a different view from what we held before. At first we said that if one of them loved, both were friends: but now, if both do not love, neither is a friend. It looks like it, he said. So there is no such thing as a friend for the lover who is not loved in return. Apparently not. And so we find no horse-lovers where the horses do not love in return, no quail-lovers, dog-lovers, wine-lovers, or sport-lovers on such terms, nor any lovers of wisdom if she returns not their love. Or does each person love these things, while yet failing to make friends of them, and was it a lying poet who said—

Happy to have your children as friends, and your trampling horses,
    Scent-snuffing hounds, and a host when you travel abroad?[1]

I do not think so, he said. But do you think he spoke the truth? Yes. Then the loved object is a friend to the lover, it would seem, Menexenus, alike whether it loves or hates: for instance, new-born children, who have either not begun to love,

[1] Solon, 21. 2.

PLATO

σοῦντα, ὅταν κολάζηται ὑπὸ τῆς μητρὸς ἢ ὑπὸ τοῦ πατρός, ὅμως καὶ μισοῦντα ἐν ἐκείνῳ τῷ χρόνῳ πάντων μάλιστά ἐστι τοῖς γονεῦσι φίλτατα. Ἔμοιγε δοκεῖ, ἔφη, οὕτως ἔχειν. Οὐκ ἄρα ὁ φιλῶν φίλος ἐκ τούτου τοῦ λόγου, ἀλλ' ὁ φιλούμενος. Ἔοικεν. Καὶ ὁ μισούμενος ἐχθρὸς ἄρα, ἀλλ' οὐχ ὁ μισῶν. Φαίνεται. Πολλοὶ ἄρα ὑπὸ τῶν ἐχθρῶν φιλοῦνται, ὑπὸ δὲ τῶν φίλων μισοῦνται, καὶ τοῖς μὲν ἐχθροῖς φίλοι εἰσί, τοῖς δὲ φίλοις ἐχθροί, εἰ τὸ φιλούμενον φίλον ἐστὶν ἀλλὰ μὴ τὸ φιλοῦν. καίτοι πολλὴ ἀλογία, ὦ φίλε ἑταῖρε, μᾶλλον δέ, οἶμαι, καὶ ἀδύνατον, τῷ τε φίλῳ ἐχθρὸν καὶ τῷ ἐχθρῷ φίλον εἶναι. Ἀληθῆ, ἔφη, ἔοικας λέγειν, ὦ Σώκρατες. Οὐκοῦν εἰ τοῦτ' ἀδύνατον, τὸ φιλοῦν ἂν εἴη φίλον τοῦ φιλουμένου. Φαίνεται. Τὸ μισοῦν ἄρα πάλιν ἐχθρὸν τοῦ μισουμένου. Ἀνάγκη. Οὐκοῦν ταὐτὰ ἡμῖν συμβήσεται ἀναγκαῖον εἶναι ὁμολογεῖν, ἅπερ ἐπὶ τῶν πρότερον, πολλάκις φίλον εἶναι μὴ φίλου, πολλάκις δὲ καὶ ἐχθροῦ, ὅταν ἢ μὴ φιλοῦν τις φιλῇ ἢ καὶ μισοῦν φιλῇ· πολλάκις δ' ἐχθρὸν εἶναι μὴ ἐχθροῦ ἢ καὶ φίλου, ὅταν ἢ μὴ μισοῦν τις μισῇ ἢ καὶ φιλοῦν μισῇ. Κινδυνεύει, ἔφη. Τί οὖν δὴ χρησώμεθα, ἦν δ' ἐγώ, εἰ μήτε οἱ φιλοῦντες φίλοι ἔσονται μήτε οἱ φιλούμενοι μήτε οἱ φιλοῦντές τε καὶ φιλούμενοι, ἀλλὰ καὶ παρὰ ταῦτα ἄλλους τινὰς ἔτι φήσομεν εἶναι φίλους ἀλλήλοις γιγνομένους; Οὐ

---

[1] In this argument Socrates makes play, like one of the "eristic" sophists, with the ambiguous meaning of φίλος ("friend" or "dear") and ἐχθρός ("enemy" or "hateful"). Beneath his immediate purpose of puzzling the young man lies the intention of pointing out the obscurity of the very terms "friend" and "enemy."

LYSIS

or already hate, if punished by their mother or their father, are yet at that very moment, and in spite of their hate, especially and pre-eminently friends to their parents. I think, he said, that is the case. Then this argument shows that it is not the lover who is a friend, but the loved. Apparently. And it is the hated who is an enemy, not the hater. Evidently. Then people must often be loved by their enemies, and hated by their friends, and be friends to their enemies and enemies to their friends, if the loved object is a friend rather than the loving agent. And yet it is a gross absurdity, my dear friend—I should say rather, an impossibility— that one should be an enemy to one's friend and a friend to one's enemy. You appear to be right there, Socrates, he said. Then if that is impossible, it is the loving that must be a friend of the loved. Evidently. And so the hating, on the other hand, will be an enemy of the hated. Necessarily. Hence in the end we shall find ourselves compelled to agree to the same statement as we made before, that frequently a man is a friend of one who is no friend, and frequently even of an enemy, when he loves one who loves not, or even hates; while frequently a man may be an enemy of one who is no enemy or even a friend, when he hates one who hates not, or even loves.[1] It looks like it, he said. What then are we to make of it, I asked, if neither the loving are to be friends, nor the loved, nor both the loving and loved together?[2] For apart from these, are there any others left for us to cite as becoming friends to one another? For my part, Socrates,

[2] Socrates cannot be said to have disposed of this third proposition.

μὰ τὸν Δία, ἔφη, ὦ Σώκρατες, οὐ πάνυ εὐπορῶ
D ἔγωγε. Ἆρα μή, ἦν δ' ἐγώ, ὦ Μενέξενε, τὸ
παράπαν οὐκ ὀρθῶς ἐζητοῦμεν; Οὐκ ἔμοιγε δοκεῖ,
ἔφη, ὦ Σώκρατες, ὁ Λύσις. καὶ ἅμα εἰπὼν
ἠρυθρίασεν· ἐδόκει γάρ μοι ἄκοντ' αὐτὸν ἐκφεύ-
γειν τὸ λεχθὲν διὰ τὸ σφόδρα προσέχειν τὸν νοῦν
τοῖς λεγομένοις· δῆλος δ' ἦν καὶ ὅτε ἠκροᾶτο
οὕτως ἔχων.

Ἐγὼ οὖν βουλόμενος τόν τε Μενέξενον ἀναπαῦ-
σαι καὶ ἐκείνου ἡσθεὶς τῇ φιλοσοφίᾳ, οὕτω μεταβαλὼν πρὸς τὸν Λύσιν ἐποιούμην τοὺς λόγους,
E καὶ εἶπον· Ὦ Λύσι, ἀληθῆ μοι δοκεῖς λέγειν ὅτι
εἰ ὀρθῶς ἡμεῖς ἐσκοποῦμεν, οὐκ ἄν ποτε οὕτως
ἐπλανώμεθα. ἀλλὰ ταύτῃ μὲν μηκέτι ἴωμεν·
καὶ γὰρ χαλεπή τίς μοι φαίνεται ὥσπερ ὁδὸς ἡ
σκέψις· ᾗ δὲ ἐτράπημεν, δοκεῖ μοι χρῆναι ἰέναι,
214 σκοποῦντα[1] κατὰ τοὺς ποιητάς· οὗτοι γὰρ ἡμῖν
ὥσπερ πατέρες τῆς σοφίας εἰσὶ καὶ ἡγεμόνες.
λέγουσι δὲ δήπου οὐ φαύλως ἀποφαινόμενοι περὶ
τῶν φίλων, οἳ τυγχάνουσιν ὄντες· ἀλλὰ τὸν θεὸν
αὐτόν φασι ποιεῖν φίλους αὐτούς, ἄγοντα παρ'
ἀλλήλους. λέγουσι δέ πως ταῦτα, ὡς ἐγᾦμαι,
ὡδί·

αἰεί τοι τὸν ὅμοιον ἄγει θεὸς ὡς τὸν ὅμοιον

B καὶ ποιεῖ γνώριμον· ἢ οὐκ ἐντετύχηκας τούτοις
τοῖς ἔπεσιν; Ἔγωγε, ἔφη. Οὐκοῦν καὶ τοῖς
τῶν σοφωτάτων συγγράμμασιν ἐντετύχηκας ταῦτα
αὐτὰ λέγουσιν, ὅτι τὸ ὅμοιον τῷ ὁμοίῳ ἀνάγκη
ἀεὶ φίλον εἶναι; εἰσὶ δέ που οὗτοι οἱ περὶ φύσεώς

---

[1] τὰ post σκοποῦντα secl. Heindorf.

LYSIS

he said, I declare I can see no sort of shift. Can it be, Menexenus, I asked, that all through there has been something wrong with our inquiry? I think there has, Socrates, said Lysis, and blushed as soon as he said it; for it struck me that the words escaped him unintentionally, through his closely applying his mind to our talk—as he had noticeably done all the time he was listening.

So then, as I wanted to give Menexenus a rest, and was delighted with the other's taste for philosophy, I took occasion to shift the discussion over to Lysis, and said: Lysis, I think your remark is true, that if we were inquiring correctly we could never have gone so sadly astray. Well, let us follow our present line no further, since our inquiry looks to me a rather hard sort of path: I think we had best make for the point where we turned off, and be guided by the poets; for they are our fathers, as it were, and conductors in wisdom. They, of course, express themselves in no mean sort on the subject of friends, where they happen to be found; even saying that God himself makes them friends by drawing them to each other. The way they put it, I believe, is something like this:

Yea, ever like and like together God doth draw,[1]

and so brings them acquainted; or have you not come across these verses? Yes, I have, he replied. And you have also come across those writings of eminent sages, which tell us this very thing — that like must needs be always friend to like? I refer, of course, to those who debate or write about

[1] Homer, *Od.* xvii. 218.

τε καὶ τοῦ ὅλου διαλεγόμενοι καὶ γράφοντες. Ἀληθῆ, ἔφη, λέγεις. Ἆρ᾽ οὖν, ἦν δ᾽ ἐγώ, εὖ λέγουσιν; Ἴσως, ἔφη. Ἴσως, ἦν δ᾽ ἐγώ, τὸ ἥμισυ αὐτοῦ, ἴσως δὲ καὶ πᾶν, ἀλλ᾽ ἡμεῖς οὐ συνίεμεν. δοκεῖ γὰρ ἡμῖν ὅ γε πονηρὸς τῷ πονηρῷ, C ὅσῳ ἂν ἐγγυτέρω προσίῃ καὶ μᾶλλον ὁμιλῇ, τοσούτῳ ἐχθίων γίγνεσθαι. ἀδικεῖ γάρ· ἀδικοῦντας δὲ καὶ ἀδικουμένους ἀδύνατόν που φίλους εἶναι. οὐχ οὕτως; Ναί, ἦ δ᾽ ὅς. Ταύτῃ μὲν ἂν τοίνυν τοῦ λεγομένου τὸ ἥμισυ οὐκ ἀληθὲς εἴη, εἴπερ οἱ πονηροὶ ἀλλήλοις ὅμοιοι. Ἀληθῆ λέγεις. Ἀλλά μοι δοκοῦσι λέγειν τοὺς ἀγαθοὺς ὁμοίους εἶναι ἀλλήλοις καὶ φίλους, τοὺς δὲ κακούς, ὅπερ καὶ λέγεται περὶ αὐτῶν, μηδέποτε ὁμοίους μηδ᾽ D αὐτοὺς αὑτοῖς εἶναι, ἀλλ᾽ ἐμπλήκτους τε καὶ ἀσταθμήτους· ὃ δὲ αὐτὸ αὑτῷ ἀνόμοιον εἴη καὶ διάφορον, σχολῇ γέ τῳ ἄλλῳ ὅμοιον ἢ φίλον γένοιτο· ἢ οὐ καὶ σοὶ δοκεῖ οὕτως; Ἔμοιγε, ἔφη. Τοῦτο τοίνυν αἰνίττονται, ὡς ἐμοὶ δοκοῦσιν, ὦ ἑταῖρε, οἱ τὸ ὅμοιον τῷ ὁμοίῳ φίλον λέγοντες, ὡς ὁ ἀγαθὸς τῷ ἀγαθῷ μόνος μόνῳ φίλος, ὁ δὲ κακὸς οὔτ᾽ ἀγαθῷ οὔτε κακῷ οὐδέποτε εἰς ἀληθῆ φιλίαν ἔρχεται. συνδοκεῖ σοι; Κατένευσεν.
E Ἔχομεν ἄρα ἤδη τίνες εἰσὶν οἱ φίλοι· ὁ γὰρ λόγος ἡμῖν σημαίνει ὅτι οἳ ἂν ὦσιν ἀγαθοί. Πάνυ γε, ἔφη, δοκεῖ.

Καὶ ἐμοί, ἦν δ᾽ ἐγώ· καίτοι δυσχεραίνω τί γε ἐν αὐτῷ· φέρε οὖν, ὦ πρὸς Διός, ἴδωμεν τί καὶ ὑποπτεύω. ὁ ὅμοιος τῷ ὁμοίῳ καθ᾽ ὅσον ὅμοιος φίλος, καὶ ἔστι χρήσιμος ὁ τοιοῦτος τῷ τοιούτῳ;

LYSIS

nature and the universe.[1] Quite so, he said. Well now, I went on, are they right in what they say? Perhaps, he replied. Perhaps in one half of it, I said; perhaps in even the whole; only we do not comprehend it. We suppose that the nearer a wicked man approaches to a wicked man, and the more he consorts with him, the more hateful he becomes; for he injures him, and we consider it impossible that injurer and injured should be friends. Is it not so? Yes, he answered. On this showing, therefore, half of the saying cannot be true, if the wicked are like one another. Quite so. What I believe they mean is that the good are like one another, and are friends, while the bad—as is also said of them—are never like even their own selves, being so ill-balanced and unsteady; and when a thing is unlike itself and variable it can hardly become like or friend to anything else. You must surely agree to that? I do, he said. Hence I conclude there is a hidden meaning, dear friend, intended by those who say that like is friend to like, namely that the good alone is friend to the good alone, while the bad never enters into true friendship with either good or bad. Do you agree? He nodded assent. So now we can tell what friends are; since our argument discloses that they are any persons who may be good. I quite think so, said he.

And I also, said I; and yet there is a point in it that makes me uneasy: so come, in Heaven's name, let us make out what it is that I suspect. Is like friend to like in so far as he is like, and is such an one useful to his fellow? Let me put it

[1] The attraction of like for like was an important force in the cosmology of Empedocles (*c.* 475–415 B.C.).

μᾶλλον δὲ ὧδε· ὁτιοῦν ὅμοιον ὁτῳοῦν ὁμοίῳ τίν' ὠφέλειαν ἔχειν ἢ τίνα βλάβην ἂν ποιῆσαι δύναιτο, ὃ μὴ καὶ αὐτὸ αὑτῷ; ἢ τί ἂν παθεῖν, ὃ μὴ καὶ ὑφ' αὑτοῦ πάθοι; τὰ δὴ τοιαῦτα πῶς ἂν ὑπ' ἀλλήλων ἀγαπηθείη, μηδεμίαν ἐπικουρίαν ἀλλήλοις ἔχοντα; ἔστιν ὅπως; Οὐκ ἔστιν. Ὁ δὲ μὴ ἀγαπῷτο, πῶς φίλον; Οὐδαμῶς. Ἀλλὰ δὴ ὁ μὲν ὅμοιος τῷ ὁμοίῳ οὐ φίλος· ὁ δὲ ἀγαθὸς τῷ ἀγαθῷ καθ' ὅσον ἀγαθός, οὐ καθ' ὅσον ὅμοιος, φίλος ἂν εἴη; Ἴσως. Τί δέ; οὐχ ὁ ἀγαθός, καθ' ὅσον ἀγαθός, κατὰ τοσοῦτον ἱκανὸς ἂν εἴη αὑτῷ; Ναί. Ὁ δέ γε ἱκανὸς οὐδενὸς δεόμενος κατὰ τὴν ἱκανότητα. Πῶς γὰρ οὔ; Ὁ δὲ μή του δεόμενος οὐδέ τι ἀγαπῴη ἄν. Οὐ γὰρ οὖν. Ὁ δὲ μὴ ἀγαπῴη, οὐδ' ἂν φιλοῖ. Οὐ δῆτα. Ὁ δὲ μὴ φιλῶν γε οὐ φίλος. Οὐ φαίνεται. Πῶς οὖν οἱ ἀγαθοὶ τοῖς ἀγαθοῖς ἡμῖν φίλοι ἔσονται τὴν ἀρχήν, οἳ μήτε ἀπόντες ποθεινοὶ ἀλλήλοις—ἱκανοὶ γὰρ ἑαυτοῖς καὶ χωρὶς ὄντες—μήτε παρόντες χρείαν αὑτῶν ἔχουσι; τοὺς δὴ τοιούτους τίς μηχανὴ περὶ πολλοῦ ποιεῖσθαι ἀλλήλους; Οὐδεμία, ἔφη. Φίλοι δέ γε οὐκ ἂν εἶεν μὴ περὶ πολλοῦ ποιούμενοι ἑαυτούς. Ἀληθῆ.

Ἄθρει δή, ὦ Λύσι, πῇ παρακρουόμεθα. ἆρά γε ὅλῳ τινὶ ἐξαπατώμεθα; Πῶς δή; ἔφη. Ἤδη ποτέ του ἤκουσα λέγοντος, καὶ ἄρτι ἀναμιμνήσκομαι, ὅτι τὸ μὲν ὅμοιον τῷ ὁμοίῳ καὶ οἱ ἀγαθοὶ τοῖς ἀγαθοῖς πολεμιώτατοι εἶεν· καὶ

---

[1] Socrates seems to pass unwarrantably from the limited to the unlimited meaning of "sufficient."

LYSIS

another way: when anything whatever is like anything else, what benefit can it offer, or what harm can it do, to its like, which it could not offer or do to itself? Or what could be done to it that could not be done to it by itself? How can such things be cherished by each other, when they can bring no mutual succour? Is it at all possible? No. And how can that be a friend, which is not cherished? By no means. But, granting that like is not friend to like, the good may still be friend to the good in so far as he is good, not as he is like? Perhaps. But again, will not the good, in so far as he is good, be in that measure sufficient for himself? Yes. And the sufficient has no need of anything, by virtue of his sufficiency.[1] Of course; And if a man has no need of anything he will not cherish anything. Presumably not. And that which does not cherish will not love. I should think not. And one who loves not is no friend. Evidently. So how can we say that the good will be friends to the good at all, when neither in absence do they long for one another—for they are sufficient for themselves even when apart—nor in presence have they need of one another? How can it be contrived that such persons shall value each other highly? By no means, he said. And if they do not set a high value on each other, they cannot be friends. True.

Now observe, Lysis, how we are missing the track. Can it be, indeed, that we are deceived in the whole matter? How so? he asked. Once on a time I heard somebody say, and I have just recollected it, that like was most hostile to like, and so were good men to good men; and what is more, he

PLATO

δὴ καὶ τὸν Ἡσίοδον ἐπήγετο μάρτυρα, λέγων ὡς ἄρα

καὶ κεραμεὺς κεραμεῖ κοτέει καὶ ἀοιδὸς ἀοιδῷ
καὶ πτωχὸς πτωχῷ,

καὶ τἆλλα δὴ πάντα οὕτως ἔφη ἀναγκαῖον εἶναι μάλιστα τὰ ὁμοιότατα πρὸς ἄλληλα φθόνου τε καὶ φιλονικίας καὶ ἔχθρας ἐμπίπλασθαι, τὰ δ' ἀνομοιότατα φιλίας. τὸν γὰρ πένητα τῷ πλουσίῳ ἀναγκάζεσθαι φίλον εἶναι καὶ τὸν ἀσθενῆ τῷ ἰσχυρῷ τῆς ἐπικουρίας ἕνεκα, καὶ τὸν κάμνοντα τῷ ἰατρῷ· καὶ πάντα δὴ τὸν μὴ εἰδότα ἀγαπᾶν τὸν εἰδότα καὶ φιλεῖν. καὶ δὴ καὶ ἔτι ἐπεξῄει τῷ λόγῳ μεγαλοπρεπέστερον, λέγων ὡς ἄρα παντὸς δέοι τὸ ὅμοιον τῷ ὁμοίῳ φίλον εἶναι, ἀλλ' αὐτὸ τὸ ἐναντίον εἴη τούτου· τὸ γὰρ ἐναντιώτατον τῷ ἐναντιωτάτῳ εἶναι μάλιστα φίλον. ἐπιθυμεῖν γὰρ τοῦ τοιούτου ἕκαστον, ἀλλ' οὐ τοῦ ὁμοίου· τὸ μὲν γὰρ ξηρὸν ὑγροῦ, τὸ δὲ ψυχρὸν θερμοῦ, τὸ δὲ πικρὸν γλυκέος, τὸ δὲ ὀξὺ ἀμβλέος, τὸ δὲ κενὸν πληρώσεως, καὶ τὸ πλῆρες δὲ κενώσεως· καὶ τἆλλα οὕτω κατὰ τὸν αὐτὸν λόγον. τροφὴν γὰρ εἶναι τὸ ἐναντίον τῷ ἐναντίῳ· τὸ γὰρ ὅμοιον τοῦ ὁμοίου οὐδὲν ἂν ἀπολαῦσαι. καὶ μέντοι, ὦ ἑταῖρε, καὶ κομψὸς ἐδόκει εἶναι ταῦτα λέγων· εὖ γὰρ ἔλεγεν. ὑμῖν δέ, ἦν δ' ἐγώ, πῶς δοκεῖ λέγειν; Εὖ γε, ἔφη ὁ Μενέξενος, ὥς γε οὑτωσὶ ἀκοῦσαι. Φῶμεν ἄρα τὸ ἐναντίον τῷ ἐναντίῳ μάλιστα φίλον εἶναι; Πάνυ γε. Εἶεν, ἦν δ' ἐγώ· οὐκ ἀλλόκοτον, ὦ Μενέξενε; καὶ ἡμῖν εὐθὺς ἅσμενοι ἐπιπηδήσονται οὗτοι οἱ πάσσοφοι ἄνδρες, οἱ ἀντιλογικοί, καὶ ἐρήσονται εἰ οὐκ ἐναντιώτα-

LYSIS

put forward Hesiod as witness, by quoting his words—

> See potter wroth with potter, bard with bard,
> Beggar with beggar,[1]

and in all other cases it was the same, he said; likest things must needs be filled with envy, contention, and hatred against each other, but the unlikest things with friendship: since the poor man must needs be friendly to the rich, and the weak to the strong, for the sake of their assistance, and also the sick man to the doctor; and every ignorant person had to cherish the well-informed, and love him. And then the speaker pursued his theme to this further and more imposing point—that like could not in the slightest degree be friendly to like, but was in just the opposite case: for it was between things most opposed that friendship was chiefly to be found, since everything desired its opposite, not its like. Thus dry desired wet, cold hot, bitter sweet, sharp blunt, empty fullness, full emptiness, and likewise the rest on the same principle: for the opposite was food for its opposite, as the like could have no enjoyment of its like. And I must say, my good friend, his argument seemed a smart one, for he expressed it well. But you, I asked—how does it strike you? It sounds all right, said Menexenus, at least on the moment's hearing. Then are we to say that the opposite is most friendly to its opposite? Certainly. Well, I exclaimed, is it not monstrous, Menexenus? Why, at once these all-accomplished logic-choppers will delightedly pounce on us and ask whether hatred is not the most opposite thing to friendship. And

[1] *Works and Days*, 25.

PLATO

τον ἔχθρα φιλίᾳ; οἷς τί ἀποκρινούμεθα; ἢ οὐκ ἀνάγκη ὁμολογεῖν ὅτι ἀληθῆ λέγουσιν; Ἀνάγκη. Ἆρ' οὖν, φήσουσι, τὸ ἐχθρὸν τῷ φίλῳ φίλον ἢ τὸ φίλον τῷ ἐχθρῷ; Οὐδέτερα, ἔφη. Ἀλλὰ τὸ δίκαιον τῷ ἀδίκῳ, ἢ τὸ σῶφρον τῷ ἀκολάστῳ, ἢ τὸ ἀγαθὸν τῷ κακῷ; Οὐκ ἄν μοι δοκεῖ οὕτως ἔχειν. Ἀλλὰ μέντοι, ἦν δ' ἐγώ, εἴπερ γε κατὰ τὴν ἐναντιότητά τί τῳ φίλον[1] ἐστίν, ἀνάγκη καὶ ταῦτα φίλα εἶναι. Ἀνάγκη. Οὔτε ἄρα τὸ ὅμοιον τῷ ὁμοίῳ οὔτε τὸ ἐναντίον τῷ ἐναντίῳ φίλον. Οὐκ ἔοικεν.

Ἔτι δὲ καὶ τόδε σκεψώμεθα, μὴ ἔτι μᾶλλον ἡμᾶς λανθάνει τὸ φίλον ὡς ἀληθῶς οὐδὲν τούτων ὄν, ἀλλὰ τὸ μήτε ἀγαθὸν μήτε κακὸν φίλον οὕτω ποτὲ γιγνόμενον τοῦ ἀγαθοῦ. Πῶς, ἦ δ' ὅς, λέγεις; Ἀλλὰ μὰ Δία, ἦν δ' ἐγώ, οὐκ οἶδα, ἀλλὰ τῷ ὄντι αὐτὸς εἰλιγγιῶ ὑπὸ τῆς τοῦ λόγου ἀπορίας, καὶ κινδυνεύει κατὰ τὴν ἀρχαίαν παροιμίαν τὸ καλὸν φίλον εἶναι. ἔοικε γοῦν μαλακῷ τινι καὶ λείῳ καὶ λιπαρῷ· διὸ καὶ ἴσως ῥᾳδίως διολισθαίνει καὶ διαδύεται ἡμᾶς, ἅτε τοιοῦτον ὄν. λέγω γὰρ τἀγαθὸν καλὸν εἶναι· σὺ δ' οὐκ οἴει; Ἔγωγε. Λέγω τοίνυν ἀπομαντευόμενος, τοῦ καλοῦ τε καὶ ἀγαθοῦ φίλον εἶναι τὸ μήτε ἀγαθὸν μήτε κακόν· πρὸς ἃ δὲ λέγων μαντεύομαι, ἄκουσον. δοκεῖ μοι ὡσπερεὶ τρία ἄττα εἶναι γένη, τὸ μὲν ἀγαθόν, τὸ δὲ κακόν, τὸ δ' οὔτ' ἀγαθὸν οὔτε κακόν· τί δὲ σοί; Καὶ ἐμοί, ἔφη. Καὶ οὔτε τἀγαθὸν τἀγαθῷ οὔτε τὸ κακὸν τῷ

---

[1] τῳ φίλον Cornarius : τῷ φίλῳ φίλον, τῷ φίλον φίλον MSS.

---

[1] The proverb, of course, used φίλον in the sense of "dear."

LYSIS

what answer shall we give them? Shall we not be forced to admit that what they say is true? We shall. So then, they will demand, is a hating thing friend to the friendly thing, or the friendly to the hating? Neither, he replied. But is the just a friend to the unjust, or the temperate to the profligate, or the good to the bad? I do not think that could be so. But yet, I urged, if one thing is friend to another on this principle of opposition, these things too must needs be friends. They must. So neither is like friend to like, nor opposite friend to opposite. It seems not.

But there is still this point to consider; for perhaps we are yet more mistaken, and the friendly has really nothing to do with all this: it may rather be something neither good nor bad that will prove after all to be what we call friend of the good. How do you mean? he asked. For the life of me, I said, I cannot tell: the fact is, I am quite dizzy myself with the puzzle of our argument, and am inclined to agree with the ancient proverb that the beautiful is friendly.[1] It certainly resembles something soft and smooth and sleek; that is why, I daresay, it so easily slides and dives right into us, by virtue of those qualities. For I declare that the good is beautiful: do you not agree? I do. Then I will be a diviner for once, and state that what is neither good nor bad is friendly to what is beautiful and good; and what it is that prompts me to this divination, you must now hear. My view is that there are three separate kinds, as it were—the good, the bad, and what is neither good nor bad; and what is yours? Mine is the same, he replied. And that neither is the good friendly to the good, nor

κακῷ οὔτε τἀγαθὸν τῷ κακῷ φίλον εἶναι, ὥσπερ οὐδ' ὁ ἔμπροσθεν λόγος ἐᾷ· λείπεται δή, εἴπερ τῴ τί ἐστι φίλον, τὸ μήτε ἀγαθὸν μήτε κακὸν φίλον εἶναι ἢ τοῦ ἀγαθοῦ ἢ τοῦ τοιούτου οἷον αὐτό ἐστιν. οὐ γὰρ ἄν που τῷ κακῷ φίλον ἄν τι γένοιτο. Ἀληθῆ. Οὐδὲ μὴν τὸ ὅμοιον τῷ ὁμοίῳ ἔφαμεν ἄρτι· ἢ γάρ; Ναί. Οὐκ ἄρα ἔσται τῷ μήτε ἀγαθῷ μήτε κακῷ τὸ τοιοῦτον φίλον οἷον αὐτό. Οὐ φαίνεται. Τῷ ἀγαθῷ ἄρα τὸ μήτε ἀγαθὸν μήτε κακὸν μόνῳ μόνον συμβαίνει γίγνεσθαι φίλον. Ἀνάγκη, ὡς ἔοικεν.

Ἆρ' οὖν καὶ καλῶς, ἦν δ' ἐγώ, ὦ παῖδες, ὑφηγεῖται ἡμῖν τὸ νῦν λεγόμενον; εἰ γοῦν θέλοιμεν ἐννοῆσαι τὸ ὑγιαῖνον σῶμα, οὐδὲν ἰατρικῆς δεῖται οὐδ' ὠφελίας· ἱκανῶς γὰρ ἔχει, ὥστε ὑγιαίνων οὐδεὶς ἰατρῷ φίλος διὰ τὴν ὑγίειαν. ἢ γάρ; Οὐδείς. Ἀλλ' ὁ κάμνων, οἶμαι, διὰ τὴν νόσον. Πῶς γὰρ οὔ; Νόσος μὲν δὴ κακόν, ἰατρικὴ δὲ ὠφέλιμον καὶ ἀγαθόν. Ναί. Σῶμα δέ γέ που κατὰ τὸ σῶμα εἶναι οὔτ' ἀγαθὸν οὔτε κακόν. Οὕτως. Ἀναγκάζεται δέ γε σῶμα διὰ νόσον ἰατρικὴν ἀσπάζεσθαι καὶ φιλεῖν. Δοκεῖ μοι. Τὸ μήτε κακὸν ἄρα μήτ' ἀγαθὸν φίλον γίγνεται τοῦ ἀγαθοῦ διὰ κακοῦ παρουσίαν. Ἔοικεν. Δῆλον δέ γε ὅτι πρὶν γενέσθαι αὐτὸ κακὸν ὑπὸ τοῦ κακοῦ οὗ ἔχει. οὐ γὰρ δή γε κακὸν γεγονὸς ἔτι ἄν τι[1] τοῦ ἀγαθοῦ ἐπιθυμοῖ καὶ φίλον εἴη· ἀδύνατον γὰρ ἔφαμεν κακὸν ἀγαθῷ φίλον εἶναι. Ἀδύνατον γάρ. Σκέψασθε δὴ ὃ λέγω. λέγω γὰρ ὅτι ἔνια μέν, οἷον

---

[1] ἄν τι C. Schmidt: ἀντὶ MSS.

LYSIS

the bad to the bad, nor the good to the bad; so much our previous argument already forbids. One view then remains: if anything is friendly to anything, that which is neither good nor bad is friendly to either the good or what is of the same quality as itself. For I presume nothing could be found friendly to the bad. True. Nor, however, can like be friendly to like: this we stated just now, did we not? Yes. So what is neither good nor bad can have no friendship with the same sort of thing as itself. Apparently not. Then only what is neither good nor bad proves to be friendly to the good, and to that only. That must be so, it seems.

Then can we rely further on this present statement, my boys, I said, as a sure guide? For instance, we have only to consider a body in health to see that it has no need of doctoring or assistance: it is well enough as it is, and so no one in health is friend to a doctor, on account of his health. You agree? Yes. But the sick man is, I imagine, on account of his disease. Certainly. Now disease is a bad thing, and medicine is beneficial and good. Yes. And a body, of course, taken as body, is neither good nor bad. That is so. But a body is compelled by disease to welcome and love medicine. I think so. Thus what is neither bad nor good becomes a friend of the good because of the presence of evil. So it seems. But clearly this must be before it is itself made evil by the evil which it has; for surely, when once it has been made evil, it can no longer have any desire or love for the good; since we agreed it was impossible for bad to be a friend of good. Yes, impossible. Now observe what I say. Some things are of the same sort as

51

PLATO

ἂν ᾖ τὸ παρόν, τοιαῦτά ἐστι καὶ αὐτά, ἔνια δὲ οὔ. ὥσπερ εἰ ἐθέλοι τις χρώματί τῳ ὁτιοῦν ἀλεῖψαι, πάρεστί που τῷ ἀλειφθέντι τὸ ἐπαλειφθέν. Πάνυ γε. Ἆρ' οὖν καὶ ἔστι τότε τοιοῦτον τὴν χρόαν τὸ ἀλειφθέν,[1] οἷον τὸ ἐπιόν[2]; Οὐ μανθάνω, ἦ D δ' ὅς. Ἀλλ' ὧδε, ἦν δ' ἐγώ. εἴ τίς σου ξανθὰς οὔσας τὰς τρίχας ψιμυθίῳ ἀλείψειε, πότερον τότε[3] λευκαὶ εἶεν ἢ φαίνοιντ' ἄν; Φαίνοιντ' ἄν, ἦ δ' ὅς. Καὶ μὴν παρείη γ' ἂν αὐταῖς λευκότης. Ναί. Ἀλλ' ὅμως οὐδέν τι μᾶλλον ἂν εἶεν λευκαί πω, ἀλλὰ παρούσης λευκότητος οὔτε τι λευκαὶ οὔτε μέλαιναί εἰσιν. Ἀληθῆ. Ἀλλ' ὅταν δή, ὦ φίλε, τὸ γῆρας αὐταῖς ταὐτὸν τοῦτο χρῶμα ἐπαγάγῃ, τότε ἐγένοντο E οἷόνπερ τὸ παρόν, λευκοῦ παρουσίᾳ λευκαί. Πῶς γὰρ οὔ; Τοῦτο τοίνυν ἐρωτῶ νῦν δή, εἰ ᾧ ἄν τι παρῇ, τοιοῦτον ἔσται τὸ ἔχον οἷον τὸ παρόν· ἢ ἐὰν μὲν κατά τινα τρόπον παρῇ, ἔσται, ἐὰν δὲ μή, οὔ; Οὕτω μᾶλλον, ἔφη. Καὶ τὸ μήτε κακὸν ἄρα μήτ' ἀγαθὸν ἐνίοτε κακοῦ παρόντος οὔπω κακόν ἐστιν, ἔστι δ' ὅτε ἤδη [τὸ][4] τοιοῦτον γέγονεν. Πάνυ γε. Οὐκοῦν ὅταν μήπω κακὸν ᾖ κακοῦ παρόντος, αὕτη μὲν ἡ παρουσία ἀγαθοῦ αὐτὸ ποιεῖ ἐπιθυμεῖν· ἡ δὲ κακὸν ποιοῦσα ἀποστερεῖ αὐτὸ τῆς τε ἐπιθυμίας ἅμα καὶ τῆς φιλίας τοῦ ἀγαθοῦ. οὐ γὰρ ἔτι ἐστὶν 218 οὔτε κακὸν οὔτε ἀγαθόν, ἀλλὰ κακόν· φίλον δὲ ἀγαθῷ κακὸν[5] οὐκ ἦν. Οὐ γὰρ οὖν. Διὰ ταῦτα δὴ φαῖμεν ἂν καὶ τοὺς ἤδη σοφοὺς μηκέτι φιλο-

---

[1] ἀλειφθέν Heindorf: ἐπαλειφθέν MSS.
[2] ἐπιόν Heindorf: ἔτι ὄν MSS.
[3] τότε Heindorf: ποτε MSS.
[4] τὸ seclusi.
[5] ἀγαθῷ κακὸν Heindorf: ἀγαθῶν κακῷ T: ἀγαθὸν κακῷ Bt.

LYSIS

those that are present with them, and some are not. For example, if you chose to dye something a certain colour, the substance of the dye is present, I presume, with the thing dyed. Certainly. Then is the thing dyed of the same sort, in point of colour, as the substance that is added? I do not understand, he said. Well, try it this way, I went on: suppose some one tinged your golden locks with white lead, would they then be or appear to be white? They would appear so, he replied. And, in fact, whiteness would be present with them? Yes. But all the same they would not be any the more white as yet; for though whiteness be present, they are not at all white, any more than they are at all black. True. But when, my dear boy, old age has cast that same colour upon them, they have then come to be of the same sort as that which is present—white through presence of white. To be sure. So this is the question I have been trying to put to you—whether a thing that has something present with it is to be held of the same sort as that present thing; or is it only when that thing is present in a particular way, but otherwise not? More likely the latter, he said. So that what is neither bad nor good is sometimes, when bad is present, not bad as yet, but sometimes it has had time to become such. Certainly. When therefore it is not bad as yet, though bad is present, this presence makes it desire good; but the presence makes it bad, and deprives it equally of its desire and its love for the good. For it is no longer neither bad nor good, but bad; and we found that bad was no friend to good. No, indeed. And consequently we may say that those who are already

PLATO

σοφεῖν, εἴτε θεοὶ εἴτε ἄνθρωποί εἰσιν οὗτοι· οὐδ' αὖ ἐκείνους φιλοσοφεῖν τοὺς οὕτως ἄγνοιαν ἔχοντας ὥστε κακοὺς εἶναι· κακὸν γὰρ καὶ ἀμαθῆ οὐδένα φιλοσοφεῖν. λείπονται δὴ οἱ ἔχοντες μὲν τὸ κακὸν τοῦτο, τὴν ἄγνοιαν, μήπω δὲ ὑπ' αὐτοῦ ὄντες ἀγνώμονες μηδὲ ἀμαθεῖς, ἀλλ' ἔτι ἡγούμενοι μὴ εἰδέναι ἃ B μὴ ἴσασι. διὸ δὴ καὶ φιλοσοφοῦσιν οἱ οὔτε ἀγαθοὶ οὔτε κακοί πω ὄντες· ὅσοι δὲ κακοί, οὐ φιλοσοφοῦσιν, οὐδὲ οἱ ἀγαθοί· οὔτε γὰρ τὸ ἐναντίον τοῦ ἐναντίου οὔτε τὸ ὅμοιον τοῦ ὁμοίου φίλον ἡμῖν ἐφάνη ἐν τοῖς ἔμπροσθεν λόγοις. ἦ οὐ μέμνησθε; Πάνυ γε, ἐφάτην. Νῦν ἄρα, ἦν δ' ἐγώ, ὦ Λύσι τε καὶ Μενέξενε, παντὸς μᾶλλον ἐξηυρήκαμεν ὃ ἔστι τὸ φίλον καὶ οὔ. φαμὲν γὰρ αὐτό, καὶ κατὰ τὴν C ψυχὴν καὶ κατὰ τὸ σῶμα καὶ πανταχοῦ, τὸ μήτε κακὸν μήτε ἀγαθὸν διὰ κακοῦ παρουσίαν τοῦ ἀγαθοῦ φίλον εἶναι. Παντάπασιν ἐφάτην τε καὶ συνεχωρείτην οὕτω τοῦτ' ἔχειν.

Καὶ δὴ καὶ αὐτὸς ἐγὼ πάνυ ἔχαιρον, ὥσπερ θηρευτής τις, ἔχων ἀγαπητῶς ὃ ἐθηρευόμην. κἄπειτ' οὐκ οἶδ' ὁπόθεν μοι ἀτοπωτάτη τις ὑποψία εἰσῆλθεν, ὡς οὐκ ἀληθῆ εἴη τὰ ὡμολογημένα ἡμῖν· καὶ εὐθὺς ἀχθεσθεὶς εἶπον· Βαβαί, ὦ Λύσι τε καὶ Μενέξενε, κινδυνεύομεν ὄναρ πεπλουτηκέναι.
D Τί μάλιστα; ἔφη ὁ Μενέξενος.

Φοβοῦμαι, ἦν δ' ἐγώ, μὴ ὥσπερ ἀνθρώποις ἀλαζόσι λόγοις τισὶ τοιούτοις [ψευδέσιν][1] ἐντετυχήκαμεν περὶ τοῦ φίλου.

Πῶς δή; ἔφη.

[1] ψευδέσιν secl. Heindorf.

LYSIS

wise no longer love wisdom, whether they be gods or men; nor again can those be lovers of wisdom who are in such ignorance as to be bad : for we know that a bad and stupid man is no lover of wisdom. And now there remain those who, while possessing this bad thing, ignorance, are not yet made ignorant or stupid, but are still aware of not knowing the things they do not know. It follows, then, that those who are as yet neither good nor bad are lovers of wisdom, while all who are bad, and all the good, are not : for, as we found in our previous discussion, neither is opposite friend to opposite, nor like to like. You remember, do you not ? To be sure we do, they both replied. So now, Lysis and Menexenus, I said, we can count on having discovered what is the friendly and what is not. For we say that, in the soul and the body and everywhere, just that which is neither bad nor good, but has the presence of bad, is thereby friend of the good. To this statement they said that they entirely agreed.

And, beyond that, I was myself filled with delight, like a hunter, at the satisfaction of getting hold of what I was hunting ; when somehow or other a most unaccountable suspicion came over me that the conclusion to which we had agreed was not true. So at once I exclaimed in vexation : Alack-a-day, Lysis and Menexenus ! I fear our new-gotten riches are all a dream.

How on earth is that ? said Menexenus.

I am afraid, I replied, that in our search for friendship we have struck up with arguments that are no better than a set of braggarts.

How so ? he asked.

PLATO

Ὧδε, ἦν δ' ἐγώ, σκοπῶμεν· φίλος ὃς ἂν εἴη, πότερόν ἐστί τῳ φίλος ἢ οὔ; Ἀνάγκη, ἔφη. Πότερον οὖν οὐδενὸς ἕνεκα καὶ δι' οὐδέν, ἢ ἕνεκά του καὶ διά τι; Ἕνεκά του καὶ διά τι. Πότερον φίλου ὄντος ἐκείνου τοῦ πράγματος, οὗ ἕνεκα φίλος ὁ φίλος τῷ φίλῳ, ἢ οὔτε φίλου οὔτε ἐχθροῦ; Οὐ E πάνυ, ἔφη, ἕπομαι. Εἰκότως γε, ἦν δ' ἐγώ· ἀλλ' ὧδε ἴσως ἀκολουθήσεις, οἶμαι δὲ καὶ ἐγὼ μᾶλλον εἴσομαι ὅ τι λέγω. ὁ κάμνων, νῦν δὴ ἔφαμεν,[1] τοῦ ἰατροῦ φίλος· οὐχ οὕτως; Ναί. Οὐκοῦν διὰ νόσον ἕνεκα ὑγιείας τοῦ ἰατροῦ φίλος; Ναί. Ἡ δέ γε νόσος κακόν; Πῶς δ' οὔ; Τί δὲ ὑγίεια; ἦν δ' ἐγώ· ἀγαθὸν ἢ κακὸν ἢ οὐδέτερα; Ἀγαθόν, 219 ἔφη. Ἐλέγομεν δ' ἄρα, ὡς ἔοικεν, ὅτι τὸ σῶμα, οὔτε ἀγαθὸν οὔτε κακὸν ⟨ὄν⟩,[2] διὰ τὴν νόσον, τοῦτο δὲ διὰ τὸ κακόν, τῆς ἰατρικῆς φίλον ἐστίν· ἀγαθὸν δὲ ἰατρική· ἕνεκα δὲ τῆς ὑγιείας τὴν φιλίαν ἡ ἰατρικὴ ἀνῄρηται· ἡ δὲ ὑγίεια ἀγαθόν. ἦ γάρ; Ναί. Φίλον δὲ ἢ οὐ φίλον ἡ ὑγίεια; Φίλον. Ἡ δὲ νόσος ἐχθρόν. Πάνυ γε. Τὸ οὔτε κακὸν οὔτε B ἀγαθὸν ἄρα διὰ τὸ κακὸν καὶ τὸ ἐχθρὸν τοῦ ἀγαθοῦ φίλον ἐστὶν ἕνεκα τοῦ ἀγαθοῦ καὶ φίλου. Φαίνεται. Ἕνεκ' ἄρα τοῦ φίλου ⟨τοῦ φίλου⟩[3] τὸ φίλον φίλον διὰ τὸ ἐχθρόν. Ἔοικεν.

Εἶεν, ἦν δ' ἐγώ. ἐπειδὴ ἐνταῦθα ἥκομεν, ὦ παῖδες, πρόσχωμεν τὸν νοῦν μὴ ἐξαπατηθῶμεν. ὅτι μὲν γὰρ φίλον τοῦ φίλου τὸ φίλον γέγονεν, ἐῶ

[1] ἔφαμεν Heindorf : φαμὲν MSS.
[2] ὄν add. Heindorf.
[3] τοῦ φίλου add. Burnet : post τὸ φίλον add. Hermann.

LYSIS

Just consider a moment, I said. When a man is a friend, is he friend to some one or not? He needs must be, he replied. Then is he so for the sake of nothing and because of nothing, or for the sake of something and because of something? For the sake of something, and because of something. Is it a friend—that thing for whose sake he is a friend to his friend—or is it neither friend nor foe? I do not quite follow, he said. Naturally enough, said I; but perhaps you will keep up if we try it another way, and I expect that I too will better understand what I am saying. The sick man, we said just now, is a friend to the doctor; is not that so? Yes. Then is it because of disease, for the sake of health, that he is a friend of the doctor? Yes. And disease is a bad thing? Of course. But what is health? I asked: a good thing, or a bad, or neither? A good thing, he said. And we were saying, I believe, that the body, being neither good nor bad, was a friend of medicine—that is, of a good thing—because of disease—that is, because of a bad thing; and it is for the sake of health that medicine has acquired this friendship, and health is a good thing. You agree? Yes. Is health a friend or not? A friend. And disease is a foe? Certainly. So what is neither bad nor good is a friend to the good because of what is bad and a foe, for the sake of what is good and a friend. Apparently. Hence the friend is a friend of its friend for the sake of its friend and because of its foe. So it seems.

Very well, I said: since we have reached this point, my boys, let us take good heed not to be deceived. I pass over without remark the fact that the friend has become a friend to the friend,

PLATO

χαίρειν, καὶ τοῦ ὁμοίου γε τὸ ὅμοιον φίλον γίγνεται, ὃ ἔφαμεν ἀδύνατον εἶναι· ἀλλ' ὅμως τόδε σκεψώμεθα, μὴ ἡμᾶς ἐξαπατήσῃ τὸ νῦν λεγόμενον. ἡ ἰατρική, φαμέν, ἕνεκα τῆς ὑγιείας φίλον. Ναί. Οὐκοῦν καὶ ἡ ὑγίεια φίλον; Πάνυ γε. Εἰ ἄρα φίλον, ἕνεκά του. Ναί. Φίλου γέ τινος δή, εἴπερ ἀκολουθήσει τῇ πρόσθεν ὁμολογίᾳ. Πάνυ γε. Οὐκοῦν καὶ ἐκεῖνο φίλον αὖ ἔσται ἕνεκα φίλου; Ναί. Ἆρ' οὖν οὐκ ἀνάγκη ἀπειπεῖν ἡμᾶς οὕτως ἰόντας, ἢ ἀφικέσθαι ἐπί τινα ἀρχήν, ἢ οὐκέτ' ἐπανοίσει ἐπ' ἄλλο φίλον, ἀλλ' ἥξει ἐπ' ἐκεῖνο ὅ ἐστι πρῶτον φίλον, οὗ ἕνεκα καὶ τὰ ἄλλα φαμὲν πάντα φίλα εἶναι; Ἀνάγκη. Τοῦτο δή ἐστιν ὃ λέγω, μὴ ἡμᾶς τὰ ἄλλα πάντα ἃ εἴπομεν ἐκείνου ἕνεκα φίλα εἶναι, ὥσπερ εἴδωλα ἄττα ὄντα αὐτοῦ, ἐξαπατᾷ, ᾖ δ' ἐκεῖνο τὸ πρῶτον, ὃ ὡς ἀληθῶς ἐστὶ φίλον. ἐννοήσωμεν γὰρ οὑτωσί· ὅταν[1] τίς τι περὶ πολλοῦ ποιῆται, οἷόνπερ ἐνίοτε πατὴρ υἱὸν ἀντὶ πάντων τῶν ἄλλων χρημάτων προτιμᾷ, ὁ δὴ τοιοῦτος ἕνεκα τοῦ τὸν υἱὸν περὶ παντὸς ἡγεῖσθαι ἆρα καὶ ἄλλο τι ἂν περὶ πολλοῦ ποιοῖτο; οἷον εἰ αἰσθάνοιτο αὐτὸν κώνειον πεπωκότα, ἆρα περὶ πολλοῦ ποιοῖτ' ἂν οἶνον, εἴπερ τοῦτο ἡγοῖτο τὸν υἱὸν σώσειν; Τί μήν; ἔφη. Οὐκοῦν καὶ τὸ ἀγγεῖον, ἐν ᾧ ὁ οἶνος ἐνείη; Πάνυ γε. Ἆρ' οὖν τότε οὐδὲν περὶ πλείονος ποιεῖται, κύλικα κεραμέαν ἢ τὸν υἱὸν τὸν αὑτοῦ, οὐδὲ τρεῖς κοτύλας οἴνου ἢ τὸν

---

[1] ὅταν Stephanus : ὃ ἂν mss.

LYSIS

and thus the like becomes a friend to the like, which we said was impossible. There is, however, a further point which we must examine, if we are not to find our present argument a mere deception. Medicine, we say, is a friend for the sake of health. Yes. Then is health a friend also? Certainly. And if it is a friend, it is so for the sake of something. Yes. And that something is a friend, if it is to conform to our previous agreement. Quite so. Then will that something be, on its part also, a friend for the sake of a friend? Yes. Now are we not bound to weary ourselves with going on in this way, unless we can arrive at some first principle which will not keep leading us on from one friend to another, but will reach the one original friend, for whose sake all the other things can be said to be friends? We must. So you see what I am afraid of—that all the other things, which we cited as friends for the sake of that one thing, may be deceiving us like so many phantoms of it, while that original thing may be the veritable friend. For suppose we view the matter thus: when a man highly values a thing, as in the common case of a father who prizes his son above all his possessions, will such a man, for the sake of placing his son before everything, value anything else highly at the same time? For instance, on learning that he had drunk some hemlock, would he value wine highly if he believed it would save his son's life? Why, of course, he said. And the vessel too which contained the wine? Certainly. Now does he make no distinction in value, at that moment, between a cup of earthenware and his own son, or between three pints of wine and his

PLATO

υἱόν; ἢ ὡδέ πως ἔχει· πᾶσα ἡ τοιαύτη σπουδὴ οὐκ ἐπὶ τούτοις ἐστὶν ἐσπουδασμένη, ἐπὶ τοῖς ἕνεκά του παρασκευαζομένοις, ἀλλ' ἐπ' ἐκείνῳ, οὗ ἕνεκα πάντα τὰ τοιαῦτα παρασκευάζεται. οὐχ ὅτι πολλάκις λέγομεν, ὡς περὶ πολλοῦ ποιούμεθα χρυσίον καὶ ἀργύριον· ἀλλὰ μὴ οὐδέν τι μᾶλλον οὕτω τό γε ἀληθὲς ἔχῃ, ἀλλ' ἐκεῖνό ἐστιν ὃ περὶ παντὸς ποιούμεθα, ὃ ἂν φανῇ ὄν, ὅτου ἕνεκα καὶ χρυσίον καὶ πάντα τὰ παρασκευαζόμενα παρασκευάζεται. ἆρ' οὕτως φήσομεν; Πάνυ γε. Οὐκοῦν καὶ περὶ τοῦ φίλου ὁ αὐτὸς λόγος; ὅσα γάρ φαμεν φίλα εἶναι ἡμῖν ἕνεκα φίλου τινὸς ἑτέρου,[1] ῥήματι φαινόμεθα λέγοντες αὐτό· φίλον δὲ τῷ ὄντι κινδυνεύει ἐκεῖνο αὐτὸ εἶναι, εἰς ὃ πᾶσαι αὗται αἱ λεγόμεναι φιλίαι τελευτῶσιν. Κινδυνεύει οὕτως, ἔφη, ἔχειν. Οὐκοῦν τό γε τῷ ὄντι φίλον οὐ φίλου τινὸς ἕνεκα φίλον ἐστίν; Ἀληθῆ.

Τοῦτο μὲν δὴ ἀπήλλακται, μὴ φίλου τινὸς ἕνεκα τὸ φίλον φίλον εἶναι· ἀλλ' ἆρα τὸ ἀγαθόν ἐστι φίλον; Ἔμοιγε δοκεῖ. Ἆρ' οὖν διὰ τὸ κακὸν τὸ ἀγαθὸν φιλεῖται, καὶ ἔχει ὡδε· εἰ τριῶν ὄντων ὧν νῦν δὴ ἐλέγομεν, ἀγαθοῦ καὶ κακοῦ καὶ μήτε ἀγαθοῦ μήτε κακοῦ, τὰ δύο λειφθείη, τὸ δὲ κακὸν ἐκποδὼν ἀπέλθοι καὶ μηδενὸς ἐφάπτοιτο μήτε σώματος μήτε ψυχῆς μήτε τῶν ἄλλων, ἃ δή φαμεν αὐτὰ καθ' αὑτὰ οὔτε κακὰ εἶναι οὔτ' ἀγαθά, ἆρα τότε οὐδὲν ἂν ἡμῖν χρήσιμον εἴη τὸ ἀγαθόν, ἀλλ' ἄχρηστον ἂν γεγονὸς εἴη; εἰ γὰρ μηδὲν ἡμᾶς ἔτι βλάπτοι, οὐδὲν ἂν οὐδεμιᾶς ὠφελίας δεοίμεθα, καὶ οὕτω δὴ ἂν τότε

[1] ἑτέρου Hermann : ἑτέρῳ MSS.

---

[1] Socrates here strangely confuses the cause (τὸ διά τι) with the object in view (τὸ ἕνεκά του), which he carefully distinguished in the case of medicine (219 A).

LYSIS

son? Or may we perhaps state it thus: all such concern is not entertained for the actual things which are applied for the sake of something, but for that something for whose sake all the rest are applied? I know that we often talk of setting great value on gold and silver: but surely we are no nearer the truth of the matter for that; what we rather value above everything is the thing—whatever it may prove to be—for whose sake gold and all the other commodities are applied. May we state it so? By all means. Then shall we not give the same account of a friend? In speaking of all the things that are friends to us for the sake of some other friend, we find ourselves uttering a mere phrase; whereas in reality " friend " appears to be simply and solely the thing in which all these so-called friendships terminate. So it appears, he said. Then the real friend is a friend for the sake of nothing else that is a friend? True.

So we have got rid of this, and it is not for the sake of some friendly thing that the friend is friendly. But now, is the good a friend? I should say so. And further, it is because of the bad that the good is loved[1]; let me state the case as follows: there are three things of which we have just been speaking —good, bad, and what is neither good nor bad. If but two of these remained after evil had been cleared away, so that it had no contact with anything, whether body or soul or any of the other things that we count neither bad nor good in themselves, would the result be that good would be of no use to us, but would have become quite a useless thing? For if there were nothing left to harm us, we should feel no want of any assistance; and thus we should

PLATO

γένοιτο κατάδηλον ὅτι διὰ τὸ κακὸν τἀγαθὸν ἠγαπῶ-
μεν καὶ ἐφιλοῦμεν, ὡς φάρμακον ὂν τοῦ κακοῦ τὸ
ἀγαθόν, τὸ δὲ κακὸν νόσημα· νοσήματος δὲ μὴ
ὄντος οὐδὲν δεῖ φαρμάκου. ἆρ' οὕτω πέφυκέ τε καὶ
φιλεῖται τἀγαθὸν διὰ τὸ κακὸν ὑφ' ἡμῶν, τῶν μεταξὺ
ὄντων τοῦ κακοῦ τε καὶ τἀγαθοῦ, αὐτὸ δὲ ἑαυτοῦ
ἕνεκα οὐδεμίαν χρείαν ἔχει; Ἔοικεν, ἦ δ' ὅς,
οὕτως ἔχειν. Τὸ ἄρα φίλον ἡμῖν ἐκεῖνο, εἰς ὃ
E ἐτελεύτα πάντα τὰ ἄλλα—ἕνεκα ἑτέρου φίλου φίλα
ἔφαμεν εἶναι ἐκεῖνα—οὐδὲν [δὲ]¹ τούτοις ἔοικεν.
ταῦτα μὲν γὰρ φίλου ἕνεκα φίλα κέκληται, τὸ δὲ τῷ
ὄντι φίλον πᾶν τοὐναντίον τούτου φαίνεται πεφυκός·
φίλον γὰρ ἡμῖν ἀνεφάνη ὂν ἐχθροῦ ἕνεκα· εἰ δὲ τὸ
ἐχθρὸν ἀπέλθοι, οὐκέτι, ὡς ἔοικ', ἔσθ' ἡμῖν φίλον.
Οὔ μοι δοκεῖ, ἔφη, ὥς γε νῦν λέγεται. Πότερον,
ἦν δ' ἐγώ, πρὸς Διός, ἐὰν τὸ κακὸν ἀπόληται, οὐδὲ
221 πεινῆν ἔτι ἔσται οὐδὲ διψῆν οὐδὲ ἄλλο οὐδὲν τῶν
τοιούτων; ἢ πείνη μὲν ἔσται, ἐάνπερ ἄνθρωποί τε
καὶ τἆλλα ζῷα ᾖ, οὐ μέντοι βλαβερά γε; καὶ δίψα
δὴ καὶ αἱ ἄλλαι ἐπιθυμίαι, ἀλλ' οὐ κακαί, ἅτε τοῦ
κακοῦ ἀπολωλότος; ἢ γελοῖον τὸ ἐρώτημα, ὅ τί
ποτ' ἔσται τότε ἢ μὴ ἔσται; τίς γὰρ οἶδεν; ἀλλ'
οὖν τόδε γε ἴσμεν, ὅτι καὶ νῦν ἔστι πεινῶντα βλά-
πτεσθαι, ἔστι δὲ καὶ ὠφελεῖσθαι. ἦ γάρ; Πάνυ γε.
Οὐκοῦν καὶ διψῶντα καὶ τῶν ἄλλων τῶν τοιούτων
B πάντων ἐπιθυμοῦντα ἔστιν ἐνίοτε μὲν ὠφελίμως
ἐπιθυμεῖν, ἐνίοτε δὲ βλαβερῶς, ἐνίοτε δὲ μηδέτερα;
Σφόδρα γε. Οὐκοῦν ἐὰν ἀπολλύηται τὰ κακά,

¹ δὲ om. Cornarius: δὴ Heindorf.

LYSIS

have to face the fact that it was because of the bad that we felt such a friendly affection for the good, since the good is a cure for the bad, while the bad is an ailment, and if there is no ailment there is no need for a cure. Is not this the nature of the good—to be loved because of the bad by us who are midway between the bad and the good, whereas separately and for its own sake it is of no use? Apparently so, he said. Then our " friend," in which all the other things terminated—we called them " friends for the sake of some other friend "—has no resemblance to these. For they are described as friends for the sake of a friend: but the real friend appears to have quite the opposite character; for we found it to be a friend for the sake of a foe, and if the foe should be removed we have no friend, it seems, any more. I should say not, he assented, to judge by our present argument. Tell me, I beg of you, I went on, if evil is abolished, will it be impossible any longer to feel hunger or thirst or other such conditions? Or will hunger exist, so long as men and animals exist, but without being hurtful? Thirst, too, and all other desires—will these exist without being bad, because the bad will have been abolished? Or is this a ridiculous question—as to what will exist or not exist in such a case? For who can tell? Yet this, at all events, we do know—that, as things are now, it is possible for a man to feel hunger as a hurt, and also to be benefited by it. You agree? Certainly. And so, when a man feels thirst or any other desire of the sort, he may have that desire sometimes with benefit, sometimes with harm, and sometimes with neither? Quite so. Now if evil things are abolished, is there any reason

63

ἅ γε μὴ τυγχάνει ὄντα κακά, τί προσήκει τοῖς κακοῖς συναπόλλυσθαι; Οὐδέν. Ἔσονται ἄρα αἱ μήτε ἀγαθαὶ μήτε κακαὶ ἐπιθυμίαι καὶ ἐὰν ἀπόληται τὰ κακά. Φαίνεται. Οἷόν τε οὖν ἐστὶν ἐπιθυμοῦντα καὶ ἐρῶντα τούτου οὗ ἐπιθυμεῖ καὶ ἐρᾷ μὴ φιλεῖν; Οὐκ ἔμοιγε δοκεῖ. Ἔσται ἄρα καὶ τῶν κακῶν ἀπολομένων, ὡς ἔοικε, φίλ᾽ ἄττα.
C Ναί. Οὐκ ἄν, εἴ γε τὸ κακὸν αἴτιον ἦν τοῦ φίλον τι εἶναι, οὐκ ἂν ἦν τούτου ἀπολομένου φίλον ἕτερον ἑτέρῳ. αἰτίας γὰρ ἀπολομένης ἀδύνατόν που ἦν ἔτ᾽ ἐκεῖνο εἶναι, οὗ ἦν αὕτη ἡ αἰτία. Ὀρθῶς λέγεις. Οὐκοῦν ὡμολόγηται ἡμῖν τὸ φίλον φιλεῖν τι καὶ διά τι· καὶ ᾠήθημεν τότε γε διὰ τὸ κακὸν τὸ μήτε ἀγαθὸν μήτε κακὸν τὸ ἀγαθὸν
D φιλεῖν; Ἀληθῆ. Νῦν δέ γε, ὡς ἔοικε, φαίνεται ἄλλη τις αἰτία τοῦ φιλεῖν τε καὶ φιλεῖσθαι. Ἔοικεν. Ἆρ᾽ οὖν τῷ ὄντι, ὥσπερ ἄρτι ἐλέγομεν, ἡ ἐπιθυμία τῆς φιλίας αἰτία, καὶ τὸ ἐπιθυμοῦν φίλον ἐστὶ τούτῳ οὗ ἐπιθυμεῖ καὶ τότε ὅταν ἐπιθυμῇ, ὃ δὲ τὸ πρότερον ἐλέγομεν φίλον εἶναι, ὕθλος τις ἦν, ὥσπερ ποίημα μακρὸν συγκείμενον; Κινδυνεύει, ἔφη. Ἀλλὰ μέντοι, ἦν δ᾽ ἐγώ, τό γε ἐπιθυμοῦν,
E οὗ ἂν ἐνδεὲς ᾖ, τούτου ἐπιθυμεῖ. ἦ γάρ; Ναί. Τὸ δ᾽ ἐνδεὲς ἄρα φίλον ἐκείνου οὗ ἂν ἐνδεὲς ᾖ; Δοκεῖ μοι. Ἐνδεὲς δὲ γίγνεται οὗ ἄν τι[1] ἀφαιρῆται. Πῶς δ᾽ οὔ; Τοῦ οἰκείου δή, ὡς ἔοικεν, ὅ τε ἔρως καὶ ἡ φιλία καὶ ἡ ἐπιθυμία τυγχάνει οὖσα, ὡς φαίνεται, ὦ Μενέξενέ τε καὶ Λύσι. Συνεφάτην.

[1] τι Stephanus : τις mss.

---

[1] *i.e.* things that are proper or congenial to one.

LYSIS

why the things that are not evil should be abolished along with the evil? None. So that those desires which are neither good nor bad will exist even when the bad things are abolished. Apparently. Now is it possible for a man, when he desires and loves, to have no friendly feeling towards that which he desires and loves? I think not. Thus certain things will continue to be friendly, it seems, when evil things are abolished. Yes. It cannot be that, if evil were the cause of a thing being friendly, one thing should be friendly to another when evil is abolished. For when a cause is abolished, that thing can no longer exist, I presume, which had this as its cause. You are right. Now we have agreed that the friend has a friendly feeling for something and because of something; and we supposed, just then, that it was because of evil that what was neither good nor bad loved the good. True. But now, it seems, we make out a different cause of loving and being loved. It seems so. Can it really be then, as we were saying just now, that desire is the cause of friendship, and the desiring thing is a friend to what which it desires, and is so at any time of desiring; while our earlier statement about friends was all mere drivel, like a poem strung out for mere length? It looks like it, he said. But still, I went on, the desiring thing desires that in which it is deficient, does it not? Yes. And the deficient is a friend to that in which it is deficient? I suppose so. And it becomes deficient in that of which it suffers a deprivation. To be sure. So it is one's own belongings,[1] it seems, that are the objects of love and friendship and desire; so it appears, Menexenus and Lysis. They both

PLATO

221 Ὑμεῖς ἄρα εἰ φίλοι ἐστὸν ἀλλήλοις, φύσει πῃ οἰκεῖοί ἐσθ' ὑμῖν αὐτοῖς. Κομιδῇ, ἐφάτην. Καὶ 222 εἰ ἄρα τις ἕτερος ἑτέρου ἐπιθυμεῖ, ἦν δ' ἐγώ, ὦ παῖδες, ἢ ἐρᾷ, οὐκ ἄν ποτε ἐπεθύμει οὐδὲ ἤρα οὐδὲ ἐφίλει, εἰ μὴ οἰκεῖός πῃ τῷ ἐρωμένῳ ἐτύγχανεν ὢν ἢ κατὰ τὴν ψυχὴν ἢ κατά τι τῆς ψυχῆς ἦθος ἢ τρόπους ἢ εἶδος. Πάνυ γε, ἔφη ὁ Μενέξενος· ὁ δὲ Λύσις ἐσίγησεν. Εἶεν, ἦν δ' ἐγώ. τὸ μὲν δὴ φύσει οἰκεῖον ἀναγκαῖον ἡμῖν πέφανται φιλεῖν. Ἔοικεν, ἔφη. Ἀναγκαῖον ἄρα τῷ γνησίῳ ἐραστῇ καὶ μὴ προσποιήτῳ φιλεῖσθαι ὑπὸ B τῶν παιδικῶν. ὁ μὲν οὖν Λύσις καὶ ὁ Μενέξενος μόγις πως ἐπενευσάτην, ὁ δὲ Ἱπποθάλης ὑπὸ τῆς ἡδονῆς παντοδαπὰ ἠφίει χρώματα.

Καὶ ἐγὼ εἶπον, βουλόμενος τὸν λόγον ἐπισκέψασθαι, Εἰ μέν τι τὸ οἰκεῖον τοῦ ὁμοίου διαφέρει, λέγοιμεν ἄν τι, ὡς ἐμοὶ δοκεῖ, ὦ Λύσι τε καὶ Μενέξενε, περὶ φίλου, ὃ ἔστιν· εἰ δὲ ταὐτὸν τυγχάνει ὂν ὅμοιόν τε καὶ οἰκεῖον, οὐ ῥᾴδιον ἀποβαλεῖν τὸν πρόσθεν λόγον, ὡς οὐ τὸ ὅμοιον τῷ ὁμοίῳ κατὰ τὴν ὁμοιότητα ἄχρηστον· τὸ δὲ ἄχρηστον φίλον C ὁμολογεῖν πλημμελές. βούλεσθ' οὖν, ἦν δ' ἐγώ, ἐπειδὴ ὥσπερ μεθύομεν ὑπὸ τοῦ λόγου, συγχωρήσωμεν καὶ φῶμεν ἕτερόν τι εἶναι τὸ οἰκεῖον τοῦ ὁμοίου; Πάνυ γε. Πότερον οὖν καὶ τἀγαθὸν οἰκεῖον θήσομεν παντί, τὸ δὲ κακὸν ἀλλότριον εἶναι; ἢ τὸ μὲν κακὸν τῷ κακῷ οἰκεῖον, τῷ δὲ ἀγαθῷ τὸ ἀγαθόν, τῷ δὲ μήτε ἀγαθῷ μήτε κακῷ τὸ μήτε ἀγαθὸν μήτε κακόν; Οὕτως ἐφάτην δοκεῖν σφίσιν ἕκαστον ἑκάστῳ οἰκεῖον εἶναι. Πάλιν

66

LYSIS

agreed. Then if you two are friends to each other, by some natural bond you belong to one another. Precisely, they said. And in a case where one person desires another, my boys, or loves him, he would never be desiring or loving or befriending him, unless he somehow belonged to his beloved either in soul, or in some disposition, demeanour or cast of soul. Yes, to be sure, said Menexenus; but Lysis was silent. Very well, said I: what belongs to us by nature has been shown to be something we needs must befriend. It seems so, he said. Then the genuine, not the pretended, lover must needs be befriended by his favourite. To this Lysis and Menexenus gave but a faint nod of assent; while Hippothales, in his delight, turned all manner of colours.

So then, with the design of reviewing the argument, I proceeded: If there is any difference between what belongs and what is like, it seems to me, Lysis and Menexenus, that we might give some account of the meaning of "friend." But if "like" and "belonging" are the same, it is not easy to get rid of our former statement, that the like is useless to the like in so far as they have likeness; and to admit that the useless is friendly would be a gross mistake. So how if we agree now, I said, since our argument has made us quite tipsy, to say that the belonging and the like are two different things? By all means. Then shall we maintain that the good itself belongs to every one, while the bad is alien? Or does the bad belong to the bad, the good to the good, and what is neither good nor bad to what is neither good nor bad? They agreed that the last three pairs belong together. So here again, boys,

PLATO

D ἆρα, ἦν δ' ἐγώ, ὦ παῖδες, οὓς τὸ πρῶτον λόγους ἀπεβαλόμεθα περὶ φιλίας, εἰς τούτους εἰσπεπτώκαμεν· ὁ γὰρ ἄδικος τῷ ἀδίκῳ καὶ ὁ κακὸς τῷ κακῷ οὐδὲν ἧττον φίλος ἔσται ἢ ὁ ἀγαθὸς τῷ ἀγαθῷ. Ἔοικεν, ἔφη. Τί δέ; τὸ ἀγαθὸν καὶ τὸ οἰκεῖον ἂν ταὐτὸν φῶμεν εἶναι, ἄλλο τι ἢ ὁ ἀγαθὸς τῷ ἀγαθῷ μόνον φίλος; Πάνυ γε. Ἀλλὰ μὴν καὶ τοῦτό γε ᾠόμεθα ἐξελέγξαι ἡμᾶς αὐτούς· ἢ οὐ μέμνησθε; Μεμνήμεθα.

E Τί οὖν ἂν ἔτι χρησαίμεθα τῷ λόγῳ; ἢ δῆλον ὅτι οὐδέν; δέομαι οὖν, ὥσπερ οἱ σοφοὶ ἐν τοῖς δικαστηρίοις, τὰ εἰρημένα ἅπαντα ἀναπεμπάσασθαι. εἰ γὰρ μήτε οἱ φιλούμενοι μήτε οἱ φιλοῦντες μήτε οἱ ὅμοιοι μήτε οἱ ἀνόμοιοι μήτε οἱ ἀγαθοὶ μήτε οἱ οἰκεῖοι μήτε τὰ ἄλλα ὅσα διεληλύθαμεν—οὐ γὰρ ἔγωγε ἔτι μέμνημαι ὑπὸ τοῦ πλήθους—ἀλλ' εἰ μηδὲν τούτων φίλον ἐστίν, ἐγὼ μὲν οὐκέτι ἔχω τί λέγω.

223 Ταῦτα δ' εἰπὼν ἐν νῷ εἶχον ἄλλον ἤδη τινὰ τῶν πρεσβυτέρων κινεῖν· κᾆτα, ὥσπερ δαίμονές τινες, προσελθόντες οἱ παιδαγωγοί, ὅ τε τοῦ Μενεξένου καὶ ὁ τοῦ Λύσιδος, ἔχοντες αὐτῶν τοὺς ἀδελφούς, παρεκάλουν καὶ ἐκέλευον αὐτοὺς οἴκαδε ἀπιέναι· ἤδη γὰρ ἦν ὀψέ. τὸ μὲν οὖν πρῶτον καὶ ἡμεῖς καὶ οἱ περιεστῶτες αὐτοὺς ἀπηλαύνομεν· ἐπειδὴ δὲ οὐδὲν ἐφρόντιζον ἡμῶν, ἀλλ' ὑποβαρβαρίζοντες ἠγανάκτουν τε καὶ οὐδὲν ἧττον ἐκάλουν, ἀλλ' ἐδόB κουν ἡμῖν ὑποπεπωκότες ἐν τοῖς Ἑρμαίοις ἄποροι εἶναι προσφέρεσθαι, ἡττηθέντες οὖν αὐτῶν δι-

---

[1] The word "belonging" seems to throw some light on "friend," but even if we distinguish it from "like" it turns

68

LYSIS

I said, we have dropped into the very statements regarding friendship which we rejected at first; for now the unjust will be as much a friend of the unjust, and the bad of the bad, as the good of the good.[1] So it seems, he said. And what is more, if we say that the good and the belonging are the same, we cannot avoid making the good a friend only to the good. To be sure. But this again, you know, is a view of which we thought we had disabused ourselves; you remember, do you not? We do.

So what more can we do with our argument? Obviously, I think, nothing. I can only ask you, accordingly, like the professional pleaders in the law courts, to perpend the whole of what has been said. If neither the loved nor the loving, nor the like nor the unlike, nor the good nor the belonging, nor all the rest that we have tried in turn—they are so many that I, for one, fail to remember any more—well, if none of these is a friend, I am at a loss for anything further to say.

Having thus spoken, I was minded to stir up somebody else among the older people there; when, like spirits from another world, there came upon us the tutors of Menexenus and Lysis: they were bringing along the boys' brothers, and called out to them the order to go home; for it was quite late. At first we tried, with the help of the group around us, to drive the tutors off; but they took no notice of us at all, and went on angrily calling, as before, in their foreign accent. We decided that they had taken a drop too much at the festival and might be awkward customers; so we gave in

---

out to be just as indifferent to good and bad, and therefore just as remote from the moral significance of "friend."

ἐλύσαμεν τὴν συνουσίαν. ὅμως δ' ἔγωγε ἤδη ἀπιόντων αὐτῶν, Νῦν μέν, ἦν δ' ἐγώ, ὦ Λύσι τε καὶ Μενέξενε, καταγέλαστοι γεγόναμεν ἐγώ τε, γέρων ἀνήρ, καὶ ὑμεῖς. ἐροῦσι γὰρ οἵδε ἀπιόντες ὡς οἰόμεθα ἡμεῖς ἀλλήλων φίλοι εἶναι—καὶ ἐμὲ γὰρ ἐν ὑμῖν τίθημι—οὔπω δὲ ὅ τι ἔστιν ὁ φίλος οἷοί τε ἐγενόμεθα ἐξευρεῖν.

LYSIS

to them, and broke up our party. However, just as they were moving off, I remarked: To-day, Lysis and Menexenus, we have made ourselves ridiculous—I, an old man, as well as you. For these others will go away and tell how we believe we are friends of one another—for I count myself in with you—but what a " friend " is, we have not yet succeeded in discovering.

SYMPOSIUM

INTRODUCTION TO THE *SYMPOSIUM*

THE *Symposium* of Plato holds an acknowledged place among those few masterpieces of human art which unveil and interpret something of the central mystery of life. It has been a source of light and inspiration to successive ages since the revival of learning, and is revisited by the same reader at different times of life with fresh wonder and praise. Like other great works of art, it provides its own introduction; so perfectly is the scene set and presented that even at the distance of twenty-three centuries we are able to catch the various tones of the speakers, first in the ripple of their casual talk, and then in the flow of their competitive eloquence. But while the modern reader can hardly miss the main effect of the simple narrative, as it develops the lively drama in which the sparkle of satiric wit is made to enhance the glow of high poetic rapture, there are one or two points to which attention may be usefully directed, in order that the work may convey the fullest possible measure of its meaning and value.

Its theme is the passion of personal love, so often the subject or occasion of literary art, but rarely examined in its moral aspect with any true perception or profit. Love is here treated with a sense of its universal importance and with a reach and certainty of insight which do not appear in any other of the

INTRODUCTION TO THE *SYMPOSIUM*

great religious or moral teachers. This confident mastery was one of the extraordinary powers of Socrates which Plato at this stage of his writing was intent on portraying ; it was one of the strangely memorable impressions which the elder man left on his associates, in spite of his simple, inquisitive manner and his constant avowals of ignorance. In some of his more positive moods he described himself as an inveterate " lover," in the sense of a declared and devout worshipper of the great energy of Nature which in its various workings amongst men was called by the general name of " Eros." Often he would feign, in his playful, paradoxical way, to put himself on a level with ordinary sensual men, and by discussing their views—if they had any, and consented to state them—would endeavour to lead the talk on to his own conception of love, where it was to be approached on the loftiest and most serious plane of thought. For the very purpose of a telling contrast with the common attitude to the matter, he would make a humorous use of the terms of ordinary love-passion to produce a sudden surprise in his hearers, when they found that his own pursuit of intellectual refinement through friendly or affectionate intercourse was independent of the outward attractions of sense. So much of explanation may perhaps be necessary, and may just suffice, for a right understanding of his banter with Alcibiades in this dialogue.

It is one of the great dramatic excellences of Plato that he shows us how Socrates adapted his tone and language to the characters of his hearers and to the several stages of his argument or exposition. This ready sense of the daily lives and thoughts of his companions, no less than the half-logical,

INTRODUCTION TO THE *SYMPOSIUM*

half-mystical bent of his energetic mind, led him to the knowledge that, however easily or completely he might have freed his own faculties from the confusing trammels of carnal appetite, the mass of mankind was subject to the sway of bodily beauty; and that no theory of love could be satisfactory which did not take due account of this elemental fact of human nature. So he seizes this favourable moment in the talk at Agathon's party to suggest that visible beauty is the most obvious and distinct reflection in our terrene life of an eternal, immutable Beauty, perceived not with the eye but with the mind. He preaches no avoidance of the contest with appetite, but rather the achievement of a definite victory over the lower elements of love-passion, and the pursuit of beauty on higher and higher levels until, as in a sudden flash, its ultimate and all-rewarding essence is revealed. His modest attribution of the theory to his instructress, the wise woman of Mantinea, is probably meant to indicate that we are passing beyond the bounds of Socratic thought and listening really to Plato; but it is quite possible and reasonable to suppose Socrates is relating the actual results of his own cogitation after a discussion with some revered and impressive counsellor.

In this dialogue the theory is only adumbrated for an exalted moment in convivial talk: its far-reaching developments in psychology and metaphysics are set forth in the *Republic*, *Phaedrus*, *Phaedo*, and elsewhere. Here, through the glow of poetic speculation, we get a glimpse, not merely of a logical theory, but of a whole philosophy or way of life—a progress towards complete enlighten-

INTRODUCTION TO THE *SYMPOSIUM*

ment which is commended to all who have opened their eyes enough to see that they walk in the shades of ignorance. The final stages, it seems, may be too difficult even for Socrates himself to comprehend: thus with many hesitations and apologies the great master of inquiry seeks to communicate a thrilling adventure of his thought—a wondering recognition of the general " idea " or immaterial form which presides over all similar appearances in the material world. An absorbing thought, we are told, kept him standing in the street for some time before he joined the dinner-party: so here he shows us something of his endeavours to reach the summit of wisdom, and to move in a realm of absolute being which perhaps is beyond the utmost flight of philosophy. But the main thesis seeks to show how through the slavish trance of sensual charm we may pass with ever wakening and widening powers to the best and freest activity of our faculties, the contemplation of invisible, eternal verity. The lowest is linked with the highest; and it is noteworthy that Alcibiades' eulogy of Socrates serves to fix attention on the practical beginnings of the progress, by demonstrating that a rare intellectual communion may be built on the defeat of mere sensual aims.

In the proportions of its design and the texture of its style the *Symposium* stands out from even the best writings of Plato as a marvel of artistic ease and grace. Translations have frequently succeeded in presenting his vivid picture of the social manners of the place and time, and much of the beauty of his eloquence; but they have failed to transmit his brilliant characterization of the individual speakers in the style of their addresses. An

INTRODUCTION TO THE *SYMPOSIUM*

attempt has been made here to indicate in different sorts and degrees the "euphuistic" influence of Sicilian rhetoric in the speeches of Phaedrus, Pausanias, and Agathon; the "medical college" manner of Eryximachus; the racy, extravagant humour of Aristophanes; the lofty solemnity of Diotima; and the frank, unbosoming tone of Alcibiades.

The date of the opening conversation is about 400 B.C.; the banquet itself was in 416 B.C. Apollodorus, whom we meet also in the *Phaedrus* (59), was noted for his enthusiastic attachment to Socrates in his last years; Aristodemus, who related to him the story of the banquet, was the Master's intimate of an earlier time. Agathon, the brilliant and courteous host, has just won the prize with the first part of a "tetralogy" or group of four plays at a dramatic festival: he was born about 447 B.C., and studied rhetoric under Gorgias and Prodicus. Phaedrus, who makes the first speech at the party, was a disciple of Hippias (*Protag.* 315 c), and a friend of Plato, who gave his name to the other dialogue (the *Phaedrus*) which especially deals with the subject of love. Pausanias, the next speaker, was a disciple of Prodicus (*Protag.* 315 D) and a passionate admirer of Agathon; his speech is a typical exhibition of the plausible, ornamental rhetoric of the literary sophists. Eryximachus, son of the physician Acumenus, followed his father's profession and belonged to the great medical guild of the Asclepiadae. He has the unbending gravity and cold, dogmatic utterance of the student and upholder of science. Aristophanes, the great comic poet and close contemporary of Agathon, had seized on the originality which distinguished Socrates from

INTRODUCTION TO THE *SYMPOSIUM*

the ordinary sophists, and also on his scientific learning and argumentative subtlety, to make him the central figure of fun in the *Clouds* (423 B.C.). Here he makes the theme of love the occasion for a satirical sketch, in his own fantastic spirit and brilliant style, of physiological theories of the day. Alcibiades (*c.* 450–404 B.C.) is shown at the height of his popularity, a year before he sailed with the Sicilian Expedition. The tipsy immodesty of his mood throws into noble relief the passionate warmth of his admiration for the character of Socrates.

ΣΥΜΠΟΣΙΟΝ

ΑΠΟΛΛΟΔΩΡΟΣ ΕΤΑΙΡΟΣ

ΑΠ. Δοκῶ μοι περὶ ὧν πυνθάνεσθε οὐκ ἀμελέτητος εἶναι. καὶ γὰρ ἐτύγχανον πρῴην εἰς ἄστυ οἴκοθεν ἀνιὼν Φαληρόθεν· τῶν οὖν γνωρίμων τις ὄπισθεν κατιδών με πόρρωθεν ἐκάλεσε, καὶ παίζων ἅμα τῇ κλήσει, Ὦ Φαληρεύς, ἔφη, οὗτος Ἀπολλόδωρος, οὐ περιμενεῖς; κἀγὼ ἐπιστὰς περιέμεινα· καὶ ὅς, Ἀπολλόδωρε, ἔφη, καὶ μὴν καὶ ἔναγχός σε ἐζήτουν βουλόμενος διαπυθέσθαι τὴν Ἀγάθωνος συνουσίαν καὶ Σωκράτους καὶ Ἀλκιβιάδου καὶ τῶν ἄλλων τῶν τότε ἐν τῷ συνδείπνῳ παραγενομένων, περὶ τῶν ἐρωτικῶν λόγων τίνες ἦσαν. ἄλλος γάρ τίς μοι διηγεῖτο ἀκηκοὼς Φοίνικος τοῦ Φιλίππου, ἔφη δὲ καὶ σὲ εἰδέναι. ἀλλὰ γὰρ οὐδὲν εἶχε σαφὲς λέγειν· σὺ οὖν μοι διήγησαι· δικαιότατος γὰρ εἶ τοὺς τοῦ ἑταίρου λόγους ἀπαγγέλλειν. πρότερον δέ μοι, ἦ δ' ὅς, εἰπέ, σὺ αὐτὸς παρεγένου τῇ συνουσίᾳ ταύτῃ ἢ οὔ; κἀγὼ εἶπον ὅτι Παντάπασιν ἔοικέ σοι οὐδὲν διηγεῖσθαι σαφὲς ὁ διηγούμενος, εἰ νεωστὶ ἡγῇ τὴν συνουσίαν γεγονέναι ταύτην ἣν

---

[1] Nothing is known of this man.

THE SYMPOSIUM

Apollodorus tells his Companions how he heard about the Banquet

AP. I believe I have got the story you inquire of pretty well by heart. The day before yesterday I chanced to be going up to town from my house in Phalerum, when one of my acquaintance caught sight of me from behind, some way off, and called in a bantering tone — "Hullo, Phalerian ! I say, Apollodorus, wait a moment." So I stopped and waited. Then, "Apollodorus," he said, "do you know, I have just been looking for you, as I want to hear all about the banquet that brought together Agathon and Socrates and Alcibiades and the rest of that party, and what were the speeches they delivered upon love. For somebody else was relating to me the account he had from Phoenix,[1] son of Philip, and he mentioned that you knew it too. But he could not tell it at all clearly ; so you must give me the whole story, for you are the most proper reporter of your dear friend's discourses. But first tell me this," he went on ; "were you at that party yourself, or not ?" To which my answer was : "You have had anything but a clear account from your informant, if you suppose the party you are asking about to have been such a recent affair

ἐρωτᾷς, ὥστε καὶ ἐμὲ παραγενέσθαι. Ἔγωγε δή, ἔφη.[1] Πόθεν, ἦν δ' ἐγώ, ὦ Γλαύκων; οὐκ οἶσθ' ὅτι πολλῶν ἐτῶν Ἀγάθων ἐνθάδε οὐκ ἐπιδεδήμηκεν, ἀφ' οὗ δ' ἐγὼ Σωκράτει συνδιατρίβω καὶ ἐπιμελὲς πεποίημαι ἑκάστης ἡμέρας εἰδέναι ὅ τι ἂν λέγῃ ἢ πράττῃ, οὐδέπω τρία ἔτη ἐστίν; πρὸ τοῦ δὲ περιτρέχων ὅπη τύχοιμι καὶ οἰόμενος τὶ ποιεῖν ἀθλιώτερος ἦ ὁτουοῦν, οὐχ ἧττον ἢ σὺ νυνί, οἰόμενος δεῖν πάντα μᾶλλον πράττειν ἢ φιλοσοφεῖν. καὶ ὅς, Μὴ σκῶπτ', ἔφη, ἀλλ' εἰπέ μοι πότε ἐγένετο ἡ συνουσία αὕτη. κἀγὼ εἶπον ὅτι Παίδων ὄντων ἡμῶν ἔτι, ὅτε τῇ πρώτῃ τραγῳδίᾳ ἐνίκησεν Ἀγάθων, τῇ ὑστεραίᾳ ᾗ τὰ ἐπινίκια ἔθυεν αὐτός τε καὶ οἱ χορευταί. Πάνυ, ἔφη, ἄρα πάλαι, ὡς ἔοικεν. ἀλλὰ τίς σοι διηγεῖτο; ἢ αὐτὸς Σωκράτης; Οὐ μὰ τὸν Δία, ἦν δ' ἐγώ, ἀλλ' ὅσπερ Φοίνικι· Ἀριστόδημος ἦν τις, Κυδαθηναιεύς, σμικρός, ἀνυπόδητος ἀεί· παραγεγόνει δ' ἐν τῇ συνουσίᾳ, Σωκράτους ἐραστὴς ὢν ἐν τοῖς μάλιστα τῶν τότε, ὡς ἐμοὶ δοκεῖ. οὐ μέντοι ἀλλὰ καὶ Σωκράτη γε ἔνια ἤδη ἀνηρόμην ὧν ἐκείνου ἤκουσα, καί μοι ὡμολόγει καθάπερ ἐκεῖνος διηγεῖτο. Τί οὖν, ἔφη, οὐ διηγήσω μοι; πάντως δὲ ἡ ὁδὸς ἡ εἰς ἄστυ ἐπιτηδεία πορευομένοις καὶ λέγειν καὶ ἀκούειν.

Οὕτω δὴ ἰόντες ἅμα τοὺς λόγους περὶ αὐτῶν ἐποιούμεθα, ὥστε, ὅπερ ἀρχόμενος εἶπον, οὐκ ἀμελετήτως ἔχω. εἰ οὖν δεῖ καὶ ὑμῖν διηγήσασθαι, ταῦτα χρὴ ποιεῖν. καὶ γὰρ ἔγωγε καὶ ἄλλως,

[1] ἔφη add. Burnet.

---

[1] Probably Plato's brother (*Rep.* 368 A).

SYMPOSIUM

that I could be included." "So I did suppose," he said. "How so, Glaucon[1]?" said I. "You must know it is many a year that Agathon has been away from home and country, and not yet three years that I have been consorting with Socrates and making it my daily care to know whatever he says or does. Before that time, what with running about at random and thinking I did things, I was the wretchedest man alive; just as you are at present, thinking philosophy is none of your business." "Instead of jeering at me," he said, "tell me when it was that this party took place." "When you and I were only children," I told him; "on the occasion of Agathon's victory with his first tragedy: the day after that of the dedicatory feast which he and his players held for its celebration." "Ah, quite a long while ago, it would seem," said he; "but who gave you the account of it? Socrates himself?" "Goodness, no!" I answered. "It was the person who told Phoenix—Aristodemus of Cydathenaeum, a little man, who went always barefoot. He was of the company there, being one of the chief among Socrates' lovers at that time, I believe. But all the same, I have since questioned Socrates on some details of the story I had from his friend, and he acknowledged them to be in accordance with his account." "Come then," he said, "let me have it now; and in fact the road up to town is well suited for telling and hearing as we go along."

So on we went, discoursing the while of this affair; and hence, as I began by saying, I have it pretty well by heart. So, friends, if you too must hear the whole story, I had better tell it. For my

PLATO

ὅταν μέν τινας περὶ φιλοσοφίας λόγους ἢ αὐτὸς ποιῶμαι ἢ ἄλλων ἀκούω, χωρὶς τοῦ οἴεσθαι ὠφελεῖσθαι ὑπερφυῶς ὡς χαίρω· ὅταν δὲ ἄλλους τινάς, ἄλλως τε καὶ τοὺς ὑμετέρους τοὺς τῶν πλουσίων καὶ χρηματιστικῶν, αὐτός τε ἄχθομαι ὑμᾶς τε τοὺς ἑταίρους ἐλεῶ, ὅτι οἴεσθε τὶ ποιεῖν οὐδὲν D ποιοῦντες. καὶ ἴσως αὖ ὑμεῖς ἐμὲ ἡγεῖσθε κακοδαίμονα εἶναι, καὶ οἴομαι ὑμᾶς ἀληθῆ οἴεσθαι· ἐγὼ μέντοι ὑμᾶς οὐκ οἴομαι ἀλλ' εὖ οἶδα.

ΕΤ. Ἀεὶ ὅμοιος εἶ, ὦ Ἀπολλόδωρε· ἀεὶ γὰρ σαυτόν τε κακηγορεῖς καὶ τοὺς ἄλλους, καὶ δοκεῖς μοι ἀτεχνῶς πάντας ἀθλίους ἡγεῖσθαι πλὴν Σωκράτους, ἀπὸ σαυτοῦ ἀρξάμενος. καὶ ὁπόθεν ποτὲ ταύτην τὴν ἐπωνυμίαν ἔλαβες τὸ μανικὸς καλεῖσθαι, οὐκ οἶδα ἔγωγε· ἐν μὲν γὰρ τοῖς λόγοις ἀεὶ τοιοῦτος εἶ· σαυτῷ τε καὶ τοῖς ἄλλοις ἀγριαίνεις πλὴν Σωκράτους.

E ΑΠ. Ὦ φίλτατε, καὶ δῆλόν γε δὴ ὅτι οὕτω διανοούμενος καὶ περὶ ἐμαυτοῦ καὶ περὶ ὑμῶν μαίνομαι καὶ παραπαίω;

ΕΤ. Οὐκ ἄξιον περὶ τούτων, Ἀπολλόδωρε, νῦν ἐρίζειν· ἀλλ' ὅπερ ἐδεόμεθά σου, μὴ ἄλλως ποιήσῃς, ἀλλὰ διήγησαι τίνες ἦσαν οἱ λόγοι.

ΑΠ. Ἦσαν τοίνυν ἐκεῖνοι τοιοίδε τινές· μᾶλλον 174 δ' ἐξ ἀρχῆς ὑμῖν ὡς ἐκεῖνος διηγεῖτο καὶ ἐγὼ πειράσομαι διηγήσασθαι.

---

[1] His companion means: "I expect you quite deserve your name of crazy fanatic (for your general absorption in

SYMPOSIUM

own part, indeed, I commonly find that, setting aside the benefit I conceive they do me, I take an immense delight in any philosophic discourses, whether I speak them myself or hear them from others: whereas in the case of other sorts of talk—especially that of your wealthy, money-bag friends—I am not only annoyed myself but sorry for dear intimates like you, who think you are doing a great deal when you really do nothing at all. From your point of view, I daresay, I seem a hapless creature, and I think your thought is true. I, however, do not think it of you: I know it for sure.

COMP. You are the same as ever, Apollodorus,—always defaming your self and every one else! Your view, I take it, is that all men alike are miserable, save Socrates, and that your own plight is the worst. How you may have come by your title of "crazy,"[1] I do not know: though, of course, you are always like that in your way of speech—raging against yourself and everybody except Socrates.

AP. My dear sir, obviously it must be a mere crazy aberration in me, to hold this opinion of myself and of you all!

COMP. It is waste of time, Apollodorus, to wrangle about such matters now. Come, without more ado, comply with our request and relate how the speeches went.

AP. Well then, they were somewhat as follows,—but stay, I must try and tell you all in order from the beginning, just as my friend told it to me.

philosophy), because your vehement censure of yourself and others suggests it to me."

PLATO

Ἔφη γὰρ οἱ Σωκράτη ἐντυχεῖν λελουμένον τε καὶ τὰς βλαύτας ὑποδεδεμένον, ἃ ἐκεῖνος ὀλιγάκις ἐποίει· καὶ ἐρέσθαι αὐτὸν ὅποι ἴοι οὕτω καλὸς γεγενημένος.

Καὶ τὸν εἰπεῖν ὅτι Ἐπὶ δεῖπνον εἰς Ἀγάθωνος. χθὲς γὰρ αὐτὸν διέφυγον τοῖς ἐπινικίοις, φοβηθεὶς τὸν ὄχλον· ὡμολόγησα δ' εἰς τήμερον παρέσεσθαι. ταῦτα δὴ ἐκαλλωπισάμην, ἵνα καλὸς παρὰ καλὸν ἴω. ἀλλὰ σύ, ἦ δ' ὅς, πῶς ἔχεις πρὸς τὸ ἐθέλειν ἂν ἰέναι ἄκλητος ἐπὶ δεῖπνον;

Κἀγώ, ἔφη, εἶπον ὅτι Οὕτως ὅπως ἂν σὺ κελεύῃς.

Ἕπου τοίνυν, ἔφη, ἵνα καὶ τὴν παροιμίαν διαφθείρωμεν μεταβάλλοντες, ὡς ἄρα καὶ "Ἀγάθων'[1] ἐπὶ δαῖτας ἴασιν αὐτόματοι ἀγαθοί." Ὅμηρος μὲν γὰρ κινδυνεύει οὐ μόνον διαφθεῖραι ἀλλὰ καὶ ὑβρίσαι εἰς ταύτην τὴν παροιμίαν· ποιήσας γὰρ τὸν Ἀγαμέμνονα διαφερόντως ἀγαθὸν ἄνδρα τὰ πολεμικά, τὸν δὲ Μενέλεων "μαλθακὸν αἰχμητήν," θυσίαν ποιουμένου καὶ ἑστιῶντος τοῦ Ἀγαμέμνονος ἄκλητον ἐποίησεν ἐλθόντα τὸν Μενέλεων ἐπὶ τὴν θοίνην, χείρω ὄντα ἐπὶ τὴν τοῦ ἀμείνονος.

Ταῦτ' ἀκούσας εἰπεῖν ἔφη Ἴσως μέντοι κινδυνεύσω καὶ ἐγὼ οὐχ ὡς σὺ λέγεις, ὦ Σώκρατες, ἀλλὰ καθ' Ὅμηρον φαῦλος ὢν ἐπὶ σοφοῦ ἀνδρὸς

[1] Ἀγάθων' Lachmann: ἀγαθῶν MSS.

---

[1] The name *Agathon* resembles the Greek for *good men's* in the proverb, which seems to have been: αὐτόματοι δ' ἀγαθοὶ ἀγαθῶν ἐπὶ δαῖτας ἴασι (Athen. i. 8 A: Bacchyl. *fr.* 33). The "corruption" consists in putting the dative Ἀγάθων(ι) for ἀγαθῶν; though perhaps the reference is to another form of the proverb which had δειλῶν (cravens') instead of ἀγαθῶν.

SYMPOSIUM

How Aristodemus fell in with Socrates and came to the Banquet

He said that he met with Socrates fresh from the bath and wearing his best pair of slippers—quite rare events with him—and asked him whither he was bound in such fine trim.

"To dinner at Agathon's," he answered. "I evaded him and his celebrations yesterday, fearing the crowd; but I agreed to be present to-day. So I got myself up in this handsome style in order to be a match for my handsome host. Now tell me," said he, "do you feel in the mood for going unasked to dinner?"

"For anything," he said he replied, "that you may bid me do."

"Come along then," he said; "let us corrupt the proverb with a new version:

> What if they go of their own accord,
> The good men to our Goodman's[1] board?

Though indeed Homer[2] may be said to have not merely corrupted the adage, but debauched it: for after setting forth Agamemnon as a man eminently good at warfare, and Menelaus as only 'a spearman spiritless,' he makes the latter come unbidden to the banquet of the former, who was offering sacrifice and holding a feast; so the worse man was the guest of the better."

To this my friend's answer, as he told me, was: "I am afraid mine, most likely, is a case that fits not your version, Socrates, but Homer's—a dolt coming unbidden to the banquet of a scholar. Be

[2] *Il.* xvii. 587 Μενέλαον ὑπετρέσας, ὃς τὸ πάρος γε μαλθακὸς αἰχμητής, and ii. 408 αὐτόματος δέ οἱ ἦλθε βοὴν ἀγαθὸς Μενέλαος.

ἰέναι θοίνην ἄκλητος. ὅρα οὖν ἄγων με τί[1] ἀπολογήσῃ, ὡς ἐγὼ μὲν οὐχ ὁμολογήσω ἄκλητος ἥκειν, ἀλλ' ὑπὸ σοῦ κεκλημένος.

"Σύν τε δύ'," ἔφη, "ἐρχομένω πρὸ ὁ τοῦ" βουλευσόμεθα ὅ τι ἐροῦμεν. ἀλλὰ ἴωμεν.

Τοιαῦτ' ἄττα σφᾶς ἔφη διαλεχθέντας ἰέναι. τὸν οὖν Σωκράτη ἑαυτῷ πως προσέχοντα τὸν νοῦν κατὰ τὴν ὁδὸν πορεύεσθαι ὑπολειπόμενον, καὶ περιμένοντος οὗ κελεύειν προϊέναι εἰς τὸ πρόσθεν. ἐπειδὴ δὲ γενέσθαι ἐπὶ τῇ οἰκίᾳ τῇ Ἀγάθωνος, ἀνεῳγμένην καταλαμβάνειν τὴν θύραν, καί τι ἔφη αὐτόθι γελοῖον παθεῖν. οἷ μὲν γὰρ εὐθὺς παῖδά τινα ἔνδοθεν ἀπαντήσαντα ἄγειν οὗ κατέκειντο οἱ ἄλλοι, καὶ καταλαμβάνειν ἤδη μέλλοντας δειπνεῖν· εὐθὺς δ' οὖν ὡς ἰδεῖν τὸν Ἀγάθωνα, Ὦ, φάναι, Ἀριστόδημε, εἰς καλὸν ἥκεις ὅπως συνδειπνήσῃς· εἰ δ' ἄλλου τινὸς ἕνεκα ἦλθες, εἰς αὖθις ἀναβαλοῦ, ὡς καὶ χθὲς ζητῶν σε ἵνα καλέσαιμι οὐχ οἷός τ' ἦ ἰδεῖν. ἀλλὰ Σωκράτη ἡμῖν πῶς οὐκ ἄγεις;

Καὶ ἐγώ, ἔφη, μεταστρεφόμενος οὐδαμοῦ ὁρῶ Σωκράτη ἑπόμενον· εἶπον οὖν ὅτι καὶ αὐτὸς μετὰ Σωκράτους ἥκοιμι, κληθεὶς ὑπ' ἐκείνου δεῦρ' ἐπὶ δεῖπνον.

Καλῶς γ', ἔφη, ποιῶν σύ· ἀλλὰ ποῦ ἔστιν οὗτος;

Ὄπισθεν ἐμοῦ ἄρτι εἰσῄει· ἀλλὰ θαυμάζω καὶ αὐτὸς ποῦ ἂν εἴη.

Οὐ σκέψῃ, ἔφη, παῖ, φάναι τὸν Ἀγάθωνα, καὶ

[1] ὅρα . . . τί Badham: ἄρα, ἄρα . . . τι, . . . τί MSS.

SYMPOSIUM

sure, then, to have your excuse quite ready when you bring me; for I shall not confess to coming unasked, but only on your invitation."

"'If two go along together,'" he remarked, "'there's one before another'[1] in devising what we are to say. Well, let's go."

After some such conversation, he told me, they started off. Then Socrates, becoming absorbed in his own thoughts by the way, fell behind him as they went; and when my friend began to wait for him he bade him go on ahead. So he came to Agathon's house, and found the door open; where he found himself in a rather ridiculous position. For he was met immediately by a servant from within, who took him where the company was reclining, and he found them just about to dine. However, as soon as Agathon saw him—"Ha, Aristodemus," he cried, "right welcome to a place at table with us! If you came on some other errand, put it off to another time: only yesterday I went round to invite you, but failed to see you. But how is it you do not bring us Socrates?"

At that I turned back for Socrates, he said, but saw no sign of him coming after me: so I told them how I myself had come along with Socrates, since he had asked me to dine with them.

"Very good of you to come," he said, "but where is the man?"

"He was coming in just now behind me: I am wondering myself where he can be."

"Go at once," said Agathon to the servant, "and

---

[1] *Cf. Il.* x. 224 σύν τε δύ' ἐρχομένω, καί τε πρὸ ὃ τοῦ ἐνόησεν ὅππως κέρδος ἔῃ, "if two go along together, there's one to espy before another how a profit may be had."

89

εἰσάξεις Σωκράτη; σὺ δ', ἦ δ' ὅς, Ἀριστόδημε, παρ' Ἐρυξίμαχον κατακλίνου.

Καὶ ἓ μὲν[1] ἔφη ἀπονίζειν τὸν παῖδα, ἵνα κατακέοιτο· ἄλλον δέ τινα τῶν παίδων ἥκειν ἀγγέλλοντα ὅτι Σωκράτης οὗτος ἀναχωρήσας ἐν τῷ τῶν γειτόνων προθύρῳ ἕστηκε καὶ οὗ καλοῦντος οὐκ ἐθέλει εἰσιέναι.

Ἄτοπόν γ', ἔφη, λέγεις· οὔκουν καλεῖς αὐτὸν καὶ μὴ ἀφήσεις;

Καὶ ὃς ἔφη εἰπεῖν Μηδαμῶς, ἀλλ' ἐᾶτε αὐτόν. ἔθος γάρ τι τοῦτ' ἔχει· ἐνίοτε ἀποστὰς ὅποι ἂν τύχῃ ἕστηκεν. ἥξει δὲ αὐτίκα, ὡς ἐγὼ οἶμαι. μὴ οὖν κινεῖτε, ἀλλ' ἐᾶτε.

Ἀλλ' οὕτω χρὴ ποιεῖν, εἰ σοὶ δοκεῖ, ἔφη φάναι τὸν Ἀγάθωνα. ἀλλ' ἡμᾶς, ὦ παῖδες, τοὺς ἄλλους ἑστιᾶτε. πάντως παρατίθετε ὅ τι ἂν βούλησθε, ἐπειδάν τις ὑμῖν μὴ ἐφεστήκῃ (ὃ ἐγὼ οὐδεπώποτε ἐποίησα)· νῦν οὖν, νομίζοντες καὶ ἐμὲ ὑφ' ὑμῶν κεκλῆσθαι ἐπὶ δεῖπνον καὶ τούσδε τοὺς ἄλλους, θεραπεύετε, ἵνα ὑμᾶς ἐπαινῶμεν.

Μετὰ ταῦτα ἔφη σφᾶς μὲν δειπνεῖν, τὸν δὲ Σωκράτη οὐκ εἰσιέναι. τὸν οὖν Ἀγάθωνα πολλάκις κελεύειν μεταπέμψασθαι τὸν Σωκράτη, ἓ δὲ οὐκ ἐᾶν. ἥκειν οὖν αὐτὸν οὐ πολὺν χρόνον, ὡς εἰώθει, διατρίψαντα, ἀλλὰ μάλιστα σφᾶς μεσοῦν δειπνοῦντας. τὸν οὖν Ἀγάθωνα, τυγχάνειν γὰρ ἔσχατον κατακείμενον μόνον, Δεῦρ', ἔφη φάναι, Σώκρατες, παρ' ἐμὲ κατάκεισο, ἵνα καὶ τοῦ σοφοῦ ἁπτόμενός σου ἀπολαύσω, ὅ σοι προσέστη ἐν τοῖς

---

[1] ἓ μὲν Bast: ἐμὲ MSS.

SYMPOSIUM

see if you can fetch in Socrates. You, Aristodemus, take a place by Eryximachus."

So the attendant washed him and made him ready for reclining, when another of the servants came in with the news that our good Socrates had retreated into their neighbours' porch; there he was standing, and when bidden to come in, he refused.

"How strange!" said Agathon, "you must go on bidding him, and by no means let him go."

But this Aristodemus forbade: "No," said he, "let him alone; it is a habit he has. Occasionally he turns aside, anywhere at random, and there he stands. He will be here presently, I expect. So do not disturb him; let him be."

"Very well then," said Agathon, "as you judge best. Come, boys," he called to the servants, "serve the feast for the rest of us. You are to set on just whatever you please, when you find no one to direct you (this method I have never tried before).[1] To-day you are to imagine that I and all the company here have come on your invitation: so look after us, and earn our compliments."

Thereupon, he said, they all began dinner, but Socrates did not arrive; and though Agathon ever and anon gave orders that they should go and fetch him, my friend would not allow it. When he did come, it was after what, for him, was no great delay, as they were only about half-way through dinner. Then Agathon, who happened to be sitting alone in the lowest place, said: "Here, Socrates, come sit by me, so that by contact with you I may have some benefit from that piece of wisdom that occurred to you there in the porch. Clearly you have made

[1] This clause is probably an "aside" to his guests.

προθύροις. δῆλον γὰρ ὅτι ηὗρες αὐτὸ καὶ ἔχεις· οὐ γὰρ ἂν προαπέστης.

Καὶ τὸν Σωκράτη καθίζεσθαι καὶ εἰπεῖν ὅτι Εὖ ἂν ἔχοι, φάναι, ὦ Ἀγάθων, εἰ τοιοῦτον εἴη ἡ σοφία, ὥστ᾽ ἐκ τοῦ πληρεστέρου εἰς τὸν κενώτερον ῥεῖν ἡμῶν, ἐὰν ἁπτώμεθα ἀλλήλων, ὥσπερ τὸ ἐν ταῖς κύλιξιν ὕδωρ τὸ διὰ τοῦ ἐρίου ῥέον ἐκ τῆς πληρεστέρας εἰς τὴν κενωτέραν. εἰ γὰρ οὕτως ἔχει καὶ ἡ σοφία, πολλοῦ τιμῶμαι τὴν παρὰ σοὶ Ε κατάκλισιν· οἶμαι γάρ με παρὰ σοῦ πολλῆς καὶ καλῆς σοφίας πληρωθήσεσθαι. ἡ μὲν γὰρ ἐμὴ φαύλη τις ἂν εἴη καὶ ἀμφισβητήσιμος, ὥσπερ ὄναρ οὖσα, ἡ δὲ σὴ λαμπρά τε καὶ πολλὴν ἐπίδοσιν ἔχουσα, ἥ γε παρὰ σοῦ νέου ὄντος οὕτω σφόδρα ἐξέλαμψε καὶ ἐκφανὴς ἐγένετο πρῴην ἐν μάρτυσι τῶν Ἑλλήνων πλέον ἢ τρισμυρίοις.

Ὑβριστὴς εἶ, ἔφη, ὦ Σώκρατες, ὁ Ἀγάθων. καὶ ταῦτα μὲν καὶ ὀλίγον ὕστερον διαδικασόμεθα ἐγώ τε καὶ σὺ περὶ τῆς σοφίας, δικαστῇ χρώμενοι τῷ Διονύσῳ· νῦν δὲ πρὸς τὸ δεῖπνον πρῶτα τρέπου.

176 Μετὰ ταῦτα, ἔφη, κατακλινέντος τοῦ Σωκράτους καὶ δειπνήσαντος καὶ τῶν ἄλλων, σπονδάς τε σφᾶς ποιήσασθαι καὶ ᾄσαντας τὸν θεὸν καὶ τἆλλα τὰ νομιζόμενα τρέπεσθαι πρὸς τὸν πότον· τὸν οὖν Παυσανίαν ἔφη λόγου τοιούτου τινὸς κατάρχειν. Εἶεν, ἄνδρες, φάναι, τίνα τρόπον ῥᾷστα πιόμεθα; ἐγὼ μὲν οὖν λέγω ὑμῖν, ὅτι τῷ ὄντι πάνυ χαλεπῶς ἔχω ὑπὸ τοῦ χθὲς πότου καὶ δέομαι ἀναψυχῆς τινος, οἶμαι δὲ καὶ ὑμῶν τοὺς πολλούς· παρῆστε γὰρ χθές· σκοπεῖσθε οὖν, τίνι Β τρόπῳ ἂν ὡς ῥᾷστα πίνοιμεν.

Τὸν οὖν Ἀριστοφάνη εἰπεῖν, Τοῦτο μέντοι εὖ

SYMPOSIUM

the discovery and got hold of it; for you would not have come away before."

Then Socrates sat down, and—" How fine it would be, Agathon," he said, " if wisdom were a sort of thing that could flow out of the one of us who is fuller into him who is emptier, by our mere contact with each other, as water will flow through wool from the fuller cup into the emptier. If such is indeed the case with wisdom, I set a great value on my sitting next to you: I look to be filled with excellent wisdom drawn in abundance out of you. My own is but meagre, as disputable as a dream; but yours is bright and expansive, as the other day we saw it shining forth from your youth, strong and splendid, in the eyes of more than thirty thousand Greeks."

" You rude mocker, Socrates!" said Agathon. " A little later on you and I shall go to law on this matter of our wisdom, and Dionysus shall be our judge. For the present, let the dinner be your first concern."

After this, it seems, when Socrates had taken his place and had dined with the rest, they made libation and sang a chant to the god and so forth, as custom bids, till they betook them to drinking. Then Pausanias opened a conversation after this manner: " Well, gentlemen, what mode of drinking will suit us best? For my part, to tell the truth, I am in very poor form as a result of yesterday's bout, and I claim a little relief; it is so, I believe, with most of you, for you were at yesterday's party: so consider what method of drinking would suit us best."

On this Aristophanes observed: " Now that,

λέγεις, ὦ Παυσανία, τὸ παντὶ τρόπῳ παρασκευάσασθαι ῥᾳστώνην τινὰ τῆς πόσεως· καὶ γὰρ αὐτός εἰμι τῶν χθὲς βεβαπτισμένων.

Ἀκούσαντα οὖν αὐτῶν ἔφη Ἐρυξίμαχον τὸν Ἀκουμενοῦ, Ἦ καλῶς, φάναι, λέγετε. καὶ ἔτι ἑνὸς δέομαι ὑμῶν ἀκοῦσαι, πῶς ἔχει πρὸς τὸ ἐρρῶσθαι πίνειν Ἀγάθων.

Οὐδαμῶς, φάναι, οὐδ' αὐτὸς ἔρρωμαι.

C Ἕρμαιον ἂν εἴη ἡμῖν, ᾗ δ' ὅς, ὡς ἔοικεν, ἐμοί τε καὶ Ἀριστοδήμῳ καὶ Φαίδρῳ καὶ τοῖσδε, εἰ ὑμεῖς οἱ δυνατώτατοι πίνειν νῦν ἀπειρήκατε· ἡμεῖς μὲν γὰρ ἀεὶ ἀδύνατοι. Σωκράτη δ' ἐξαιρῶ λόγου· ἱκανὸς γὰρ καὶ ἀμφότερα, ὥστ' ἐξαρκέσει αὐτῷ ὁπότερ' ἂν ποιῶμεν. ἐπειδὴ οὖν μοι δοκεῖ οὐδεὶς τῶν παρόντων προθύμως ἔχειν πρὸς τὸ πολὺν πίνειν οἶνον, ἴσως ἂν ἐγὼ περὶ τοῦ μεθύσκεσθαι οἷόν ἐστι τἀληθῆ λέγων ἧττον ἂν εἴην ἀηδής. ἐμοὶ γὰρ δὴ τοῦτό γε οἶμαι κατάδηλον
D γεγονέναι ἐκ τῆς ἰατρικῆς, ὅτι χαλεπὸν τοῖς ἀνθρώποις ἡ μέθη ἐστί· καὶ οὔτε αὐτὸς ἑκὼν εἶναι πόρρω ἐθελήσαιμι ἂν πιεῖν οὔτε ἄλλῳ συμβουλεύσαιμι, ἄλλως τε καὶ κραιπαλῶντα ἔτι ἐκ τῆς προτεραίας.

Ἀλλὰ μήν, ἔφη φάναι ὑπολαβόντα Φαῖδρον τὸν Μυρρινούσιον, ἔγωγέ σοι εἴωθα πείθεσθαι ἄλλως τε καὶ ἅττ' ἂν περὶ ἰατρικῆς λέγῃς· νῦν δ', ἂν εὖ βουλεύωνται, καὶ οἱ λοιποί. ταῦτα δὴ ἀκούσαν-
E τας συγχωρεῖν πάντας μὴ διὰ μέθης ποιήσασθαι τὴν ἐν τῷ παρόντι συνουσίαν, ἀλλ' οὕτω πίνοντας πρὸς ἡδονήν.

SYMPOSIUM

Pausanias, is a good suggestion of yours, that we make a point of consulting our comfort in our cups: for I myself am one of those who got such a soaking yesterday."

When Eryximachus, son of Acumenus, heard this; "You are quite right, sirs," he said; "and there is yet one other question on which I request your opinion, as to what sort of condition Agathon finds himself in for drinking."

"No, no," said Agathon, "I am not in good condition for it either."

"It would be a piece of luck for us, I take it," the other went on, "that is, for me, Aristodemus, Phaedrus, and our friends here, if you who are the stoutest drinkers are now feeling exhausted. We, of course, are known weaklings. Socrates I do not count in the matter: he is fit either way, and will be content with whichever choice we make. Now as it appears that nobody here present is eager for copious draughts, perhaps it will be the less irksome to you if I speak of intoxication, and tell you truly what it is. The practice of medicine, I find, has made this clear to me—that drunkenness is harmful to mankind; and neither would I myself agree, if I could help it, to an excess of drinking, nor would I recommend it to another, especially when his head is still heavy from a bout of the day before."

Here Phaedrus of Myrrhinus intervened with these words: "Why, you know I always obey you, above all in medical matters; and so now will the rest of us, if they are well advised." Then all of them, on hearing this, consented not to make their present meeting a tipsy affair, but to drink just as it might serve their pleasure.

Ἐπειδὴ τοίνυν, φάναι τὸν Ἐρυξίμαχον, τοῦτο μὲν δέδοκται, πίνειν ὅσον ἂν ἕκαστος βούληται, ἐπάναγκες δὲ μηδὲν εἶναι, τὸ μετὰ τοῦτο εἰσηγοῦμαι τὴν μὲν ἄρτι εἰσελθοῦσαν αὐλητρίδα χαίρειν ἐᾶν, αὐλοῦσαν ἑαυτῇ ἢ ἂν βούληται ταῖς γυναιξὶ ταῖς ἔνδον, ἡμᾶς δὲ διὰ λόγων ἀλλήλοις συνεῖναι τὸ τήμερον· καὶ δι' οἵων λόγων, εἰ βούλεσθε, ἐθέλω ὑμῖν εἰσηγήσασθαι.

Φάναι δὴ πάντας καὶ βούλεσθαι, καὶ κελεύειν αὐτὸν εἰσηγεῖσθαι. εἰπεῖν οὖν τὸν Ἐρυξίμαχον ὅτι Ἡ μέν μοι ἀρχὴ τοῦ λόγου ἐστὶ κατὰ τὴν Εὐριπίδου Μελανίππην· οὐ γὰρ ἐμὸς ὁ μῦθος, ἀλλὰ Φαίδρου τοῦδε, ὃν μέλλω λέγειν. Φαῖδρος γὰρ ἑκάστοτε πρός με ἀγανακτῶν λέγει Οὐ δεινόν, φησίν, ὦ Ἐρυξίμαχε, ἄλλοις μέν τισι θεῶν ὕμνους καὶ παιῶνας εἶναι ὑπὸ τῶν ποιητῶν πεποιημένους, τῷ δὲ Ἔρωτι, τηλικούτῳ ὄντι καὶ τοσούτῳ θεῷ, μηδὲ ἕνα πώποτε τοσούτων γεγονότων ποιητῶν πεποιηκέναι μηδὲν ἐγκώμιον· εἰ δὲ βούλει αὖ σκέψασθαι τοὺς χρηστοὺς σοφιστάς, Ἡρακλέους μὲν καὶ ἄλλων ἐπαίνους καταλογάδην συγγράφειν, ὥσπερ ὁ βέλτιστος Πρόδικος· καὶ τοῦτο μὲν ἧττον καὶ θαυμαστόν, ἀλλ' ἔγωγε ἤδη τινὶ ἐνέτυχον βιβλίῳ, ἐν ᾧ ἐνῆσαν ἅλες ἔπαινον θαυμάσιον ἔχοντες πρὸς ὠφέλειαν, καὶ ἄλλα τοιαῦτα συχνὰ ἴδοις ἂν ἐγκεκωμιασμένα· τὸ οὖν τοιούτων μὲν πέρι πολλὴν σπουδὴν ποιήσασθαι, Ἔρωτα δὲ μηδένα πω ἀνθρώπων τετολμηκέναι εἰς ταυτηνὶ

---

[1] Eurip. *fr.* 488 οὐκ ἐμὸς ὁ μῦθος, ἀλλ' ἐμῆς μητρὸς πάρα, "not mine the tale; my mother taught it me."
[2] The moralizing sophist, famous for his parable of *The*

SYMPOSIUM

"Since it has been resolved, then," said Eryximachus, "that we are to drink only so much as each desires, with no constraint on any, I next propose that the flute-girl who came in just now be dismissed: let her pipe to herself or, if she likes, to the women-folk within, but let us seek our entertainment to-day in conversation. I am ready, if you so desire, to suggest what sort of discussion it should be."

Eryximachus proposes the Theme of Love

They all said they did so desire, and bade him make his proposal. So Eryximachus proceeded: "The beginning of what I have to say is in the words of Euripides' Melanippe, for 'not mine the tale'[1] that I intend to tell; it comes from Phaedrus here. He is constantly complaining to me and saying,— Is it not a curious thing, Eryximachus, that while other gods have hymns and psalms indited in their honour by the poets, the god of Love, so ancient and so great, has had no song of praise composed for him by a single one of all the many poets that ever have been? And again, pray consider our worthy professors, and the eulogies they frame of Hercules and others in prose,—for example, the excellent Prodicus.[2] This indeed is not so surprising; but I recollect coming across a book by somebody, in which I found Salt superbly lauded for its usefulness, and many more such matters I could show you celebrated there. To think of all this bustle about such trifles, and not a single man ever essaying till this day to make a fitting hymn

Choice of Heracles (Xen. *Mem.* ii. 1. 21), where the appeal of Virtue prevails over that of Vice.

τὴν ἡμέραν ἀξίως ὑμνῆσαι· ἀλλ' οὕτως ἠμέληται τοσοῦτος θεός. ταῦτα δή μοι δοκεῖ εὖ λέγειν Φαῖδρος. ἐγὼ οὖν ἐπιθυμῶ ἅμα μὲν τούτῳ ἔρανον εἰσενεγκεῖν καὶ χαρίσασθαι, ἅμα δ' ἐν τῷ παρόντι πρέπον μοι δοκεῖ εἶναι ἡμῖν τοῖς παροῦσι κοσμῆσαι τὸν θεόν. εἰ οὖν συνδοκεῖ καὶ ὑμῖν, γένοιτ' ἂν ἡμῖν ἐν λόγοις ἱκανὴ διατριβή· δοκεῖ γάρ μοι χρῆναι ἕκαστον ἡμῶν λόγον εἰπεῖν ἔπαινον Ἔρωτος ἐπὶ δεξιὰ ὡς ἂν δύνηται κάλλιστον, ἄρχειν δὲ Φαῖδρον πρῶτον, ἐπειδὴ καὶ πρῶτος κατάκειται καὶ ἔστιν ἅμα πατὴρ τοῦ λόγου.

Οὐδείς σοι, ὦ Ἐρυξίμαχε, φάναι τὸν Σωκράτη, ἐναντία ψηφιεῖται. οὔτε γὰρ ἄν που ἐγὼ ἀποφήσαιμι, ὃς οὐδέν φημι ἄλλο ἐπίστασθαι ἢ τὰ ἐρωτικά, οὔτε που Ἀγάθων καὶ Παυσανίας, οὐδὲ μὴν Ἀριστοφάνης, ᾧ περὶ Διόνυσον καὶ Ἀφροδίτην πᾶσα ἡ διατριβή, οὐδὲ ἄλλος οὐδεὶς τουτωνὶ ὧν ἐγὼ ὁρῶ. καίτοι οὐκ ἐξ ἴσου γίγνεται ἡμῖν τοῖς ὑστάτοις κατακειμένοις· ἀλλ' ἐὰν οἱ πρόσθεν ἱκανῶς καὶ καλῶς εἴπωσιν, ἐξαρκέσει ἡμῖν. ἀλλὰ τύχῃ ἀγαθῇ καταρχέτω Φαῖδρος καὶ ἐγκωμιαζέτω τὸν Ἔρωτα.

Ταῦτα δὴ καὶ οἱ ἄλλοι πάντες ἄρα συνέφασάν τε καὶ ἐκέλευον ἅπερ ὁ Σωκράτης. πάντων μὲν οὖν ἃ ἕκαστος εἶπεν, οὔτε πάνυ ὁ Ἀριστόδημος ἐμέμνητο οὔτ' αὖ ἐγὼ ἃ ἐκεῖνος ἔλεγε πάντα· ἃ δὲ μάλιστα καὶ ὧν ἔδοξέ μοι ἀξιομνημόνευτον, τούτων ὑμῖν ἐρῶ ἑκάστου τὸν λόγον.

Πρῶτον μὲν γάρ, ὥσπερ λέγω, ἔφη Φαῖδρον ἀρξάμενον ἐνθένδε ποθὲν λέγειν, ὅτι μέγας θεὸς

to Love! So great a god, and so neglected! Now I think Phaedrus's protest a very proper one. Accordingly I am not only desirous of obliging him with a contribution of my own, but I also pronounce the present to be a fitting occasion for us here assembled to honour the god. So if you on your part approve, we might pass the time well enough in discourses; for my opinion is that we ought each of us to make a speech in turn, from left to right, praising Love as beautifully as he can. Phaedrus shall open first; for he has the topmost place at table, and besides is father of our debate."

"No one, Eryximachus," said Socrates, "will vote against you: I do not see how I could myself decline, when I set up to understand nothing but love-matters; nor could Agathon and Pausanias either, nor yet Aristophanes, who divides his time between Dionysus and Aphrodite; nor could any other of the persons I see before me. To be sure, we who sit at the bottom do not get a fair chance: but if the earlier speakers rise nobly to the occasion, we shall be quite content. So now let Phaedrus, with our best wishes, make a beginning and give us a eulogy of Love."

To this they assented one and all, bidding him do as Socrates said. Now the entire speech in each case was beyond Aristodemus's recollection, and so too the whole of what he told me is beyond mine: but those parts which, on account also of the speakers, I deemed most memorable, I will tell you successively as they were delivered.

The Speech of Phaedrus

First then, as I said, he told me that the speech of Phaedrus began with points of this sort—that

PLATO

εἴη ὁ Ἔρως καὶ θαυμαστὸς ἐν ἀνθρώποις τε καὶ
θεοῖς, πολλαχῇ μὲν καὶ ἄλλῃ, οὐχ ἥκιστα δὲ
B κατὰ τὴν γένεσιν. τὸ γὰρ ἐν τοῖς πρεσβύτατον
εἶναι τὸν θεὸν τίμιον, ᾗ δ' ὅς· τεκμήριον δὲ τού-
του· γονῆς γὰρ Ἔρωτος οὔτ' εἰσὶν οὔτε λέγονται
ὑπ' οὐδενὸς οὔτε ἰδιώτου οὔτε ποιητοῦ, ἀλλ'
Ἡσίοδος πρῶτον μὲν χάος φησὶ γενέσθαι,

αὐτὰρ ἔπειτα
Γαῖ' εὐρύστερνος, πάντων ἕδος ἀσφαλὲς αἰεί,
ἠδ' Ἔρος.

Ἡσιόδῳ δὲ καὶ Ἀκουσίλεως ὁμολογεῖ.[1] φησὶ μετὰ
τὸ χάος δύο τούτω γενέσθαι, Γῆν τε καὶ Ἔρωτα.
Παρμενίδης δὲ τὴν Γένεσιν λέγει

πρώτιστον μὲν Ἔρωτα θεῶν μητίσατο πάντων.

C Οὕτω πολλαχόθεν ὁμολογεῖται ὁ Ἔρως ἐν τοῖς
πρεσβύτατος εἶναι. πρεσβύτατος δὲ ὢν μεγίστων ἀγαθῶν ἡμῖν αἴτιός ἐστιν. οὐ γὰρ ἔγωγ'
ἔχω εἰπεῖν ὅ τι μεῖζόν ἐστιν ἀγαθὸν εὐθὺς νέῳ
ὄντι ἢ ἐραστὴς χρηστὸς καὶ ἐραστῇ παιδικά. ὃ
γὰρ χρὴ ἀνθρώποις ἡγεῖσθαι παντὸς τοῦ βίου τοῖς
μέλλουσι καλῶς βιώσεσθαι, τοῦτο οὔτε συγγένεια
οἷά τε ἐμποιεῖν οὕτω καλῶς οὔτε τιμαὶ οὔτε πλοῦ-
D τος οὔτ' ἄλλο οὐδὲν ὡς ἔρως. λέγω δὲ δὴ τί
τοῦτο; τὴν ἐπὶ μὲν τοῖς αἰσχροῖς αἰσχύνην, ἐπὶ
δὲ τοῖς καλοῖς φιλοτιμίαν· οὐ γὰρ ἔστιν ἄνευ τούτων οὔτε πόλιν οὔτε ἰδιώτην μεγάλα καὶ καλὰ
ἔργα ἐξεργάζεσθαι. φημὶ τοίνυν ἐγὼ ἄνδρα ὅστις
ἐρᾷ, εἴ τι αἰσχρὸν ποιῶν κατάδηλος γίγνοιτο ἢ

---

[1] Ἡσιόδῳ . . . ὁμολογεῖ (post πάντων) huc transp. Schanz.

SYMPOSIUM

Love was a great god, among men and gods a marvel; and this appeared in many ways, but notably in his birth. " Of the most venerable are the honours of this god, and the proof of it is this : parents of Love there are none, nor are any recorded in either prose or verse. Hesiod says that Chaos came first into being—

> and thereafter rose
> Broad-breasted Earth, sure seat of all for aye,
> And Love.[1]

Acusilaus[2] also agrees with Hesiod, saying that after Chaos were born these two, Earth and Love. Parmenides says of Birth that she 'invented Love before all other gods.'[3]

" Thus Love is by various authorities allowed to be of most venerable standing ; and as most venerable, he is the cause of all our highest blessings. I for my part am at a loss to say what greater blessing a man can have in earliest youth than an honourable lover, or a lover than an honourable favourite. For the guiding principle we should choose for all our days, if we are minded to live a comely life, cannot be acquired either by kinship or office or wealth or anything so well as by Love. What shall I call this power ? The shame that we feel for shameful things, and ambition for what is noble ; without which it is impossible for city or person to perform any high and noble deeds. Let me then say that a man in love, should he be detected in some shameful act or in a cowardly submission to shameful treat-

[1] Hesiod, *Theog.* 116 foll.
[2] An Argive compiler of genealogies in the first part of the fifth century B.C.
[3] Parmen. *fr.* 132 ; Aristot. *Met.* i. 4, 984 b.

πάσχων ὑπό του δι᾽ ἀνανδρίαν μὴ ἀμυνόμενος, οὔτ᾽ ἂν ὑπὸ πατρὸς ὀφθέντα οὕτως ἀλγῆσαι οὔτε ὑπὸ ἑταίρων οὔτε ὑπ᾽ ἄλλου οὐδενὸς ὡς ὑπὸ παιδικῶν. Ε ταὐτὸν δὲ τοῦτο καὶ τὸν ἐρώμενον ὁρῶμεν, ὅτι διαφερόντως τοὺς ἐραστὰς αἰσχύνεται, ὅταν ὀφθῇ ἐν αἰσχρῷ τινὶ ὤν. εἰ οὖν μηχανή τις γένοιτο ὥστε πόλιν γενέσθαι ἢ στρατόπεδον ἐραστῶν τε καὶ παιδικῶν, οὐκ ἔστιν ὅπως ἂν ἄμεινον οἰκήσειαν τὴν ἑαυτῶν ἢ ἀπεχόμενοι πάντων τῶν αἰ-
179 σχρῶν καὶ φιλοτιμούμενοι πρὸς ἀλλήλους· καὶ μαχόμενοί γ᾽ ἂν μετ᾽ ἀλλήλων οἱ τοιοῦτοι νικῷεν ἂν ὀλίγοι ὄντες, ὡς ἔπος εἰπεῖν, πάντας ἀνθρώπους. ἐρῶν γὰρ ἀνὴρ ὑπὸ παιδικῶν ὀφθῆναι ἢ λιπὼν τάξιν ἢ ὅπλα ἀποβαλὼν ἧττον ἂν δήπου δέξαιτο ἢ ὑπὸ πάντων τῶν ἄλλων, καὶ πρὸ τούτου τεθνάναι ἂν πολλάκις ἕλοιτο· καὶ μὴν ἐγκαταλιπεῖν γε τὰ παιδικὰ ἢ μὴ βοηθῆσαι κινδυνεύοντι, οὐδεὶς οὕτω κακὸς ὅντινα οὐκ ἂν αὐτὸς ὁ Ἔρως ἔνθεον ποιήσειε πρὸς ἀρετήν, ὥσθ᾽ ὅμοιον εἶναι τῷ ἀρί-
Β στῳ φύσει. καὶ ἀτεχνῶς, ὃ ἔφη Ὅμηρος, "μένος ἐμπνεῦσαι" ἐνίοις τῶν ἡρώων τὸν θεόν, τοῦτο ὁ Ἔρως τοῖς ἐρῶσι παρέχει γιγνόμενον παρ᾽ αὐτοῦ.

Καὶ μὴν ὑπεραποθνῄσκειν γε μόνοι ἐθέλουσιν οἱ ἐρῶντες, οὐ μόνον ὅτι ἄνδρες, ἀλλὰ καὶ αἱ γυναῖκες. τούτου δὲ καὶ ἡ Πελίου θυγάτηρ Ἄλκηστις ἱκανὴν μαρτυρίαν παρέχεται ὑπὲρ τοῦδε τοῦ λόγου εἰς τοὺς Ἕλληνας, ἐθελήσασα μόνη ὑπὲρ τοῦ αὑτῆς ἀνδρὸς ἀποθανεῖν, ὄντων αὐτῷ

SYMPOSIUM

ment at another's hands, would not feel half so much distress at anyone observing it, whether father or comrade or anyone in the world, as when his favourite did; and in the selfsame way we see how the beloved is especially ashamed before his lovers when he is observed to be about some shameful business. So that if we could somewise contrive to have a city or an army composed of lovers and their favourites,[1] they could not be better citizens of their country than by thus refraining from all that is base in a mutual rivalry for honour; and such men as these, when fighting side by side, one might almost consider able to make even a little band victorious over all the world. For a man in love would surely choose to have all the rest of the host rather than his favourite see him forsaking his station or flinging away his arms; sooner than this, he would prefer to die many deaths: while, as for leaving his favourite in the lurch, or not succouring him in his peril, no man is such a craven that Love's own influence cannot inspire him with a valour that makes him equal to the bravest born; and without doubt what Homer calls a 'fury inspired'[2] by a god in certain heroes is the effect produced on lovers by Love's peculiar power.

"Furthermore, only such as are in love will consent to die for others; not merely men will do it, but women too. Sufficient witness is borne to this statement before the people of Greece by Alcestis, daughter of Pelias, who alone was willing to die for her husband, though he had both father

---

[1] There was such a "sacred band" (ἱερὸς λόχος) at Thebes, which distinguished itself at Leuctra (371 B.C.).
[2] Homer, *Il.* x. 482, xv. 262.

πατρός τε καὶ μητρός· οὓς ἐκείνη τοσοῦτον ὑπερεβάλετο τῇ φιλίᾳ διὰ τὸν ἔρωτα, ὥστε ἀποδεῖξαι αὐτοὺς ἀλλοτρίους ὄντας τῷ υἱεῖ καὶ ὀνόματι μόνον προσήκοντας· καὶ τοῦτ' ἐργασαμένη τὸ ἔργον οὕτω καλὸν ἔδοξεν ἐργάσασθαι οὐ μόνον ἀνθρώποις ἀλλὰ καὶ θεοῖς, ὥστε πολλῶν πολλὰ καὶ καλὰ ἐργασαμένων εὐαριθμήτοις δή τισιν ἔδοσαν τοῦτο γέρας οἱ θεοί, ἐξ Ἅιδου ἀνεῖναι πάλιν τὴν ψυχήν, ἀλλὰ τὴν ἐκείνης ἀνεῖσαν ἀγασθέντες τῷ ἔργῳ· οὕτω καὶ θεοὶ τὴν περὶ τὸν ἔρωτα σπουδήν τε καὶ ἀρετὴν μάλιστα τιμῶσιν. Ὀρφέα δὲ τὸν Οἰάγρου ἀτελῆ ἀπέπεμψαν ἐξ Ἅιδου, φάσμα δείξαντες τῆς γυναικὸς ἐφ' ἣν ἧκεν, αὐτὴν δὲ οὐ δόντες, ὅτι μαλθακίζεσθαι ἐδόκει, ἅτε ὢν κιθαρῳδός, καὶ οὐ τολμᾶν ἕνεκα τοῦ ἔρωτος ἀποθνῄσκειν ὥσπερ Ἄλκηστις, ἀλλὰ διαμηχανᾶσθαι ζῶν εἰσιέναι εἰς Ἅιδου. τοιγάρτοι διὰ ταῦτα δίκην αὐτῷ ἐπέθεσαν, καὶ ἐποίησαν τὸν θάνατον αὐτοῦ ὑπὸ γυναικῶν γενέσθαι, οὐχ ὥσπερ Ἀχιλλέα τὸν τῆς Θέτιδος υἱὸν ἐτίμησαν καὶ εἰς μακάρων νήσους ἀπέπεμψαν, ὅτι πεπυσμένος παρὰ τῆς μητρὸς ὡς ἀποθανοῖτο ἀποκτείνας Ἕκτορα, μὴ ἀποκτείνας δὲ τοῦτον οἴκαδ' ἐλθὼν γηραιὸς τελευτήσοι, ἐτόλμησεν ἑλέσθαι βοηθήσας τῷ ἐραστῇ Πατρόκλῳ καὶ τιμωρήσας οὐ μόνον ὑπεραποθανεῖν ἀλλὰ καὶ ἐπαποθανεῖν τετελευτηκότι· ὅθεν δὴ καὶ ὑπεραγασθέντες οἱ θεοὶ διαφερόντως αὐτὸν ἐτίμησαν, ὅτι τὸν ἐραστὴν οὕτω περὶ πολλοῦ ἐποιεῖτο. Αἰ-

and mother. So high did her love exalt her over them in kindness, that they were proved alien to their son and but nominal relations; and when she achieved this deed, it was judged so noble by gods as well as men that, although among all the many doers of noble deeds they are few and soon counted to whom the gods have granted the privilege of having their souls sent up again from Hades, hers they thus restored in admiration of her act. In this manner even the gods give special honour to zeal and courage in concerns of love. But Orpheus, son of Oeagrus, they sent back with failure from Hades, showing him only a wraith of the woman for whom he came; her real self they would not bestow, for he was accounted to have gone upon a coward's quest, too like the minstrel that he was, and to have lacked the spirit to die as Alcestis did for the sake of love, when he contrived the means of entering Hades alive. Wherefore they laid upon him the penalty he deserved, and caused him to meet his death at the hands of women: whereas Achilles, son of Thetis, they honoured and sent to his place in the Isles of the Blest,[1] because having learnt from his mother that he would die as surely as he slew Hector,[2] but if he slew him not, would return home and end his days an aged man, he bravely chose to go and rescue his lover Patroclus, avenged him, and sought death not merely in his behalf but in haste to be joined with him whom death had taken. For this the gods so highly admired him that they gave him distinguished honour, since he set so great a value on his lover.

---

[1] Pindar, *Ol.* ii. 78 foll. (Homer, *Od.* xi. 467 foll., places him in Hades). [2] Homer, *Il.* xviii. 96.

PLATO

σχύλος δὲ φλυαρεῖ φάσκων Ἀχιλλέα Πατρόκλου ἐρᾶν, ὃς ἦν καλλίων οὐ μόνον Πατρόκλου ἀλλὰ καὶ τῶν ἡρώων ἁπάντων, καὶ ἔτι ἀγένειος, ἔπειτα νεώτερος πολύ, ὥς φησιν Ὅμηρος. ἀλλὰ γὰρ τῷ ὄντι μάλιστα μὲν ταύτην τὴν ἀρετὴν οἱ θεοὶ τιμῶσι τὴν περὶ τὸν ἔρωτα, μᾶλλον μέντοι θαυμάζουσι καὶ ἄγανται καὶ εὖ ποιοῦσιν, ὅταν ὁ ἐρώμενος τὸν ἐραστὴν ἀγαπᾷ, ἢ ὅταν ὁ ἐραστὴς τὰ παιδικά. θειότερον γὰρ ἐραστὴς παιδικῶν· ἔνθεος γάρ ἐστι. διὰ ταῦτα καὶ τὸν Ἀχιλλέα τῆς Ἀλκήστιδος μᾶλλον ἐτίμησαν, εἰς μακάρων νήσους ἀποπέμψαντες.

Οὕτω δὴ ἔγωγέ φημι· Ἔρωτα θεῶν καὶ πρεσβύτατον καὶ τιμιώτατον καὶ κυριώτατον εἶναι εἰς ἀρετῆς καὶ εὐδαιμονίας κτῆσιν ἀνθρώποις καὶ ζῶσι καὶ τελευτήσασιν.

Φαῖδρον μὲν τοιοῦτόν τινα λόγον ἔφη εἰπεῖν, μετὰ δὲ Φαῖδρον ἄλλους τινὰς εἶναι, ὧν οὐ πάνυ διεμνημόνευεν· οὓς παρεὶς τὸν Παυσανίου λόγον διηγεῖτο. εἰπεῖν δ' αὐτὸν ὅτι Οὐ καλῶς μοι δοκεῖ, ὦ Φαῖδρε, προβεβλῆσθαι ἡμῖν ὁ λόγος, τὸ ἁπλῶς οὕτως παρηγγέλθαι ἐγκωμιάζειν Ἔρωτα. εἰ μὲν γὰρ εἷς ἦν ὁ Ἔρως, καλῶς ἂν εἶχε· νῦν δὲ οὐ γάρ ἐστιν εἷς· μὴ ὄντος δὲ ἑνὸς ὀρθότερόν ἐστι πρότερον προρρηθῆναι ὁποῖον δεῖ ἐπαινεῖν. ἐγὼ οὖν πειράσομαι τοῦτο ἐπανορθώσασθαι, πρῶτον μὲν Ἔρωτα φράσαι ὃν δεῖ ἐπαινεῖν, ἔπειτα ἐπαινέσαι ἀξίως τοῦ θεοῦ. πάντες γὰρ ἴσμεν ὅτι οὐκ

SYMPOSIUM

And Aeschylus[1] talks nonsense when he says that it was Achilles who was in love with Patroclus; for he excelled in beauty not Patroclus alone but assuredly all the other heroes, being still beardless and, moreover, much the younger, by Homer's account.[2] For in truth there is no sort of valour more respected by the gods than this which comes of love; yet they are even more admiring and delighted and beneficent when the beloved is fond of his lover than when the lover is fond of his favourite; since a lover, filled as he is with a god, surpasses his favourite in divinity. This is the reason why they honoured Achilles above Alcestis, giving him his abode in the Isles of the Blest.

"So there is my description of Love—that he is the most venerable and valuable of the gods, and that he has sovereign power to provide all virtue and happiness for men whether living or departed."

The Speech of Pausanias

Such in the main was Phaedrus' speech as reported to me. It was followed by several others, which my friend could not recollect at all clearly; so he passed them over and related that of Pausanias, which ran as follows: "I do not consider, Phaedrus, our plan of speaking a good one, if the rule is simply that we are to make eulogies of Love. If Love were only one, it would be right; but, you see, he is not one, and this being the case, it would be more correct to have it previously announced what sort we ought to praise. Now this defect I will endeavour to amend, and will first decide on a Love who deserves our praise, and then will praise him in terms worthy of his godhead. We are all aware that there is no

---

[1] Aesch. *Myrm. fr.* 135-136. [2] Homer, *Il.* xi. 786.

ἔστιν ἄνευ Ἔρωτος Ἀφροδίτη. μιᾶς μὲν οὖν
οὔσης εἷς ἂν ἦν Ἔρως· ἐπεὶ δὲ δὴ δύο ἐστόν, δύο
ἀνάγκη καὶ Ἔρωτε εἶναι. πῶς δ' οὐ δύο τὼ θεά;
ἡ μέν γέ που πρεσβυτέρα καὶ ἀμήτωρ Οὐρανοῦ
θυγάτηρ, ἣν δὴ καὶ Οὐρανίαν ἐπονομάζομεν· ἡ δὲ
νεωτέρα Διὸς καὶ Διώνης, ἣν δὴ Πάνδημον καλοῦμεν. ἀναγκαῖον δὴ καὶ Ἔρωτα τὸν μὲν τῇ ἑτέρᾳ
συνεργὸν Πάνδημον ὀρθῶς καλεῖσθαι, τὸν δὲ
Οὐράνιον. ἐπαινεῖν μὲν οὖν δεῖ πάντας θεούς, ἃ
δ' οὖν ἑκάτερος εἴληχε πειρατέον εἰπεῖν. πᾶσα
γὰρ πρᾶξις ὧδ' ἔχει· αὐτὴ ἐφ' ἑαυτῆς πραττο-
μένη οὔτε καλὴ οὔτε αἰσχρά. οἷον ὃ νῦν ἡμεῖς
ποιοῦμεν, ἢ πίνειν ἢ ᾄδειν ἢ διαλέγεσθαι, οὐκ ἔστι
τούτων αὐτὸ καλὸν οὐδέν, ἀλλ' ἐν τῇ πράξει, ὡς
ἂν πραχθῇ, τοιοῦτον ἀπέβη· καλῶς μὲν γὰρ πραττόμενον καὶ ὀρθῶς καλὸν γίγνεται, μὴ ὀρθῶς δὲ
αἰσχρόν. οὕτω δὴ καὶ τὸ ἐρᾶν καὶ ὁ Ἔρως οὐ πᾶς
ἐστι καλὸς οὐδὲ ἄξιος ἐγκωμιάζεσθαι, ἀλλ' ὁ
καλῶς προτρέπων ἐρᾶν.

Ὁ μὲν οὖν τῆς Πανδήμου Ἀφροδίτης ὡς
ἀληθῶς πάνδημός ἐστι καὶ ἐξεργάζεται ὅ τι ἂν
τύχῃ· καὶ οὗτός ἐστιν ὃν οἱ φαῦλοι τῶν ἀνθρώπων
ἐρῶσιν. ἐρῶσι δὲ οἱ τοιοῦτοι πρῶτον μὲν οὐχ
ἧττον γυναικῶν ἢ παίδων, ἔπειτα ὧν καὶ ἐρῶσι
τῶν σωμάτων μᾶλλον ἢ τῶν ψυχῶν, ἔπειτα ὡς ἂν
δύνωνται ἀνοητοτάτων, πρὸς τὸ διαπράξασθαι
μόνον βλέποντες, ἀμελοῦντες δὲ τοῦ καλῶς ἢ μή.

SYMPOSIUM

Aphrodite or Love-passion without a Love. True, if that goddess were one, then Love would be one: but since there are two of her, there must needs be two Loves also. Does anyone doubt that she is double? Surely there is the elder, of no mother born, but daughter of Heaven, whence we name her Heavenly;[1] while the younger was the child of Zeus and Dione, and her we call Popular.[2] It follows then that of the two Loves also the one ought to be called Popular, as fellow-worker with the one of those goddesses, and the other Heavenly. All gods, of course, ought to be praised: but none the less I must try to describe the faculties of each of these two. For of every action it may be observed that as acted by itself it is neither noble nor base. For instance, in our conduct at this moment, whether we drink or sing or converse, none of these things is noble in itself; each only turns out to be such in the doing, as the manner of doing it may be. For when the doing of it is noble and right, the thing itself becomes noble; when wrong, it becomes base. So also it is with loving, and Love is not in every case noble or worthy of celebration, but only when he impels us to love in a noble manner.

"Now the Love that belongs to the Popular Aphrodite is in very truth popular and does his work at haphazard: this is the Love we see in the meaner sort of men; who, in the first place, love women as well as boys; secondly, where they love, they are set on the body more than the soul; and thirdly, they choose the most witless people they can find, since they look merely to the accomplishment and care not if the manner be noble or no.

[1] Herod. i. 105, 131; Pausan. i. 146.   [2] Pausan. i. 22. 3.

PLATO

ὅθεν δὴ συμβαίνει αὐτοῖς, ὅ τι ἂν τύχωσι, τοῦτο πράττειν, ὁμοίως μὲν ἀγαθόν, ὁμοίως δὲ τοὐναντίον. ἔστι γὰρ καὶ ἀπὸ τῆς θεοῦ νεωτέρας τε οὔσης πολὺ ἢ τῆς ἑτέρας, καὶ μετεχούσης ἐν τῇ γενέσει καὶ θήλεος καὶ ἄρρενος. ὁ δὲ τῆς Οὐρανίας πρῶτον μὲν οὐ μετεχούσης θήλεος ἀλλ' ἄρρενος μόνον· [καὶ ἔστιν οὗτος ὁ τῶν παίδων ἔρως·][1] ἔπειτα πρεσβυτέρας, ὕβρεως ἀμοίρου· ὅθεν δὴ ἐπὶ τὸ ἄρρεν τρέπονται οἱ ἐκ τούτου τοῦ ἔρωτος ἔπιπνοι, τὸ φύσει ἐρρωμενέστερον καὶ νοῦν μᾶλλον ἔχον ἀγαπῶντες. καί τις ἂν γνοίη καὶ ἐν αὐτῇ τῇ παιδεραστίᾳ τοὺς εἰλικρινῶς ὑπὸ τούτου τοῦ ἔρωτος ὡρμημένους· οὐ γὰρ ἐρῶσι παίδων, ἀλλ' ἐπειδὰν ἤδη ἄρχωνται νοῦν ἴσχειν· τοῦτο δὲ πλησιάζει τῷ γενειάσκειν. παρεσκευασμένοι γάρ, οἶμαι, εἰσὶν οἱ ἐντεῦθεν ἀρχόμενοι ἐρᾶν ὡς τὸν βίον ἅπαντα συνεσόμενοι καὶ κοινῇ συμβιωσόμενοι, ἀλλ' οὐκ ἐξαπατήσαντες, ἐν ἀφροσύνῃ λαβόντες ὡς νέον, καταγελάσαντες οἰχήσεσθαι ἐπ' ἄλλον ἀποτρέχοντες. χρῆν δὲ καὶ νόμον εἶναι μὴ ἐρᾶν παίδων, ἵνα μὴ εἰς ἄδηλον πολλὴ σπουδὴ ἀνηλίσκετο· τὸ γὰρ τῶν παίδων τέλος ἄδηλον οἷ τελευτᾷ κακίας καὶ ἀρετῆς ψυχῆς τε πέρι καὶ σώματος. οἱ μὲν οὖν ἀγαθοὶ τὸν νόμον τοῦτον αὐτοὶ αὑτοῖς ἑκόντες τίθενται, χρῆν δὲ καὶ τούτους τοὺς πανδήμους ἐραστὰς προσαναγκάζειν τὸ τοιοῦτον, ὥσπερ καὶ τῶν ἐλευθέρων γυναικῶν προσαναγκάζομεν αὐτοὺς καθ' ὅσον δυνάμεθα μὴ ἐρᾶν. οὗτοι γάρ εἰσιν οἱ καὶ τὸ ὄνειδος πεποιηκότες, ὥστε τινὰς τολμᾶν λέγειν ὡς αἰσχρὸν χαρίζεσθαι ἐρασταῖς· λέγουσι δὲ εἰς τούτους ἀποβλέποντες, ὁρῶντες

---

[1] καὶ ... ἔρως secl. Schütz.

SYMPOSIUM

Hence they find themselves doing everything at haphazard, good or its opposite, without distinction: for this Love proceeds from the goddess who is far the younger of the two, and who in her origin partakes of both female and male. But the other Love springs from the Heavenly goddess who, firstly, partakes not of the female but only of the male; and secondly, is the elder, untinged with wantonness: wherefore those who are inspired by this Love betake them to the male, in fondness for what has the robuster nature and a larger share of mind. Even in the passion for boys you may note the way of those who are under the single incitement of this Love: they love boys only when they begin to acquire some mind—a growth associated with that of down on their chins. For I conceive that those who begin to love them at this age are prepared to be always with them and share all with them as long as life shall last: they will not take advantage of a boy's green thoughtlessness to deceive him and make a mock of him by running straight off to another. Against this love of boys a law should have been enacted, to prevent the sad waste of attentions paid to an object so uncertain: for who can tell where a boy will end at last, vicious or virtuous in body and soul? Good men, however, voluntarily make this law for themselves, and it is a rule which those 'popular' lovers ought to be forced to obey, just as we force them, so far as we can, to refrain from loving our freeborn women. These are the persons responsible for the scandal which prompts some to say it is a shame to gratify one's lover: such are the cases they have in view,

PLATO

αὐτῶν τὴν ἀκαιρίαν καὶ ἀδικίαν, ἐπεὶ οὐ δήπου κοσμίως γε καὶ νομίμως ὁτιοῦν πραττόμενον ψόγον ἂν δικαίως φέροι.

Καὶ δὴ καὶ ὁ περὶ τὸν ἔρωτα νόμος ἐν μὲν ταῖς ἄλλαις πόλεσι νοῆσαι ῥᾴδιος· ἁπλῶς γὰρ ὥρισται· ὁ δ' ἐνθάδε [καὶ ἐν Λακεδαίμονι][1] ποικίλος. ἐν Ἤλιδι μὲν γὰρ καὶ ἐν Βοιωτοῖς, καὶ οὗ μὴ σοφοὶ λέγειν, ἁπλῶς νενομοθέτηται καλὸν τὸ χαρίζεσθαι ἐρασταῖς, καὶ οὐκ ἄν τις εἴποι οὔτε νέος οὔτε παλαιὸς ὡς αἰσχρόν, ἵνα, οἶμαι, μὴ πράγματ' ἔχωσι λόγῳ πειρώμενοι πείθειν τοὺς νέους, ἅτε ἀδύνατοι λέγειν· τῆς δὲ Ἰωνίας καὶ ἄλλοθι πολλαχοῦ αἰσχρὸν νενόμισται, ὅσοι ὑπὸ βαρβάροις οἰκοῦσι. τοῖς γὰρ βαρβάροις διὰ τὰς τυραννίδας αἰσχρὸν τοῦτό τε καὶ ἥ γε φιλοσοφία καὶ ἡ φιλογυμναστία· οὐ γάρ, οἶμαι, συμφέρει τοῖς ἄρχουσι φρονήματα μεγάλα ἐγγίγνεσθαι τῶν ἀρχομένων, οὐδὲ φιλίας ἰσχυρὰς καὶ κοινωνίας, ὃ δὴ μάλιστα φιλεῖ τά τε ἄλλα πάντα καὶ ὁ ἔρως ἐμποιεῖν. ἔργῳ δὲ τοῦτο ἔμαθον καὶ οἱ ἐνθάδε τύραννοι· ὁ γὰρ Ἀριστογείτονος ἔρως καὶ ἡ Ἁρμοδίου φιλία βέβαιος γενομένη κατέλυσεν αὐτῶν τὴν ἀρχήν. οὕτως οὗ μὲν αἰσχρὸν ἐτέθη χαρίζεσθαι ἐρασταῖς, κακίᾳ τῶν θεμένων κεῖται, τῶν μὲν ἀρχόντων πλεονεξίᾳ, τῶν δὲ ἀρχομένων ἀνανδρίᾳ· οὗ δὲ καλὸν ἁπλῶς ἐνομίσθη, διὰ τὴν τῶν θεμένων τῆς ψυχῆς ἀργίαν. ἐνθάδε δὲ πολὺ τούτων κάλλιον νενομοθέτηται, καὶ ὅπερ εἶπον, οὐ ῥᾴδιον κατανοῆσαι.

Ἐνθυμηθέντι γὰρ ὅτι λέγεται κάλλιον τὸ

---

[1] καὶ ἐν Λακεδαίμονι secl. Winckelmann.

SYMPOSIUM

for they observe all their reckless and wrongful doings; and surely, whatsoever is done in an orderly and lawful manner can never justly bring reproach.

"Further, it is easy to note the rule with regard to love in other cities: there it is laid down in simple terms, while ours here is complicated. For in Elis and Boeotia and where there is no skill in speech they have simply an ordinance that it is seemly to gratify lovers, and no one whether young or old will call it shameful, in order, I suppose, to save themselves the trouble of trying what speech can do to persuade the youths; for they have no ability for speaking. But in Ionia and many other regions where they live under foreign sway, it is counted a disgrace. Foreigners hold this thing, and all training in philosophy and sports, to be disgraceful, because of their despotic government; since, I presume, it is not to the interest of their princes to have lofty notions engendered in their subjects, or any strong friendships and communions; all of which Love is pre-eminently apt to create. It is a lesson that our despots learnt by experience; for Aristogeiton's love and Harmodius's friendship grew to be so steadfast that it wrecked their power. Thus where it was held a disgrace to gratify one's lover, the tradition is due to the evil ways of those who made such a law—that is, to the encroachments of the rulers and to the cowardice of the ruled. But where it was accepted as honourable without any reserve, this was due to a sluggishness of mind in the law-makers. In our city we have far better regulations, which, as I said, are not so easily grasped.

"Consider, for instance, our saying that it is more

PLATO

φανερῶς ἐρᾶν τοῦ λάθρᾳ, καὶ μάλιστα τῶν γεν-
ναιοτάτων καὶ ἀρίστων, κἂν αἰσχίους ἄλλων ὦσι,
καὶ ὅτι αὖ ἡ παρακέλευσις τῷ ἐρῶντι παρὰ πάντων θαυμαστή. οὐχ ὥς τι αἰσχρὸν ποιοῦντι, καὶ
ἑλόντι τε καλὸν δοκεῖ εἶναι καὶ μὴ ἑλόντι αἰσχρόν,
καὶ πρὸς τὸ ἐπιχειρεῖν ἑλεῖν ἐξουσίαν ὁ νόμος
δέδωκε τῷ ἐραστῇ θαυμαστὰ ἔργα ἐργαζομένῳ
ἐπαινεῖσθαι, ἃ εἴ τις τολμῴη ποιεῖν ἄλλ' ὁτιοῦν
διώκων καὶ βουλόμενος διαπράξασθαι πλὴν τοῦτο
[φιλοσοφίας],[1] τὰ μέγιστα καρποῖτ' ἂν ὀνείδη· εἰ
γὰρ ἢ χρήματα βουλόμενος παρά του λαβεῖν ἢ
ἀρχὴν ἄρξαι ἤ τιν' ἄλλην δύναμιν ἐθέλοι ποιεῖν
οἷάπερ οἱ ἐρασταὶ πρὸς τὰ παιδικά, ἱκετείας τε
καὶ ἀντιβολήσεις ἐν ταῖς δεήσεσι ποιούμενοι, καὶ
ὅρκους ὀμνύντες, καὶ κοιμήσεις ἐπὶ θύραις, καὶ
ἐθέλοντες δουλείας δουλεύειν οἵας οὐδ' ἂν δοῦλος
οὐδείς, ἐμποδίζοιτο ἂν μὴ πράττειν οὕτω τὴν
πρᾶξιν καὶ ὑπὸ φίλων καὶ ὑπὸ ἐχθρῶν, τῶν μὲν
ὀνειδιζόντων κολακείας καὶ ἀνελευθερίας, τῶν δὲ
νουθετούντων καὶ αἰσχυνομένων ὑπὲρ αὐτῶν· τῷ
δ' ἐρῶντι πάντα ταῦτα ποιοῦντι χάρις ἔπεστι, καὶ
δέδοται ὑπὸ τοῦ νόμου ἄνευ ὀνείδους πράττειν, ὡς
πάγκαλόν τι πρᾶγμα διαπραττομένου· ὃ δὲ δει-
νότατον, ὥς γε λέγουσιν οἱ πολλοί, ὅτι καὶ ὀμνύντι
μόνῳ συγγνώμη παρὰ θεῶν ἐκβάντι τὸν ὅρκον·
ἀφροδίσιον γὰρ ὅρκον οὔ φασιν εἶναι· οὕτω καὶ οἱ
θεοὶ καὶ οἱ ἄνθρωποι πᾶσαν ἐξουσίαν πεποιήκασι

[1] φιλοσοφίας secl. Schleiermacher.

SYMPOSIUM

honourable to love openly than in secret, especially when the beloved excels not so much in beauty as in nobility and virtue; and again, what a wonderful encouragement a lover gets from us all: we have no thought of his doing anything unseemly, and success in his pursuit is counted honourable and failure disgraceful; and how in his endeavours for success our law leaves him a free hand for performing such admirable acts as may win him praise; while the same acts, if attempted for any other purpose or effect to which one might be inclined, would bring one nothing in return but the sharpest reproach. For suppose that with the view of gaining money from another, or some office, or any sort of influence, a man should allow himself to behave as lovers commonly do to their favourites—pressing their suit with supplications and entreaties, binding themselves with vows, sleeping on doorsteps, and submitting to such slavery as no slave would ever endure—both the friends and the enemies of such a man would hinder his behaving in such fashion; for while the latter would reproach him with adulation and ill-breeding, the former would admonish him and feel ashamed of his conduct. But in a lover all such doings only win him favour: by free grant of our law he may behave thus without reproach, as compassing a most honourable end. Strangest of all, he alone in the vulgar opinion has indulgence from the gods when he forsakes the vow he has sworn; for the vow of love-passion, they say, is no vow.[1] So true it is that both gods and men have given absolute licence to the lover,

---

[1] *Cf.* Sophocles, *fr.* 694 ὅρκους δὲ μοιχῶν εἰς τέφραν ἐγὼ γράφω, " the lecher's vows in ashes I record."

PLATO

τῷ ἐρῶντι, ὡς ὁ νόμος φησὶν ὁ ἐνθάδε. ταύτῃ μὲν οὖν οἰηθείη ἄν τις πάγκαλον νομίζεσθαι ἐν τῇδε τῇ πόλει καὶ τὸ ἐρᾶν καὶ τὸ φίλους γίγνεσθαι τοῖς ἐρασταῖς. ἐπειδὰν δὲ παιδαγωγοὺς ἐπιστήσαντες οἱ πατέρες τοῖς ἐρωμένοις μὴ ἐῶσι διαλέγεσθαι τοῖς ἐρασταῖς, καὶ τῷ παιδαγωγῷ ταῦτα προστεταγμένα ᾖ, ἡλικιῶται δὲ καὶ ἑταῖροι[1] ὀνειδίζωσιν, ἐάν τι ὁρῶσι τοιοῦτο γιγνόμενον, καὶ τοὺς ὀνειδίζοντας αὖ οἱ πρεσβύτεροι μὴ διακωλύωσι μηδὲ λοιδορῶσιν ὡς οὐκ ὀρθῶς λέγοντας, εἰς δὲ ταῦτά τις αὖ βλέψας ἡγήσαιτ' ἂν πάλιν αἴσχιστον τὸ τοιοῦτον ἐνθάδε νομίζεσθαι. τὸ δέ, οἶμαι, ὧδ' ἔχει· οὐχ ἁπλοῦν ἐστίν, ὅπερ ἐξ ἀρχῆς ἐλέχθη, οὔτε καλὸν εἶναι αὐτὸ καθ' αὑτὸ οὔτε αἰσχρόν, ἀλλὰ καλῶς μὲν πραττόμενον καλόν, αἰσχρῶς δὲ αἰσχρόν. αἰσχρῶς μὲν οὖν ἐστὶ πονηρῷ τε καὶ πονηρῶς χαρίζεσθαι, καλῶς δὲ χρηστῷ τε καὶ καλῶς. πονηρὸς δ' ἐστὶν ἐκεῖνος ὁ ἐραστὴς ὁ πάνδημος, ὁ τοῦ σώματος μᾶλλον ἢ τῆς ψυχῆς ἐρῶν· καὶ γὰρ οὐδὲ μόνιμός ἐστιν, ἅτε οὐ μονίμου ἐρῶν πράγματος. ἅμα γὰρ τῷ τοῦ σώματος ἄνθει λήγοντι, οὗπερ ἤρα, "οἴχεται ἀποπτάμενος," πολλοὺς λόγους καὶ ὑποσχέσεις καταισχύνας· ὁ δὲ τοῦ ἤθους χρηστοῦ ὄντος ἐραστὴς διὰ βίου μένει, ἅτε μονίμῳ συντακείς. τούτους δὴ βούλεται ὁ ἡμέτερος νόμος εὖ καὶ καλῶς βασανίζειν, καὶ τοῖς μὲν χαρίσασθαι, τοὺς δὲ διαφεύγειν. διὰ ταῦτα οὖν τοῖς μὲν διώκειν παρακελεύεται, τοῖς δὲ φεύγειν, ἀγωνοθετῶν καὶ βασανίζων ποτέ-

---

[1] ἑταῖροι Heindorf: ἕτεροι mss.

[1] So Agamemnon speaks of the dream which brought him a message through the lips of Nestor (Homer, *Il.* ii. 71).

SYMPOSIUM

as our Athenian law provides. Thus far, then, we have ground for supposing that here in our city both loving some one and showing affection to one's lover are held in highest honour. But it happens that fathers put tutors in charge of their boys when they are beloved, to prevent them from conversing with their lovers: the tutor has strict injunctions on the matter, and when they observe a boy to be guilty of such a thing his playmates and fellows reproach him, while his reproachers are not in their turn withheld or upbraided by their elders as speaking amiss; and from this it might rather be inferred that his behaviour is held to be a great disgrace in Athens. Yet the truth of it, I think, is this: the affair is no simple thing; you remember we said that by itself it was neither noble nor base, but that it was noble if nobly conducted, and base if basely. To do the thing basely is to gratify a wicked man in a wicked manner: 'nobly' means having to do with a good man in a noble manner. By 'wicked' we mean that popular lover, who craves the body rather than the soul: as he is not in love with what abides, he himself is not abiding. As soon as the bloom of the body he so loved begins to fade he 'flutters off and is gone,'[1] leaving all his speeches and promises dishonoured: whereas the lover of a nature that is worthy abides throughout life, as being fused into one with the abiding.

"Now our law has a sure and excellent test for the trial of these persons, showing which are to be favoured and which to be shunned. In the one case, accordingly, it encourages pursuit, but flight in the other, applying ordeals and tests in each case,

PLATO

ρων ποτέ ἐστιν ὁ ἐρῶν καὶ ποτέρων ὁ ἐρώμενος. οὕτω δὴ ὑπὸ ταύτης τῆς αἰτίας πρῶτον μὲν τὸ ἁλίσκεσθαι ταχὺ αἰσχρὸν νενόμισται, ἵνα χρόνος ἐγγένηται, ὃς δὴ δοκεῖ τὰ πολλὰ καλῶς βασανίζειν· ἔπειτα τὸ ὑπὸ χρημάτων καὶ ὑπὸ πολιτικῶν B δυνάμεων ἁλῶναι αἰσχρόν, ἐάν τε κακῶς πάσχων πτήξῃ καὶ μὴ καρτερήσῃ, ἄν τ' εὐεργετούμενος εἰς χρήματα ἢ εἰς διαπράξεις πολιτικὰς μὴ καταφρονήσῃ· οὐδὲν γὰρ δοκεῖ τούτων οὔτε βέβαιον οὔτε μόνιμον εἶναι, χωρὶς τοῦ μηδὲ πεφυκέναι ἀπ' αὐτῶν γενναίαν φιλίαν· μία δὴ λείπεται τῷ ἡμετέρῳ νόμῳ ὁδός, εἰ μέλλει καλῶς χαριεῖσθαι C ἐραστῇ παιδικά. ἔστι γὰρ ἡμῖν νόμος, ὥσπερ ἐπὶ τοῖς ἐρασταῖς ἦν δουλεύειν ἐθέλοντα ἡντινοῦν δουλείαν παιδικοῖς μὴ κολακείαν εἶναι μηδὲ ἐπονείδιστον, οὕτω δὴ καὶ ἄλλη μία μόνη δουλεία ἑκούσιος λείπεται οὐκ ἐπονείδιστος· αὕτη δέ ἐστιν ἡ περὶ τὴν ἀρετήν.

Νενόμισται γὰρ δὴ ἡμῖν, ἐάν τις ἐθέλῃ τινὰ θεραπεύειν ἡγούμενος δι' ἐκεῖνον ἀμείνων ἔσεσθαι ἢ κατὰ σοφίαν τινὰ ἢ κατὰ ἄλλο ὁτιοῦν μέρος ἀρετῆς, αὕτη αὖ ἡ ἐθελοδουλεία οὐκ αἰσχρὰ εἶναι οὐδὲ κολακεία. δεῖ δὴ τὼ νόμω τούτω συμβαλεῖν D εἰς ταὐτόν, τόν τε περὶ τὴν παιδεραστίαν καὶ τὸν περὶ τὴν φιλοσοφίαν τε καὶ τὴν ἄλλην ἀρετήν, εἰ μέλλει συμβῆναι καλὸν γενέσθαι τὸ ἐραστῇ παιδικὰ χαρίσασθαι. ὅταν γὰρ εἰς τὸ αὐτὸ ἔλθωσιν ἐραστής τε καὶ παιδικά, νόμον ἔχων ἑκάτερος, ὁ μὲν χαρισαμένοις παιδικοῖς ὑπηρετῶν ὁτιοῦν δικαίως ἂν ὑπηρετεῖν, ὁ δὲ τῷ ποιοῦντι αὐτὸν

whereby we are able to rank the lover and the beloved on this side or on that. And so it is for this reason that our convention regards a quick capitulation as a disgrace: for there ought, first, to be a certain interval — the generally approved touchstone — of time; and, second, it is disgraceful if the surrender is due to gold or public preferment, or is a mere cowering away from the endurance of ill-treatment, or shows the youth not properly contemptuous of such benefits as he may receive in pelf or political success. For in these there appears nothing steadfast or abiding, unless it be the impossibility of their producing a noble friendship. One way remains in our custom whereby a favourite may rightly gratify his lover: it is our rule that, just as in the case of the lovers it was counted no flattery or scandal for them to be willingly and utterly enslaved to their favourites, so there is left one sort of voluntary thraldom which is not scandalous; I mean, in the cause of virtue.

" It is our settled tradition that when a man freely devotes his service to another in the belief that his friend will make him better in point of wisdom, it may be, or in any of the other parts of virtue, this willing bondage also is no sort of baseness or flattery. Let us compare the two rules — one dealing with the passion for boys, and the other with the love of wisdom and all virtuous ways: by this we shall see if we are to conclude it a good thing that a favourite should gratify his lover. For when lover and favourite come together, each guided by his own rule—on the one side, of being justified in doing any service to the favourite who has obliged him, and on the other, of being justified in showing

PLATO

σοφόν τε καὶ ἀγαθὸν δικαίως αὖ ὁτιοῦν ἂν ὑπουργῶν ⟨ὑπουργεῖν⟩,[1] καὶ ὁ μὲν δυνάμενος εἰς φρόνησιν καὶ τὴν ἄλλην ἀρετὴν συμβάλλεσθαι, ὁ δὲ δεόμενος εἰς παίδευσιν καὶ τὴν ἄλλην σοφίαν κτᾶσθαι, τότε δὴ τούτων συνιόντων εἰς ταὐτὸν τῶν νόμων μοναχοῦ ἐνταῦθα συμπίπτει τὸ καλὸν εἶναι παιδικὰ ἐραστῇ χαρίσασθαι, ἄλλοθι δὲ οὐδαμοῦ. ἐπὶ τούτῳ καὶ ἐξαπατηθῆναι οὐδὲν αἰσχρόν· ἐπὶ δὲ τοῖς ἄλλοις πᾶσι καὶ ἐξαπατωμένῳ αἰσχύνην φέρει καὶ μή. εἰ γάρ τις ἐραστῇ ὡς πλουσίῳ πλούτου ἕνεκα χαρισάμενος ἐξαπατηθείη καὶ μὴ λάβοι χρήματα, ἀναφανέντος τοῦ ἐραστοῦ πένητος, οὐδὲν ἧττον αἰσχρόν· δοκεῖ γὰρ ὁ τοιοῦτος τό γε αὑτοῦ ἐπιδεῖξαι, ὅτι ἕνεκα χρημάτων ὁτιοῦν ἂν ὁτῳοῦν ὑπηρετοῖ, τοῦτο δὲ οὐ καλόν. κατὰ τὸν αὐτὸν δὴ λόγον κἂν εἴ τις ὡς ἀγαθῷ χαρισάμενος καὶ αὐτὸς ὡς ἀμείνων ἐσόμενος διὰ τὴν φιλίαν τοῦ ἐραστοῦ ἐξαπατηθείη, ἀναφανέντος ἐκείνου κακοῦ καὶ οὐ κεκτημένου ἀρετήν, ὅμως καλὴ ἡ ἀπάτη· δοκεῖ γὰρ αὖ καὶ οὗτος τὸ καθ' αὑτὸν δεδηλωκέναι, ὅτι ἀρετῆς γ' ἕνεκα καὶ τοῦ βελτίων γενέσθαι πᾶν ἂν παντὶ προθυμηθείη, τοῦτο δὲ αὖ πάντων κάλλιστον· οὕτω πάντως γε καλὸν ἀρετῆς ἕνεκα χαρίζεσθαι.

Οὗτός ἐστιν ὁ τῆς οὐρανίας θεοῦ ἔρως καὶ οὐράνιος καὶ πολλοῦ ἄξιος καὶ πόλει καὶ ἰδιώταις, πολλὴν ἐπιμέλειαν ἀναγκάζων ποιεῖσθαι πρὸς ἀρετὴν τόν τε ἐρῶντα αὐτὸν αὑτοῦ καὶ τὸν ἐρώμενον· οἱ

[1] ὑπουργῶν ⟨ὑπουργεῖν⟩ Baiter.

SYMPOSIUM

any attentions to the friend who makes him wise and good; the elder of his plenty contributing to intellectual and all other excellence, the younger in his paucity acquiring education and all learned arts: only then, at the meeting of these two principles in one place, only then and there, and in no other case, can it befall that a favourite may honourably indulge his lover. To have such hopes deceived is no disgrace; while those of any other sort must be disgraceful, whether deceived or not. For suppose that a youth had a lover he deemed to be wealthy and, after obliging him for the sake of his wealth, were to find himself deceived and no money to be got, since the lover proved to be poor; this would be disgraceful all the same; since the youth may be said to have revealed his character, and shown himself ready to do anyone any service for pelf, and this is not honourable. By the same token, when a youth gratifies a friend, supposing him to be a good man and expecting to be made better himself as a result of his lover's affection, and then finds he is deceived, since his friend proves to be vile and destitute of virtue; even so the deception is honourable. For this youth is also held to have discovered his nature, by showing that he would make anyone the object of his utmost ardour for the sake of virtuous improvement; and this by contrast is supremely honourable. Thus by all means it is right to bestow this favour for the sake of virtue.

" This is the Love that belongs to the Heavenly Goddess, heavenly itself and precious to both public and private life: for this compels lover and beloved alike to feel a zealous concern for their own virtue.

PLATO

δ' ἕτεροι πάντες τῆς ἑτέρας, τῆς πανδήμου. ταῦτά σοι, ἔφη, ὡς ἐκ τοῦ παραχρῆμα, ὦ Φαῖδρε, περὶ Ἔρωτος συμβάλλομαι.

Παυσανίου δὲ παυσαμένου, διδάσκουσι γάρ με ἴσα λέγειν οὑτωσὶ οἱ σοφοί, ἔφη ὁ Ἀριστόδημος δεῖν μὲν Ἀριστοφάνη λέγειν, τυχεῖν δὲ αὐτῷ τινὰ ἢ ὑπὸ πλησμονῆς ἢ ὑπό τινος ἄλλου λύγγα ἐπιπεπτωκυῖαν καὶ οὐχ οἷόν τε εἶναι λέγειν, ἀλλ' εἰπεῖν αὐτόν—ἐν τῇ κάτω γὰρ αὐτοῦ τὸν ἰατρὸν Ἐρυξίμαχον κατακεῖσθαι—Ὦ Ἐρυξίμαχε, δίκαιος εἶ ἢ παῦσαί με τῆς λυγγὸς ἢ λέγειν ὑπὲρ ἐμοῦ, ἕως ἂν ἐγὼ παύσωμαι. καὶ τὸν Ἐρυξίμαχον εἰπεῖν Ἀλλὰ ποιήσω ἀμφότερα ταῦτα, ἐγὼ μὲν γὰρ ἐρῶ ἐν τῷ σῷ μέρει, σὺ δ' ἐπειδὰν παύσῃ, ἐν τῷ ἐμῷ· ἐν ᾧ δ' ἂν ἐγὼ λέγω, ἐὰν μέν σοι ἐθέλῃ ἀπνευστὶ ἔχοντι πολὺν χρόνον παύεσθαι ἡ λύγξ· εἰ δὲ μή, ὕδατι ἀνακογχυλίασον. εἰ δ' ἄρα πάνυ ἰσχυρά ἐστιν, ἀναλαβών τι τοιοῦτον οἵῳ κνήσαις[1] ἂν τὴν ῥῖνα, πτάρε· καὶ ἐὰν τοῦτο ποιήσῃς ἅπαξ ἢ δίς, καὶ εἰ πάνυ ἰσχυρά ἐστι, παύσεται. Οὐκ ἂν φθάνοις λέγων, φάναι τὸν Ἀριστοφάνη· ἐγὼ δὲ ταῦτα ποιήσω.

Εἰπεῖν δὴ τὸν Ἐρυξίμαχον, Δοκεῖ τοίνυν μοι ἀναγκαῖον εἶναι, ἐπειδὴ Παυσανίας ὁρμήσας ἐπὶ τὸν λόγον καλῶς οὐχ ἱκανῶς ἀπετέλεσε, δεῖν ἐμὲ πειρᾶσθαι τέλος ἐπιθεῖναι τῷ λόγῳ. τὸ μὲν γὰρ διπλοῦν εἶναι τὸν Ἔρωτα δοκεῖ μοι καλῶς διελέσθαι· ὅτι δὲ οὐ μόνον ἐστὶν ἐπὶ ταῖς ψυχαῖς

[1] κνήσαις Wyttenbach : κινήσαις MSS.

---

[1] The punning assonance alludes to those sophists who developed the etymological suggestions of Heraclitus and Aeschylus into mere sound-effects for prose. A more serious philological development is discussed in *Cratylus*, 396.

SYMPOSIUM

But lovers of the other sort belong all to the other Goddess, the Popular. Such, Phaedrus, is the contribution I am able to offer you, on the spur of the moment, towards the discussion of Love."

Pausanias' praise made a pause with this phrase—you see what jingles the schoolmen are teaching me![1] The next speaker, so Aristodemus told me, was to have been Aristophanes: but a surfeit or some other cause had chanced to afflict him with a hiccough, which prevented him from speaking; and he could only just say to Eryximachus the doctor, whose place was next below him, "I look to you, Eryximachus, either to stop my hiccough, or to speak in my stead until I can stop it." "Why, I will do both," replied Eryximachus "for I will take your turn for speaking, and when you have stopped it, you shall take mine. But during my speech, if on your holding your breath a good while the hiccough chooses to stop, well and good; otherwise, you must gargle with some water. If, however, it is a very stubborn one, take something that will tickle your nostrils, and sneeze: do this once or twice, and though it be of the stubbornest, it will stop." "Start away with your speech," said Aristophanes, "and I will do as you advise."

The Speech of Eryximachus

Then Eryximachus spoke as follows: "Well then, since Pausanias did not properly finish off the speech he began so well, I must do my best to append a conclusion thereto. His division of Love into two sorts appears to me a good one: but medicine, our great mystery, has taught me to observe that Love is not merely an impulse of human souls towards

123

τῶν ἀνθρώπων πρὸς τοὺς καλοὺς ἀλλὰ καὶ πρὸς ἄλλα πολλὰ καὶ ἐν τοῖς ἄλλοις, τοῖς τε σώμασι τῶν πάντων ζῴων καὶ τοῖς ἐν τῇ γῇ φυομένοις καὶ ὡς ἔπος εἰπεῖν ἐν πᾶσι τοῖς οὖσι, καθεωρακέναι μοι δοκῶ ἐκ τῆς ἰατρικῆς, τῆς ἡμετέρας τέχνης,
B ὡς μέγας καὶ θαυμαστὸς καὶ ἐπὶ πᾶν ὁ θεὸς τείνει καὶ κατ' ἀνθρώπινα καὶ κατὰ θεῖα πράγματα. ἄρξομαι δὲ ἀπὸ τῆς ἰατρικῆς λέγων, ἵνα καὶ πρεσβεύωμεν τὴν τέχνην. ἡ γὰρ φύσις τῶν σωμάτων τὸν διπλοῦν Ἔρωτα τοῦτον ἔχει. τὸ γὰρ ὑγιὲς τοῦ σώματος καὶ τὸ νοσοῦν ὁμολογουμένως ἕτερόν τε καὶ ἀνόμοιόν ἐστι, τὸ δὲ ἀνόμοιον ἀνομοίων ἐπιθυμεῖ καὶ ἐρᾷ. ἄλλος μὲν οὖν ὁ ἐπὶ τῷ ὑγιεινῷ ἔρως, ἄλλος δὲ ὁ ἐπὶ τῷ νοσώδει. ἔστι δή, ὥσπερ ἄρτι Παυσανίας ἔλεγε τοῖς μὲν ἀγαθοῖς καλὸν
C χαρίζεσθαι τῶν ἀνθρώπων, τοῖς δὲ ἀκολάστοις αἰσχρόν, οὕτω καὶ ἐν αὐτοῖς τοῖς σώμασι τοῖς μὲν ἀγαθοῖς ἑκάστου τοῦ σώματος καὶ ὑγιεινοῖς καλὸν χαρίζεσθαι καὶ δεῖ, καὶ τοῦτό ἐστιν ᾧ ὄνομα τὸ ἰατρικόν, τοῖς δὲ κακοῖς καὶ νοσώδεσιν αἰσχρόν τε καὶ δεῖ ἀχαριστεῖν, εἰ μέλλει τις τεχνικὸς εἶναι. ἔστι γὰρ ἰατρική, ὡς ἐν κεφαλαίῳ εἰπεῖν, ἐπιστήμη τῶν τοῦ σώματος ἐρωτικῶν πρὸς πλησμονὴν καὶ
D κένωσιν, καὶ ὁ διαγιγνώσκων ἐν τούτοις τὸν καλόν τε καὶ αἰσχρὸν ἔρωτα, οὗτός ἐστιν ὁ ἰατρικώτατος, καὶ ὁ μεταβάλλειν ποιῶν, ὥστε ἀντὶ τοῦ ἑτέρου ἔρωτος τὸν ἕτερον κτᾶσθαι, καὶ οἷς μὴ ἔνεστιν ἔρως, δεῖ δ' ἐγγενέσθαι, ἐπιστάμενος ἐμποιῆσαι καὶ ἐνόντα ἐξελεῖν, ἀγαθὸς ἂν εἴη δημιουργός. δεῖ γὰρ δὴ τὰ ἔχθιστα ὄντα ἐν τῷ σώματι φίλα

beautiful men but the attraction of all creatures to a great variety of things, which works in the bodies of all animals and all growths upon the earth, and practically in everything that is; and I have learnt how mighty and wonderful and universal is the sway of this god over all affairs both human and divine.[1] Reverence for my profession prompts me to begin with the witness of medicine. This double Love belongs to the nature of all bodies: for between bodily health and sickness there is an admitted difference or dissimilarity, and what is dissimilar craves and loves dissimilar things. And so the desire felt by a sound body is quite other than that of a sickly one. Now I agree with what Pausanias was just saying, that it is right to gratify good men, base to gratify the dissolute: similarly, in treating actual bodies it is right and necessary to gratify the good and healthy elements of each, and this is what we term the physician's skill; but it is a disgrace to do aught but disappoint the bad and sickly parts, if one aims at being an adept. For the art of medicine may be summarily described as a knowledge of the love-matters of the body in regard to repletion and evacuation; and the master-physician is he who can distinguish there between the nobler and baser Loves, and can effect such alteration that the one passion is replaced by the other; and he will be deemed a good practitioner who is expert in producing Love where it ought to flourish but exists not, and in removing it from where it should not be. Indeed he must be able to make friends

[1] This cosmic theory was derived from Empedocles, who spoke of Love as the combining, and Strife as the disruptive, force pervading the universe.

οἷόν τ' εἶναι ποιεῖν καὶ ἐρᾶν ἀλλήλων· ἔστι δὲ ἔχθιστα τὰ ἐναντιώτατα, ψυχρὸν θερμῷ, πικρὸν γλυκεῖ, ξηρὸν ὑγρῷ, πάντα τὰ τοιαῦτα· τούτοις ἐπιστηθεὶς ἔρωτα ἐμποιῆσαι καὶ ὁμόνοιαν ὁ ἡμέτερος πρόγονος Ἀσκληπιός, ὥς φασιν οἵδε οἱ ποιηταὶ καὶ ἐγὼ πείθομαι, συνέστησε τὴν ἡμετέραν τέχνην. ἥ τε οὖν ἰατρική, ὥσπερ λέγω, πᾶσα διὰ τοῦ θεοῦ τούτου κυβερνᾶται, ὡσαύτως δὲ καὶ γυμναστικὴ καὶ γεωργία· μουσικὴ δὲ καὶ παντὶ κατάδηλος τῷ καὶ σμικρὸν προσέχοντι τὸν νοῦν ὅτι κατὰ ταὐτὰ ἔχει τούτοις, ὥσπερ ἴσως καὶ Ἡράκλειτος βούλεται λέγειν, ἐπεὶ τοῖς γε ῥήμασιν οὐ καλῶς λέγει. τὸ ἓν γάρ φησι " διαφερόμενον αὐτὸ αὑτῷ συμφέρεσθαι, ὥσπερ ἁρμονίαν τόξου τε καὶ λύρας." ἔστι δὲ πολλὴ ἀλογία ἁρμονίαν φάναι διαφέρεσθαι ἢ ἐκ διαφερομένων ἔτι εἶναι. ἀλλ' ἴσως τόδε ἐβούλετο λέγειν, ὅτι ἐκ διαφερομένων πρότερον τοῦ ὀξέος καὶ βαρέος, ἔπειτα ὕστερον ὁμολογησάντων γέγονεν ὑπὸ τῆς μουσικῆς τέχνης. οὐ γὰρ δήπου ἐκ διαφερομένων γε ἔτι τοῦ ὀξέος καὶ βαρέος ἁρμονία ἂν εἴη. ἡ γὰρ ἁρμονία συμφωνία ἐστί, συμφωνία δὲ ὁμολογία τις· ὁμολογίαν δὲ ἐκ διαφερομένων, ἕως ἂν διαφέρωνται, ἀδύνατον εἶναι· διαφερόμενον δὲ αὖ καὶ μὴ ὁμολογεῖν ἀδυνατοῦν ⟨δυνατὸν⟩[1] ἁρμόσαι, ὥσπερ γε καὶ ὁ ῥυθμὸς ἐκ τοῦ ταχέος καὶ βραδέος διενηνεγμένων πρότερον, ὕστερον δὲ ὁμολογησάντων γέγονε. τὴν δὲ ὁμολογίαν πᾶσι τούτοις, ὥσπερ ἐκεῖ ἡ ἰατρική, ἐνταῦθα ἡ μουσικὴ ἐντίθησιν, ἔρωτα καὶ

---

[1] ὁμολογεῖν ἀδυνατοῦν ⟨δυνατὸν⟩ Bury: ὁμολογοῦν ἀδύνατον MSS.

SYMPOSIUM

and happy lovers of the keenest opponents in the body. Now the most contrary qualities are most hostile to each other — cold and hot, bitter and sweet, dry and moist, and the rest of them. It was by knowing how to foster love and unanimity in these that, as our two poets[1] here relate, and as I myself believe, our forefather Asclepius composed this science of ours. And so not merely is all medicine governed, as I propound it, through the influence of this god, but likewise athletics and agriculture. Music also, as is plain to any the least curious observer, is in the same sort of case: perhaps Heracleitus intends as much by those perplexing words, 'The One at variance with itself is drawn together, like harmony of bow or lyre.'[2] Now it is perfectly absurd to speak of a harmony at variance, or as formed from things still varying. Perhaps he meant, however, that from the grave and acute which were varying before, but which afterwards came to agreement, the harmony was by musical art created. For surely there can be no harmony of acute and grave while still at variance: harmony is consonance, and consonance is a kind of agreement; and agreement of things varying, so long as they are at variance, is impossible. On the other hand, when a thing varies with no disability of agreement, then it may be harmonized; just as rhythm is produced by fast and slow, which in the beginning were at variance but later came to agree. In all these cases the agreement is brought about by music which, like medicine in the former instance,

[1] Aristophanes and Agathon.
[2] Heracl. fr. 45 (Bywater). The universe is held together by the strain of opposing forces, just as the right use of bow or lyre depends on opposite tension.

PLATO

ὁμόνοιαν ἀλλήλων ἐμποιήσασα· καὶ ἔστιν αὖ μουσικὴ περὶ ἁρμονίαν καὶ ῥυθμὸν ἐρωτικῶν ἐπιστήμη. καὶ ἐν μέν γε αὐτῇ τῇ συστάσει ἁρμονίας τε καὶ ῥυθμοῦ οὐδὲν χαλεπὸν τὰ ἐρωτικὰ διαγιγνώσκειν, οὐδὲ ὁ διπλοῦς ἔρως ἐνταῦθά πω[1] ἐστιν· ἀλλ' ἐπειδὰν δέῃ πρὸς τοὺς ἀνθρώπους καταχρῆσθαι ῥυθμῷ τε καὶ ἁρμονίᾳ ἢ ποιοῦντα, ὃ δὴ μελοποιίαν καλοῦσιν, ἢ χρώμενον ὀρθῶς τοῖς πεποιημένοις μέλεσί τε καὶ μέτροις, ὃ δὴ παιδεία ἐκλήθη, ἐνταῦθα δὴ καὶ χαλεπὸν καὶ ἀγαθοῦ δημιουργοῦ δεῖ. πάλιν γὰρ ἥκει ὁ αὐτὸς λόγος, ὅτι τοῖς μὲν κοσμίοις τῶν ἀνθρώπων, καὶ ὡς ἂν κοσμιώτεροι γίγνοιντο οἱ μήπω ὄντες, δεῖ χαρίζεσθαι καὶ φυλάττειν τὸν τούτων ἔρωτα, καὶ οὗτός ἐστιν ὁ καλός, ὁ οὐράνιος, ὁ τῆς Οὐρανίας μούσης Ἔρως· ὁ δὲ Πολυμνίας ὁ πάνδημος, ὃν δεῖ εὐλαβούμενον προσφέρειν οἷς ἂν προσφέρῃ, ὅπως ἂν τὴν μὲν ἡδονὴν αὐτοῦ καρπώσηται, ἀκολασίαν δὲ μηδεμίαν ἐμποιήσῃ, ὥσπερ ἐν τῇ ἡμετέρᾳ τέχνῃ μέγα ἔργον ταῖς περὶ τὴν ὀψοποιικὴν τέχνην ἐπιθυμίαις καλῶς χρῆσθαι, ὥστ' ἄνευ νόσου τὴν ἡδονὴν καρπώσασθαι. καὶ ἐν μουσικῇ δὴ καὶ ἐν ἰατρικῇ καὶ ἐν τοῖς ἄλλοις πᾶσι καὶ τοῖς ἀνθρωπείοις καὶ τοῖς θείοις, καθ' ὅσον παρείκει, φυλακτέον ἑκάτερον τὸν Ἔρωτα· ἔνεστον γάρ.

Ἐπεὶ καὶ ἡ τῶν ὡρῶν τοῦ ἐνιαυτοῦ σύστασις μεστή ἐστιν ἀμφοτέρων τούτων, καὶ ἐπειδὰν μὲν πρὸς ἄλληλα τοῦ κοσμίου τύχῃ ἔρωτος ἃ νῦν δὴ ἐγὼ ἔλεγον, τά τε θερμὰ καὶ τὰ ψυχρὰ καὶ ξηρὰ καὶ ὑγρά, καὶ ἁρμονίαν καὶ κρᾶσιν λάβῃ σώφρονα, ἥκει φέροντα εὐετηρίαν τε καὶ ὑγίειαν ἀνθρώποις

---
[1] πω Badham: πῶς mss.

SYMPOSIUM

introduces a mutual love and unanimity. Hence in its turn music is found to be a knowledge of love-matters relating to harmony and rhythm. In the actual system of harmony or rhythm we can easily distinguish these love-matters; as yet the double Love is absent: but when we come to the application of rhythm and harmony to social life, whether we construct what are called 'melodies' or render correctly, by what is known as 'training,' tunes and measures already constructed, we find here a certain difficulty and require a good craftsman. Round comes the same conclusion: well-ordered men, and the less regular only so as to bring them to better order, should be indulged in this Love, and this is the sort we should preserve; this is the noble, the Heavenly Love, sprung from the Heavenly Muse. But the Popular Love comes from the Queen of Various Song; in applying him we must proceed with all caution, that no debauchery be implanted with the reaping of his pleasure, just as in our craft we set high importance on a right use of the appetite for dainties of the table, that we may cull the pleasure without disease. Thus in music and medicine and every other affair whether human or divine, we must be on the watch as far as may be for either sort of Love; for both are there.

" Note how even the system of the yearly seasons is full of these two forces; how the qualities I mentioned just now, heat and cold, drought and moisture, when brought together by the orderly Love, and taking on a temperate harmony as they mingle, become bearers of ripe fertility and health

PLATO

καὶ τοῖς ἄλλοις ζῴοις τε καὶ φυτοῖς, καὶ οὐδὲν
ἠδίκησεν· ὅταν δὲ ὁ μετὰ τῆς ὕβρεως Ἔρως ἐγ-
κρατέστερος περὶ τὰς τοῦ ἐνιαυτοῦ ὥρας γένηται,
B διαφθείρει τε πολλὰ καὶ ἠδίκησεν. οἵ τε γὰρ λοι-
μοὶ φιλοῦσι γίγνεσθαι ἐκ τῶν τοιούτων καὶ ἄλλ᾽
ἀνόμοια πολλὰ νοσήματα καὶ τοῖς θηρίοις καὶ τοῖς
φυτοῖς· καὶ γὰρ πάχναι καὶ χάλαζαι καὶ ἐρυσῖβαι
ἐκ πλεονεξίας καὶ ἀκοσμίας περὶ ἄλληλα τῶν τοιούτων γίγνεται ἐρωτικῶν, ὧν ἐπιστήμη περὶ ἄστρων
τε φορὰς καὶ ἐνιαυτῶν ὥρας ἀστρονομία καλεῖται.
ἔτι τοίνυν καὶ αἱ θυσίαι πᾶσαι καὶ οἷς μαντικὴ
C ἐπιστατεῖ—ταῦτα δ᾽ ἐστὶν ἡ περὶ θεούς τε καὶ
ἀνθρώπους πρὸς ἀλλήλους κοινωνία—οὐ περὶ ἄλλο
τί ἐστιν ἢ περὶ Ἔρωτος φυλακήν τε καὶ ἴασιν.
πᾶσα γὰρ [ἡ]¹ ἀσέβεια φιλεῖ γίγνεσθαι, ἐὰν μή τις
τῷ κοσμίῳ Ἔρωτι χαρίζηται μηδὲ τιμᾷ τε αὐτὸν
καὶ πρεσβεύῃ ἐν παντὶ ἔργῳ, ἀλλὰ [περὶ]² τὸν ἕτερον, καὶ περὶ γονέας καὶ ζῶντας καὶ τετελευτηκό-
τας καὶ περὶ θεούς· ἃ δὴ προστέτακται τῇ μαντικῇ
ἐπισκοπεῖν τοὺς Ἔρωτας καὶ ἰατρεύειν, καὶ ἔστιν
D αὖ ἡ μαντικὴ φιλίας θεῶν καὶ ἀνθρώπων δημιουρ-
γὸς τῷ ἐπίστασθαι τὰ κατὰ ἀνθρώπους ἐρωτικά,
ὅσα τείνει πρὸς θέμιν καὶ εὐσέβειαν.³

Οὕτω πολλὴν καὶ μεγάλην, μᾶλλον δὲ πᾶσαν
δύναμιν ἔχει συλλήβδην μὲν ὁ πᾶς Ἔρως, ὁ δὲ
περὶ τἀγαθὰ μετὰ σωφροσύνης καὶ δικαιοσύνης
ἀποτελούμενος καὶ παρ᾽ ἡμῖν καὶ παρὰ θεοῖς,
οὗτος τὴν μεγίστην δύναμιν ἔχει καὶ πᾶσαν ἡμῖν
εὐδαιμονίαν παρασκευάζει καὶ ἀλλήλοις δυναμέ-
νους ὁμιλεῖν καὶ φίλους εἶναι καὶ τοῖς κρείττοσιν

¹ ἡ om. Stob. ² περὶ om. Stob.
³ εὐσέβειαν Stob.: ἀσέβειαν MSS.

SYMPOSIUM

to men and animals and plants, and are guilty of no wrong. But when the wanton-spirited Love gains the ascendant in the seasons of the year, great destruction and wrong does he wreak. For at these junctures are wont to arise pestilences and many other varieties of disease in beasts and herbs; likewise hoar-frosts, hails, and mildews, which spring from mutual encroachments and disturbances in such love-connexions as are studied in relation to the motions of the stars and the yearly seasons by what we term astronomy. So further, all sacrifices and ceremonies controlled by divination, namely, all means of communion between gods and men, are only concerned with either the preservation or the cure of Love. For impiety is usually in each case the result of refusing to gratify the orderly Love or to honour and prefer him in all our affairs, and of yielding to the other in questions of duty towards one's parents whether alive or dead, and also towards the gods. To divination is appointed the task of supervising and treating the health of these Loves; wherefore that art, as knowing what human love-affairs will lead to seemliness and pious observance, is indeed a purveyor of friendship betwixt gods and men.

"Thus Love, conceived as a single whole, exerts a wide, a strong, nay, in short, a complete power: but that which is consummated for a good purpose, temperately and justly, both here on earth and in heaven above, wields the mightiest power of all and provides us with a perfect bliss; so that we are able to consort with one another and have friendship also with the gods who are above us. It may well

131

E ἡμῶν θεοῖς. ἴσως μὲν οὖν καὶ ἐγὼ τὸν Ἔρωτα ἐπαινῶν πολλὰ παραλείπω, οὐ μέντοι ἑκών γε. ἀλλ' εἴ τι ἐξέλιπον, σὸν ἔργον, ὦ Ἀριστόφανες, ἀναπληρῶσαι· ἢ εἴ πως ἄλλως ἐν νῷ ἔχεις ἐγκωμιάζειν τὸν θεόν, ἐγκωμίαζε, ἐπειδὴ καὶ τῆς λυγγὸς πέπαυσαι.

189 Ἐκδεξάμενον οὖν ἔφη εἰπεῖν τὸν Ἀριστοφάνη ὅτι Καὶ μάλ' ἐπαύσατο, οὐ μέντοι πρίν γε τὸν πταρμὸν προσενεχθῆναι αὐτῇ, ὥστε με θαυμάζειν εἰ τὸ κόσμιον τοῦ σώματος ἐπιθυμεῖ τοιούτων ψόφων καὶ γαργαλισμῶν, οἷον καὶ ὁ πταρμός ἐστι· πάνυ γὰρ εὐθὺς ἐπαύσατο, ἐπειδὴ αὐτῷ τὸν πταρμὸν προσήνεγκα.

Καὶ τὸν Ἐρυξίμαχον, Ὦ 'γαθέ, φάναι, Ἀριστόφανες, ὅρα τί ποιεῖς. γελωτοποιεῖς μέλλων λέγειν,
B καὶ φύλακά με τοῦ λόγου ἀναγκάζεις γίγνεσθαι τοῦ σεαυτοῦ, ἐάν τι γελοῖον εἴπῃς, ἐξόν σοι ἐν εἰρήνῃ λέγειν.

Καὶ τὸν Ἀριστοφάνη γελάσαντα εἰπεῖν Εὖ λέγεις, ὦ Ἐρυξίμαχε, καί μοι ἔστω ἄρρητα τὰ εἰρημένα. ἀλλὰ μή με φύλαττε, ὡς ἐγὼ φοβοῦμαι περὶ τῶν μελλόντων ῥηθήσεσθαι, οὔ τι μὴ γελοῖα εἴπω, τοῦτο μὲν γὰρ ἂν κέρδος εἴη καὶ τῆς ἡμετέρας μούσης ἐπιχώριον, ἀλλὰ μὴ καταγέλαστα.

Βαλών γε, φάναι, ὦ Ἀριστόφανες, οἴει ἐκφεύξεσθαι· ἀλλὰ πρόσεχε τὸν νοῦν καὶ οὕτω λέγε ὡς
C δώσων λόγον· ἴσως μέντοι, ἂν δόξῃ μοι, ἀφήσω σε.

Καὶ μήν, ὦ Ἐρυξίμαχε, εἰπεῖν τὸν Ἀριστοφάνη, ἄλλῃ γέ πῃ ἐν νῷ ἔχω λέγειν, ἢ ᾗ σύ τε

be that with the best will in the world I have omitted many points in the praise I owe to Love; but any gaps which I may have left it is your business, Aristophanes, to fill: or if you intend some different manner of glorifying the god, let us hear your eulogy, for you have stopped your hiccough now."

Then, as my friend related, Aristophanes took up the word and said: "Yes, it has stopped, though not until it was treated with a course of sneezing, such as leaves me wondering that the orderly principle of the body should call for the noises and titillations involved in sneezing; you see, it stopped the very moment I applied the sneeze to it."

"My good Aristophanes," replied Eryximachus, "take heed what you are about. Here are you buffooning before ever you begin, and compelling me to be on the watch for the first absurdity in your own speech, when you might deliver it in peace."

At this Aristophanes laughed, and—"Quite right, Eryximachus," he said; "I unsay all that I have said. Do not keep a watch on me; for as to what is going to be said, my fear is not so much of saying something absurd—since that would be all to the good and native to my Muse—as something utterly ridiculous."

"You think you can just let fly, Aristophanes, and get off unscathed! Have a good care to speak only what you can defend; though perhaps I may be pleased to let you off altogether."

The Speech of Aristophanes

"It is indeed my intention, Eryximachus," said Aristophanes, "to speak in somewhat different

καὶ Παυσανίας εἰπέτην. ἐμοὶ γὰρ δοκοῦσιν οἱ ἄνθρωποι παντάπασι τὴν τοῦ ἔρωτος δύναμιν οὐκ ᾐσθῆσθαι, ἐπεὶ αἰσθανόμενοί γε μέγιστ' ἂν αὐτοῦ ἱερὰ κατασκευάσαι καὶ βωμούς, καὶ θυσίας ἂν ποιεῖν μεγίστας, οὐχ ὥσπερ νῦν τούτων οὐδὲν γίγνεται περὶ αὐτόν, δέον πάντων μάλιστα γίγνεσθαι. D ἔστι γὰρ θεῶν φιλανθρωπότατος, ἐπίκουρός τε ὢν τῶν ἀνθρώπων καὶ ἰατρὸς τούτων, ὧν ἰαθέντων μεγίστη εὐδαιμονία ἂν τῷ ἀνθρωπείῳ γένει εἴη. ἐγὼ οὖν πειράσομαι ὑμῖν εἰσηγήσασθαι τὴν δύναμιν αὐτοῦ, ὑμεῖς δὲ τῶν ἄλλων διδάσκαλοι ἔσεσθε. δεῖ δὲ πρῶτον ὑμᾶς μαθεῖν τὴν ἀνθρωπίνην φύσιν καὶ τὰ παθήματα αὐτῆς. ἡ γὰρ πάλαι ἡμῶν φύσις οὐχ αὕτη ἦν, ἥπερ νῦν, ἀλλ' ἀλλοία. πρῶτον μὲν γὰρ τρία ἦν τὰ γένη τὰ τῶν ἀνθρώπων, E οὐχ ὥσπερ νῦν δύο, ἄρρεν καὶ θῆλυ, ἀλλὰ καὶ τρίτον προσῆν κοινὸν ὂν ἀμφοτέρων τούτων, οὗ νῦν ὄνομα λοιπόν, αὐτὸ δὲ ἠφάνισται· ἀνδρόγυνον γὰρ ἓν τότε μὲν ἦν καὶ εἶδος καὶ ὄνομα ἐξ ἀμφοτέρων κοινὸν τοῦ τε ἄρρενος καὶ θήλεος, νῦν δ' οὐκ ἔστιν ἀλλ' ἢ ἐν ὀνείδει ὄνομα κείμενον. ἔπειτα ὅλον ἦν ἑκάστου τοῦ ἀνθρώπου τὸ εἶδος στρογγύλον, νῶτον καὶ πλευρὰς κύκλῳ ἔχον, χεῖρας δὲ τέτταρας εἶχε, καὶ σκέλη τὰ ἴσα ταῖς χερσί, καὶ πρόσωπα δύ' ἐπ' 190 αὐχένι κυκλοτερεῖ, ὅμοια πάντῃ· κεφαλὴν δ' ἐπ' ἀμφοτέροις τοῖς προσώποις ἐναντίοις κειμένοις μίαν, καὶ ὦτα τέτταρα, καὶ αἰδοῖα δύο, καὶ τἆλλα πάντα ὡς ἀπὸ τούτων ἄν τις εἰκάσειεν. ἐπορεύετο δὲ καὶ ὀρθὸν ὥσπερ νῦν, ὁποτέρωσε βουληθείη· καὶ ὁπότε ταχὺ ὁρμήσειε θεῖν, ὥσπερ οἱ κυβιστῶν-

SYMPOSIUM

strain from you and Pausanias. For in my opinion humanity has entirely failed to perceive the power of Love: if men did perceive it, they would have provided him with splendid temples and altars, and would splendidly honour him with sacrifice ; whereas we see none of these things done for him, though they are especially his due. He of all gods is most friendly to men ; he succours mankind and heals those ills whose cure must be the highest happiness of the human race. Hence I shall try and introduce you to his power, that you may transmit this teaching to the world at large. You must begin your lesson with the nature of man and its development. For our original nature was by no means the same as it is now. In the first place, there were three kinds of human beings, not merely the two sexes, male and female, as at present: there was a third kind as well, which had equal shares of the other two, and whose name survives though the thing itself has vanished. For 'man-woman'[1] was then a unity in form no less than name, composed of both sexes and sharing equally in male and female ; whereas now it has come to be merely a name of reproach. Secondly, the form of each person was round all over, with back and sides encompassing it every way ; each had four arms, and legs to match these, and two faces perfectly alike on a cylindrical neck. There was one head to the two faces, which looked opposite ways ; there were four ears, two privy members, and all the other parts, as may be imagined, in proportion. The creature walked upright as now, in either direction as it pleased ; and whenever it started running fast, it went like our acrobats,

---

[1] *i.e.* "hermaphrodite" ; *cf.* Lucret. v. 837 foll.

τες καὶ εἰς ὀρθὸν τὰ σκέλη περιφερόμενοι κυβι-
στῶσι κύκλῳ, ὀκτὼ τότε οὖσι τοῖς μέλεσιν ἀπερει-
δόμενοι ταχὺ ἐφέροντο κύκλῳ. ἦν δὲ διὰ ταῦτα
τρία τὰ γένη καὶ τοιαῦτα, ὅτι τὸ μὲν ἄρρεν ἦν τοῦ
ἡλίου τὴν ἀρχὴν ἔκγονον, τὸ δὲ θῆλυ τῆς γῆς, τὸ
δὲ ἀμφοτέρων μετέχον τῆς σελήνης, ὅτι καὶ ἡ
σελήνη ἀμφοτέρων μετέχει· περιφερῆ δὲ δὴ ἦν
καὶ αὐτὰ καὶ ἡ πορεία αὐτῶν διὰ τὸ τοῖς γονεῦσιν
ὅμοια εἶναι. ἦν οὖν τὴν ἰσχὺν δεινὰ καὶ τὴν
ῥώμην, καὶ τὰ φρονήματα μεγάλα εἶχον, ἐπεχεί-
ρησαν δὲ τοῖς θεοῖς, καὶ ὃ λέγει Ὅμηρος περὶ
Ἐφιάλτου τε καὶ Ὤτου, περὶ ἐκείνων λέγεται, τὸ
εἰς τὸν οὐρανὸν ἀνάβασιν ἐπιχειρεῖν ποιεῖν, ὡς
ἐπιθησομένων τοῖς θεοῖς.

Ὁ οὖν Ζεὺς καὶ οἱ ἄλλοι θεοὶ ἐβουλεύοντο,
ὅ τι χρὴ αὐτοὺς ποιῆσαι, καὶ ἠπόρουν· οὔτε γὰρ
ὅπως ἀποκτείναιεν εἶχον καὶ ὥσπερ τοὺς γίγαντας
κεραυνώσαντες τὸ γένος ἀφανίσαιεν—αἱ τιμαὶ γὰρ
αὐτοῖς καὶ ἱερὰ τὰ παρὰ τῶν ἀνθρώπων ἠφανίζετο
—οὔθ' ὅπως ἐῷεν ἀσελγαίνειν. μόγις δὴ ὁ Ζεὺς
ἐννοήσας λέγει ὅτι Δοκῶ μοι, ἔφη, ἔχειν μηχανήν,
ὡς ἂν εἶέν τε ἄνθρωποι καὶ παύσαιντο τῆς ἀκολασίας ἀσθενέστεροι γενόμενοι. νῦν μὲν γὰρ αὐτούς,
ἔφη, διατεμῶ δίχα ἕκαστον, καὶ ἅμα μὲν ἀσθενέστεροι ἔσονται, ἅμα δὲ χρησιμώτεροι ἡμῖν διὰ τὸ
πλείους τὸν ἀριθμὸν γεγονέναι· καὶ βαδιοῦνται
ὀρθοὶ ἐπὶ δυοῖν σκελοῖν· ἐὰν δ' ἔτι δοκῶσιν ἀσελγαίνειν καὶ μὴ ἐθέλωσιν ἡσυχίαν ἄγειν, πάλιν αὖ,

SYMPOSIUM

whirling over and over with legs stuck out straight; only then they had eight limbs to support and speed them swiftly round and round. The number and features of these three sexes were owing to the fact that the male was originally the offspring of the sun, and the female of the earth; while that which partook of both sexes was born of the moon, for the moon also partakes of both.[1] They were globular in their shape as in their progress, since they took after their parents. Now, they were of surprising strength and vigour, and so lofty in their notions that they even conspired against the gods; and the same story is told of them as Homer relates of Ephialtes and Otus,[2] that scheming to assault the gods in fight they essayed to mount high heaven.

"Thereat Zeus and the other gods debated what they should do, and were perplexed: for they felt they could not slay them like the Giants, whom they had abolished root and branch with strokes of thunder—it would be only abolishing the honours and observances they had from men; nor yet could they endure such sinful rioting. Then Zeus, putting all his wits together, spake at length and said: 'Methinks I can contrive that men, without ceasing to exist, shall give over their iniquity through a lessening of their strength. I propose now to slice every one of them in two, so that while making them weaker we shall find them more useful by reason of their multiplication; and they shall walk erect upon two legs. If they continue turbulent and do not choose to keep quiet, I will do it again,'

---

[1] The double sex of the moon is mentioned in an Orphic hymn (ix. 4): *cf*. Macrob. iii. 8.
[2] Homer, *Od*. xi. 305 foll.; *Il*. v. 385 foll.

PLATO

ἔφη, τεμῶ δίχα, ὥστ' ἐφ' ἑνὸς πορεύσονται σκέλους ἀσκωλίζοντες· ταῦτα εἰπὼν ἔτεμνε τοὺς ἀνθρώπους δίχα, ὥσπερ οἱ τὰ ὄα τέμνοντες καὶ μέλλοντες ταριχεύειν, ἢ ὥσπερ οἱ τὰ ᾠὰ ταῖς θριξίν· ὅντινα δὲ τέμοι, τὸν Ἀπόλλω ἐκέλευε τό τε πρόσωπον μεταστρέφειν καὶ τὸ τοῦ αὐχένος ἥμισυ πρὸς τὴν τομήν, ἵνα θεώμενος τὴν αὑτοῦ τμῆσιν κοσμιώτερος εἴη ὁ ἄνθρωπος, καὶ τἆλλα ἰᾶσθαι ἐκέλευεν. ὁ δὲ τό τε πρόσωπον μετέστρεφε, καὶ συνέλκων πανταχόθεν τὸ δέρμα ἐπὶ τὴν γαστέρα νῦν καλουμένην, ὥσπερ τὰ σύσπαστα βαλλάντια, ἓν στόμα ποιῶν ἀπέδει κατὰ μέσην τὴν γαστέρα, ὃ δὴ τὸν ὀμφαλὸν καλοῦσι. καὶ τὰς μὲν ἄλλας ῥυτίδας τὰς πολλὰς ἐξελέαινε καὶ τὰ στήθη διήρθρου, ἔχων τι τοιοῦτον ὄργανον οἷον οἱ σκυτοτόμοι περὶ τὸν καλόποδα λεαίνοντες τὰς τῶν σκυτῶν ῥυτίδας· ὀλίγας δὲ κατέλιπε, τὰς περὶ αὐτὴν τὴν γαστέρα καὶ τὸν ὀμφαλόν, μνημεῖον εἶναι τοῦ παλαιοῦ πάθους. ἐπειδὴ οὖν ἡ φύσις δίχα ἐτμήθη, ποθοῦν ἕκαστον τὸ ἥμισυ τὸ αὑτοῦ συνῄει, καὶ περιβάλλοντες τὰς χεῖρας καὶ συμπλεκόμενοι ἀλλήλοις, ἐπιθυμοῦντες συμφῦναι, ἀπέθνησκον ὑπὸ λιμοῦ καὶ τῆς ἄλλης ἀργίας διὰ τὸ μηδὲν ἐθέλειν χωρὶς ἀλλήλων ποιεῖν. καὶ ὁπότε τι ἀποθάνοι τῶν ἡμίσεων, τὸ δὲ λειφθείη, τὸ λειφθὲν ἄλλο ἐζήτει καὶ συνεπλέκετο, εἴτε γυναικὸς τῆς ὅλης ἐντύχοι ἡμίσει, ὃ δὴ νῦν γυναῖκα καλοῦμεν, εἴτε ἀνδρός· καὶ οὕτως ἀπώλλυντο. ἐλεήσας δὲ ὁ Ζεὺς ἄλλην μηχανὴν πορίζεται, καὶ μετατίθησιν αὐτῶν τὰ αἰδοῖα εἰς τὸ πρόσθεν· τέως γὰρ καὶ ταῦτα ἐκτὸς εἶχον, καὶ ἐγέννων καὶ ἔτικτον οὐκ

SYMPOSIUM

said he; 'I will slice every person in two, and then they must go their ways on one leg, hopping.' So saying, he sliced each human being in two, just as they slice sorb-apples to make a dry preserve, or eggs with hairs; and at the cleaving of each he bade Apollo turn its face and half-neck to the section side, in order that every one might be made more orderly by the sight of the knife's work upon him; this done, the god was to heal them up. Then Apollo turned their faces about, and pulled their skin together from the edges over what is now called the belly, just like purses which you draw close with a string; the little opening he tied up in the middle of the belly, so making what we know as the navel. For the rest, he smoothed away most of the puckers and figured out the breast with some such instrument as shoemakers use in smoothing the wrinkles of leather on the last; though he left there a few which we have just about the belly and navel, to remind us of our early fall. Now when our first form had been cut in two, each half in longing for its fellow would come to it again; and then would they fling their arms about each other and in mutual embraces yearn to be grafted together, till they began to perish of hunger and general indolence, through refusing to do anything apart. And whenever on the death of one half the other was left alone, it went seeking and embracing either any half of the whole woman (which now we call a woman), or any half of the whole man on which it might happen. In this plight they were perishing away, when Zeus in his pity provided a fresh device. He moved their privy parts to the front—for until then they had these, like all else, on the outside, and

εἰς ἀλλήλους ἀλλ' εἰς γῆν, ὥσπερ οἱ τέττιγες· μετέθηκέ τε οὖν οὕτω ⟨ταῦτ'⟩[1] αὐτῶν εἰς τὸ πρόσθεν καὶ διὰ τούτων τὴν γένεσιν ἐν ἀλλήλοις ἐποίησε, διὰ τοῦ ἄρρενος ἐν τῷ θήλει, τῶνδε ἕνεκα, ἵνα ἐν τῇ συμπλοκῇ ἅμα μὲν εἰ ἀνὴρ γυναικὶ ἐντύχοι, γεννῷεν καὶ γίγνοιτο τὸ γένος, ἅμα δ' εἰ καὶ ἄρρην ἄρρενι, πλησμονὴ γοῦν γίγνοιτο τῆς συνουσίας καὶ διαπαύοιντο καὶ ἐπὶ τὰ ἔργα τρέποιντο καὶ τοῦ ἄλλου βίου ἐπιμελοῖντο. ἔστι δὴ οὖν ἐκ τόσου ὁ ἔρως ἔμφυτος ἀλλήλων τοῖς ἀνθρώποις καὶ τῆς ἀρχαίας φύσεως συναγωγεὺς καὶ ἐπιχειρῶν ποιῆσαι ἓν ἐκ δυοῖν καὶ ἰάσασθαι τὴν φύσιν τὴν ἀνθρωπίνην.

Ἕκαστος οὖν ἡμῶν ἐστὶν ἀνθρώπου σύμβολον, ἅτε τετμημένος ὥσπερ αἱ ψῆτται, ἐξ ἑνὸς δύο. ζητεῖ δὴ ἀεὶ τὸ αὑτοῦ ἕκαστος σύμβολον. ὅσοι μὲν οὖν τῶν ἀνδρῶν τοῦ κοινοῦ τμῆμά εἰσιν, ὃ δὴ τότε ἀνδρόγυνον ἐκαλεῖτο, φιλογύναικές τ' εἰσὶ καὶ οἱ πολλοὶ τῶν μοιχῶν ἐκ τούτου τοῦ γένους γεγόνασι, καὶ ὅσαι αὖ γυναῖκες φίλανδροί τε καὶ μοιχεύτριαι, ἐκ τούτου τοῦ γένους γίγνονται. ὅσαι δὲ τῶν γυναικῶν γυναικὸς τμῆμά εἰσιν, οὐ πάνυ αὗται τοῖς ἀνδράσι τὸν νοῦν προσέχουσιν, ἀλλὰ μᾶλλον πρὸς τὰς γυναῖκας τετραμμέναι εἰσί, καὶ αἱ ἑταιρίστριαι ἐκ τούτου τοῦ γένους γίγνονται. ὅσοι δὲ ἄρρενος τμῆμά εἰσι, τὰ ἄρρενα διώκουσι, καὶ τέως μὲν ἂν παῖδες ὦσιν, ἅτε τεμάχια ὄντα τοῦ ἄρρενος, φιλοῦσι τοὺς ἄνδρας καὶ χαίρουσι συγκατακείμενοι καὶ συμπεπλεγμένοι τοῖς

[1] ⟨ταῦτ'⟩ Bury.

SYMPOSIUM

did their begetting and bringing forth not on each other but on the earth, like the crickets. These parts he now shifted to the front, to be used for propagating on each other—in the female member by means of the male; so that if in their embracements a man should happen on a woman there might be conception and continuation of their kind; and also, if male met with male they might have some satiety of their union and a relief, and so might turn their hands to their labours and their interest to ordinary life. Thus anciently is mutual love ingrained in mankind, reassembling our early estate and endeavouring to combine two in one and heal the human sore.

"Each of us, then, is but a tally[1] of a man, since every one shows like a flat-fish the traces of having been sliced in two; and each is ever searching for the tally that will fit him. All the men who are sections of that composite sex that at first was called man-woman are woman-courters; our adulterers are mostly descended from that sex, whence likewise are derived our man-courting women and adulteresses. All the women who are sections of the woman have no great fancy for men: they are inclined rather to women, and of this stock are the she-minions. Men who are sections of the male pursue the masculine, and so long as their boyhood lasts they show themselves to be slices of the male by making friends with men and delighting to lie with them and to be clasped in men's

[1] A tally, or notched stick matching another, is the nearest English equivalent for σύμβολον, which was a half of a broken die given and kept as a token of friendship; see below, 193 A (λίσπαι).

ἀνδράσι, καί εἰσιν οὗτοι βέλτιστοι τῶν παίδων καὶ μειρακίων, ἅτε ἀνδρειότατοι ὄντες φύσει. φασὶ δὲ δή τινες αὐτοὺς ἀναισχύντους εἶναι, ψευδόμενοι· οὐ γὰρ ὑπ' ἀναισχυντίας τοῦτο δρῶσιν, ἀλλ' ὑπὸ θάρρους καὶ ἀνδρείας καὶ ἀρρενωπίας, τὸ ὅμοιον αὑτοῖς ἀσπαζόμενοι. μέγα δὲ τεκμήριον· καὶ γὰρ τελεωθέντες μόνοι ἀποβαίνουσιν εἰς τὰ πολιτικὰ ἄνδρες οἱ τοιοῦτοι. ἐπειδὰν δὲ ἀνδρω-
B θῶσι, παιδεραστοῦσι καὶ πρὸς γάμους καὶ παιδοποιίας οὐ προσέχουσι τὸν νοῦν φύσει, ἀλλὰ ὑπὸ τοῦ νόμου ἀναγκάζονται· ἀλλ' ἐξαρκεῖ αὐτοῖς μετ' ἀλλήλων καταζῆν ἀγάμοις. πάντως μὲν οὖν ὁ τοιοῦτος παιδεραστής τε καὶ φιλεραστὴς γίγνεται, ἀεὶ τὸ συγγενὲς ἀσπαζόμενος. ὅταν μὲν οὖν καὶ αὐτῷ ἐκείνῳ ἐντύχῃ τῷ αὑτοῦ ἡμίσει καὶ ὁ παιδεραστὴς
C καὶ ἄλλος πᾶς, τότε καὶ θαυμαστὰ ἐκπλήττονται φιλίᾳ τε καὶ οἰκειότητι καὶ ἔρωτι, οὐκ ἐθέλοντες, ὡς ἔπος εἰπεῖν, χωρίζεσθαι ἀλλήλων οὐδὲ σμικρὸν χρόνον. καὶ οἱ διατελοῦντες μετ' ἀλλήλων διὰ βίου οὗτοί εἰσιν, οἳ οὐδ' ἂν ἔχοιεν εἰπεῖν ὅ τι βούλονται σφίσι παρ' ἀλλήλων γίγνεσθαι. οὐδενὶ[1] γὰρ ἂν δόξειε τοῦτ' εἶναι ἡ τῶν ἀφροδισίων συνουσία, ὡς ἄρα τούτου ἕνεκα ἕτερος ἑτέρῳ χαίρει συνὼν οὕτως ἐπὶ μεγάλης σπουδῆς· ἀλλ' ἄλλο τι βουλομένη ἑκατέρου ἡ ψυχὴ δήλη ἐστίν, ὃ οὐ δύνα-
D ται εἰπεῖν, ἀλλὰ μαντεύεται ὃ βούλεται, καὶ αἰνίττεται. καὶ εἰ αὐτοῖς ἐν τῷ αὐτῷ κατακειμένοις ἐπιστὰς ὁ Ἥφαιστος, ἔχων τὰ ὄργανα, ἔροιτο· Τί ἔσθ' ὃ βούλεσθε, ὦ ἄνθρωποι, ὑμῖν παρ' ἀλλήλων

[1] οὐδενὶ Stob.: οὐδὲν mss.: οὐδὲ, recc.

embraces; these are the finest boys and striplings, for they have the most manly nature. Some say they are shameless creatures, but falsely: for their behaviour is due not to shamelessness but to daring, manliness, and virility, since they are quick to welcome their like. Sure evidence of this is the fact that on reaching maturity these alone prove in a public career to be men. So when they come to man's estate they are boy-lovers, and have no natural interest in wiving and getting children, but only do these things under stress of custom; they are quite contented to live together unwedded all their days. A man of this sort is at any rate born to be a lover of boys or the willing mate of a man, eagerly greeting his own kind. Well, when one of them—whether he be a boy-lover or a lover of any other sort—happens on his own particular half, the two of them are wondrously thrilled with affection and intimacy and love, and are hardly to be induced to leave each other's side for a single moment. These are they who continue together throughout life, though they could not even say what they would have of one another. No one could imagine this to be the mere amorous connexion, or that such alone could be the reason why each rejoices in the other's company with so eager a zest: obviously the soul of each is wishing for something else that it cannot express, only divining and darkly hinting what it wishes. Suppose that, as they lay together, Hephaestus should come and stand over them, and showing his implements [1] should ask: 'What is it, good mortals, that you would have of one another?'

---

[1] *i.e.* his anvil (*Od.* viii. 274), bellows, tongs, and hammer (*Il.* xviii. 372 foll., 474 foll.).

γενέσθαι; καὶ εἰ ἀποροῦντας αὐτοὺς πάλιν ἔροιτο
*Ἆρά γε τοῦδε ἐπιθυμεῖτε, ἐν τῷ αὐτῷ γενέσθαι ὅτι
μάλιστα ἀλλήλοις, ὥστε καὶ νύκτα καὶ ἡμέραν
E μὴ ἀπολείπεσθαι ἀλλήλων; εἰ γὰρ τούτου ἐπιθυμεῖτε, ἐθέλω ὑμᾶς συντῆξαι καὶ συμφυσῆσαι εἰς τὸ
αὐτό, ὥστε δύ᾽ ὄντας ἕνα γεγονέναι καὶ ἕως τ᾽ ἂν
ζῆτε, ὡς ἕνα ὄντα, κοινῇ ἀμφοτέρους ζῆν, καὶ
ἐπειδὰν ἀποθάνητε, ἐκεῖ αὖ ἐν Ἅιδου ἀντὶ δυοῖν
ἕνα εἶναι κοινῇ τεθνεῶτε· ἀλλ᾽ ὁρᾶτε εἰ τούτου
ἐρᾶτε καὶ ἐξαρκεῖ ὑμῖν ἂν τούτου τύχητε· ταῦτα
ἀκούσας ἴσμεν ὅτι οὐδ᾽ ἂν εἷς ἐξαρνηθείη οὐδ᾽
ἄλλο τι ἂν φανείη βουλόμενος, ἀλλ᾽ ἀτεχνῶς οἴοιτ᾽
ἂν ἀκηκοέναι τοῦτο ὃ πάλαι ἄρα ἐπεθύμει, συν-
ελθὼν καὶ συντακεὶς τῷ ἐρωμένῳ ἐκ δυοῖν εἷς
γενέσθαι.

Τοῦτο γάρ ἐστι τὸ αἴτιον, ὅτι ἡ ἀρχαία φύσις
ἡμῶν ἦν αὕτη καὶ ἦμεν ὅλοι· τοῦ ὅλου οὖν τῇ
193 ἐπιθυμίᾳ καὶ διώξει ἔρως ὄνομα. καὶ πρὸ τοῦ,
ὥσπερ λέγω, ἓν ἦμεν· νυνὶ δὲ διὰ τὴν ἀδικίαν
διῳκίσθημεν ὑπὸ τοῦ θεοῦ, καθάπερ Ἀρκάδες
ὑπὸ Λακεδαιμονίων. φόβος οὖν ἔστιν, ἐὰν μὴ
κόσμιοι ὦμεν πρὸς τοὺς θεούς, ὅπως μὴ καὶ αὖθις
διασχισθησόμεθα, καὶ περίιμεν ἔχοντες ὥσπερ οἱ
ἐν ταῖς στήλαις καταγραφὴν ἐκτετυπωμένοι, δια-
πεπρισμένοι κατὰ τὰς ῥῖνας, γεγονότες ὥσπερ
λίσπαι. ἀλλὰ τούτων ἕνεκα πάντ᾽ ἄνδρα χρὴ ἅπαντα παρακελεύεσθαι εὐσεβεῖν περὶ θεούς, ἵνα τὰ
B μὲν ἐκφύγωμεν, τῶν δὲ τύχωμεν, ὡς ὁ Ἔρως ἡμῖν

SYMPOSIUM

—and suppose that in their perplexity he asked them again: 'Do you desire to be joined in the closest possible union, so that you shall not be divided by night or by day? If that is your craving, I am ready to fuse and weld you together in a single piece, that from being two you may be made one; that so long as you live, the pair of you, being as one, may share a single life; and that when you die you may also in Hades yonder be one instead of two, having shared a single death. Bethink yourselves if this is your heart's desire, and if you will be quite contented with this lot.' Not one on hearing this, we are sure, would demur to it or would be found wishing for anything else: each would unreservedly deem that he had been offered just what he was yearning for all the time, namely, to be so joined and fused with his beloved that the two might be made one.

"The cause of it all is this, that our original form was as I have described, and we were entire; and the craving and pursuit of that entirety is called Love. Formerly, as I have said, we were one; but now for our sins we are all dispersed by God, as the Arcadians were by the Lacedaemonians[1]; and we may well be afraid that if we are disorderly towards Heaven we may once more be cloven asunder and may go about in the shape of those outline-carvings on the tombs, with our noses sawn down the middle, and may thus become like tokens of split dice. Wherefore we ought all to exhort others to a pious observance of the gods in all things, so that we may escape harm and attain to bliss under the

[1] Probably referring to the dispersal of Mantinea into villages in 385 B.C. (Xenophon, *Hell.* v. 2. 1 foll.).

ἡγεμὼν καὶ στρατηγός. ᾧ μηδεὶς ἐναντία πραττέτω· πράττει δ' ἐναντία, ὅστις θεοῖς ἀπεχθάνεται· φίλοι γὰρ γενόμενοι καὶ διαλλαγέντες τῷ θεῷ ἐξευρήσομέν τε καὶ ἐντευξόμεθα τοῖς παιδικοῖς τοῖς ἡμετέροις αὐτῶν, ὃ τῶν νῦν ὀλίγοι ποιοῦσι. καὶ μή μοι ὑπολάβῃ Ἐρυξίμαχος κωμῳδῶν τὸν λόγον, ὡς Παυσανίαν καὶ Ἀγάθωνα λέγω· ἴσως μὲν γὰρ καὶ οὗτοι τούτων τυγχάνουσιν ὄντες καὶ εἰσὶν ἀμφότεροι τὴν φύσιν ἄρρενες· λέγω δὲ οὖν ἔγωγε καθ' ἁπάντων καὶ ἀνδρῶν καὶ γυναικῶν, ὅτι οὕτως ἂν ἡμῶν τὸ γένος εὔδαιμον γένοιτο, εἰ ἐκτελέσαιμεν τὸν ἔρωτα καὶ τῶν παιδικῶν τῶν αὑτοῦ ἕκαστος τύχοι εἰς τὴν ἀρχαίαν ἀπελθὼν φύσιν. εἰ δὲ τοῦτο ἄριστον, ἀναγκαῖον καὶ τῶν νῦν παρόντων τὸ τούτου ἐγγυτάτω ἄριστον εἶναι· τοῦτο δ' ἐστὶ παιδικῶν τυχεῖν κατὰ νοῦν αὐτῷ πεφυκότων· οὗ δὴ τὸν αἴτιον θεὸν ὑμνοῦντες δικαίως ἂν ὑμνοῖμεν Ἔρωτα, ὃς ἔν τε τῷ παρόντι ἡμᾶς πλεῖστα ὀνίνησιν εἰς τὸ οἰκεῖον ἄγων, καὶ εἰς τὸ ἔπειτα ἐλπίδας μεγίστας παρέχεται, ἡμῶν παρεχομένων πρὸς θεοὺς εὐσέβειαν, καταστήσας ἡμᾶς εἰς τὴν ἀρχαίαν φύσιν καὶ ἰασάμενος μακαρίους καὶ εὐδαίμονας ποιῆσαι.

Οὗτος, ἔφη, ὦ Ἐρυξίμαχε, ὁ ἐμὸς λόγος ἐστὶ περὶ Ἔρωτος, ἀλλοῖος ἢ ὁ σός. ὥσπερ οὖν ἐδεήθην σου, μὴ κωμῳδήσῃς αὐτόν, ἵνα καὶ τῶν λοιπῶν ἀκούσωμεν τί ἕκαστος ἐρεῖ, μᾶλλον δὲ τί ἑκάτερος· Ἀγάθων γὰρ καὶ Σωκράτης λοιποί.

Ἀλλὰ πείσομαί σοι, ἔφη φάναι τὸν Ἐρυξίμαχον· καὶ γάρ μοι ὁ λόγος ἡδέως ἐρρήθη. καὶ εἰ μὴ συνῄδη Σωκράτει τε καὶ Ἀγάθωνι δεινοῖς

SYMPOSIUM

gallant leadership of Love. Let none in act oppose him—and it is opposing him to incur the hate of Heaven: if we make friends with the god and are reconciled, we shall have the fortune that falls to few in our day, of discovering our proper favourites. And let not Eryximachus retort on my speech with a comic mock, and say I refer to Pausanias and Agathon; it may be they do belong to the fortunate few, and are both of them males by nature; what I mean is—and this applies to the whole world of men and women—that the way to bring happiness to our race is to give our love its true fulfilment: let every one find his own favourite, and so revert to his primal estate. If this be the best thing of all, the nearest approach to it among all acts open to us now must accordingly be the best to choose; and that is, to find a favourite whose nature is exactly to our mind. Love is the god who brings this about; he fully deserves our hymns. For not only in the present does he bestow the priceless boon of bringing us to our very own, but he also supplies this excellent hope for the future, that if we will supply the gods with reverent duty he will restore us to our ancient life and heal and help us into the happiness of the blest.

"There, Eryximachus, is my discourse on Love, of a different sort from yours. As I besought you, make no comic sport of it, for we want to hear what the others will say in their turn—I rather mean the other two, since only Agathon and Socrates are left."

"Well, I will obey you," said Eryximachus, "for in fact I enjoyed your speech. Had I not reason to know the prowess of Socrates and Agathon in

193

οὖσι περὶ τὰ ἐρωτικά, πάνυ ἂν ἐφοβούμην μὴ ἀπορήσωσι λόγων διὰ τὸ πολλὰ καὶ παντοδαπὰ εἰρῆσθαι· νῦν δὲ ὅμως θαρρῶ.

Τὸν οὖν Σωκράτη εἰπεῖν Καλῶς γὰρ αὐτὸς 194 ἠγώνισαι, ὦ Ἐρυξίμαχε· εἰ δὲ γένοιο οὗ νῦν ἐγώ εἰμι, μᾶλλον δὲ ἴσως οὗ ἔσομαι, ἐπειδὰν καὶ Ἀγάθων εἴπῃ, εὖ καὶ μάλ' ἂν φοβοῖο καὶ ἐν παντὶ εἴης ὥσπερ ἐγὼ νῦν.

Φαρμάττειν βούλει με, ὦ Σώκρατες, εἰπεῖν τὸν Ἀγάθωνα, ἵνα θορυβηθῶ διὰ τὸ οἴεσθαι τὸ θέατρον προσδοκίαν μεγάλην ἔχειν ὡς εὖ ἐροῦντος ἐμοῦ.

Ἐπιλήσμων μεντἂν εἴην, ὦ Ἀγάθων, εἰπεῖν B τὸν Σωκράτη, εἰ ἰδὼν τὴν σὴν ἀνδρείαν καὶ μεγαλοφροσύνην ἀναβαίνοντος ἐπὶ τὸν ὀκρίβαντα μετὰ τῶν ὑποκριτῶν, καὶ βλέψαντος ἐναντία τοσούτῳ θεάτρῳ, μέλλοντος ἐπιδείξεσθαι σαυτοῦ λόγους, καὶ οὐδ' ὁπωστιοῦν ἐκπλαγέντος, νῦν οἰηθείην σε θορυβηθήσεσθαι ἕνεκα ἡμῶν ὀλίγων ἀνθρώπων.

Τί δέ, ὦ Σώκρατες; τὸν Ἀγάθωνα φάναι, οὐ δήπου με οὕτω θεάτρου μεστὸν ἡγῇ, ὥστε καὶ ἀγνοεῖν, ὅτι νοῦν ἔχοντι ὀλίγοι ἔμφρονες πολλῶν ἀφρόνων φοβερώτεροι;

Οὐ μεντἂν καλῶς ποιοίην, φάναι τὸν Σωκράτη, C ὦ Ἀγάθων, περὶ σοῦ τι ἐγὼ ἄγροικον δοξάζων· ἀλλ' εὖ οἶδα, ὅτι εἴ τισιν ἐντύχοις οὓς ἡγοῖο σοφούς, μᾶλλον ἂν αὐτῶν φροντίζοις ἢ τῶν πολλῶν· ἀλλὰ μὴ οὐχ οὗτοι ἡμεῖς ὦμεν· ἡμεῖς μὲν γὰρ

SYMPOSIUM

love-matters, I should have great fears of their being at a loss for eloquence after we have heard it in such copious variety: but you see, my confidence is unshaken."

Whereon Socrates remarked: "Your own performance, Eryximachus, made a fine hit: but if you could be where I am now—or rather, I should say, where I shall be when Agathon has spoken—you would be fitly and sorely afraid, and would be as hard put to it as I am."

"You want to throw a spell over me, Socrates," said Agathon, "so that I may be flustered with the consciousness of the high expectations the audience has formed of my discourse."

"Nay, Agathon, how forgetful I should be," replied Socrates, "if after noticing your high and manly spirit as you stepped upon the platform with your troupe—how you sent a straight glance at that vast assembly to show that you meant to do yourself credit with your production, and how you were not dismayed in the slightest—if I should now suppose you could be flustered on account of a few fellows like us."

"Why, Socrates," said Agathon, "I hope you do not always fancy me so puffed up with the playhouse as to forget that an intelligent speaker is more alarmed at a few men of wit than at a host of fools."

"No, Agathon, it would be wrong of me indeed," said Socrates, "to associate you with any such clownish notion: I am quite sure that on finding yourself with a few persons whom you considered clever you would make more account of them than of the multitude. Yet we, perhaps, are not the

PLATO

καὶ ἐκεῖ παρῆμεν καὶ ἦμεν τῶν πολλῶν· εἰ δὲ ἄλλοις ἐντύχοις σοφοῖς, τάχ' ἂν αἰσχύνοιο αὐτούς, εἴ τι ἴσως οἴοιο αἰσχρὸν ὂν ποιεῖν· ἢ πῶς λέγεις;

D Ἀληθῆ λέγεις, φάναι.

Τοὺς δὲ πολλοὺς οὐκ ἂν αἰσχύνοιο, εἴ τι οἴοιο αἰσχρὸν ποιεῖν;

Καὶ τὸν Φαῖδρον ἔφη ὑπολαβόντα εἰπεῖν Ὦ φίλε Ἀγάθων, ἐὰν ἀποκρίνῃ Σωκράτει, οὐδὲν ἔτι διοίσει αὐτῷ ὁπηοῦν τῶν ἐνθάδε ὁτιοῦν γίγνεσθαι, ἐὰν μόνον ἔχῃ ὅτῳ διαλέγηται, ἄλλως τε καὶ καλῷ. ἐγὼ δὲ ἡδέως μὲν ἀκούω Σωκράτους διαλεγομένου, ἀναγκαῖον δέ μοι ἐπιμεληθῆναι τοῦ ἐγκωμίου τῷ Ἔρωτι καὶ ἀποδέξασθαι παρ' ἑνὸς ἑκάστου ὑμῶν τὸν λόγον· ἀποδοὺς οὖν ἑκάτερος τῷ θεῷ οὕτως ἤδη διαλεγέσθω.

Ἀλλὰ καλῶς λέγεις, ὦ Φαῖδρε, φάναι τὸν
E Ἀγάθωνα, καὶ οὐδέν με κωλύει λέγειν· Σωκράτει γὰρ καὶ αὖθις ἔσται πολλάκις διαλέγεσθαι.

Ἐγὼ δὲ δὴ βούλομαι πρῶτον μὲν εἰπεῖν ὡς χρή με εἰπεῖν, ἔπειτα εἰπεῖν. δοκοῦσι γάρ μοι πάντες οἱ πρόσθεν εἰρηκότες οὐ τὸν θεὸν ἐγκωμιάζειν, ἀλλὰ τοὺς ἀνθρώπους εὐδαιμονίζειν τῶν ἀγαθῶν ὧν ὁ θεὸς αὐτοῖς αἴτιος· ὁποῖος δέ
195 τις αὐτὸς ὢν ταῦτα ἐδωρήσατο, οὐδεὶς εἴρηκεν. εἷς δὲ τρόπος ὀρθὸς παντὸς ἐπαίνου περὶ παντός, λόγῳ διελθεῖν οἷος οἵων[1] αἴτιος ὢν τυγχάνει περὶ

[1] οἷος οἵων Schanz: οἷος ὢν mss.

former; for we were there too, as part of the crowd: but suppose you found yourself with other folk who were clever, you would probably feel ashamed that they should witness any shameful act you might feel yourself to be doing. Will you agree to that?"

"Quite true," he said.

"Whereas before the multitude you would not be ashamed if you felt you were doing anything shameful?"

Here Phaedrus interposed: "My dear Agathon, if you go on answering Socrates he will be utterly indifferent to the fate of our present business, so long as he has some one to argue with, especially some one handsome. For my part, I enjoy listening to Socrates' arguments; but I am responsible for our eulogy of Love, and must levy his speech from every one of you in turn. Let each of you two, then, give the god his meed before you have your argument."

"You are quite right, Phaedrus," said Agathon, "and there is nothing to hinder my speaking; for I shall find many other occasions for arguing with Socrates."

The Speech of Agathon

"I propose first to speak of the plan most proper for my speaking, and after that to speak. Every one of the previous speakers, instead of eulogizing the god, has merely, as it seems to me, felicitated humanity on the benefits he bestows: not one of them has told us what is the nature of the benefactor himself. There is but one correct method of giving anyone any kind of praise, namely to make the words unfold the character of him, and of the bless-

PLATO

οὗ ἂν ὁ λόγος ᾖ. οὕτω δὴ τὸν Ἔρωτα καὶ ἡμᾶς δίκαιον ἐπαινέσαι πρῶτον αὐτὸν οἷός ἐστιν, ἔπειτα τὰς δόσεις.

Φημὶ οὖν ἐγὼ πάντων θεῶν εὐδαιμόνων ὄντων Ἔρωτα, εἰ θέμις καὶ ἀνεμέσητον εἰπεῖν, εὐδαιμονέστατον εἶναι αὐτῶν, κάλλιστον ὄντα καὶ ἄριστον. ἔστι δὲ κάλλιστος ὢν τοιόσδε. πρῶτον μὲν νεώτατος θεῶν, ὦ Φαῖδρε. μέγα δὲ τεκμήριον B τῷ λόγῳ αὐτὸς παρέχεται, φεύγων φυγῇ τὸ γῆρας, ταχὺ ὂν δῆλον ὅτι· θᾶττον γοῦν τοῦ δέοντος ἡμῖν προσέρχεται. ὃ δὴ πέφυκεν Ἔρως μισεῖν καὶ οὐδ᾽ ἐντὸς[1] πολλοῦ πλησιάζειν. μετὰ δὲ νέων ἀεὶ σύνεστί τε καὶ ἔστιν· ὁ γὰρ παλαιὸς λόγος εὖ ἔχει, ὡς ὅμοιον ὁμοίῳ ἀεὶ πελάζει. ἐγὼ δὲ Φαίδρῳ πολλὰ ἄλλα ὁμολογῶν τοῦτο οὐχ ὁμολογῶ, ὡς Ἔρως Κρόνου καὶ Ἰαπετοῦ ἀρχαιότερός ἐστιν, ἀλλὰ φημὶ νεώτατον αὐτὸν εἶναι θεῶν καὶ ἀεὶ νέον, τὰ C δὲ παλαιὰ πράγματα περὶ θεούς, ἃ Ἡσίοδος καὶ Παρμενίδης λέγουσιν, Ἀνάγκῃ καὶ οὐκ Ἔρωτι γεγονέναι, εἰ ἐκεῖνοι ἀληθῆ ἔλεγον· οὐ γὰρ ἂν ἐκτομαὶ οὐδὲ δεσμοὶ ἀλλήλων ἐγίγνοντο καὶ ἄλλα πολλὰ καὶ βίαια, εἰ Ἔρως ἐν αὐτοῖς ἦν, ἀλλὰ φιλία καὶ εἰρήνη, ὥσπερ νῦν, ἐξ οὗ Ἔρως τῶν θεῶν βασιλεύει. νέος μὲν οὖν ἐστί, πρὸς δὲ τῷ νέῳ ἁπαλός· ποιητοῦ δ᾽ ἔστιν ἐνδεὴς οἷος ἦν Ὅμηρος πρὸς τὸ ἐπιδεῖξαι θεοῦ ἁπαλότητα. D Ὅμηρος γὰρ Ἄτην θεόν τέ φησιν εἶναι καὶ

[1] οὐδ᾽ ἐντὸς Stob.: οὐ δόντος, οὐδ᾽ ὄντος MSS.

SYMPOSIUM

ings brought by him, who is to be our theme. Hence it is meet that we praise him first for what he is and then for what he gives.

"So I say that, while all gods are blissful, Love—with no irreverence or offence be it spoken—is the most blissful, as being the most beautiful and the best. How most beautiful, I will explain. First of all, Phaedrus, he is youngest of the gods. He himself supplies clear evidence of this; for he flies and flees from old age—a swift thing obviously, since it gains on us too quickly for our liking. Love hates it by nature, and refuses to come within any distance of it. He is ever consorting with the young, and such also is he: well says the old saw, 'Like and like together strike.'[1] And though in much else I agree with Phaedrus, in this I agree not, that Love by his account is more ancient than Cronos and Iapetus[2]: I say he is youngest of the gods and ever young, while those early dealings with the gods which Hesiod[3] and Parmenides relate, I take to have been the work of Necessity, not of Love, if there is any truth in those stories. For there would have been no gelding or fettering of each other, nor any of those various violences, if Love had been amongst them; rather only amity and peace, such as now subsist ever since Love has reigned over the gods. So then he is young, and delicate withal: he requires a poet such as Homer to set forth his delicacy divine. Homer it is who tells of Ate as

---

[1] So Homer, *Od.* xvii. 218 "Heaven ever bringeth like and like together."

[2] These two Titans were proverbially the original inhabitants of the world. For Phaedrus' view see 178 c.

[3] Hesiod, *Theog.* 176 foll., 746 foll. There are no such stories in the remaining fragments of Parmenides.

PLATO

ἁπαλήν—τοὺς γοῦν πόδας αὐτῆς ἁπαλοὺς εἶναι—
λέγων

τῆς μένθ' ἁπαλοὶ πόδες· οὐ γὰρ ἐπ' οὔδεος
πίλναται, ἀλλ' ἄρα ἥ γε κατ' ἀνδρῶν κράατα βαίνει.

καλῷ οὖν δοκεῖ μοι τεκμηρίῳ τὴν ἁπαλότητα
ἀποφαίνειν, ὅτι οὐκ ἐπὶ σκληροῦ βαίνει, ἀλλ' ἐπὶ
μαλθακοῦ. τῷ αὐτῷ δὴ καὶ ἡμεῖς χρησώμεθα
τεκμηρίῳ περὶ Ἔρωτα ὅτι ἁπαλός. οὐ γὰρ ἐπὶ
γῆς βαίνει οὐδ' ἐπὶ κρανίων, ἅ ἐστιν οὐ πάνυ
μαλακά, ἀλλ' ἐν τοῖς μαλακωτάτοις τῶν ὄντων
καὶ βαίνει καὶ οἰκεῖ. ἐν γὰρ ἤθεσι καὶ ψυχαῖς
θεῶν καὶ ἀνθρώπων τὴν οἴκησιν ἵδρυται, καὶ οὐκ
αὖ ἑξῆς ἐν πάσαις ταῖς ψυχαῖς, ἀλλ' ᾗτινι ἂν
σκληρὸν ἦθος ἐχούσῃ ἐντύχῃ, ἀπέρχεται, ᾗ δ'
ἂν μαλακόν, οἰκίζεται. ἁπτόμενον οὖν ἀεὶ καὶ
ποσὶ καὶ πάντῃ ἐν μαλακωτάτοις τῶν μαλακωτά-
των, ἁπαλώτατον ἀνάγκη εἶναι. νεώτατος μὲν
δή ἐστι καὶ ἁπαλώτατος, πρὸς δὲ τούτοις ὑγρὸς
τὸ εἶδος. οὐ γὰρ ἂν οἷός τ' ἦν πάντῃ περιπτύσ-
σεσθαι οὐδὲ διὰ πάσης ψυχῆς καὶ εἰσιὼν τὸ πρῶτον
λανθάνειν καὶ ἐξιών, εἰ σκληρὸς ἦν. συμμέτρου
δὲ καὶ ὑγρᾶς ἰδέας μέγα τεκμήριον ἡ εὐσχημοσύνη,
ὃ δὴ διαφερόντως ἐκ πάντων ὁμολογουμένως
Ἔρως ἔχει· ἀσχημοσύνη γὰρ καὶ Ἔρωτι πρὸς
ἀλλήλους ἀεὶ πόλεμος. χρόας δὲ κάλλος ἡ κατ'
ἄνθη δίαιτα τοῦ θεοῦ σημαίνει· ἀνανθεῖ γὰρ καὶ
ἀπηνθηκότι καὶ σώματι καὶ ψυχῇ καὶ ἄλλῳ ὁτῳοῦν
οὐκ ἐνίζει Ἔρως, οὗ δ' ἂν εὐανθής τε καὶ εὐώδης
τόπος ᾖ, ἐνταῦθα καὶ ἵζει καὶ μένει.

154

SYMPOSIUM

both divine and delicate; you recollect those delicate feet of hers, where he says—

> Yet delicate are her feet, for on the ground
> She speeds not, only on the heads of men.[1]

So I hold it convincing proof of her delicacy that she goes not on hard things but on soft. The same method will serve us to prove the delicacy of Love. Not upon earth goes he, nor on our crowns, which are not very soft;[2] but takes his way and abode in the softest things that exist. The tempers and souls of gods and men are his chosen habitation: not indeed any soul as much as another; when he comes upon one whose temper is hard, away he goes, but if it be soft, he makes his dwelling there. So if with feet and every way he is wont ever to get hold of the softest parts of the softest creatures, he needs must be most delicate. Youngest, then, and most delicate is he, and withal pliant of form: for he would never contrive to fold himself about us every way, nor steal in at first and pass out of every soul so secretly, if he were hard. Clear evidence of his fit proportion and pliancy of form is found in his shapely grace, a quality wherein Love is in every quarter allowed to excel: unshapeliness and Love are ever at war with one another. Beauty of hue in this god is evinced by his haunting among flowers: for Love will not settle on body or soul or aught else that is flowerless or whose flower has faded away; while he has only to light on a plot of sweet blossoms and scents to settle there and stay.

[1] Homer, *Il.* xix. 92-93.
[2] Perhaps here he smiles at or touches the bald head of Socrates.

Περὶ μὲν οὖν κάλλους τοῦ θεοῦ καὶ ταῦθ' ἱκανὰ καὶ ἔτι πολλὰ λείπεται, περὶ δὲ ἀρετῆς Ἔρωτος μετὰ ταῦτα λεκτέον, τὸ μὲν μέγιστον ὅτι Ἔρως οὔτ' ἀδικεῖ οὔτ' ἀδικεῖται οὔθ' ὑπὸ θεοῦ οὔτε θεόν, οὔθ' ὑπ' ἀνθρώπου οὔτε ἄνθρωπον. οὔτε γὰρ αὐτὸς βίᾳ πάσχει, εἴ τι πάσχει· βία γὰρ Ἔρωτος οὐχ ἅπτεται· οὔτε ποιῶν ποιεῖ· πᾶς γὰρ ἑκὼν Ἔρωτι πᾶν ὑπηρετεῖ, ἃ δ' ἂν ἑκὼν ἑκόντι ὁμολογήσῃ, φασὶν "οἱ πόλεως βασιλῆς νόμοι" δίκαια εἶναι. πρὸς δὲ τῇ δικαιοσύνῃ σωφροσύνης πλείστης μετέχει. εἶναι γὰρ ὁμολογεῖται σωφροσύνη τὸ κρατεῖν ἡδονῶν καὶ ἐπιθυμιῶν, Ἔρωτος δὲ μηδεμίαν ἡδονὴν κρείττω εἶναι· εἰ δὲ ἥττους, κρατοῖντ' ἂν ὑπὸ Ἔρωτος, ὁ δὲ κρατοῖ, κρατῶν δὲ ἡδονῶν καὶ ἐπιθυμιῶν ὁ Ἔρως διαφερόντως ἂν σωφρονοῖ. καὶ μὴν εἴς γε ἀνδρείαν Ἔρωτι "οὐδ' Ἄρης ἀνθίσταται." οὐ γὰρ ἔχει Ἔρωτα Ἄρης, ἀλλ' Ἔρως Ἄρη, Ἀφροδίτης, ὡς λόγος· κρείττων δὲ ὁ ἔχων τοῦ ἐχομένου· τοῦ δ' ἀνδρειοτάτου τῶν ἄλλων κρατῶν πάντων ἂν ἀνδρειότατος εἴη. περὶ μὲν οὖν δικαιοσύνης καὶ σωφροσύνης καὶ ἀνδρείας τοῦ θεοῦ εἴρηται, περὶ δὲ σοφίας λείπεται· ὅσον οὖν δυνατόν, πειρατέον μὴ ἐλλείπειν. καὶ πρῶτον μέν, ἵν' αὖ καὶ ἐγὼ τὴν ἡμετέραν τέχνην τιμήσω ὥσπερ Ἐρυξίμαχος τὴν αὑτοῦ, ποιητὴς ὁ θεὸς σοφὸς οὕτως ὥστε καὶ ἄλλον ποιῆσαι· πᾶς γοῦν ποιητὴς γίγνεται, "κἂν ἄμουσος ᾖ τὸ πρίν," οὗ ἂν Ἔρως ἅψηται. ᾧ δὴ πρέπει ἡμᾶς μαρτυρίῳ χρῆσθαι, ὅτι ποιητὴς ὁ Ἔρως

---

[1] Quoted from Alcidamas, a stylist of the school of Gorgias; Aristot. *Rhet.* iii. 1406 a.

SYMPOSIUM

"Enough has now been said, though much remains unsaid, of the beauty of our god; next shall Love's goodness be my theme. The strongest plea for this is that neither to a god he gives nor from a god receives any injury, nor from men receives it nor to men gives it. For neither is the usage he himself gets a violent usage, since violence takes not hold of Love; nor is there violence in his dealings, since Love wins all men's willing service; and agreements on both sides willingly made are held to be just by 'our city's sovereign, the law.'[1] Then, over and above his justice, he is richly endowed with temperance. We all agree that temperance is a control of pleasures and desires, while no pleasure is stronger than Love: if they are the weaker, they must be under Love's control, and he is their controller; so that Love, by controlling pleasures and desires, must be eminently temperate. And observe how in valour 'not even the God of War withstands'[2] Love; for we hear, not of Love caught by Ares, but of Ares caught by Love—of Aphrodite. The captor is stronger than the caught; and as he controls what is braver than any other, he must be bravest of all. So much for justice and temperance and valour in the god: it remains to speak of skill; and here I must try my best to be adequate. First, if I in turn may dignify our craft as Eryximachus did his, the god is a composer so accomplished that he is a cause of composing in others: every one, you know, becomes a poet, 'though alien to the Muse before,'[3] when Love gets hold of him. This we may fitly take for a testimony that Love

---

[2] Sophocl. *Thyest. fr.* 235 "Necessity, whom not the God of War withstands."   [3] Eurip. *Stheneb. fr.* 663.

PLATO

ἀγαθὸς ἐν κεφαλαίῳ πᾶσαν ποίησιν τὴν κατὰ μουσικήν· ἃ γάρ τις ἢ μὴ ἔχει ἢ μὴ οἶδεν, οὔτ' ἂν ἑτέρῳ δοίη οὔτ' ἂν ἄλλον διδάξειε. καὶ μὲν δὴ τήν γε τῶν ζῴων ποίησιν πάντων τίς ἐναντιώσεται μὴ οὐχὶ Ἔρωτος εἶναι σοφίαν, ᾗ γίγνεταί τε καὶ φύεται πάντα τὰ ζῷα; ἀλλὰ τὴν τῶν τεχνῶν δημιουργίαν οὐκ ἴσμεν, ὅτι οὗ μὲν ἂν ὁ θεὸς οὗτος διδάσκαλος γένηται, ἐλλόγιμος καὶ φανὸς ἀπέβη, οὗ δ' ἂν Ἔρως μὴ ἐφάψηται, σκοτεινός; τοξικήν γε μὴν καὶ ἰατρικὴν καὶ μαντικὴν Ἀπόλλων ἀνεῦρεν ἐπιθυμίας καὶ ἔρωτος ἡγεμονεύσαντος, ὥστε καὶ οὗτος Ἔρωτος ἂν εἴη μαθητής, καὶ Μοῦσαι μουσικῆς καὶ Ἥφαιστος χαλκείας καὶ Ἀθηνᾶ ἱστουργίας καὶ Ζεὺς " κυβερνᾶν θεῶν τε καὶ ἀνθρώπων." ὅθεν δὴ καὶ κατεσκευάσθη τῶν θεῶν τὰ πράγματα Ἔρωτος ἐγγενομένου, δῆλον ὅτι κάλλους· αἴσχει γὰρ οὐκ ἔπι Ἔρως· πρὸ τοῦ δέ, ὥσπερ ἐν ἀρχῇ εἶπον, πολλὰ καὶ δεινὰ θεοῖς ἐγίγνετο, ὡς λέγεται, διὰ τὴν τῆς Ἀνάγκης βασιλείαν· ἐπειδὴ δ' ὁ θεὸς οὗτος ἔφυ, ἐκ τοῦ ἐρᾶν τῶν καλῶν πάντ' ἀγαθὰ γέγονε καὶ θεοῖς καὶ ἀνθρώποις.

Οὕτως ἐμοὶ δοκεῖ, ὦ Φαῖδρε, Ἔρως πρῶτος αὐτὸς ὢν κάλλιστος καὶ ἄριστος μετὰ τοῦτο τοῖς ἄλλοις ἄλλων τοιούτων αἴτιος εἶναι. ἐπέρχεται δέ μοί τι καὶ ἔμμετρον εἰπεῖν, ὅτι οὗτός ἐστιν ὁ ποιῶν

εἰρήνην μὲν ἐν ἀνθρώποις, πελάγει δὲ γαλήνην
νηνεμίαν,—ἀνέμων κοίτην ὕπνον τ' ἐνὶ κήδει·

---

[1] Agathon here strains the meaning of ποιητής back to the original and wider one of " maker," " creator." *Cf.* below, 205 B, C.

[2] Homer, *Il.* ii. 827, i. 72; above, 190 E.

SYMPOSIUM

is a poet well skilled—I speak summarily—in all composing that has to do with music; for whatever we have not or know not we can neither give to another nor teach our neighbour. And who, let me ask, will gainsay that the composing[1] of all forms of life is Love's own craft, whereby all creatures are begotten and produced? Again, in artificial manufacture, do we not know that a man who has this god for teacher turns out a brilliant success, whereas he on whom Love has laid no hold is obscure? If Apollo invented archery and medicine[2] and divination, it was under the guidance of Desire and Love; so that he too may be deemed a disciple of Love, as likewise may the Muses in music, Hephaestus in metal-work, Athene in weaving and Zeus 'in pilotage of gods and men.'[3] Hence also those dealings of the gods were contrived by Love— clearly love of beauty—astir in them, for Love has no concern with ugliness; though aforetime, as I began by saying, there were many strange doings among the gods, as legend tells, because of the dominion of Necessity. But since this god arose, the loving of beautiful things has brought all kinds of benefits both to gods and to men.

"Thus I conceive, Phaedrus, that Love was originally of surpassing beauty and goodness, and is latterly the cause of similar excellences in others. And now I am moved to summon the aid of verse, and tell how it is he who makes—

> Peace among men, and a windless waveless main;
> Repose for winds, and slumber in our pain.[4]

[3] *Cf.* Parmen. (Diels² 123) δαίμων ἡ πάντα κυβερνᾷ.
[4] *Cf. Od.* v. 391 "Then ceased the wind, and came a windless calm." Agathon is here displaying his own poetic skill, not quoting.

PLATO

D οὗτος δὲ ἡμᾶς ἀλλοτριότητος μὲν κενοῖ, οἰκειότητος δὲ πληροῖ, τὰς τοιάσδε συνόδους μετ' ἀλλήλων πάσας τιθεὶς συνιέναι, ἐν ἑορταῖς, ἐν χοροῖς, ἐν θυσίαις γιγνόμενος ἡγεμών· πρᾳότητα μὲν πορίζων, ἀγριότητα δ' ἐξορίζων· φιλόδωρος εὐμενείας, ἄδωρος δυσμενείας· ἵλεως ἀγανός·[1] θεατὸς σοφοῖς, ἀγαστὸς θεοῖς· ζηλωτὸς ἀμοίροις, κτητὸς εὐμοίροις· τρυφῆς, ἁβρότητος, χλιδῆς, χαρίτων, ἱμέρου, πόθου πατήρ· ἐπιμελὴς ἀγαθῶν, ἀμελὴς κακῶν·
E ἐν πόνῳ, ἐν φόβῳ, ἐν πότῳ,[2] ἐν λόγῳ κυβερνήτης, ἐπιβάτης, παραστάτης τε καὶ σωτὴρ ἄριστος, συμπάντων τε θεῶν καὶ ἀνθρώπων κόσμος, ἡγεμὼν κάλλιστος καὶ ἄριστος, ᾧ χρὴ ἕπεσθαι πάντα ἄνδρα ἐφυμνοῦντα καλῶς, ᾠδῆς μετέχοντα ἣν ᾄδει θέλγων πάντων θεῶν τε καὶ ἀνθρώπων νόημα.

Οὗτος, ἔφη, ὁ παρ' ἐμοῦ λόγος, ὦ Φαῖδρε, τῷ θεῷ ἀνακείσθω, τὰ μὲν παιδιᾶς, τὰ δὲ σπουδῆς μετρίας, καθ' ὅσον ἐγὼ δύναμαι, μετέχων.

198 Εἰπόντος δὲ τοῦ Ἀγάθωνος πάντας ἔφη ὁ Ἀριστόδημος ἀναθορυβῆσαι τοὺς παρόντας, ὡς πρεπόντως τοῦ νεανίσκου εἰρηκότος καὶ αὑτῷ καὶ τῷ θεῷ. τὸν οὖν Σωκράτη εἰπεῖν βλέψαντα εἰς τὸν Ἐρυξίμαχον, Ἆρά σοι δοκῶ, φάναι, ὦ παῖ Ἀκουμενοῦ, ἀδεὲς πάλαι δέος δεδιέναι, ἀλλ' οὐ μαντικῶς ἃ νῦν δὴ ἔλεγον εἰπεῖν, ὅτι Ἀγάθων θαυμαστῶς ἐροῖ, ἐγὼ δ' ἀπορήσοιμι;

Τὸ μὲν ἕτερον, φάναι τὸν Ἐρυξίμαχον, μαντικῶς
B μοι δοκεῖς εἰρηκέναι, ὅτι Ἀγάθων εὖ ἐρεῖ· τὸ δὲ σὲ ἀπορήσειν, οὐκ οἶμαι.

---
[1] ἀγανός Usen.: ἀγαθός mss.: ἀγαθοῖς Stob.
[2] πότῳ Bury: πόθῳ mss.

SYMPOSIUM

He it is who casts alienation out, draws intimacy in; he brings us together in all such friendly gatherings as the present; at feasts and dances and oblations he makes himself our leader; politeness contriving, moroseness outdriving; kind giver of amity, giving no enmity; gracious, benign; a marvel to the wise, a delight to the gods; coveted of such as share him not, treasured of such as good share have got; father of luxury, tenderness, elegance, graces and longing and yearning; careful of the good, careless of the bad; in toil and fear, in drink and discourse, our trustiest helmsman, boatswain, champion, deliverer; ornament of all gods and men; leader fairest and best, whom every one should follow, joining tunefully in the burthen of his song, wherewith he enchants the thought of every god and man.

"There, Phaedrus," he said, "is the speech I would offer at his shrine: I have done my best to mingle amusement with a decent gravity."

At the end of Agathon's speech, as Aristodemus told me, there was tumultuous applause from all present, at hearing the youngster speak in terms so appropriate to himself and to the god. Then Socrates, with a glance at Eryximachus, said: "Son of Acumenus, do you really call it an unfearful fear that has all this while affrighted me, and myself no prophet in saying just now that Agathon would make a marvellous speech, and I be hard put to it?"

"In one part of your statement, that he would speak finely," replied Eryximachus, "I think you were a true prophet; but as to your being hard put to it, I do not agree."

PLATO

Καὶ πῶς, ὦ μακάριε, εἰπεῖν τὸν Σωκράτη, οὐ μέλλω ἀπορεῖν καὶ ἐγὼ καὶ ἄλλος ὁστισοῦν, μέλλων λέξειν μετὰ καλὸν οὕτω καὶ παντοδαπὸν λόγον ῥηθέντα; καὶ τὰ μὲν ἄλλα οὐχ ὁμοίως μὲν θαυμαστά· τὸ δ' ἐπὶ τελευτῆς τοῦ κάλλους τῶν ὀνομάτων καὶ ῥημάτων τίς οὐκ ἂν ἐξεπλάγη ἀκούων; ἐπεὶ ἔγωγε ἐνθυμούμενος, ὅτι αὐτὸς οὐχ οἷός τ' ἔσομαι οὐδ' C ἐγγὺς τούτων οὐδὲν καλὸν εἰπεῖν, ὑπ' αἰσχύνης ὀλίγου ἀποδρὰς ᾠχόμην, εἴ πῃ εἶχον. καὶ γάρ με Γοργίου ὁ λόγος ἀνεμίμνησκεν, ὥστε ἀτεχνῶς τὸ τοῦ Ὁμήρου ἐπεπόνθη· ἐφοβούμην μή μοι τελευτῶν ὁ Ἀγάθων Γοργίου κεφαλὴν δεινοῦ λέγειν ἐν τῷ λόγῳ ἐπὶ τὸν ἐμὸν λόγον πέμψας αὐτόν με λίθον τῇ ἀφωνίᾳ ποιήσειε. καὶ ἐνενόησα τότε ἄρα καταγέλαστος ὤν, ἡνίκα ὑμῖν ὡμολόγουν ἐν τῷ μέρει μεθ' ὑμῶν ἐγκωμιάσεσθαι D τὸν Ἔρωτα καὶ ἔφην εἶναι δεινὸς τὰ ἐρωτικά, οὐδὲν εἰδὼς ἄρα τοῦ πράγματος, ὡς ἔδει ἐγκωμιάζειν ὁτιοῦν. ἐγὼ μὲν γὰρ ὑπ' ἀβελτερίας ᾤμην δεῖν τἀληθῆ λέγειν περὶ ἑκάστου τοῦ ἐγκωμιαζομένου, καὶ τοῦτο μὲν ὑπάρχειν, ἐξ αὐτῶν δὲ τούτων τὰ κάλλιστα ἐκλεγομένους ὡς εὐπρεπέστατα τιθέναι· καὶ πάνυ δὴ μέγα ἐφρόνουν ὡς εὖ ἐρῶν, ὡς εἰδὼς τὴν ἀλήθειαν [τοῦ ἐπαινεῖν ὁτιοῦν].[1] τὸ δὲ ἄρα, ὡς ἔοικεν, οὐ τοῦτο ἦν τὸ καλῶς ἐπαινεῖν E ὁτιοῦν, ἀλλὰ τὸ ὡς μέγιστα ἀνατιθέναι τῷ πράγματι καὶ ὡς κάλλιστα, ἐάν τε ᾖ οὕτως ἔχοντα ἐάν

[1] τοῦ ... ὁτιοῦν secl. Badham. Fort. τοῦ πράγματος. Cf. supra, οὐδὲν εἰδὼς ἄρα τοῦ πρ.

SYMPOSIUM

"But surely, my good sir," said Socrates, "I am bound to be hard put, I or anyone else in the world who should have to speak after such a fine assortment of eloquence. The greater part of it was not quite so astounding; but when we drew towards the close, the beauty of the words and phrases could not but take one's breath away. For myself, indeed, I was so conscious that I should fail to say anything half as fine, that for very shame I was on the point of slinking away, had I had any chance. For his speech so reminded me of Gorgias that I was exactly in the plight described by Homer:[1] I feared that Agathon in his final phrases would confront me with the eloquent Gorgias' head, and by opposing his speech to mine would turn me thus dumbfounded into stone. And so in that moment I realized what a ridiculous fool I was to fall in with your proposal that I should take my turn in your eulogies of Love, and to call myself an expert in love-matters, when really I was ignorant of the method in which eulogies ought to be made at all. For I was such a silly wretch as to think that one ought in each case to speak the truth about the person eulogized; on this assumption I hoped we might pick out the fairest of the facts and set these forth in their comeliest guise. I was quite elated with the notion of what a fine speech I should make, for I felt that I knew the truth. But now, it appears that this is not what is meant by a good speech of praise; which is rather an ascription of all the highest and fairest qualities, whether the case be

[1] *Od.* xi. 632, where Odysseus is sore afraid that Persephone will send up the Gorgon's head among the crowd of ghosts from Hades. Agathon has just displayed his addiction to the elegant rhetoric of Gorgias.

PLATO

τε μή· εἰ δὲ ψευδῆ, οὐδὲν ἄρ' ἦν πρᾶγμα. προύρ-
ρήθη γάρ, ὡς ἔοικεν, ὅπως ἕκαστος ἡμῶν τὸν
Ἔρωτα ἐγκωμιάζειν δόξει,[1] οὐχ ὅπως ἐγκωμιάσεται.
διὰ ταῦτα δή, οἶμαι, πάντα λόγον κινοῦντες ἀνα-
τίθετε τῷ Ἔρωτι, καί φατε αὐτὸν τοιοῦτόν τε
εἶναι καὶ τοσούτων αἴτιον, ὅπως ἂν φαίνηται ὡς
κάλλιστος καὶ ἄριστος, δῆλον ὅτι τοῖς μὴ γιγνώ-
σκουσιν—οὐ γάρ που τοῖς γε εἰδόσι—καὶ καλῶς
γ' ἔχει καὶ σεμνῶς ὁ ἔπαινος. ἀλλὰ γὰρ ἐγὼ οὐκ
ᾔδη τὸν τρόπον τοῦ ἐπαίνου, οὐδ' εἰδὼς ὑμῖν
ὡμολόγησα καὶ αὐτὸς ἐν τῷ μέρει ἐπαινέσεσθαι.
ἡ γλῶσσα οὖν ὑπέσχετο, ἡ δὲ φρὴν οὔ· χαιρέτω δή.
οὐ γὰρ ἔτι ἐγκωμιάζω τοῦτον τὸν τρόπον· οὐ γὰρ
ἂν δυναίμην· οὐ μέντοι ἀλλὰ τά γε ἀληθῆ, εἰ βούλεσθε, ἐθέλω εἰπεῖν κατ' ἐμαυτόν, οὐ πρὸς τοὺς
ὑμετέρους λόγους, ἵνα μὴ γέλωτα ὄφλω. ὅρα
οὖν, ὦ Φαῖδρε, εἴ τι καὶ τοιούτου λόγου δέῃ, περὶ
Ἔρωτος τἀληθῆ λεγόμενα ἀκούειν, ὀνόμασι δὲ
καὶ θέσει ῥημάτων τοιαύτῃ ὁποία δὴ ἄν τις τύχῃ
ἐπελθοῦσα.

Τὸν οὖν Φαῖδρον ἔφη καὶ τοὺς ἄλλους κελεύειν
λέγειν, ὅπῃ αὐτὸς οἴοιτο δεῖν εἰπεῖν, ταύτῃ.

Ἔτι τοίνυν, φάναι, ὦ Φαῖδρε, πάρες μοι Ἀγάθωνα σμίκρ' ἄττα ἐρέσθαι, ἵνα ἀνομολογησά-
μενος παρ' αὐτοῦ οὕτως ἤδη λέγω.

Ἀλλὰ παρίημι, φάναι τὸν Φαῖδρον, ἀλλ' ἐρώτα.
μετὰ ταῦτα δὴ τὸν Σωκράτη ἔφη ἐνθένδε ποθὲν
ἄρξασθαι.

[1] δόξει Steph.: δόξῃ mss.

SYMPOSIUM

so or not; it is really no matter if they are untrue. Our arrangement, it seems, was that each should appear to eulogize Love, not that he should make a real eulogy. Hence it is, sirs, I suppose, that you muster every kind of phrase for your tribute to Love, declaring such and such to be his character and influence, in order to present him in the best and fairest light; successfully, of course, before those who do not observe him, though it must be otherwise before those who know; your praise has such a fine impressive air! No, I find I was quite mistaken as to the method required; it was in ignorance that I agreed to take my turn in the round of praising. 'The tongue,' you see, undertook, 'the mind' did not;[1] so good-bye to my bond. I am not to be called upon now as an eulogist in your sense; for such I cannot be. Nevertheless I am ready, if you like, to speak the mere truth in my own way; not to rival your discourses, and so be your laughing-stock. Decide then, Phaedrus, whether you have any need of such a speech besides, and would like to hear the truth told about Love in whatsoever style of terms and phrases may chance to occur by the way."

So Phaedrus and the others bade him speak, just in any manner he himself should think fit.

"Then allow me further, Phaedrus, to put some little questions to Agathon, so as to secure his agreement before I begin my speech."

"You have my leave," said Phaedrus; "so ask him." After that, my friend told me, Socrates started off in this sort of way:

[1] Eurip. *Hippol.* 612 "The tongue hath sworn; the mind is yet unsworn."

PLATO

Καὶ μήν, ὦ φίλε Ἀγάθων, καλῶς μοι ἔδοξας καθηγήσασθαι τοῦ λόγου, λέγων ὅτι πρῶτον μὲν δέοι αὐτὸν ἐπιδεῖξαι ὁποῖός τίς ἐστιν ὁ Ἔρως, ὕστερον δὲ τὰ ἔργα αὐτοῦ. ταύτην τὴν ἀρχὴν πάνυ ἄγαμαι. ἴθι οὖν μοι περὶ Ἔρωτος, ἐπειδὴ καὶ τἆλλα καλῶς καὶ μεγαλοπρεπῶς διῆλθες οἷός D ἐστι, καὶ τόδε εἰπέ· πότερόν ἐστι τοιοῦτος οἷος εἶναι τινὸς ὁ Ἔρως ἔρως, ἢ οὐδενός; ἐρωτῶ δ᾽ οὐκ εἰ μητρός τινος ἢ πατρός ἐστι—γελοῖον γὰρ ἂν εἴη τὸ ἐρώτημα, εἰ Ἔρως ἐστὶν ἔρως μητρὸς ἢ πατρός—ἀλλ᾽ ὥσπερ ἂν εἰ αὐτὸ τοῦτο πατέρα ἠρώτων, ἆρα ὁ πατήρ ἐστι πατὴρ τινὸς ἢ οὔ; εἶπες ἂν δήπου μοι, εἰ ἐβούλου καλῶς ἀποκρίνασθαι, ὅτι ἔστιν υἱέος γε ἢ θυγατρὸς ὁ πατὴρ πατήρ· ἢ οὔ;

Πάνυ γε, φάναι τὸν Ἀγάθωνα.

Οὐκοῦν καὶ ἡ μήτηρ ὡσαύτως; Ὁμολογεῖσθαι καὶ τοῦτο.

E Ἔτι τοίνυν, εἰπεῖν τὸν Σωκράτη, ἀπόκριναι ὀλίγῳ πλείω, ἵνα μᾶλλον καταμάθῃς ὃ βούλομαι. εἰ γὰρ ἐροίμην, τί δέ; ἀδελφός, αὐτὸ τοῦθ᾽ ὅπερ ἔστι, ἔστι τινὸς ἀδελφὸς ἢ οὔ; Φάναι εἶναι.

Οὐκοῦν ἀδελφοῦ ἢ ἀδελφῆς; Ὁμολογεῖν.

Πειρῶ δή, φάναι, καὶ τὸν ἔρωτα εἰπεῖν. ὁ Ἔρως ἔρως ἐστὶν οὐδενὸς ἢ τινός;

200 Πάνυ μὲν οὖν ἔστιν.

Τοῦτο μὲν τοίνυν, εἰπεῖν τὸν Σωκράτη, φύλαξον παρὰ σαυτῷ μεμνημένος ὅτου· τοσόνδε δὲ εἰπέ, πότερον ὁ Ἔρως ἐκείνου, οὗ ἔστιν ἔρως, ἐπιθυμεῖ αὐτοῦ ἢ οὔ;

Πάνυ γε, φάναι.

SYMPOSIUM

"I must say, my dear Agathon, you gave your speech an excellent introduction, by stating that your duty was first to display the character of Love, and then to treat of his acts. Those opening words I thoroughly admire. So come now, complete your beautiful and magnificent description of Love, and tell me this: Are we so to view his character as to take Love to be love of some object, or of none? My question is not whether he is love of a mother or a father—how absurd it would be to ask whether Love is love of mother or father!—but as though I were asking about our notion of 'father,' whether one's father is a father of somebody or not. Surely you would say, if you wished to give the proper answer, that the father is father of son or of daughter, would you not?"

"Yes, of course," said Agathon.

"And you would say the same of the mother?" He agreed to this too.

"Then will you give me just a few more answers," said Socrates, "so that you may the better grasp my meaning? Suppose I were to ask you, 'Well now, a brother, viewed in the abstract, is he brother of somebody or not?'"

"He is," said Agathon.

"That is, of brother or of sister?" He agreed.

"Now try and tell me about Love: is he a love of nothing or of something?"

"Of something, to be sure."

"Now then," said Socrates, "keep carefully in mind what is the object of Love, and only tell me whether he desires the particular thing that is his object."

"Yes, to be sure," he replied.

PLATO

Πότερον ἔχων αὐτὸ οὗ ἐπιθυμεῖ τε καὶ ἐρᾷ, εἶτα ἐπιθυμεῖ τε καὶ ἐρᾷ, ἢ οὐκ ἔχων;

Οὐκ ἔχων, ὡς τὸ εἰκός γε, φάναι.

Σκόπει δή, εἰπεῖν τὸν Σωκράτη, ἀντὶ τοῦ εἰκότος εἰ ἀνάγκη οὕτως, τὸ ἐπιθυμοῦν ἐπιθυμεῖν οὗ ἐνδεές ἐστιν, ἢ μὴ ἐπιθυμεῖν, ἐὰν μὴ ἐνδεὲς ᾖ; ἐμοὶ μὲν γὰρ θαυμαστῶς δοκεῖ, ὦ Ἀγάθων, ὡς ἀνάγκη εἶναι· σοὶ δὲ πῶς;

Κἀμοί, φάναι, δοκεῖ.

Καλῶς λέγεις. ἆρ᾽ οὖν βούλοιτ᾽ ἄν τις μέγας ὢν μέγας εἶναι, ἢ ἰσχυρὸς ὢν ἰσχυρός;

Ἀδύνατον ἐκ τῶν ὡμολογημένων.

Οὐ γάρ που ἐνδεὴς ἂν εἴη τούτων ὅ γε ὤν.

Ἀληθῆ λέγεις.

Εἰ γὰρ καὶ ἰσχυρὸς ὢν βούλοιτο ἰσχυρὸς εἶναι, φάναι τὸν Σωκράτη, καὶ ταχὺς ὢν ταχύς, καὶ ὑγιὴς ὢν ὑγιής—ἴσως γὰρ ἄν τις ταῦτα οἰηθείη καὶ πάντα τὰ τοιαῦτα, τοὺς ὄντας τε τοιούτους καὶ ἔχοντας ταῦτα τούτων ἅπερ ἔχουσι καὶ ἐπιθυμεῖν, ἵν᾽ οὖν μὴ ἐξαπατηθῶμεν, τούτου ἕνεκα λέγω—τούτοις γάρ, ὦ Ἀγάθων, εἰ ἐννοεῖς, ἔχειν μὲν ἕκαστα τούτων ἐν τῷ παρόντι ἀνάγκη ἃ ἔχουσιν, ἐάν τε βούλωνται ἐάν τε μή, καὶ τούτου γε δήπου τίς ἂν ἐπιθυμήσειεν; ἀλλ᾽ ὅταν τις λέγῃ ὅτι ἐγὼ ὑγιαίνων βούλομαι καὶ ὑγιαίνειν, καὶ πλουτῶν βούλομαι καὶ πλουτεῖν, καὶ ἐπιθυμῶ αὐτῶν τούτων ἃ ἔχω, εἴποιμεν ἂν αὐτῷ ὅτι σύ, ὦ ἄνθρωπε, πλοῦτον κεκτημένος καὶ ὑγίειαν καὶ ἰσχὺν βούλει καὶ εἰς τὸν ἔπειτα χρόνον ταῦτα κεκτῆσθαι, ἐπεὶ ἐν τῷ γε νῦν παρόντι, εἴτε βούλει εἴτε μή, ἔχεις· σκόπει οὖν, ὅταν τοῦτο λέγῃς, ὅτι ἐπιθυμῶ τῶν παρόντων, εἰ ἄλλο τι λέγεις ἢ τόδε,

SYMPOSIUM

"Has he or has he not the object of his desire and love before he desires and loves it?"

"He does not have it, most likely," he said.

"Not as a likelihood," said Socrates, "but as a necessity, consider if the desiring subject must have desire for something it lacks, and again, no desire if it has no lack. I at least, Agathon, am perfectly sure it is a necessity. How does it strike you?"

"I am sure of it also," said he.

"Very good. Now could a tall man wish to be tall, or a strong man to be strong?"

"By what has been admitted, this is impossible."

"Since, I suppose, the man in each case would not be lacking the quality mentioned."

"True."

"For if, being strong, he should wish to be strong," said Socrates, "or being swift, to be swift, or being healthy, to be healthy,—since we are apt to *suppose* in these and all such cases that men of this or that sort, possessing these qualities, do also desire what they have already: I put this in, to prevent our being deceived; these men, Agathon, if you consider, are bound to have at the very moment each thing that they have whether they wish it or not; and how, I ask, is a man going to desire that? No, when a person says, 'I being healthy, want to be healthy; being rich, I want to be rich; I desire the very things that I have'—we shall tell him, 'My good sir, riches you possess, and health and strength, which you would like to possess in the future also: for the time now present you have them whether you would or no. When you say— *I desire these present things*—we suggest you are

169

ὅτι βούλομαι τὰ νῦν παρόντα καὶ εἰς τὸν ἔπειτα χρόνον παρεῖναι· ἄλλο τι ὁμολογοῖ ἄν; Συμφάναι ἔφη τὸν Ἀγάθωνα.

Εἰπεῖν δὴ τὸν Σωκράτη, Οὐκοῦν τοῦτό γ' ἐστὶν ἐκείνου ἐρᾶν, ὃ οὔπω ἕτοιμον αὐτῷ ἐστιν οὐδὲ ἔχει, τὸ εἰς τὸν ἔπειτα χρόνον ταῦτα εἶναι αὐτῷ σωζόμενα καὶ ἀεὶ[1] παρόντα;

Πάνυ γε, φάναι.

Ε Καὶ οὗτος ἄρα καὶ ἄλλος πᾶς ὁ ἐπιθυμῶν τοῦ μὴ ἑτοίμου ἐπιθυμεῖ καὶ τοῦ μὴ παρόντος, καὶ ὃ μὴ ἔχει καὶ ὃ μὴ ἔστιν αὐτὸς καὶ οὗ ἐνδεής ἐστι, τοιαῦτ' ἄττα ἐστὶν ὧν ἡ ἐπιθυμία τε καὶ ὁ ἔρως ἐστίν;

Πάνυ γ', εἰπεῖν.

Ἴθι δή, φάναι τὸν Σωκράτη, ἀνομολογησώμεθα τὰ εἰρημένα. ἄλλο τι ἔστιν ὁ Ἔρως πρῶτον μὲν τινῶν, ἔπειτα τούτων ὧν ἂν ἔνδεια παρῇ αὐτῷ;

Ναί, φάναι.

201 Ἐπὶ δὴ τούτοις ἀναμνήσθητι τίνων ἔφησθα ἐν τῷ λόγῳ εἶναι τὸν Ἔρωτα· εἰ δὲ βούλει, ἐγώ σε ἀναμνήσω. οἶμαι γάρ σε οὑτωσί πως εἰπεῖν, ὅτι τοῖς θεοῖς κατεσκευάσθη τὰ πράγματα δι' ἔρωτα καλῶν· αἰσχρῶν γὰρ οὐκ εἴη ἔρως. οὐχ οὑτωσί πως ἔλεγες;

Εἶπον γάρ, φάναι τὸν Ἀγάθωνα.

Καὶ ἐπιεικῶς γε λέγεις, ὦ ἑταῖρε, φάναι τὸν Σωκράτη· καὶ εἰ τοῦτο οὕτως ἔχει, ἄλλο τι ὁ Ἔρως κάλλους ἂν εἴη ἔρως, αἴσχους δ' οὔ; Ὡμολόγει.

Β Οὐκοῦν ὡμολόγηται, οὗ ἐνδεής ἐστι καὶ μὴ ἔχει, τούτου ἐρᾶν;

[1] καὶ ἀεί Bury: καὶ μοι MSS.

merely saying—*I wish these things now present to be present also in the future.* Would he not admit our point?" To this Agathon assented.

"And so," continued Socrates, "a man may be said to love a thing not yet provided or possessed, when he would have the presence of certain things secured to him for ever in the future."

"Certainly," he said.

"Then such a person, and in general all who feel desire, feel it for what is not provided or present; for something they have not or are not or lack; and that sort of thing is the object of desire and love?"

"Assuredly," he said.

"Now then," said Socrates, "let us agree to what we have so far concluded. First, is not Love directed to certain things; of which, in the second place, he has a want?"

"Yes," he said.

"Then, granting this, recollect what things you named in our discussion as the objects of Love: if you like, I will remind you. What you said, I believe, was to the effect that the gods contrived the world from a love of beautiful things, for of ugly there was no love. Did you not say something of the sort?"

"Yes, I did," said Agathon.

"And quite properly, my friend," said Socrates; "then, such being the case, must not Love be only love of beauty, and not of ugliness?" He assented.

"Well then, we have agreed that he loves what he lacks and has not?"

Ναί, εἰπεῖν.

Ἐνδεὴς ἄρ᾽ ἐστὶ καὶ οὐκ ἔχει ὁ Ἔρως κάλλος.

Ἀνάγκη, φάναι.

Τί δέ; τὸ ἐνδεὲς κάλλους καὶ μηδαμῇ κεκτημένον κάλλος ἆρα λέγεις σὺ καλὸν εἶναι;

Οὐ δῆτα.

Ἔτι οὖν ὁμολογεῖς Ἔρωτα καλὸν εἶναι, εἰ ταῦτα οὕτως ἔχει;

Καὶ τὸν Ἀγάθωνα εἰπεῖν Κινδυνεύω, ὦ Σώκρατες, οὐδὲν εἰδέναι ὧν τότε εἶπον.

C Καὶ μὴν καλῶς γε εἶπες, φάναι, ὦ Ἀγάθων. ἀλλὰ σμικρὸν ἔτι εἰπέ· τἀγαθὰ οὐ καὶ καλὰ δοκεῖ σοι εἶναι;

Ἔμοιγε.

Εἰ ἄρα ὁ Ἔρως τῶν καλῶν ἐνδεής ἐστι, τὰ δὲ ἀγαθὰ καλά, κἂν τῶν ἀγαθῶν ἐνδεὴς εἴη.

Ἐγώ, φάναι, ὦ Σώκρατες, σοὶ οὐκ ἂν δυναίμην ἀντιλέγειν, ἀλλ᾽ οὕτως ἐχέτω ὡς σὺ λέγεις.

Οὐ μὲν οὖν τῇ ἀληθείᾳ, φάναι, ὦ φιλούμενε
D Ἀγάθων, δύνασαι ἀντιλέγειν, ἐπεὶ Σωκράτει γε οὐδὲν χαλεπόν.

Καὶ σὲ μέν γε ἤδη ἐάσω· τὸν δὲ λόγον τὸν περὶ τοῦ Ἔρωτος, ὅν ποτ᾽ ἤκουσα γυναικὸς Μαντινικῆς Διοτίμας, ἣ ταῦτά τε σοφὴ ἦν καὶ ἄλλα πολλά, καὶ Ἀθηναίοις ποτὲ θυσαμένοις πρὸ τοῦ λοιμοῦ δέκα ἔτη ἀναβολὴν ἐποίησε τῆς νόσου, ἣ δὴ καὶ ἐμὲ τὰ ἐρωτικὰ ἐδίδαξεν—ὃν οὖν ἐκείνη ἔλεγε λόγον, πειράσομαι ὑμῖν διελθεῖν ἐκ τῶν

"Yes," he replied.

"And what Love lacks and has not is beauty?"

"That needs must be," he said.

"Well now, will you say that what lacks beauty, and in no wise possesses it, is beautiful?"

"Surely not."

"So can you still allow Love to be beautiful, if this is the case?"

Whereupon Agathon said, "I greatly fear, Socrates, I knew nothing of what I was talking about."

"Ah, your words were beautiful enough, Agathon; but pray give me one or two more: you hold, do you not, that good things are beautiful?"

"I do."

"Then if Love lacks beautiful things, and good things are beautiful, he must lack good things too."

"I see no means, Socrates, of contradicting you," he replied; "let it be as you say."

"No, it is Truth, my lovable Agathon, whom you cannot contradict: Socrates you easily may."

The Speech of Socrates

"And now I shall let you alone, and proceed with the discourse upon Love which I heard one day from a Mantinean woman named Diotima:[1] in this subject she was skilled, and in many others too; for once, by bidding the Athenians offer sacrifices ten years before the plague, she procured them so much delay in the advent of the sickness. Well, I also had my lesson from her in love-matters; so now I will try and follow up the points on which

[1] These names suggest a connexion respectively with prophecy and with the favour of Heaven.

ὡμολογημένων ἐμοὶ καὶ Ἀγάθωνι, αὐτὸς ἐπ᾽ ἐμαυτοῦ, ὅπως ἂν δύνωμαι. δεῖ δή, ὦ Ἀγάθων, E ὥσπερ σὺ διηγήσω, διελθεῖν αὐτὸν πρῶτον, τίς ἐστιν ὁ Ἔρως καὶ ποῖός τις, ἔπειτα τὰ ἔργα αὐτοῦ. δοκεῖ οὖν μοι ῥᾷστον εἶναι οὕτω διελθεῖν, ὥς ποτέ με ἡ ξένη ἀνακρίνουσα διῄει. σχεδὸν γάρ τι καὶ ἐγὼ πρὸς αὐτὴν ἕτερα τοιαῦτα ἔλεγον, οἷάπερ νῦν πρὸς ἐμὲ Ἀγάθων, ὡς εἴη ὁ Ἔρως μέγας θεός, εἴη δὲ τῶν καλῶν· ἤλεγχε δή με τούτοις τοῖς λόγοις οἷσπερ ἐγὼ τοῦτον, ὡς οὔτε καλὸς εἴη κατὰ τὸν ἐμὸν λόγον οὔτε ἀγαθός.

Καὶ ἐγώ, Πῶς λέγεις, ἔφην, ὦ Διοτίμα; αἰσχρὸς ἄρα ὁ Ἔρως ἐστὶ καὶ κακός;

Καὶ ἥ, Οὐκ εὐφημήσεις; ἔφη· ἢ οἴει, ὅ τι ἂν μὴ καλὸν ᾖ, ἀναγκαῖον αὐτὸ εἶναι αἰσχρόν;

202 Μάλιστά γε.

Ἦ καὶ ἂν μὴ σοφόν, ἀμαθές; ἢ οὐκ ᾔσθησαι ὅτι ἔστι τι μεταξὺ σοφίας καὶ ἀμαθίας;

Τί τοῦτο;

Τὸ ὀρθὰ δοξάζειν καὶ ἄνευ τοῦ ἔχειν λόγον δοῦναι οὐκ οἶσθ᾽, ἔφη, ὅτι οὔτε ἐπίστασθαί ἐστιν· ἄλογον γὰρ πρᾶγμα πῶς ἂν εἴη ἐπιστήμη; οὔτε ἀμαθία· τὸ γὰρ τοῦ ὄντος τυγχάνον πῶς ἂν εἴη ἀμαθία; ἔστι δὲ δήπου τοιοῦτον ἡ ὀρθὴ δόξα, μεταξὺ φρονήσεως καὶ ἀμαθίας.

Ἀληθῆ, ἦν δ᾽ ἐγώ, λέγεις.

B Μὴ τοίνυν ἀνάγκαζε ὃ μὴ καλόν ἐστιν αἰσχρὸν

SYMPOSIUM

Agathon and I have just agreed by narrating to you all on my own account, as well as I am able, the speech she delivered to me. So first, Agathon, I must unfold, in your manner of exposition, who and what sort of being is Love, and then I shall tell of his works. The readiest way, I think, will be to give my description that form of question and answer which the stranger woman used for hers that day. For I spoke to her in much the same terms as Agathon addressed just now to me, saying Love was a great god, and was of beautiful things; and she refuted me with the very arguments I have brought against our young friend, showing that by my account that god was neither beautiful nor good.

"'How do you mean, Diotima?' said I; 'is Love then ugly and bad?'

"'Peace, for shame!' she replied: 'or do you imagine that whatever is not beautiful must needs be ugly?'

"'To be sure I do.'

"'And what is not skilled, ignorant? Have you not observed that there is something halfway between skill and ignorance?'

"'What is that?'

"'You know, of course, that to have correct opinion, if you can give no reason for it, is neither full knowledge—how can an unreasoned thing be knowledge?—nor yet ignorance; for what hits on the truth cannot be ignorance. So correct opinion, I take it, is just in that position, between understanding and ignorance.'

"'Quite true,' I said.

"'Then do not compel what is not beautiful to be

175

PLATO

εἶναι, μηδὲ ὃ μὴ ἀγαθόν, κακόν. οὕτω δὲ καὶ τὸν Ἔρωτα ἐπειδὴ αὐτὸς ὁμολογεῖς μὴ εἶναι ἀγαθὸν μηδὲ καλόν, μηδέν τι μᾶλλον οἴου δεῖν αὐτὸν αἰσχρὸν καὶ κακὸν εἶναι, ἀλλά τι μεταξύ, ἔφη, τούτοιν.

Καὶ μήν, ἦν δ' ἐγώ, ὁμολογεῖταί γε παρὰ πάντων μέγας θεὸς εἶναι.

Τῶν μὴ εἰδότων, ἔφη, πάντων λέγεις, ἢ καὶ τῶν εἰδότων;

Συμπάντων μὲν οὖν.

C Καὶ ἣ γελάσασα, Καὶ πῶς ἄν, ἔφη, ὦ Σώκρατες, ὁμολογοῖτο μέγας θεὸς εἶναι παρὰ τούτων, οἳ φασιν αὐτὸν οὐδὲ θεὸν εἶναι;

Τίνες οὗτοι; ἦν δ' ἐγώ.

Εἷς μέν, ἔφη, σύ, μία δ' ἐγώ.

Κἀγὼ εἶπον, Πῶς τοῦτο, ἔφην, λέγεις;

Καὶ ἥ, Ῥαδίως, ἔφη. λέγε γάρ μοι, οὐ πάντας θεοὺς φῂς εὐδαίμονας εἶναι καὶ καλούς; ἢ τολμήσαις ἄν τινα μὴ φάναι καλόν τε καὶ εὐδαίμονα θεῶν εἶναι;

Μὰ Δί' οὐκ ἔγωγ', ἔφην.

Εὐδαίμονας δὲ δὴ λέγεις οὐ τοὺς τἀγαθὰ καὶ τὰ καλὰ κεκτημένους;

D Πάνυ γε.

Ἀλλὰ μὴν Ἔρωτά γε ὡμολόγηκας δι' ἔνδειαν τῶν ἀγαθῶν καὶ καλῶν ἐπιθυμεῖν αὐτῶν τούτων ὧν ἐνδεής ἐστιν.

Ὡμολόγηκα γάρ.

Πῶς ἂν οὖν θεὸς εἴη ὅ γε τῶν καλῶν καὶ ἀγαθῶν ἄμοιρος;

Οὐδαμῶς, ὥς γ' ἔοικεν.

Ὁρᾷς οὖν, ἔφη, ὅτι καὶ σὺ Ἔρωτα οὐ θεὸν νομίζεις;

SYMPOSIUM

ugly,' she said, ' or what is not good to be bad. Likewise of Love, when you find yourself admitting that he is not good nor beautiful, do not therefore suppose he must be ugly and bad, but something betwixt the two.'

" ' And what of the notion,' I asked, ' to which every one agrees, that he is a great god ? '

" ' Every one ? People who do not know,' she rejoined, ' or those who know also ? '

" ' I mean everybody in the world.'

" At this she laughed and said, ' But how, Socrates, can those agree that he is a great god who say he is no god at all ? '

" ' What persons are they ? ' I asked.

" ' You are one,' she replied, ' and I am another.'

" ' How do you make that out ? ' I said.

" ' Easily,' said she ; ' tell me, do you not say that all gods are happy and beautiful ? Or will you dare to deny that any god is beautiful and happy ? '

" ' Bless me ! ' I exclaimed, ' not I.'

" ' And do you not call those happy who possess good and beautiful things ? '

" ' Certainly I do.'

" ' But you have admitted that Love, from lack of good and beautiful things, desires these very things that he lacks.'

" ' Yes, I have.'

" ' How then can he be a god, if he is devoid of things beautiful and good ? '

" ' By no means, it appears.'

" ' So you see,' she said, ' you are a person who does not consider Love to be a god.'

202

Τί οὖν ἄν, ἔφην, εἴη ὁ Ἔρως; θνητός;

Ἥκιστά γε.

E Ἀλλὰ τί μήν;

Ὥσπερ τὰ πρότερα ἔφην, μεταξὺ θνητοῦ καὶ ἀθανάτου.

Τί οὖν, ὦ Διοτίμα;

Δαίμων μέγας, ὦ Σώκρατες· καὶ γὰρ πᾶν τὸ δαιμόνιον μεταξύ ἐστι θεοῦ τε καὶ θνητοῦ.

Τίνα, ἦν δ' ἐγώ, δύναμιν ἔχον;

Ἑρμηνεῦον καὶ διαπορθμεῦον θεοῖς τὰ παρ' ἀνθρώπων καὶ ἀνθρώποις τὰ παρὰ θεῶν, τῶν μὲν τὰς δεήσεις καὶ θυσίας, τῶν δὲ τὰς ἐπιτάξεις τε καὶ ἀμοιβὰς [τῶν θυσιῶν],[1] ἐν μέσῳ δὲ ὂν ἀμφοτέρων συμπληροῖ, ὥστε τὸ πᾶν αὐτὸ αὑτῷ συνδεδέσθαι. διὰ τούτου καὶ ἡ μαντικὴ πᾶσα χωρεῖ καὶ ἡ τῶν ἱερέων τέχνη τῶν τε περὶ τὰς θυσίας καὶ 203 τὰς τελετὰς καὶ τὰς ἐπῳδὰς καὶ τὴν μαντείαν πᾶσαν καὶ γοητείαν. θεὸς δὲ ἀνθρώπῳ οὐ μίγνυται, ἀλλὰ διὰ τούτου πᾶσά ἐστιν ἡ ὁμιλία καὶ ἡ διάλεκτος θεοῖς πρὸς ἀνθρώπους ⟨καὶ πρὸς θεοὺς ἀνθρώποις⟩,[2] καὶ ἐγρηγορόσι καὶ καθεύδουσι· καὶ ὁ μὲν περὶ τὰ τοιαῦτα σοφὸς δαιμόνιος ἀνήρ, ὁ δὲ ἄλλο τι σοφὸς ὢν ἢ περὶ τέχνας ἢ χειρουργίας τινὰς βάναυσος. οὗτοι δὴ οἱ δαίμονες πολλοὶ καὶ παντοδαποί εἰσιν, εἷς δὲ τούτων ἐστὶ καὶ ὁ Ἔρως.

Πατρὸς δέ, ἦν δ' ἐγώ, τίνος ἐστὶ καὶ μητρός;

B Μακρότερον μέν, ἔφη, διηγήσασθαι· ὅμως δέ σοι ἐρῶ. ὅτε γὰρ ἐγένετο ἡ Ἀφροδίτη, εἱστιῶντο οἱ θεοί, οἵ τε ἄλλοι καὶ ὁ τῆς Μήτιδος υἱὸς Πόρος· ἐπειδὴ δὲ ἐδείπνησαν, προσαιτήσουσα οἷον δὴ

---

[1] τῶν θυσιῶν om. Pollux, secl. Schanz.
[2] ⟨καὶ πρὸς θεοὺς ἀνθρώποις⟩ Wolf.

178

SYMPOSIUM

"'What then,' I asked, 'can Love be? A mortal?'"

"'Anything but that.'"

"'Well what?'"

"'As I previously suggested, between a mortal and an immortal.'"

"'And what is that, Diotima?'"

"'A great spirit, Socrates: for the whole of the spiritual[1] is between divine and mortal.'"

"'Possessing what power?' I asked."

"'Interpreting and transporting human things to the gods and divine things to men; entreaties and sacrifices from below, and ordinances and requitals from above: being midway between, it makes each to supplement the other, so that the whole is combined in one. Through it are conveyed all divination and priestcraft concerning sacrifice and ritual and incantations, and all soothsaying and sorcery. God with man does not mingle: but the spiritual is the means of all society and converse of men with gods and of gods with men, whether waking or asleep. Whosoever has skill in these affairs is a spiritual man; to have it in other matters, as in common arts and crafts, is for the mechanical. Many and multifarious are these spirits, and one of them is Love.'"

"'From what father and mother sprung?' I asked."

"'That is rather a long story,' she replied; 'but still, I will tell it you. When Aphrodite was born, the gods made a great feast, and among the company was Resource the son of Cunning. And when they had banqueted there came Poverty abegging, as

[1] Δαίμονες and τὸ δαιμόνιον represent the mysterious agencies and influences by which the gods communicate with mortals.

εὐωχίας οὔσης ἀφίκετο ἡ Πενία, καὶ ἦν περὶ τὰς θύρας. ὁ οὖν Πόρος μεθυσθεὶς τοῦ νέκταρος, οἶνος γὰρ οὔπω ἦν, εἰς τὸν τοῦ Διὸς κῆπον εἰσελθὼν βεβαρημένος ηὗδεν. ἡ οὖν Πενία ἐπιβουλεύουσα διὰ τὴν αὑτῆς ἀπορίαν παιδίον ποιήσασθαι ἐκ τοῦ Πόρου, κατακλίνεταί τε παρ' αὐτῷ καὶ ἐκύησε τὸν Ἔρωτα. διὸ δὴ καὶ τῆς Ἀφροδίτης ἀκόλουθος καὶ θεράπων γέγονεν ὁ Ἔρως, γεννηθεὶς ἐν τοῖς ἐκείνης γενεθλίοις, καὶ ἅμα φύσει ἐραστὴς ὢν περὶ τὸ καλὸν καὶ τῆς Ἀφροδίτης καλῆς οὔσης. ἅτε οὖν Πόρου καὶ Πενίας υἱὸς ὢν ὁ Ἔρως ἐν τοιαύτῃ τύχῃ καθέστηκε. πρῶτον μὲν πένης ἀεί ἐστι, καὶ πολλοῦ δεῖ ἁπαλός τε καὶ καλός, οἷον οἱ πολλοὶ οἴονται, ἀλλὰ σκληρὸς καὶ αὐχμηρὸς καὶ ἀνυπόδητος καὶ ἄοικος, χαμαιπετὴς ἀεὶ ὢν καὶ ἄστρωτος, ἐπὶ θύραις καὶ ἐν ὁδοῖς ὑπαίθριος κοιμώμενος, τὴν τῆς μητρὸς φύσιν ἔχων, ἀεὶ ἐνδείᾳ σύνοικος. κατὰ δὲ αὖ τὸν πατέρα ἐπίβουλός ἐστι τοῖς καλοῖς καὶ τοῖς ἀγαθοῖς, ἀνδρεῖος ὢν καὶ ἴτης καὶ σύντονος, θηρευτὴς δεινός, ἀεί τινας πλέκων μηχανάς, καὶ φρονήσεως ἐπιθυμητὴς καὶ πόριμος, φιλοσοφῶν διὰ παντὸς τοῦ βίου, δεινὸς γόης καὶ φαρμακεὺς καὶ σοφιστής· καὶ οὔτε ὡς ἀθάνατος πέφυκεν οὔτε ὡς θνητός, ἀλλὰ τοτὲ μὲν τῆς αὐτῆς ἡμέρας θάλλει τε καὶ ζῇ, ὅταν εὐπορήσῃ, τοτὲ δὲ ἀποθνῄσκει, πάλιν δὲ ἀναβιώσκεται διὰ τὴν τοῦ πατρὸς φύσιν, τὸ δὲ ποριζόμενον ἀεὶ ὑπεκρεῖ· ὥστε οὔτε ἀπορεῖ Ἔρως ποτὲ οὔτε πλουτεῖ, σοφίας τε αὖ καὶ ἀμαθίας ἐν μέσῳ ἐστίν. ἔχει γὰρ ὧδε. θεῶν οὐδεὶς φιλοσοφεῖ οὐδ' ἐπιθυμεῖ σοφὸς

SYMPOSIUM

well she might in an hour of good cheer, and hung about the door. Now Resource, grown tipsy with nectar — for wine as yet there was none — went into the garden of Zeus, and there, overcome with heaviness, slept. Then Poverty, being of herself so resourceless devised the scheme of having a child by Resource, and lying down by his side she conceived Love. Hence it is that Love from the beginning has been attendant and minister to Aphrodite, since he was begotten on the day of her birth, and is, moreover, by nature a lover bent on beauty since Aphrodite is beautiful. Now, as the son of Resource and Poverty, Love is in a peculiar case. First, he is ever poor, and far from tender or beautiful as most suppose him: rather is he hard and parched, shoeless and homeless; on the bare ground always he lies with no bedding, and takes his rest on doorsteps and waysides in the open air; true to his mother's nature, he ever dwells with want. But he takes after his father in scheming for all that is beautiful and good; for he is brave, impetuous and high-strung, a famous hunter, always weaving some stratagem; desirous and competent of wisdom, throughout life ensuing the truth; a master of jugglery, witchcraft, and artful speech. By birth neither immortal nor mortal, in the selfsame day he is flourishing and alive at the hour when he is abounding in resource; at another he is dying, and then reviving again by force of his father's nature: yet the resources that he gets will ever be ebbing away; so that Love is at no time either resourceless or wealthy, and furthermore, he stands midway betwixt wisdom and ignorance. The position is this: no gods ensue wisdom or desire to be

204 γενέσθαι· ἔστι γάρ· οὐδ' εἴ τις ἄλλος σοφός, οὐ φιλοσοφεῖ. οὐδ' αὖ οἱ ἀμαθεῖς φιλοσοφοῦσιν οὐδ' ἐπιθυμοῦσι σοφοὶ γενέσθαι· αὐτὸ γὰρ τοῦτό ἐστι χαλεπὸν ἀμαθία, τὸ μὴ ὄντα καλὸν κἀγαθὸν μηδὲ φρόνιμον δοκεῖν αὑτῷ εἶναι ἱκανόν· οὔκουν ἐπιθυμεῖ ὁ μὴ οἰόμενος ἐνδεὴς εἶναι οὗ ἂν μὴ οἴηται ἐπιδεῖσθαι.

Τίνες οὖν, ἔφην ἐγώ, ὦ Διοτίμα, οἱ φιλοσοφοῦντες, εἰ μήτε οἱ σοφοὶ μήτε οἱ ἀμαθεῖς;

B Δῆλον, ἔφη, τοῦτό γε ἤδη καὶ παιδί, ὅτι οἱ μεταξὺ τούτων ἀμφοτέρων, ὧν ἂν καὶ ὁ Ἔρως. ἔστι γὰρ δὴ τῶν καλλίστων ἡ σοφία, Ἔρως δ' ἐστὶν ἔρως περὶ τὸ καλόν, ὥστε ἀναγκαῖον Ἔρωτα φιλόσοφον εἶναι, φιλόσοφον δὲ ὄντα μεταξὺ εἶναι σοφοῦ καὶ ἀμαθοῦς. αἰτία δ' αὐτῷ καὶ τούτων ἡ γένεσις· πατρὸς μὲν γὰρ σοφοῦ ἐστι καὶ εὐπόρου, μητρὸς δὲ οὐ σοφῆς καὶ ἀπόρου. ἡ μὲν οὖν φύσις τοῦ δαίμονος, ὦ φίλε Σώκρατες, αὕτη· ὃν δὲ σὺ ᾠήθης Ἔρωτα

C εἶναι, θαυμαστὸν οὐδὲν ἔπαθες. ᾠήθης δέ, ὡς ἐμοὶ δοκεῖ τεκμαιρομένῃ ἐξ ὧν σὺ λέγεις, τὸ ἐρώμενον Ἔρωτα εἶναι, οὐ τὸ ἐρῶν. διὰ ταῦτά σοι, οἶμαι, πάγκαλος ἐφαίνετο ὁ Ἔρως. καὶ γὰρ ἔστι τὸ ἐραστὸν τὸ τῷ ὄντι καλὸν καὶ ἁβρὸν καὶ τέλεον καὶ μακαριστόν· τὸ δέ γε ἐρῶν ἄλλην ἰδέαν τοιαύτην ἔχον, οἵαν ἐγὼ διῆλθον.

Καὶ ἐγὼ εἶπον, Εἶεν δή, ὦ ξένη· καλῶς γὰρ λέγεις· τοιοῦτος ὢν ὁ Ἔρως τίνα χρείαν ἔχει τοῖς ἀνθρώποις;

D Τοῦτο δὴ μετὰ ταῦτ', ἔφη, ὦ Σώκρατες, πει-

SYMPOSIUM

made wise; such they are already; nor does anyone else that is wise ensue it. Neither do the ignorant ensue wisdom, nor desire to be made wise: in this very point is ignorance distressing, that a person who is not enlightened or intelligent should be satisfied with himself. The man who does not feel himself defective has no desire for that whereof he feels no defect.'

"'Who then, Diotima,' I asked, 'are the followers of wisdom, if they are neither the wise nor the ignorant?'

"'Why, a child could tell by this time,' she answered, 'that they are the intermediate sort, and amongst these also is Love. For wisdom has to do with the fairest things, and Love is a love directed to what is fair; so that Love must needs be a friend of wisdom, and, as such, must be between wise and ignorant. This again is a result for which he has to thank his origin: for while he comes of a wise and resourceful father, his mother is unwise and resourceless. Such, my good Socrates, is the nature of this spirit. That you should have formed your other notion of Love is no surprising accident. You supposed, if I am to take your own words as evidence, that the beloved and not the lover was Love. This led you, I fancy, to hold that Love is all-beautiful. The lovable, indeed, is the truly beautiful, tender, perfect, and heaven-blest; but the lover is of a different type, in accordance with the account I have given.'

"Upon this I observed: 'Very well then, madam, you are right; but if Love is such as you describe him, of what use is he to mankind?'

"'That is the next question, Socrates,' she

ράσομαί σε διδάξαι. ἔστι μὲν γὰρ δὴ τοιοῦτος
καὶ οὕτω γεγονὼς ὁ Ἔρως, ἔστι δὲ τῶν καλῶν,
ὡς σὺ φῄς. εἰ δέ τις ἡμᾶς ἔροιτο· τί τῶν καλῶν
ἐστὶν ὁ Ἔρως, ὦ Σώκρατές τε καὶ Διοτίμα; ὧδε
δὲ σαφέστερον ἐρῶ· ὁ ἐρῶν τῶν καλῶν τί ἐρᾷ;

Καὶ ἐγὼ εἶπον ὅτι Γενέσθαι αὑτῷ.

Ἀλλ' ἔτι ποθεῖ, ἔφη, ἡ ἀπόκρισις ἐρώτησιν
τοιάνδε· τί ἔσται ἐκείνῳ ᾧ ἂν γένηται τὰ καλά;

Οὐ πάνυ ἔφην ἔτι ἔχειν ἐγὼ πρὸς ταύτην τὴν
ἐρώτησιν προχείρως ἀποκρίνασθαι.

Ἀλλ', ἔφη, ὥσπερ ἂν εἴ τις μεταβαλὼν ἀντὶ τοῦ
καλοῦ τῷ ἀγαθῷ χρώμενος πυνθάνοιτο· φέρε, ὦ
Σώκρατες, ἐρῶ· ὁ ἐρῶν τῶν ἀγαθῶν τί ἐρᾷ;

Γενέσθαι, ἦν δ' ἐγώ, αὑτῷ.

Καὶ τί ἔσται ἐκείνῳ ᾧ ἂν γένηται τἀγαθά;

Τοῦτ' εὐπορώτερον, ἦν δ' ἐγώ, ἔχω ἀποκρίνασθαι, ὅτι εὐδαίμων ἔσται.

Κτήσει γάρ, ἔφη, ἀγαθῶν οἱ εὐδαίμονες εὐδαίμονες, καὶ οὐκέτι προσδεῖ ἐρέσθαι, ἵνα τί δὲ
βούλεται εὐδαίμων εἶναι ὁ βουλόμενος, ἀλλὰ τέλος
δοκεῖ ἔχειν ἡ ἀπόκρισις.

Ἀληθῆ λέγεις, εἶπον ἐγώ.

Ταύτην δὲ τὴν βούλησιν καὶ τὸν ἔρωτα τοῦτον
πότερα κοινὸν οἴει εἶναι πάντων ἀνθρώπων, καὶ
πάντας τἀγαθὰ βούλεσθαι αὑτοῖς εἶναι ἀεί, ἢ
πῶς λέγεις;

Οὕτως, ἦν δ' ἐγώ· κοιν`ν εἶναι πάντων.

Τί δὴ οὖν, ἔφη, ὦ Σώκρατες, οὐ πάντας ἐρᾶν

SYMPOSIUM

replied, 'on which I will try to enlighten you. While Love is of such nature and origin as I have related, he is also set on beautiful things, as you say. Now, suppose some one were to ask us: In what respect is he Love of beautiful things, Socrates and Diotima? But let me put the question more clearly thus: What is the love of the lover of beautiful things?'

"'That they may be his,' I replied.

"'But your answer craves a further query,' she said, 'such as this: What will he have who gets beautiful things?'

"This question I declared I was quite unable now to answer offhand.

"'Well,' she proceeded, 'imagine that the object is changed, and the inquiry is made about the good instead of the beautiful. Come, Socrates (I shall say), what is the love of the lover of good things?'

"'That they may be his,' I replied.

"'And what will he have who gets good things?'

"'I can make more shift to answer this,' I said; 'he will be happy.'

"'Yes,' she said, 'the happy are happy by acquisition of good things, and we have no more need to ask for what end a man wishes to be happy, when such is his wish: the answer seems to be ultimate.'

"'Quite true,' I said.

"'Now do you suppose this wish or this love to be common to all mankind, and that every one always wishes to have good things? Or what do you say?'

"'Even so,' I said; 'it is common to all.'

"'Well then, Socrates,' she said, 'we do not

φαμέν, εἴπερ γε πάντες τῶν αὐτῶν ἐρῶσι καὶ ἀεί, ἀλλά τινάς φαμεν ἐρᾶν, τοὺς δ' οὔ;

Θαυμάζω, ἦν δ' ἐγώ, καὶ αὐτός.

Ἀλλὰ μὴ θαύμαζ', ἔφη· ἀφελόντες γὰρ τοῦ ἔρωτός τι εἶδος ὀνομάζομεν, τὸ τοῦ ὅλου ἐπιτιθέντες ὄνομα, ἔρωτα, τὰ δὲ ἄλλα ἄλλοις καταχρώμεθα ὀνόμασιν.

Ὥσπερ τί; ἦν δ' ἐγώ.

Ὥσπερ τόδε. οἶσθ' ὅτι ποίησίς ἐστί τι πολύ· ἡ γάρ τοι ἐκ τοῦ μὴ ὄντος εἰς τὸ ὂν ἰόντι ὁτῳοῦν αἰτία πᾶσά ἐστι ποίησις, ὥστε καὶ αἱ ὑπὸ πάσαις ταῖς τέχναις ἐργασίαι ποιήσεις εἰσὶ καὶ οἱ τούτων δημιουργοὶ πάντες ποιηταί.

Ἀληθῆ λέγεις.

Ἀλλ' ὅμως, ἦ δ' ἥ, οἶσθ' ὅτι οὐ καλοῦνται ποιηταὶ ἀλλ' ἄλλα ἔχουσιν ὀνόματα, ἀπὸ δὲ πάσης τῆς ποιήσεως ἓν μόριον ἀφορισθὲν τὸ περὶ τὴν μουσικὴν καὶ τὰ μέτρα τῷ τοῦ ὅλου ὀνόματι προσαγορεύεται. ποίησις γὰρ τοῦτο μόνον καλεῖται, καὶ οἱ ἔχοντες τοῦτο τὸ μόριον τῆς ποιήσεως ποιηταί.

Ἀληθῆ λέγεις, ἔφην.

Οὕτω τοίνυν καὶ περὶ τὸν ἔρωτα· τὸ μὲν κεφάλαιόν ἐστι πᾶσα ἡ τῶν ἀγαθῶν ἐπιθυμία καὶ τοῦ εὐδαιμονεῖν, "ὁ μέγιστός τε καὶ δολερὸς ἔρως παντί"· ἀλλ' οἱ μὲν ἄλλῃ τρεπόμενοι πολλαχῇ ἐπ' αὐτόν, ἢ κατὰ χρηματισμὸν ἢ κατὰ φιλογυμναστίαν ἢ κατὰ φιλοσοφίαν, οὔτ' ἐρᾶν καλοῦνται οὔτ' ἐρασταί, οἱ δὲ κατὰ ἕν τι εἶδος ἰόντες τε καὶ

SYMPOSIUM

mean that all men love, when we say that all men love the same things always; we mean that some people love and others do not?'

"'I am wondering myself,' I replied.

"'But you should not wonder,' she said; 'for we have singled out a certain form of love, and applying thereto the name of the whole, we call it love; and there are other names that we commonly abuse.'

"'As, for example —— ?' I asked.

"'Take the following: you know that *poetry*[1] is more than a single thing. For of anything whatever that passes from not being into being the whole cause is composing or poetry; so that the productions of all arts are kinds of poetry, and their craftsmen are all poets.'

"'That is true.'

"'But still, as you are aware,' said she, 'they are not called poets: they have other names, while a single section disparted from the whole of poetry—merely the business of music and metres—is entitled with the name of the whole. This and no more is called poetry; those only who possess this branch of the art are poets.'

"'Quite true,' I said.

"'Well, it is just the same with love. Generically, indeed, it is all that desire of good things and of being happy[2]—Love most mighty and all-beguiling. Yet, whereas those who resort to him in various other ways—in money-making, an inclination to sports, or philosophy—are not described either as loving or as lovers, all those who pursue him seriously in one of his several forms

[1] *Cf.* above, 197 A.
[2] *Cf.* above, 204 E-205 A.

PLATO

ἐσπουδακότες τὸ τοῦ ὅλου ὄνομα ἴσχουσιν [ἔρωτά τε]¹ καὶ ἐρᾶν καὶ ἐρασταί.

Κινδυνεύεις ἀληθῆ, ἔφην ἐγώ, λέγειν.

Καὶ λέγεται μέν γέ τις, ἔφη, λόγος, ὡς οἳ ἂν τὸ ἥμισυ ἑαυτῶν ζητῶσιν, οὗτοι ἐρῶσιν· ὁ δ' ἐμὸς λόγος οὔθ' ἡμίσεός φησιν εἶναι τὸν ἔρωτα οὔθ' ὅλου, ἐὰν μὴ τυγχάνῃ γέ που, ὦ ἑταῖρε, ἀγαθὸν ὄν· ἐπεὶ αὑτῶν γε καὶ πόδας καὶ χεῖρας ἐθέλουσιν ἀποτέμνεσθαι οἱ ἄνθρωποι, ἐὰν αὐτοῖς δοκῇ τὰ ἑαυτῶν πονηρὰ εἶναι. οὐ γὰρ τὸ ἑαυτῶν, οἶμαι, ἕκαστοι ἀσπάζονται, εἰ μὴ εἴ τις τὸ μὲν ἀγαθὸν οἰκεῖον καλεῖ καὶ ἑαυτοῦ, τὸ δὲ κακὸν ἀλλότριον· ὡς οὐδέν γε ἄλλο ἐστὶν οὗ ἐρῶσιν ἄνθρωποι ἢ τοῦ ἀγαθοῦ· ἢ σοὶ δοκοῦσιν;

Μὰ Δί' οὐκ ἔμοιγε, ἦν δ' ἐγώ.

Ἆρ' οὖν, ἦ δ' ἥ, οὕτως ἁπλοῦν ἐστὶ λέγειν, ὅτι οἱ ἄνθρωποι τοῦ ἀγαθοῦ ἐρῶσιν;

Ναί, ἔφην.

Τί δέ; οὐ προσθετέον, ἔφη, ὅτι καὶ εἶναι τὸ ἀγαθὸν αὑτοῖς ἐρῶσιν;

Προσθετέον.

Ἆρ' οὖν, ἔφη, καὶ οὐ μόνον εἶναι, ἀλλὰ καὶ ἀεὶ εἶναι;

Καὶ τοῦτο προσθετέον.

Ἔστιν ἄρα συλλήβδην, ἔφη, ὁ ἔρως τοῦ τὸ ἀγαθὸν αὑτῷ εἶναι ἀεί.

Ἀληθέστατα, ἔφην ἐγώ, λέγεις.

Ὅτε δὴ τούτου² ὁ ἔρως ἐστὶν ἀεί, ἦ δ' ἥ, τῶν τίνα τρόπον διωκόντων αὐτὸ καὶ ἐν τίνι πράξει ἡ σπουδὴ καὶ ἡ σύντασις ἔρως ἂν

---
¹ ἔρωτά τε seclusi : ἔρωτά . . . ἐρασταί secl. Schanz.
² τούτου Bast : τοῦτο MSS.

SYMPOSIUM

obtain, as loving and as lovers, the name of the whole.'

"'I fancy you are right,' I said.

"'And certainly there runs a story,' she continued, 'that all who go seeking their other half[1] are in love; though by my account love is neither for half nor for whole, unless, of course, my dear sir, this happens to be something good. For men are prepared to have their own feet and hands cut off if they feel these belongings to be harmful. The fact is, I suppose, that each person does not cherish his belongings except where a man calls the good his own property and the bad another's; since what men love is simply and solely the good. Or is your view otherwise?'

"'Faith, no,' I said.

"'Then we may state unreservedly that men love the good?'

"'Yes,' I said.

"'Well now, must we not extend it to this, that they love the good to be theirs?'

"'We must.'

"'And do they love it to be not merely theirs but theirs always?'

"'Include that also.'

"'Briefly then,' said she, 'love loves the good to be one's own for ever.'

"'That is the very truth,' I said.

"'Now if love is always for this,' she proceeded, 'what is the method of those who pursue it, and what is the behaviour whose eagerness and straining

[1] A "prophetic" allusion to Aristophanes' speech, 192 foll.

PLATO

καλοῖτο; τί τοῦτο τυγχάνει ὂν τὸ ἔργον; ἔχεις εἰπεῖν;

Οὐ μεντἂν σέ, ἔφην ἐγώ, ὦ Διοτίμα, ἐθαύμαζον ἐπὶ σοφίᾳ καὶ ἐφοίτων παρὰ σὲ αὐτὰ ταῦτα μαθησόμενος.

'Αλλ' ἐγώ σοι, ἔφη, ἐρῶ. ἔστι γὰρ τοῦτο τόκος ἐν καλῷ καὶ κατὰ τὸ σῶμα καὶ κατὰ τὴν ψυχήν. Μαντείας, ἦν δ' ἐγώ, δεῖται ὅ τί ποτε λέγεις, καὶ οὐ μανθάνω.

C 'Αλλ' ἐγώ, ἦ δ' ἥ, σαφέστερον ἐρῶ. κυοῦσι γάρ, ἔφη, ὦ Σώκρατες, πάντες ἄνθρωποι καὶ κατὰ τὸ σῶμα καὶ κατὰ τὴν ψυχήν, καὶ ἐπειδὰν ἔν τινι ἡλικίᾳ γένωνται, τίκτειν ἐπιθυμεῖ ἡμῶν ἡ φύσις. τίκτειν δὲ ἐν μὲν αἰσχρῷ οὐ δύναται, ἐν δὲ τῷ καλῷ. ἡ γὰρ ἀνδρὸς καὶ γυναικὸς συνουσία τόκος ἐστίν. ἔστι δὲ τοῦτο θεῖον τὸ πρᾶγμα, καὶ τοῦτο ἐν θνητῷ ὄντι τῷ ζῴῳ ἀθάνατον ἔνεστιν, ἡ κύησις καὶ ἡ γέννησις. τὰ δ' ἐν τῷ ἀναρμόστῳ ἀδύνατον
D γενέσθαι. ἀνάρμοστον δ' ἐστὶ τὸ αἰσχρὸν παντὶ τῷ θείῳ, τὸ δὲ καλὸν ἁρμόττον. Μοῖρα οὖν καὶ Εἰλείθυια ἡ Καλλονή ἐστι τῇ γενέσει. διὰ ταῦτα ὅταν μὲν καλῷ προσπελάζῃ τὸ κυοῦν, ἵλεών τε γίγνεται καὶ εὐφραινόμενον διαχεῖται καὶ τίκτει τε καὶ γεννᾷ· ὅταν δὲ αἰσχρῷ, σκυθρωπόν τε καὶ λυπούμενον συσπειρᾶται καὶ ἀποτρέπεται καὶ ἀνείλλεται καὶ οὐ γεννᾷ, ἀλλὰ ἴσχον τὸ κύημα χαλεπῶς φέρει. ὅθεν δὴ τῷ κυοῦντί τε καὶ ἤδη
E σπαργῶντι πολλὴ ἡ πτοίησις γέγονε περὶ τὸ

SYMPOSIUM

are to be termed love ? What actually is this effort ? Can you tell me ? '

" ' Ah, Diotima,' I said; ' in that case I should hardly be admiring you and your wisdom, and sitting at your feet to be enlightened on just these questions.'

" ' Well, I will tell you,' said she ; ' it is begetting on a beautiful thing by means of both the body and the soul.'

" ' It wants some divination to make out what you mean,' I said ; ' I do not understand.'

" ' Let me put it more clearly,' she said. ' All men are pregnant, Socrates, both in body and in soul: on reaching a certain age our nature yearns to beget. This it cannot do upon an ugly person, but only on the beautiful : the conjunction of man and woman is a begetting for both.[1] It is a divine affair, this engendering and bringing to birth, an immortal element in the creature that is mortal ; and it cannot occur in the discordant. The ugly is discordant with whatever is divine, whereas the beautiful is accordant. Thus Beauty presides over birth as Fate and Lady of Travail ; and hence it is that when the pregnant approaches the beautiful it becomes not only gracious but so exhilarate, that it flows over with begetting and bringing forth ; though when it meets the ugly it coils itself close in a sullen dismay : rebuffed and repressed, it brings not forth, but goes in labour with the burden of its young. Therefore when a person is big and teeming-ripe he feels himself in a sore flutter for the beautiful, because its possessor can relieve him

[1] The argument requires the application of " begetting " and other such terms indifferently to either sex.

PLATO

καλὸν διὰ τὸ μεγάλης ὠδῖνος ἀπολύειν τὸν ἔχοντα. ἔστι γάρ, ὦ Σώκρατες, ἔφη, οὐ τοῦ καλοῦ ὁ ἔρως, ὡς σὺ οἴει.

Ἀλλὰ τί μήν;

Τῆς γεννήσεως καὶ τοῦ τόκου ἐν τῷ καλῷ.

Εἶεν, ἦν δ' ἐγώ.

Πάνυ μὲν οὖν, ἔφη. τί δὴ οὖν τῆς γεννήσεως; ὅτι ἀειγενές ἐστι καὶ ἀθάνατον ὡς θνητῷ ἡ γέννησις. ἀθανασίας δὲ ἀναγκαῖον ἐπιθυμεῖν μετὰ ἀγαθοῦ ἐκ τῶν ὡμολογημένων, εἴπερ τοῦ ἀγαθὸν[1] ἑαυτῷ εἶναι ἀεὶ ἔρως ἐστίν. ἀναγκαῖον δὴ ἐκ τούτου τοῦ λόγου καὶ τῆς ἀθανασίας τὸν ἔρωτα εἶναι.

Ταῦτά τε οὖν πάντα ἐδίδασκέ με, ὁπότε περὶ τῶν ἐρωτικῶν λόγους ποιοῖτο, καί ποτε ἤρετο Τί οἴει, ὦ Σώκρατες, αἴτιον εἶναι τούτου τοῦ ἔρωτος καὶ τῆς ἐπιθυμίας; ἢ οὐκ αἰσθάνῃ ὡς δεινῶς διατίθεται πάντα τὰ θηρία, ἐπειδὰν γεννᾶν ἐπιθυμήσῃ, καὶ τὰ πεζὰ καὶ τὰ πτηνά, νοσοῦντά τε πάντα καὶ ἐρωτικῶς διατιθέμενα, πρῶτον μὲν περὶ τὸ συμμιγῆναι ἀλλήλοις, ἔπειτα περὶ τὴν τροφὴν τοῦ γενομένου, καὶ ἕτοιμά ἐστιν ὑπὲρ τούτων καὶ διαμάχεσθαι τὰ ἀσθενέστατα τοῖς ἰσχυροτάτοις καὶ ὑπεραποθνῄσκειν, καὶ αὐτὰ τῷ λιμῷ παρατεινόμενα ὥστ' ἐκεῖνα ἐκτρέφειν, καὶ ἄλλο πᾶν ποιοῦντα; τοὺς μὲν γὰρ ἀνθρώπους, ἔφη, οἴοιτ' ἄν τις ἐκ λογισμοῦ ταῦτα ποιεῖν· τὰ δὲ θηρία τίς αἰτία οὕτως ἐρωτικῶς διατίθεσθαι; ἔχεις λέγειν;

Καὶ ἐγὼ αὖ ἔλεγον ὅτι οὐκ εἰδείην· ἣ δ' εἶπε, Διανοῇ οὖν δεινός ποτε γενήσεσθαι τὰ ἐρωτικά ἐὰν ταῦτα μὴ ἐννοῇς;

---
[1] ἀγαθὸν Bury: ἀγαθοῦ, τἀγαθὸν mss.

SYMPOSIUM

of his heavy pangs. For you are wrong, Socrates, in supposing that love is of the beautiful.'

"'What then is it?'

"'It is of engendering and begetting upon the beautiful.'

"'Be it so,' I said.

"'To be sure it is,' she went on; 'and how of engendering? Because this is something ever-existent and immortal in our mortal life. From what has been admitted, we needs must yearn for immortality no less than for good, since love loves good to be one's own for ever. And hence it necessarily follows that love is of immortality.'

"All this instruction did I get from her at various times when she discoursed of love-matters; and one time she asked me, 'What do you suppose, Socrates, to be the cause of this love and desire? For you must have observed the strange state into which all the animals are thrown, whether going on earth or winging the air, when they desire to beget: they are all sick and amorously disposed, first to have union one with another, and next to find food for the new-born; in whose behalf they are ready to fight hard battles, even the weakest against the strongest, and to sacrifice their lives; to be racked with starvation themselves if they can but nurture their young, and be put to any sort of shift. As for men,' said she, 'one might suppose they do these things on the promptings of reason; but what is the cause of this amorous condition in the animals? Can you tell me?'

"Once more I replied that I did not know; so she proceeded: 'How do you design ever to become a master of love-matters, if you can form no notion of this?'

'Αλλὰ διὰ ταῦτά τοι, ὦ Διοτίμα, ὅπερ νῦν δὴ εἶπον, παρὰ σὲ ἥκω, γνοὺς ὅτι διδασκάλων δέομαι. ἀλλά μοι λέγε καὶ τούτων τὴν αἰτίαν καὶ τῶν ἄλλων τῶν περὶ τὰ ἐρωτικά.

Εἰ τοίνυν, ἔφη, πιστεύεις ἐκείνου εἶναι φύσει τὸν ἔρωτα, οὗ πολλάκις ὡμολογήκαμεν, μὴ θαύμαζε. ἐνταῦθα γὰρ τὸν αὐτὸν ἐκείνῳ λόγον ἡ θνητὴ φύσις ζητεῖ κατὰ τὸ δυνατὸν ἀεὶ τὸ εἶναι ἀθάνατος. δύναται δὲ ταύτῃ μόνον, τῇ γενέσει, ὅτι ἀεὶ καταλείπει ἕτερον νέον ἀντὶ τοῦ παλαιοῦ, ἐπεὶ καὶ ἐν ᾧ ἓν ἕκαστον τῶν ζῴων ζῆν καλεῖται καὶ εἶναι τὸ αὐτό, οἷον ἐκ παιδαρίου ὁ αὐτὸς λέγεται ἕως ἂν πρεσβύτης γένηται· οὗτος μέντοι οὐδέποτε τὰ αὐτὰ ἔχων ἐν αὑτῷ ὅμως ὁ αὐτὸς καλεῖται, ἀλλὰ νέος ἀεὶ γιγνόμενος, τὰ δὲ ἀπολλύς, καὶ κατὰ τὰς τρίχας καὶ σάρκα καὶ ὀστᾶ καὶ αἷμα καὶ σύμπαν τὸ σῶμα. καὶ μὴ ὅτι κατὰ τὸ σῶμα, ἀλλὰ καὶ κατὰ τὴν ψυχὴν οἱ τρόποι, τὰ ἤθη, δόξαι, ἐπιθυμίαι, ἡδοναί, λῦπαι, φόβοι, τούτων ἕκαστα οὐδέποτε τὰ αὐτὰ πάρεστιν ἑκάστῳ, ἀλλὰ τὰ μὲν γίγνεται, τὰ δὲ ἀπόλλυται. πολὺ δὲ τούτων ἀτοπώτερον ἔτι, ὅτι καὶ αἱ ἐπιστῆμαι μὴ ὅτι αἱ μὲν γίγνονται, αἱ δὲ ἀπόλλυνται ἡμῖν, καὶ οὐδέποτε οἱ αὐτοί ἐσμεν οὐδὲ κατὰ τὰς ἐπιστήμας, ἀλλὰ καὶ μία ἑκάστη τῶν ἐπιστημῶν ταὐτὸν πάσχει. ὃ γὰρ καλεῖται μελετᾶν, ὡς ἐξιούσης ἐστὶ τῆς ἐπιστήμης· λήθη γὰρ ἐπιστήμης ἔξοδος, μελέτη δὲ πάλιν καινὴν ἐμποιοῦσα ἀντὶ τῆς ἀπ-

SYMPOSIUM

"'Why, it is just for this, I tell you, Diotima—as I stated a moment ago—that I have come to see you, because I noted my need of an instructor. Come, tell me the cause of these effects as well as of the others that have relation to love-matters.'

"'Well then,' she said, 'if you believe that love is by nature bent on what we have repeatedly admitted, you may cease to wonder. For here, too, on the same principle as before, the mortal nature ever seeks, as best it can, to be immortal. In one way only can it succeed, and that is by generation; since so it can always leave behind it a new creature in place of the old. It is only for a while that each live thing can be described as alive and the same, as a man is said to be the same person from childhood until he is advanced in years: yet though he is called the same he does not at any time possess the same properties; he is continually becoming a new person, and there are things also which he loses, as appears by his hair, his flesh, his bones, and his blood and body altogether. And observe that not only in his body but in his soul besides we find none of his manners or habits, his opinions, desires, pleasures, pains or fears, ever abiding the same in his particular self; some things grow in him, while others perish. And here is a yet stranger fact: with regard to the possessions of knowledge, not merely do some of them grow and others perish in us, so that neither in what we know are we ever the same persons; but a like fate attends each single sort of knowledge. What we call *conning* implies that our knowledge is departing; since forgetfulness is an egress of knowledge, while conning substitutes a fresh one in place of that

PLATO

ἰούσης [μνήμην]¹ σώζει τὴν ἐπιστήμην, ὥστε τὴν αὐτὴν δοκεῖν εἶναι. τούτῳ γὰρ τῷ τρόπῳ πᾶν τὸ θνητὸν σώζεται, οὐ τῷ παντάπασι τὸ αὐτὸ ἀεὶ εἶναι ὥσπερ τὸ θεῖον, ἀλλὰ τῷ τὸ ἀπιὸν καὶ παλαιούμενον ἕτερον νέον ἐγκαταλείπειν οἷον αὐτὸ ἦν. ταύτῃ τῇ μηχανῇ, ὦ Σώκρατες, ἔφη, θνητὸν ἀθανασίας μετέχει,² καὶ σῶμα καὶ τἆλλα πάντα· ἀδύνατον³ δὲ ἄλλῃ. μὴ οὖν θαύμαζε εἰ τὸ αὑτοῦ ἀποβλάστημα φύσει πᾶν τιμᾷ· ἀθανασίας γὰρ χάριν παντὶ αὕτη ἡ σπουδὴ καὶ ὁ ἔρως ἕπεται.

Καὶ ἐγὼ ἀκούσας τὸν λόγον ἐθαύμασά τε καὶ εἶπον Εἶεν, ἦν δ' ἐγώ, ὦ σοφωτάτη Διοτίμα, ταῦτα ὡς ἀληθῶς οὕτως ἔχει;

Καὶ ἥ, ὥσπερ οἱ τέλεοι σοφισταί, Εὖ ἴσθι, ἔφη, ὦ Σώκρατες· ἐπεί γε καὶ τῶν ἀνθρώπων εἰ ἐθέλεις εἰς τὴν φιλοτιμίαν βλέψαι, θαυμάζοις ἂν τῆς ἀλογίας [πέρι]⁴ ἃ ἐγὼ εἴρηκα εἰ μὴ ἐννοεῖς, ἐνθυμηθεὶς ὡς δεινῶς διάκεινται ἔρωτι τοῦ ὀνομαστοὶ γενέσθαι "καὶ κλέος εἰς τὸν ἀεὶ χρόνον ἀθάνατον καταθέσθαι," καὶ ὑπὲρ τούτου κινδύνους τε κινδυνεύειν ἕτοιμοί εἰσι πάντας ἔτι μᾶλλον ἢ ὑπὲρ τῶν παίδων, καὶ χρήματ' ἀναλίσκειν καὶ πόνους πονεῖν οὑστινασοῦν καὶ ὑπεραποθνῄσκειν. ἐπεὶ οἴει σύ, ἔφη, Ἄλκηστιν ὑπὲρ Ἀδμήτου ἀποθανεῖν ἄν, ἢ Ἀχιλλέα Πατρόκλῳ ἐπαποθανεῖν, ἢ προαποθανεῖν τὸν ὑμέτερον Κόδρον ὑπὲρ τῆς βασιλείας τῶν παίδων,

---
¹ μνήμην secl. Baiter.
² μετέχει Steph. : μετέχειν MSS.
³ ἀδύνατον Creuzer : ἀθάνατον MSS.
⁴ πέρι secl. Ast.

SYMPOSIUM

which departs, and so preserves our knowledge enough to make it seem the same. Every mortal thing is preserved in this way; not by keeping it exactly the same for ever, like the divine, but by replacing what goes off or is antiquated with something fresh, in the semblance of the original. Through this device, Socrates, a mortal thing partakes of immortality, both in its body and in all other respects; by no other means can it be done. So do not wonder if everything naturally values its own offshoot; since all are beset by this eagerness and this love with a view to immortality.'

"On hearing this argument I wondered, and said: 'Really, can this in truth be so, most wise Diotima?'

"Whereat she, like our perfect professors, said: 'Be certain of it, Socrates; only glance at the ambition of the men around you, and you will have to wonder at the unreasonableness of what I have told you, unless you are careful to consider how singularly they are affected with the love of winning a name, "and laying up fame immortal for all time to come."[1] For this, even more than for their children, they are ready to run all risks, to expend money, perform any kind of task, and sacrifice their lives. Do you suppose,' she asked, 'that Alcestis would have died for Admetus, or Achilles have sought death on the corpse of Patroclus, or your own Codrus[2] have welcomed it to save the kingdom of his children, if they had not expected to

[1] Diotima, like Agathon, breaks into verse of her own composing.
[2] A legendary king of Athens who exposed his life because an oracle had said that the Dorian invaders would conquer if they did not slay the Athenian king.

PLATO

μὴ οἰομένους "ἀθάνατον μνήμην ἀρετῆς πέρι" ἑαυτῶν ἔσεσθαι, ἣν νῦν ἡμεῖς ἔχομεν; πολλοῦ γε δεῖ, ἔφη, ἀλλ', οἶμαι, ὑπὲρ ἀρετῆς ἀθανάτου καὶ τοιαύτης δόξης εὐκλεοῦς πάντες πάντα ποιοῦσιν, ὅσῳ ἂν ἀμείνους ὦσι, τοσούτῳ μᾶλλον· τοῦ γὰρ ἀθανάτου ἐρῶσιν. οἱ μὲν οὖν ἐγκύμονες, ἔφη, κατὰ σώματα ὄντες πρὸς τὰς γυναῖκας μᾶλλον τρέπονται καὶ ταύτῃ ἐρωτικοί εἰσι, διὰ παιδογονίας ἀθανασίαν καὶ μνήμην καὶ εὐδαιμονίαν, ὡς οἴονται, αὑτοῖς "εἰς τὸν ἔπειτα χρόνον πάντα ποριζόμενοι." οἱ δὲ κατὰ τὴν ψυχήν—εἰσὶ γὰρ οὖν, ἔφη, οἳ ἐν ταῖς ψυχαῖς κυοῦσιν ἔτι μᾶλλον ἢ ἐν τοῖς σώμασιν, ἃ ψυχῇ προσήκει καὶ κυῆσαι καὶ τεκεῖν·[1] τί οὖν προσήκει; φρόνησίν τε καὶ τὴν ἄλλην ἀρετήν· ὧν δή εἰσι καὶ οἱ ποιηταὶ πάντες γεννήτορες καὶ τῶν δημιουργῶν ὅσοι λέγονται εὑρετικοὶ εἶναι· πολὺ δὲ μεγίστη, ἔφη, καὶ καλλίστη τῆς φρονήσεως ἡ περὶ τὰς τῶν πόλεών τε καὶ οἰκήσεων διακοσμήσεις, ᾗ δὴ ὄνομά ἐστι σωφροσύνη τε καὶ δικαιοσύνη· τούτων αὖ ὅταν τις ἐκ νέου ἐγκύμων ᾖ τὴν ψυχὴν θεῖος ὤν, καὶ ἡκούσης τῆς ἡλικίας τίκτειν τε καὶ γεννᾶν ἤδη ἐπιθυμῇ, ζητεῖ δή, οἶμαι, καὶ οὗτος περιιὼν τὸ καλὸν ἐν ᾧ ἂν γεννήσειεν· ἐν τῷ γὰρ αἰσχρῷ οὐδέποτε γεννήσει. τά τε οὖν σώματα τὰ καλὰ μᾶλλον ἢ τὰ αἰσχρὰ ἀσπάζεται ἅτε κυῶν, καὶ ἐὰν ἐντύχῃ ψυχῇ καλῇ καὶ γενναίᾳ καὶ εὐφυεῖ, πάνυ δὴ ἀσπάζεται τὸ συναμφότερον, καὶ πρὸς τοῦτον τὸν ἄνθρωπον εὐθὺς εὐπορεῖ λόγων περὶ ἀρετῆς καὶ περὶ οἷον χρὴ εἶναι τὸν ἄνδρα τὸν ἀγαθὸν καὶ ἃ ἐπιτηδεύειν, καὶ

[1] τεκεῖν Hug: κυεῖν MSS.

SYMPOSIUM

win 'a deathless memory for valour,' which now we keep? Of course not. I hold it is for immortal distinction and for such illustrious renown as this that they all do all they can, and so much the more in proportion to their excellence. They are in love with what is immortal. Now those who are teeming in body betake them rather to women, and are amorous on this wise: by getting children they acquire an immortality, a memorial, and a state of bliss, which in their imagining they "for all succeeding time procure." But pregnancy of soul—for there are persons,' she declared, 'who in their souls still more than in their bodies conceive those things which are proper for soul to conceive and bring forth; and what are those things? Prudence, and virtue in general; and of these the begetters are all the poets and those craftsmen who are styled *inventors*. Now by far the highest and fairest part of prudence is that which concerns the regulation of cities and habitations; it is called sobriety and justice. So when a man's soul is so far divine that it is made pregnant with these from his youth, and on attaining manhood immediately desires to bring forth and beget, he too, I imagine, goes about seeking the beautiful object whereon he may do his begetting, since he will never beget upon the ugly. Hence it is the beautiful rather than the ugly bodies that he welcomes in his pregnancy, and if he chances also on a soul that is fair and noble and well-endowed, he gladly cherishes the two combined in one; and straightway in addressing such a person he is resourceful in discoursing of virtue and of what should be the good man's character and what his pursuits; and so he takes

PLATO

ἐπιχειρεῖ παιδεύειν. ἁπτόμενος γάρ, οἶμαι, τοῦ καλοῦ καὶ ὁμιλῶν αὐτῷ, ἃ πάλαι ἐκύει τίκτει καὶ γεννᾷ, καὶ παρὼν καὶ ἀπὼν μεμνημένος, καὶ τὸ γεννηθὲν συνεκτρέφει κοινῇ μετ' ἐκείνου, ὥστε πολὺ μείζω κοινωνίαν τῆς τῶν παίδων πρὸς ἀλλήλους οἱ τοιοῦτοι ἴσχουσι καὶ φιλίαν βεβαιοτέραν, ἅτε καλλιόνων καὶ ἀθανατωτέρων παίδων κεκοινωνηκότες. καὶ πᾶς ἂν δέξαιτο ἑαυτῷ τοιούτους παῖδας μᾶλλον γεγονέναι ἢ τοὺς ἀνθρωπίνους, καὶ εἰς Ὅμηρον ἀποβλέψας καὶ Ἡσίοδον καὶ τοὺς ἄλλους ποιητὰς τοὺς ἀγαθοὺς ζηλῶν οἷα ἔκγονα ἑαυτῶν καταλείπουσιν, ἃ ἐκείνοις ἀθάνατον κλέος καὶ μνήμην παρέχεται αὐτὰ τοιαῦτα ὄντα· εἰ δὲ βούλει, ἔφη, οἵους Λυκοῦργος παῖδας κατελίπετο ἐν Λακεδαίμονι σωτῆρας τῆς Λακεδαίμονος καὶ ὡς ἔπος εἰπεῖν τῆς Ἑλλάδος. τίμιος δὲ παρ' ὑμῖν καὶ Σόλων διὰ τὴν τῶν νόμων γέννησιν, καὶ ἄλλοι ἄλλοθι πολλαχοῦ ἄνδρες, καὶ ἐν Ἕλλησι καὶ ἐν βαρβάροις, πολλὰ καὶ καλὰ ἀποφηνάμενοι ἔργα, γεννήσαντες παντοίαν ἀρετήν· ὧν καὶ ἱερὰ πολλὰ ἤδη γέγονε διὰ τοὺς τοιούτους παῖδας, διὰ δὲ τοὺς ἀνθρωπίνους οὐδενός πω.

Ταῦτα μὲν οὖν τὰ ἐρωτικὰ ἴσως, ὦ Σώκρατες, κἂν σὺ μυηθείης· τὰ δὲ τέλεα καὶ ἐποπτικά, ὧν ἕνεκα καὶ ταῦτα ἔστιν, ἐάν τις ὀρθῶς μετίῃ, οὐκ οἶδ' εἰ οἷός τ' ἂν εἴης. ἐρῶ μὲν οὖν, ἔφη, ἐγὼ καὶ προθυμίας οὐδὲν ἀπολείψω· πειρῶ δὲ ⟨καὶ σὺ⟩[1] ἕπεσθαι, ἂν οἷός τε ᾖς. δεῖ

[1] ⟨καὶ σὺ⟩ Oxyrh. Pap.

SYMPOSIUM

in hand the other's education. For I hold that by contact with the fair one and by consorting with him he bears and brings forth his long-felt conception, because in presence or absence he remembers his fair. Equally too with him he shares the nurturing of what is begotten, so that men in this condition enjoy a far fuller community with each other than that which comes with children, and a far surer friendship, since the children of their union are fairer and more deathless. Every one would choose to have got children such as these rather than the human sort—merely from turning a glance upon Homer and Hesiod and all the other good poets, and envying the fine offspring they leave behind to procure them a glory immortally renewed in the memory of men. Or only look,' she said, 'at the fine children whom Lycurgus[1] left behind him in Lacedaemon to deliver his country and—I may almost say —the whole of Greece; while Solon is highly esteemed among you for begetting his laws; and so are divers men in divers other regions, whether among the Greeks or among foreign peoples, for the number of goodly deeds shown forth in them, the manifold virtues they begot. In their name has many a shrine been reared because of their fine children; whereas for the human sort never any man obtained this honour.

"'Into these love-matters even you, Socrates, might haply be initiated; but I doubt if you could approach the rites and revelations to which these, for the properly instructed, are merely the avenue. However I will speak of them,' she said, 'and will not stint my best endeavours; only you on your part must try your best to follow. He who would

[1] The legendary creator of Spartan laws and customs.

γάρ, ἔφη, τὸν ὀρθῶς ἰόντα ἐπὶ τοῦτο τὸ πρᾶγμα ἄρχεσθαι μὲν νέον ὄντα ἰέναι ἐπὶ τὰ καλὰ σώματα, καὶ πρῶτον μέν, ἐὰν ὀρθῶς ἡγῆται ὁ ἡγούμενος, ἑνὸς αὐτὸν σώματος ἐρᾶν καὶ ἐνταῦθα γεννᾶν λόγους καλούς, ἔπειτα δὲ αὐτὸν κατανοῆσαι, ὅτι τὸ κάλλος τὸ ἐπὶ ὁτῳοῦν σώματι τῷ ἐπὶ ἑτέρῳ σώματι ἀδελφόν ἐστι, καὶ εἰ δεῖ διώκειν τὸ ἐπ᾽ εἴδει καλόν, πολλὴ ἄνοια μὴ οὐχ ἕν τε καὶ ταὐτὸν ἡγεῖσθαι τὸ ἐπὶ πᾶσι τοῖς σώμασι κάλλος· τοῦτο δ᾽ ἐννοήσαντα καταστῆναι πάντων τῶν καλῶν σωμάτων ἐραστήν, ἑνὸς δὲ τὸ σφόδρα τοῦτο χαλάσαι καταφρονήσαντα καὶ σμικρὸν ἡγησάμενον· μετὰ δὲ ταῦτα τὸ ἐν ταῖς ψυχαῖς κάλλος τιμιώτερον ἡγήσασθαι τοῦ ἐν τῷ σώματι, ὥστε καὶ ἐὰν ἐπιεικὴς ὢν τὴν ψυχήν τις κἂν σμικρὸν ἄνθος ἔχῃ, ἐξαρκεῖν αὐτῷ καὶ ἐρᾶν καὶ κήδεσθαι καὶ τίκτειν λόγους τοιούτους καὶ ζητεῖν οἵτινες ποιήσουσι βελτίους τοὺς νέους, ἵνα ἀναγκασθῇ αὖ θεάσασθαι τὸ ἐν τοῖς ἐπιτηδεύμασι καὶ τοῖς νόμοις καλὸν καὶ τοῦτ᾽ ἰδεῖν ὅτι πᾶν αὐτὸ αὑτῷ συγγενές ἐστιν, ἵνα τὸ περὶ τὸ σῶμα καλὸν σμικρόν τι ἡγήσηται εἶναι· μετὰ δὲ τὰ ἐπιτηδεύματα ἐπὶ τὰς ἐπιστήμας ἀγαγεῖν, ἵνα ἴδῃ αὖ ἐπιστημῶν κάλλος, καὶ βλέπων πρὸς πολὺ ἤδη τὸ καλὸν μηκέτι τῷ παρ᾽ ἑνί, ὥσπερ οἰκέτης, ἀγαπῶν παιδαρίου κάλλος ἢ ἀνθρώπου τινὸς ἢ ἐπιτηδεύματος ἑνός, δουλεύων φαῦλος ᾖ καὶ σμικρολόγος, ἀλλ᾽ ἐπὶ τὸ πολὺ πέλαγος τετραμμένος τοῦ καλοῦ καὶ θεωρῶν πολλοὺς καὶ καλοὺς λόγους καὶ μεγαλοπρεπεῖς τίκτῃ

proceed rightly in this business must not merely begin from his youth to encounter beautiful bodies. In the first place, indeed, if his conductor guides him aright, he must be in love with one particular body, and engender beautiful converse therein; but next he must remark how the beauty attached to this or that body is cognate to that which is attached to any other, and that if he means to ensue beauty in form, it is gross folly not to regard as one and the same the beauty belonging to all; and so, having grasped this truth, he must make himself a lover of all beautiful bodies, and slacken the stress of his feeling for one by contemning it and counting it a trifle. But his next advance will be to set a higher value on the beauty of souls than on that of the body, so that however little the grace that may bloom in any likely soul it shall suffice him for loving and caring, and for bringing forth and soliciting such converse as will tend to the betterment of the young; and that finally he may be constrained to contemplate the beautiful as appearing in our observances and our laws, and to behold it all bound together in kinship and so estimate the body's beauty as a slight affair. From observances he should be led on to the branches of knowledge, that there also he may behold a province of beauty, and by looking thus on beauty in the mass may escape from the mean, meticulous slavery of a single instance, where he must centre all his care, like a lackey, upon the beauty of a particular child or man or single observance; and turning rather towards the main ocean of the beautiful may by contemplation of this bring forth in all their splendour many fair fruits of discourse and meditation in a

καὶ διανοήματα ἐν φιλοσοφίᾳ ἀφθόνῳ, ἕως ἂν ἐνταῦθα ῥωσθεὶς καὶ αὐξηθεὶς κατίδῃ τινὰ ἐπιστήμην μίαν τοιαύτην, ἥ ἐστι καλοῦ τοιοῦδε. πειρῶ δέ μοι, ἔφη, τὸν νοῦν προσέχειν ὡς οἷόν τε μάλιστα.

Ὃς γὰρ ἂν μέχρι ἐνταῦθα πρὸς τὰ ἐρωτικὰ παιδαγωγηθῇ, θεώμενος ἐφεξῆς τε καὶ ὀρθῶς τὰ καλά, πρὸς τέλος ἤδη ἰὼν τῶν ἐρωτικῶν ἐξαίφνης κατόψεταί τι θαυμαστὸν τὴν φύσιν καλόν, τοῦτο ἐκεῖνο, ὦ Σώκρατες, οὗ δὴ ἕνεκεν καὶ οἱ ἔμπροσθεν πάντες πόνοι ἦσαν, πρῶτον μὲν ἀεὶ ὂν καὶ οὔτε γιγνόμενον οὔτε ἀπολλύμενον, οὔτε αὐξανόμενον οὔτε φθῖνον, ἔπειτα οὐ τῇ μὲν καλόν, τῇ δ' αἰσχρόν, οὐδὲ τοτὲ μέν, τοτὲ δ' οὔ, οὐδὲ πρὸς μὲν τὸ καλόν, πρὸς δὲ τὸ αἰσχρόν, οὐδ' ἔνθα μὲν καλόν, ἔνθα δὲ αἰσχρόν, ὡς τισὶ μὲν ὂν καλόν, τισὶ δὲ αἰσχρόν· οὐδ' αὖ φαντασθήσεται αὐτῷ τὸ καλὸν οἷον πρόσωπόν τι οὐδὲ χεῖρες οὐδὲ ἄλλο οὐδὲν ὧν σῶμα μετέχει, οὐδέ τις λόγος οὐδέ τις ἐπιστήμη, οὐδέ που ὂν ἐν ἑτέρῳ τινί, οἷον ἐν ζῴῳ ἢ ἐν γῇ ἢ ἐν οὐρανῷ ἢ ἔν τῳ ἄλλῳ, ἀλλὰ αὐτὸ καθ' αὑτὸ μεθ' αὑτοῦ μονοειδὲς ἀεὶ ὄν, τὰ δὲ ἄλλα πάντα καλὰ ἐκείνου μετέχοντα τρόπον τινὰ τοιοῦτον, οἷον γιγνομένων τε τῶν ἄλλων καὶ ἀπολλυμένων μηδὲν ἐκεῖνο μήτε τι πλέον μήτε ἔλαττον γίγνεσθαι μηδὲ πάσχειν μηδέν. ὅταν δή τις ἀπὸ τῶνδε διὰ τὸ ὀρθῶς παιδεραστεῖν ἐπανιὼν ἐκεῖνο τὸ καλὸν ἄρχηται καθορᾶν, σχεδὸν ἄν τι ἅπτοιτο τοῦ τέλους. τοῦτο γὰρ δή ἐστι τὸ ὀρθῶς ἐπὶ τὰ ἐρωτικὰ ἰέναι ἢ ὑπ' ἄλλου ἄγεσθαι, ἀρχόμενον ἀπὸ

SYMPOSIUM

plenteous crop of philosophy; until with the strength and increase there acquired he descries a certain single knowledge connected with a beauty which has yet to be told. And here, I pray you,' said she, ' give me the very best of your attention.

"' When a man has been thus far tutored in the lore of love, passing from view to view of beautiful things, in the right and regular ascent, suddenly he will have revealed to him, as he draws to the close of his dealings in love, a wondrous vision, beautiful in its nature; and this, Socrates, is the final object of all those previous toils. First of all, it is ever-existent and neither comes to be nor perishes, neither waxes nor wanes; next, it is not beautiful in part and in part ugly, nor is it such at such a time and other at another, nor in one respect beautiful and in another ugly, nor so affected by position as to seem beautiful to some and ugly to others. Nor again will our initiate find the beautiful presented to him in the guise of a face or of hands or any other portion of the body, nor as a particular description or piece of knowledge, nor as existing somewhere in another substance, such as an animal or the earth or sky or any other thing; but existing ever in singularity of form independent by itself, while all the multitude of beautiful things partake of it in such wise that, though all of them are coming to be and perishing, it grows neither greater nor less, and is affected by nothing. So when a man by the right method of boy-loving ascends from these particulars and begins to descry that beauty, he is almost able to lay hold of the final secret. Such is the right approach or induction to love-matters.

PLATO

τῶνδε τῶν καλῶν ἐκείνου ἕνεκα τοῦ καλοῦ ἀεὶ
ἐπανιέναι, ὥσπερ ἐπαναβαθμοῖς χρώμενον, ἀπὸ
ἑνὸς ἐπὶ δύο καὶ ἀπὸ δυοῖν ἐπὶ πάντα τὰ καλὰ
σώματα, καὶ ἀπὸ τῶν καλῶν σωμάτων ἐπὶ τὰ
καλὰ ἐπιτηδεύματα, καὶ ἀπὸ τῶν ἐπιτηδευμάτων
ἐπὶ τὰ καλὰ μαθήματα, καὶ ἀπὸ τῶν μαθημάτων
ἐπ' ἐκεῖνο τὸ μάθημα τελευτῆσαι,[1] ὅ ἐστιν οὐκ
ἄλλου ἢ αὐτοῦ ἐκείνου τοῦ καλοῦ μάθημα, ἵνα[2] γνῷ
D αὐτὸ τελευτῶν ὃ ἔστι καλόν. ἐνταῦθα τοῦ βίου,
ὦ φίλε Σώκρατες, ἔφη ἡ Μαντινικὴ ξένη, εἴπερ
που ἄλλοθι, βιωτὸν ἀνθρώπῳ, θεωμένῳ αὐτὸ τὸ
καλόν. ὃ ἐάν ποτε ἴδῃς, οὐ κατὰ χρυσίον τε καὶ
ἐσθῆτα καὶ τοὺς καλοὺς παῖδάς τε καὶ νεανίσκους
δόξει σοι εἶναι, οὓς νῦν ὁρῶν ἐκπέπληξαι καὶ ἕτοι-
μος εἶ καὶ σὺ καὶ ἄλλοι πολλοί, ὁρῶντες τὰ παιδικὰ καὶ συνόντες ἀεὶ αὐτοῖς, εἴ πως οἷόν τ' ἦν,
μήτε ἐσθίειν μήτε πίνειν, ἀλλὰ θεᾶσθαι μόνον καὶ
E συνεῖναι. τί δῆτα, ἔφη, οἰόμεθα, εἴ τῳ γένοιτο
αὐτὸ τὸ καλὸν ἰδεῖν εἰλικρινές, καθαρόν, ἄμικτον,
ἀλλὰ μὴ ἀνάπλεων σαρκῶν τε ἀνθρωπίνων καὶ
χρωμάτων καὶ ἄλλης πολλῆς φλυαρίας θνητῆς,
ἀλλ' αὐτὸ τὸ θεῖον καλὸν δύναιτο μονοειδὲς κατ-
212 ιδεῖν; ἆρ' οἴει, ἔφη, φαῦλον βίον γίγνεσθαι ἐκεῖσε
βλέποντος ἀνθρώπου καὶ ἐκεῖνο ᾧ δεῖ θεωμένου
καὶ συνόντος αὐτῷ; ἢ οὐκ ἐνθυμῇ, ἔφη, ὅτι
ἐνταῦθα αὐτῷ μοναχοῦ γενήσεται, ὁρῶντι ᾧ
ὁρατὸν τὸ καλόν, τίκτειν οὐκ εἴδωλα ἀρετῆς,
ἅτε οὐκ εἰδώλου ἐφαπτομένῳ, ἀλλ' ἀληθῆ,
ἅτε τοῦ ἀληθοῦς ἐφαπτομένῳ· τεκόντι δὲ ἀρετὴν
ἀληθῆ καὶ θρεψαμένῳ ὑπάρχει θεοφιλεῖ γενέσθαι,

---

[1] τελευτῆσαι Usener : τελευτήσῃ MSS.
[2] ἵνα Usener : καὶ MSS.

SYMPOSIUM

Beginning from obvious beauties he must for the sake of that highest beauty be ever climbing aloft, as on the rungs of a ladder, from one to two, and from two to all beautiful bodies; from personal beauty he proceeds to beautiful observances, from observance to beautiful learning, and from learning at last to that particular study which is concerned with the beautiful itself and that alone; so that in the end he comes to know the very essence of beauty. In that state of life above all others, my dear Socrates,' said the Mantinean woman, 'a man finds it truly worth while to live, as he contemplates essential beauty. This, when once beheld, will outshine your gold and your vesture, your beautiful boys and striplings, whose aspect now so astounds you and makes you and many another, at the sight and constant society of your darlings, ready to do without either food or drink if that were any way possible, and only gaze upon them and have their company. But tell me, what would happen if one of you had the fortune to look upon essential beauty entire, pure and unalloyed; not infected with the flesh and colour of humanity, and ever so much more of mortal trash? What if he could behold the divine beauty itself, in its unique form? Do you call it a pitiful life for a man to lead—looking that way, observing that vision by the proper means, and having it ever with him? Do but consider,' she said, ' that there only will it befall him, as he sees the beautiful through that which makes it visible, to breed not illusions but true examples of virtue, since his contact is not with illusion but with truth. So when he has begotten a true virtue and has reared it up he is destined to win

καὶ εἴπερ τῳ ἄλλῳ ἀνθρώπων ἀθανάτῳ καὶ ἐκείνῳ;

B Ταῦτα δὴ, ὦ Φαῖδρέ τε καὶ οἱ ἄλλοι, ἔφη μὲν Διοτίμα, πέπεισμαι δ' ἐγώ· πεπεισμένος δὲ πειρῶμαι καὶ τοὺς ἄλλους πείθειν, ὅτι τούτου τοῦ κτήματος τῇ ἀνθρωπείᾳ φύσει συνεργὸν ἀμείνω Ἔρωτος οὐκ ἄν τις ῥᾳδίως λάβοι. διὸ δὴ ἔγωγέ φημι χρῆναι πάντα ἄνδρα τὸν Ἔρωτα τιμᾶν, καὶ αὐτὸς τιμῶ τὰ ἐρωτικὰ καὶ διαφερόντως ἀσκῶ καὶ τοῖς ἄλλοις παρακελεύομαι, καὶ νῦν τε καὶ ἀεὶ ἐγκωμιάζω τὴν δύναμιν καὶ ἀνδρείαν τοῦ
C Ἔρωτος καθ' ὅσον οἷός τ' εἰμί. τοῦτον οὖν τὸν λόγον, ὦ Φαῖδρε, εἰ μὲν βούλει, ὡς ἐγκώμιον εἰς Ἔρωτα νόμισον εἰρῆσθαι, εἰ δέ, ὅ τι καὶ ὅπῃ χαίρεις ὀνομάζων, τοῦτο ὀνόμαζε.

Εἰπόντος δὲ ταῦτα τοῦ Σωκράτους τοὺς μὲν ἐπαινεῖν, τὸν δὲ Ἀριστοφάνη λέγειν τι ἐπιχειρεῖν, ὅτι ἐμνήσθη αὐτοῦ λέγων ὁ Σωκράτης περὶ τοῦ λόγου· καὶ ἐξαίφνης τὴν αὔλιον θύραν κρουομένην πολὺν ψόφον παρασχεῖν ὡς κωμαστῶν, καὶ αὐλητρίδος φωνὴν ἀκούειν. τὸν οὖν Ἀγά-
D θωνα, Παῖδες, φάναι, οὐ σκέψεσθε; καὶ ἐὰν μέν τις τῶν ἐπιτηδείων ᾖ, καλεῖτε· εἰ δὲ μή, λέγετε ὅτι οὐ πίνομεν, ἀλλὰ ἀναπαυόμεθα ἤδη.

Καὶ οὐ πολὺ ὕστερον Ἀλκιβιάδου τὴν φωνὴν ἀκούειν ἐν τῇ αὐλῇ σφόδρα μεθύοντος καὶ μέγα βοῶντος, ἐρωτῶντος ὅπου Ἀγάθων καὶ κελεύοντος ἄγειν παρ' Ἀγάθωνα. ἄγειν οὖν αὐτὸν παρὰ σφᾶς τήν τε αὐλητρίδα ὑπολαβοῦσαν καὶ ἄλλους τινὰς τῶν ἀκολούθων, καὶ ἐπιστῆναι ἐπὶ τὰς θύρας
E ἐστεφανωμένον αὐτὸν κιττῷ τέ τινι στεφάνῳ δασεῖ καὶ ἴων, καὶ ταινίας ἔχοντα ἐπὶ τῆς κεφαλῆς

SYMPOSIUM

the friendship of Heaven; he, above all men, is immortal.'

"This, Phaedrus and you others, is what Diotima told me, and I am persuaded of it; in which persuasion I pursue my neighbours, to persuade them in turn that towards this acquisition the best helper that our human nature can hope to find is Love. Wherefore I tell you now that every man should honour Love, as I myself do honour all love-matters with especial devotion, and exhort all other men to do the same; both now and always do I glorify Love's power and valour as far as I am able. So I ask you, Phaedrus, to be so good as to consider this account as a eulogy bestowed on Love, or else to call it by any name that pleases your fancy."

After Socrates had thus spoken, there was applause from all the company except Aristophanes, who was beginning to remark on the allusion which Socrates' speech had made to his own;[1] when suddenly there was a knocking at the outer door, which had a noisy sound like that of revellers, and they heard notes of a flute-girl. "Go and see to it," said Agathon to the servants; "and if it be one of our intimates, invite him in: otherwise, say we are not drinking, but just about to retire."

A few moments after, they heard the voice of Alcibiades in the forecourt, very drunken and bawling loud, to know where Agathon was, and bidding them bring him to Agathon. So he was brought into the company by the flute-girl and some others of his people supporting him: he stood at the door, crowned with a bushy wreath of ivy and violets, and wearing a great array of ribands

[1] See 205 E.

PLATO

πάνυ πολλάς, καὶ εἰπεῖν· Ἄνδρες, χαίρετε· μεθύοντα ἄνδρα πάνυ σφόδρα δέξεσθε συμπότην, ἢ ἀπίωμεν ἀναδήσαντες μόνον Ἀγάθωνα, ἐφ' ᾧπερ ἤλθομεν; ἐγὼ γάρ τοι, φάναι, χθὲς μὲν οὐχ οἷός τ' ἐγενόμην ἀφικέσθαι, νῦν δὲ ἥκω ἐπὶ τῇ κεφαλῇ ἔχων τὰς ταινίας, ἵνα ἀπὸ τῆς ἐμῆς κεφαλῆς τὴν τοῦ σοφωτάτου καὶ καλλίστου κεφαλὴν, ἐὰν εἴπω[1]—οὑτωσὶ ἀναδήσω. ἆρα καταγελάσεσθέ μου ὡς μεθύοντος; ἐγὼ δέ, κἂν ὑμεῖς γελᾶτε, ὅμως εὖ οἶδ' ὅτι ἀληθῆ λέγω. ἀλλά μοι λέγετε αὐτόθεν, ἐπὶ ῥητοῖς εἰσίω ἢ μή; συμπίεσθε ἢ οὔ;

Πάντας οὖν ἀναθορυβῆσαι καὶ κελεύειν εἰσιέναι καὶ κατακλίνεσθαι, καὶ τὸν Ἀγάθωνα καλεῖν αὐτόν. καὶ τὸν ἰέναι ἀγόμενον ὑπὸ τῶν ἀνθρώπων, καὶ περιαιρούμενον ἅμα τὰς ταινίας ὡς ἀναδήσοντα, ἐπίπροσθεν τῶν ὀφθαλμῶν ἔχοντα οὐ κατιδεῖν τὸν Σωκράτη, ἀλλὰ καθίζεσθαι παρὰ τὸν Ἀγάθωνα ἐν μέσῳ Σωκράτους τε καὶ ἐκείνου· παραχωρῆσαι γὰρ τὸν Σωκράτη ὡς ἐκεῖνον κατιδεῖν.[2] παρακαθεζόμενον δὲ αὐτὸν ἀσπάζεσθαί τε τὸν Ἀγάθωνα καὶ ἀναδεῖν.

Εἰπεῖν οὖν τὸν Ἀγάθωνα Ὑπολύετε, παῖδες, Ἀλκιβιάδην, ἵνα ἐκ τρίτων κατακέηται.

Πάνυ γε, εἰπεῖν τὸν Ἀλκιβιάδην· ἀλλὰ τίς ἡμῖν ὅδε τρίτος συμπότης; καὶ ἅμα μεταστρεφόμενοι αὐτὸν ὁρᾶν τὸν Σωκράτη, ἰδόντα δὲ ἀναπηδῆσαι καὶ εἰπεῖν Ὦ Ἡράκλεις, τουτὶ τί ἦν; Σωκράτης

---

[1] ἐὰν εἴπω MSS.: ἀνειπὼν Winckelm.: ἐὰν εἰσίω Bergk.
[2] κατιδεῖν scripsi: κατιδε(ν) Oxyrh. Pap. (cf. 174 E ὡς ἰδεῖν) καθίζειν MSS.

SYMPOSIUM

on his head. "Good evening, sirs," he said; "will you admit to your drinking a fellow very far gone in liquor, or shall we simply set a wreath on Agathon—which indeed is what we came for—and so away? I tell you, sir, I was hindered from getting to you yesterday; but now I am here with these ribands on my head, so that I can pull them off mine and twine them about the head of the cleverest, the handsomest, if I may speak the—see, like this![1] Ah, you would laugh at me because I am drunk? Well, for my part, laugh as you may, I am sure I am speaking the truth. Come, tell me straight out, am I to enter on the terms stated or not? Will you take a cup with me or no?"

At this they all boisterously acclaimed him, bidding him enter and take a seat, and Agathon also invited him. So he came along with the assistance of his people; and while unwinding the ribands for his purpose of wreathing his friend he so held them before his eyes that he failed to notice Socrates, and actually took a seat next to Agathon, between Socrates and him: for Socrates had moved up when he caught sight of Alcibiades. So there he sat, and he saluted Agathon and began to twine his head.

Then Agathon said to the servants, "Take off Alcibiades' shoes, so that he can recline here with us two."

"By all means," said Alcibiades; "but who is our third at table?" With that he turned about and saw Socrates, and the same moment leapt up and cried, "Save us, what a surprise! Socrates

[1] His drunken gesture interrupts what he means to say and resumes later,—"If I may speak the truth."

211

PLATO

οὗτος; ἐλλοχῶν αὖ με ἐνταῦθα κατέκεισο, ὥσπερ εἰώθεις ἐξαίφνης ἀναφαίνεσθαι ὅπου ἐγὼ ᾤμην ἥκιστά σε ἔσεσθαι. καὶ νῦν τί ἥκεις; καὶ τί αὖ ἐνταῦθα κατεκλίνης, καὶ[1] οὐ παρὰ Ἀριστοφάνει οὐδὲ εἴ τις ἄλλος γελοῖος ἔστι τε καὶ βούλεται, ἀλλὰ διεμηχανήσω ὅπως παρὰ τῷ καλλίστῳ τῶν ἔνδον κατακείσῃ;

Καὶ τὸν Σωκράτη, Ἀγάθων, φάναι, ὅρα εἴ μοι ἐπαμύνεις· ὡς ἐμοὶ ὁ τούτου ἔρως τοῦ ἀνθρώπου οὐ φαῦλον πρᾶγμα γέγονεν. ἀπ' ἐκείνου γὰρ τοῦ χρόνου, ἀφ' οὗ τούτου ἠράσθην, οὐκέτι ἔξεστί μοι οὔτε προσβλέψαι οὔτε διαλεχθῆναι καλῷ οὐδ' ἑνί, ἢ οὑτοσὶ ζηλοτυπῶν με καὶ φθονῶν θαυμαστὰ ἐργάζεται καὶ λοιδορεῖταί τε καὶ τὼ χεῖρε μόγις ἀπέχεται. ὅρα οὖν μή τι καὶ νῦν ἐργάσηται, ἀλλὰ διάλλαξον ἡμᾶς, ἢ ἐὰν ἐπιχειρῇ βιάζεσθαι, ἐπάμυνε, ὡς ἐγὼ τὴν τούτου μανίαν τε καὶ φιλεραστίαν πάνυ ὀρρωδῶ.

Ἀλλ' οὐκ ἔστι, φάναι τὸν Ἀλκιβιάδην, ἐμοὶ καὶ σοὶ διαλλαγή. ἀλλὰ τούτων μὲν εἰσαῦθίς σε τιμωρήσομαι· νῦν δέ μοι, Ἀγάθων, φάναι, μετάδος τῶν ταινιῶν, ἵνα ἀναδήσω καὶ τὴν τούτου ταυτηνὶ τὴν θαυμαστὴν κεφαλήν, καὶ μή μοι μέμφηται ὅτι σὲ μὲν ἀνέδησα, αὐτὸν δὲ νικῶντα ἐν λόγοις πάντας ἀνθρώπους, οὐ μόνον πρώην ὥσπερ σύ, ἀλλ' ἀεί, ἔπειτα οὐκ ἀνέδησα. καὶ ἅμ' αὐτὸν λαβόντα τῶν ταινιῶν ἀναδεῖν τὸν Σωκράτη καὶ κατακλίνεσθαι.

Ἐπειδὴ δὲ κατεκλίνη, εἰπεῖν· Εἶεν δή, ἄνδρες· δοκεῖτε γάρ μοι νήφειν· οὐκ ἐπιτρεπτέον ὑμῖν, ἀλλὰ ποτέον· ὡμολόγηται γὰρ ταῦθ' ἡμῖν. ἄρχοντα οὖν αἱροῦμαι τῆς πόσεως, ἕως ἂν ὑμεῖς

[1] καὶ Hermann: ὡς MSS.

SYMPOSIUM

here! So it was to lie in wait for me again that you were sitting there—your old trick of turning up on a sudden where least I expected you! Well, what are you after now? Tell me, I say, why you took a seat here and not by Aristophanes or some one else who is absurd and means to be? Why did you intrigue to get a seat beside the handsomest person in the room?"

Then Socrates said, "Agathon, do your best to protect me, for I have found my love for this fellow no trifling affair. From the time when I fell in love with him I have not had a moment's liberty either to look upon or converse with a single handsome person, but the fellow flies into a spiteful jealousy which makes him treat me in a monstrous fashion, girding at me and hardly keeping his hands to himself. So take care that he does no mischief now: pray reconcile us; or if he sets about using force, protect me, for I shudder with alarm at his amorous frenzy."

"No," said Alcibiades; "no reconcilement for you and me. I will have my revenge on you for this another time: for the present, Agathon, give me some of your ribands, that I may also deck this person's head, this astonishing head. He shall not reproach me with having made a garland for you and then, though he conquers every one in discourse —not once in a while, like you the other day, but always—bestowing none upon him." So saying he took some of the ribands and, after decking the head of Socrates, resumed his seat.

Reclining there, he proceeded: "Now then, gentlemen, you look sober: I cannot allow this; you must drink, and fulfil our agreement. So I appoint as president of this bout, till you have

ἱκανῶς πίητε, ἐμαυτόν. ἀλλὰ φερέτω, Ἀγάθων,[1] εἴ τι ἔστιν ἔκπωμα μέγα. μᾶλλον δὲ οὐδὲν δεῖ, ἀλλὰ φέρε, παῖ, φάναι, τὸν ψυκτῆρα ἐκεῖνον, ἰδόντα αὐτὸν πλέον ἢ ὀκτὼ κοτύλας χωροῦντα. τοῦτον ἐμπλησάμενον πρῶτον μὲν αὐτὸν ἐκπιεῖν, ἔπειτα τῷ Σωκράτει κελεύειν ἐγχεῖν καὶ ἅμα εἰπεῖν· Πρὸς μὲν Σωκράτη, ὦ ἄνδρες, τὸ σόφισμά μοι οὐδέν· ὁπόσον γὰρ ἂν κελεύῃ τις, τοσοῦτον ἐκπιὼν οὐδὲν μᾶλλον μή ποτε μεθυσθῇ.

Τὸν μὲν οὖν Σωκράτη ἐγχέαντος τοῦ παιδὸς πίνειν· τὸν δ' Ἐρυξίμαχον Πῶς οὖν, φάναι, ὦ Ἀλκιβιάδη, ποιοῦμεν; οὕτως οὔτε τι λέγομεν ἐπὶ τῇ κύλικι οὔτ' ἐπᾴδομεν, ἀλλ' ἀτεχνῶς ὥσπερ οἱ διψῶντες πιόμεθα;

Τὸν οὖν Ἀλκιβιάδην εἰπεῖν Ὦ Ἐρυξίμαχε, βέλτιστε βελτίστου πατρὸς καὶ σωφρονεστάτου, χαῖρε.

Καὶ γὰρ σύ, φάναι τὸν Ἐρυξίμαχον· ἀλλὰ τί ποιῶμεν;

Ὅ τι δἂν[2] σὺ κελεύῃς. δεῖ γάρ σοι πείθεσθαι·

ἰητρὸς γὰρ ἀνὴρ πολλῶν ἀντάξιος ἄλλων·

ἐπίταττε οὖν ὅ τι βούλει.

Ἄκουσον δή, εἰπεῖν τὸν Ἐρυξίμαχον. ἡμῖν πρὶν σὲ εἰσελθεῖν ἔδοξε χρῆναι ἐπὶ δεξιὰ ἕκαστον ἐν μέρει λόγον περὶ Ἔρωτος εἰπεῖν ὡς δύναιτο κάλλιστον, καὶ ἐγκωμιάσαι. οἱ μὲν οὖν ἄλλοι πάντες ἡμεῖς εἰρήκαμεν· σὺ δ' ἐπειδὴ οὐκ εἴρηκας καὶ ἐκπέπωκας, δίκαιος εἶ εἰπεῖν, εἰπὼν δ' ἐπιτάξαι Σωκράτει ὅ τι ἂν βούλῃ, καὶ τοῦτον τῷ ἐπὶ δεξιὰ καὶ οὕτω τοὺς ἄλλους.

[1] φερέτω, Ἀγάθων distinxit Burnet.
[2] δἂν Burnet: δ' ἂν T.

SYMPOSIUM

had a reasonable drink—myself. Agathon, let the boy bring me as large a goblet as you have. Ah well, do not trouble," he said; "boy, bring me that cooler there,"—for he saw it would hold a good half-gallon and more. This he got filled to the brim, and after quaffing it off himself bade them fill up for Socrates, saying, "Against Socrates, sirs, my crafty plan is as nought. However large the bumper you order him, he will quaff it all off and never get tipsy with it."

Socrates drank as soon as the boy had filled: but—"What procedure is this, Alcibiades?" asked Eryximachus. "Are we to have nothing to say or sing over the cup? Are we going to drink just like any thirsty folk?"

To this Alcibiades answered: "Ha, Eryximachus, 'of noblest, soberest sire most noble son'; all hail!"

"And the same to you," said Eryximachus: "but what are we to do?"

"Whatever you command, for we are bound to obey you:

> One learned leech is worth the multitude.[1]

So prescribe what you please."

"Then listen," said Eryximachus. "We resolved, before your arrival, that each in order from left to right should make the finest speech he could upon Love, and glorify his name. Now all of us here have spoken; so you, since you have made no speech and have drained the cup, must do your duty and speak. This done, you shall prescribe what you like for Socrates, and he for his neighbour on the right, and so on with the rest."

[1] Homer, *Il.* xi. 514.

Ἀλλά, φάναι, ὦ Ἐρυξίμαχε, τὸν Ἀλκιβιάδην καλῶς μὲν λέγεις, μεθύοντα δὲ ἄνδρα παρὰ νηφόντων λόγους παραβάλλειν μὴ οὐκ ἐξ ἴσου ᾖ. καὶ ἅμα, ὦ μακάριε, πείθει τί σε Σωκράτης ὧν ἄρτι εἶπεν; ἢ οἶσθα ὅτι τοὐναντίον ἐστὶ πᾶν ἢ ὃ ἔλεγεν; οὗτος γάρ, ἐάν τινα ἐγὼ ἐπαινέσω τούτου παρόντος ἢ θεὸν ἢ ἄνθρωπον ἄλλον ἢ τοῦτον, οὐκ ἀφέξεταί μου τὼ χεῖρε.

Οὐκ εὐφημήσεις; φάναι τὸν Σωκράτη.

Μὰ τὸν Ποσειδῶ, εἰπεῖν τὸν Ἀλκιβιάδην, μηδὲν λέγε πρὸς ταῦτα, ὡς ἐγὼ οὐδ' ἂν ἕνα ἄλλον ἐπαινέσαιμι σοῦ παρόντος.

Ἀλλ' οὕτω ποίει, φάναι τὸν Ἐρυξίμαχον, εἰ βούλει· Σωκράτη ἐπαίνεσον.

Πῶς λέγεις; εἰπεῖν τὸν Ἀλκιβιάδην· δοκεῖ χρῆναι, ὦ Ἐρυξίμαχε; ἐπιθῶμαι τῷ ἀνδρὶ καὶ τιμωρήσωμαι ὑμῶν ἐναντίον;

Οὗτος, φάναι τὸν Σωκράτη, τί ἐν νῷ ἔχεις; ἐπὶ τὰ γελοιότερά με ἐπαινέσαι,[1] ἢ τί ποιήσεις;

Τἀληθῆ ἐρῶ. ἀλλ' ὅρα εἰ παρίης.

Ἀλλὰ μέντοι, φάναι, τά γε ἀληθῆ παρίημι καὶ κελεύω λέγειν.

Οὐκ ἂν φθάνοιμι, εἰπεῖν τὸν Ἀλκιβιάδην. καὶ μέντοι οὑτωσὶ ποίησον. ἐάν τι μὴ ἀληθὲς λέγω, μεταξὺ ἐπιλαβοῦ, ἂν βούλῃ, καὶ εἰπὲ ὅτι τοῦτο ψεύδομαι· ἑκὼν γὰρ εἶναι οὐδὲν ψεύσομαι. ἐὰν μέντοι ἀναμιμνησκόμενος ἄλλο ἄλλοθεν λέγω, μηδὲν θαυμάσῃς· οὐ γάρ τι ῥᾴδιον τὴν σὴν ἀτοπίαν ὧδ' ἔχοντι εὐπόρως καὶ ἐφεξῆς καταριθμῆσαι.

[1] ἐπαινέσαι Burnet: ἐπαινέσεις MSS.

SYMPOSIUM

"Very good, Eryximachus," said Alcibiades; "but to pit a drunken man against sober tongues is hardly fair. Besides, my gifted friend, you are surely not convinced by anything that Socrates has just told you? You must know the case is quite the contrary of what he was saying. It is he who, if I praise any god in his presence or any person other than himself, will not keep his hands off me."

"Come, enough of this," said Socrates.

"On the honour of a gentleman," said Alcibiades, "it is no use your protesting, for I could not praise anyone else in your presence."

"Well, do that if you like," said Eryximachus; "praise Socrates."

"You mean it?" said Alcibiades; "you think I had better, Eryximachus? Am I to set upon the fellow and have my revenge before you all?"

"Here," said Socrates; "what are you about,—to make fun of me with your praises, or what?"

"I shall speak the truth; now, will you permit me?"

"Ah well, so long as it is the truth, I permit you and command you to speak."

"You shall hear it this moment," said Alcibiades; "but there is something you must do. If I say anything that is false, have the goodness to take me up short and say that there I am lying; for I will not lie if I can help it. Still, you are not to be surprised if I tell my reminiscences at haphazard; it is anything but easy for a man in my condition to give a fluent and regular enumeration of your oddities."

PLATO

Σωκράτη δ' ἐγὼ ἐπαινεῖν, ὦ ἄνδρες, οὕτως ἐπιχειρήσω, δι' εἰκόνων. οὗτος μὲν οὖν ἴσως οἰήσεται ἐπὶ τὰ γελοιότερα, ἔσται δ' ἡ εἰκὼν τοῦ ἀληθοῦς ἕνεκα, οὐ τοῦ γελοίου. φημὶ γὰρ δὴ ὁμοιότατον αὐτὸν εἶναι τοῖς σιληνοῖς τούτοις τοῖς ἐν τοῖς ἑρμογλυφείοις καθημένοις, οὕς τινας ἐργάζονται οἱ δημιουργοὶ σύριγγας ἢ αὐλοὺς ἔχοντας, οἳ διχάδε διοιχθέντες φαίνονται ἔνδοθεν ἀγάλματα ἔχοντες θεῶν. καὶ φημὶ αὖ ἐοικέναι αὐτὸν τῷ σατύρῳ τῷ Μαρσύᾳ. ὅτι μὲν οὖν τό γε εἶδος ὅμοιος εἶ τούτοις, ὦ Σώκρατες, οὐδ' αὐτὸς ἄν[1] που ἀμφισβητήσαις· ὡς δὲ καὶ τἆλλα ἔοικας, μετὰ τοῦτο ἄκουε. ὑβριστὴς εἶ ἢ οὔ; ἐὰν γὰρ μὴ ὁμολογῇς, μάρτυρας παρέξομαι. ἀλλ' οὐκ αὐλητής; πολύ γε θαυμασιώτερος ἐκείνου. ὁ μέν γε δι' ὀργάνων ἐκήλει τοὺς ἀνθρώπους τῇ ἀπὸ τοῦ στόματος δυνάμει, καὶ ἔτι νυνὶ ὃς ἂν τὰ ἐκείνου αὐλῇ. ἃ γὰρ Ὄλυμπος ηὔλει, Μαρσύου λέγω τοῦ[2] διδάξαντος. τὰ οὖν ἐκείνου ἐάν τε ἀγαθὸς αὐλητὴς αὐλῇ ἐάν τε φαύλη αὐλητρίς, μόνα κατέχεσθαι ποιεῖ καὶ δηλοῖ τοὺς τῶν θεῶν τε καὶ τελετῶν δεομένους διὰ τὸ θεῖα εἶναι. σὺ δ' ἐκείνου τοσοῦτον μόνον διαφέρεις, ὅτι ἄνευ ὀργάνων ψιλοῖς λόγοις ταὐτὸν τοῦτο ποιεῖς. ἡμεῖς γοῦν ὅταν μέν του ἄλλου ἀκούωμεν λέγοντος καὶ πάνυ ἀγαθοῦ ῥήτορος ἄλλους λόγους, οὐδὲν μέλει ὡς ἔπος εἰπεῖν οὐδενί· ἐπειδὰν δὲ σοῦ τις ἀκούῃ ἢ τῶν σῶν λόγων

[1] ἄν Baiter: δή MSS.
[2] τοῦ Badham: τούτου MSS.

SYMPOSIUM

Alcibiades' praise of Socrates

"The way I shall take, gentlemen, in my praise of Socrates, is by similitudes. Probably he will think I do this for derision; but I choose my similitude for the sake of truth, not of ridicule. For I say he is likest to the Silenus-figures that sit in the statuaries' shops; those, I mean, which our craftsmen make with pipes or flutes in their hands: when their two halves are pulled open, they are found to contain images of gods. And I further suggest that he resembles the satyr Marsyas. Now, as to your likeness, Socrates, to these in figure, I do not suppose even you yourself will dispute it; but I have next to tell you that you are like them in every other respect. You are a fleering fellow, eh? If you will not confess it, I have witnesses at hand. Are you not a piper? Why, yes, and a far more marvellous one than the satyr. His lips indeed had power to entrance mankind by means of instruments; a thing still possible to-day for anyone who can pipe his tunes: for the music of Olympus's flute belonged, I may tell you, to Marysas his teacher. So that if anyone, whether a fine flute-player or paltry flute-girl, can but flute his tunes, they have no equal for exciting a ravishment, and will indicate by the divinity that is in them who are apt recipients of the deities and their sanctifications. You differ from him in one point only—that you produce the same effect with simple prose unaided by instruments. For example, when we hear any other person—quite an excellent orator, perhaps—pronouncing one of the usual discourses, no one, I venture to say, cares a jot; but so soon as we hear you, or your discourses in the mouth of another,—

PLATO

ἄλλου λέγοντος, κἂν πάνυ φαῦλος ᾖ ὁ λέγων, ἐάν τε γυνὴ ἀκούῃ ἐάν τε ἀνὴρ ἐάν τε μειράκιον, ἐκπεπληγμένοι ἐσμὲν καὶ κατεχόμεθα. ἐγὼ γοῦν, ὦ ἄνδρες, εἰ μὴ ἔμελλον κομιδῇ δόξειν μεθύειν, εἶπον ὀμόσας ἂν ὑμῖν, οἷα δὴ πέπονθα αὐτὸς ὑπὸ τῶν τούτου λόγων καὶ πάσχω ἔτι καὶ νυνί. ὅταν E γὰρ ἀκούω, πολύ μοι μᾶλλον ἢ τῶν κορυβαντιώντων ἥ τε καρδία πηδᾷ καὶ δάκρυα ἐκχεῖται ὑπὸ τῶν λόγων τῶν τούτου· ὁρῶ δὲ καὶ ἄλλους παμπόλλους τὰ αὐτὰ πάσχοντας. Περικλέους δὲ ἀκούων καὶ ἄλλων ἀγαθῶν ῥητόρων εὖ μὲν ἡγούμην λέγειν, τοιοῦτον δ' οὐδὲν ἔπασχον, οὐδ' ἐτεθορύβητό μου ἡ ψυχὴ οὐδ' ἠγανάκτει ὡς ἀνδραποδωδῶς διακειμένου· ἀλλ' ὑπὸ τουτουῒ τοῦ Μαρσύου πολλάκις 216 δὴ οὕτω διετέθην, ὥστε μοι δόξαι μὴ βιωτὸν εἶναι ἔχοντι ὡς ἔχω. καὶ ταῦτα, Σώκρατες, οὐκ ἐρεῖς ὡς οὐκ ἀληθῆ. καὶ ἔτι γε νῦν σύνοιδ' ἐμαυτῷ, ὅτι εἰ ἐθέλοιμι παρέχειν τὰ ὦτα, οὐκ ἂν καρτερήσαιμι, ἀλλὰ ταὐτὰ ἂν πάσχοιμι. ἀναγκάζει γάρ με ὁμολογεῖν, ὅτι πολλοῦ ἐνδεὴς ὢν αὐτὸς ἔτι ἐμαυτοῦ μὲν ἀμελῶ, τὰ δ' Ἀθηναίων πράττω. βίᾳ οὖν ὥσπερ ἀπὸ τῶν Σειρήνων ἐπισχόμενος τὰ ὦτα οἴχομαι φεύγων, ἵνα μὴ αὐτοῦ καθήμενος παρὰ B τούτῳ καταγηράσω. πέπονθα δὲ πρὸς τοῦτον μόνον ἀνθρώπων, ὃ οὐκ ἄν τις οἴοιτο ἐν ἐμοὶ ἐνεῖναι, τὸ αἰσχύνεσθαι ὁντινοῦν· ἐγὼ δὲ τοῦτον μόνον αἰσχύνομαι. σύνοιδα γὰρ ἐμαυτῷ ἀντιλέγειν μὲν οὐ δυναμένῳ, ὡς οὐ δεῖ ποιεῖν ἃ οὗτος κελεύει, ἐπειδὰν δὲ ἀπέλθω, ἡττημένῳ τῆς τιμῆς

220

SYMPOSIUM

though such person be ever so poor a speaker, and whether the hearer be a woman or a man or a youngster—we are all astounded and entranced. As for myself, gentlemen, were it not that I might appear to be absolutely tipsy, I would have affirmed on oath all the strange effects I personally have felt from his words, and still feel even now. For when I hear him I am worse than any wild fanatic; I find my heart leaping and my tears gushing forth at the sound of his speech, and I see great numbers of other people having the same experience. When I listened to Pericles and other skilled orators I thought them eloquent, but I never felt anything like this; my spirit was not left in a tumult and had not to complain of my being in the condition of a common slave: whereas the influence of our Marsyas here has often thrown me into such a state that I thought my life not worth living on these terms. In all this, Socrates, there is nothing that you can call untrue. Even now I am still conscious that if I consented to lend him my ear, I could not resist him, but would have the same feeling again. For he compels me to admit that, sorely deficient as I am, I neglect myself while I attend to the affairs of Athens. So I withhold my ears perforce as from the Sirens, and make off as fast as I can, for fear I should go on sitting beside him till old age was upon me. And there is one experience I have in presence of this man alone, such as nobody would expect in me,—to be made to feel ashamed by anyone; he alone can make me feel it. For he brings home to me that I cannot disown the duty of doing what he bids me, but that as soon as I turn from his company I fall a victim to the favours

PLATO

τῆς ὑπὸ τῶν πολλῶν. δραπετεύω οὖν αὐτὸν καὶ
C φεύγω, καὶ ὅταν ἴδω, αἰσχύνομαι τὰ ὡμολογημένα. καὶ πολλάκις μὲν ἡδέως ἂν ἴδοιμι αὐτὸν
μὴ ὄντα ἐν ἀνθρώποις· εἰ δ' αὖ τοῦτο γένοιτο, εὖ
οἶδα ὅτι πολὺ μεῖζον ἂν ἀχθοίμην, ὥστε οὐκ ἔχω
ὅ τι χρήσωμαι τούτῳ τῷ ἀνθρώπῳ.

Καὶ ὑπὸ μὲν δὴ τῶν αὐλημάτων καὶ ἐγὼ καὶ
ἄλλοι πολλοὶ τοιαῦτα πεπόνθασιν ὑπὸ τοῦδε τοῦ
σατύρου· ἄλλα δὲ ἐμοῦ ἀκούσατε ὡς ὅμοιός τ'
ἐστὶν οἷς ἐγὼ ᾔκασα αὐτὸν καὶ τὴν δύναμιν
ὡς θαυμασίαν ἔχει. εὖ γὰρ ἴστε ὅτι οὐδεὶς
D ὑμῶν τοῦτον γιγνώσκει· ἀλλὰ ἐγὼ δηλώσω,
ἐπείπερ ἠρξάμην. ὁρᾶτε γὰρ ὅτι Σωκράτης ἐρωτικῶς διάκειται τῶν καλῶν καὶ ἀεὶ περὶ τούτους
ἐστὶ καὶ ἐκπέπληκται, καὶ αὖ ἀγνοεῖ πάντα καὶ
οὐδὲν οἶδεν, ὡς τὸ σχῆμα αὐτοῦ. τοῦτο οὐ σιληνῶδες; σφόδρα γε. τοῦτο γὰρ οὗτος ἔξωθεν
περιβέβληται, ὥσπερ ὁ γεγλυμμένος σιληνός· ἔνδοθεν δὲ ἀνοιχθεὶς πόσης οἴεσθε γέμει, ὦ ἄνδρες
συμπόται, σωφροσύνης; ἴστε ὅτι οὔτ' εἴ τις καλός
ἐστι μέλει αὐτῷ οὐδέν, ἀλλὰ καταφρονεῖ τοσοῦτον
E ὅσον οὐδ' ἂν εἷς οἰηθείη, οὔτ' εἴ τις πλούσιος, οὔτ'
εἰ ἄλλην τινὰ τιμὴν ἔχων τῶν ὑπὸ πλήθους μακαριζομένων· ἡγεῖται δὲ πάντα ταῦτα τὰ κτήματα
οὐδενὸς ἄξια καὶ ἡμᾶς οὐδὲν εἶναι,—λέγω ὑμῖν,—
εἰρωνευόμενος δὲ καὶ παίζων πάντα τὸν βίον πρὸς
τοὺς ἀνθρώπους διατελεῖ. σπουδάσαντος δὲ αὐτοῦ
καὶ ἀνοιχθέντος οὐκ οἶδα εἴ τις ἑώρακε τὰ ἐντὸς
ἀγάλματα· ἀλλ' ἐγὼ ἤδη ποτ' εἶδον, καί μοι ἔδοξεν
217 οὕτω θεῖα καὶ χρυσᾶ εἶναι καὶ πάγκαλα καὶ
θαυμαστά, ὥστε ποιητέον εἶναι ἔμβραχυ[1] ὅ τι

[1] ἔμβραχυ Cobet, al.: ἐν βραχεῖ mss.

SYMPOSIUM

of the crowd. So I take a runaway's leave of him and flee away; when I see him again I think of those former admissions, and am ashamed. Often I could wish he had vanished from this world; yet again, should this befall, I am sure I should be more distressed than ever; so I cannot tell what to do with the fellow at all.

"Such then is the effect that our satyr can work upon me and many another with his piping; but let me tell you how like he is in other respects to the figures of my comparison, and what a wondrous power he wields. I assure you, not one of you knows him; well, I shall reveal him, now that I have begun. Observe how Socrates is amorously inclined to handsome persons; with these he is always busy and enraptured. Again, he is utterly stupid and ignorant, as he affects. Is not this like a Silenus? Exactly. It is an outward casing he wears, similarly to the sculptured Silenus. But if you opened his inside, you cannot imagine how full he is, good cup-companions, of sobriety. I tell you, all the beauty a man may have is nothing to him; he despises it more than any of you can believe; nor does wealth attract him, nor any sort of honour that is the envied prize of the crowd. All these possessions he counts as nothing worth, and all of us as nothing, I assure you; he spends his whole life in chaffing and making game of his fellow-men. Whether anyone else has caught him in a serious moment and opened him, and seen the images inside, I know not; but I saw them one day, and thought them so divine and golden, so perfectly fair and wondrous, that I

PLATO

κελεύοι Σωκράτης. ἡγούμενος δὲ αὐτὸν ἐσπουδακέναι ἐπὶ τῇ ἐμῇ ὥρᾳ ἕρμαιον ἡγησάμην εἶναι καὶ εὐτύχημα ἐμὸν θαυμαστόν, ὡς ὑπάρχον μοι χαρισαμένῳ Σωκράτει πάντ' ἀκοῦσαι ὅσαπερ οὗτος ᾔδει· ἐφρόνουν γὰρ δὴ ἐπὶ τῇ ὥρᾳ θαυμάσιον ὅσον. ταῦτα οὖν διανοηθείς, πρὸ τοῦ οὐκ εἰωθὼς ἄνευ ἀκολούθου μόνος μετ' αὐτοῦ γίγνεσθαι, τότε ἀποπέμπων τὸν ἀκόλουθον μόνος συνεγιγνόμην· δεῖ γὰρ πρὸς ὑμᾶς πάντα τἀληθῆ εἰπεῖν· ἀλλὰ προσέχετε τὸν νοῦν, καὶ εἰ ψεύδομαι, Σώκρατες, ἐξέλεγχε. συνεγιγνόμην γάρ, ὦ ἄνδρες, μόνος μόνῳ, καὶ ᾤμην αὐτίκα διαλέξεσθαι αὐτόν μοι ἅπερ ἂν ἐραστὴς παιδικοῖς ἐν ἐρημίᾳ διαλεχθείη, καὶ ἔχαιρον. τούτων δ' οὐ μάλα ἐγίγνετο οὐδέν, ἀλλ' ὥσπερ εἰώθει διαλεχθεὶς ἄν μοι καὶ συνημερεύσας ᾤχετο ἀπιών. μετὰ ταῦτα συγγυμνάζεσθαι προὐκαλούμην αὐτὸν καὶ συνεγυμναζόμην, ὥς τι ἐνταῦθα περανῶν. συνεγυμνάζετο οὖν μοι καὶ προσεπάλαιε πολλάκις οὐδενὸς παρόντος· καὶ τί δεῖ λέγειν; οὐδὲν γάρ μοι πλέον ἦν. ἐπειδὴ δὲ οὐδαμῇ ταύτῃ ἤνυτον, ἔδοξέ μοι ἐπιθετέον εἶναι τῷ ἀνδρὶ κατὰ τὸ καρτερὸν καὶ οὐκ ἀνετέον, ἐπειδήπερ ἐγκεχειρήκη, ἀλλὰ ἰστέον ἤδη τί ἐστι τὸ πρᾶγμα. προκαλοῦμαι δὴ αὐτὸν πρὸς τὸ συνδειπνεῖν, ἀτεχνῶς ὥσπερ ἐραστὴς παιδικοῖς ἐπιβουλεύων. καί μοι οὐδὲ τοῦτο ταχὺ ὑπήκουσεν, ὅμως δ' οὖν χρόνῳ ἐπείσθη. ἐπειδὴ δὲ ἀφίκετο τὸ πρῶτον, δειπνήσας ἀπιέναι ἐβούλετο. καὶ τότε μὲν αἰσχυνόμενος ἀφῆκα αὐτόν· αὖθις δὲ ἐπιβουλεύσας, ἐπειδὴ ἐδεδειπνήκεμεν,[1] διελεγόμην πόρρω τῶν νυκτῶν,

---

[1] ἐδεδειπνήκεμεν Burnet: ἐδεδειπνήκει MSS.

SYMPOSIUM

simply had to do as Socrates bade me. And believing he had a serious affection for my youthful bloom, I supposed I had here a godsend and a rare stroke of luck, thinking myself free at any time by gratifying his desires to hear all that our Socrates knew; for I was enormously proud of my youthful charms. So with this design I dismissed the attendant whom till then I invariably brought to my meetings with Socrates, and I would go and meet him alone: I am to tell you the whole truth; you must all mark my words, and, Socrates, you shall refute me if I lie. Yes, gentlemen, I went and met him, and the two of us would be alone; and I thought he would seize the chance of talking to me as a lover does to his dear one in private, and I was glad. But nothing of the sort occurred at all: he would merely converse with me in his usual manner, and when he had spent the day with me he would leave me and go his way. After that I proposed he should go with me to the trainer's, and I trained with him, expecting to gain my point there. So he trained and wrestled with me many a time when no one was there. The same story! I got no further with the affair. Then, as I made no progress that way, I resolved to charge full tilt at the man, and not to throw up the contest once I had entered upon it: I felt I must clear up the situation. Accordingly I invited him to dine with me, for all the world like a lover scheming to ensnare his favourite. Even this he was backward to accept; however, he was eventually persuaded. The first time he came, he wanted to leave as soon as he had dined. On that occasion I was ashamed and let him go. The second time I devised a scheme: when we had dined I went on talking with him far

PLATO

καὶ ἐπειδὴ ἐβούλετο ἀπιέναι, σκηπτόμενος ὅτι ὀψὲ εἴη, προσηνάγκασα αὐτὸν μένειν. ἀνεπαύετο οὖν ἐν τῇ ἐχομένῃ ἐμοῦ κλίνῃ, ἐν ᾗπερ ἐδείπνει, καὶ οὐδεὶς ἐν τῷ οἰκήματι ἄλλος καθηῦδεν ἢ ἡμεῖς.

Μέχρι μὲν οὖν δὴ δεῦρο τοῦ λόγου καλῶς ἂν ἔχοι καὶ πρὸς ὁντινοῦν λέγειν· τὸ δ' ἐντεῦθεν οὐκ ἂν μου ἠκούσατε λέγοντος, εἰ μὴ πρῶτον μέν, τὸ λεγόμενον, οἶνος ἄνευ τε παίδων καὶ μετὰ παίδων ἦν ἀληθής, ἔπειτα ἀφανίσαι Σωκράτους ἔργον ὑπερήφανον εἰς ἔπαινον ἐλθόντα ἄδικόν μοι φαίνεται. ἔτι δὲ τὸ τοῦ δηχθέντος ὑπὸ τοῦ ἔχεως πάθος κἀμὲ ἔχει. φασὶ γάρ πού τινα τοῦτο παθόντα οὐκ ἐθέλειν λέγειν οἷον ἦν πλὴν τοῖς δεδηγμένοις, ὡς μόνοις γνωσομένοις τε καὶ συγγνωσομένοις, εἰ πᾶν ἐτόλμα δρᾶν τε καὶ λέγειν ὑπὸ τῆς ὀδύνης. ἐγὼ οὖν δεδηγμένος τε ὑπὸ ἀλγεινοτέρου καὶ τὸ ἀλγεινότατον ὧν ἄν τις δηχθείη—τὴν καρδίαν γὰρ ἢ ψυχὴν ἢ ὅ τι δεῖ αὐτὸ ὀνομάσαι πληγείς τε καὶ δηχθεὶς ὑπὸ τῶν ἐν φιλοσοφίᾳ λόγων, οἳ ἔχονται ἐχίδνης ἀγριώτερον, νέου ψυχῆς μὴ ἀφυοῦς ὅταν λάβωνται, καὶ ποιοῦσι δρᾶν τε καὶ λέγειν ὁτιοῦν —καὶ ὁρῶν αὖ Φαίδρους, Ἀγάθωνας, Ἐρυξιμάχους, Παυσανίας, Ἀριστοδήμους τε καὶ Ἀριστοφάνας· Σωκράτη δὲ αὐτὸν τί δεῖ λέγειν, καὶ ὅσοι ἄλλοι; πάντες γὰρ κεκοινωνήκατε τῆς φιλοσόφου μανίας τε καὶ βακχείας· διὸ πάντες ἀκούσεσθε· συγγνώσεσθε γὰρ τοῖς τε τότε πραχθεῖσι καὶ τοῖς

---

[1] The usual proverb of the truthfulness of wine (οἶνος καὶ ἀλήθεια) was sometimes extended to οἶνος καὶ παῖδες ἀληθεῖς—"Truthful are wine and children."

SYMPOSIUM

into the night, and when he wanted to go I made a pretext of the lateness of the hour and constrained him to stay. So he sought repose on the couch next to me, on which he had been sitting at dinner, and no one was sleeping in the room but ourselves.

"Now up to this point my tale could fairly be told to anybody; but from here onwards I would not have continued in your hearing were it not, in the first place, that wine, as the saying goes, whether you couple 'children' with it or no, is 'truthful';[1] and in the second, I consider it dishonest, when I have started on the praise of Socrates, to hide his deed of lofty disdain. Besides, I share the plight of the man who was bitten by the snake: you know it is related of one in such a plight that he refused to describe his sensations to any but persons who had been bitten themselves, since they alone would understand him and stand up for him if he should give way to wild words and actions in his agony. Now I have been bitten by a more painful creature, in the most painful way that one can be bitten: in my heart, or my soul, or whatever one is to call it, I am stricken and stung by his philosophic discourses, which adhere more fiercely than any adder when once they lay hold of a young and not ungifted soul, and force it to do or say whatever they will; I have only to look around me, and there is a Phaedrus, an Agathon, an Eryximachus, a Pausanias, an Aristodemus, and an Aristophanes—I need not mention Socrates himself —and all the rest of them; every one of you has had his share of philosophic frenzy and transport, so all of you shall hear. You shall stand up alike for what then was done and for what now is spoken.

227

PLATO

νῦν λεγομένοις· οἱ δὲ οἰκέται, καὶ εἴ τις ἄλλος ἐστὶ
βέβηλός τε καὶ ἄγροικος, πύλας πάνυ μεγάλας τοῖς
ὠσὶν ἐπίθεσθε.

Ἐπειδὴ γὰρ οὖν, ὦ ἄνδρες, ὅ τε λύχνος
C ἀπεσβήκει καὶ οἱ παῖδες ἔξω ἦσαν, ἔδοξέ μοι
χρῆναι μηδὲν ποικίλλειν πρὸς αὐτόν, ἀλλ' ἐλευ-
θέρως εἰπεῖν ἅ μοι ἐδόκει· καὶ εἶπον κινήσας αὐτόν,
Σώκρατες, καθεύδεις;

Οὐ δῆτα, ἦ δ' ὅς.

Οἶσθα οὖν ἅ μοι δέδοκται;

Τί μάλιστα, ἔφη.

Σὺ ἐμοὶ δοκεῖς, ἦν δ' ἐγώ, ἐμοῦ ἐραστὴς ἄξιος
γεγονέναι μόνος, καί μοι φαίνῃ ὀκνεῖν μνησθῆναι
πρός με· ἐγὼ δὲ οὑτωσὶ ἔχω· πάνυ ἀνόητον ἡγοῦμαι
εἶναι σοὶ μὴ οὐ καὶ τοῦτο χαρίζεσθαι καὶ εἴ τι
D ἄλλο ἢ τῆς οὐσίας τῆς ἐμῆς δέοιο ἢ τῶν φίλων
τῶν ἐμῶν. ἐμοὶ μὲν γὰρ οὐδέν ἐστι πρεσβύτερον
τοῦ ὡς ὅτι βέλτιστον ἐμὲ γενέσθαι, τούτου δὲ
οἶμαί μοι συλλήπτορα οὐδένα κυριώτερον εἶναι σοῦ.
ἐγὼ δὴ τοιούτῳ ἀνδρὶ πολὺ μᾶλλον ἂν μὴ χαριζόμενος αἰσχυνοίμην τοὺς φρονίμους, ἢ χαριζόμενος
τούς τε πολλοὺς καὶ ἄφρονας.

Καὶ οὗτος ἀκούσας μάλα εἰρωνικῶς καὶ σφόδρα
ἑαυτοῦ τε καὶ εἰωθότως ἔλεξεν Ὦ φίλε Ἀλκιβιάδη,
κινδυνεύεις τῷ ὄντι οὐ φαῦλος εἶναι, εἴπερ ἀληθῆ
E τυγχάνει ὄντα ἃ λέγεις περὶ ἐμοῦ, καί τις ἔστ' ἐν
ἐμοὶ δύναμις, δι' ἧς ἂν σὺ γένοιο ἀμείνων· ἀμή-
χανόν τοι κάλλος ὁρῴης ἂν ἐν ἐμοὶ καὶ τῆς παρὰ
σοὶ εὐμορφίας πάμπολυ διαφέρον. εἰ δὴ καθορῶν
αὐτὸ κοινώσασθαί τέ μοι ἐπιχειρεῖς καὶ ἀλλάξασθαι
κάλλος ἀντὶ κάλλους, οὐκ ὀλίγῳ μου πλεονεκτεῖν
διανοῇ, ἀλλ' ἀντὶ δόξης ἀλήθειαν καλῶν κτᾶσθαι

SYMPOSIUM

But the domestics, and all else profane and clownish, must clap the heaviest of doors upon their ears.

"Well, gentlemen, when the lamp had been put out and the servants had withdrawn, I determined not to mince matters with him, but to speak out freely what I intended. So I shook him and said, 'Socrates, are you asleep?'

"'Why, no,' he replied.

"'Let me tell you what I have decided.'

"'What is the matter?' he asked.

"'I consider,' I replied, 'that you are the only worthy lover I have had, and it looks to me as if you were shy of mentioning it to me. My position is this: I count it sheer folly not to gratify you in this as in any other need you may have of either my property or that of my friends. To me nothing is more important than the attainment of the highest possible excellence, and in this aim I believe I can find no abler ally than you. So I should feel a far worse shame before sensible people for not gratifying such a friend than I should before the senseless multitude for gratifying him.'

"When he heard this, he put on that innocent air which habit has made so characteristic of him, and remarked: 'My dear Alcibiades, I daresay you are not really a dolt, if what you say of me is the actual truth, and there is a certain power in me that could help you to be better; for then what a stupendous beauty you must see in me, vastly superior to your comeliness! And if on espying this you are trying for a mutual exchange of beauty for beauty, it is no slight advantage you are counting on—you are trying to get genuine in return for reputed beauties, and in fact are designing to fetch

PLATO

219 ἐπιχειρεῖς καὶ τῷ ὄντι " χρύσεα χαλκείων " διαμείβεσθαι νοεῖς. ἀλλ', ὦ μακάριε, ἄμεινον σκόπει, μή σε λανθάνω οὐδὲν ὤν. ἤ τοι τῆς διανοίας ὄψις ἄρχεται ὀξὺ βλέπειν ὅταν ἡ τῶν ὀμμάτων τῆς ἀκμῆς λήγειν ἐπιχειρῇ· σὺ δὲ τούτων ἔτι πόρρω.

Κἀγὼ ἀκούσας, Τὰ μὲν παρ' ἐμοῦ, ἔφην, ταῦτ' ἐστίν, ὧν οὐδὲν ἄλλως εἴρηται ἢ ὡς διανοοῦμαι· σὺ δὲ αὐτὸς οὕτω βουλεύου ὅ τι σοί τε ἄριστον καὶ ἐμοὶ ἡγῇ.

Ἀλλ', ἔφη, τοῦτό γε εὖ λέγεις· ἐν γὰρ τῷ ἐπιόντι
B χρόνῳ βουλευόμενοι πράξομεν ὃ ἂν φαίνηται νῶν περί τε τούτων καὶ περὶ τῶν ἄλλων ἄριστον.

Ἐγὼ μὲν δὴ ταῦτα ἀκούσας τε καὶ εἰπών, καὶ ἀφεὶς ὥσπερ βέλη, τετρῶσθαι αὐτὸν ᾤμην· καὶ ἀναστάς γε, οὐδὲ ἐπιτρέψας τούτῳ εἰπεῖν οὐδὲν ἔτι, ἀμφιέσας τὸ ἱμάτιον τὸ ἐμαυτοῦ τοῦτον—καὶ γὰρ ἦν χειμών—ὑπὸ τὸν τρίβωνα κατακλινεὶς τὸν
C τούτου, περιβαλὼν τὼ χεῖρε τούτῳ τῷ δαιμονίῳ ὡς ἀληθῶς καὶ θαυμαστῷ, κατεκείμην τὴν νύκτα ὅλην. καὶ οὐδὲ ταῦτα αὖ, ὦ Σώκρατες, ἐρεῖς ὅτι ψεύδομαι. ποιήσαντος δὲ δὴ ταῦτα ἐμοῦ οὗτος τοσοῦτον περιεγένετό τε καὶ κατεφρόνησε καὶ κατεγέλασε τῆς ἐμῆς ὥρας καὶ ὕβρισε καὶ περὶ ἐκεῖνο ὅ[1] γε ᾤμην τὶ εἶναι, ὦ ἄνδρες δικασταί· δικασταὶ γάρ ἐστε τῆς Σωκράτους ὑπερηφανίας. εὖ γὰρ ἴστε μὰ θεούς, μὰ θεάς, οὐδὲν περιττότερον κατα-
D δεδαρθηκὼς ἀνέστην μετὰ Σωκράτους, ἢ εἰ μετὰ πατρὸς καθηῦδον ἢ ἀδελφοῦ πρεσβυτέρου.

Τὸ δὴ μετὰ τοῦτο τίνα οἴεσθέ με διάνοιαν

[1] καὶ περὶ ἐκεῖνο ⟨ὅ⟩ γε Bury : περὶ ἐκεῖνο γε Oxyrh. Pap. : καίπερ ἐκεῖνό γε TW : καίπερ κεῖνο γε B.

SYMPOSIUM

off the old bargain of *gold for bronze*.[1] But be more wary, my gifted friend: you may be deceived and I may be worthless. Remember, the intellectual sight begins to be keen when the visual is entering on its wane; but you are a long way yet from that time.'

"To this I answered: 'You have heard what I had to say; not a word differed from the feeling in my mind: it is for you now to consider what you judge to be best for you and me.'

"Ah, there you speak to some purpose,' he said: 'for in the days that are to come we shall consider and do what appears to be best for the two of us in this and our other affairs.'

"Well, after I had exchanged these words with him and, as it were, let fly my shafts, I fancied he felt the wound: so up I got, and without suffering the man to say a word more I wrapped my own coat about him—it was winter-time; drew myself under his cloak, so; wound my arms about this truly spiritual and miraculous creature; and lay thus all the night long. Here too, Socrates, you are unable to give me the lie. When I had done all this, he showed such superiority and contempt, laughing my youthful charms to scorn, and flouting the very thing on which I prided myself, gentlemen of the jury—for you are here to try Socrates for his lofty disdain: you may be sure, by gods—and goddesses—that when I arose I had in no more particular sense slept a night with Socrates than if it had been with my father or my elder brother.

"After that, you can imagine what a state of

[1] Homer, *Il.* vi. 236 — Glaucus foolishly exchanging his golden armour for the bronze armour of Diomedes.

ἔχειν, ἡγούμενον μὲν ἠτιμάσθαι, ἀγάμενον δὲ τὴν τούτου φύσιν τε καὶ σωφροσύνην καὶ ἀνδρείαν, ἐντετυχηκότα ἀνθρώπῳ τοιούτῳ οἵῳ ἐγὼ οὐκ ἂν ᾤμην ποτὲ ἐντυχεῖν εἰς φρόνησιν καὶ εἰς καρτερίαν; ὥστε οὔθ' ὅπως οὖν ὀργιζοίμην εἶχον καὶ ἀποστερηθείην τῆς τούτου συνουσίας, οὔθ' ὅπῃ E προσαγαγοίμην αὐτὸν ηὐπόρουν. εὖ γὰρ ᾔδη ὅτι χρήμασί τε πολὺ μᾶλλον ἄτρωτος ἦν πανταχῇ ἢ σιδήρῳ ὁ Αἴας, ᾧ τε ᾤμην αὐτὸν μόνῳ ἁλώσεσθαι, διεπεφεύγει με. ἠπόρουν δή, καταδεδουλωμένος τε ὑπὸ τοῦ ἀνθρώπου ὡς οὐδεὶς ὑπ' οὐδενὸς ἄλλου περιῇα. ταῦτά τε γάρ μοι ἅπαντα προὐγεγόνει, καὶ μετὰ ταῦτα στρατεία ἡμῖν εἰς Ποτίδαιαν ἐγένετο κοινῇ καὶ συνεσιτοῦμεν ἐκεῖ. πρῶτον μὲν οὖν τοῖς πόνοις οὐ μόνον ἐμοῦ περιῆν, ἀλλὰ καὶ τῶν ἄλλων ἁπάντων· ὁπότ' ἀναγκασθεῖημεν ἀπο-
220 ληφθέντες που, οἷα δὴ ἐπὶ στρατείας, ἀσιτεῖν, οὐδὲν ἦσαν οἱ ἄλλοι πρὸς τὸ καρτερεῖν· ἔν τ' αὖ ταῖς εὐωχίαις μόνος ἀπολαύειν οἷός τ' ἦν τά τ' ἄλλα καὶ πίνειν οὐκ ἐθέλων, ὁπότε ἀναγκασθείη, πάντας ἐκράτει, καὶ ὃ πάντων θαυμαστότατον, Σωκράτη μεθύοντα οὐδεὶς πώποτε ἑώρακεν ἀνθρώπων. τούτου μὲν οὖν μοι δοκεῖ καὶ αὐτίκα ὁ ἔλεγχος ἔσεσθαι. πρὸς δὲ αὖ τὰς τοῦ χειμῶνος B καρτερήσεις—δεινοὶ γὰρ αὐτόθι χειμῶνες—θαυμάσια εἰργάζετο τά τε ἄλλα, καί ποτε ὄντος πάγου οἵου δεινοτάτου, καὶ πάντων ἢ οὐκ ἐξιόντων ἔνδοθεν ἤ, εἴ τις ἐξίοι, ἠμφιεσμένων τε θαυμαστὰ

SYMPOSIUM

mind I was in, feeling myself affronted, yet marvelling at the sobriety and integrity of his nature: for I had lighted on a man such as I never would have dreamt of meeting—so sensible and so resolute. Hence I could find neither a reason for being angry and depriving myself of his society nor a ready means of enticing him. For I was well aware that he was far more proof against money on every side than Ajax against a spear;[1] and in what I thought was my sole means of catching him he had eluded me. So I was at a loss, and wandered about in the most abject thraldom to this man that ever was known. Now all this, you know, had already happened to me when we later went on a campaign together to Potidaea;[2] and there we were messmates. Well, first of all, he surpassed not me only but every one else in bearing hardships; whenever we were cut off in some place and were compelled, as often in campaigns, to go without food, the rest of us were nowhere in point of endurance. Then again, when we had plenty of good cheer, he alone could enjoy it to the full, and though unwilling to drink, when once overruled he used to beat us all; and, most surprising of all, no man has ever yet seen Socrates drunk. Of this power I expect we shall have a good test in a moment. But it was in his endurance of winter —in those parts the winters are awful—that I remember, among his many marvellous feats, how once there came a frost about as awful as can be: we all preferred not to stir abroad, or if any of us did, we wrapped ourselves up with prodigious

---

[1] Referring to the sevenfold shield of Ajax: *cf.* Pindar, *Isth.* v. 45; Soph. *Aj.* 576.
[2] 432 B.C.

PLATO

δὴ ὅσα καὶ ὑποδεδεμένων καὶ ἐνειλιγμένων τοὺς
πόδας εἰς πίλους καὶ ἀρνακίδας, οὗτος δ' ἐν τούτοις
ἐξῄει ἔχων ἱμάτιον μὲν τοιοῦτον οἷόνπερ καὶ πρότερον εἰώθει φορεῖν, ἀνυπόδητος δὲ διὰ τοῦ κρυσ-
τάλλου ῥᾷον ἐπορεύετο ἢ οἱ ἄλλοι ὑποδεδεμένοι. οἱ
δὲ στρατιῶται ὑπέβλεπον αὐτὸν ὡς καταφρονοῦντα
σφῶν.

Καὶ ταῦτα μὲν δὴ ταῦτα·

οἷον δ' αὖ τόδ' ἔρεξε καὶ ἔτλη καρτερὸς ἀνὴρ

ἐκεῖ ποτὲ ἐπὶ στρατιᾶς,[1] ἄξιον ἀκοῦσαι. συννοήσας
γὰρ αὐτόθι ἕωθέν τι εἱστήκει σκοπῶν, καὶ ἐπειδὴ
οὐ προὐχώρει αὐτῷ, οὐκ ἀνίει ἀλλὰ εἱστήκει ζητῶν.
καὶ ἤδη ἦν μεσημβρία, καὶ ἄνθρωποι[2] ᾐσθάνοντο,
καὶ θαυμάζοντες ἄλλος ἄλλῳ ἔλεγεν ὅτι Σωκράτης
ἐξ ἑωθινοῦ φροντίζων τι ἕστηκε. τελευτῶντες δέ
τινες τῶν Ἰώνων, ἐπειδὴ ἑσπέρα ἦν, δειπνήσαντες
—καὶ γὰρ θέρος τότε γ' ἦν—χαμεύνια ἐξενεγκά-
μενοι ἅμα μὲν ἐν τῷ ψύχει καθηῦδον, ἅμα δὲ
ἐφύλαττον αὐτὸν εἰ καὶ τὴν νύκτα ἑστήξοι. ὁ δὲ
εἱστήκει μέχρι ἕως ἐγένετο καὶ ἥλιος ἀνέσχεν·
ἔπειτα ᾤχετ' ἀπιὼν προσευξάμενος τῷ ἡλίῳ.

Εἰ δὲ βούλεσθε ἐν ταῖς μάχαις· τοῦτο γὰρ δὴ
δίκαιόν γε αὐτῷ ἀποδοῦναι· ὅτε γὰρ ἡ μάχη ἦν,
ἐξ ἧς ἐμοὶ καὶ τἀριστεῖα ἔδοσαν οἱ στρατηγοί,
οὐδεὶς ἄλλος ἐμὲ ἔσωσεν ἀνθρώπων ἢ οὗτος, τετρω-
μένον οὐκ ἐθέλων ἀπολιπεῖν, ἀλλὰ συνδιέσωσε καὶ
τὰ ὅπλα καὶ αὐτὸν ἐμέ. καὶ ἐγὼ μέν, ὦ Σώκρατες,
καὶ τότε ἐκέλευον σοὶ διδόναι τἀριστεῖα τοὺς στρα-
τηγούς, καὶ τοῦτό γέ μοι οὔτε μέμψῃ οὔτε ἐρεῖς

[1] στρατιᾶς Oxyrh. Pap., Cobet: στρατείας MSS.
[2] ἄνθρωποι Mehler: ἄνθρωποι MSS.

care, and after putting on our shoes we muffled up our feet with felt and little fleeces. But he walked out in that weather, clad in just such a coat as he was always wont to wear, and he made his way more easily over the ice unshod than the rest of us did in our shoes. The soldiers looked askance at him, thinking that he despised them.

'So much for that: 'but next, the valiant deed our strong-souled hero dared'[1] on service there one day, is well worth hearing. Immersed in some problem at dawn, he stood in the same spot considering it; and when he found it a tough one, he would not give it up but stood there trying. The time drew on to midday, and the men began to notice him, and said to one another in wonder: 'Socrates has been standing there in a study ever since dawn!' The end of it was that in the evening some of the Ionians after they had supped—this time it was summer—brought out their mattresses and rugs and took their sleep in the cool; thus they waited to see if he would go on standing all night too. He stood till dawn came and the sun rose; then walked away, after offering a prayer to the Sun.

"Then, if you care to hear of him in battle—for there also he must have his due—on the day of the fight in which I gained my prize for valour from our commanders, it was he, out of the whole army, who saved my life: I was wounded, and he would not forsake me, but helped me to save both my armour and myself. I lost no time, Socrates, in urging the generals to award the prize for valour to you; and here I think you will neither rebuke

[1] Homer, *Od.* iv. 242.

ὅτι ψεύδομαι· ἀλλὰ γὰρ τῶν στρατηγῶν πρὸς τὸ
ἐμὸν ἀξίωμα ἀποβλεπόντων καὶ βουλομένων ἐμοὶ
διδόναι τἀριστεῖα, αὐτὸς προθυμότερος ἐγένου τῶν
στρατηγῶν ἐμὲ λαβεῖν ἢ σαυτόν. ἔτι τοίνυν, ὦ
ἄνδρες, ἄξιον ἦν θεάσασθαι Σωκράτη, ὅτε ἀπὸ
Δηλίου φυγῇ ἀνεχώρει τὸ στρατόπεδον· ἔτυχον
γὰρ παραγενόμενος ἵππον ἔχων, οὗτος δὲ ὅπλα.
ἀνεχώρει οὖν ἐσκεδασμένων ἤδη τῶν ἀνθρώπων
οὗτός τε ἅμα καὶ Λάχης· καὶ ἐγὼ περιτυγχάνω,
καὶ ἰδὼν εὐθὺς παρακελεύομαί τε αὐτοῖν θαρρεῖν,
καὶ ἔλεγον ὅτι οὐκ ἀπολείψω αὐτώ. ἐνταῦθα δὴ
καὶ κάλλιον ἐθεασάμην Σωκράτη ἢ ἐν Ποτιδαίᾳ·
αὐτὸς γὰρ ἧττον ἐν φόβῳ ἦ διὰ τὸ ἐφ᾽ ἵππου εἶναι·
πρῶτον μὲν ὅσον περιῆν Λάχητος τῷ ἔμφρων
εἶναι· ἔπειτα ἔμοιγε ἐδόκει, ὦ Ἀριστόφανες, τὸ
σὸν δὴ τοῦτο, καὶ ἐκεῖ διαπορεύεσθαι ὥσπερ καὶ
ἐνθάδε, "βρενθυόμενος καὶ τὠφθαλμὼ παρα-
βάλλων," ἠρέμα παρασκοπῶν καὶ τοὺς φιλίους καὶ
τοὺς πολεμίους, δῆλος ὢν παντὶ καὶ πάνυ πόρρωθεν, ὅτι εἴ τις ἅψεται τούτου τοῦ ἀνδρός, μάλα
ἐρρωμένως ἀμυνεῖται. διὸ καὶ ἀσφαλῶς ἀπῄει καὶ
οὗτος καὶ ὁ ἑταῖρος.[1] σχεδὸν γάρ τι τῶν οὕτω
διακειμένων ἐν τῷ πολέμῳ οὐδὲ ἅπτονται, ἀλλὰ
τοὺς προτροπάδην φεύγοντας διώκουσι.

Πολλὰ μὲν οὖν ἄν τις καὶ ἄλλα ἔχοι Σωκράτη
ἐπαινέσαι καὶ θαυμάσια· ἀλλὰ τῶν μὲν ἄλλων
ἐπιτηδευμάτων τάχ᾽ ἄν τις καὶ περὶ ἄλλου τοιαῦτα
εἴποι, τὸ δὲ μηδενὶ ἀνθρώπων ὅμοιον εἶναι, μήτε
τῶν παλαιῶν μήτε τῶν νῦν ὄντων, τοῦτο ἄξιον

---

[1] ἑταῖρος Aristid. : ἕτερος MSS.

SYMPOSIUM

me nor give me the lie. For when the generals, out of regard for my consequence, were inclined to award the prize to me, you outdid them in urging that I should have it rather than you. And further let me tell you, gentlemen, what a notable figure he made when the army was retiring in flight from Delium[1]: I happened to be there on horseback, while he marched under arms. The troops were in utter disorder, and he was retreating along with Laches, when I chanced to come up with them and, as soon as I saw them, passed them the word to have no fear, saying I would not abandon them. Here, indeed, I had an even finer view of Socrates than at Potidaea — for personally I had less reason for alarm, as I was mounted; and I noticed, first, how far he outdid Laches in collectedness, and next I felt—to use a phrase of yours, Aristophanes—how there he stepped along, as his wont is in our streets, 'strutting like a proud marsh-goose, with ever a sidelong glance,'[2] turning a calm sidelong look on friend and foe alike, and convincing anyone even from afar that whoever cares to touch this person will find he can put up a stout enough defence. The result was that both he and his comrade got away unscathed: for, as a rule, people will not lay a finger on those who show this disposition in war; it is men flying in headlong rout that they pursue.

"There are many more quite wonderful things that one could find to praise in Socrates: but although there would probably be as much to say about any other one of his habits, I select his unlikeness to anybody else, whether in the ancient or in the

---

[1] The Athenians were defeated by the Thebans, 424 B.C.: cf. Thuc. iv. 76 foll. [2] Aristoph. *Clouds*, 362.

PLATO

παντὸς θαύματος. οἷος γὰρ Ἀχιλλεὺς ἐγένετο, ἀπεικάσειεν ἄν τις καὶ Βρασίδαν καὶ ἄλλους, καὶ οἷος αὖ Περικλῆς, καὶ Νέστορα καὶ Ἀντήνορα, εἰσὶ δὲ καὶ ἕτεροι· καὶ τοὺς ἄλλους κατὰ ταῦτ' ἄν τις ἀπεικάζοι· οἷος δὲ οὑτοσὶ γέγονε τὴν ἀτοπίαν ἄνθρωπος,[1] καὶ αὐτὸς καὶ οἱ λόγοι αὐτοῦ, οὐδ' ἐγγὺς ἂν εὕροι τις ζητῶν, οὔτε τῶν νῦν οὔτε τῶν παλαιῶν, εἰ μὴ ἄρα εἰ οἷς ἐγὼ λέγω ἀπεικάζοι τις αὐτόν, ἀνθρώπων μὲν μηδενί, τοῖς δὲ σιληνοῖς καὶ σατύροις, αὐτὸν καὶ τοὺς λόγους.

Καὶ γὰρ οὖν καὶ τοῦτο ἐν τοῖς πρώτοις παρέλιπον, ὅτι καὶ οἱ λόγοι αὐτοῦ ὁμοιότατοί εἰσι τοῖς σιληνοῖς τοῖς διοιγομένοις. εἰ γὰρ ἐθέλει τις τῶν Σωκράτους ἀκούειν λόγων, φανεῖεν ἂν πάνυ γελοῖοι τὸ πρῶτον· τοιαῦτα καὶ ὀνόματα καὶ ῥήματα ἔξωθεν περιαμπέχονται, σατύρου δή[2] τινα ὑβριστοῦ δοράν. ὄνους γὰρ κανθηλίους λέγει καὶ χαλκέας τινὰς καὶ σκυτοτόμους καὶ βυρσοδέψας, καὶ ἀεὶ διὰ τῶν αὐτῶν ταὐτὰ φαίνεται λέγειν, ὥστε ἄπειρος καὶ ἀνόητος ἄνθρωπος πᾶς ἂν τῶν λόγων καταγελάσειεν. διοιγομένους δὲ ἰδὼν αὖ[3] τις καὶ ἐντὸς αὐτῶν γιγνόμενος πρῶτον μὲν νοῦν ἔχοντας ἔνδον μόνους εὑρήσει τῶν λόγων, ἔπειτα θειοτάτους καὶ πλεῖστ' ἀγάλματ' ἀρετῆς ἐν αὑτοῖς ἔχοντας καὶ ἐπὶ πλεῖστον τείνοντας, μᾶλλον δὲ ἐπὶ πᾶν ὅσον προσήκει σκοπεῖν τῷ μέλλοντι καλῷ κἀγαθῷ ἔσεσθαι.

Ταῦτ' ἐστίν, ὦ ἄνδρες, ἃ ἐγὼ Σωκράτη ἐπαινῶ· καὶ αὖ ἃ μέμφομαι συμμίξας ὑμῖν εἶπον ἅ με

---

[1] ἄνθρωπος Sauppe : ἄνθρωπος MSS.
[2] δή Baiter : ἄν T.
[3] αὖ Bekker : ἂν MSS.

SYMPOSIUM

modern world, as calling for our greatest wonder. You may take the character of Achilles and see his parallel in Brasidas or others; you may couple Nestor, Antenor, or others I might mention, with Pericles; and in the same order you may liken most great men; but with the odd qualities of this person, both in himself and in his conversation, you would not come anywhere near finding a comparison if you searched either among men of our day or among those of the past, unless perhaps you borrowed my words and matched him, not with any human being, but with the Silenuses and satyrs, in his person and his speech.

"For there is a point I omitted when I began—how his talk most of all resembles the Silenuses that are made to open. If you chose to listen to Socrates' discourses you would feel them at first to be quite ridiculous; on the outside they are clothed with such absurd words and phrases—all, of course, the hide of a mocking satyr. His talk is of pack-asses, smiths, cobblers, and tanners, and he seems always to be using the same terms for the same things; so that anyone inexpert and thoughtless might laugh his speeches to scorn. But when these are opened, and you obtain a fresh view of them by getting inside, first of all you will discover that they are the only speeches which have any sense in them; and secondly, that none are so divine, so rich in images of virtue, so largely—nay, so completely—intent on all things proper for the study of such as would attain both grace and worth.

"This, gentlemen, is the praise I give to Socrates: at the same time, I have seasoned it with a little fault-finding, and have told you his rude behaviour

ὕβρισεν. καὶ μέντοι οὐκ ἐμὲ μόνον ταῦτα πεποίηκεν, ἀλλὰ καὶ Χαρμίδην τὸν Γλαύκωνος καὶ Εὐθύδημον τὸν Διοκλέους καὶ ἄλλους πάνυ πολλούς, οὓς οὗτος ἐξαπατῶν ὡς ἐραστὴς παιδικὰ μᾶλλον αὐτὸς καθίσταται ἀντ' ἐραστοῦ. ἃ δὴ καὶ σοὶ λέγω, ὦ Ἀγάθων, μὴ ἐξαπατᾶσθαι ὑπὸ τούτου, ἀλλ' ἀπὸ τῶν ἡμετέρων παθημάτων γνόντα εὐλαβηθῆναι, καὶ μὴ κατὰ τὴν παροιμίαν ὥσπερ νήπιον παθόντα γνῶναι.

Εἰπόντος δὴ ταῦτα τοῦ Ἀλκιβιάδου γέλωτα γενέσθαι ἐπὶ τῇ παρρησίᾳ αὐτοῦ, ὅτι ἐδόκει ἔτι ἐρωτικῶς ἔχειν τοῦ Σωκράτους. τὸν οὖν Σωκράτη, Νήφειν μοι δοκεῖς, φάναι, ὦ Ἀλκιβιάδη. οὐ γὰρ ἄν ποθ' οὕτω κομψῶς κύκλῳ περιβαλλόμενος ἀφανίσαι ἐνεχείρεις οὗ ἕνεκα ταῦτα πάντα εἴρηκας καί, ὡς ἐν παρέργῳ δὴ λέγων ἐπὶ τελευτῆς αὐτὸ ἔθηκας, ὡς οὐ πάντα τούτου ἕνεκα εἰρηκώς, τοῦ ἐμὲ καὶ Ἀγάθωνα διαβάλλειν, οἰόμενος δεῖν ἐμὲ μὲν σοῦ ἐρᾶν καὶ μηδενὸς ἄλλου, Ἀγάθωνα δὲ ὑπὸ σοῦ ἐρᾶσθαι καὶ μηδ' ὑφ' ἑνὸς ἄλλου. ἀλλ' οὐκ ἔλαθες, ἀλλὰ τὸ σατυρικόν σου δρᾶμα τοῦτο καὶ σιληνικὸν κατάδηλον ἐγένετο. ἀλλ', ὦ φίλε Ἀγάθων, μηδὲν πλέον αὐτῷ γένηται, ἀλλὰ παρασκευάζου ὅπως ἐμὲ καὶ σὲ μηδεὶς διαβαλεῖ.[1]

Τὸν οὖν Ἀγάθωνα εἰπεῖν, Καὶ μήν, ὦ Σώκρατες, κινδυνεύεις ἀληθῆ λέγειν. τεκμαίρομαι δὲ καὶ ὡς κατεκλίνη ἐν μέσῳ ἐμοῦ τε καὶ σοῦ, ἵνα χωρὶς ἡμᾶς διαλάβῃ. οὐδὲν οὖν πλέον αὐτῷ ἔσται, ἀλλ' ἐγὼ παρὰ σὲ ἐλθὼν κατακλινήσομαι.

---

[1] διαβαλεῖ Hirschig: διαβαλει Oxyrh. Pap.: διαβάλῃ MSS.

SYMPOSIUM

towards me. However, I am not the only person he has treated thus: there are Charmides, son of Glaucon, Euthydemus, son of Diocles, and any number of others who have found his way of loving so deceitful that he might rather be their favourite than their lover. I tell you this, Agathon, to save you from his deceit, that by laying our sad experiences to heart you may be on your guard and escape learning by your own pain, like the loon in the adage."[1]

When Alcibiades had thus spoken, there was some laughter at his frankness, which showed him still amorously inclined to Socrates; who then remarked: "I believe you are sober, Alcibiades; else you would never have enfolded yourself so charmingly all about, trying to screen from sight your object in all this talk, nor would have put it in as a mere incident at the end. The true object of all you have said was to stir up a quarrel between me and Agathon: for you think you must keep me as your undivided lover, and Agathon as the undivided object of your love. But now you are detected: your *Satyric* or *Silenic* play-scene is all shown up. Dear Agathon, do not let his plot succeed, but take measures to prevent anyone from setting you and me at odds."

To which Agathon replied: "Do you know, Socrates, I fancy you have hit on the truth. Besides, I take his sitting down between us two as an obvious attempt to draw us apart. See, he shall not gain his point: I will come and sit by your side."

[1] Homer, *Il.* xvii. 33 ῥεχθὲν δέ τε νήπιος ἔγνω, " fools get their lesson from the deed done."

PLATO

Πάνυ γε, φάναι τὸν Σωκράτη, δεῦρο ὑποκάτω ἐμοῦ κατακλίνου.

Ὦ Ζεῦ, εἰπεῖν τὸν Ἀλκιβιάδην, οἷα αὖ πάσχω ὑπὸ τοῦ ἀνθρώπου. οἴεταί μου δεῖν πανταχῇ περιεῖναι. ἀλλ᾽ εἰ μή τι ἄλλο, ὦ θαυμάσιε, ἐν μέσῳ ἡμῶν ἔα Ἀγάθωνα κατακεῖσθαι.

Ἀλλ᾽ ἀδύνατον, φάναι τὸν Σωκράτη. σὺ μὲν γὰρ ἐμὲ ἐπῄνεσας, δεῖ δ᾽ ἐμὲ αὖ τὸν ἐπὶ δεξί᾽ ἐπαινεῖν. ἐὰν οὖν ὑπὸ σοὶ κατακλινῇ Ἀγάθων, οὐ δήπου ἐμὲ πάλιν ἐπαινέσεται, πρὶν ὑπ᾽ ἐμοῦ μᾶλλον ἐπαινεθῆναι; ἀλλ᾽ ἔασον, ὦ δαιμόνιε, καὶ μὴ φθονήσῃς τῷ μειρακίῳ ὑπ᾽ ἐμοῦ ἐπαινεθῆναι· καὶ γὰρ πάνυ ἐπιθυμῶ αὐτὸν ἐγκωμιάσαι.

Ἰοὺ ἰού, φάναι τὸν Ἀγάθωνα, Ἀλκιβιάδη, οὐκ ἔσθ᾽ ὅπως ἂν ἐνθάδε μείναιμι, ἀλλὰ παντὸς μᾶλλον μεταναστήσομαι, ἵνα ὑπὸ Σωκράτους ἐπαινεθῶ.

Ταῦτα ἐκεῖνα, φάναι τὸν Ἀλκιβιάδην, τὰ εἰωθότα· Σωκράτους παρόντος τῶν καλῶν μεταλαβεῖν ἀδύνατον ἄλλῳ. καὶ νῦν ὡς εὐπόρως καὶ πιθανὸν λόγον εὗρεν, ὥστε παρ᾽ ἑαυτῷ τουτονὶ κατακεῖσθαι.

Τὸν μὲν οὖν Ἀγάθωνα ὡς κατακεισόμενον παρὰ τῷ Σωκράτει ἀνίστασθαι· ἐξαίφνης δὲ κωμαστὰς ἥκειν παμπόλλους ἐπὶ τὰς θύρας, καὶ ἐπιτυχόντας ἀνεῳγμέναις ἐξιόντος τινὸς εἰς τὸ ἄντικρυς πορεύεσθαι παρὰ σφᾶς καὶ κατακλίνεσθαι, καὶ θορύβου μεστὰ πάντα εἶναι, καὶ οὐκέτι ἐν κόσμῳ οὐδενὶ ἀναγκάζεσθαι πίνειν πάμπολυν οἶνον. τὸν μὲν οὖν Ἐρυξίμαχον καὶ τὸν Φαῖδρον καὶ ἄλλους τινὰς ἔφη ὁ Ἀριστόδημος οἴχεσθαι ἀπιόντας, ἓ δὲ ὕπνον λαβεῖν, καὶ κατα-

SYMPOSIUM

"By all means," said Socrates; "here is a place for you beyond me."

"Good God!" said Alcibiades, "here's the fellow at me again. He has set his heart on having the better of me every way. But at least, you surprising person, do allow Agathon to sit between us."

"That cannot be," said Socrates: "you have praised me, and so it behoves me to praise my neighbour on the right.[1] Thus if Agathon sits beyond you, he must surely be praising me again, before receiving his due praises from me. So let him be, my good soul, and do not grudge the lad those praises of mine: for I am most eager to pronounce his eulogy."

"Ha, ha! Alcibiades," said Agathon; "there can be no question of my staying here: I shall jump up and change at once, if that will make Socrates praise me."

"There you are," said Alcibiades; "just as usual: when Socrates is present, nobody else has a chance with the handsome ones. You see how resourceful he was in devising a plausible reason why our young friend should sit beside him."

So Agathon was getting up in order to seat himself by Socrates, when suddenly a great crowd of revellers arrived at the door, which they found just opened for some one who was going out. They marched straight into the party and seated themselves: the whole place was in an uproar and, losing all order, they were forced to drink a vast amount of wine. Then, as Aristodemus related, Eryximachus, Phaedrus, and some others took their leave and departed;

---

[1] At § 214 c it was only agreed that each should impose *what topic he pleased* upon his neighbour.

PLATO

δαρθεῖν πάνυ πολύ, ἅτε μακρῶν τῶν νυκτῶν οὐσῶν, ἐξεγρέσθαι δὲ πρὸς ἡμέραν ἤδη ἀλεκτρυόνων ᾀδόντων, ἐξεγρόμενος δὲ ἰδεῖν τοὺς μὲν ἄλλους καθεύδοντας καὶ οἰχομένους, Ἀγάθωνα δὲ καὶ Ἀριστοφάνη καὶ Σωκράτη ἔτι μόνους ἐγρηγορέναι καὶ πίνειν ἐκ φιάλης μεγάλης ἐπὶ δεξιά. τὸν οὖν Σωκράτη αὐτοῖς διαλέγεσθαι· καὶ τὰ μὲν ἄλλα ὁ Ἀριστόδημος οὐκ ἔφη μεμνῆσθαι τῶν λόγων· οὔτε γὰρ ἐξ ἀρχῆς παραγενέσθαι ὑπονυστάζειν τε· τὸ μέντοι κεφάλαιον, ἔφη, προσαναγκάζειν τὸν Σωκράτη ὁμολογεῖν αὐτοὺς τοῦ αὐτοῦ ἀνδρὸς εἶναι κωμῳδίαν καὶ τραγῳδίαν ἐπίστασθαι ποιεῖν, καὶ τὸν τέχνῃ τραγῳδιοποιὸν ὄντα ⟨καὶ⟩[1] κωμῳδιοποιὸν εἶναι. ταῦτα δὴ ἀναγκαζομένους αὐτοὺς καὶ οὐ σφόδρα ἑπομένους νυστάζειν, καὶ πρῶτον μὲν καταδαρθεῖν τὸν Ἀριστοφάνη, ἤδη δὲ ἡμέρας γιγνομένης τὸν Ἀγάθωνα. τὸν οὖν Σωκράτη, κατακοιμήσαντ᾽ ἐκείνους, ἀναστάντα ἀπιέναι,—καὶ ⟨ἓ⟩[2] ὥσπερ εἰώθει ἕπεσθαι,—καὶ ἐλθόντα εἰς Λύκειον, ἀπονιψάμενον, ὥσπερ ἄλλοτε τὴν ἄλλην ἡμέραν διατρίβειν, καὶ οὕτω διατρίψαντα εἰς ἑσπέραν οἴκοι ἀναπαύεσθαι.

[1] ⟨καὶ⟩ Vindob.   [2] ⟨ἓ⟩ Hermann.

SYMPOSIUM

while he himself fell asleep, and slumbered a great while, for the nights were long. He awoke towards dawn, as the cocks were crowing; and immediately he saw that all the company were either sleeping or gone, except Agathon, Aristophanes, and Socrates, who alone remained awake and were drinking out of a large vessel, from left to right; and Socrates was arguing with them. As to most of the talk, Aristodemus had no recollection, for he had missed the beginning and was also rather drowsy; but the substance of it was, he said, that Socrates was driving them to the admission that the same man could have the knowledge required for writing comedy and tragedy—that the fully skilled tragedian could be a comedian as well. While they were being driven to this, and were but feebly following it, they began to nod; first Aristophanes dropped into a slumber, and then, as day began to dawn, Agathon also. When Socrates had seen them comfortable, he rose and went away,—followed in the usual manner by my friend; on arriving at the Lyceum, he washed himself, and then spent the rest of the day in his ordinary fashion; and so, when the day was done, he went home for the evening and reposed.

GORGIAS

INTRODUCTION TO THE *GORGIAS*

The *Gorgias* marks an important stage in Plato's thought and art. If we read it, in the probable sequence of composition, after the *Protagoras, Meno*, and *Euthydemus*, we soon become aware of a new and lofty impulse animating the whole work, and stimulating the personal fervour and determination of the writer beneath the proceedings of his lively drama. The unjust execution of Socrates in 399 B.C., when Plato was a young man of twenty-eight, filled him with horror and amazement. He left Athens for some years; but although he had lost all hope of taking any useful part in the government of his city, and remained sorely convinced of the errors of her rulers, it was not till about 387 B.C., when he founded the Academy, that he definitely cut himself off from the political world. Either some further misdeed occurred that specially disgusted him, or else the decision came, as he rather implies in his seventh *Letter*, from his own judgement on the general trend of affairs in Athens. At any rate, he produced the *Gorgias* as his manifesto towards the time when, at forty years of age, he embarked on his great experiment in philosophic education. The design of attracting the attention of the ordinary man of some culture is evident, first

INTRODUCTION TO THE *GORGIAS*

in the choice of the venerable Gorgias—famed all over Greece for his ingenious wit and jingling eloquence—as the figure-head of the piece; then in the fierce attack on rhetoric, so flourishing and influential in forensic and political debate; and lastly in the proud renunciation of the pomps and vanities of the world, and in the passionate insistence on the claims of truth and right. The *Gorgias* achieved its immediate object, for Plato was quickly surrounded by a band of earnest students: the effect of the dialogue on a Corinthian farmer is thus described by Themistius (*Or.* xxiii. 356)—" he left forthwith his fields and vines, and committing his soul to Plato sowed and raised his teacher's doctrines for crops."

The scheme of the work is simple. In the first of its three main divisions (447–460) Socrates, accompanied, as often, by the eager, eccentric Chaerephon (*cf. Charm.* 153 B; Aristoph. *Clouds*, 503), is greeted in the streets by Callicles, who had been expecting him at his house for a rhetorical display: this has just been given there by Gorgias, who is now on his second visit to Athens and about eighty years of age. However, Socrates and his friend are taken into the house, where they find both Gorgias and his ardent disciple Polus among the company; and immediately Socrates begins to question Gorgias on the nature of his profession, in such a way as to show the need of an accurate definition of it, and of some satisfactory rule for its proper use. He points out that the true rhetorician, if he is to train men (as he professes to do) for public as well as private life, must himself be just and good. But Gorgias has agreed that rhetoric may be abused

INTRODUCTION TO THE *GORGIAS*

—that some rhetoricians may be unjust or wicked—and he admits the inconsistency. Socrates hints (458 E) that he may not be treating Gorgias fairly; but the aged professor is tired after the performance he has previously given, and it is left to Polus to enter a vehement protest against this unfair treatment of his master, and to give a more controversial tone to the discussion.

In this second division (461-480, the scene between Socrates and Polus) we consider rhetoric—on which Polus had published a treatise—in its place among the various arts which provide for man's body and soul, viz. cookery, self-adornment, medicine and gymnastic for the one, and rhetoric, sophistry, judicature, and legislation for the other. Four of these arts—two, medicine and gymnastic, in one sphere, and two, judicature and legislation, in the other—are genuine arts, aiming at our good; but the other two pairs—cookery and self-adornment, rhetoric and sophistry—are mere flatteries or cajoleries. This classification of the arts (462-465) is only dwelt on so far as to show that Polus, at any rate, has not come near thinking out the basis of his work in life, and to serve as an easy transition to the main business of the dialogue. For it leads at once to the subject of power, as acquired by the flattering art of persuasion, and to the question of what we are to regard as true happiness. Is it absolute liberty to do what one likes, without regard to what is good? Socrates applies his favourite thesis, that nobody wishes to do evil, although many do evil, thinking it to be for their good; such people do not know what is their real ultimate good, or how to get it. This end of all action is a matter of knowledge

INTRODUCTION TO THE *GORGIAS*

—but the doctrine " virtue is knowledge " is not put forward here. The arrogant young lecturer thinks to crush Socrates with the instance of Archelaus, the deeply criminal usurper of the Macedonian throne: surely everyone would like to be in his place! But Socrates enunciates the famous paradoxes (*a*) that it is better to suffer than to do wrong: this he is prepared to maintain though all the rest of the world be against him; and (*b*) that the unjust man is less unhappy if he is punished than if he escapes and thrives. As regards (*a*), Polus makes the fatal admission (474 c) that doing wrong is more disgraceful than suffering it, for this must mean that it is also more evil; and on (*b*) he has to agree (477 A) that a just punishment is an honourable thing, and therefore good. Punishment, he is told, is a release from evil, though of course it is better to be just and have no need of it. Rhetoric may have its use here, in enabling one to accuse oneself of crime and so to get one's punishment; perhaps also, to excuse an enemy whom one wishes to suffer the disaster of going unpunished for his wickedness. This refinement of revenge amazes Callicles (481), the typical Athenian democrat, who in mind and body follows his instinctive desires, obeying only the law of nature, and cultivating literature and philosophy for mere amusement (484).

With the protest of Callicles we enter upon the third and most important section of the dialogue (481–end). Plato's aim is now quite clear—to vindicate his own choice of the philosophic and educational life in preference to the political career that lay open to the ablest men of his time. Callicles

INTRODUCTION TO THE *GORGIAS*

(like Thrasymachus in the *Republic*) maintains the supremacy of force over all things, and concludes by urging Socrates to pursue a practical career. Socrates thanks him for his outspoken friendliness (487 A), and again, after he has driven Callicles to a fuller and more downright statement of his position, he compliments him on the freedom with which he speaks what most men think but will not say (492 D). Socrates proceeds to show by parable his notion of true happiness, which involves temperance or self-control; and he exposes the vile results of an unbridled, undiscriminating pursuit of pleasure as opposed to good, from which it must be clearly distinguished (497). Callicles here would retire from the argument; but he is persuaded by Gorgias to continue, and is shown that badness in a man has nothing to do with his experience of pain, and that good, not pleasure, is the real end of action (499). Socrates now repeats his distinction between true arts and "flatteries," and among the latter he places poetry along with rhetoric (502 D). On the analogy of the arts, the virtue that we seek in the soul, as in the body, is a certain order or harmony (504). From this point Callicles cares only to get the argument finished, and Socrates indulges in longer speeches for his eloquent exposition of the true rule of life. Temperance of mind and body is extolled as the great principle; for order, truth, and art are the necessary means to virtue of any kind (506), and so to happiness (508—*cf.* the conception of " justice " in the *Republic*). It is unfortunate that the bad man often has the power, and uses it, to destroy the good man: but rhetoric is only one of many arts which may save a man from death, and what we

INTRODUCTION TO THE *GORGIAS*

want to know is whether such-and-such a person *ought* to be saved (511-512). Callicles is too intent on popularity to be permanently affected by Socrates' eloquence on behalf of virtue (513); but he is induced to agree with Socrates that the citizens must somehow be trained to virtue by persons properly qualified (514). Pericles and other great Athenians did nothing of the sort, rather the contrary (516-519). Callicles again urges Socrates to serve the state and avoid unpopularity; Socrates replies that he is himself about the only real politician in Athens, though he has no other supporter but truth to protect him. He tells a story of the judgement of the dead, to show that the philosopher need have no fear of death (523-524). Most men who have had great power in life fare very ill when life is done. He ends with an eloquent plea for individual dissent and aspiration.

Such is the bare outline of the discussion. The upshot has little to show of strictly reasoned proof, but the cumulative effect of Socrates' pleading, as it works its way through playful comparisons and startling paradoxes to the bitterness and pride, tempered with regretful sympathy, which give a strangely noble glow to the conclusion, is deeply memorable and inspiring. Plato's dramatic art is at its height: not only are the disputants intensely alive, but the very statements—especially when recalled, and reconsidered or reinforced—seem for the moment to become active participators in the contest; and " the truth," " the good," and " the just " are similarly invested with a certain august personality. The characters of the three men who in turn oppose Socrates are ingeniously chosen for the

INTRODUCTION TO THE *GORGIAS*

progressive broadening and deepening of the issue and its interest to the ordinary person. Gorgias, although some of his pretensions are absurd, is a man of fine sense and integrity, and he acknowledges the claims of moral rectitude; but his outlook is cramped by professional success. Polus is immature and headstrong, easily trapped in argument, and in danger of going astray through thoughtless vanity rather than any decided inclination. Callicles is an uncompromising champion of worldly success and ruthless self-seeking: he represents the solid mass of opinion which confronts the single mind of Socrates. Though this brave assailant has every prospect of being shattered for the time, the wall of prejudice seems to quiver and open—thanks to the immortality which Plato has bestowed on his hero—under the continual impact of his teaching from that day to ours.

As the conversation proceeds, it becomes increasingly evident that Plato is speaking through the mouth of Socrates to the world at large, and especially to the critics who objected to his abandonment of the political sphere. The supposed date of the meeting is 405 B.C. (see 474 A, note), when Socrates was sixty-four; and yet Callicles exhorts him almost as though he were a young man of promise who had still a career to choose. There is also good reason to think that the theory of order or harmony as the secret of virtue was of Plato's own invention (on a hint from the Pythagoreans), as it is quite distinct from the Socratic "virtue is knowledge," and is developed, to lengths far beyond the analytical powers of Socrates, in the *Republic* and the *Philebus*. And we should note that in sketching here the

INTRODUCTION TO THE *GORGIAS*

independent standing and high devotion of the philosopher—a picture that he elaborated afterwards in the *Theaetetus*—he leaves out the duty of cross-examining every casual person of one's acquaintance which Socrates proclaims in the *Apology*. The *Gorgias*, in fact, as has been well said, is Plato's own " Apology " : we may, in fact,—

> See there the olive grove of Academe,
> Plato's retirement,—

and this explains the peculiar severity of his attitude and language towards statesmen of the past and the present. In the *Protagoras* and the *Meno*, it should be remembered, Pericles and Themistocles were examples of wisdom. As Plato tells us himself in his seventh *Letter*, " I found myself obliged to say, in praise of the right kind of philosophy, that this alone can give us insight into public and private justice ; and that consequently the human kind in every land will have no cessation from evil until either the kind of men who rightly and truly pursue philosophy shall acquire authority in the state, or the ruling statesmen shall by some divine dispensation be real philosophers." The *Gorgias* and the *Republic* (which must have been begun about the same time, 390–387 B.C.) show us how he actually said it. Both dialogues are remarkable for a new certainty of conviction and statement (*cf. Gorg.* 509 A), and for an enthusiastic fluency which is hardly in keeping with Socrates' avowed dislike of lengthy speeches (*cf. Gorg.* 519 D, where Socrates tries to excuse his " harangue "). We hear also in the *Gorgias* (*cf.* 499 A) the unmistakable tone of the teacher who is intent on pure logic : the purview is no longer

INTRODUCTION TO THE *GORGIAS*

limited to the ethical outlook of Socrates, but is expanding into the region of metaphysics.

ΓΟΡΓΙΑΣ

[Η ΠΕΡΙ ΡΗΤΟΡΙΚΗΣ· ΑΝΑΤΡΕΠΤΙΚΟΣ]

ΤΑ ΤΟΥ ΔΙΑΛΟΓΟΥ ΠΡΟΣΩΠΑ

ΚΑΛΛΙΚΛΗΣ, ΣΩΚΡΑΤΗΣ, ΧΑΙΡΕΦΩΝ, ΓΟΡΓΙΑΣ, ΠΩΛΟΣ

ΚΑΛΛ. Πολέμου καὶ μάχης φασὶ χρῆναι, ὦ Σώκρατες, οὕτω μεταλαγχάνειν.

ΣΩ. Ἀλλ' ἦ τὸ λεγόμενον κατόπιν ἑορτῆς ἥκομεν [καὶ ὑστεροῦμεν]¹;

ΚΑΛΛ. Καὶ μάλα γε ἀστείας ἑορτῆς. πολλὰ γὰρ καὶ καλὰ Γοργίας ἡμῖν ὀλίγον πρότερον ἐπεδείξατο.

ΣΩ. Τούτων μέντοι, ὦ Καλλίκλεις, αἴτιος Χαιρεφῶν ὅδε, ἐν ἀγορᾷ ἀναγκάσας ἡμᾶς διατρῖψαι.

ΧΑΙΡ. Οὐδὲν πρᾶγμα, ὦ Σώκρατες· ἐγὼ γὰρ καὶ ἰάσομαι. φίλος γάρ μοι Γοργίας, ὥστ' ἐπιδείξεται ἡμῖν, εἰ μὲν δοκεῖ, νῦν, ἐὰν δὲ βούλῃ, εἰσαῦθις.

ΚΑΛΛ. Τί δέ, ὦ Χαιρεφῶν; ἐπιθυμεῖ Σωκράτης ἀκοῦσαι Γοργίου;

ΧΑΙΡ. Ἐπ' αὐτό γέ τοι τοῦτο πάρεσμεν.

ΚΑΛΛ. Οὐκοῦν ὅταν βούλησθε παρ' ἐμὲ ἥκειν

¹ καὶ ὑστεροῦμεν secl. Cobet.

GORGIAS

[or ON RHETORIC; REFUTATIVE]

CHARACTERS

CALLICLES, SOCRATES, CHAEREPHON, GORGIAS, POLUS

CALL. To join in a fight or a fray, as the saying is, Socrates, you have chosen your time well enough.

SOC. Do you mean, according to the proverb, we have come too late for a feast?[1]

CALL. Yes, a most elegant feast; for Gorgias gave us a fine and varied display but a moment ago.

SOC. But indeed, Callicles, it is Chaerephon here who must take the blame for this; he forced us to spend our time in the market-place.

CHAER. No matter, Socrates: I will take the curing of it too; for Gorgias is a friend of mine, so that he will give us a display now, if you think fit, or if you prefer, on another occasion.

CALL. What, Chaerephon? Has Socrates a desire to hear Gorgias?

CHAER. Yes, it is for that very purpose we are here.

CALL. Then whenever you have a mind to pay me

[1] *Cf.* Shakespeare, 1 *K. H. IV.* iv. 2. 74: "To the latter end of a fray and the beginning of a feast, Fits a dull fighter and a keen guest."

οἴκαδε· παρ' ἐμοὶ γὰρ Γοργίας καταλύει καὶ ἐπιδείξεται ὑμῖν.

ΣΩ. Εὖ λέγεις, ὦ Καλλίκλεις. ἀλλ' ἆρα ἐθε-
C λήσειεν ἂν ἡμῖν διαλεχθῆναι; βούλομαι γὰρ πυθέσθαι παρ' αὐτοῦ, τίς ἡ δύναμις τῆς τέχνης τοῦ ἀνδρός, καὶ τί ἐστιν ὃ ἐπαγγέλλεταί τε καὶ διδάσκει· τὴν δὲ ἄλλην ἐπίδειξιν εἰσαῦθις, ὥσπερ σὺ λέγεις, ποιησάσθω.

ΚΑΛΛ. Οὐδὲν οἷον τὸ αὐτὸν ἐρωτᾶν, ὦ Σώκρατες. καὶ γὰρ αὐτῷ ἓν τοῦτ' ἦν τῆς ἐπιδείξεως· ἐκέλευε γοῦν νῦν δὴ ἐρωτᾶν ὅ τι τις βούλοιτο τῶν ἔνδον ὄντων, καὶ πρὸς ἅπαντα ἔφη ἀποκρινεῖσθαι.

ΣΩ. Ἦ καλῶς λέγεις. ὦ Χαιρεφῶν, ἐροῦ αὐτόν.

ΧΑΙΡ. Τί ἔρωμαι;

ΣΩ. Ὅστις ἐστίν.

ΧΑΙΡ. Πῶς λέγεις;

D ΣΩ. Ὥσπερ ἂν εἰ ἐτύγχανεν ὢν ὑποδημάτων δημιουργός, ἀπεκρίνατο ἂν δήπου σοι ὅτι σκυτοτόμος· ἢ οὐ μανθάνεις ὡς λέγω;

ΧΑΙΡ. Μανθάνω καὶ ἐρήσομαι. εἰπέ μοι, ὦ Γοργία, ἀληθῆ λέγει Καλλικλῆς ὅδε, ὅτι ἐπαγγέλλῃ ἀποκρίνεσθαι ὅ τι ἄν τίς σε ἐρωτᾷ;

ΓΟΡΓ. Ἀληθῆ, ὦ Χαιρεφῶν· καὶ γὰρ νῦν δὴ αὐτὰ ταῦτα ἐπηγγελλόμην, καὶ λέγω ὅτι οὐδείς μέ πω ἠρώτηκε καινὸν οὐδὲν πολλῶν ἐτῶν.

ΧΑΙΡ. Ἦ που ἄρα ῥᾳδίως ἀποκρινῇ, ὦ Γοργία.

ΓΟΡΓ. Πάρεστι τούτου πεῖραν, ὦ Χαιρεφῶν, λαμβάνειν.

ΠΩΛ. Νὴ Δία· ἂν δέ γε βούλῃ, ὦ Χαιρεφῶν, ἐμοῦ. Γοργίας μὲν γὰρ καὶ ἀπειρηκέναι μοι δοκεῖ· πολλὰ γὰρ ἄρτι διελήλυθεν.

GORGIAS

a call—Gorgias is staying with me, and he will give you a display.

soc. Thank you, Callicles: but would he consent to discuss with us? For I want to find out from the man what is the function of his art, and what it is that he professes and teaches. As for the rest of his performance, he must give it us, as you suggest, on another occasion.

CALL. The best way is to ask our friend himself, Socrates: for indeed that was one of the features of his performance. Why, only this moment he was pressing for whatever questions anyone in the house might like to ask, and saying he would answer them all.

soc. What a good idea! Ask him, Chaerephon.

CHAER. What am I to ask?

soc. What he is.

CHAER. How do you mean?

soc. Just as, if he chanced to be in the shoemaking business, his answer would have been, I presume, "a shoemaker." Now, don't you see my meaning?

CHAER. I see, and will ask him. Tell me, Gorgias, is Callicles here correct in saying that you profess to answer any questions one may ask you?

GORG. He is, Chaerephon; indeed, I was just now making this very profession, and I may add that nobody has asked me anything new for many years now.

CHAER. So I presume you will easily answer, Gorgias.

GORG. You are free to make trial of that, Chaerephon.

POL. Yes, to be sure; and, if you like, Chaerephon, of me. For I think Gorgias must be quite tired out, after the long discourse he has just delivered.

ΧΑΙΡ. Τί δέ, ὦ Πῶλε; οἴει σὺ κάλλιον ἂν Γοργίου ἀποκρίνασθαι;

ΠΩΛ. Τί δὲ τοῦτο, ἐὰν σοί γε ἱκανῶς;

ΧΑΙΡ. Οὐδέν· ἀλλ' ἐπειδὴ σὺ βούλει, ἀποκρίνου.

ΠΩΛ. Ἐρώτα.

ΧΑΙΡ. Ἐρωτῶ δή. εἰ ἐτύγχανε Γοργίας ἐπιστήμων ὢν τῆς τέχνης ἧσπερ ὁ ἀδελφὸς αὐτοῦ Ἡρόδικος, τίνα ἂν αὐτὸν ὠνομάζομεν δικαίως; οὐχ ὅπερ ἐκεῖνον;

ΠΩΛ. Πάνυ γε.

ΧΑΙΡ. Ἰατρὸν ἄρα φάσκοντες αὐτὸν εἶναι καλῶς ἂν ἐλέγομεν.

ΠΩΛ. Ναί.

ΧΑΙΡ. Εἰ δέ γε ἧσπερ Ἀριστοφῶν ὁ Ἀγλαοφῶντος ἢ ὁ ἀδελφὸς αὐτοῦ ἔμπειρος ἦν τέχνης, τίνα ἂν αὐτὸν ὀρθῶς ἐκαλοῦμεν;

ΠΩΛ. Δῆλον ὅτι ζωγράφον.

ΧΑΙΡ. Νῦν δ' ἐπειδὴ τίνος τέχνης ἐπιστήμων ἐστί, τίνα ἂν καλοῦντες αὐτὸν ὀρθῶς καλοῖμεν;

ΠΩΛ. Ὦ Χαιρεφῶν, πολλαὶ τέχναι ἐν ἀνθρώποις εἰσὶν ἐκ τῶν ἐμπειριῶν ἐμπείρως ηὑρημέναι· ἐμπειρία μὲν γὰρ ποιεῖ τὸν αἰῶνα ἡμῶν πορεύεσθαι κατὰ τέχνην, ἀπειρία δὲ κατὰ τύχην. ἑκάστων δὲ τούτων μεταλαμβάνουσιν ἄλλοι ἄλλων ἄλλως, τῶν δὲ ἀρίστων οἱ ἄριστοι· ὧν καὶ Γοργίας ἐστὶν ὅδε, καὶ μετέχει τῆς καλλίστης τῶν τεχνῶν.

ΣΩ. Καλῶς γε, ὦ Γοργία, φαίνεται Πῶλος παρεσκευάσθαι εἰς λόγους· ἀλλὰ γὰρ ὃ ὑπέσχετο Χαιρεφῶντι οὐ ποιεῖ.

GORGIAS

CHAER. Why, Polus, do you suppose you could answer more excellently than Gorgias?

POL. And what does that matter, if I should satisfy you?

CHAER. Not at all; since it is your wish, answer.

POL. Ask.

CHAER. Then I ask you, if Gorgias chanced to be skilled in the same art as his brother Herodicus, what should we be justified in calling him? What we call his brother, should we not?

POL. Certainly.

CHAER. Then we should make a right statement if we described him as a doctor.

POL. Yes.

CHAER. And if he were expert in the same art as Aristophon, son of Aglaophon, or his brother,[1] what name should we rightly give him?

POL. Obviously that of painter.

CHAER. But as it is, we would like to know in what art he is skilled, and hence by what name we should rightly call him.

POL. Chaerephon, there are many arts amongst mankind that have been discovered experimentally, as the result of experiences: for experience conducts the course of our life according to art, but inexperience according to chance. Of these several arts various men partake in various ways, and the best men of the best. Gorgias here is one of these, and he is a partner in the finest art of all.

SOC. Fine, at any rate, Gorgias, is the equipment for discourse that Polus seems to have got: but still he is not performing his promise to Chaerephon.

[1] Polygnotus, the famous painter who decorated public buildings in Athens from about 470 B.C.

448

ΓΟΡΓ. Τί μάλιστα, ὦ Σώκρατες;

ΣΩ. Τὸ ἐρωτώμενον οὐ πάνυ μοι φαίνεται ἀποκρίνεσθαι.

ΓΟΡΓ. Ἀλλὰ σύ, εἰ βούλει, ἐροῦ αὐτόν.

ΣΩ. Οὔκ, εἰ αὐτῷ γε σοὶ βουλομένῳ ἐστὶν ἀποκρίνεσθαι, ἀλλὰ πολὺ ἂν ἥδιον σέ. δῆλος γάρ E μοι Πῶλος καὶ ἐξ ὧν εἴρηκεν, ὅτι τὴν καλουμένην ῥητορικὴν μᾶλλον μεμελέτηκεν ἢ διαλέγεσθαι.

ΠΩΛ. Τί δή, ὦ Σώκρατες;

ΣΩ. Ὅτι, ὦ Πῶλε, ἐρομένου Χαιρεφῶντος τίνος Γοργίας ἐπιστήμων τέχνης, ἐγκωμιάζεις μὲν αὐτοῦ τὴν τέχνην ὥσπερ τινὸς ψέγοντος, ἥτις δέ ἐστιν οὐκ ἀπεκρίνω.

ΠΩΛ. Οὐ γὰρ ἀπεκρινάμην ὅτι εἴη ἡ καλλίστη;

ΣΩ. Καὶ μάλα γε. ἀλλ' οὐδεὶς ἠρώτα ποία τις εἴη ἡ Γοργίου τέχνη, ἀλλὰ τίς καὶ ὅντινα δέοι καλεῖν τὸν Γοργίαν· ὥσπερ τὰ ἔμπροσθέν σοι 449 ὑπετείνατο Χαιρεφῶν καὶ αὐτῷ καλῶς καὶ διὰ βραχέων ἀπεκρίνω· καὶ νῦν οὕτως εἰπὲ τίς ἡ τέχνη καὶ τίνα Γοργίαν καλεῖν χρὴ ἡμᾶς. μᾶλλον δέ, ὦ Γοργία, αὐτὸς ἡμῖν εἰπέ, τίνα σε χρὴ καλεῖν ὡς τίνος ἐπιστήμονα τέχνης.

ΓΟΡΓ. Τῆς ῥητορικῆς, ὦ Σώκρατες.

ΣΩ. Ῥήτορα ἄρα χρή σε καλεῖν;

ΓΟΡΓ. Ἀγαθόν γε, ὦ Σώκρατες, εἰ δὴ ὅ γε εὔχομαι εἶναι, ὡς ἔφη Ὅμηρος, βούλει με καλεῖν.

ΣΩ. Ἀλλὰ βούλομαι.

ΓΟΡΓ. Κάλει δή.

GORGIAS

GORG. How exactly, Socrates?

SOC. He does not seem to me to be quite answering what he is asked.

GORG. Well, will you please ask him?

SOC. No, if you yourself will be so good as to answer, why, I would far rather ask you. For I see plainly, from what he has said, that Polus has had more practice in what is called rhetoric than in discussion.

POL. How so, Socrates?

SOC. Because, Polus, when Chaerephon has asked in what art Gorgias is skilled, you merely eulogize his art as though it were under some censure, instead of replying what it is.

POL. Why, did I not reply that it was the finest?

SOC. You certainly did: but nobody asked what was the quality of his art, only what it was, and by what name we ought to call Gorgias. Just as Chaerephon laid out the lines for you at first, and you answered him properly in brief words, in the same way you must now state what is that art, and what we ought to call Gorgias; or rather, Gorgias, do you tell us yourself in what art it is you are skilled, and hence, what we ought to call you.

GORG. Rhetoric, Socrates.

SOC. So we are to call you a rhetorician?

GORG. Yes, and a good one, if you are pleased to call me what—to use Homer's phrase—" I vaunt myself to be."[1]

SOC. Well, I am pleased to do so.

GORG. Then call me such.

---

[1] The regular phrase of a Homeric hero in boasting of his valour, parentage, etc.; *cf. Il.* vi. 211, xiv. 113.

PLATO

449

Β ΣΩ. Οὐκοῦν καὶ ἄλλους σε φῶμεν δυνατὸν εἶναι ποιεῖν;

ΓΟΡΓ. Ἐπαγγέλλομαί γε δὴ ταῦτα οὐ μόνον ἐνθάδε ἀλλὰ καὶ ἄλλοθι.

ΣΩ. Ἆρ' οὖν ἐθελήσαις ἄν, ὦ Γοργία, ὥσπερ νῦν διαλεγόμεθα, διατελέσαι τὸ μὲν ἐρωτῶν, τὸ δ' ἀποκρινόμενος, τὸ δὲ μῆκος τῶν λόγων τοῦτο, οἷον καὶ Πῶλος ἤρξατο, εἰσαῦθις ἀποθέσθαι; ἀλλ' ὅπερ ὑπισχνῇ, μὴ ψεύσῃ, ἀλλὰ ἐθέλησον κατὰ βραχὺ τὸ ἐρωτώμενον ἀποκρίνεσθαι.

ΓΟΡΓ. Εἰσὶ μέν, ὦ Σώκρατες, ἔνιαι τῶν ἀποκρίσεων ἀναγκαῖαι διὰ μακρῶν τοὺς λόγους ποιεῖ-
C σθαι· οὐ μὴν ἀλλὰ πειράσομαί γε ὡς διὰ βραχυτάτων. καὶ γὰρ αὖ καὶ τοῦτο ἕν ἐστιν ὧν φημί, μηδένα ἂν ἐν βραχυτέροις ἐμοῦ τὰ αὐτὰ εἰπεῖν.

ΣΩ. Τούτου μὴν δεῖ, ὦ Γοργία· καί μοι ἐπίδειξιν αὐτοῦ τούτου ποίησαι, τῆς βραχυλογίας, μακρολογίας δὲ εἰσαῦθις.

ΓΟΡΓ. Ἀλλὰ ποιήσω, καὶ οὐδενὸς φήσεις βραχυλογωτέρου ἀκοῦσαι.

ΣΩ. Φέρε δή· ῥητορικῆς γὰρ φῂς ἐπιστήμων
D τέχνης εἶναι καὶ ποιῆσαι ἂν καὶ ἄλλον ῥήτορα· ἡ ῥητορικὴ περὶ τί τῶν ὄντων τυγχάνει οὖσα; ὥσπερ ἡ ὑφαντικὴ περὶ τὴν τῶν ἱματίων ἐργασίαν· ἢ γάρ;

ΓΟΡΓ. Ναί.

ΣΩ. Οὐκοῦν καὶ ἡ μουσικὴ περὶ τὴν τῶν μελῶν ποίησιν;

ΓΟΡΓ. Ναί.

ΣΩ. Νὴ τὴν Ἥραν, ὦ Γοργία, ἄγαμαί γε τὰς ἀποκρίσεις, ὅτι ἀποκρίνῃ ὡς οἷόν τε διὰ βραχυτάτων.

GORGIAS

soc. And are we to say that you are able to make others like yourself?

gorg. Yes, that is what I profess to do, not only here, but elsewhere also.

soc. Then would you be willing, Gorgias, to continue this present way of discussion, by alternate question and answer, and defer to some other time that lengthy style of speech in which Polus made a beginning? Come, be true to your promise, and consent to answer each question briefly.

gorg. There are some answers, Socrates, that necessitate a lengthy expression: however, I will try to be as brief as possible; for indeed it is one of my claims that no one could express the same thing in briefer terms than myself.

soc. That is just what I want, Gorgias: give me a display of this very skill—in brevity of speech; your lengthy style will do another time.

gorg. Well, I will do that, and you will admit that you never heard anyone speak more briefly.

soc. Come then; since you claim to be skilled in rhetorical art, and to be able to make anyone else a rhetorician, tell me with what particular thing rhetoric is concerned: as, for example, weaving is concerned with the manufacture of clothes, is it not?

gorg. Yes.

soc. And music, likewise, with the making of tunes?

gorg. Yes.

soc. Upon my word, Gorgias, I do admire your answers! You make them as brief as they well can be.

449

ΓΟΡΓ. Πάνυ γὰρ οἶμαι, ὦ Σώκρατες, ἐπιεικῶς τοῦτο ποιεῖν.

ΣΩ. Εὖ λέγεις. ἴθι δή μοι ἀπόκριναι οὕτω καὶ περὶ τῆς ῥητορικῆς, περὶ τί τῶν ὄντων ἐστὶν ἐπιστήμη;

ΓΟΡΓ. Περὶ λόγους.

Ε ΣΩ. Ποίους τούτους, ὦ Γοργία; ἆρα οἳ δηλοῦσι τοὺς κάμνοντας, ὡς ἂν διαιτώμενοι ὑγιαίνοιεν;

ΓΟΡΓ. Οὔ.

ΣΩ. Οὐκ ἄρα περὶ πάντας γε τοὺς λόγους ἡ ῥητορική ἐστιν.

ΓΟΡΓ. Οὐ δῆτα.

ΣΩ. Ἀλλὰ μὴν λέγειν γε ποιεῖ δυνατούς.

ΓΟΡΓ. Ναί.

ΣΩ. Οὐκοῦν περὶ ὧνπερ λέγειν, καὶ φρονεῖν;

ΓΟΡΓ. Πῶς γὰρ οὔ;

450 ΣΩ. Ἆρ' οὖν, ἣν νῦν δὴ ἐλέγομεν, ἡ ἰατρικὴ περὶ τῶν καμνόντων ποιεῖ δυνατοὺς εἶναι φρονεῖν καὶ λέγειν;

ΓΟΡΓ. Ἀνάγκη.

ΣΩ. Καὶ ἡ ἰατρικὴ ἄρα, ὡς ἔοικε, περὶ λόγους ἐστίν.

ΓΟΡΓ. Ναί.

ΣΩ. Τούς γε περὶ τὰ νοσήματα;

ΓΟΡΓ. Μάλιστα.

ΣΩ. Οὐκοῦν καὶ ἡ γυμναστικὴ περὶ λόγους ἐστὶ τοὺς περὶ εὐεξίαν τε τῶν σωμάτων καὶ καχεξίαν;

ΓΟΡΓ. Πάνυ γε.

ΣΩ. Καὶ μὴν καὶ αἱ ἄλλαι τέχναι, ὦ Γοργία, Β οὕτως ἔχουσιν· ἑκάστη αὐτῶν περὶ λόγους ἐστὶ τούτους, οἳ τυγχάνουσιν ὄντες περὶ τὸ πρᾶγμα, οὗ ἑκάστη ἐστὶν ἡ τέχνη.

GORGIAS

GORG. Yes, Socrates, I consider myself a very fair hand at that.

SOC. You are right there. Come now, answer me in the same way about rhetoric: with what particular thing is its skill concerned?

GORG. With speech.

SOC. What kind of speech, Gorgias? Do you mean that which shows by what regimen sick people could get well?

GORG. No.

SOC. Then rhetoric is not concerned with all kinds of speech.

GORG. No, I say.

SOC. Yet it does make men able to speak.

GORG. Yes.

SOC. And to understand also the things about which they speak.

GORG. Of course.

SOC. Now, does the medical art, which we mentioned just now, make men able to understand and speak about the sick?

GORG. It must.

SOC. Hence the medical art also, it seems, is concerned with speech.

GORG. Yes.

SOC. That is, speech about diseases?

GORG. Certainly.

SOC. Now, is gymnastic also concerned with speech about the good and bad condition of our bodies?

GORG. Quite so.

SOC. And moreover it is the same, Gorgias, with all the other arts; each of them is concerned with that kind of speech which deals with the subject matter of that particular art.

PLATO

ΓΟΡΓ. Φαίνεται.

ΣΩ. Τί οὖν δή ποτε τὰς ἄλλας τέχνας οὐ ῥητορικὰς καλεῖς, οὔσας περὶ λόγους, εἴπερ ταύτην ῥητορικὴν καλεῖς, ἣ ἂν ᾖ περὶ λόγους;

ΓΟΡΓ. Ὅτι, ὦ Σώκρατες, τῶν μὲν ἄλλων τεχνῶν περὶ χειρουργίας τε καὶ τοιαύτας πράξεις, ὡς ἔπος εἰπεῖν, πᾶσά ἐστιν ἡ ἐπιστήμη, τῆς δὲ ῥητορικῆς οὐδέν ἐστι τοιοῦτον χειρούργημα, ἀλλὰ πᾶσα ἡ πρᾶξις καὶ ἡ κύρωσις διὰ λόγων ἐστίν. διὰ ταῦτ' ἐγὼ τὴν ῥητορικὴν τέχνην ἀξιῶ εἶναι περὶ λόγους, ὀρθῶς λέγων, ὡς ἐγώ φημι.

ΣΩ. Ἆρ' οὖν μανθάνω οἵαν αὐτὴν βούλει καλεῖν; τάχα δὲ εἴσομαι σαφέστερον. ἀλλ' ἀπόκριναι· εἰσὶν ἡμῖν τέχναι. ἦ γάρ;

ΓΟΡΓ. Ναί.

ΣΩ. Πασῶν δή, οἶμαι, τῶν τεχνῶν τῶν μὲν ἐργασία τὸ πολύ ἐστι καὶ λόγου βραχέος δέονται, ἔνιαι δὲ οὐδενός, ἀλλὰ τὸ τῆς τέχνης περαίνοιτο ἂν καὶ διὰ σιγῆς, οἷον γραφικὴ καὶ ἀνδριαντοποιία καὶ ἄλλαι πολλαί. τὰς τοιαύτας μοι δοκεῖς λέγειν, περὶ ἃς οὐ φῂς τὴν ῥητορικὴν εἶναι· ἢ οὔ;

ΓΟΡΓ. Πάνυ μὲν οὖν καλῶς ὑπολαμβάνεις, ὦ Σώκρατες.

ΣΩ. Ἕτεραι δέ γέ εἰσι τῶν τεχνῶν αἳ διὰ λόγου πᾶν περαίνουσι, καὶ ἔργου, ὡς ἔπος εἰπεῖν, ἢ οὐδενὸς προσδέονται ἢ βραχέος πάνυ, οἷον ἀριθμητικὴ καὶ λογιστικὴ καὶ γεωμετρικὴ καὶ πεττευτική γε καὶ ἄλλαι πολλαὶ τέχναι, ὧν ἔνιαι σχεδόν τι ἴσους τοὺς λόγους ἔχουσι ταῖς πράξεσιν, αἱ δὲ πολλαὶ πλείους, καὶ τὸ παράπαν πᾶσα ἡ πρᾶξις καὶ

GORGIAS

GORG. Apparently.

SOC. Then why, pray, do you not give the name "rhetorical" to those other arts, when they are concerned with speech, if you call that "rhetoric" which has to do with speech?

GORG. Because, Socrates, the skill in those other arts is almost wholly concerned with manual work and similar activities, whereas in rhetoric there is no such manual working, but its whole activity and efficacy is by means of speech. For this reason I claim for the rhetorical art that it is concerned with speech, and it is a correct description, I maintain.

SOC. Now, do I understand what sort of art you choose to call it? Perhaps, however, I shall get to know this more clearly. But answer me this: we have arts, have we not?

GORG. Yes.

SOC. Then amongst the various arts some, I take it, consist mainly of work, and so require but brief speech; while others require none, for the art's object may be achieved actually in silence, as with painting, sculpture, and many other arts. It is to such as these that I understand you to refer when you say rhetoric has no concern with them; is not that so?

GORG. Your supposition is quite correct, Socrates.

SOC. But there is another class of arts which achieve their whole purpose through speech and—to put it roughly—require either no action to aid them, or very little; for example, numeration, calculation, geometry, draught-playing, and many other arts: some of these have the speech in about equal proportion to the action, but most have it as the larger part, or absolutely the whole of their operation

271

PLATO

450

τὸ κῦρος αὐταῖς διὰ λόγων ἐστί. τῶν τοιούτων
E τινά μοι δοκεῖς λέγειν τὴν ῥητορικήν.

ΓΟΡΓ. Ἀληθῆ λέγεις.

ΣΩ. Ἀλλ᾽ οὔτοι τούτων γε οὐδεμίαν οἶμαί σε
βούλεσθαι ῥητορικὴν καλεῖν, οὐχ ὅτι τῷ ῥήματι
οὕτως εἶπες, ὅτι ἡ διὰ λόγου τὸ κῦρος ἔχουσα
ῥητορική ἐστι, καὶ ὑπολάβοι ἄν τις, εἰ βούλοιτο
δυσχεραίνειν ἐν τοῖς λόγοις, τὴν ἀριθμητικὴν ἄρα
ῥητορικήν, ὦ Γοργία, λέγεις; ἀλλ᾽ οὐκ οἶμαί σε
οὔτε τὴν ἀριθμητικὴν οὔτε τὴν γεωμετρίαν ῥητορικὴν λέγειν.

451 ΓΟΡΓ. Ὀρθῶς γὰρ οἴει, ὦ Σώκρατες, καὶ δικαίως
ὑπολαμβάνεις.

ΣΩ. Ἴθι νῦν καὶ σὺ τὴν ἀπόκρισιν ἣν ἠρόμην
διαπέρανον. ἐπεὶ γὰρ ἡ ῥητορικὴ τυγχάνει μὲν
οὖσα τούτων τις τῶν τεχνῶν τῶν τὸ πολὺ λόγῳ
χρωμένων, τυγχάνουσι δὲ καὶ ἄλλαι τοιαῦται
οὖσαι, πειρῶ εἰπεῖν, ἡ περὶ τί ἐν λόγοις τὸ κῦρος
ἔχουσα ῥητορική ἐστιν. ὥσπερ ἂν εἴ τίς με ἔροιτο
ὧν νῦν δὴ ἔλεγον περὶ ἡστινοσοῦν τῶν τεχνῶν· ὦ
Σώκρατες, τίς ἐστιν ἡ ἀριθμητικὴ τέχνη; εἴποιμ᾽
B ἂν αὐτῷ, ὥσπερ σὺ ἄρτι, ὅτι τῶν διὰ λόγου τις τὸ
κῦρος ἐχουσῶν· καὶ εἴ με ἐπανέροιτο· τῶν περὶ τί;
εἴποιμ᾽ ἂν ὅτι τῶν περὶ τὸ ἄρτιόν τε καὶ περιττὸν
[γνῶσις],[1] ὅσα ἂν ἑκάτερα τυγχάνῃ ὄντα. εἰ δ᾽
αὖ ἔροιτο· τὴν δὲ λογιστικὴν τίνα καλεῖς τέχνην,
εἴποιμ᾽ ἂν ὅτι καὶ αὕτη ἐστὶ τῶν λόγῳ τὸ πᾶν
κυρουμένων· καὶ εἰ ἐπανέροιτο· ἡ περὶ τί; εἴποιμ᾽
C ἂν ὥσπερ οἱ ἐν τῷ δήμῳ συγγραφόμενοι, ὅτι τὰ
μὲν ἄλλα καθάπερ ἡ ἀριθμητικὴ ἡ λογιστικὴ ἔχει

---
[1] γνῶσις secl. Bekker.

GORGIAS

and effect is by means of speech. It is one of this class of arts that I think you refer to as rhetoric.

GORG. You are right.

SOC. But, mind you, I do not think it is any one of these that you mean to call rhetoric; though, so far as your expression went, you did say that the art which has its effect through speech is rhetoric, and one might retort, if one cared to strain at mere words: So, Gorgias, you call numeration rhetoric! But I do not believe it is either numeration or geometry that you call rhetoric.

GORG. Your belief is correct, Socrates, and your retort just.

SOC. Come now, and do your part in finishing off the answer to my question. Since rhetoric is in fact one of these arts which depend mainly on speech, and there are likewise other arts of the same nature, try if you can tell me with what this rhetoric, which has its effect in speech, is concerned. For instance, suppose some one asked me about one or other of the arts which I was mentioning just now: Socrates, what is the art of numeration? I should tell him, as you did me a moment ago, that it is one of those which have their effect through speech. And suppose he went on to ask: With what is its speech concerned? I should say: With the odd and even numbers, whatever may chance to be the amount of each. And if he asked again: What art is it that you call calculation? I should say that this also is one of those which achieve their whole effect by speech. And if he proceeded to ask: With what is it concerned? I should say—in the manner of those who draft amendments in the Assembly—that " in all else " calculation " corresponds " with

273

PLATO

περὶ τὸ αὐτὸ γάρ ἐστι, τό τε ἄρτιον καὶ τὸ περιττόν· διαφέρει δὲ τοσοῦτον, ὅτι καὶ πρὸς αὑτὰ καὶ πρὸς ἄλληλα πῶς ἔχει πλήθους ἐπισκοπεῖ τὸ περιττὸν καὶ τὸ ἄρτιον ἡ λογιστική. καὶ εἴ τις τὴν ἀστρονομίαν ἀνέροιτο, ἐμοῦ λέγοντος ὅτι καὶ αὕτη λόγῳ κυροῦται τὰ πάντα, οἱ δὲ λόγοι οἱ τῆς ἀστρονομίας, εἰ φαίη, περὶ τί εἰσιν, ὦ Σώκρατες; εἴποιμ' ἂν ὅτι περὶ τὴν τῶν ἄστρων φορὰν καὶ ἡλίου καὶ σελήνης, πῶς πρὸς ἄλληλα τάχους ἔχει.

ΓΟΡΓ. Ὀρθῶς γε λέγων σύ, ὦ Σώκρατες.

ΣΩ. Ἴθι δὴ καὶ σύ, ὦ Γοργία. τυγχάνει μὲν γὰρ δὴ ἡ ῥητορικὴ οὖσα τῶν λόγῳ τὰ πάντα διαπραττομένων τε καὶ κυρουμένων· ἦ γάρ;

ΓΟΡΓ. Ἔστι ταῦτα.

ΣΩ. Λέγε δὴ τῶν περὶ τί; τί[1] ἐστι τοῦτο τῶν ὄντων, περὶ οὗ οὗτοι οἱ λόγοι εἰσίν, οἷς ἡ ῥητορικὴ χρῆται;

ΓΟΡΓ. Τὰ μέγιστα τῶν ἀνθρωπείων πραγμάτων ὦ Σώκρατες, καὶ ἄριστα.

ΣΩ. Ἀλλ', ὦ Γοργία, ἀμφισβητήσιμον καὶ τοῦτο λέγεις καὶ οὐδέν πω σαφές. οἴομαι γάρ σε ἀκηκοέναι ἐν τοῖς συμποσίοις ᾀδόντων ἀνθρώπων τοῦτο τὸ σκολιόν, ἐν ᾧ καταριθμοῦνται ᾄδοντες ὅτι ὑγιαίνειν μὲν ἄριστόν ἐστι, τὸ δὲ δεύτερον καλὸν γενέσθαι, τρίτον δέ, ὥς φησιν ὁ ποιητὴς τοῦ σκολιοῦ, τὸ πλουτεῖν ἀδόλως.

ΓΟΡΓ. Ἀκήκοα γάρ· ἀλλὰ πρὸς τί τοῦτο λέγεις;

ΣΩ. Ὅτι εἴ σοι αὐτίκα παρασταῖεν οἱ δημιουργοὶ τούτων ὧν ἐπῄνεσεν ὁ τὸ σκολιὸν ποιήσας, ἰατρός τε καὶ παιδοτρίβης καὶ χρηματιστής, καὶ εἴποι

[1] τί add. Heindorf.

numeration, for both are concerned with the same thing, the odd and the even; but that they differ to this extent, that calculation considers the numerical values of odd and even numbers not merely in themselves but in relation to each other. And suppose, on my saying that astronomy also achieves its whole effect by speech, he were to ask me: And the speech of astronomy, with what is it concerned? I should say: With the courses of the stars and sun and moon, and their relative speeds.

GORG. And you would be right, Socrates.

SOC. Come then and do your part, Gorgias: rhetoric is one of those arts, is it not, which carry out their work and achieve their effect by speech?

GORG. That is so.

SOC. Then tell me what they deal with: what subject is it, of all in the world, that is dealt with by this speech employed by rhetoric?

GORG. The greatest of human affairs, Socrates, and the best.

SOC. But that also, Gorgias, is ambiguous, and still by no means clear. I expect you have heard people singing over their cups the old catch, in which the singers enumerate the best things in life,—first health, then beauty, and thirdly, as the author of the catch puts it, wealth got without guile.[1]

GORG. Yes, I have heard it; but what is the point of your quotation?

SOC. I mean that, supposing the producers of those blessings which the author of the catch commends —namely, the doctor, the trainer, and the money-

[1] Bergk, *Poet. Lyr. Gr.* viii., gives four lines of the (anonymous) song: ὑγιαίνειν μὲν ἄριστον ἀνδρὶ θνατῷ, δεύτερον δὲ φυὰν καλὸν γενέσθαι, τὸ τρίτον δὲ πλουτεῖν ἀδόλως, καὶ τὸ τέταρτον ἡβᾶν μετὰ τῶν φίλων.

PLATO

πρῶτον μὲν ὁ ἰατρὸς ὅτι ὦ Σώκρατες, ἐξαπατᾷ σε Γοργίας· οὐ γάρ ἐστιν ἡ τούτου τέχνη περὶ τὸ μέγιστον ἀγαθὸν τοῖς ἀνθρώποις, ἀλλ' ἡ ἐμή· εἰ οὖν αὐτὸν ἐγὼ ἐροίμην· σὺ δὲ τίς ὢν ταῦτα λέγεις; εἴποι ἂν ἴσως ὅτι ἰατρός. τί οὖν λέγεις; ἢ τὸ τῆς σῆς τέχνης ἔργον μέγιστόν ἐστιν ἀγαθόν; πῶς γὰρ οὔ, φαίη ἂν ἴσως, ὦ Σώκρατες, ὑγίεια; τί δ' B ἐστὶ μεῖζον ἀγαθὸν ἀνθρώποις ὑγιείας· εἰ δ' αὖ μετὰ τοῦτον ὁ παιδοτρίβης εἴποι ὅτι θαυμάζοιμι τἂν, ὦ Σώκρατες, καὶ αὐτός, εἴ σοι ἔχοι Γοργίας μεῖζον ἀγαθὸν ἐπιδεῖξαι τῆς αὑτοῦ τέχνης ἢ ἐγὼ τῆς ἐμῆς· εἴποιμ' ἂν αὖ καὶ πρὸς τοῦτον· σὺ δὲ δὴ τίς εἶ, ὦ ἄνθρωπε, καὶ τί τὸ σὸν ἔργον; παιδοτρίβης, φαίη ἄν, τὸ δ' ἔργον μού ἐστι καλούς τε καὶ ἰσχυροὺς ποιεῖν τοὺς ἀνθρώπους τὰ σώματα. μετὰ δὲ τὸν παιδοτρίβην εἴποι ἂν ὁ χρηματιστής, ὡς C ἐγᾦμαι, πάνυ καταφρονῶν ἁπάντων· σκόπει δῆτα, ὦ Σώκρατες, ἐάν σοι πλούτου φανῇ τι μεῖζον ἀγαθὸν ὂν ἢ παρὰ Γοργίᾳ ἢ παρ' ἄλλῳ ὁτῳοῦν. φαῖμεν ἂν οὖν πρὸς αὐτόν· τί δὲ δή; ἦ σὺ τούτου δημιουργός; φαίη ἄν. τίς ὤν; χρηματιστής. τί οὖν; κρίνεις σὺ μέγιστον ἀνθρώποις ἀγαθὸν εἶναι πλοῦτον; φήσομεν. πῶς γὰρ οὔκ· ἐρεῖ. καὶ μὴν ἀμφισβητεῖ γε Γοργίας ὅδε τὴν παρ' αὑτῷ τέχνην μείζονος ἀγαθοῦ αἰτίαν εἶναι ἢ τὴν σήν, φαῖμεν ἂν ἡμεῖς. δῆλον οὖν ὅτι τὸ μετὰ τοῦτο ἔροιτ' ἄν· D καὶ τί ἐστι τοῦτο τὸ ἀγαθόν; ἀποκρινάσθω Γοργίας. ἴθι οὖν νομίσας, ὦ Γοργία, ἐρωτᾶσθαι καὶ ὑπ' ἐκείνων καὶ ὑπ' ἐμοῦ, ἀπόκριναι τί ἐστι τοῦτο ὃ φῂς σὺ μέγιστον ἀγαθὸν εἶναι τοῖς ἀνθρώποις καὶ σὲ δημιουργὸν εἶναι αὐτοῦ.

GORGIAS

getter—were to stand before you this moment, and the doctor first should say: "Gorgias is deceiving you, Socrates; for it is not his art, but mine, that deals with man's greatest good." Then supposing I were to ask him: "And who are you, to say so?" He would probably reply: "A doctor." "Well, what do you mean? That the work of your art is the greatest good?" "What else, Socrates," I expect he would reply, "is health? What greater good is there for men than health?" And supposing the trainer came next and said: "I also should be surprised indeed, Socrates, if Gorgias could show you a greater good in his art than I can in mine." Again I should say to him in his turn: "And who are you, sir? What is your work?" "A trainer," he would reply, "and my work is making men's bodies beautiful and strong." After the trainer would come the money-getter, saying—with, I fancy, a fine contempt for every one: "Pray consider, Socrates, if you can find a good that is greater than wealth, either on Gorgias' showing or on that of anyone else at all." "Why then," we should say to him, "are you a producer of that?" "Yes," he would say. "And who are you?" "A money-getter." "Well then," we shall say to him, "do you judge wealth to be the greatest good for men?" "Of course," he will reply. "But look here," we should say; "our friend Gorgias contends that his own art is a cause of greater good than yours." Then doubtless his next question would be: "And what is that good? Let Gorgias answer." Now come, Gorgias; imagine yourself being questioned by those persons and by me, and tell us what is this thing that you say is the greatest good for men, and that you claim to produce.

ΓΟΡΓ. Ὅπερ ἐστίν, ὦ Σώκρατες, τῇ ἀληθείᾳ μέγιστον ἀγαθὸν καὶ αἴτιον ἅμα μὲν ἐλευθερίας αὐτοῖς τοῖς ἀνθρώποις, ἅμα δὲ τοῦ ἄλλων ἄρχειν ἐν τῇ αὑτοῦ πόλει ἑκάστῳ.

ΣΩ. Τί οὖν δὴ τοῦτο λέγεις;

ΓΟΡΓ. Τὸ πείθειν ἔγωγ' οἷόν τ' εἶναι τοῖς λόγοις καὶ ἐν δικαστηρίῳ δικαστὰς καὶ ἐν βουλευτηρίῳ βουλευτὰς καὶ ἐν ἐκκλησίᾳ ἐκκλησιαστὰς καὶ ἐν ἄλλῳ συλλόγῳ παντί, ὅστις ἂν πολιτικὸς σύλλογος γίγνηται. καίτοι ἐν ταύτῃ τῇ δυνάμει δοῦλον μὲν ἕξεις τὸν ἰατρόν, δοῦλον δὲ τὸν παιδοτρίβην· ὁ δὲ χρηματιστὴς οὗτος ἄλλῳ ἀναφανήσεται χρηματιζόμενος καὶ οὐχ αὑτῷ, ἀλλὰ σοὶ τῷ δυναμένῳ λέγειν καὶ πείθειν τὰ πλήθη.

ΣΩ. Νῦν μοι δοκεῖς δηλῶσαι, ὦ Γοργία, ἐγγύτατα τὴν ῥητορικὴν ἥντινα τέχνην ἡγῇ εἶναι, καὶ εἴ τι ἐγὼ συνίημι, λέγεις ὅτι πειθοῦς δημιουργός ἐστιν ἡ ῥητορική, καὶ ἡ πραγματεία αὐτῆς ἅπασα καὶ τὸ κεφάλαιον εἰς τοῦτο τελευτᾷ· ἢ ἔχεις τι λέγειν ἐπὶ πλέον τὴν ῥητορικὴν δύνασθαι ἢ πειθὼ τοῖς ἀκούουσιν ἐν τῇ ψυχῇ ποιεῖν;

ΓΟΡΓ. Οὐδαμῶς, ὦ Σώκρατες, ἀλλά μοι δοκεῖς ἱκανῶς ὁρίζεσθαι· ἔστι γὰρ τοῦτο τὸ κεφάλαιον αὐτῆς.

ΣΩ. Ἄκουσον δή, ὦ Γοργία. ἐγὼ γὰρ εὖ ἴσθ' ὅτι, ὡς ἐμαυτὸν πείθω, εἴπερ τις ἄλλος ἄλλῳ διαλέγεται βουλόμενος εἰδέναι αὐτὸ τοῦτο περὶ ὅτου ὁ λόγος ἐστί, καὶ ἐμὲ εἶναι τούτων ἕνα· ἀξιῶ δὲ καὶ σέ.

ΓΟΡΓ. Τί οὖν δή, ὦ Σώκρατες;

ΣΩ. Ἐγὼ ἐρῶ νῦν. ἐγὼ τὴν ἀπὸ τῆς ῥητορικῆς πειθώ, ἥ τίς ποτ' ἐστὶν ἣν σὺ λέγεις καὶ περὶ

GORGIAS

GORG. A thing, Socrates, which in truth is the greatest good, and a cause not merely of freedom to mankind at large, but also of dominion to single persons in their several cities.

SOC. Well, and what do you call it?

GORG. I call it the ability to persuade with speeches either judges in the law courts or statesmen in the council-chamber or the commons in the Assembly or an audience at any other meeting that may be held on public affairs. And I tell you that by virtue of this power you will have the doctor as your slave, and the trainer as your slave; your money-getter will turn out to be making money not for himself, but for another,—in fact for you, who are able to speak and persuade the multitude.

SOC. I think now, Gorgias, you have come very near to showing us the art of rhetoric as you conceive it, and if I at all take your meaning, you say that rhetoric is a producer of persuasion, and has therein its whole business and main consummation. Or can you tell us of any other function it can have beyond that of effecting persuasion in the minds of an audience?

GORG. None at all, Socrates; your definition seems to me satisfactory; that is the main substance of the art.

SOC. Then listen, Gorgias: I, let me assure you, for so I persuade myself—if ever there was a man who debated with another from a desire of knowing the truth of the subject discussed, I am such a man; and so, I trust, are you.

GORG. Well, what then, Socrates?

SOC. I will now tell you. What the real nature of the persuasion is that you speak of as resulting

279

PLATO

ὧντινων πραγμάτων ἐστὶ πειθώ, σαφῶς μὲν εὖ
ἴσθ' ὅτι οὐκ οἶδα, οὐ μὴν ἀλλ' ὑποπτεύω γε ἣν
οἶμαί σε λέγειν καὶ περὶ ὧν· οὐδὲν μέντοι ἧττον
ἐρήσομαί σε, τίνα ποτὲ λέγεις τὴν πειθὼ τὴν ἀπὸ
C τῆς ῥητορικῆς καὶ περὶ τίνων αὐτὴν εἶναι. τοῦ
οὖν ἕνεκα δὴ αὐτὸς ὑποπτεύων σὲ ἐρήσομαι, ἀλλ'
οὐκ αὐτὸς λέγω; οὐ σοῦ ἕνεκα, ἀλλὰ τοῦ λόγου,
ἵνα οὕτω προΐῃ, ὡς μάλιστ' ἂν ἡμῖν καταφανὲς
ποιοῖ περὶ ὅτου λέγεται. σκόπει γὰρ εἴ σοι δοκῶ
δικαίως ἀνερωτᾶν σε, ὥσπερ ἂν εἰ ἐτύγχανόν σε
ἐρωτῶν τίς ἐστι τῶν ζωγράφων Ζεῦξις, εἴ μοι
εἶπες ὅτι ὁ τὰ ζῷα γράφων, ἆρ' οὐκ ἂν δικαίως
σε ἠρόμην ὁ τὰ ποῖα τῶν ζῴων γράφων καὶ
ποῦ;

ΓΟΡΓ. Πάνυ γε.

D ΣΩ. Ἆρα διὰ τοῦτο, ὅτι καὶ ἄλλοι εἰσὶ ζωγράφοι
γράφοντες ἄλλα πολλὰ ζῷα;

ΓΟΡΓ. Ναί.

ΣΩ. Εἰ δέ γε μηδεὶς ἄλλος ἢ Ζεῦξις ἔγραφε,
καλῶς ἄν σοι ἀπεκέκριτο;

ΓΟΡΓ. Πῶς γὰρ οὔ;

ΣΩ. Ἴθι δὴ καὶ περὶ τῆς ῥητορικῆς εἰπέ· πότερόν
σοι δοκεῖ πειθὼ ποιεῖν ἡ ῥητορικὴ μόνη ἢ καὶ
ἄλλαι τέχναι; λέγω δὲ τὸ τοιόνδε· ὅστις διδάσκει
ὁτιοῦν πρᾶγμα, πότερον ὃ διδάσκει πείθει ἢ οὔ;

ΓΟΡΓ. Οὐ δῆτα, ὦ Σώκρατες, ἀλλὰ πάντων
μάλιστα πείθει.

E ΣΩ. Πάλιν δὴ ἐπὶ τῶν αὐτῶν τεχνῶν λέγωμεν

GORGIAS

from rhetoric, and what the matters are with which persuasion deals, I assure you I do not clearly understand; though I may have my suspicions as to what I suppose you to mean by it, and with what things you think it deals. But nevertheless I will ask you what you do mean by the persuasion that results from rhetoric, and with what matters you think it deals. Now why is it that, having a suspicion of my own, I am going to ask you this, instead of stating it myself? It is not on your account, but with a view to the argument, and to such a progress in it as may best reveal to us the point we are discussing. Just see if you do not think it fair of me to press you with my question: suppose I happened to ask you what Zeuxis was among painters, and you said "a figure painter," would it not be fair of me to ask you what sort of figures he painted, and where?

GORG. Certainly.

SOC. Would this be the reason—that there are also other painters who depict a variety of other figures?

GORG. Yes.

SOC. But if no one besides Zeuxis were a painter, your answer would have been right?

GORG. Yes, of course.

SOC. Come then, tell me now about rhetoric: do you think rhetoric alone effects persuasion, or can other arts do it as well? I mean, for example, when a man teaches anything, does he persuade in his teaching? Or do you think not?

GORG. No, to be sure, Socrates, I think he most certainly does persuade.

SOC. Then let us repeat our question with reference

453

ὥνπερ νῦν δή· ἡ ἀριθμητικὴ οὐ διδάσκει ἡμᾶς, ὅσα ἐστὶ τὰ τοῦ ἀριθμοῦ, καὶ ὁ ἀριθμητικὸς ἄνθρωπος;

ΓΟΡΓ. Πάνυ γε.

ΣΩ. Οὐκοῦν καὶ πείθει;

ΓΟΡΓ. Ναί.

ΣΩ. Πειθοῦς ἄρα δημιουργός ἐστι καὶ ἡ ἀριθμητική.

ΓΟΡΓ. Φαίνεται.

ΣΩ. Οὐκοῦν ἐάν τις ἐρωτᾷ ἡμᾶς, ποίας πειθοῦς καὶ περὶ τί, ἀποκρινούμεθά που αὐτῷ ὅτι τῆς διδασκαλικῆς τῆς περὶ τὸ ἄρτιόν τε καὶ τὸ περιττὸν ὅσον ἐστί· καὶ τὰς ἄλλας ἃς νῦν δὴ ἐλέγομεν τέχνας ἁπάσας ἕξομεν ἀποδεῖξαι πειθοῦς δημιουργοὺς οὔσας καὶ ἧστινος καὶ περὶ ὅ τι· ἢ οὔ;

ΓΟΡΓ. Ναί.

ΣΩ. Οὐκ ἄρα ῥητορικὴ μόνη πειθοῦς ἐστι δημιουργός.

ΓΟΡΓ. Ἀληθῆ λέγεις.

ΣΩ. Ἐπειδὴ τοίνυν οὐ μόνη ἀπεργάζεται τοῦτο τὸ ἔργον, ἀλλὰ καὶ ἄλλαι, δικαίως ὥσπερ περὶ τοῦ ζωγράφου μετὰ τοῦτο ἐπανεροίμεθ᾽ ἂν τὸν λέγοντα, ποίας δὴ πειθοῦς καὶ τῆς περὶ τί πειθοῦς ἡ ῥητορικὴ ἐστὶ τέχνη; ἢ οὐ δοκεῖ σοι δίκαιον εἶναι ἐπανερέσθαι;

ΓΟΡΓ. Ἔμοιγε.

ΣΩ. Ἀπόκριναι δή, ὦ Γοργία, ἐπειδή γε καὶ σοὶ δοκεῖ οὕτως.

ΓΟΡΓ. Ταύτης τοίνυν τῆς πειθοῦς λέγω, ὦ Σώκρατες, τῆς ἐν τοῖς δικαστηρίοις καὶ ἐν τοῖς

GORGIAS

to the same arts that we spoke of just now : does not numeration, or the person skilled in numeration, teach us all that pertains to number ?

GORG. Certainly.

SOC. And persuades also ?

GORG. Yes.

SOC. So that numeration also is a producer of persuasion ?

GORG. Apparently.

SOC. Then if we are asked what kind of persuasion, and dealing with what, we shall reply, I suppose : The instructive kind, which deals with the amount of an odd or an even number ; and we shall be able to demonstrate that all the other arts which we mentioned just now are producers of persuasion, and what kind it is, and what it deals with, shall we not ?

GORG. Yes.

SOC. Hence rhetoric is not the only producer of persuasion.

GORG. You are right.

SOC. Since then it is not the only one that achieves this effect, but others can also, we should be justified in putting this further question to the speaker, as we did concerning the painter : Then of what kind of persuasion, and of persuasion dealing with what, is rhetoric the art ? Or do you not consider that such a further question would be justified ?

GORG. Yes, I do.

SOC. Then answer me, Gorgias, since you agree with me on that.

GORG. Well then, I mean that kind of persuasion, Socrates, which you find in the law-courts and in

283

PLATO

ἄλλοις ὄχλοις, ὥσπερ καὶ ἄρτι ἔλεγον, καὶ περὶ τούτων ἅ ἐστι δίκαιά τε καὶ ἄδικα.

ΣΩ. Καὶ ἐγώ τοι ὑπώπτευον ταύτην σε λέγειν τὴν πειθὼ καὶ περὶ τούτων, ὦ Γοργία· ἀλλ' ἵνα μὴ θαυμάζῃς, ἐὰν ὀλίγον ὕστερον τοιοῦτόν τί σε ἀνέρωμαι, ὃ δοκεῖ μὲν δῆλον εἶναι, ἐγὼ δ' ἐπανερωτῶ· ὅπερ γὰρ λέγω, τοῦ ἑξῆς ἕνεκα περαίνεσθαι τὸν λόγον ἐρωτῶ, οὐ σοῦ ἕνεκα, ἀλλ' ἵνα μὴ ἐθιζώμεθα ὑπονοοῦντες προαρπάζειν ἀλλήλων τὰ λεγόμενα, ἀλλὰ σὺ τὰ σαυτοῦ κατὰ τὴν ὑπόθεσιν ὅπως ἂν βούλῃ περαίνῃς.

ΓΟΡΓ. Καὶ ὀρθῶς γέ μοι δοκεῖς ποιεῖν, ὦ Σώκρατες.

ΣΩ. Ἴθι δὴ καὶ τόδε ἐπισκεψώμεθα. καλεῖς τι μεμαθηκέναι;

ΓΟΡΓ. Καλῶ.

ΣΩ. Τί δέ; πεπιστευκέναι;

ΓΟΡΓ. Ἔγωγε.

ΣΩ. Πότερον οὖν ταὐτὸν δοκεῖ σοι εἶναι μεμαθηκέναι καὶ πεπιστευκέναι, καὶ μάθησις καὶ πίστις, ἢ ἄλλο τι;

ΓΟΡΓ. Οἶμαι μὲν ἔγωγε, ὦ Σώκρατες, ἄλλο.

ΣΩ. Καλῶς γὰρ οἴει· γνώσῃ δὲ ἐνθένδε. εἰ γάρ τίς σε ἔροιτο· ἆρ' ἔστι τις, ὦ Γοργία, πίστις ψευδὴς καὶ ἀληθής; φαίης ἄν, ὡς ἐγὼ οἶμαι.

ΓΟΡΓ. Ναί.

ΣΩ. Τί δέ; ἐπιστήμη ἐστὶ ψευδὴς καὶ ἀληθής;

ΓΟΡΓ. Οὐδαμῶς.

ΣΩ. Δῆλον ἄρ' αὖ[1] ὅτι οὐ ταὐτόν ἐστιν.

---

[1] ἆρ' αὖ Burnet: γὰρ αὖ MSS.

GORGIAS

any public gatherings, as in fact I said just now; and it deals with what is just and unjust.

soc. I, too, I may tell you, had a suspicion that it was this persuasion that you meant, and as dealing with those things, Gorgias; but you must not be surprised if I ask you by-and-by some such question as may seem to be obvious, though I persist in it; for, as I say, I ask my questions with a view to an orderly completion of our argument—I am not aiming at you, but only anxious that we do not fall into a habit of snatching at each other's words with a hasty guess, and that you may complete your own statement in your own way, as the premises may allow.

gorg. And I think you are quite right in doing so, Socrates.

soc. Come then, let us consider another point. Is there something that you call " having learnt."

gorg. There is.

soc. And again, " having believed " ?

gorg. Yes.

soc. Then do you think that having learnt and having believed, or learning and belief, are the same thing, or different ?

gorg. In my opinion, Socrates, they are different.

soc. And your opinion is right, as you can prove in this way : if some one asked you—Is there, Gorgias, a false and a true belief ?—you would say, Yes, I imagine.

gorg. I should.

soc. But now, is there a false and a true knowledge ?

gorg. Surely not.

soc. So it is evident again that they[1] are not the same.

---

[1] *i.e.* knowledge and belief.

285

ΓΟΡΓ. Ἀληθῆ λέγεις.

ΣΩ. Ἀλλὰ μὴν οἵ τέ γε μεμαθηκότες πεπεισμένοι εἰσὶ καὶ οἱ πεπιστευκότες.

ΓΟΡΓ. Ἔστι ταῦτα.

ΣΩ. Βούλει οὖν δύο εἴδη θῶμεν πειθοῦς, τὸ μὲν πίστιν παρεχόμενον ἄνευ τοῦ εἰδέναι, τὸ δ' ἐπιστήμην;

ΓΟΡΓ. Πάνυ γε.

ΣΩ. Ποτέραν οὖν ἡ ῥητορικὴ πειθὼ ποιεῖ ἐν δικαστηρίοις τε καὶ τοῖς ἄλλοις ὄχλοις περὶ τῶν δικαίων τε καὶ ἀδίκων; ἐξ ἧς τὸ πιστεύειν γίγνεται ἄνευ τοῦ εἰδέναι ἢ ἐξ ἧς τὸ εἰδέναι;

ΓΟΡΓ. Δῆλον δήπου, ὦ Σώκρατες, ὅτι ἐξ ἧς τὸ πιστεύειν.

ΣΩ. Ἡ ῥητορικὴ ἄρα, ὡς ἔοικε, πειθοῦς δημιουργός ἐστι πιστευτικῆς, ἀλλ' οὐ διδασκαλικῆς περὶ τὸ δίκαιόν τε καὶ ἄδικον.

ΓΟΡΓ. Ναί.

ΣΩ. Οὐδ' ἄρα διδασκαλικὸς ὁ ῥήτωρ ἐστὶ δικαστηρίων τε καὶ τῶν ἄλλων ὄχλων δικαίων τε πέρι καὶ ἀδίκων, ἀλλὰ πειστικὸς μόνον. οὐ γὰρ δήπου ὄχλον γ' ἂν δύναιτο τοσοῦτον ἐν ὀλίγῳ χρόνῳ διδάξαι οὕτω μεγάλα πράγματα.

ΓΟΡΓ. Οὐ δῆτα.

ΣΩ. Φέρε δή, ἴδωμεν τί ποτε καὶ λέγομεν περὶ τῆς ῥητορικῆς· ἐγὼ μὲν γάρ τοι οὐδ' αὐτός πω δύναμαι κατανοῆσαι ὅ τι λέγω. ὅταν περὶ ἰατρῶν αἱρέσεως ᾖ τῇ πόλει σύλλογος ἢ περὶ ναυπηγῶν ἢ περὶ ἄλλου τινὸς δημιουργικοῦ ἔθνους, ἄλλο τι ἢ τότε ὁ ῥητορικὸς οὐ συμβουλεύσει; δῆλον γὰρ ὅτι ἐν ἑκάστῃ αἱρέσει τὸν τεχνικώτατον δεῖ αἱρεῖσθαι. οὐδ' ὅταν τειχῶν περὶ οἰκοδομήσεως ἢ λιμένων

GORGIAS

GORG. You are right.

SOC. But yet those who have learnt have been persuaded, as well as those who have believed.

GORG. That is so.

SOC. Then would you have us assume two forms of persuasion—one providing belief without knowledge, and the other sure knowledge?

GORG. Certainly.

SOC. Now which kind of persuasion is it that rhetoric creates in law courts or any public meeting on matters of right and wrong? The kind from which we get belief without knowledge, or that from which we get knowledge?

GORG. Obviously, I presume, Socrates, that from which we get belief.

SOC. Thus rhetoric, it seems, is a producer of persuasion for belief, not for instruction in the matter of right and wrong.

GORG. Yes.

SOC. And so the rhetorician's business is not to instruct a law court or a public meeting in matters of right and wrong, but only to make them believe; since, I take it, he could not in a short while instruct such a mass of people in matters so important.

GORG. No, to be sure.

SOC. Come then, let us see what actually is our account of rhetoric: for I confess I am not yet able to distinguish what my own account of it is. When the city holds a meeting to appoint doctors or shipbuilders or any other set of craftsmen, there is no question then, is there, of the rhetorician giving advice? And clearly this is because in each appointment we have to elect the most skilful person. Again, in a case of building walls or con-

κατασκευῆς ἢ νεωρίων, ἀλλ' οἱ ἀρχιτέκτονες· οὐδ'
αὖ ὅταν στρατηγῶν αἱρέσεως πέρι ἢ τάξεώς τινος
πρὸς πολεμίους ἢ χωρίων καταλήψεως συμβουλὴ
ᾖ, ἀλλ' οἱ στρατηγικοὶ τότε συμβουλεύσουσιν, οἱ
ῥητορικοὶ δὲ οὔ· ἢ πῶς λέγεις, ὦ Γοργία, τὰ
τοιαῦτα; ἐπειδὴ γὰρ αὐτός τε φῂς ῥήτωρ εἶναι καὶ
ἄλλους ποιεῖν ῥητορικούς, εὖ ἔχει τὰ τῆς σῆς
τέχνης παρὰ σοῦ πυνθάνεσθαι. καὶ ἐμὲ νῦν νόμισον
καὶ τὸ σὸν σπεύδειν· ἴσως γὰρ καὶ τυγχάνει τις
τῶν ἔνδον ὄντων μαθητής σου βουλόμενος γενέσθαι,
ὡς ἐγώ τινας σχεδὸν καὶ συχνοὺς αἰσθάνομαι, οἳ
ἴσως αἰσχύνοιντ' ἄν σε ἀνερέσθαι· ὑπ' ἐμοῦ οὖν
ἀνερωτώμενος νόμισον καὶ ὑπ' ἐκείνων ἀνερωτᾶ-
σθαι· τί ἡμῖν, ὦ Γοργία, ἔσται, ἐάν σοι συνῶμεν;
περὶ τίνων τῇ πόλει συμβουλεύειν οἷοί τε ἐσόμεθα;
πότερον περὶ δικαίου μόνον καὶ ἀδίκου ἢ καὶ περὶ
ὧν νῦν δὴ Σωκράτης ἔλεγεν; πειρῶ οὖν αὐτοῖς
ἀποκρίνεσθαι.

ΓΟΡΓ. Ἀλλ' ἐγώ σοι πειράσομαι, ὦ Σώκρατες,
σαφῶς ἀποκαλύψαι τὴν τῆς ῥητορικῆς δύναμιν
ἅπασαν· αὐτὸς γὰρ καλῶς ὑφηγήσω. οἶσθα γὰρ
δήπου ὅτι τὰ νεώρια ταῦτα καὶ τὰ τείχη τὰ Ἀθηναίων καὶ ἡ τῶν λιμένων κατασκευὴ ἐκ τῆς
Θεμιστοκλέους συμβουλῆς γέγονε, τὰ δ' ἐκ τῆς
Περικλέους, ἀλλ' οὐκ ἐκ τῶν δημιουργῶν.

ΣΩ. Λέγεται ταῦτα, ὦ Γοργία, περὶ Θεμιστο-
κλέους· Περικλέους δὲ καὶ αὐτὸς ἤκουον ὅτε
συνεβούλευεν ἡμῖν περὶ τοῦ διὰ μέσου τείχους.

---

[1] Built about 440 B.C. between the two walls built in 456 B.C., one connecting the Piraeus, and the other Phalerum, with Athens. The "middle wall" ran parallel to the former, and secured from hostile attack a narrow strip of land

structing harbours or arsenals, our only advisers are the master-builders; or in consulting on the appointment of generals, or on a manœuvre against the enemy, or on a military occupation, it is the general staff who will then advise us, and not the rhetoricians. Or what do you say, Gorgias, to these instances? For as you claim to be an orator yourself and to make orators of others, it is proper to inquire of you concerning your own craft. And here you must regard me as furthering your own interest: for it is quite likely that some one within these walls has a wish to become your pupil—indeed I fancy I perceive more than one, yes, a number of them, who, perhaps, would be ashamed to press you with questions. So, when you are being pressed with mine, consider that you are being questioned by them as well: "What shall we get, Gorgias, by coming to hear you? On what matters shall we be enabled to give advice to the state? Will it be only on right and wrong, or on those things besides which Socrates was mentioning just now?" So try to give them an answer.

GORG. Well, I will try, Socrates, to reveal to you clearly the whole power of rhetoric: and in fact you have correctly shown the way to it yourself. You know, I suppose, that these great arsenals and walls of Athens, and the construction of your harbours, are due to the advice of Themistocles, and in part to that of Pericles, not to your craftsmen.

SOC. So we are told, Gorgias, of Themistocles; and as to Pericles, I heard him myself when he was advising us about the middle wall.[1]

between Athens and the Piraeus. Socrates was born in 469 B.C.

PLATO

456 ΓΟΡΓ. Καὶ ὅταν γέ τις αἵρεσις ᾖ ὧν δὴ σὺ ἔλεγες, ὦ Σώκρατες, ὁρᾷς ὅτι οἱ ῥήτορές εἰσιν οἱ συμβουλεύοντες καὶ οἱ νικῶντες τὰς γνώμας περὶ τούτων.

ΣΩ. Ταῦτα καὶ θαυμάζων, ὦ Γοργία, πάλαι ἐρωτῶ ἥτις ποτε ἡ δύναμίς ἐστι τῆς ῥητορικῆς. δαιμονία γάρ τις ἔμοιγε καταφαίνεται τὸ μέγεθος οὕτω σκοποῦντι.

ΓΟΡΓ. Εἰ πάντα γε εἰδείης, ὦ Σώκρατες, ὅτι ὡς ἔπος εἰπεῖν ἁπάσας τὰς δυνάμεις συλλαβοῦσα ὑφ' B αὑτῇ ἔχει. μέγα δέ σοι τεκμήριον ἐρῶ· πολλάκις γὰρ ἤδη ἔγωγε μετὰ τοῦ ἀδελφοῦ καὶ μετὰ τῶν ἄλλων ἰατρῶν εἰσελθὼν παρά τινα τῶν καμνόντων οὐχὶ ἐθέλοντα ἢ φάρμακον πιεῖν ἢ τεμεῖν ἢ καῦσαι παρασχεῖν τῷ ἰατρῷ, οὐ δυναμένου τοῦ ἰατροῦ πεῖσαι, ἐγὼ ἔπεισα, οὐκ ἄλλῃ τέχνῃ ἢ τῇ ῥητορικῇ. φημὶ δὲ καὶ εἰς πόλιν ὅπῃ βούλει ἐλθόντα ῥητορικὸν ἄνδρα καὶ ἰατρόν, εἰ δέοι λόγῳ διαγωνίζεσθαι ἐν ἐκκλησίᾳ ἢ ἐν ἄλλῳ τινὶ συλλόγῳ, ὁπότερον δεῖ αἱρεθῆναι ἰατρόν, οὐδαμοῦ ἂν φανῆναι τὸν ἰατρόν, C ἀλλ' αἱρεθῆναι ἂν τὸν εἰπεῖν δυνατόν, εἰ βούλοιτο. καὶ εἰ πρὸς ἄλλον γε δημιουργὸν ὁντιναοῦν ἀγωνίζοιτο, πείσειεν ἂν αὑτὸν ἑλέσθαι ὁ ῥητορικὸς μᾶλλον ἢ ἄλλος ὁστισοῦν· οὐ γὰρ ἔστι περὶ ὅτου οὐκ ἂν πιθανώτερον εἴποι ὁ ῥητορικὸς ἢ ἄλλος ὁστισοῦν τῶν δημιουργῶν ἐν πλήθει. ἡ μὲν οὖν δύναμις τοσαύτη ἐστὶ καὶ τοιαύτη τῆς τέχνης· δεῖ μέντοι, ὦ Σώκρατες, τῇ ῥητορικῇ χρῆσθαι

GORGIAS

GORG. So whenever there is an election of such persons as you were referring to, Socrates, you see it is the orators who give the advice and get resolutions carried in these matters.

SOC. That is just what surprises me, Gorgias, and has made me ask you all this time what in the world the power of rhetoric can be. For, viewed in this light, its greatness comes over me as something supernatural.

GORG. Ah yes, if you knew all, Socrates,—how it comprises in itself practically all powers at once! And I will tell you a striking proof of this: many and many a time have I gone with my brother or other doctors to visit one of their patients, and found him unwilling either to take medicine or submit to the surgeon's knife or cautery; and when the doctor failed to persuade him I succeeded, by no other art than that of rhetoric. And I further declare that, if a rhetorician and a doctor were to enter any city you please, and there had to contend in speech before the Assembly or some other meeting as to which of the two should be appointed physician, you would find the physician was nowhere, while the master of speech would be appointed if he wished. And if he had to contend with a member of any other profession whatsoever, the rhetorician would persuade the meeting to appoint him before anyone else in the place: for there is no subject on which the rhetorician could not speak more persuasively than a member of any other profession whatsoever, before a multitude. So great, so strange, is the power of this art. At the same time, Socrates, our use of rhetoric should be like our use of any

ὥσπερ τῇ ἄλλῃ πάσῃ ἀγωνίᾳ. καὶ γὰρ τῇ ἄλλῃ ἀγωνίᾳ οὐ τούτου ἕνεκα δεῖ πρὸς ἅπαντας χρῆσθαι ἀνθρώπους, ὅτι ἔμαθε πυκτεύειν τε καὶ παγκρατιάζειν καὶ ἐν ὅπλοις μάχεσθαι, ὥστε κρείττων εἶναι καὶ φίλων καὶ ἐχθρῶν· οὐ τούτου ἕνεκα τοὺς φίλους δεῖ τύπτειν οὐδὲ κεντεῖν τε καὶ ἀποκτιννύναι. οὐδέ γε μὰ Δία ἐάν τις εἰς παλαίστραν φοιτήσας, εὖ ἔχων τὸ σῶμα καὶ πυκτικὸς γενόμενος, ἔπειτα τὸν πατέρα τύπτῃ καὶ τὴν μητέρα ἢ ἄλλον τινὰ τῶν οἰκείων ἢ τῶν φίλων, οὐ τούτου ἕνεκα δεῖ τοὺς παιδοτρίβας καὶ τοὺς ἐν τοῖς ὅπλοις διδάσκοντας μάχεσθαι μισεῖν τε καὶ ἐκβάλλειν ἐκ τῶν πόλεων. ἐκεῖνοι μὲν γὰρ παρέδοσαν ἐπὶ τῷ δικαίως χρῆσθαι τούτοις πρὸς τοὺς πολεμίους καὶ τοὺς ἀδικοῦντας, ἀμυνομένους, μὴ ὑπάρχοντας· οἱ δὲ μεταστρέψαντες χρῶνται τῇ ἰσχύϊ καὶ τῇ τέχνῃ οὐκ ὀρθῶς. οὔκουν οἱ διδάξαντες πονηροί, οὐδὲ ἡ τέχνη οὔτε αἰτία οὔτε πονηρὰ τούτου ἕνεκά ἐστιν, ἀλλ᾽ οἱ μὴ χρώμενοι, οἶμαι, ὀρθῶς. ὁ αὐτὸς δὴ λόγος καὶ περὶ τῆς ῥητορικῆς. δυνατὸς μὲν γὰρ πρὸς ἅπαντάς ἐστιν ὁ ῥήτωρ καὶ περὶ παντὸς λέγειν, ὥστε πιθανώτερος εἶναι ἐν τοῖς πλήθεσιν ἔμβραχυ περὶ ὅτου ἂν βούληται· ἀλλ᾽ οὐδέν τι μᾶλλον τούτου ἕνεκα δεῖ οὔτε τοὺς ἰατροὺς τὴν δόξαν ἀφαιρεῖσθαι —ὅτι δύναιτο ἂν τοῦτο ποιῆσαι—οὔτε τοὺς ἄλλους δημιουργούς, ἀλλὰ δικαίως καὶ τῇ ῥητορικῇ χρῆσθαι, ὥσπερ καὶ τῇ ἀγωνίᾳ. ἐὰν δέ, οἶμαι, ῥητορικὸς γενόμενός τις κᾆτα ταύτῃ τῇ δυνάμει καὶ τῇ τέχνῃ ἀδικῇ, οὐ τὸν διδάξαντα δεῖ μισεῖν τε καὶ ἐκβάλλειν ἐκ τῶν πόλεων. ἐκεῖνος μὲν γὰρ ἐπὶ δικαίᾳ χρείᾳ παρέδωκεν, ὁ δ᾽ ἐναντίως χρῆται. τὸν οὖν οὐκ ὀρθῶς χρώμενον μισεῖν

GORGIAS

other sort of exercise. For other exercises are not to be used against all and sundry, just because one has learnt boxing or wrestling or fighting in armour so well as to vanquish friend and foe alike: this gives one no right to strike one's friends, or stab them to death. Nor, in all conscience, if a man took lessons at a wrestling-school, and having got himself into good condition and learnt boxing he proceeded to strike his father and mother, or some other of his relations or friends, should that be a reason for hating athletic trainers and teachers of fighting in armour, and expelling them from our cities. For they imparted their skill with a view to its rightful use against enemies and wrongdoers, in self-defence, not provocation; whereas the others have perverted their strength and art to an improper use. So it is not the teachers who are wicked, nor is the art either guilty or wicked on this account, but rather, to my thinking, those who do not use it properly. Now the same argument applies also to rhetoric: for the orator is able, indeed, to speak against every one and on every question in such a way as to win over the votes of the multitude, practically in any matter he may choose to take up: but he is no whit the more entitled to deprive the doctors of their credit, just because he could do so, or other professionals of theirs; he must use his rhetoric fairly, as in the case of athletic exercise. And, in my opinion, if a man becomes a rhetorician and then uses this power and this art unfairly, we ought not to hate his teacher and cast him out of our cities. For he imparted that skill to be used in all fairness, whilst this man puts it to an opposite use. Thus it is the man who does not use it aright

δίκαιον καὶ ἐκβάλλειν καὶ ἀποκτιννύναι, ἀλλ' οὐ τὸν διδάξαντα.

ΣΩ. Οἶμαι, ὦ Γοργία, καὶ σὲ ἔμπειρον εἶναι πολλῶν λόγων καὶ καθεωρακέναι ἐν αὐτοῖς τὸ τοιόνδε, ὅτι οὐ ῥᾳδίως δύνανται περὶ ὧν ἂν ἐπιχειρήσωσι διαλέγεσθαι διορισάμενοι πρὸς ἀλλήλους καὶ μαθόντες καὶ διδάξαντες ἑαυτούς, οὕτω διαλύεσθαι τὰς συνουσίας, ἀλλ' ἐὰν περί του ἀμφισβητήσωσι καὶ μὴ φῇ ὁ ἕτερος τὸν ἕτερον ὀρθῶς λέγειν ἢ μὴ σαφῶς, χαλεπαίνουσί τε καὶ κατὰ φθόνον οἴονται τὸν ἑαυτῶν λέγειν, φιλονικοῦντας ἀλλ' οὐ ζητοῦντας τὸ προκείμενον ἐν τῷ λόγῳ· καὶ ἔνιοί γε τελευτῶντες αἴσχιστα ἀπαλλάττονται, λοιδορηθέντες τε καὶ εἰπόντες καὶ ἀκούσαντες περὶ σφῶν αὐτῶν τοιαῦτα, οἷα καὶ τοὺς παρόντας ἄχθεσθαι ὑπὲρ σφῶν αὐτῶν, ὅτι τοιούτων ἀνθρώπων ἠξίωσαν ἀκροαταὶ γενέσθαι. τοῦ δὴ ἕνεκα λέγω ταῦτα; ὅτι νῦν ἐμοὶ δοκεῖς σὺ οὐ πάνυ ἀκόλουθα λέγειν οὐδὲ σύμφωνα οἷς τὸ πρῶτον ἔλεγες περὶ τῆς ῥητορικῆς. φοβοῦμαι οὖν διελέγχειν σε, μή με ὑπολάβῃς οὐ πρὸς τὸ πρᾶγμα φιλονικοῦντα λέγειν τοῦ καταφανὲς γενέσθαι, ἀλλὰ πρὸς σέ. ἐγὼ οὖν, εἰ μὲν καὶ σὺ εἶ τῶν ἀνθρώπων ὧνπερ καὶ ἐγώ, ἡδέως ἄν σε διερωτῴην· εἰ δὲ μή, ἐῴην ἄν. ἐγὼ δὲ τίνων εἰμί; τῶν ἡδέως μὲν ἂν ἐλεγχθέντων, εἴ τι μὴ ἀληθὲς λέγω, ἡδέως δ' ἂν ἐλεγξάντων, εἴ τίς τι μὴ ἀληθὲς λέγοι, οὐκ ἀηδέστερον μέντ' ἂν ἐλεγχθέντων ἢ ἐλεγξάντων· μεῖζον γὰρ αὐτὸ ἀγαθὸν ἡγοῦμαι, ὅσῳπερ μεῖζον ἀγαθὸν

GORGIAS

who deserves to be hated and expelled and put to death, and not his teacher.

soc. I expect, Gorgias, that you as well as I have had no small practice in arguments, and have observed the following fact about them, that it is not easy for people to define to each other the matters which they take in hand to discuss, and to make such exchange of instruction as will fairly bring their debate to an end: no, if they find that some point is in dispute between them, and one of them says that the other is speaking incorrectly or obscurely, they are annoyed and think the remark comes from jealousy of themselves, and in a spirit of contention rather than of inquiry into the matter proposed for discussion. In some cases, indeed, they end by making a most disgraceful scene, with such abusive expressions on each side that the rest of the company are vexed on their own account that they allowed themselves to listen to such fellows. Well, what is my reason for saying this? It is because your present remarks do not seem to me quite in keeping or accord with what you said at first about rhetoric. Now I am afraid to refute you, lest you imagine I am contentiously neglecting the point and its elucidation, and merely attacking you. I therefore, if you are a person of the same sort as myself, should be glad to continue questioning you: if not, I can let it drop. Of what sort am I? One of those who would be glad to be refuted if I say anything untrue, and glad to refute anyone else who might speak untruly; but just as glad, mind you, to be refuted as to refute, since I regard the former as the greater benefit, in proportion as it is a greater benefit for oneself to be delivered

ἐστιν αὐτὸν ἀπαλλαγῆναι κακοῦ τοῦ μεγίστου ἢ ἄλλον ἀπαλλάξαι. οὐδὲν γὰρ οἶμαι τοσοῦτον κακὸν εἶναι ἀνθρώπῳ, ὅσον δόξα ψευδὴς περὶ ὧν τυγχάνει νῦν ἡμῖν ὁ λόγος ὤν. εἰ μὲν οὖν καὶ σὺ φῇς τοιοῦτος εἶναι, διαλεγώμεθα. εἰ δὲ καὶ δοκεῖ χρῆναι ἐᾶν, ἐῶμεν ἤδη χαίρειν καὶ διαλύωμεν τὸν λόγον.

ΓΟΡΓ. Ἀλλὰ φημὶ μὲν ἔγωγε, ὦ Σώκρατες, καὶ αὐτὸς τοιοῦτος εἶναι οἷον σὺ ὑφηγῇ· ἴσως μέντοι χρῆν ἐννοεῖν καὶ τὸ τῶν παρόντων. πάλαι γάρ τοι, πρὶν καὶ ὑμᾶς ἐλθεῖν, ἐγὼ τοῖς παροῦσι πολλὰ ἐπεδειξάμην, καὶ νῦν ἴσως πόρρω ἀποτενοῦμεν, ἢν διαλεγώμεθα. σκοπεῖν οὖν χρὴ καὶ τὸ τούτων, μή τινας αὐτῶν κατέχομεν βουλομένους τι καὶ ἄλλο πράττειν.

ΧΑΙΡ. Τοῦ μὲν θορύβου, ὦ Γοργία τε καὶ Σώκρατες, αὐτοὶ ἀκούετε τούτων τῶν ἀνδρῶν, βουλομένων ἀκούειν, ἐάν τι λέγητε· ἐμοὶ δ' οὖν καὶ αὐτῷ μὴ γένοιτο τοσαύτη ἀσχολία, ὥστε τοιούτων λόγων καὶ οὕτω λεγομένων ἀφεμένῳ προὐργιαίτερόν τι γενέσθαι ἄλλο πράττειν.

ΚΑΛΛ. Νὴ τοὺς θεούς, ὦ Χαιρεφῶν, καὶ μὲν δὴ καὶ αὐτὸς πολλοῖς ἤδη λόγοις παραγενόμενος οὐκ οἶδ' εἰ πώποτε ἥσθην οὕτως ὥσπερ νυνί· ὥστ' ἔμοιγε, κἂν τὴν ἡμέραν ὅλην ἐθέλητε διαλέγεσθαι, χαριεῖσθε.

ΣΩ. Ἀλλὰ μήν, ὦ Καλλίκλεις, τό γ' ἐμὸν οὐδὲν κωλύει, εἴπερ ἐθέλει Γοργίας.

GORGIAS

from the greatest evil than to deliver some one else. For I consider that a man cannot suffer any evil so great as a false opinion on the subjects of our actual argument. Now if you say that you too are of that sort, let us go on with the conversation; but if you think we had better drop it, let us have done with it at once and make an end of the discussion.

GORG. Nay, I too, Socrates, claim to be of the sort you indicate; though perhaps we should have taken thought also for the wishes of our company. For, let me tell you, some time before you and your friend arrived, I gave the company a performance of some length; and if we now have this conversation I expect we shall seriously protract our sitting. We ought, therefore, to consider their wishes as well, in case we are detaining any of them who may want to do something else.

CHAER. You hear for yourselves, Gorgias and Socrates, the applause by which these gentlemen show their desire to hear anything you may say; for my own part, however, Heaven forbid that I should ever be so busy as to give up a discussion so interesting and so conducted, because I found it more important to attend to something else.

CALL. Yes, by all that's holy, Chaerephon; and let me say, moreover, for myself that among the many discussions which I have attended in my time I doubt if there was one that gave me such delight as this present one. So, for my part, I shall count it a favour even if you choose to continue it all day long.

SOC. Why, Callicles, I assure you there s no hindrance on my side, if Gorgias is willing.

297

PLATO

ΓΟΡΓ. Αἰσχρὸν δὴ τὸ λοιπόν, ὦ Σώκρατες γίγνεται ἐμέ γε μὴ ἐθέλειν, αὐτὸν ἐπαγγειλάμενον ἐρωτᾶν ὅ τι τις βούλεται. ἀλλ' εἰ δοκεῖ τουτοισί, διαλέγου τε καὶ ἐρώτα ὅ τι βούλει.

ΣΩ. Ἄκουε δή, ὦ Γοργία, ἃ θαυμάζω ἐν τοῖς λεγομένοις ὑπὸ σοῦ· ἴσως γάρ τοι σοῦ ὀρθῶς λέγοντος ἐγὼ οὐκ ὀρθῶς ὑπολαμβάνω. ῥητορικὸν φὴς ποιεῖν οἷός τ' εἶναι, ἐάν τις βούληται παρὰ σοῦ μανθάνειν;

ΓΟΡΓ. Ναί.

ΣΩ. Οὐκοῦν περὶ πάντων ὥστ' ἐν ὄχλῳ πιθανὸν εἶναι, οὐ διδάσκοντα ἀλλὰ πείθοντα;

ΓΟΡΓ. Πάνυ μὲν οὖν.

ΣΩ. Ἔλεγές τοι νῦν δὴ ὅτι καὶ περὶ τοῦ ὑγιεινοῦ τοῦ ἰατροῦ πιθανώτερος ἔσται ὁ ῥήτωρ.

ΓΟΡΓ. Καὶ γὰρ ἔλεγον, ἔν γε ὄχλῳ.

ΣΩ. Οὐκοῦν τὸ ἐν ὄχλῳ τοῦτό ἐστιν, ἐν τοῖς μὴ εἰδόσιν; οὐ γὰρ δήπου ἔν γε τοῖς εἰδόσι τοῦ ἰατροῦ πιθανώτερος ἔσται.

ΓΟΡΓ. Ἀληθῆ λέγεις.

ΣΩ. Οὐκοῦν εἴπερ τοῦ ἰατροῦ πιθανώτερος ἔσται, τοῦ εἰδότος πιθανώτερος γίγνεται;

ΓΟΡΓ. Πάνυ γε.

ΣΩ. Οὐκ ἰατρός γε ὤν· ἦ γάρ;

ΓΟΡΓ. Ναί.

ΣΩ. Ὁ δὲ μὴ ἰατρός γε δήπου ἀνεπιστήμων ὧν ὁ ἰατρὸς ἐπιστήμων.

ΓΟΡΓ. Δῆλον ὅτι.

GORGIAS

GORG. After that, Socrates, it would be shameful indeed if I were unwilling, when it was I who challenged everybody to ask what questions they pleased. But if our friends here are so minded, go on with the conversation and ask me anything you like.

SOC. Hark you then, Gorgias, to what surprises me in your statements: to be sure, you may possibly be right, and I may take your meaning wrongly. You say you are able to make a rhetorician of any man who chooses to learn from you?

GORG. Yes.

SOC. Now, do you mean, to make him carry conviction to the crowd on all subjects, not by teaching them, but by persuading?

GORG. Certainly I do.

SOC. You were saying just now, you know, that even in the matter of health the orator will be more convincing than the doctor.

GORG. Yes, indeed, I was—meaning, to the crowd.

SOC. And "to the crowd" means "to the ignorant"? For surely, to those who know, he will not be more convincing than the doctor.

GORG. You are right.

SOC. And if he is to be more convincing than the doctor, he thus becomes more convincing than he who knows?

GORG. Certainly.

SOC. Though not himself a doctor, you agree?

GORG. Yes.

SOC. But he who is not a doctor is surely without knowledge of that whereof the doctor has knowledge.

GORG. Clearly

ΣΩ. Ὁ οὐκ εἰδὼς ἄρα τοῦ εἰδότος ἐν οὐκ εἰδόσι πιθανώτερος ἔσται, ὅταν ὁ ῥήτωρ τοῦ ἰατροῦ πιθανώτερος ᾖ. τοῦτο συμβαίνει ἢ ἄλλο τι;

ΓΟΡΓ. Τοῦτο ἐνταῦθά γε συμβαίνει.

ΣΩ. Οὐκοῦν καὶ περὶ τὰς ἄλλας ἁπάσας τέχνας ὡσαύτως ἔχει ὁ ῥήτωρ καὶ ἡ ῥητορική· αὐτὰ μὲν τὰ πράγματα οὐδὲν δεῖ αὐτὴν εἰδέναι ὅπως ἔχει, μηχανὴν δέ τινα πειθοῦς εὑρηκέναι, ὥστε φαίνεσθαι τοῖς οὐκ εἰδόσι μᾶλλον εἰδέναι τῶν εἰδότων.

ΓΟΡΓ. Οὐκοῦν πολλὴ ῥᾳστώνη, ὦ Σώκρατες, γίγνεται, μὴ μαθόντα τὰς ἄλλας τέχνας, ἀλλὰ μίαν ταύτην, μηδὲν ἐλαττοῦσθαι τῶν δημιουργῶν;

ΣΩ. Εἰ μὲν ἐλαττοῦται ἢ μὴ ἐλαττοῦται ὁ ῥήτωρ τῶν ἄλλων διὰ τὸ οὕτως ἔχειν, αὐτίκα ἐπισκεψόμεθα, ἐάν τι ἡμῖν πρὸς λόγου ᾖ· νῦν δὲ τόδε πρότερον σκεψώμεθα, ἆρα τυγχάνει περὶ τὸ δίκαιον καὶ τὸ ἄδικον καὶ τὸ αἰσχρὸν καὶ τὸ καλὸν καὶ ἀγαθὸν καὶ κακὸν οὕτως ἔχων ὁ ῥητορικὸς ὡς περὶ τὸ ὑγιεινὸν καὶ περὶ τὰ ἄλλα ὧν αἱ ἄλλαι τέχναι, αὐτὰ μὲν οὐκ εἰδώς, τί ἀγαθὸν ἢ τί κακόν ἐστιν ἢ τί καλὸν ἢ τί αἰσχρὸν ἢ δίκαιον ἢ ἄδικον, πειθὼ δὲ περὶ αὐτῶν μεμηχανημένος, ὥστε δοκεῖν εἰδέναι οὐκ εἰδὼς ἐν οὐκ εἰδόσι μᾶλλον τοῦ εἰδότος; ἢ ἀνάγκη εἰδέναι, καὶ δεῖ προεπιστάμενον ταῦτα ἀφικέσθαι παρὰ σὲ τὸν μέλλοντα μαθήσεσθαι τὴν ῥητορικήν; εἰ δὲ μή, σὺ ὁ τῆς ῥητορικῆς διδάσκαλος τούτων μὲν οὐδὲν διδάξεις τὸν ἀφικνούμενον—οὐ γὰρ σὸν ἔργον—ποιήσεις δ᾽ ἐν τοῖς πολλοῖς

GORGIAS

soc. So he who does not know will be more convincing to those who do not know than he who knows, supposing the orator to be more convincing than the doctor. Is that, or something else, the consequence?

gorg. In this case it does follow.

soc. Then the case is the same in all the other arts for the orator and his rhetoric: there is no need to know the truth of the actual matters, but one merely needs to have discovered some device of persuasion which will make one appear to those who do not know to know better than those who know.

gorg. Well, and is it not a great convenience, Socrates, to make oneself a match for the professionals by learning just this single art and omitting all the others?

soc. Whether the orator is or is not a match for the rest of them by reason of that skill, is a question we shall look into presently, if our argument so requires: for the moment let us consider first whether the rhetorician is in the same relation to what is just and unjust, base and noble, good and bad, as to what is healthful, and to the various objects of all the other arts; he does not know what is really good or bad, noble or base, just or unjust, but he has devised a persuasion to deal with these matters so as to appear to those who, like himself, do not know to know better than he who knows. Or is it necessary to know, and must anyone who intends to learn rhetoric have a previous knowledge of these things when he comes to you? Or if not, are you, as the teacher of rhetoric, to teach the person who comes to you nothing about them—for it is not your business—but only to

δοκεῖν εἰδέναι αὐτὸν τὰ τοιαῦτα οὐκ εἰδότα καὶ δοκεῖν ἀγαθὸν εἶναι οὐκ ὄντα; ἢ τὸ παράπαν οὐχ οἷός τε ἔσῃ διδάξαι αὐτὸν τὴν ῥητορικήν, ἐὰν μὴ προειδῇ περὶ τούτων τὴν ἀλήθειαν; ἢ πῶς τὰ τοιαῦτα ἔχει, ὦ Γοργία; καὶ πρὸς Διός, ὥσπερ ἄρτι εἶπες, ἀποκαλύψας τῆς ῥητορικῆς εἰπὲ τίς ποθ' ἡ δύναμίς ἐστιν.

ΓΟΡΓ. Ἀλλ' ἐγὼ μὲν οἶμαι, ὦ Σώκρατες, ἐὰν τύχῃ μὴ εἰδώς, καὶ ταῦτα παρ' ἐμοῦ μαθήσεται.

ΣΩ. Ἔχε δή· καλῶς γὰρ λέγεις. ἐάνπερ ῥητορικὸν σύ τινα ποιήσῃς, ἀνάγκη αὐτὸν εἰδέναι τὰ δίκαια καὶ τὰ ἄδικα ἤτοι πρότερόν γε ἢ ὕστερον μαθόντα παρὰ σοῦ.

ΓΟΡΓ. Πάνυ γε.

ΣΩ. Τί οὖν; ὁ τὰ τεκτονικὰ μεμαθηκὼς τεκτονικός, ἢ οὔ;

ΓΟΡΓ. Ναί.

ΣΩ. Οὐκοῦν καὶ ὁ τὰ μουσικὰ μουσικός;

ΓΟΡΓ. Ναί.

ΣΩ. Καὶ ὁ τὰ ἰατρικὰ ἰατρικός, καὶ τἆλλα οὕτω κατὰ τὸν αὐτὸν λόγον, ὁ μεμαθηκὼς ἕκαστα τοιοῦτός ἐστιν οἷον ἡ ἐπιστήμη ἕκαστον ἀπεργάζεται;

ΓΟΡΓ. Πάνυ γε.

ΣΩ. Οὐκοῦν κατὰ τοῦτον τὸν λόγον καὶ ὁ τὰ δίκαια μεμαθηκὼς δίκαιος;

ΓΟΡΓ. Πάντως δήπου.

ΣΩ. Ὁ δὲ δίκαιος δίκαιά που πράττει.

ΓΟΡΓ. Ναί.

ΣΩ. Οὐκοῦν ἀνάγκη τὸν [ῥητορικὸν δίκαιον εἶναι, τὸν δὲ][1] δίκαιον βούλεσθαι δίκαια πράττειν;

---

[1] ῥητορικὸν δίκαιον εἶναι, τὸν δὲ secl. Hirschig.

GORGIAS

make him appear in the eyes of the multitude to know things of this sort when he does not know, and to appear to be good when he is not? Or will you be utterly unable to teach him rhetoric unless he previously knows the truth about these matters? Or what is the real state of the case, Gorgias? For Heaven's sake, as you proposed just now, draw aside the veil and tell us what really is the function of rhetoric.

GORG. Why, I suppose, Socrates, if he happens not to know these things he will learn them too from me.

SOC. Stop there: I am glad of that statement. If you make a man a rhetorician he must needs know what is just and unjust either previously or by learning afterwards from you.

GORG. Quite so.

SOC. Well now, a man who has learnt building is a builder, is he not?

GORG. Yes.

SOC. And he who has learnt music, a musician?

GORG. Yes.

SOC. Then he who has learnt medicine is a medical man, and so on with the rest on the same principle; anyone who has learnt a certain art has the qualification acquired by his particular knowledge?

GORG. Certainly.

SOC. And so, on this principle, he who has learnt what is just is just?

GORG. Absolutely, I presume.

SOC. And the just man, I suppose, does what is just.

GORG. Yes.

SOC. Now the just man must *wish* to do what is just?

PLATO

ΓΟΡΓ. Φαίνεταί γε.

ΣΩ. Οὐδέποτε ἄρα βουλήσεται ὅ γε δίκαιος ἀδικεῖν.

ΓΟΡΓ. Ἀνάγκη.

ΣΩ. Τὸν δὲ ῥητορικὸν ἀνάγκη ἐκ τοῦ λόγου δίκαιον εἶναι.

ΓΟΡΓ. Ναί.

ΣΩ. Οὐδέποτε ἄρα βουλήσεται ὁ ῥητορικὸς ἀδικεῖν.

ΓΟΡΓ. Οὐ φαίνεταί γε.

ΣΩ. Μέμνησαι οὖν λέγων ὀλίγῳ πρότερον, ὅτι
D οὐ δεῖ τοῖς παιδοτρίβαις ἐγκαλεῖν οὐδ' ἐκβάλλειν ἐκ τῶν πόλεων, ἐὰν ὁ πύκτης τῇ πυκτικῇ χρῆταί τε καὶ ἀδικῇ; ὡσαύτως δὲ οὕτω καὶ ἐὰν ὁ ῥήτωρ τῇ ῥητορικῇ ἀδίκως χρῆται, μὴ τῷ διδάξαντι ἐγκαλεῖν μηδὲ ἐξελαύνειν ἐκ τῆς πόλεως, ἀλλὰ τῷ ἀδικοῦντι καὶ οὐκ ὀρθῶς χρωμένῳ τῇ ῥητορικῇ; ἐρρήθη ταῦτα ἢ οὔ;

ΓΟΡΓ. Ἐρρήθη.

E ΣΩ. Νῦν δέ γε ὁ αὐτὸς οὗτος φαίνεται, ὁ ῥητορικός, οὐκ ἄν ποτε ἀδικήσας. ἢ οὔ;

ΓΟΡΓ. Φαίνεται.

ΣΩ. Καὶ ἐν τοῖς πρώτοις γε, ὦ Γοργία, λόγοις ἐλέγετο, ὅτι ἡ ῥητορικὴ περὶ λόγους εἴη οὐ τοὺς τοῦ ἀρτίου καὶ περιττοῦ, ἀλλὰ τοὺς τοῦ δικαίου καὶ ἀδίκου· ἦ γάρ;

ΓΟΡΓ. Ναί.

ΣΩ. Ἐγὼ τοίνυν σου τότε ταῦτα λέγοντος ὑπέλαβον, ὡς οὐδέποτ' ἂν εἴη ἡ ῥητορικὴ ἄδικον πρᾶγμα, ὅ γ' ἀεὶ περὶ δικαιοσύνης τοὺς λόγους ποιεῖται· ἐπειδὴ δὲ ὀλίγον ὕστερον ἔλεγες, ὅτι ὁ

GORGIAS

GORG. Apparently.

SOC. Hence the just man will never wish to act unjustly?

GORG. That must needs be so.

SOC. But it follows from our statements [1] that the rhetorician must be just.

GORG. Yes.

SOC. Hence the rhetorician will never wish to do wrong.

GORG. Apparently not.

SOC. Then do you remember saying a little while ago that we ought not to complain against the trainers or expel them from our cities, if a boxer makes not merely use, but an unfair use, of his boxing? So in just the same way, if an orator uses his rhetoric unfairly, we should not complain against his teacher or banish him from our city, but the man who does the wrong and misuses his rhetoric. Was that said or not?

GORG. It was.

SOC. But now we find that this very person, the rhetorician, could never be guilty of wrongdoing, do we not?

GORG. We do.

SOC. And in our first statements, Gorgias, we said that rhetoric dealt with speech, not on even and odd, but on the just and unjust, did we not?

GORG. Yes.

SOC. Well then, I supposed at the time when you were saying this that rhetoric could never be an unjust thing, since the speeches it made were always about justice; but when a little later you

---

[1] *i.e.* that he must know what is just, and that he who knows this must be just (see §§ A and B above).

PLATO

461 ῥήτωρ τῇ ῥητορικῇ κἂν ἀδίκως χρῷτο, οὕτω θαυμάσας καὶ ἡγησάμενος οὐ συνᾴδειν τὰ λεγόμενα ἐκείνους εἶπον τοὺς λόγους, ὅτι εἰ μὲν κέρδος ἡγοῖο εἶναι τὸ ἐλέγχεσθαι ὥσπερ ἐγώ, ἄξιον εἴη διαλέγεσθαι, εἰ δὲ μή, ἐᾶν χαίρειν· ὕστερον δὲ ἡμῶν ἐπισκοπουμένων ὁρᾷς δὴ καὶ αὐτὸς ὅτι αὖ ὁμολογεῖται τὸν ῥητορικὸν ἀδύνατον εἶναι ἀδίκως χρῆσθαι τῇ ῥητορικῇ καὶ ἐθέλειν ἀδικεῖν. ταῦτα οὖν ὅπῃ

B ποτὲ ἔχει, μὰ τὸν κύνα, ὦ Γοργία, οὐκ ὀλίγης συνουσίας ἐστὶν ὥστε ἱκανῶς διασκέψασθαι.

ΠΩΛ. Τί δέ, ὦ Σώκρατες; οὕτω καὶ σὺ περὶ τῆς ῥητορικῆς δοξάζεις ὥσπερ νῦν λέγεις; ἢ οἴει, ὅτι Γοργίας ᾐσχύνθη σοι μὴ προσομολογῆσαι τὸν ῥητορικὸν ἄνδρα μὴ οὐχὶ καὶ τὰ δίκαια εἰδέναι καὶ τὰ καλὰ καὶ τὰ ἀγαθά, καὶ ἐὰν μὴ ἔλθῃ ταῦτα εἰδὼς παρ' αὐτόν, αὐτὸς διδάξειν, ἔπειτα ἐκ ταύτης

C ἴσως τῆς ὁμολογίας ἐναντίον τι συνέβη ἐν τοῖς λόγοις, τοῦθ' ὃ δὴ ἀγαπᾷς, αὐτὸς ἀγαγὼν ἐπὶ τοιαῦτα ἐρωτήματα—ἐπεὶ τίνα οἴει ἀπαρνήσεσθαι μὴ οὐχὶ καὶ αὐτὸν ἐπίστασθαι τὰ δίκαια καὶ ἄλλους διδάξειν; ἀλλ' εἰς τὰ τοιαῦτα ἄγειν πολλὴ ἀγροικία ἐστὶ τοὺς λόγους.

ΣΩ. Ὦ κάλλιστε Πῶλε, ἀλλά τοι ἐξεπίτηδες κτώμεθα ἑταίρους καὶ ὑιεῖς, ἵνα ἐπειδὰν αὐτοὶ πρεσβύτεροι γιγνόμενοι σφαλλώμεθα, παρόντες ὑμεῖς οἱ νεώτεροι ἐπανορθῶτε ἡμῶν τὸν βίον κα

---

[1] This favourite oath of Socrates was derived from Egypt where the god Anubis was represented with a dog's head cf. 482 B.

[2] The defective construction of this sentence is probably

GORGIAS

told us that the orator might make even an unjust use of his rhetoric, that indeed surprised me, and thinking the two statements were not in accord I made those proposals,—that if, like myself, you counted it a gain to be refuted, it was worth while to have the discussion, but if not, we had better have done with it. And now that we have come to examine the matter, you see for yourself that we agree once more that it is impossible for the rhetorician to use his rhetoric unjustly or consent to do wrong Now, to distinguish properly which way the truth of the matter lies will require, by the Dog,[1] Gorgias, no short sitting.

POL. How is this, Socrates? Is that really your opinion of rhetoric, as you now express it? Or, think you, because Gorgias was ashamed not to admit your point that the rhetorician knows what is just and noble and good, and will himself teach these to anyone who comes to him without knowing them; and then from this admission I daresay there followed some inconsistency in the statements made —the result that you are so fond of—when it was yourself who led him into that set of questions![2] For who do you think will deny that he has a knowledge of what is just and can also teach it to others? I call it very bad taste to lead the discussion in such a direction.

SOC. Ah, sweet Polus, of course it is for this very purpose we possess ourselves of companions and sons, that when the advance of years begins to make us stumble, you younger ones may be at hand to set our lives upright again in words as well

intended to mark the agitated manner of Polus in making his protest.

307

ἐν ἔργοις καὶ ἐν λόγοις. καὶ νῦν εἴ τι ἐγὼ καὶ Γοργίας ἐν τοῖς λόγοις σφαλλόμεθα, σὺ παρὼν ἐπανόρθου· δίκαιος δ' εἶ· καὶ ἐγὼ ἐθέλω τῶν ὡμολογημένων εἴ τί σοι δοκεῖ μὴ καλῶς ὡμολογῆσθαι, ἀναθέσθαι ὅ τι ἂν σὺ βούλῃ, ἐάν μοι ἓν μόνον φυλάττῃς.

ΠΩΛ. Τί τοῦτο λέγεις;

ΣΩ. Τὴν μακρολογίαν, ὦ Πῶλε, ἣν καθέρξῃς, ᾗ τὸ πρῶτον ἐπεχείρησας χρῆσθαι.

ΠΩΛ. Τί δέ; οὐκ ἐξέσται μοι λέγειν ὁπόσα ἂν βούλωμαι;

ΣΩ. Δεινὰ μέντ' ἂν πάθοις, ὦ βέλτιστε, εἰ Ἀθήναζε ἀφικόμενος, οὗ τῆς Ἑλλάδος πλείστη ἐστὶν ἐξουσία τοῦ λέγειν, ἔπειτα σὺ ἐνταῦθα τούτου μόνος ἀτυχήσαις. ἀλλὰ ἀντίθες τοι· σοῦ μακρὰ λέγοντος καὶ μὴ ἐθέλοντος τὸ ἐρωτώμενον ἀποκρίνεσθαι, οὐ δεινὰ ἂν αὖ ἐγὼ πάθοιμι, εἰ μὴ ἐξέσται μοι ἀπιέναι καὶ μὴ ἀκούειν σου; ἀλλ' εἴ τι κήδῃ τοῦ λόγου τοῦ εἰρημένου καὶ ἐπανορθώσασθαι αὐτὸν βούλει, ὥσπερ νῦν δὴ ἔλεγον, ἀναθέμενος ὅ τι σοι δοκεῖ, ἐν τῷ μέρει ἐρωτῶν τε καὶ ἐρωτώμενος, ὥσπερ ἐγώ τε καὶ Γοργίας, ἔλεγχέ τε καὶ ἐλέγχου. φῂς γὰρ δήπου καὶ σὺ ἐπίστασθαι ἅπερ Γοργίας· ἢ οὔ;

ΠΩΛ. Ἔγωγε.

ΣΩ. Οὐκοῦν καὶ σὺ κελεύεις σαυτὸν ἐρωτᾶν ἑκάστοτε ὅ τι ἄν τις βούληται, ὡς ἐπιστάμενος ἀποκρίνεσθαι;

ΠΩΛ. Πάνυ μὲν οὖν.

ΣΩ. Καὶ νῦν δὴ τούτων ὁπότερον βούλει ποίει, ἐρώτα ἢ ἀποκρίνου.

GORGIAS

as deeds. So now if Gorgias and I are stumbling in our words, you are to stand by and set us up again—it is only your duty; and for my part I am willing to revoke at your pleasure anything that you think has been wrongly admitted, if you will kindly observe one condition.

POL. What do you mean by that?

SOC. That you keep a check on that lengthy way of speaking, Polus, which you tried to employ at first.

POL. Why, shall I not be at liberty to say as much as I like?

SOC. It would indeed be a hard fate for you, my excellent friend, if having come to Athens, where there is more freedom of speech than anywhere in Greece, you should be the one person there who could not enjoy it. But as a set-off to that, I ask you if it would not be just as hard on me, while you spoke at length and refused to answer my questions, not to be free to go away and avoid listening to you. No, if you have any concern for the argument that we have carried on, and care to set it on its feet again, revoke whatever you please, as I suggested just now; take your turn in questioning and being questioned, like me and Gorgias; and thus either refute or be refuted. For you claim, I understand, that you yourself know all that Gorgias knows, do you not?

POL. I do.

SOC. Then are you with him also in bidding us ask at each point any questions we like of you, as one who knows how to answer?

POL. Certainly I am.

SOC. So now, take whichever course you like: either put questions, or answer them.

PLATO

ΠΩΛ. Ἀλλὰ ποιήσω ταῦτα. καί μοι ἀπόκριναι, ὦ Σώκρατες· ἐπειδὴ Γοργίας ἀπορεῖν σοι δοκεῖ περὶ τῆς ῥητορικῆς, σὺ αὐτὴν τίνα φῂς εἶναι;

ΣΩ. Ἆρα ἐρωτᾷς ἥντινα τέχνην φημὶ εἶναι;

ΠΩΛ. Ἔγωγε.

ΣΩ. Οὐδεμία ἔμοιγε δοκεῖ, ὦ Πῶλε, ὥς γε πρὸς σὲ τἀληθῆ εἰρῆσθαι.

ΠΩΛ. Ἀλλὰ τί σοι δοκεῖ ἡ ῥητορικὴ εἶναι;

C ΣΩ. Πρᾶγμα ὃ φῂς σὺ ποιῆσαι τέχνην ἐν τῷ συγγράμματι ὃ ἐγὼ ἔναγχος ἀνέγνων.

ΠΩΛ. Τί τοῦτο λέγεις;

ΣΩ. Ἐμπειρίαν ἔγωγέ τινα.

ΠΩΛ. Ἐμπειρία ἄρα σοι δοκεῖ ἡ ῥητορικὴ εἶναι;

ΣΩ. Ἔμοιγε, εἰ μή τι σὺ ἄλλο λέγεις.

ΠΩΛ. Τίνος ἐμπειρία;

ΣΩ. Χάριτός τινος καὶ ἡδονῆς ἀπεργασίας.

ΠΩΛ. Οὐκοῦν καλόν σοι δοκεῖ ἡ ῥητορικὴ εἶναι, χαρίζεσθαι οἷόν τ' εἶναι ἀνθρώποις;

ΣΩ. Τί δέ, ὦ Πῶλε; ἤδη πέπυσαι παρ' ἐμοῦ,
D ὅ τι φημὶ αὐτὴν εἶναι, ὥστε τὸ μετὰ τοῦτο ἐρωτᾷς, εἰ οὐ καλή μοι δοκεῖ εἶναι;

ΠΩΛ. Οὐ γὰρ πέπυσμαι ὅτι ἐμπειρίαν τινὰ αὐτὴν φῂς εἶναι;

ΣΩ. Βούλει οὖν, ἐπειδὴ τιμᾷς τὸ χαρίζεσθαι, σμικρόν τί μοι χαρίσασθαι;

ΠΩΛ. Ἔγωγε.

ΣΩ. Ἐροῦ νῦν με, ὀψοποιία ἥτις μοι δοκεῖ τέχνη εἶναι.

ΠΩΛ. Ἐρωτῶ δή, τίς τέχνη ὀψοποιία;

ΣΩ. Οὐδεμία, ὦ Πῶλε.

ΠΩΛ. Ἀλλὰ τί; φάθι.

ΣΩ. Φημὶ δή, ἐμπειρία τις.

GORGIAS

POL. Well, I will do as you say. So answer me this, Socrates: since you think that Gorgias is at a loss about rhetoric, what is your own account of it?

SOC. Are you asking what art I call it?

POL. Yes.

SOC. None at all, I consider, Polus, if you would have the honest truth.

POL. But what do you consider rhetoric to be?

SOC. A thing which you say—in the treatise which I read of late—" made art."

POL. What thing do you mean?

SOC. I mean a certain habitude.

POL. Then do you take rhetoric to be a habitude?

SOC. I do, if you have no other suggestion.

POL. Habitude of what?

SOC. Of producing a kind of gratification and pleasure.

POL. Then you take rhetoric to be something fine—an ability to gratify people?

SOC. How now, Polus? Have you as yet heard me tell you what I say it is, that you ask what should follow that—whether I do not take it to be fine?

POL. Why, did I not hear you call it a certain habitude?

SOC. Then please—since you value "gratification"—be so good as gratify me in a small matter.

POL. I will.

SOC. Ask me now what art I take cookery to be.

POL. Then I ask you, what art is cookery?

SOC. None at all, Polus.

POL. Well, what is it? Tell me.

SOC. Then I reply, a certain habitude.

311

πωλ. Τίνος; φάθι.

σω. Φημὶ δή, χάριτος καὶ ἡδονῆς ἀπεργασίας, ὦ Πῶλε.

πωλ. Ταὐτὸν ἄρ' ἐστὶν ὀψοποιία καὶ ῥητορική;

σω. Οὐδαμῶς γε, ἀλλὰ τῆς αὐτῆς μὲν ἐπιτηδεύσεως μόριον.

πωλ. Τίνος λέγεις ταύτης;

σω. Μὴ ἀγροικότερον ᾖ τὸ ἀληθὲς εἰπεῖν· ὀκνῶ γὰρ Γοργίου ἕνεκα λέγειν, μὴ οἴηταί με διακωμῳδεῖν τὸ ἑαυτοῦ ἐπιτήδευμα· ἐγὼ δέ, εἰ μὲν τοῦτό ἐστιν ἡ ῥητορικὴ ἣν Γοργίας ἐπιτηδεύει, οὐκ οἶδα· καὶ γὰρ ἄρτι ἐκ τοῦ λόγου οὐδὲν ἡμῖν καταφανὲς ἐγένετο, τί ποτε οὗτος ἡγεῖται· ὃ δ' ἐγὼ καλῶ τὴν ῥητορικήν, πράγματός τινός ἐστι μόριον οὐδενὸς τῶν καλῶν.

γοργ. Τίνος, ὦ Σώκρατες; εἰπέ, μηδὲν ἐμὲ αἰσχυνθείς.

σω. Δοκεῖ τοίνυν μοι, ὦ Γοργία, εἶναί τι ἐπιτήδευμα τεχνικὸν μὲν οὔ, ψυχῆς δὲ στοχαστικῆς καὶ ἀνδρείας καὶ φύσει δεινῆς προσομιλεῖν τοῖς ἀνθρώποις· καλῶ δὲ αὐτοῦ ἐγὼ τὸ κεφάλαιον κολακείαν. ταύτης μοι δοκεῖ τῆς ἐπιτηδεύσεως πολλὰ μὲν καὶ ἄλλα μόρια εἶναι, ἓν δὲ καὶ ἡ ὀψοποιική· ὃ δοκεῖ μὲν εἶναι τέχνη, ὡς δὲ ὁ ἐμὸς λόγος, οὐκ ἔστι τέχνη, ἀλλ' ἐμπειρία καὶ τριβή. ταύτης μόριον καὶ τὴν ῥητορικὴν ἐγὼ καλῶ καὶ τήν γε κομμωτικὴν καὶ τὴν σοφιστικήν, τέτταρα ταῦτα μόρια ἐπὶ τέτταρσι πράγμασιν. εἰ οὖν βούλεται Πῶλος πυνθάνεσθαι, πυνθανέσθω· οὐ γάρ πω πέπυσται, ὁποῖόν φημι ἐγὼ τῆς κολακείας μόριον εἶναι τὴν ῥητορικήν, ἀλλ' αὐτὸν λέληθα οὔπω ἀποκεκριμένος, ὁ δὲ ἐπανερωτᾷ,

GORGIAS

POL. Of what? Tell me.

SOC. Then I reply, of production of gratification and pleasure, Polus.

POL. So cookery and rhetoric are the same thing?

SOC. Not at all, only parts of the same practice.

POL. What practice do you mean?

SOC. I fear it may be too rude to tell the truth; for I shrink from saying it on Gorgias' account, lest he suppose I am making satirical fun of his own pursuit. Yet indeed I do not know whether this is the rhetoric which Gorgias practises, for from our argument just now we got no very clear view as to how he conceives it; but what I call rhetoric is a part of a certain business which has nothing fine about it.

GORG. What is that, Socrates? Tell us, without scruple on my account.

SOC. It seems to me then, Gorgias, to be a pursuit that is not a matter of art, but showing a shrewd, gallant spirit which has a natural bent for clever dealing with mankind, and I sum up its substance in the name *flattery*. This practice, as I view it, has many branches, and one of them is cookery; which appears indeed to be an art but, by my account of it, is not an art but a habitude or knack. I call rhetoric another branch of it, as also personal adornment and sophistry—four branches of it for four kinds of affairs. So if Polus would inquire, let him inquire: he has not yet been informed to what sort of branch of flattery I assign rhetoric; but without noticing that I have not yet answered that, he proceeds to ask whether I do not consider it a

PLATO

εἰ οὐ καλὸν ἡγοῦμαι εἶναι. ἐγὼ δὲ αὐτῷ οὐκ ἀποκρινοῦμαι πρότερον, εἴτε καλὸν εἴτε αἰσχρὸν ἡγοῦμαι εἶναι τὴν ῥητορικήν, πρὶν ἂν πρῶτον ἀποκρίνωμαι ὅ τι ἐστίν, οὐ γὰρ δίκαιον, ὦ Πῶλε· ἀλλ' εἴπερ βούλει πυθέσθαι, ἐρώτα, ὁποῖον μόριον τῆς κολακείας φημὶ εἶναι τὴν ῥητορικήν.

ΠΩΛ. Ἐρωτῶ δή, καὶ ἀπόκριναι, ὁποῖον μόριον.

ΣΩ. Ἆρ' οὖν ἂν μάθοις ἀποκριναμένου; ἔστι D γὰρ ἡ ῥητορικὴ κατὰ τὸν ἐμὸν λόγον πολιτικῆς μορίου εἴδωλον.

ΠΩΛ. Τί οὖν; καλὸν ἢ αἰσχρὸν λέγεις αὐτὴν εἶναι;

ΣΩ. Αἰσχρὸν ἔγωγε· τὰ γὰρ κακὰ αἰσχρὰ καλῶ· ἐπειδὴ δεῖ σοι ἀποκρίνασθαι ὡς ἤδη εἰδότι ἃ ἐγὼ λέγω.

ΓΟΡΓ. Μὰ τὸν Δία, ὦ Σώκρατες, ἀλλ' ἐγὼ οὐδὲ E αὐτὸς συνίημι ὅ τι λέγεις.

ΣΩ. Εἰκότως γε, ὦ Γοργία· οὐδὲν γάρ πω σαφὲς λέγω, Πῶλος δὲ ὅδε νέος ἐστὶ καὶ ὀξύς.

ΓΟΡΓ. Ἀλλὰ τοῦτον μὲν ἔα, ἐμοὶ δ' εἰπέ, πῶς λέγεις πολιτικῆς μορίου εἴδωλον εἶναι τὴν ῥητορικήν.

ΣΩ. Ἀλλ' ἐγὼ πειράσομαι φράσαι, ὅ γέ μοι φαίνεται εἶναι ἡ ῥητορική· εἰ δὲ μὴ τυγχάνει ὂν τοῦτο, Πῶλος ὅδε ἐλέγξει. σῶμά που καλεῖς τι καὶ ψυχήν;

ΓΟΡΓ. Πῶς γὰρ οὔ;

ΣΩ. Οὐκοῦν καὶ τούτων οἴει τινὰ εἶναι ἑκατέρου εὐεξίαν;

ΓΟΡΓ. Ἔγωγε.

GORGIAS

fine thing. But I am not going to reply to the question whether I consider rhetoric a fine or a base thing, until I have first answered what it is; for it would not be fair, Polus: but if you want the information, ask me what sort of branch of flattery I assert rhetoric to be.

POL. I ask you then; so answer, what sort of branch it is.

SOC. Now, will you understand when I answer? Rhetoric, by my account, is a semblance[1] of a branch of politics.

POL. Well then, do you call it a fine or a base thing?

SOC. A base one, I call it—for all that is bad I call base—since I am to answer you as one who already understands my meaning.

GORG. But I myself, upon my word, Socrates, do not grasp your meaning either.

SOC. And no wonder, Gorgias, for as yet my statement is not at all clear; but Polus[2] here is so young and fresh!

GORG. Ah, do not mind him; but tell me what you mean by rhetoric being a semblance of a branch of politics.

SOC. Well, I will try to express what rhetoric appears to me to be: if it is not in fact what I say, Polus here will refute me. There are things, I suppose, that you call body and soul?

GORG. Of course.

SOC. And each of these again you believe to have a good condition?

GORG. I do.

---

[1] *i.e.* an unreal image or counterfeit: Quintilian (ii. 15. 25) renders *simulacrum*.

[2] Socrates alludes to the meaning of πῶλος (a colt).

PLATO

ΣΩ. Τί δέ; δοκοῦσαν μὲν εὐεξίαν, οὖσαν δ' οὔ; οἷον τοιόνδε λέγω· πολλοὶ δοκοῦσιν εὖ ἔχειν τὰ σώματα, οὓς οὐκ ἂν ῥᾳδίως αἴσθοιτό τις, ὅτι οὐκ εὖ ἔχουσιν, ἀλλ' ἢ ἰατρός τε καὶ τῶν γυμναστικῶν τις.

ΓΟΡΓ. Ἀληθῆ λέγεις.

ΣΩ. Τὸ τοιοῦτον λέγω καὶ ἐν σώματι εἶναι καὶ ἐν ψυχῇ, ὃ ποιεῖ μὲν δοκεῖν εὖ ἔχειν τὸ σῶμα καὶ τὴν ψυχήν, ἔχει δὲ οὐδὲν μᾶλλον.

ΓΟΡΓ. Ἔστι ταῦτα.

ΣΩ. Φέρε δή σοι, ἐὰν δύνωμαι, σαφέστερον ἐπιδείξω ὃ λέγω. δυοῖν ὄντοιν τοῖν πραγμάτοιν δύο λέγω τέχνας· τὴν μὲν ἐπὶ τῇ ψυχῇ πολιτικὴν καλῶ, τὴν δὲ ἐπὶ σώματι μίαν μὲν οὕτως ὀνομάσαι οὐκ ἔχω σοι, μιᾶς δὲ οὔσης τῆς τοῦ σώματος θεραπείας δύο μόρια λέγω, τὴν μὲν γυμναστικήν, τὴν δὲ ἰατρικήν· τῆς δὲ πολιτικῆς ἀντὶ μὲν τῆς γυμναστικῆς τὴν νομοθετικήν, ἀντίστροφον δὲ τῇ ἰατρικῇ τὴν δικαιοσύνην. ἐπικοινωνοῦσι μὲν δὴ ἀλλήλαις, ἅτε περὶ τὸ αὐτὸ οὖσαι, ἑκάτεραι τούτων, ἥ τε ἰατρικὴ τῇ γυμναστικῇ καὶ ἡ δικαιοσύνη τῇ νομοθετικῇ· ὅμως δὲ διαφέρουσί τι ἀλλήλων. τεττάρων δὴ τούτων οὐσῶν, καὶ ἀεὶ πρὸς τὸ βέλτιστον θεραπευουσῶν τῶν μὲν τὸ σῶμα, τῶν δὲ τὴν ψυχήν, ἡ κολακευτικὴ αἰσθομένη, οὐ γνοῦσα λέγω ἀλλὰ στοχασαμένη, τέτραχα ἑαυτὴν διανείμασα, ὑποδῦσα ὑπὸ ἕκαστον τῶν μορίων, προσποιεῖται εἶναι τοῦτο ὅπερ ὑπέδυ, καὶ τοῦ μὲν βελτίστου οὐδὲν φροντίζει, τῷ δὲ

GORGIAS

soc. And again, a good condition that may seem so, but is not? As an example, let me give the following: many people seem to be in good bodily condition when it would not be easy for anyone but a doctor, or one of the athletic trainers, to perceive that they are not so.

gorg. You are right.

soc. Something of this sort I say there is in body and in soul, which makes the body or the soul seem to be in good condition, though it is none the more so in fact.

gorg. Quite so.

soc. Now let me see if I can explain my meaning to you more clearly. There are two different affairs to which I assign two different arts: the one, which has to do with the soul, I call politics; the other, which concerns the body, though I cannot give you a single name for it offhand, is all one business, the tendance of the body, which I can designate in two branches as gymnastic and medicine. Under politics I set legislation in the place of gymnastic, and justice to match medicine. In each of these pairs, of course—medicine and gymnastic, justice and legislation—there is some intercommunication, as both deal with the same thing; at the same time they have certain differences. Now these four, which always bestow their care for the best advantage respectively of the body and the soul, are noticed by the art of flattery which, I do not say with knowledge, but by speculation, divides herself into four parts, and then, insinuating herself into each of those branches, pretends to be that into which she has crept, and cares nothing for what is the best, but dangles what is most pleasant for the

PLATO

ἀεὶ ἡδίστῳ θηρεύεται τὴν ἄνοιαν καὶ ἐξαπατᾷ, ὥστε δοκεῖ πλείστου ἀξία εἶναι. ὑπὸ μὲν οὖν τὴν ἰατρικὴν ἡ ὀψοποιικὴ ὑποδέδυκε, καὶ προσποιεῖται τὰ βέλτιστα σιτία τῷ σώματι εἰδέναι, ὥστ' εἰ δέοι ἐν παισὶ διαγωνίζεσθαι ὀψοποιόν τε καὶ ἰατρὸν ἢ ἐν ἀνδράσιν οὕτως ἀνοήτοις ὥσπερ οἱ παῖδες, πότερος ἐπαΐει περὶ τῶν χρηστῶν σιτίων καὶ πονηρῶν, ὁ ἰατρὸς ἢ ὁ ὀψοποιός, λιμῷ ἂν ἀποθανεῖν τὸν ἰατρόν. κολακείαν μὲν οὖν αὐτὸ καλῶ, καὶ αἰσχρόν φημι εἶναι τὸ τοιοῦτον, ὦ Πῶλε— τοῦτο γὰρ πρὸς σὲ λέγω—ὅτι τοῦ ἡδέος στοχάζεται ἄνευ τοῦ βελτίστου· τέχνην δὲ αὐτὴν οὔ φημι εἶναι ἀλλ' ἐμπειρίαν, ὅτι οὐκ ἔχει λόγον οὐδένα ὧν προσφέρει,[1] ὁποῖ' ἄττα τὴν φύσιν ἐστίν, ὥστε τὴν αἰτίαν ἑκάστου μὴ ἔχειν εἰπεῖν. ἐγὼ δὲ τέχνην οὐ καλῶ, ὃ ἂν ᾖ ἄλογον πρᾶγμα· τούτων δὲ πέρι εἰ ἀμφισβητεῖς, ἐθέλω ὑποσχεῖν λόγον. τῇ μὲν οὖν ἰατρικῇ, ὥσπερ λέγω, ἡ ὀψοποιικὴ κολακεία ὑπόκειται· τῇ δὲ γυμναστικῇ κατὰ τὸν αὐτὸν τρόπον τοῦτον ἡ κομμωτική, κακοῦργός τε οὖσα καὶ ἀπατηλὴ καὶ ἀγεννὴς καὶ ἀνελεύθερος, σχήμασι καὶ χρώμασι καὶ λειότητι καὶ ἐσθῆσει[2] ἀπατῶσα, ὥστε ποιεῖν ἀλλότριον κάλλος ἐφελκομένους τοῦ οἰκείου τοῦ διὰ τῆς γυμναστικῆς ἀμελεῖν. ἵν' οὖν μὴ μακρολογῶ, ἐθέλω σοι εἰπεῖν ὥσπερ οἱ γεωμέτραι—ἤδη γὰρ ἂν ἴσως ἀκολουθήσαις—[ὅτι ὃ κομμωτικὴ πρὸς γυμναστικήν, τοῦτο ὀψοποιικὴ πρὸς ἰατρικήν· μᾶλλον δὲ ὧδε],[3] ὅτι ὃ κομμωτικὴ πρὸς γυμναστικήν, τοῦτο σοφιστικὴ πρὸς νομοθετικήν, καὶ ὅτι ὃ ὀψοποιικὴ

[1] ὧν προσφέρει Cornarius: ᾧ προσφέρει ἃ προσφέρει MSS.
[2] ἐσθῆσει Coraes: αἰσθήσει, ἐσθῆσι MSS.

GORGIAS

moment as a bait for folly, and deceives it into thinking that she is of the highest value. Thus cookery assumes the form of medicine, and pretends to know what foods are best for the body; so that if a cook and a doctor had to contend before boys, or before men as foolish as boys, as to which of the two, the doctor or the cook, understands the question of sound and noxious foods, the doctor would starve to death. Flattery, however, is what I call it, and I say that this sort of thing is a disgrace, Polus—for here I address you—because it aims at the pleasant and ignores the best; and I say it is not an art, but a habitude, since it has no account to give of the real nature of the things it applies, and so cannot tell the cause of any of them. I refuse to give the name of art to anything that is irrational: if you dispute my views, I am ready to give my reasons. However, as I put it, cookery is flattery disguised as medicine; and in just the same manner self-adornment personates gymnastic: with its rascally, deceitful, ignoble, and illiberal nature it deceives men by forms and colours, polish and dress, so as to make them, in the effort of assuming an extraneous beauty, neglect the native sort that comes through gymnastic. Well, to avoid prolixity, I am willing to put it to you like a geometer [1]—for by this time I expect you can follow me: as self-adornment is to gymnastic, so is sophistry to legislation; and as

[1] *i.e.* in the concise mathematical manner, such as that which later appeared in the writings of Euclid.

---

[2] ὅτι . . . ὧδε secl. Thompson.

PLATO

πρὸς ἰατρικήν, τοῦτο ῥητορικὴ πρὸς δικαιοσύνην. ὅπερ μέντοι λέγω, διέστηκε μὲν οὕτω φύσει· ἅτε δ' ἐγγὺς ὄντων φύρονται ἐν τῷ αὐτῷ καὶ περὶ ταὐτὰ σοφισταὶ καὶ ῥήτορες, καὶ οὐκ ἔχουσιν ὅ τι χρήσονται οὔτε αὐτοὶ ἑαυτοῖς οὔτε οἱ ἄλλοι ἄνθρωποι τούτοις. καὶ γὰρ ἄν, εἰ μὴ ἡ ψυχὴ τῷ σώματι ἐπεστάτει, ἀλλ' αὐτὸ αὑτῷ, καὶ μὴ ὑπὸ ταύτης D κατεθεωρεῖτο καὶ διεκρίνετο ἥ τε ὀψοποιικὴ καὶ ἡ ἰατρική, ἀλλ' αὐτὸ τὸ σῶμα ἔκρινε σταθμώμενον ταῖς χάρισι ταῖς πρὸς αὐτό, τὸ τοῦ Ἀναξαγόρου ἂν πολὺ ἦν, ὦ φίλε Πῶλε—σὺ γὰρ τούτων ἔμπειρος—ὁμοῦ ἂν πάντα χρήματα ἐφύρετο ἐν τῷ αὐτῷ, ἀκρίτων ὄντων τῶν τε ἰατρικῶν καὶ ὑγιεινῶν καὶ ὀψοποιικῶν. ὃ μὲν οὖν ἐγώ φημι τὴν ῥητορικὴν εἶναι, ἀκήκοας· ἀντίστροφον ὀψοποιίας ἐν ψυχῇ, ὡς ἐκεῖνο ἐν σώματι. ἴσως μὲν οὖν ἄτοπον E πεποίηκα, ὅτι σε οὐκ ἐῶν μακροὺς λόγους λέγειν αὐτὸς συχνὸν λόγον ἀποτέτακα. ἄξιον μὲν οὖν ἐμοὶ συγγνώμην ἔχειν ἐστίν· λέγοντος γάρ μου βραχέα οὐκ ἐμάνθανες, οὐδὲ χρῆσθαι τῇ ἀποκρίσει, ἥν σοι ἀπεκρινάμην, οὐδὲν οἷός τ' ἦσθα, ἀλλ' ἐδέου διηγήσεως. ἐὰν μὲν οὖν καὶ ἐγώ σου ἀποκρινομένου μὴ ἔχω ὅ τι χρήσωμαι, ἀπότεινε 466 καὶ σὺ λόγον, ἐὰν δὲ ἔχω, ἔα με χρῆσθαι· δίκαιον γάρ. καὶ νῦν ταύτῃ τῇ ἀποκρίσει εἴ τι ἔχεις χρῆσθαι, χρῶ.

ΠΩΛ. Τί οὖν φῄς; κολακεία δοκεῖ σοι εἶναι ἡ ῥητορική;

---

[1] Administrative justice is here specially meant.
[2] *i.e.* sophistry and rhetoric.

GORGIAS

cookery is to medicine, so is rhetoric to justice.[1] But although, as I say, there is this natural distinction between them,[2] they are so nearly related that sophists and orators are jumbled up as having the same field and dealing with the same subjects, and neither can they tell what to make of each other, nor the world at large what to make of them. For indeed, if the soul were not in command of the body, but the latter had charge of itself, and so cookery and medicine were not surveyed and distinguished by the soul, but the body itself were the judge, forming its own estimate of them by the gratifications they gave it, we should have a fine instance of what Anaxagoras described, my dear Polus,— for you are versed in these matters: everything would be jumbled together, without distinction as between medicinal and healthful and tasty concoctions. Well now, you have heard what I state rhetoric to be—the counterpart of cookery in the soul, acting here as that does on the body. It may, indeed, be absurd of me, when I do not allow you to make long speeches, to have extended mine to so considerable a length. However, I can fairly claim indulgence: for when I spoke briefly you did not understand me; you were unable to make any use of the answer I gave you, but required a full exposition. Now if I on my part cannot tell what use to make of any answers you may give me, you shall extend your speech also; but if I can make some use of them, allow me to do it; that will only be fair. And now, if you can make any use of this answer of mine, do so.

POL. Then what is it you say? Do you take rhetoric to be flattery?

PLATO

ΣΩ. Κολακείας μὲν οὖν ἔγωγε εἶπον μόριον. ἀλλ' οὐ μνημονεύεις τηλικοῦτος ὤν, ὦ Πῶλε; τί τάχα δράσεις;

ΠΩΛ. ῏Αρ' οὖν δοκοῦσί σοι ὡς κόλακες ἐν ταῖς πόλεσι φαῦλοι νομίζεσθαι οἱ ἀγαθοὶ ῥήτορες;

ΣΩ. Ἐρώτημα τοῦτ' ἐρωτᾷς ἢ λόγου τινὸς ἀρχὴν λέγεις;

ΠΩΛ. Ἐρωτῶ ἔγωγε.

ΣΩ. Οὐδὲ νομίζεσθαι ἔμοιγε δοκοῦσιν.

ΠΩΛ. Πῶς οὐ νομίζεσθαι; οὐ μέγιστον δύνανται ἐν ταῖς πόλεσιν;

ΣΩ. Οὔκ, εἰ τὸ δύνασθαί γε λέγεις ἀγαθόν τι εἶναι τῷ δυναμένῳ.

ΠΩΛ. Ἀλλὰ μὴν[1] λέγω γε.

ΣΩ. Ἐλάχιστον τοίνυν μοι δοκοῦσι τῶν ἐν τῇ πόλει δύνασθαι οἱ ῥήτορες.

ΠΩΛ. Τί δέ; οὐχ, ὥσπερ οἱ τύραννοι, ἀποκτιννύασί τε ὃν ἂν βούλωνται, καὶ ἀφαιροῦνται χρήματα καὶ ἐκβάλλουσιν ἐκ τῶν πόλεων ὃν ἂν δοκῇ αὐτοῖς;

ΣΩ. Νὴ τὸν κύνα, ἀμφιγνοῶ μέντοι, ὦ Πῶλε, ἐφ' ἑκάστου ὧν λέγεις, πότερον αὐτὸς ταῦτα λέγεις καὶ γνώμην σαυτοῦ ἀποφαίνει, ἢ ἐμὲ ἐρωτᾷς.

ΠΩΛ. Ἀλλ' ἔγωγε σὲ ἐρωτῶ.

ΣΩ. Εἶεν, ὦ φίλε· ἔπειτα δύο ἅμα με ἐρωτᾷς,

ΠΩΛ. Πῶς δύο;

ΣΩ. Οὐκ ἄρτι οὕτω πως ἔλεγες, εἰ οὐχὶ ἀποκτιννύασιν οἱ ῥήτορες οὓς ἂν βούλωνται, ὥσπερ οἱ τύραννοι, καὶ χρήματα ἀφαιροῦνται καὶ ἐξελαύνουσιν ἐκ τῶν πόλεων ὃν ἂν δοκῇ αὐτοῖς;

[1] μὴν Burnet: μὴν δὴ MSS.

GORGIAS

soc. Well, I said rather a branch of flattery. Why, at your age, Polus, have you no memory? What will you do later on?

pol. Then do you think that good orators are considered to be flatterers in their cities, and so worthless?

soc. Is that a question you are asking, or are you beginning a speech?

pol. I am asking a question.

soc. To my mind, they are not considered at all.

pol. How not considered? Have they not the chief power in their cities?

soc. No, if you mean power in the sense of something good for him who has it.

pol. Why, of course I mean that.

soc. Then, to my thinking, the orators have the smallest power of all who are in their city.

pol. What? Are they not like the despots, in putting to death anyone they please, and depriving anyone of his property and expelling him from their cities as they may think fit?

soc. By the Dog, I fear I am still in two minds, Polus, at everything you say, as to whether this is a statement on your own part, and a declaration of your own opinion, or a question you are putting to me.

pol. Why, I am asking you.

soc. Very well, my friend: then are you asking me two things at once?

pol. How two?

soc. Were you not this moment saying something like this: Is it not the case that the orators put to death anyone they wish, like the despots, and deprive people of property and expel them from their cities as they may think fit?

PLATO

ΠΩΛ. Ἔγωγε.

ΣΩ. Λέγω τοίνυν σοι, ὅτι δύο ταῦτ' ἐστὶ τὰ ἐρωτήματα, καὶ ἀποκρινοῦμαί γέ σοι πρὸς ἀμφότερα. φημὶ γάρ, ὦ Πῶλε, ἐγὼ καὶ τοὺς ῥήτορας καὶ τοὺς τυράννους δύνασθαι μὲν ἐν ταῖς πόλεσι σμικρότατον, ὥσπερ νῦν δὴ ἔλεγον· οὐδὲν γὰρ ποιεῖν ὧν βούλονται, ὡς ἔπος εἰπεῖν· ποιεῖν μέντοι ὅ τι ἂν αὐτοῖς δόξῃ βέλτιστον εἶναι.

ΠΩΛ. Οὐκοῦν τοῦτο ἔστι τὸ μέγα δύνασθαι;

ΣΩ. Οὔχ, ὥς γέ φησι Πῶλος.

ΠΩΛ. Ἐγὼ οὔ φημι; φημὶ μὲν οὖν ἔγωγε.

ΣΩ. Μὰ τὸν—οὐ σύ γε, ἐπεὶ τὸ μέγα δύνασθαι ἔφης ἀγαθὸν εἶναι τῷ δυναμένῳ.

ΠΩΛ. Φημὶ γὰρ οὖν.

ΣΩ. Ἀγαθὸν οὖν οἴει εἶναι, ἐάν τις ποιῇ ταῦτα, ἃ ἂν δοκῇ αὐτῷ βέλτιστα εἶναι, νοῦν μὴ ἔχων, καὶ τοῦτο καλεῖς μέγα δύνασθαι;

ΠΩΛ. Οὐκ ἔγωγε.

ΣΩ. Οὐκοῦν ἀποδείξεις τοὺς ῥήτορας νοῦν ἔχοντας καὶ τέχνην τὴν ῥητορικὴν ἀλλὰ μὴ κολακείαν, ἐμὲ ἐξελέγξας; εἰ δὲ με ἐάσεις ἀνέλεγκτον, οἱ ῥήτορες οἱ ποιοῦντες ἐν ταῖς πόλεσιν ἃ δοκεῖ αὐτοῖς καὶ οἱ τύραννοι οὐδὲν ἀγαθὸν τοῦτο κεκτήσονται, εἰ δὴ[1] δύναμίς ἐστιν, ὡς σὺ φῄς, ἀγαθόν, τὸ δὲ ποιεῖν ἄνευ νοῦ ἃ δοκεῖ καὶ σὺ ὁμολογεῖς κακὸν εἶναι· ἢ οὔ;

ΠΩΛ. Ἔγωγε.

ΣΩ. Πῶς ἂν οὖν οἱ ῥήτορες μέγα δύναιντο ἢ οἱ τύραννοι ἐν ταῖς πόλεσιν, ἐὰν μὴ Σωκράτης ἐξελεγχθῇ ὑπὸ Πώλου ὅτι ποιοῦσιν ἃ βούλονται;

ΠΩΛ. Οὗτος ἀνήρ—

[1] εἰ δὴ Heindorf: ἢ δὲ MSS.

GORGIAS

POL. I was.

SOC. Then I tell you that there are two questions here, and I will give you answers to them both. For I say, Polus, that the orators and the despots alike have the least power in their cities, as I stated just now; since they do nothing that they wish to do, practically speaking, though they do whatever they think to be best.

POL. Well, and is not that a great power to have?

SOC. No, judging at least by what Polus says.

POL. I say no! Pardon me, I say yes.

SOC. No, by the ——, you do not; for you said that great power is a good to him who has it.

POL. Yes, and I maintain it.

SOC. Then do you regard it as a good, when a man does what he thinks to be best, without having intelligence? Is that what you call having a great power?

POL. No, I do not.

SOC. Then will you prove that the orators have intelligence, and that rhetoric is an art, not a flattery, and so refute me? Else, if you are going to leave me unrefuted, the orators who do what they think fit in their cities, and the despots, will find they have got no good in doing that, if indeed power is, as you say, a good, but doing what one thinks fit without intelligence is—as you yourself admit, do you not?—an evil.

POL. Yes, I do.

SOC. How then can the orators or the despots have great power in their cities, unless Socrates is refuted by Polus, and admits that they do what they wish?

POL. Hark at the man——!

ΣΩ. Οὔ φημι ποιεῖν αὐτοὺς ἃ βούλονται· ἀλλά μ' ἔλεγχε.

ΠΩΛ. Οὐκ ἄρτι ὡμολόγεις ποιεῖν ἃ δοκεῖ αὐτοῖς βέλτιστα εἶναι [τούτου πρόσθεν][1];

ΣΩ. Καὶ γὰρ νῦν ὁμολογῶ.

ΠΩΛ. Οὐκ οὖν ποιοῦσιν ἃ βούλονται;

ΣΩ. Οὔ φημι.

ΠΩΛ. Ποιοῦντες δὲ ἃ δοκεῖ αὐτοῖς;

ΣΩ. Φημί.

ΠΩΛ. Σχέτλιά γε λέγεις καὶ ὑπερφυῆ, ὦ Σώκρατες.

ΣΩ. Μὴ κατηγόρει, ὦ λῷστε Πῶλε, ἵνα προσείπω σε κατὰ σέ· ἀλλ' εἰ μὲν ἔχεις ἐμὲ ἐρωτᾶν, ἐπίδειξον ὅτι ψεύδομαι, εἰ δὲ μή, αὐτὸς ἀποκρίνου.

ΠΩΛ. Ἀλλ' ἐθέλω ἀποκρίνεσθαι, ἵνα καὶ εἰδῶ ὅ τι λέγεις.

ΣΩ. Πότερον οὖν σοι δοκοῦσιν οἱ ἄνθρωποι τοῦτο βούλεσθαι, ὃ ἂν πράττωσιν ἑκάστοτε, ἢ ἐκεῖνο, οὗ ἕνεκα πράττουσι τοῦθ' ὃ πράττουσιν; οἷον οἱ τὰ φάρμακα πίνοντες παρὰ τῶν ἰατρῶν πότερόν σοι δοκοῦσι τοῦτο βούλεσθαι, ὅπερ ποιοῦσι, πίνειν τὸ φάρμακον καὶ ἀλγεῖν, ἢ ἐκεῖνο, τὸ ὑγιαίνειν, οὗ ἕνεκα πίνουσιν;

ΠΩΛ. Δῆλον ὅτι τὸ ὑγιαίνειν.

ΣΩ. Οὐκοῦν καὶ οἱ πλέοντές τε καὶ τὸν ἄλλον χρηματισμὸν χρηματιζόμενοι οὐ τοῦτό ἐστιν ὃ βούλονται, ὃ ποιοῦσιν ἑκάστοτε· τίς γὰρ βούλεται πλεῖν τε καὶ κινδυνεύειν καὶ πράγματ' ἔχειν;

---

[1] τούτου πρόσθεν secl. Schleiermacher.

GORGIAS

soc. I deny that they do what they wish: there, refute me.

pol. Did you not admit just now that they do what they think best?

soc. Yes, and I admit it now.

pol. Then do they not do what they wish?

soc. I say no.

pol. When they do what they think fit?

soc. Yes.

pol. What shocking, nay, monstrous answers, Socrates!

soc. Spare your invective, peerless Polus—if I may address you in your own style:[1] but if you have a question to ask me, expose my falsehood; otherwise, make answer yourself.

pol. Well, I am ready to answer, in order that I may know what you mean.

soc. Then is it your view that people wish merely that which they do each time, or that which is the object of their doing what they do? For instance, do those who take medicine by doctor's orders wish, in your opinion, merely what they do,—to take the medicine and suffer the pain of it,—or rather to be healthy, which is the object of their taking it?

pol. To be healthy, without a doubt.

soc. And so with seafarers and such as pursue profit generally in trade; what they wish is not what they are doing at each moment—for who wishes to go on a voyage, and incur all its danger

---

[1] The assonance in ὦ λῷστε Πῶλε is a mocking allusion to the nicely balanced clauses and jingling phrases which Polus imitated from his master Gorgias. Something of this style appears in Polus's speech above, 448 c.

ἀλλ' ἐκεῖνο, οἶμαι, οὗ ἕνεκα πλέουσι, πλουτεῖν· πλούτου γὰρ ἕνεκα πλέουσιν.

ΠΩΛ. Πάνυ γε.

ΣΩ. Ἄλλο τι οὖν οὕτω καὶ περὶ πάντων, ἐάν τίς τι πράττῃ ἕνεκά του, οὐ τοῦτο βούλεται, ὃ πράττει, ἀλλ' ἐκεῖνο, οὗ ἕνεκα πράττει;

ΠΩΛ. Ναί.

ΣΩ. Ἆρ' οὖν ἔστι τι τῶν ὄντων, ὃ οὐχὶ ἤτοι ἀγαθόν γ' ἐστὶν ἢ κακὸν ἢ μεταξὺ τούτων, οὔτε ἀγαθὸν οὔτε κακόν;

ΠΩΛ. Πολλὴ ἀνάγκη, ὦ Σώκρατες.

ΣΩ. Οὐκοῦν λέγεις εἶναι ἀγαθὸν μὲν σοφίαν τε καὶ ὑγίειαν καὶ πλοῦτον καὶ τἆλλα τὰ τοιαῦτα, κακὰ δὲ τἀναντία τούτων;

ΠΩΛ. Ἔγωγε.

ΣΩ. Τὰ δὲ μήτε ἀγαθὰ μήτε κακὰ ἆρα τοιάδε λέγεις, ἃ ἐνίοτε μὲν μετέχει τοῦ ἀγαθοῦ, ἐνίοτε δὲ τοῦ κακοῦ, ἐνίοτε δὲ οὐδετέρου, οἷον καθῆσθαι καὶ βαδίζειν καὶ τρέχειν καὶ πλεῖν, καὶ οἷον αὖ λίθους καὶ ξύλα καὶ τἆλλα τὰ τοιαῦτα; οὐ ταῦτα λέγεις; ἢ ἄλλ' ἄττα καλεῖς τὰ μήτε ἀγαθὰ μήτε κακά;

ΠΩΛ. Οὔκ, ἀλλὰ ταῦτα.

ΣΩ. Πότερον οὖν τὰ μεταξὺ ταῦτα ἕνεκεν τῶν ἀγαθῶν πράττουσιν, ὅταν πράττωσιν, ἢ τἀγαθὰ τῶν μεταξύ;

ΠΩΛ. Τὰ μεταξὺ δήπου τῶν ἀγαθῶν.

ΣΩ. Τὸ ἀγαθὸν ἄρα διώκοντες καὶ βαδίζομεν, ὅταν βαδίζωμεν, οἰόμενοι βέλτιον εἶναι, καὶ τὸ ἐναντίον ἕσταμεν, ὅταν ἑστῶμεν, τοῦ αὐτοῦ ἕνεκα, τοῦ ἀγαθοῦ· ἢ οὔ;

GORGIAS

and trouble? It is rather, I conceive, the object of their voyage—to get wealth; since it is for wealth that they go on it.

POL. Certainly.

SOC. And is it not just the same in every case? If a man does something for an object, he does not wish the thing that he does, but the thing for which he does it.

POL. Yes.

SOC. Now is there any existent thing that is not either good or bad or between these—neither good nor bad?

POL. Most assuredly nothing, Socrates.

SOC. Well, do you call wisdom and health and wealth and everything else of that kind good, and their opposites bad?

POL. I do.

SOC. And by things neither good nor bad do you mean such things as sometimes partake of the good, sometimes of the bad, and sometimes of neither—for example, sitting, walking, running, and sailing, or again, stones and sticks and anything else of that sort? These are what you mean, are they not? Or are there other things that you describe as neither good nor bad?

POL. No, these are what I mean.

SOC. Then do people do these intermediate things, when they do them, for the sake of the good things, or the good things for the intermediate?

POL. The intermediate, I presume, for the good.

SOC. Thus it is in pursuit of the good that we walk, when we walk, conceiving it to be better; or on the contrary, stand, when we stand, for the sake of the same thing, the good: is it not so?

PLATO

ΠΩΛ. Ναί.

ΣΩ. Οὐκοῦν καὶ ἀποκτίννυμεν, εἴ τινα ἀποκτίννυμεν, καὶ ἐκβάλλομεν καὶ ἀφαιρούμεθα χρήματα, οἰόμενοι ἄμεινον εἶναι ἡμῖν ταῦτα ποιεῖν ἢ μή;

ΠΩΛ. Πάνυ γε.

ΣΩ. Ἕνεκ' ἄρα τοῦ ἀγαθοῦ ἅπαντα ταῦτα ποιοῦσιν οἱ ποιοῦντες.

ΠΩΛ. Φημί.

ΣΩ. Οὐκοῦν ὡμολογήσαμεν, ἃ ἕνεκά του ποιοῦμεν, μὴ ἐκεῖνα βούλεσθαι, ἀλλ' ἐκεῖνο, οὗ ἕνεκα ταῦτα ποιοῦμεν;

C ΠΩΛ. Μάλιστα.

ΣΩ. Οὐκ ἄρα σφάττειν βουλόμεθα οὐδ' ἐκβάλλειν ἐκ τῶν πόλεων οὐδὲ χρήματα ἀφαιρεῖσθαι ἁπλῶς οὕτως, ἀλλ' ἐὰν μὲν ὠφέλιμα ᾖ ταῦτα, βουλόμεθα πράττειν αὐτά, βλαβερὰ δὲ ὄντα οὐ βουλόμεθα. τὰ γὰρ ἀγαθὰ βουλόμεθα, ὡς φῂς σύ, τὰ δὲ μήτε ἀγαθὰ μήτε κακὰ οὐ βουλόμεθα, οὐδὲ τὰ κακά. ἦ γάρ; ἀληθῆ σοι δοκῶ λέγειν, ὦ Πῶλε, ἢ οὔ; τί οὐκ ἀποκρίνῃ;

ΠΩΛ. Ἀληθῆ.

D ΣΩ. Οὐκοῦν εἴπερ ταῦτα ὁμολογοῦμεν, εἴ τις ἀποκτείνει τινὰ ἢ ἐκβάλλει ἐκ πόλεως ἢ ἀφαιρεῖται χρήματα, εἴτε τύραννος ὢν εἴτε ῥήτωρ, οἰόμενος ἄμεινον εἶναι αὑτῷ, τυγχάνει δὲ ὂν κάκιον, οὗτος δήπου ποιεῖ ἃ δοκεῖ αὐτῷ· ἦ γάρ;

ΠΩΛ. Ναί.

ΣΩ. Ἆρ' οὖν καὶ ἃ βούλεται, εἴπερ τυγχάνει ταῦτα κακὰ ὄντα; τί οὐκ ἀποκρίνῃ;

ΠΩΛ. Ἀλλ' οὔ μοι δοκεῖ ποιεῖν ἃ βούλεται.

E ΣΩ. Ἔστιν οὖν ὅπως ὁ τοιοῦτος μέγα δύναται

GORGIAS

POL. Yes.

SOC. And so we put a man to death, if we do put him to death, or expel him or deprive him of his property, because we think it better for us to do this than not?

POL. Certainly.

SOC. So it is for the sake of the good that the doers of all these things do them?

POL. I agree.

SOC. And we have admitted that when we do things for an object, we do not wish those things, but the object for which we do them?

POL. Quite so.

SOC. Then we do not wish to slaughter people or expel them from our cities or deprive them of their property as an act in itself, but if these things are beneficial we wish to do them, while if they are harmful, we do not wish them. For we wish what is good, as you say; but what is neither good nor bad we do not wish, nor what is bad either, do we? Is what I say true in your opinion, Polus, or not? Why do you not answer?

POL. It is true.

SOC. Then, as we agree on this, if a man puts anyone to death or expels him from a city or deprives him of his property, whether he does it as a despot or an orator, because he thinks it better for himself though it is really worse, that man, I take it, does what he thinks fit, does he not?

POL. Yes.

SOC. Now is it also what he wishes, supposing it to be really bad? Why do you not answer?

POL. No, I do not think he does what he wishes.

SOC. Can such a man then be said to have great

331

PLATO

ἐν τῇ πόλει ταύτῃ, εἴπερ ἐστὶ τὸ μέγα **δύνασθαι** ἀγαθόν τι κατὰ τὴν σὴν ὁμολογίαν;

ΠΩΛ. Οὐκ ἔστιν.

ΣΩ. Ἀληθῆ ἄρα ἐγὼ ἔλεγον, λέγων ὅτι ἔστιν ἄνθρωπον ποιοῦντα ἐν πόλει ἃ δοκεῖ αὐτῷ μὴ **μέγα** δύνασθαι μηδὲ ποιεῖν ἃ βούλεται.

ΠΩΛ. Ὡς δὴ σύ, ὦ Σώκρατες, οὐκ ἂν δέξαιο ἐξεῖναί σοι ποιεῖν ὅ τι δοκεῖ σοι ἐν τῇ πόλει μᾶλλον ἢ μή, οὐδὲ ζηλοῖς ὅταν ἴδῃς τινὰ ἢ ἀποκτείναντα ὃν ἔδοξεν αὐτῷ ἢ ἀφελόμενον χρήματα ἢ δήσαντα.

ΣΩ. Δικαίως λέγεις ἢ ἀδίκως;

ΠΩΛ. Ὁπότερ᾽ ἂν ποιῇ, οὐκ ἀμφοτέρως ζηλωτόν ἐστιν;

ΣΩ. Εὐφήμει, ὦ Πῶλε.

ΠΩΛ. Τί δή;

ΣΩ. Ὅτι οὐ χρὴ οὔτε τοὺς ἀζηλώτους ζηλοῦν οὔτε τοὺς ἀθλίους, ἀλλ᾽ ἐλεεῖν.

ΠΩΛ. Τί δέ; οὕτω σοι δοκεῖ ἔχειν περὶ ὧν ἐγὼ λέγω τῶν ἀνθρώπων;

ΣΩ. Πῶς γὰρ οὔ;

ΠΩΛ. Ὅστις οὖν ἀποκτίννυσιν ὃν ἂν δόξῃ αὐτῷ, δικαίως ἀποκτιννύς, ἄθλιος δοκεῖ σοι εἶναι καὶ ἐλεεινός;

ΣΩ. Οὐκ ἔμοιγε, οὐδὲ μέντοι ζηλωτός.

ΠΩΛ. Οὐκ ἄρτι ἄθλιον ἔφησθα εἶναι;

ΣΩ. Τὸν ἀδίκως γε, ὦ ἑταῖρε, ἀποκτείναντα, καὶ ἐλεεινὸν δὲ πρός· τὸν δὲ δικαίως ἀζήλωτον.

ΠΩΛ. Ἦ που ὅ γε ἀποθνῄσκων ἀδίκως ἐλεεινός τε καὶ ἄθλιός ἐστιν.

ΣΩ. Ἧττον ἢ ὁ ἀποκτιννύς, ὦ Πῶλε, καὶ ἧττον ἢ ὁ δικαίως ἀποθνῄσκων.

GORGIAS

power in that city, if to have great power is something good, according to your admission?

POL. He cannot.

SOC. Then I spoke the truth when I said that it is possible for a man to do what he thinks fit in a city and yet not to have great power nor to do what he wishes.

POL. As if you, Socrates, would not accept the liberty of doing what you think fit in your city rather than not, and would not envy a man whom you observed to have put some one to death as he thought fit, or deprived him of his property or sent him to prison!

SOC. Justly, do you mean, or unjustly?

POL. Whichever way he does it, is it not enviable in either case?

SOC. Hush, Polus!

POL. Why?

SOC. Because we ought not to envy either the unenviable or the wretched, but pity them.

POL. What! Is that the state in which you consider those people, of whom I speak, to be?

SOC. Yes, for so I must.

POL. Then do you consider that a man who puts another to death as he thinks fit, and justly puts him to death, is wretched and pitiable?

SOC. Not I; but not enviable either.

POL. Did you not say just now that he was wretched?

SOC. Only he who unjustly put some one to death, my friend, and I called him pitiable as well: if he acted justly, then he is unenviable.

POL. I suppose, at any rate, the man who is put to death unjustly is both pitiable and wretched.

SOC. Less so than he who puts him to death, Polus, and less so than he who is put to death justly.

PLATO

ΠΩΛ. Πῶς δῆτα, ὦ Σώκρατες;

ΣΩ. Οὕτως, ὡς μέγιστον τῶν κακῶν τυγχάνει ὂν τὸ ἀδικεῖν.

ΠΩΛ. Ἦ γὰρ τοῦτο μέγιστον; οὐ τὸ ἀδικεῖσθαι μεῖζον;

ΣΩ. Ἥκιστά γε.

ΠΩΛ. Σὺ ἄρα βούλοιο ἂν ἀδικεῖσθαι μᾶλλον ἢ ἀδικεῖν;

ΣΩ. Βουλοίμην μὲν ἂν ἔγωγε οὐδέτερα· εἰ δ' ἀναγκαῖον εἴη ἀδικεῖν ἢ ἀδικεῖσθαι, ἑλοίμην ἂν μᾶλλον ἀδικεῖσθαι ἢ ἀδικεῖν.

ΠΩΛ. Σὺ ἄρα τυραννεῖν οὐκ ἂν δέξαιο;

ΣΩ. Οὔκ, εἰ τὸ τυραννεῖν γε λέγεις ὅπερ ἐγώ.

ΠΩΛ. Ἀλλ' ἔγωγε τοῦτο λέγω ὅπερ ἄρτι, ἐξεῖναι ἐν τῇ πόλει, ὃ ἂν δοκῇ αὐτῷ, ποιεῖν τοῦτο, καὶ ἀποκτιννύντι καὶ ἐκβάλλοντι καὶ πάντα πράττοντι κατὰ τὴν αὑτοῦ δόξαν.

ΣΩ. Ὦ μακάριε, ἐμοῦ δὴ λέγοντος τῷ λόγῳ ἐπιλαβοῦ. εἰ γὰρ ἐγὼ ἐν ἀγορᾷ πληθούσῃ λαβὼν ὑπὸ μάλης ἐγχειρίδιον λέγοιμι πρὸς σὲ ὅτι ὦ Πῶλε, ἐμοὶ δύναμίς τις καὶ τυραννὶς θαυμασία ἄρτι προσγέγονεν· ἐὰν γὰρ ἄρα ἐμοὶ δόξῃ τινὰ τουτωνὶ τῶν ἀνθρώπων ὧν σὺ ὁρᾷς αὐτίκα μάλα δεῖν τεθνάναι, τεθνήξει οὗτος ὃν ἂν δόξῃ· κἄν τινα δόξῃ μοι τῆς κεφαλῆς αὐτῶν καταγῆναι[1] δεῖν, κατεαγὼς ἔσται αὐτίκα μάλα, κἂν θοἰματίον διεσχίσθαι, διεσχισμένον ἔσται· οὕτω μέγα ἐγὼ δύναμαι ἐν τῇδε τῇ πόλει· εἰ οὖν ἀπιστοῦντί σοι δείξαιμι τὸ ἐγχειρίδιον, ἴσως ἂν εἴποις ἰδὼν ὅτι ὦ Σώκρατες, οὕτω μὲν πάντες ἂν μέγα δύναιντο, ἐπεὶ κἂν ἐμπρησθείη οἰκία τούτῳ τῷ τρόπῳ ἥντινά σοι δοκοῖ, καὶ τά γε Ἀθηναίων νεώρια

[1] καταγῆναι Burnet: κατεαγῆναι MSS.

GORGIAS

POL. In what way can that be, Socrates?

SOC. In this, that to do wrong is the greatest of evils.

POL. What, is this the greatest? Is not to suffer wrong a greater?

SOC. By no means.

POL. Then would you wish rather to suffer wrong than to do it?

SOC. I should wish neither, for my own part; but if it were necessary either to do wrong or to suffer it, I should choose to suffer rather than do it.

POL. Then you would not accept a despot's power?

SOC. No, if you mean by a despot's power the same as I do.

POL. Why, what I mean is, as I did just now, the liberty of doing anything one thinks fit in one's city—putting people to death and expelling them and doing everything at one's own discretion.

SOC. My gifted friend, let me speak, and you shall take me to task in your turn. Suppose that in a crowded market I should hide a dagger under my arm and then say to you: "Polus, I have just acquired, by a wonderful chance, the power of a despot; for if I should think fit that one of those people whom you see there should die this very instant, a dead man he will be, just as I think fit; or if I think fit that one of them shall have his head broken, broken it will be immediately; or to have his cloak torn in pieces, torn it will be: so great is my power in this city." Then suppose that on your disbelieving this I showed you my dagger; I expect when you saw it you would say: "Socrates, at this rate every one would have great power, for any house you thought fit might be set ablaze on these methods, and the Athenian arsenals also, and

335

PLATO

καὶ ⟨αἱ⟩[1] τριήρεις καὶ τὰ πλοῖα πάντα καὶ τὰ δημόσια καὶ τὰ ἴδια· ἀλλ' οὐκ ἄρα τοῦτ' ἔστι τὸ μέγα δύνασθαι, τὸ ποιεῖν ἃ δοκεῖ αὐτῷ· ἢ δοκεῖ σοι;

ΠΩΛ. Οὐ δῆτα οὕτω γε.

ΣΩ. Ἔχεις οὖν εἰπεῖν δι' ὅ τι μέμφῃ τὴν τοιαύτην δύναμιν;

ΠΩΛ. Ἔγωγε.

ΣΩ. Τί δή; λέγε.

ΠΩΛ. Ὅτι ἀναγκαῖον τὸν οὕτω πράττοντα ζημιοῦσθαί ἐστιν.

ΣΩ. Τὸ δὲ ζημιοῦσθαι οὐ κακόν;

ΠΩΛ. Πάνυ γε.

ΣΩ. Οὐκοῦν, ὦ θαυμάσιε [τὸ μέγα δύνασθαι],[2] πάλιν αὖ σοι φαίνεται, ἐὰν μὲν πράττοντι ἃ δοκεῖ ἕπηται τὸ ὠφελίμως πράττειν, ἀγαθόν τε εἶναι, καὶ τοῦτο, ὡς ἔοικεν, ἐστὶ τὸ μέγα δύνασθαι· εἰ δὲ μή, κακὸν καὶ σμικρὸν δύνασθαι. σκεψώμεθα δὲ καὶ τόδε· ἄλλο τι ἢ ὁμολογοῦμεν ἐνίοτε μὲν ἄμεινον εἶναι ταῦτα ποιεῖν ἃ νῦν δὴ ἐλέγομεν, ἀποκτιννύναι τε καὶ ἐξελαύνειν ἀνθρώπους καὶ ἀφαιρεῖσθαι χρήματα, ἐνίοτε δὲ οὔ;

ΠΩΛ. Πάνυ γε.

ΣΩ. Τοῦτο μὲν δή, ὡς ἔοικε, καὶ παρὰ σοῦ καὶ παρ' ἐμοῦ ὁμολογεῖται.

ΠΩΛ. Ναί.

ΣΩ. Πότε οὖν σὺ φῂς ἄμεινον εἶναι ταῦτα ποιεῖν; εἰπὲ τίνα ὅρον ὁρίζῃ.

ΠΩΛ. Σὺ μὲν οὖν, ὦ Σώκρατες, ἀπόκριναι [ταὐτὸ][3] τοῦτο.

ΣΩ. Ἐγὼ μὲν τοίνυν φημί, ὦ Πῶλε, εἴ σοι

[1] αἱ add. Schaefer.
[2] τὸ μέγα δύνασθαι secl. Thompson.
[3] ταὐτὸ secl. Heindorf.

the men-of-war and all the rest of the shipping, both public and private." But surely this is not what it is to have great power—merely doing what one thinks fit. Or do you think it is?

POL. Oh no, not in that way.

SOC. Then can you tell me why you disapprove of this kind of power?

POL. I can.

SOC. Why, then? Tell me.

POL. Because it is inevitable that he who acts thus will be punished.

SOC. And is it not a bad thing to be punished?

POL. Certainly.

SOC. So, my remarkable friend, you have come round again to the view that if doing what one thinks fit is attended by advantage in doing it, this is not merely a good thing but at the same time, it seems, the possession of great power; otherwise it is a bad thing and means little power. And let us consider another point besides; do we not admit that sometimes it is better to do those things that we were mentioning just now—to put people to death and banish them and deprive them of property —while sometimes it is not?

POL. To be sure.

SOC. Then here is a point, it seems, that is admitted both on your side and on mine.

POL. Yes.

SOC. Then when do you say it is better to do these things? Tell me where you draw the line.

POL. Nay, I would rather that you, Socrates, answered that.

SOC. Well then I say, Polus, if you prefer to hear

παρ' ἐμοῦ ἥδιόν ἐστιν ἀκούειν, ὅταν μὲν δικαίως τις ταῦτα ποιῇ, ἄμεινον εἶναι, ὅταν δὲ ἀδίκως, κάκιον.

πωλ. Χαλεπόν γέ σε ἐλέγξαι, ὦ Σώκρατες· ἀλλ' οὐχὶ κἂν παῖς σε ἐλέγξειεν, ὅτι οὐκ ἀληθῆ λέγεις;

σω. Πολλὴν ἄρα ἐγὼ τῷ παιδὶ χάριν ἕξω, ἴσην δὲ καὶ σοί, ἐάν με ἐλέγξῃς καὶ ἀπαλλάξῃς φλυαρίας. ἀλλὰ μὴ κάμῃς φίλον ἄνδρα εὐεργετῶν, ἀλλ' ἔλεγχε.

D πωλ. Ἀλλὰ μήν, ὦ Σώκρατες, οὐδέν γέ σε δεῖ παλαιοῖς πράγμασιν ἐλέγχειν· τὰ γὰρ ἐχθὲς καὶ πρώην γεγονότα ταῦτα ἱκανά σε ἐξελέγξαι ἐστὶ καὶ ἀποδεῖξαι, ὡς πολλοὶ ἀδικοῦντες ἄνθρωποι εὐδαίμονές εἰσιν.

σω. Τὰ ποῖα ταῦτα;

πωλ. Ἀρχέλαον δήπου τοῦτον τὸν Περδίκκου ὁρᾷς ἄρχοντα Μακεδονίας;

σω. Εἰ δὲ μή, ἀλλ' ἀκούω γε.

πωλ. Εὐδαίμων οὖν σοι δοκεῖ εἶναι ἢ ἄθλιος;

σω. Οὐκ οἶδα, ὦ Πῶλε· οὐ γάρ πω συγγέγονα τῷ ἀνδρί.

E πωλ. Τί δέ; συγγενόμενος ἂν γνοίης, ἄλλως δὲ αὐτόθεν οὐ γιγνώσκεις ὅτι εὐδαιμονεῖ;

σω. Μὰ Δί' οὐ δῆτα.

πωλ. Δῆλον δή, ὦ Σώκρατες, ὅτι οὐδὲ τὸν μέγαν βασιλέα γιγνώσκειν φήσεις εὐδαίμονα ὄντα.

σω. Καὶ ἀληθῆ γε ἐρῶ· οὐ γὰρ οἶδα παιδείας ὅπως ἔχει καὶ δικαιοσύνης.

GORGIAS

it from me, that it is better when these things are done justly, and worse when unjustly.

POL. So hard to refute you, Socrates! Nay, a mere child could do it, could he not, and prove your words are untrue?

SOC. Then I shall be most grateful to the child, and equally to you, if you refute me and rid me of foolery. Come, do not grow weary in well-doing towards your friend, but refute me.

POL. Well, to be sure, Socrates, there is no need to refute you with ancient instances; for those happenings of but a day or two ago are enough to refute you, and prove that many a wrongdoer is happy.

SOC. What sort of thing do you mean?

POL. I suppose you see that Archelaus, son of Perdiccas, is ruler of Macedonia?[1]

SOC. Well, if I do not, at any rate I hear it.

POL. Do you consider him happy or wretched?

SOC. I do not know, Polus; I have never met the man.

POL. What? Could you find out by meeting him, and cannot otherwise tell, straight off, that he is happy?

SOC. No, indeed, upon my word.

POL. Then doubtless you will say, Socrates, that you do not know that even the Great King is happy.

SOC. Yes, and I shall be speaking the truth; for I do not know how he stands in point of education and justice.

[1] Archelaus usurped the throne of Macedonia in 413 B.C., and ruled till his death in 399 B.C. Euripides, Agathon, and other distinguished Athenians were guests at his court; Socrates was also invited, but declined to visit him (Aristot. *Rhet.* ii. 23. 8), and this is probably the point of Socrates' next remark.

PLATO

470 ΠΩΛ. Τί δέ; ἐν τούτῳ ἡ πᾶσα εὐδαιμονία ἐστίν;

ΣΩ. Ὥς γε ἐγὼ λέγω, ὦ Πῶλε· τὸν μὲν γὰρ καλὸν κἀγαθὸν ἄνδρα καὶ γυναῖκα εὐδαίμονα εἶναί φημι, τὸν δὲ ἄδικον καὶ πονηρὸν ἄθλιον.

471 ΠΩΛ. Ἄθλιος ἄρα οὗτός ἐστιν ὁ Ἀρχέλαος κατὰ τὸν σὸν λόγον;

ΣΩ. Εἴπερ γε, ὦ φίλε, ἄδικος.

ΠΩΛ. Ἀλλὰ μὲν δὴ πῶς οὐκ ἄδικος; ᾧ γε προσῆκε μὲν τῆς ἀρχῆς οὐδὲν ἦν νῦν ἔχει, ὄντι ἐκ γυναικὸς ἣ ἦν δούλη Ἀλκέτου τοῦ Περδίκκου ἀδελφοῦ, καὶ κατὰ μὲν τὸ δίκαιον δοῦλος ἦν Ἀλκέτου, καὶ εἰ ἐβούλετο τὰ δίκαια ποιεῖν, ἐδούλευεν ἂν Ἀλκέτῃ καὶ ἦν εὐδαίμων κατὰ τὸν σὸν λόγον· νῦν δὲ θαυμασίως ὡς ἄθλιος γέγονεν,

B ἐπεὶ τὰ μέγιστα ἠδίκηκεν· ὅς γε πρῶτον μὲν τοῦτον αὐτὸν τὸν δεσπότην καὶ θεῖον μεταπεμψάμενος ὡς ἀποδώσων τὴν ἀρχὴν ἣν Περδίκκας αὐτὸν ἀφείλετο, ξενίσας καὶ καταμεθύσας αὐτόν τε καὶ τὸν υἱὸν αὐτοῦ Ἀλέξανδρον, ἀνεψιὸν αὑτοῦ, σχεδὸν ἡλικιώτην, ἐμβαλὼν εἰς ἅμαξαν, νύκτωρ ἐξαγαγὼν ἀπέσφαξέ τε καὶ ἠφάνισεν ἀμφοτέρους· καὶ ταῦτα ἀδικήσας ἔλαθεν ἑαυτὸν ἀθλιώτατος γενόμενος καὶ οὐ μετεμέλησεν αὐτῷ, ἀλλ' ὀλίγον

C ὕστερον τὸν ἀδελφόν, τὸν γνήσιον τοῦ Περδίκκου υἱόν, παῖδα ὡς ἑπταετῆ, οὗ ἡ ἀρχὴ ἐγίγνετο κατὰ τὸ δίκαιον, οὐκ ἐβουλήθη εὐδαίμων γενέσθαι δικαίως ἐκθρέψας καὶ ἀποδοὺς τὴν ἀρχὴν ἐκείνῳ, ἀλλ' εἰς φρέαρ ἐμβαλὼν καὶ ἀποπνίξας πρὸς τὴν μητέρα αὐτοῦ Κλεοπάτραν χῆνα ἔφη διώκοντα ἐμπεσεῖν καὶ ἀποθανεῖν. τοιγάρτοι νῦν, ἅτε μέ-

GORGIAS

POL. Why, does happiness entirely consist in that?

SOC. Yes, by my account, Polus; for a good and honourable man or woman, I say, is happy, and an unjust and wicked one is wretched.

POL. Then this Archelaus, on your statement, is wretched?

SOC. Yes, my friend, supposing he is unjust.

POL. Well, but how can he be other than unjust? He had no claim to the throne which he now occupies, being the son of a woman who was a slave of Perdiccas' brother Alcetas, and in mere justice he was Alcetas' slave; and if he wished to do what is just, he would be serving Alcetas and would be happy, by your account; but, as it is, he has become a prodigy of wretchedness, since he has done the most enormous wrong. First of all he invited this very master and uncle of his to his court, as if he were going to restore to him the kingdom of which Perdiccas had deprived him; and after entertaining him and his son Alexander—his own cousin, about the same age as himself—and making them drunk, he packed them into a carriage, drove them away by night, and murdered and made away with them both. And after all these iniquities he failed to observe that he had become a most wretched person, and had no repentance, but a while later he refused to make himself happy by bringing up, as he was justly bound, his brother, the legitimate son of Perdiccas, a boy about seven years old who had a just title to the throne, and restoring the kingdom to him; but he cast him into a well and drowned him, and then told his mother Cleopatra that he had fallen in and lost his life while chasing a goose. So now, you see, as the greatest wrongdoer in

PLATO

γιστα ἠδικηκὼς τῶν ἐν Μακεδονίᾳ, ἀθλιώτατός ἐστι πάντων Μακεδόνων, ἀλλ' οὐκ εὐδαιμονέστατος, καὶ ἴσως ἔστιν ὅστις Ἀθηναίων ἀπὸ σοῦ ἀρξάμενος δέξαιτ' ἂν ἄλλος ὁστισοῦν Μακεδόνων γενέσθαι μᾶλλον ἢ Ἀρχέλαος.

ΣΩ. Καὶ κατ' ἀρχὰς τῶν λόγων, ὦ Πῶλε, ἔγωγέ σε ἐπῄνεσα ὅτι μοι δοκεῖς εὖ πρὸς τὴν ῥητορικὴν πεπαιδεῦσθαι, τοῦ δὲ διαλέγεσθαι ἠμεληκέναι· καὶ νῦν ἄλλο τι οὗτός ἐστιν ὁ λόγος, ᾧ με καὶ ἂν παῖς ἐξελέγξειε, καὶ ἐγὼ ὑπὸ σοῦ νῦν, ὡς σὺ οἴει, ἐξελήλεγμαι τούτῳ τῷ λόγῳ, φάσκων τὸν ἀδικοῦντα οὐκ εὐδαίμονα εἶναι; πόθεν, ὦ 'γαθέ; καὶ μὴν οὐδέν γέ σοι τούτων ὁμολογῶ ὧν σὺ φῄς.

ΠΩΛ. Οὐ γὰρ ἐθέλεις, ἐπεὶ δοκεῖ γέ σοι ὡς ἐγὼ λέγω.

ΣΩ. Ὦ μακάριε, ῥητορικῶς γάρ με ἐπιχειρεῖς ἐλέγχειν, ὥσπερ οἱ ἐν τοῖς δικαστηρίοις ἡγούμενοι ἐλέγχειν. καὶ γὰρ ἐκεῖ οἱ ἕτεροι τοὺς ἑτέρους δοκοῦσιν ἐλέγχειν, ἐπειδὰν τῶν λόγων ὧν ἂν λέγωσι μάρτυρας πολλοὺς παρέχωνται καὶ εὐδοκίμους, ὁ δὲ τἀναντία λέγων ἕνα τινὰ παρέχηται ἢ μηδένα. οὗτος δὲ ὁ ἔλεγχος οὐδενὸς ἄξιός ἐστι πρὸς τὴν ἀλήθειαν· ἐνίοτε γὰρ ἂν καὶ καταψευδομαρτυρηθείη τις ὑπὸ πολλῶν καὶ δοκούντων εἶναί τι. καὶ νῦν περὶ ὧν σὺ λέγεις ὀλίγου σοι πάντες συμφήσουσι ταῦτα Ἀθηναῖοι καὶ οἱ ξένοι, ἐὰν βούλῃ κατ' ἐμοῦ μάρτυρας παρασχέσθαι, ὡς οὐκ ἀληθῆ λέγω· μαρτυρήσουσί σοι, ἐὰν μὲν βούλῃ, Νικίας ὁ Νικηράτου καὶ οἱ ἀδελφοὶ μετ' αὐτοῦ, ὧν οἱ τρίποδες οἱ ἐφεξῆς ἑστῶτές εἰσιν

GORGIAS

Macedonia, he is the most wretched of all the Macedonians, not the happiest; and I daresay some Athenians could be found who would join you in preferring to change places with any other Macedonian of them all, rather than with Archelaus!

soc. At the beginning of our discussion, Polus, I complimented you on having had, as I consider, a good training in rhetoric, while you seem to have neglected disputation; and now, accordingly, this is the argument, is it, with which any child could refute me? By this statement, you think, I now stand refuted at your hands, when I assert that the wrongdoer is not happy? How so, my good friend? Why, I tell you I do not admit a single point in what you say.

pol. No, because you do not want to; for you really agree with my statement.

soc. My gifted friend, that is because you attempt to refute me in rhetorical fashion, as they understand refuting in the law courts. For there, one party is supposed to refute the other when they bring forward a number of reputable witnesses to any statements they may make, whilst their opponent produces only one, or none. But this sort of refutation is quite worthless for getting at the truth; since occasionally a man may actually be crushed by the number and reputation of the false witnesses brought against him. And so now you will find almost everybody, Athenians and foreigners, in agreement with you on the points you state, if you like to bring forward witnesses against the truth of what I say: if you like, there is Nicias, son of Niceratus, with his brothers, whose tripods are

PLATO

ἐν τῷ Διονυσίῳ, ἐὰν δὲ βούλῃ, Ἀριστοκράτης ὁ Σκελλίου, οὗ αὖ ἔστιν ἐν Πυθίου τοῦτο τὸ καλὸν ἀνάθημα, ἐὰν δὲ βούλῃ, ἡ Περικλέους ὅλη οἰκία ἢ ἄλλη συγγένεια, ἥντινα ἂν βούλῃ τῶν ἐνθάδε ἐκλέξασθαι. ἀλλ' ἐγώ σοι εἷς ὢν οὐχ ὁμολογῶ· οὐ γάρ με σὺ ἀναγκάζεις, ἀλλὰ ψευδομάρτυρας πολλοὺς κατ' ἐμοῦ παρασχόμενος ἐπιχειρεῖς ἐκβάλλειν με ἐκ τῆς οὐσίας καὶ τοῦ ἀληθοῦς. ἐγὼ δὲ ἂν μὴ σὲ αὐτὸν ἕνα ὄντα μάρτυρα παράσχωμαι ὁμολογοῦντα περὶ ὧν λέγω, οὐδὲν οἶμαι ἄξιον λόγου μοι πεπεράνθαι περὶ ὧν ἂν ἡμῖν ὁ λόγος ᾖ· οἶμαι δὲ οὐδὲ σοί, ἐὰν μὴ ἐγώ σοι μαρτυρῶ εἷς ὢν μόνος, τοὺς δ' ἄλλους πάντας τούτους χαίρειν ἐᾷς. ἔστι μὲν οὖν οὗτός τις τρόπος ἐλέγχου, ὡς σύ τε οἴει καὶ ἄλλοι πολλοί· ἔστι δὲ καὶ ἄλλος, ὃν ἐγὼ αὖ οἶμαι. παραβαλόντες οὖν παρ' ἀλλήλους σκεψώμεθα, εἴ τι διοίσουσιν ἀλλήλων. καὶ γὰρ τυγχάνει περὶ ὧν ἀμφισβητοῦμεν οὐ πάνυ σμικρὰ ὄντα, ἀλλὰ σχεδόν τι ταῦτα, περὶ ὧν εἰδέναι τε κάλλιστον μὴ εἰδέναι τε αἴσχιστον· τὸ γὰρ κεφάλαιον αὐτῶν ἐστιν ἢ γιγνώσκειν ἢ ἀγνοεῖν, ὅστις τε εὐδαίμων ἐστὶ καὶ ὅστις μή. αὐτίκα πρῶτον, περὶ οὗ νῦν ὁ λόγος ἐστί, σὺ ἡγῇ οἷόν τε εἶναι μακάριον ἄνδρα ἀδικοῦντά τε καὶ ἄδικον ὄντα, εἴπερ Ἀρχέλαον ἄδικον μὲν ἡγῇ εἶναι, εὐδαίμονα δέ· ἄλλο τι ὡς οὕτω σου νομίζοντος διανοώμεθα;

ΠΩΛ. Πάνυ γε.

---

[1] These tripods were prizes won by dramatic performances supported as a public service by Nicias and his brothers, and they were placed in the precincts of the temple of Dionysus. The persons here mentioned are selected as instances of public men who won high reputation in their time through the pursuit of material wealth and influence.

GORGIAS

standing in a row in the Dionysium;[1] or else Aristocrates, son of Scellias, whose goodly offering again we have in the Pythium[2]; or if you choose, there is the whole house of Pericles or any other family you may like to select in this place. But I, alone here before you, do not admit it, for you fail to convince me : you only attempt, by producing a number of false witnesses against me, to oust me from my reality, the truth. But if on my part I fail to produce yourself as my one witness to confirm what I say, I consider I have achieved nothing of any account towards the matter of our discussion, whatever it may be ; nor have you either, I conceive, unless I act alone as your one witness, and you have nothing to do with all these others. Well now, this is one mode of refutation, as you and many other people conceive it; but there is also another which I on my side conceive. Let us therefore compare them with each other and consider if we find a difference between them. For indeed the points which we have at issue are by no means of slight importance : rather, one might say, they are matters on which it is most honourable to have knowledge, and most disgraceful to lack it; for in sum they involve our knowing or not knowing who is happy and who is not. To start at once with the point we are now debating, you consider it possible for a man to be happy while doing wrong, and as a wrongdoer, since you regard Archelaus as a wrongdoer, and yet happy. We are to conclude, are we not, that this is your opinion ?

POL. Certainly.

[2] The temple of Apollo to the east of the Acropolis.

345

PLATO

ΣΩ. Ἐγὼ δέ φημι ἀδύνατον. ἓν μὲν τουτὶ ἀμφισβητοῦμεν. εἶεν· ἀδικῶν δὲ δὴ εὐδαίμων ἔσται ἆρ', ἂν τυγχάνῃ δίκης τε καὶ τιμωρίας;

ΠΩΛ. Ἥκιστά γε, ἐπεὶ οὕτω γ' ἂν ἀθλιώτατος εἴη.

ΣΩ. Ἀλλ' ἐὰν ἄρα μὴ τυγχάνῃ δίκης ὁ ἀδικῶν, κατὰ τὸν σὸν λόγον εὐδαίμων ἔσται;

ΠΩΛ. Φημί.

ΣΩ. Κατὰ δέ γε τὴν ἐμὴν δόξαν, ὦ Πῶλε, ὁ ἀδικῶν τε καὶ ὁ ἄδικος πάντως μὲν ἄθλιος, ἀθλιώτερος μέντοι, ἐὰν μὴ διδῷ δίκην μηδὲ τυγχάνῃ τιμωρίας ἀδικῶν, ἧττον δὲ ἄθλιος, ἐὰν διδῷ δίκην καὶ τυγχάνῃ δίκης ὑπὸ θεῶν τε καὶ ἀνθρώπων.

ΠΩΛ. Ἄτοπά γε, ὦ Σώκρατες, ἐπιχειρεῖς λέγειν.

ΣΩ. Πειράσομαι δέ γε καὶ σὲ ποιῆσαι, ὦ ἑταῖρε, ταὐτὰ ἐμοὶ λέγειν· φίλον γάρ σε ἡγοῦμαι. νῦν μὲν οὖν ἃ διαφερόμεθα ταῦτ' ἐστίν· σκόπει δὲ καὶ σύ· εἶπον ἐγώ που ἐν τοῖς ἔμπροσθεν τὸ ἀδικεῖν τοῦ ἀδικεῖσθαι κάκιον εἶναι.

ΠΩΛ. Πάνυ γε.

ΣΩ. Σὺ δὲ τὸ ἀδικεῖσθαι.

ΠΩΛ. Ναί.

ΣΩ. Καὶ τοὺς ἀδικοῦντας ἀθλίους ἔφην εἶναι ἐγώ, καὶ ἐξηλέγχθην ὑπὸ σοῦ.

ΠΩΛ. Ναὶ μὰ Δία.

ΣΩ. Ὡς σύ γε οἴει, ὦ Πῶλε.

ΠΩΛ. Ἀληθῆ γε οἰόμενος.

ΣΩ. Ἴσως. σὺ δέ γε εὐδαίμονας αὖ τοὺς ἀδικοῦντας, ἐὰν μὴ διδῶσι δίκην.

GORGIAS

soc. And I say it is impossible. There we have one point at issue. Very good; but then, will a man be happy in wrongdoing if he comes in for requital and punishment?

pol. Not at all, since in that case he would be most wretched.

soc. But if the wrongdoer escapes requital, by your account he will be happy?

pol. Yes.

soc. Whereas in my opinion, Polus, the wrongdoer or the unjust is wretched anyhow; more wretched, however, if he does not pay the penalty and gets no punishment for his wrongdoing, but less wretched if he pays the penalty and meets with requital from gods and men.

pol. What a strange doctrine, Socrates, you are trying to maintain!

soc. Yes, and I will endeavour to make you too, my friend, maintain it with me: for I count you as a friend. Well now, these are the points on which we differ; just examine them yourself. I think I told you at an earlier stage that wrongdoing was worse than being wronged.

pol. Certainly you did.

soc. And you thought that being wronged was worse.

pol. Yes.

soc. And I said that wrongdoers were wretched, and I was refuted by you.

pol. Upon my word, yes.

soc. At least to your thinking, Polus.

pol. Yes, and true thinking too.

soc. Perhaps. But you said, on the other hand, that wrongdoers are happy, if they pay no penalty.

ΠΩΛ. Πάνυ μὲν οὖν.

ΣΩ. Ἐγὼ δὲ αὐτοὺς ἀθλιωτάτους φημί, τοὺς δὲ διδόντας δίκην ἧττον. βούλει καὶ τοῦτο ἐλέγχειν;

ΠΩΛ. Ἀλλ' ἔτι τοῦτ' ἐκείνου χαλεπώτερόν ἐστιν, ὦ Σώκρατες, ἐξελέγξαι.

ΣΩ. Οὐ δῆτα, ὦ Πῶλε, ἀλλ' ἀδύνατον· τὸ γὰρ ἀληθὲς οὐδέποτε ἐλέγχεται.

C ΠΩΛ. Πῶς λέγεις; ἐὰν ἀδικῶν ἄνθρωπος ληφθῇ τυραννίδι ἐπιβουλεύων, καὶ ληφθεὶς στρεβλῶται καὶ ἐκτέμνηται καὶ τοὺς ὀφθαλμοὺς ἐκκάηται, καὶ ἄλλας πολλὰς καὶ μεγάλας καὶ παντοδαπὰς λώβας αὐτός τε λωβηθεὶς καὶ τοὺς αὑτοῦ ἐπιδὼν παῖδάς τε καὶ γυναῖκα τὸ ἔσχατον ἀνασταυρωθῇ ἢ καταπιττωθῇ, οὗτος εὐδαιμονέστερος ἔσται, ἢ ἐὰν διαφυγὼν τύραννος καταστῇ καὶ ἄρχων ἐν τῇ πόλει διαβιῷ ποιῶν ὅ τι ἂν βούληται, ζηλωτὸς ὢν καὶ εὐδαιμονιζόμενος ὑπὸ τῶν πολιτῶν καὶ D τῶν ἄλλων ξένων; ταῦτα λέγεις ἀδύνατον εἶναι ἐξελέγχειν;

ΣΩ. Μορμολύττῃ αὖ, ὦ γενναῖε Πῶλε, καὶ οὐκ ἐλέγχεις· ἄρτι δὲ ἐμαρτύρου. ὅμως δὲ ὑπόμνησόν με σμικρόν· ἐὰν ἀδίκως ἐπιβουλεύων τυραννίδι, εἶπες;

ΠΩΛ. Ἔγωγε.

ΣΩ. Εὐδαιμονέστερος μὲν τοίνυν οὐδέποτε ἔσται οὐδέτερος αὐτῶν, οὔτε ὁ κατειργασμένος τὴν τυραννίδα ἀδίκως οὔτε ὁ διδοὺς δίκην· δυοῖν γὰρ E ἀθλίοιν εὐδαιμονέστερος μὲν οὐκ ἂν εἴη· ἀθλιώτερος μέντοι ὁ διαφεύγων καὶ τυραννεύσας. τί τοῦτο, ὦ Πῶλε; γελᾷς; ἄλλο αὖ τοῦτο εἶδος

348

GORGIAS

POL. Certainly.

SOC. Whereas I say they are most wretched, and those who pay the penalty, less so. Do you wish to refute that as well?

POL. Why, that is still harder to refute, Socrates, than the other!

SOC. Not merely so, Polus, but impossible; for the truth is never refuted.

POL. How do you mean? If a man be caught criminally plotting to make himself a despot, and he be straightway put on the rack and castrated and have his eyes burnt out, and after suffering himself, and seeing inflicted on his wife and children, a number of grievous torments of every kind, he be finally crucified or burnt in a coat of pitch, will he be happier than if he escape and make himself despot, and pass his life as the ruler in his city, doing whatever he likes, and envied and congratulated by the citizens and the foreigners besides? Impossible, do you tell me, to refute that?

SOC. You are trying to make my flesh creep this time, my spirited Polus, instead of refuting me; a moment ago you were for calling witnesses. However, please refresh my memory a little: "criminally plotting to make himself a despot," you said?

POL. I did.

SOC. Then neither of them will ever be happier than the other—neither he who has unjustly compassed the despotic power, nor he who pays the penalty; for of two wretched persons neither can be *happier*; but still more wretched is he who goes scot-free and establishes himself as despot. What is that I see, Polus? You are laughing?

PLATO

ἐλέγχου ἐστίν, ἐπειδάν τίς τι εἴπῃ, καταγελᾶν, ἐλέγχειν δὲ μή;

ΠΩΛ. Οὐκ οἴει ἐξεληλέγχθαι, ὦ Σώκρατες, ὅταν τοιαῦτα λέγῃς, ἃ οὐδεὶς ἂν φήσειεν ἀνθρώπων; ἐπεὶ ἐροῦ τινὰ τουτωνί.

ΣΩ. Ὦ Πῶλε, οὐκ εἰμὶ τῶν πολιτικῶν, καὶ πέρυσι βουλεύειν λαχών, ἐπειδὴ ἡ φυλὴ ἐπρυτάνευε καὶ ἔδει με ἐπιψηφίζειν, γέλωτα παρεῖχον καὶ οὐκ ἠπιστάμην ἐπιψηφίζειν. μὴ οὖν μηδὲ νῦν με κέλευε ἐπιψηφίζειν τοὺς παρόντας, ἀλλ' εἰ μὴ ἔχεις τούτων βελτίω ἔλεγχον, ὅπερ νῦν δὴ ἐγὼ ἔλεγον, ἐμοὶ ἐν τῷ μέρει παράδος, καὶ πείρασαι τοῦ ἐλέγχου, οἷον ἐγὼ οἶμαι δεῖν εἶναι. ἐγὼ γὰρ ὧν ἂν λέγω ἕνα μὲν παρασχέσθαι μάρτυρα ἐπίσταμαι, αὐτὸν πρὸς ὃν ἄν μοι ὁ λόγος ᾖ, τοὺς δὲ πολλοὺς ἐῶ χαίρειν, καὶ ἕνα ἐπιψηφίζειν ἐπίσταμαι, τοῖς δὲ πολλοῖς οὐδὲ διαλέγομαι. ὅρα οὖν, εἰ ἐθελήσεις ἐν τῷ μέρει διδόναι ἔλεγχον ἀποκρινόμενος τὰ ἐρωτώμενα. ἐγὼ γὰρ δὴ οἶμαι καὶ ἐμὲ καὶ σὲ καὶ τοὺς ἄλλους ἀνθρώπους τὸ ἀδικεῖν τοῦ ἀδικεῖσθαι κάκιον ἡγεῖσθαι καὶ τὸ μὴ διδόναι δίκην τοῦ διδόναι.

ΠΩΛ. Ἐγὼ δέ γε οὔτ' ἐμὲ οὔτ' ἄλλον ἀνθρώπων οὐδένα. ἐπεὶ σὺ δέξαι' ἂν μᾶλλον ἀδικεῖσθαι ἢ ἀδικεῖν;

ΣΩ. Καὶ σύ γ' ἂν καὶ οἱ ἄλλοι πάντες.

ΠΩΛ. Πολλοῦ γε δεῖ, ἀλλ' οὔτ' ἐγὼ οὔτε σὺ οὔτ' ἄλλος οὐδείς.

---

[1] Socrates refers humorously to his noble act in refusing to put to the vote an illegal proposal against the generals who fought at Arginusae, 406 B.C. By saying "last year" he fixes the supposed date of this conversation at 405 B.C.

GORGIAS

Here we have yet another form of refutation—when a statement is made, to laugh it down, instead of disproving it!

POL. Do you not think yourself utterly refuted, Socrates, when you make such statements as nobody in the world would assent to? You have only to ask anyone of the company here.

SOC. Polus, I am not one of your statesmen: indeed, last year, when I was elected a member of the Council, and, as my tribe held the Presidency, I had to put a question to the vote, I got laughed at for not understanding the procedure.[1] So do not call upon me again to take the votes of the company now; but if, as I said this moment, you have no better disproof than those, hand the work over to me in my turn, and try the sort of refutation that I think the case requires. For I know how to produce one witness in support of my statements, and that is the man himself with whom I find myself arguing; the many I dismiss: there is also one whose vote I know how to take, whilst to the multitude I have not a word to say. See therefore if you will consent to be put to the proof in your turn by answering my questions. For I think, indeed, that you and I and the rest of the world believe that doing wrong is worse than suffering it, and escaping punishment worse than incurring it.

POL. And I, that neither I nor anyone else in the world believes it. You, it seems, would choose rather to suffer wrong than to do it.

SOC. Yes, and so would you and everyone else.

POL. Far from it; neither I nor you nor anybody else.

PLATO

474

C ΣΩ. Οὐκοῦν ἀποκρινῇ;

ΠΩΛ. Πάνυ μὲν οὖν· καὶ γὰρ ἐπιθυμῶ εἰδέναι ὅ τί ποτ' ἐρεῖς.

ΣΩ. Λέγε δή μοι, ἵν' εἰδῇς, ὥσπερ ἂν εἰ ἐξ ἀρχῆς σε ἠρώτων· πότερον δοκεῖ σοι, ὦ Πῶλε, κάκιον εἶναι, τὸ ἀδικεῖν ἢ τὸ ἀδικεῖσθαι;

ΠΩΛ. Τὸ ἀδικεῖσθαι ἔμοιγε.

ΣΩ. Τί δὲ δή; αἴσχιον πότερον τὸ ἀδικεῖν ἢ τὸ ἀδικεῖσθαι; ἀποκρίνου.

ΠΩΛ. Τὸ ἀδικεῖν.

ΣΩ. Οὐκοῦν καὶ κάκιον, εἴπερ αἴσχιον.

ΠΩΛ. Ἥκιστά γε.

ΣΩ. Μανθάνω· οὐ ταὐτὸν ἡγῇ σύ, ὡς ἔοικας,
D καλόν τε καὶ ἀγαθὸν καὶ κακὸν καὶ αἰσχρόν.

ΠΩΛ. Οὐ δῆτα.

ΣΩ. Τί δὲ τόδε; τὰ καλὰ πάντα, οἷον καὶ σώματα καὶ χρώματα καὶ σχήματα καὶ φωνὰς καὶ ἐπιτηδεύματα, εἰς οὐδὲν ἀποβλέπων καλεῖς ἑκάστοτε καλά; οἷον πρῶτον τὰ σώματα τὰ καλὰ οὐχὶ ἤτοι κατὰ τὴν χρείαν λέγεις καλὰ εἶναι, πρὸς ὃ ἂν ἕκαστον χρήσιμον ᾖ, πρὸς τοῦτο, ἢ κατὰ ἡδονήν τινα, ἐὰν ἐν τῷ θεωρεῖσθαι χαίρειν ποιῇ τοὺς θεωροῦντας; ἔχεις τι ἐκτὸς τούτων λέγειν
E περὶ σώματος κάλλους;

ΠΩΛ. Οὐκ ἔχω.

ΣΩ. Οὐκοῦν καὶ τἆλλα πάντα οὕτω καὶ σχήματα καὶ χρώματα ἢ διὰ ἡδονήν τινα ἢ διὰ ὠφελίαν ἢ δι' ἀμφότερα καλὰ προσαγορεύεις;

ΠΩΛ. Ἔγωγε.

ΣΩ. Οὐ καὶ τὰς φωνὰς καὶ τὰ κατὰ τὴν μουσικὴν πάντα ὡσαύτως;

GORGIAS

soc. Then will you answer?

pol. To be sure I will, for indeed I am eager to know what on earth you will say.

soc. Well then, so that you may know, tell me, just as though I were asking you at the beginning, which of the two seems to you, Polus, to be the worse—doing wrong or suffering it?

pol. Suffering it, I say.

soc. Now again, which is fouler—doing wrong or suffering it? Answer.

pol. Doing it.

soc. And also more evil, if fouler.

pol. Not at all.

soc. I see: you hold, apparently, that fair and good are not the same, nor evil and foul.

pol. Just so.

soc. But what of this? All fair things, like bodies and colours and figures and sounds and observances—is it according to no standard that you call these fair in each case? Thus in the first place, when you say that fair bodies are fair, it must be either in view of their use for some particular purpose that each may serve, or in respect of some pleasure arising when, in the act of beholding them, they cause delight to the beholder. Have you any description to give beyond this of bodily beauty?

pol. I have not.

soc. And so with all the rest in the same way, whether they be figures or colours, is it for some pleasure or benefit or both that you give them the name of "fair"?

pol. It is.

soc. And sounds also, and the effects of music, are not these all in the same case?

ΠΩΛ. Ναί.

ΣΩ. Καὶ μὴν τά γε κατὰ τοὺς νόμους καὶ τὰ ἐπιτηδεύματα οὐ δήπου ἐκτὸς τούτων ἐστί, τὰ καλά, τοῦ ἢ ὠφέλιμα εἶναι ἢ ἡδέα ἢ ἀμφότερα.

ΠΩΛ. Οὐκ ἔμοιγε δοκεῖ.

ΣΩ. Οὐκοῦν καὶ τὸ τῶν μαθημάτων κάλλος ὡσαύτως;

ΠΩΛ. Πάνυ γε· καὶ καλῶς γε νῦν δὴ ὁρίζῃ, ὦ Σώκρατες, ἡδονῇ τε καὶ ἀγαθῷ ὁριζόμενος τὸ καλόν.

ΣΩ. Οὐκοῦν τὸ αἰσχρὸν τῷ ἐναντίῳ, λύπῃ τε καὶ κακῷ;

ΠΩΛ. Ἀνάγκη.

ΣΩ. Ὅταν ἄρα δυοῖν καλοῖν θάτερον κάλλιον ᾖ, ἢ τῷ ἑτέρῳ τούτοιν ἢ ἀμφοτέροις ὑπερβάλλον κάλλιόν ἐστιν, ἤτοι ἡδονῇ ἢ ὠφελίᾳ ἢ ἀμφοτέροις.

ΠΩΛ. Πάνυ γε.

ΣΩ. Καὶ ὅταν δὲ δὴ δυοῖν αἰσχροῖν τὸ ἕτερον αἴσχιον ᾖ, ἤτοι λύπῃ ἢ κακῷ ὑπερβάλλον αἴσχιον ἔσται· ἢ οὐκ ἀνάγκη;

ΠΩΛ. Ναί.

ΣΩ. Φέρε δή, πῶς ἐλέγετο νῦν δὴ περὶ τοῦ ἀδικεῖν καὶ ἀδικεῖσθαι; οὐκ ἔλεγες τὸ μὲν ἀδικεῖσθαι κάκιον εἶναι, τὸ δὲ ἀδικεῖν αἴσχιον;

ΠΩΛ. Ἔλεγον.

ΣΩ. Οὐκοῦν εἴπερ αἴσχιον τὸ ἀδικεῖν τοῦ ἀδικεῖσθαι, ἤτοι λυπηρότερόν ἐστι καὶ λύπῃ ὑπερβάλλον αἴσχιον ἂν εἴη ἢ κακῷ ἢ ἀμφοτέροις; οὐ καὶ τοῦτο ἀνάγκη;

ΠΩΛ. Πῶς γὰρ οὔ;

ΣΩ. Πρῶτον μὲν δὴ σκεψώμεθα, ἆρα λύπῃ ὑπερβάλλει τὸ ἀδικεῖν τοῦ ἀδικεῖσθαι, καὶ ἀλγοῦσι μᾶλλον οἱ ἀδικοῦντες ἢ οἱ ἀδικούμενοι;

GORGIAS

POL. Yes.

SOC. And further, in all that belongs to laws and observances, surely the " fairness " of them cannot lie beyond those limits of being either beneficial or pleasant or both.

POL. I think not.

SOC. And is it not just the same with the " fairness " of studies also ?

POL. Doubtless; and this time, Socrates, your definition is quite fair, when you define what is fair by pleasure and good.

SOC. And foul by their opposites, pain and evil ?

POL. That needs must follow.

SOC. Thus when of two fair things one is fairer, the cause is that it surpasses in either one or both of these effects, either in pleasure, or in benefit, or in both.

POL. Certainly.

SOC. And again, when one of two foul things is fouler, this will be due to an excess either of pain or of evil : must not that be so ?

POL. Yes.

SOC. Come then, what was it we heard just now about doing and suffering wrong ? Were you not saying that suffering wrong is more evil, but doing it fouler ?

POL. I was.

SOC. Well now, if doing wrong is fouler than suffering it, it is either more painful, and fouler by an excess of pain or evil or both ; must not this also be the case ?

POL. Yes, of course.

SOC. Then let us first consider if doing wrong exceeds suffering it in point of pain—if those who do wrong are more pained than those who suffer it.

355

ΠΩΛ. Οὐδαμῶς, ὦ Σώκρατες, τοῦτό γε.
ΣΩ. Οὐκ ἄρα λύπῃ γε ὑπερέχει.
ΠΩΛ. Οὐ δῆτα.
ΣΩ. Οὐκοῦν εἰ μὴ λύπῃ, ἀμφοτέροις μὲν οὐκ ἂν ἔτι ὑπερβάλλοι.
ΠΩΛ. Οὐ φαίνεται.
ΣΩ. Οὐκοῦν τῷ ἑτέρῳ λείπεται.
ΠΩΛ. Ναί.
ΣΩ. Τῷ κακῷ.
ΠΩΛ. Ἔοικεν.
ΣΩ. Οὐκοῦν κακῷ ὑπερβάλλον τὸ ἀδικεῖν κάκιον ἂν εἴη τοῦ ἀδικεῖσθαι.
ΠΩΛ. Δῆλον δὴ ὅτι.
ΣΩ. Ἄλλο τι οὖν ὑπὸ μὲν τῶν πολλῶν ἀνθρώπων καὶ ὑπὸ σοῦ ὡμολογεῖτο ἡμῖν ἐν τῷ ἔμπροσθεν χρόνῳ αἴσχιον εἶναι τὸ ἀδικεῖν τοῦ ἀδικεῖσθαι;
ΠΩΛ. Ναί.
ΣΩ. Νῦν δέ γε κάκιον ἐφάνη.
ΠΩΛ. Ἔοικεν.
ΣΩ. Δέξαιο ἂν οὖν σὺ μᾶλλον τὸ κάκιον καὶ τὸ αἴσχιον ἀντὶ τοῦ ἧττον; μὴ ὄκνει ἀποκρίνασθαι, ὦ Πῶλε· οὐδὲν γὰρ βλαβήσῃ· ἀλλὰ γενναίως τῷ λόγῳ ὥσπερ ἰατρῷ παρέχων ἀποκρίνου, καὶ ἢ φάθι ἢ μὴ ἃ ἐρωτῶ.
ΠΩΛ. Ἀλλ' οὐκ ἂν δεξαίμην, ὦ Σώκρατες.
ΣΩ. Ἄλλος δέ τις ἀνθρώπων;
ΠΩΛ. Οὔ μοι δοκεῖ κατά γε τοῦτον τὸν λόγον.
ΣΩ. Ἀληθῆ ἄρα ἐγὼ ἔλεγον, ὅτι οὔτ' ἂν ἐγὼ οὔτ' ἂν σὺ οὔτ' ἄλλος οὐδεὶς ἀνθρώπων δέξαιτ' ἂν μᾶλλον ἀδικεῖν ἢ ἀδικεῖσθαι· κάκιον γὰρ τυγχάνει ὄν.
ΠΩΛ. Φαίνεται.

GORGIAS

POL. Not so at all, Socrates.

SOC. Then it does not surpass in pain.

POL. No, indeed.

SOC. And so, if not in pain, it can no longer be said to exceed in both.

POL. Apparently.

SOC. It remains, then, that it exceeds in the other.

POL. Yes.

SOC. In evil.

POL. So it seems.

SOC. And so, if it exceeds in evil, doing wrong will be more evil than suffering it.

POL. Yes, obviously.

SOC. Now it is surely admitted by the mass of mankind, as it was too by you in our talk a while ago, that doing wrong is fouler than suffering it.

POL. Yes.

SOC. And now it has been found to be more evil.

POL. So it seems.

SOC. Then would you rather have the evil and foul when it is more than when it is less? Do not shrink from answering, Polus; you will get no hurt by it: but submit yourself bravely to the argument, as to a doctor, and reply yes or no to my question.

POL. Why, I should not so choose, Socrates.

SOC. And would anybody else in the world?

POL. I think not, by this argument at least.

SOC. Then I spoke the truth when I said that neither you nor anyone else in the world would choose to do wrong rather than suffer it, since it really is more evil.

POL. Apparently.

PLATO

ΣΩ. Ὁρᾷς οὖν, ὦ Πῶλε, ὁ ἔλεγχος παρὰ τὸν ἔλεγχον παραβαλλόμενος ὅτι οὐδὲν ἔοικεν, ἀλλὰ σοὶ μὲν οἱ ἄλλοι πάντες ὁμολογοῦσι πλὴν ἐμοῦ, ἐμοὶ δὲ σὺ ἐξαρκεῖς εἷς ὢν μόνος καὶ ὁμολογῶν καὶ μαρτυρῶν, καὶ ἐγὼ σὲ μόνον ἐπιψηφίζων τοὺς ἄλλους ἐῶ χαίρειν. καὶ τοῦτο μὲν ἡμῖν οὕτως ἐχέτω· μετὰ τοῦτο δὲ περὶ οὗ τὸ δεύτερον ἠμφεσβητήσαμεν σκεψώμεθα, τὸ ἀδικοῦντα διδόναι δίκην ἆρα μέγιστον τῶν κακῶν ἐστίν, ὡς σὺ ᾤου, ἢ μεῖζον τὸ μὴ διδόναι, ὡς αὖ ἐγὼ ᾤμην. σκοπώμεθα δὲ τῇδε· τὸ διδόναι δίκην καὶ τὸ κολάζεσθαι δικαίως ἀδικοῦντα ἆρα τὸ αὐτὸ καλεῖς;

ΠΩΛ. Ἔγωγε.

ΣΩ. Ἔχεις οὖν λέγειν, ὡς οὐχὶ τά γε δίκαια πάντα καλά ἐστι, καθ᾽ ὅσον δίκαια; καὶ διασκεψάμενος εἰπέ.

ΠΩΛ. Ἀλλά μοι δοκεῖ, ὦ Σώκρατες.

ΣΩ. Σκόπει δὴ καὶ τόδε· ἆρα εἴ τίς τι ποιεῖ, ἀνάγκη τι εἶναι καὶ πάσχον ὑπὸ τούτου τοῦ ποιοῦντος;

ΠΩΛ. Ἔμοιγε δοκεῖ.

ΣΩ. Ἆρα τοῦτο πάσχον, ὃ τὸ ποιοῦν ποιεῖ, καὶ τοιοῦτον, οἷον ποιεῖ τὸ ποιοῦν; λέγω δὲ τὸ τοιόνδε· εἴ τις τύπτει, ἀνάγκη τι τύπτεσθαι;

ΠΩΛ. Ἀνάγκη.

ΣΩ. Καὶ εἰ σφόδρα τύπτει ἢ ταχὺ ὁ τύπτων, οὕτω καὶ τὸ τυπτόμενον τύπτεσθαι;

ΠΩΛ. Ναί.

ΣΩ. Τοιοῦτον ἄρα πάθος τῷ τυπτομένῳ ἐστίν, οἷον ἂν τὸ τύπτον ποιῇ;

ΠΩΛ. Πάνυ γε.

GORGIAS

soc. So you see, Polus, that when one proof is contrasted with the other they have no resemblance, but whereas you have the assent of every one else except myself, I am satisfied with your sole and single assent and evidence, and I take but your vote only and disregard the rest. Now let us leave this matter where it stands, and proceed next to examine the second part on which we found ourselves at issue—whether for a wrongdoer to pay the penalty is the greatest of evils, as you supposed, or to escape it is a greater, as I on my side held. Let us look at it this way : do you call paying the just penalty, and being justly punished, for wrongdoing the same thing ?

pol. I do.

soc. And can you maintain that all just things are not fair, in so far as they are just ? Consider well before you speak.

pol. No, I think they are, Socrates.

soc. Then take another point : if a man does anything, must there be something which is also acted upon by this doer of the thing ?

pol. I think so.

soc. And does it suffer what the doer does, and is the effect such as the agent's action makes it ? I mean, for example, when one strikes a blow something must needs be struck ?

pol. It must.

soc. And if the striker strikes hard or quick, the thing struck is struck in the same way ?

pol. Yes.

soc. Hence the effect in the thing struck is such as the striker makes it ?

pol. Certainly.

PLATO

ΣΩ. Οὐκοῦν καὶ εἰ κάει τις, ἀνάγκη τι κάεσθαι;

ΠΩΛ. Πῶς γὰρ οὔ;

ΣΩ. Καὶ εἰ σφόδρα γε κάει ἢ ἀλγεινῶς, οὕτω κάεσθαι τὸ καόμενον ὡς ἂν τὸ κᾶον κάῃ;

ΠΩΛ. Πάνυ γε.

ΣΩ. Οὐκοῦν καὶ εἰ τέμνει τις, ὁ αὐτὸς λόγος; τέμνεται γάρ τι.

ΠΩΛ. Ναί.

ΣΩ. Καὶ εἰ μέγα γε ἢ βαθὺ τὸ τμῆμα ἢ ἀλγεινόν, τοιοῦτον τμῆμα τέμνεται τὸ τεμνόμενον, οἷον τὸ τέμνον τέμνει;

ΠΩΛ. Φαίνεται.

ΣΩ. Συλλήβδην δὴ ὅρα εἰ ὁμολογεῖς, ὃ ἄρτι ἔλεγον, περὶ πάντων, οἷον ἂν ποιῇ τὸ ποιοῦν, τοιοῦτον τὸ πάσχον πάσχειν.

ΠΩΛ. Ἀλλ' ὁμολογῶ.

ΣΩ. Τούτων δὴ ὁμολογουμένων, τὸ δίκην διδόναι πότερον πάσχειν τί ἐστιν ἢ ποιεῖν;

ΠΩΛ. Ἀνάγκη, ὦ Σώκρατες, πάσχειν.

ΣΩ. Οὐκοῦν ὑπό τινος ποιοῦντος;

ΠΩΛ. Πῶς γὰρ οὔ; ὑπό γε τοῦ κολάζοντος.

ΣΩ. Ὁ δὲ ὀρθῶς κολάζων δικαίως κολάζει;

ΠΩΛ. Ναί.

ΣΩ. Δίκαια ποιῶν ἢ οὔ;

ΠΩΛ. Δίκαια.

ΣΩ. Οὐκοῦν ὁ κολαζόμενος δίκην διδοὺς δίκαια πάσχει;

ΠΩΛ. Φαίνεται.

ΣΩ. Τὰ δὲ δίκαιά που καλὰ ὡμολόγηται;

ΠΩΛ. Πάνυ γε.

ΣΩ. Τούτων ἄρα ὁ μὲν ποιεῖ καλά, ὁ δὲ πάσχει, ὁ κολαζόμενος.

GORGIAS

soc. And so again, if one burns, something must be burnt?

pol. Yes, of course.

soc. And if one burns severely or sorely, the thing burnt is burnt according as the burner burns it?

pol. Certainly.

soc. And again, if one cuts, the same may be said? For something is cut.

pol. Yes.

soc. And if the cut is large or deep or sore, the cut made in the thing cut is such as the cutter cuts it?

pol. Apparently.

soc. Then putting it all in a word, see if you agree that what I was just saying applies to all cases—that the patient receives an effect of the same kind as the agent's action.

pol. I do agree.

soc. Then this being admitted, is paying the penalty suffering something, or doing it?

pol. Suffering it must be, Socrates.

soc. And at the hands of an agent?

pol. Yes, of course; at the hands of the punisher.

soc. And he who punishes aright punishes justly?

pol. Yes.

soc. Doing what is just, or not?

pol. What is just.

soc. And he who pays the penalty by being punished suffers what is just?

pol. Apparently.

soc. And what is just, I think we have agreed, is fair?

pol. Certainly.

soc. Then of these two, the one does what is fair and the other, he who is punished, suffers it.

ΠΩΛ. Ναί.

ΣΩ. Οὐκοῦν εἴπερ καλά, ἀγαθά; ἢ γὰρ ἡδέα ἢ ὠφέλιμα.

ΠΩΛ. Ἀνάγκη.

ΣΩ. Ἀγαθὰ ἄρα πάσχει ὁ δίκην διδούς;

ΠΩΛ. Ἔοικεν.

ΣΩ. Ὠφελεῖται ἄρα;

ΠΩΛ. Ναί.

ΣΩ. Ἆρα ἥνπερ ἐγὼ ὑπολαμβάνω τὴν ὠφελίαν; βελτίων τὴν ψυχὴν γίγνεται, εἴπερ δικαίως κολάζεται;

ΠΩΛ. Εἰκός γε.

ΣΩ. Κακίας ἄρα ψυχῆς ἀπαλλάττεται ὁ δίκην διδούς;

ΠΩΛ. Ναί.

ΣΩ. Ἆρ' οὖν τοῦ μεγίστου ἀπαλλάττεται κακοῦ; ὧδε δὲ σκόπει· ἐν χρημάτων κατασκευῇ ἀνθρώπου κακίαν ἄλλην τινὰ ἐνορᾷς ἢ πενίαν;

ΠΩΛ. Οὔκ, ἀλλὰ πενίαν.

ΣΩ. Τί δ' ἐν σώματος κατασκευῇ; κακίαν ἂν φήσαις ἀσθένειαν εἶναι καὶ νόσον καὶ αἶσχος καὶ τὰ τοιαῦτα;

ΠΩΛ. Ἔγωγε.

ΣΩ. Οὐκοῦν καὶ ἐν ψυχῇ πονηρίαν ἡγῇ τινὰ εἶναι;

ΠΩΛ. Πῶς γὰρ οὔ;

ΣΩ. Ταύτην οὖν οὐκ ἀδικίαν καλεῖς καὶ ἀμαθίαν καὶ δειλίαν καὶ τὰ τοιαῦτα;

ΠΩΛ. Πάνυ μὲν οὖν.

ΣΩ. Οὐκοῦν χρημάτων καὶ σώματος καὶ ψυχῆς, τριῶν ὄντων, τριττὰς εἴρηκας πονηρίας, πενίαν, νόσον, ἀδικίαν;

GORGIAS

POL. Yes.

SOC. And so, if fair, good? For that is either pleasant or beneficial.[1]

POL. It must be so.

SOC. So he who pays the penalty suffers what is good?

POL. It seems so.

SOC. Then he is benefited?

POL. Yes.

SOC. Is it the benefit I imagine—that he becomes better in soul if he is justly punished?

POL. Quite likely.

SOC. Then is he who pays the penalty relieved from badness of soul?

POL. Yes.

SOC. And so relieved from the greatest evil? Look at it this way; in a man's pecuniary resources do you perceive any other badness than poverty?

POL. No, only poverty.

SOC. And what in his bodily resources? You would say that badness there is weakness or disease or ugliness or the like?

POL. I would.

SOC. And in soul too you believe there is a certain vice?

POL. Of course.

SOC. And do you not call this injustice, ignorance, cowardice, and so forth?

POL. Certainly I do.

SOC. So now in property, body, and soul, these three, you have mentioned three vices—poverty, disease, and injustice?

---

[1] As was agreed above, 474 D, E.

ΠΩΛ. Ναί.

ΣΩ. Τίς οὖν τούτων τῶν πονηριῶν αἰσχίστη; οὐχ ἡ ἀδικία καὶ συλλήβδην ἡ τῆς ψυχῆς πονηρία;

ΠΩΛ. Πολύ γε.

ΣΩ. Εἰ δὴ αἰσχίστη, καὶ κακίστη;

ΠΩΛ. Πῶς, ὦ Σώκρατες, λέγεις;

ΣΩ. Ὡδί· ἀεὶ τὸ αἴσχιστον ἤτοι λύπην μεγίστην παρέχον ἢ βλάβην ἢ ἀμφότερα αἴσχιστόν ἐστιν ἐκ τῶν ὡμολογημένων ἐν τῷ ἔμπροσθεν.

ΠΩΛ. Μάλιστα.

ΣΩ. Αἴσχιστον δὲ ἀδικία καὶ σύμπασα ψυχῆς πονηρία νῦν δὴ ὡμολόγηται ἡμῖν;

ΠΩΛ. Ὡμολόγηται γάρ.

ΣΩ. Οὐκοῦν ἢ ἀνιαρότατόν ἐστι καὶ ἀνίᾳ ὑπερβάλλον αἴσχιστον τούτων ἐστὶν ἢ βλάβῃ ἢ ἀμφότερα;

ΠΩΛ. Ἀνάγκη.

ΣΩ. Ἆρ' οὖν ἀλγεινότερόν ἐστι τοῦ πένεσθαι καὶ κάμνειν τὸ ἄδικον εἶναι καὶ ἀκόλαστον καὶ δειλὸν καὶ ἀμαθῆ;

ΠΩΛ. Οὐκ ἔμοιγε δοκεῖ, ὦ Σώκρατες, ἀπὸ τούτων γε.

ΣΩ. Ὑπερφυεῖ τινὶ ἄρα ὡς μεγάλῃ βλάβῃ καὶ κακῷ θαυμασίῳ ὑπερβάλλουσα τἆλλα ἡ τῆς ψυχῆς πονηρία αἴσχιστόν ἐστι πάντων, ἐπειδὴ οὐκ ἀλγηδόνι γε, ὡς ὁ σὸς λόγος.

ΠΩΛ. Φαίνεται.

ΣΩ. Ἀλλὰ μήν που τό γε μεγίστῃ βλάβῃ ὑπερβάλλον μέγιστον ἂν κακὸν εἴη τῶν ὄντων.

ΠΩΛ. Ναί.

ΣΩ. Ἡ ἀδικία ἄρα καὶ ἡ ἀκολασία καὶ ἡ ἄλλη ψυχῆς πονηρία μέγιστον τῶν ὄντων κακόν ἐστιν;

GORGIAS

POL. Yes.

SOC. Then which of these vices is the foulest? Is it not injustice—in short, the vice of the soul?

POL. Far the foulest.

SOC. And if foulest, then also most evil?

POL. How do you mean, Socrates?

SOC. Just this: the foulest is foulest in each case because it produces the greatest pain or harm or both; this follows from our previous admissions.

POL. Quite so.

SOC. And foulest of all, we have just agreed, is injustice and, in general, vice of soul?

POL. Yes, we have.

SOC. So then either it is most painful, that is, foulest of these vices by an excess of painfulness, or else of harmfulness, or in both ways?

POL. Necessarily.

SOC. Then do you think that being unjust, licentious, cowardly, and ignorant is more painful than being poor and sick?

POL. No, I do not, Socrates, from what we have said.

SOC. Portentous then must be the extent of harm, and astonishing the evil, by which the soul's vice exceeds all the others so as to be foulest of all, since it is not by pain, on your view of the matter.

POL. Apparently.

SOC. But further, I suppose, whatever has an excess of harm in the greatest measure, must be the greatest evil in the world.

POL. Yes.

SOC. So injustice, licentiousness, and in general, vice of soul, are the greatest evils in the world?

PLATO

ΠΩΛ. Φαίνεται.

ΣΩ. Τίς οὖν τέχνη πενίας ἀπαλλάττει; οὐ χρηματιστική;

ΠΩΛ. Ναί.

ΣΩ. Τίς δὲ νόσου; οὐκ ἰατρική;

ΠΩΛ. Ἀνάγκη.

ΣΩ. Τίς δὲ πονηρίας καὶ ἀδικίας; εἰ μὴ οὕτως εὐπορεῖς, ὧδε σκόπει· ποῖ ἄγομεν καὶ παρὰ τίνας τοὺς κάμνοντας τὰ σώματα;

ΠΩΛ. Παρὰ τοὺς ἰατρούς, ὦ Σώκρατες.

ΣΩ. Ποῖ δὲ τοὺς ἀδικοῦντας καὶ τοὺς ἀκολασταίνοντας;

ΠΩΛ. Παρὰ τοὺς δικαστὰς λέγεις;

ΣΩ. Οὐκοῦν δίκην δώσοντας;

ΠΩΛ. Φημί.

ΣΩ. Ἆρ' οὖν οὐ δικαιοσύνῃ τινὶ χρώμενοι κολάζουσιν οἱ ὀρθῶς κολάζοντες;

ΠΩΛ. Δῆλον δή.

ΣΩ. Χρηματιστικὴ μὲν ἄρα πενίας ἀπαλλάττει, ἰατρικὴ δὲ νόσου, δίκη δὲ ἀκολασίας καὶ ἀδικίας.

ΠΩΛ. Φαίνεται.

ΣΩ. Τί οὖν τούτων κάλλιστόν ἐστιν [ὧν λέγεις][1];

ΠΩΛ. Τίνων λέγεις;

ΣΩ. Χρηματιστικῆς, ἰατρικῆς, δίκης.

ΠΩΛ. Πολὺ διαφέρει, ὦ Σώκρατες, ἡ δίκη.

ΣΩ. Οὐκοῦν αὖ ἤτοι ἡδονὴν πλείστην ποιεῖ ἢ ὠφελίαν ἢ ἀμφότερα, εἴπερ κάλλιστόν ἐστιν;

ΠΩΛ. Ναί.

ΣΩ. Ἆρ' οὖν τὸ ἰατρεύεσθαι ἡδύ ἐστι, καὶ χαίρουσιν οἱ ἰατρευόμενοι;

ΠΩΛ. Οὐκ ἔμοιγε δοκεῖ.

[1] ὧν λέγεις secl. Hermann.

GORGIAS

POL. Apparently.

SOC. Now what is the art that relieves from poverty? Is it not money-making?

POL. Yes.

SOC. And what from disease? Is it not medicine?

POL. It must be.

SOC. And what from wickedness and injustice? If you are not ready for that offhand, consider it thus: whither and to whom do we take those who are in bodily sickness?

POL. To the doctor, Socrates.

SOC. And whither the wrongdoers and libertines?

POL. To the law-court, do you mean?

SOC. Yes, and to pay the penalty?

POL. I agree.

SOC. Then is it not by employing a kind of justice that those punish who punish aright?

POL. Clearly so.

SOC. Then money-making relieves us from poverty, medicine from disease, and justice from licentiousness and injustice.

POL. Apparently.

SOC. Which then is the fairest of these things?

POL. Of what things, pray?

SOC. Money-making, medicine, justice.

POL. Justice, Socrates, is far above the others.

SOC. Now again, if it is fairest, it causes either most pleasure or benefit or both.

POL. Yes.

SOC. Well then, is it pleasant to be medically treated, and do those who undergo such treatment enjoy it?

POL. I do not think so.

ΣΩ. Ἀλλ' ὠφέλιμόν γε. ἢ γάρ;
ΠΩΛ. Ναί.
ΣΩ. Μεγάλου γὰρ κακοῦ ἀπαλλάττεται, ὥστε λυσιτελεῖ ὑπομεῖναι τὴν ἀλγηδόνα καὶ ὑγιεῖ εἶναι.
ΠΩΛ. Πῶς γὰρ οὔ;
ΣΩ. Ἆρ' οὖν οὕτως ἂν περὶ σῶμα εὐδαιμονέστατος ἄνθρωπος εἴη, ἰατρευόμενος, ἢ μηδὲ κάμνων ἀρχήν;
ΠΩΛ. Δῆλον ὅτι μηδὲ κάμνων.
ΣΩ. Οὐ γὰρ τοῦτ' ἦν εὐδαιμονία, ὡς ἔοικε, κακοῦ ἀπαλλαγή, ἀλλὰ τὴν ἀρχὴν μηδὲ κτῆσις.
ΠΩΛ. Ἔστι ταῦτα.
ΣΩ. Τί δέ; ἀθλιώτερος πότερος δυοῖν ἐχόντοιν κακὸν εἴτ' ἐν σώματι εἴτ' ἐν ψυχῇ, ὁ ἰατρευόμενος καὶ ἀπαλλαττόμενος τοῦ κακοῦ, ἢ ὁ μὴ ἰατρευόμενος, ἔχων δέ;
ΠΩΛ. Φαίνεταί μοι ὁ μὴ ἰατρευόμενος.
ΣΩ. Οὐκοῦν τὸ δίκην διδόναι μεγίστου κακοῦ ἀπαλλαγὴ ἦν, πονηρίας;
ΠΩΛ. Ἦν γάρ.
ΣΩ. Σωφρονίζει γάρ που καὶ δικαιοτέρους ποιεῖ καὶ ἰατρικὴ γίγνεται πονηρίας ἡ δίκη.
ΠΩΛ. Ναί.
ΣΩ. Εὐδαιμονέστατος μὲν ἄρα ὁ μὴ ἔχων κακίαν ἐν ψυχῇ, ἐπειδὴ τοῦτο μέγιστον τῶν κακῶν ἐφάνη.
ΠΩΛ. Δῆλον δή.
ΣΩ. Δεύτερος δήπου ὁ ἀπαλλαττόμενος.
ΠΩΛ. Ἔοικεν.
ΣΩ. Οὗτος δ' ἦν ὁ νουθετούμενός τε καὶ ἐπιπληττόμενος καὶ δίκην διδούς.
ΠΩΛ. Ναί.

GORGIAS

soc. But it is beneficial, is it not?

pol. Yes.

soc. Because one is relieved of a great evil, and hence it is worth while to endure the pain and be well.

pol. Of course.

soc. Is this then the happiest state of body for a man to be in—that of being medically treated—or that of never being ill at all?

pol. Clearly, never being ill.

soc. Yes, for what we regarded as happiness, it seems, was not this relief from evil, but its non-acquisition at any time.

pol. That is so.

soc. Well now, which is the more wretched of two persons who have something evil either in body or in soul, he who is medically treated and is relieved of the evil, or he who is not treated and keeps it?

pol. To my thinking, he who is not treated.

soc. And we found that paying the penalty is a relief from the greatest evil, wickedness?

pol. We did.

soc. Because, I suppose, the justice of the court reforms us and makes us juster, and acts as a medicine for wickedness.

pol. Yes.

soc. Happiest therefore is he who has no vice in his soul, since we found this to be the greatest of evils.

pol. Clearly so.

soc. Next after him, I take it, is he who is relieved of it.

pol. So it seems.

soc. And that was the man who is reproved, reprimanded, and made to pay the penalty.

pol. Yes.

478

ΣΩ. Κάκιστα ἄρα ζῇ ὁ ἔχων [ἀδικίαν][1] καὶ μὴ ἀπαλλαττόμενος.

ΠΩΛ. Φαίνεται.

ΣΩ. Οὐκοῦν οὗτος τυγχάνει ὢν ὃς ἂν τὰ μέγιστα ἀδικῶν καὶ χρώμενος μεγίστῃ ἀδικίᾳ διαπράξηται ὥστε μήτε νουθετεῖσθαι μήτε κολάζεσθαι 479 μήτε δίκην διδόναι, ὥσπερ σὺ φῂς Ἀρχέλαον παρεσκευάσθαι καὶ τοὺς ἄλλους τυράννους καὶ ῥήτορας καὶ δυνάστας;

ΠΩΛ. Ἔοικεν.

ΣΩ. Σχεδὸν γάρ που οὗτοι, ὦ ἄριστε, τὸ αὐτὸ διαπεπραγμένοι εἰσί, ὥσπερ ἂν εἴ τις τοῖς μεγίστοις νοσήμασι συνισχόμενος διαπράξαιτο μὴ διδόναι δίκην τῶν περὶ τὸ σῶμα ἁμαρτημάτων τοῖς ἰατροῖς μηδὲ ἰατρεύεσθαι, φοβούμενος, ὡσπερανεὶ παῖς, τὸ κάεσθαι καὶ τὸ τέμνεσθαι, ὅτι B ἀλγεινόν. ἢ οὐ δοκεῖ καὶ σοὶ οὕτως;

ΠΩΛ. Ἔμοιγε.

ΣΩ. Ἀγνοῶν γε, ὡς ἔοικεν, οἷόν ἐστιν ἡ ὑγίεια καὶ ἀρετὴ σώματος. κινδυνεύουσι γὰρ ἐκ τῶν νῦν ἡμῖν ὡμολογημένων τοιοῦτόν τι ποιεῖν καὶ οἱ τὴν δίκην φεύγοντες, ὦ Πῶλε, τὸ ἀλγεινὸν αὐτοῦ καθορᾶν, πρὸς δὲ τὸ ὠφέλιμον τυφλῶς ἔχειν καὶ ἀγνοεῖν, ὅσῳ ἀθλιώτερόν ἐστι μὴ ὑγιοῦς σώματος μὴ ὑγιεῖ ψυχῇ συνοικεῖν, ἀλλὰ σαθρᾷ καὶ ἀδίκῳ C καὶ ἀνοσίῳ· ὅθεν καὶ πᾶν ποιοῦσιν ὥστε δίκην μὴ διδόναι μηδ' ἀπαλλάττεσθαι τοῦ μεγίστου κακοῦ, καὶ χρήματα παρασκευαζόμενοι καὶ φίλους καὶ ὅπως ἂν ὦσιν ὡς πιθανώτατοι λέγειν. εἰ δὲ ἡμεῖς ἀληθῆ ὡμολογήκαμεν, ὦ Πῶλε, ἆρ' αἰσθάνῃ

[1] ἀδικίαν om. Stobaeus.

GORGIAS

soc. Hence the worst life is led by him who has the vice and is not relieved of it.

pol. Apparently.

soc. And this is the man who in committing the greatest wrongs and practising the greatest injustice has contrived to escape reproof and chastisement and penalty alike, as you say Archelaus has succeeded in doing, and the rest of the despots and orators and overlords?

pol. So it seems.

soc. Because, I conceive, my excellent friend, what these persons have contrived for themselves is very much as though a man who was the victim of the worst diseases should contrive not to submit to the doctor's penalty for his bodily transgressions and take the prescribed treatment, from a childish fear of cautery or incision, as being so painful. Or do you not agree to this view of it?

pol. I do.

soc. Since he was ignorant, it would seem, of the virtue of bodily health and fitness. For it is very probable, from what we have just agreed, that something like this is done also by those who evade their due penalty, Polus; they perceive its painfulness, but are blind to its benefits, and are unaware how much more wretched than lack of health in the body it is to dwell with a soul that is not healthy, but corrupt, unjust, and unholy; and hence it is that they do all they can to avoid paying the penalty and being relieved of the greatest of evils, by providing themselves with money and friends and the ability to excel in persuasive speech. But if what we have agreed is true, Polus, do you observe the con-

τὰ συμβαίνοντα ἐκ τοῦ λόγου; ἢ βούλει συλλογισώμεθα αὐτά;

ΠΩΛ. Εἰ μὴ σοί γε ἄλλως δοκεῖ.

ΣΩ. Ἆρ᾽ οὖν συμβαίνει μέγιστον κακὸν ἡ ἀδικία καὶ τὸ ἀδικεῖν;

ΠΩΛ. Φαίνεταί γε.

ΣΩ. Καὶ μὴν ἀπαλλαγή γε ἐφάνη τούτου τοῦ κακοῦ τὸ δίκην διδόναι;

ΠΩΛ. Κινδυνεύει.

ΣΩ. Τὸ δέ γε μὴ διδόναι ἐμμονὴ τοῦ κακοῦ;

ΠΩΛ. Ναί.

ΣΩ. Δεύτερον ἄρα ἐστὶ τῶν κακῶν μεγέθει τὸ ἀδικεῖν· τὸ δὲ ἀδικοῦντα μὴ διδόναι δίκην πάντων μέγιστόν τε καὶ πρῶτον κακῶν πέφυκεν.

ΠΩΛ. Ἔοικεν.

ΣΩ. Ἆρ᾽ οὖν περὶ τούτου, ὦ φίλε, ἠμφεσβητήσαμεν, σὺ μὲν τὸν Ἀρχέλαον εὐδαιμονίζων τὸν τὰ μέγιστα ἀδικοῦντα δίκην οὐδεμίαν διδόντα, ἐγὼ δὲ τοὐναντίον οἰόμενος, εἴτ᾽ Ἀρχέλαος εἴτ᾽ ἄλλος ἀνθρώπων ὁστισοῦν μὴ δίδωσι δίκην ἀδικῶν, τούτῳ προσήκειν ἀθλίῳ εἶναι διαφερόντως τῶν ἄλλων ἀνθρώπων, καὶ ἀεὶ τὸν ἀδικοῦντα τοῦ ἀδικουμένου ἀθλιώτερον εἶναι καὶ τὸν μὴ διδόντα δίκην τοῦ διδόντος; οὐ ταῦτ᾽ ἦν τὰ ὑπ᾽ ἐμοῦ λεγόμενα;

ΠΩΛ. Ναί.

ΣΩ. Οὐκοῦν ἀποδέδεικται ὅτι ἀληθῆ ἐλέγετο;

ΠΩΛ. Φαίνεται.

ΣΩ. Εἶεν· εἰ οὖν δὴ ταῦτα ἀληθῆ, ὦ Πῶλε, τίς ἡ μεγάλη χρεία ἐστὶ τῆς ῥητορικῆς; δεῖ μὲν

sequences of our argument? Or, if you like, shall we reckon them up together?

POL. Yes, if you do not mind.

SOC. Then does it result that injustice and wrongdoing is the greatest evil?

POL. Yes, apparently.

SOC. And further, it appeared that paying the penalty is a relief from this evil?

POL. It looks like it.

SOC. Whereas not paying it is a retention of the evil in us?

POL. Yes.

SOC. Thus wrongdoing is second of evils in greatness; but to do wrong and not pay the penalty is the greatest and takes the first place among all evils.

POL. It seems so.

SOC. Well now, my friend, was this the point at issue between us, that you counted Archelaus, who did the greatest wrong, happy because he paid no penalty, whilst I on the contrary thought that anyone—whether Archelaus or any other person you please—who pays no penalty for the wrong he has done, is peculiarly and pre-eminently wretched among men, and that it is always the wrongdoer who is more wretched than the wronged, and the unpunished than the punished? Is not this what I stated?

POL. Yes.

SOC. Then has it not been proved that this was a true statement?

POL. Apparently.

SOC. Very well: so if this is true, Polus, what is the great use of rhetoric? For you see by what

PLATO

γὰρ δὴ ἐκ τῶν νῦν ὡμολογημένων αὐτὸν ἑαυτὸν μάλιστα φυλάττειν ὅπως μὴ ἀδικήσει, ὡς ἱκανὸν κακὸν ἕξοντα. οὐ γάρ;

ΠΩΛ. Πάνυ γε.

ΣΩ. Ἐὰν δέ γε ἀδικήσῃ ἢ αὐτὸς ἢ ἄλλος τις ὧν ἂν κήδηται, αὐτὸν ἑκόντα ἰέναι ἐκεῖσε, ὅπου ὡς τάχιστα δώσει δίκην, παρὰ τὸν δικαστήν, B ὥσπερ παρὰ τὸν ἰατρόν, σπεύδοντα ὅπως μὴ ἐγχρονισθὲν τὸ νόσημα τῆς ἀδικίας ὕπουλον τὴν ψυχὴν ποιήσει καὶ ἀνίατον· ἢ πῶς λέγωμεν, ὦ Πῶλε, εἴπερ τὰ πρότερον μένει ἡμῖν ὁμολογήματα; οὐκ ἀνάγκη ταῦτα ἐκείνοις οὕτω μὲν συμφωνεῖν, ἄλλως δὲ μή;

ΠΩΛ. Τί γὰρ δὴ φῶμεν, ὦ Σώκρατες;

ΣΩ. Ἐπὶ μὲν ἄρα τὸ ἀπολογεῖσθαι ὑπὲρ τῆς ἀδικίας τῆς αὑτοῦ ἢ γονέων ἢ ἑταίρων ἢ παίδων ἢ πατρίδος ἀδικούσης οὐ χρήσιμος οὐδὲν ἡ ῥητορικὴ ἡμῖν, ὦ Πῶλε, εἰ μὴ εἴ τις ὑπολάβοι ἐπὶ C τοὐναντίον, κατηγορεῖν δεῖν μάλιστα μὲν ἑαυτοῦ, ἔπειτα δὲ καὶ τῶν οἰκείων καὶ τῶν ἄλλων, ὃς ἂν ἀεὶ τῶν φίλων τυγχάνῃ ἀδικῶν, καὶ μὴ ἀποκρύπτεσθαι, ἀλλ' εἰς τὸ φανερὸν ἄγειν τὸ ἀδίκημα, ἵνα δῷ δίκην καὶ ὑγιὴς γένηται, ἀναγκάζειν δὲ καὶ αὐτὸν καὶ τοὺς ἄλλους μὴ ἀποδειλιᾶν, ἀλλὰ παρέχειν μύσαντα καὶ ἀνδρείως, ὥσπερ τέμνειν καὶ κάειν ἰατρῷ, τὸ ἀγαθὸν καὶ καλὸν διώκοντα, μὴ ὑπολογιζόμενον τὸ ἀλγεινόν, ἐὰν μέν γε πληγῶν D ἄξια ἠδικηκὼς ᾖ, τύπτειν παρέχοντα, ἐὰν δὲ δεσμοῦ, δεῖν, ἐὰν δὲ ζημίας, ἀποτίνοντα, ἐὰν δὲ φυγῆς, φεύγοντα, ἐὰν δὲ θανάτου, ἀποθνήσκοντα,

GORGIAS

we have just agreed that a man must keep a close watch over himself so as to avoid wrongdoing, since it would bring a great deal of evil upon him; must he not?

POL. Certainly.

SOC. But if he is guilty of wrongdoing, either himself or anyone else he may care for, he must go of his own freewill where he may soonest pay the penalty, to the judge as if to his doctor, with the earnest intent that the disease of his injustice shall not become chronic and cause a deep incurable ulcer in his soul. Or what are we to say, Polus, if our former conclusions stand? Must not our later ones accord with them in this way, and in this only?

POL. Yes, what else, indeed, are we to say, Socrates?

SOC. Then for pleading in defence of injustice, whether it is oneself or one's parents or friends or children or country that has done the wrong, rhetoric is of no use to us at all, Polus; except one were to suppose, perchance, to the contrary, that a man ought to accuse himself first of all, and in the second place his relations or anyone else of his friends who may from time to time be guilty of wrong; and, instead of concealing the iniquity, to bring it to light in order that he may pay the penalty and be made healthy; and, moreover, to compel both himself and his neighbours not to cower away but to submit with closed eyes and good courage, as it were, to the cutting and burning of the surgeon, in pursuit of what is good and fair, and without reckoning in the smart: if his crimes have deserved a flogging, he must submit to the rod; if fetters, to their grip; if a fine, to its payment; if banishment, to be banished; or if

375

PLATO

αὐτὸν πρῶτον ὄντα κατήγορον καὶ αὑτοῦ καὶ τῶν ἄλλων οἰκείων καὶ ἐπὶ τοῦτο χρώμενον τῇ ῥητορικῇ, ὅπως ἂν καταδήλων τῶν ἀδικημάτων γιγνομένων ἀπαλλάττωνται τοῦ μεγίστου κακοῦ, ἀδικίας. φῶμεν οὕτως ἢ μὴ φῶμεν, ὦ Πῶλε;

ΠΩΛ. Ἄτοπα μέν, ὦ Σώκρατες, ἔμοιγε δοκεῖ, τοῖς μέντοι ἔμπροσθεν ἴσως σοι ὁμολογεῖται.

ΣΩ. Οὐκοῦν ἢ κἀκεῖνα λυτέον ἢ τάδε ἀνάγκη συμβαίνειν;

ΠΩΛ. Ναί, τοῦτό γε οὕτως ἔχει.

ΣΩ. Τοὐναντίον δέ γε αὖ μεταβαλόντα, εἰ ἄρα δεῖ τινὰ κακῶς ποιεῖν, εἴτ' ἐχθρὸν εἴτε ὁντινοῦν, ἐὰν μόνον μὴ αὐτὸς ἀδικῆται ὑπὸ τοῦ ἐχθροῦ· τοῦτο μὲν γὰρ εὐλαβητέον· ἐὰν δὲ ἄλλον ἀδικῇ ὁ ἐχθρός, παντὶ τρόπῳ παρασκευαστέον, καὶ πράττοντα καὶ λέγοντα, ὅπως μὴ δῷ δίκην μηδὲ ἔλθῃ παρὰ τὸν δικαστήν· ἐὰν δὲ ἔλθῃ, μηχανητέον, ὅπως ἂν διαφύγῃ καὶ μὴ δῷ δίκην ὁ ἐχθρός, ἀλλ' ἐάν τε χρυσίον ἡρπακὼς ᾖ πολύ, μὴ ἀποδιδῷ τοῦτο ἀλλ' ἔχων ἀναλίσκῃ[1] καὶ εἰς ἑαυτὸν καὶ εἰς τοὺς ἑαυτοῦ ἀδίκως καὶ ἀθέως, ἐάν τε θανάτου ἄξια ἠδικηκὼς ᾖ, ὅπως μὴ ἀποθανεῖται, μάλιστα μὲν μηδέποτε, ἀλλ' ἀθάνατος ἔσται πονηρὸς ὤν, εἰ δὲ μή, ὅπως ὡς πλεῖστον χρόνον βιώσεται τοιοῦτος ὤν. ἐπὶ τὰ τοιαῦτα ἔμοιγε δοκεῖ, ὦ Πῶλε, ἡ ῥητορικὴ χρήσιμος εἶναι, ἐπεὶ τῷ γε μὴ

[1] ἀναλίσκῃ L. Dindorf : ἀναλίσκηται mss.

GORGIAS

death, to die; himself to be the first accuser either of himself or of his relations, and to employ his rhetoric for the purpose of so exposing their iniquities that they may be relieved of that greatest evil, injustice. Shall this be our statement or not, Polus?

POL. An extraordinary one, Socrates, it seems to me, though perhaps you do find it agrees with what went before.

SOC. Well, either that must be upset, or this necessarily follows.

POL. Yes, that certainly is so.

SOC. And so again conversely, supposing it is our duty to injure somebody, whether an enemy or anyone else—provided only that it is not against oneself that wrong has been done by such enemy, for this we must take care to avoid[1]—but supposing our enemy has wronged some one else, we must make every exertion of act and word to prevent him from being punished or coming to trial, or if he does, we must contrive that our enemy shall escape and not be punished; nay, if he has carried off a great lot of gold, that he shall not refund it but keep and spend it on himself and his, unjustly and godlessly, or if he has committed crimes that deserve death, that he shall not die; if possible, never die, but be deathless in his villainy, or failing that, live as long a time as may be in that condition. Such are the purposes, as it seems to me, Polus, for which rhetoric is useful, since to him who has no intention of doing wrong

[1] The parenthesis humorously anticipates an objection that might be made, in a particular case, to this theory of what a really thorough enmity would be: if our enemy has robbed *us* of gold, of course we cannot, as is presently urged, take care that " he shall not refund it."

μέλλοντι ἀδικεῖν οὐ μεγάλη τίς μοι δοκεῖ ἡ χρεία αὐτῆς εἶναι, εἰ δὴ καὶ ἔστι τις χρεία, ὡς ἔν γε τοῖς πρόσθεν οὐδαμῇ ἐφάνη οὖσα.

ΚΑΛΛ. Εἰπέ μοι, ὦ Χαιρεφῶν, σπουδάζει ταῦτα Σωκράτης ἢ παίζει;

ΧΑΙΡ. Ἐμοὶ μὲν δοκεῖ, ὦ Καλλίκλεις, ὑπερφυῶς σπουδάζειν· οὐδὲν μέντοι οἷον τὸ αὐτὸν ἐρωτᾶν.

ΚΑΛΛ. Νὴ τοὺς θεοὺς ἀλλ' ἐπιθυμῶ. εἰπέ μοι, ὦ Σώκρατες, πότερόν σε θῶμεν[1] νυνὶ σπουδάζοντα ἢ παίζοντα; εἰ μὲν γὰρ σπουδάζεις τε καὶ τυγχάνει ταῦτα ἀληθῆ ὄντα ἃ λέγεις, ἄλλο τι ἢ ἡμῶν ὁ βίος ἀνατετραμμένος ἂν εἴη τῶν ἀνθρώπων καὶ πάντα τὰ ἐναντία πράττομεν, ὡς ἔοικεν, ἢ ἃ δεῖ;

ΣΩ. Ὦ Καλλίκλεις, εἰ μή τι ἦν τοῖς ἀνθρώποις πάθος, τοῖς μὲν ἄλλο τι, τοῖς δὲ ἄλλο τι τὸ αὐτό, ἀλλά τις ἡμῶν ἴδιόν τι ἔπασχε πάθος ἢ οἱ ἄλλοι, οὐκ ἂν ἦν ῥᾴδιον ἐνδείξασθαι τῷ ἑτέρῳ τὸ ἑαυτοῦ πάθημα. λέγω δ' ἐννοήσας, ὅτι ἐγώ τε καὶ σὺ νῦν τυγχάνομεν ταὐτόν τι πεπονθότες, ἐρῶντε δύο ὄντε δυοῖν ἑκάτερος, ἐγὼ μὲν Ἀλκιβιάδου τε τοῦ Κλεινίου καὶ φιλοσοφίας, σὺ δὲ δυοῖν, τοῦ τε Ἀθηναίων δήμου καὶ τοῦ Πυριλάμπους. αἰσθάνομαι οὖν σου ἑκάστοτε, καίπερ ὄντος δεινοῦ, ὅτι ὁπόσ' ἂν φῇ σου τὰ παιδικὰ καὶ ὅπως ἂν φῇ ἔχειν, οὐ δυναμένου ἀντιλέγειν, ἀλλ' ἄνω καὶ κάτω μεταβαλλομένου· ἔν τε τῇ ἐκκλησίᾳ, ἐάν τι σοῦ λέγοντος ὁ δῆμος ὁ Ἀθηναίων μὴ φῇ οὕτως ἔχειν, μεταβαλλόμενος λέγεις ἃ ἐκεῖνος

---

[1] θῶμεν Madvig: φῶμεν MSS.

GORGIAS

it is, I consider, of no great use, if indeed there is any use in it at all; for in our previous argument it was nowhere to be found.

CALL. Tell me, Chaerephon, is Socrates in earnest over this, or only joking?

CHAER. To my thinking, Callicles, prodigiously in earnest: still, there is nothing like asking him.

CALL. Upon my word, just what I want to do. Tell me, Socrates, are we to take you as serious just now, or joking? For if you are serious and what you say is really true, must not the life of us human beings have been turned upside down, and must we not be doing quite the opposite, it seems, of what we ought to do?

SOC. Callicles, if men had not certain feelings, each common to one sort of people, but each of us had a feeling peculiar to himself and apart from the rest, it would not be easy for him to indicate his own impression to his neighbour. I say this because I notice that you and I are at this moment in much the same condition, since the two of us are enamoured each of two things—I of Alcibiades, son of Cleinias, and philosophy, and you of two, the Athenian Demus, and the son of Pyrilampes.[1] Now I always observe that, for all your cleverness, you are unable to contradict your favourite, however much he may say or whatever may be his account of anything, but are ever changing over from side to side. In the Assembly, if the Athenian Demus disagrees with some statement you are making, you change over and say what it desires; and just

[1] Pyrilampes' son was named Demus, and was famous for his beauty; cf. Aristoph. *Wasps*, 97. "Demus" was the ordinary word for the "people" of a city.

379

PLATO

481

βούλεται, καὶ πρὸς τὸν Πυριλάμπους νεανίαν τὸν καλὸν τοῦτον τοιαῦτα ἕτερα πέπονθας· τοῖς γὰρ τῶν παιδικῶν βουλεύμασί τε καὶ λόγοις οὐχ οἷός τ᾽ εἶ ἐναντιοῦσθαι, ὥστε, εἴ τίς σου λέγοντος ἑκάστοτε, ἃ διὰ τούτους λέγεις, θαυμάζοι ὡς ἄτοπά ἐστιν, ἴσως εἴποις ἂν αὐτῷ, εἰ βούλοιο

482 τἀληθῆ λέγειν, ὅτι, εἰ μή τις παύσει τὰ σὰ παιδικὰ τούτων τῶν λόγων, οὐδὲ σὺ παύσει ποτὲ ταῦτα λέγων. νόμιζε τοίνυν καὶ παρ᾽ ἐμοῦ χρῆναι ἕτερα τοιαῦτα ἀκούειν, καὶ μὴ θαύμαζε ὅτι ἐγὼ ταῦτα λέγω, ἀλλὰ τὴν φιλοσοφίαν, τὰ ἐμὰ παιδικά, παῦσον ταῦτα λέγουσαν. λέγει γάρ, ὦ φίλε ἑταῖρε, ἃ νῦν ἐμοῦ ἀκούεις, καί μοί ἐστι τῶν ἑτέρων παιδικῶν πολὺ ἧττον ἔμπληκτος· ὁ μὲν γὰρ Κλεινίειος οὗτος ἄλλοτε ἄλλων ἐστὶ λόγων,

B ἡ δὲ φιλοσοφία ἀεὶ τῶν αὐτῶν· λέγει δὲ ἃ σὺ νῦν θαυμάζεις, παρῆσθα δὲ καὶ αὐτὸς λεγομένοις. ἢ οὖν ἐκείνην ἐξέλεγξον, ὅπερ ἄρτι ἔλεγον, ὡς οὐ τὸ ἀδικεῖν ἐστι καὶ ἀδικοῦντα δίκην μὴ διδόναι ἁπάντων ἔσχατον κακῶν· ἢ εἰ τοῦτο ἐάσεις ἀνέλεγκτον, μὰ τὸν κύνα τὸν Αἰγυπτίων θεόν, οὔ σοι ὁμολογήσει Καλλικλῆς, ὦ Καλλίκλεις, ἀλλὰ διαφωνήσει ἐν ἅπαντι τῷ βίῳ. καίτοι ἔγωγε οἶμαι, ὦ βέλτιστε, καὶ τὴν λύραν μοι κρεῖττον εἶναι ἀναρμοστεῖν[1] τε καὶ διαφωνεῖν, καὶ χορὸν

C ᾧ χορηγοίην, καὶ πλείστους ἀνθρώπους μὴ ὁμολογεῖν μοι ἀλλ᾽ ἐναντία λέγειν μᾶλλον ἢ ἕνα ὄντα ἐμὲ ἐμαυτῷ ἀσύμφωνον εἶναι καὶ ἐναντία λέγειν.

ΚΑΛΛ. Ὦ Σώκρατες, δοκεῖς νεανιεύεσθαι ἐν τοῖς λόγοις ὡς ἀληθῶς δημηγόρος ὤν· καὶ νῦν ταῦτα δημηγορεῖς ταὐτὸν παθόντος Πώλου πάθος,

[1] ἀναρμοστεῖν Heusde : ἀνάρμοστόν MSS.

GORGIAS

the same thing happens to you in presence of that fair youth, the son of Pyrilampes; you are unable to resist the counsels and statements of your darling, so that if anyone showed surprise at the strangeness of the things you are constantly saying under that influence, you would probably tell him, if you chose to speak the truth, that unless somebody makes your favourite stop speaking thus, you will never stop speaking thus either. Consider yourself therefore obliged to hear the same sort of remark from me now, and do not be surprised at my saying it, but make my darling, philosophy, stop talking thus. For she, my dear friend, speaks what you hear me saying now, and she is far less fickle to me than any other favourite: that son of Cleinias is ever changing his views, but philosophy always holds the same, and it is her speech that now surprises you, and she spoke it in your own presence. So you must either refute her, as I said just now, by proving that wrongdoing and impunity for wrong done is not the uttermost evil; or, if you leave that unproved, by the Dog, god of the Egyptians, there will be no agreement between you, Callicles, and Callicles, but you will be in discord with him all your life. And yet I, my very good sir, should rather choose to have my lyre, or some chorus that I might provide for the public, out of tune and discordant, or to have any number of people disagreeing with me and contradicting me, than that I should have internal discord and contradiction in my own single self.

CALL. Socrates, you seem to be roistering recklessly in your talk, like the true demagogue that you are; and you are declaiming now in this way because Polus has got into the same plight

ὅπερ Γοργίου κατηγόρει πρὸς σὲ παθεῖν. ἔφη γάρ που Γοργίαν ἐρωτώμενον ὑπὸ σοῦ, ἐὰν ἀφίκηται παρ' αὐτὸν μὴ ἐπιστάμενος τὰ δίκαια ὁ τὴν ῥητορικὴν βουλόμενος μαθεῖν, εἰ διδάξοι αὐτὸν ὁ Γοργίας, αἰσχυνθῆναι αὐτὸν καὶ φάναι διδάξειν διὰ τὸ ἔθος τῶν ἀνθρώπων, ὅτι ἀγανακτοῖεν ἂν εἴ τις μὴ φαίη—διὰ δὴ ταύτην τὴν ὁμολογίαν ἀναγκασθῆναι ἐναντία αὐτὸν αὑτῷ εἰπεῖν, σὲ δὲ αὐτὸ τοῦτο ἀγαπᾶν—καί σου καταγελᾶν, ὥς γέ μοι δοκεῖν, ὀρθῶς τότε· νῦν δὲ πάλιν αὐτὸς ταὐτὸν τοῦτο ἔπαθεν. καὶ ἔγωγε κατ' αὐτὸ τοῦτο οὐκ ἄγαμαι Πῶλον, ὅτι σοι συνεχώρησε τὸ ἀδικεῖν αἴσχιον εἶναι τοῦ ἀδικεῖσθαι· ἐκ ταύτης γὰρ αὖ τῆς ὁμολογίας αὐτὸς ὑπὸ σοῦ συμποδισθεὶς ἐν τοῖς λόγοις ἐπεστομίσθη, αἰσχυνθεὶς ἃ ἐνόει εἰπεῖν. σὺ γὰρ τῷ ὄντι, ὦ Σώκρατες, εἰς τοιαῦτα ἄγεις φορτικὰ καὶ δημηγορικά, φάσκων τὴν ἀλήθειαν διώκειν, ἃ φύσει μὲν οὐκ ἔστι καλά, νόμῳ δέ. ὡς τὰ πολλὰ δὲ ταῦτα ἐναντία ἀλλήλοις ἐστίν, ἥ τε φύσις καὶ ὁ νόμος· ἐὰν οὖν τις αἰσχύνηται καὶ μὴ τολμᾷ λέγειν ἅπερ νοεῖ, ἀναγκάζεται ἐναντία λέγειν. ὃ δὴ καὶ σὺ τοῦτο τὸ σοφὸν κατανενοηκὼς κακουργεῖς ἐν τοῖς λόγοις, ἐὰν μέν τις κατὰ νόμον λέγῃ, κατὰ φύσιν ὑπερωτῶν, ἐὰν δὲ τὰ τῆς φύσεως, τὰ τοῦ νόμου. ὥσπερ αὐτίκα ἐν τούτοις, τῷ ἀδικεῖν τε καὶ τῷ ἀδικεῖσθαι, Πώλου τὸ κατὰ νόμον αἴσχιον λέγοντος, σὺ

---

[1] The distinction between "natural," or absolute, and "conventional," or legal, right, first made by the Ionian Archelaus who taught Socrates in his youth, is developed at length in the *Republic* (i. 388 foll.), and was a constant subject of discussion among the sophists of Plato's time.

GORGIAS

as he was accusing Gorgias of letting himself be led into by you. For he said, I think, when you asked Gorgias whether, supposing a man came to him with no knowledge of justice but a desire to learn rhetoric, he would instruct the man, Gorgias showed some shame and said he would, because of the habit of mind in people which would make them indignant if refused—and so, because of this admission, he was forced to contradict himself, and that was just what suited you—and Polus was right, to my thinking, in mocking at you as he did then; but this time he has got into the very same plight himself. For my own part, where I am not satisfied with Polus is just that concession he made to you—that doing wrong is fouler than suffering it; for owing to this admission he too in his turn got entangled in your argument and had his mouth stopped, being ashamed to say what he thought. For you, Socrates, really turn the talk into such low, popular clap-trap, while you give out that you are pursuing the truth—into stuff that is "fair," not by nature, but by convention.[1] Yet for the most part these two—nature and convention—are opposed to each other, so that if a man is ashamed and dares not say what he thinks, he is forced to contradict himself. And this, look you, is the clever trick you have devised for our undoing in your discussions: when a man states anything according to convention you slip "according to nature" into your questions; and again, if he means nature, you imply convention. In the present case, for instance, of doing and suffering wrong, when Polus was speaking of what is conventionally fouler, you followed it up in the sense

383

483

τὸν λόγον[1] ἐδιώκαθες κατὰ φύσιν. φύσει μὲν γὰρ πᾶν αἴσχιόν ἐστιν ὅπερ καὶ κάκιον, τὸ ἀδικεῖσθαι, νόμῳ δὲ τὸ ἀδικεῖν. οὐδὲ γὰρ ἀνδρὸς τοῦτό γ' ἐστὶ τὸ πάθημα, τὸ ἀδικεῖσθαι, ἀλλ'
B ἀνδραπόδου τινός, ᾧ κρεῖττόν ἐστι τεθνάναι ἢ ζῆν, ὅστις ἀδικούμενος καὶ προπηλακιζόμενος μὴ οἷός τε ἐστὶν αὐτὸς αὑτῷ βοηθεῖν μηδὲ ἄλλῳ οὗ ἂν κήδηται. ἀλλ', οἶμαι, οἱ τιθέμενοι τοὺς νόμους οἱ ἀσθενεῖς ἄνθρωποί εἰσι καὶ οἱ πολλοί. πρὸς αὑτοὺς οὖν καὶ τὸ αὑτοῖς συμφέρον τούς τε νόμους τίθενται καὶ τοὺς ἐπαίνους ἐπαινοῦσι καὶ
C τοὺς ψόγους ψέγουσιν, ἐκφοβοῦντες τοὺς ἐρρωμενεστέρους τῶν ἀνθρώπων καὶ δυνατοὺς ὄντας πλέον ἔχειν, ἵνα μὴ αὐτῶν πλέον ἔχωσιν, λέγουσιν ὡς αἰσχρὸν καὶ ἄδικον τὸ πλεονεκτεῖν, καὶ τοῦτο ἔστι τὸ ἀδικεῖν, τὸ πλέον τῶν ἄλλων ζητεῖν ἔχειν· ἀγαπῶσι γάρ, οἶμαι, αὐτοὶ ἂν τὸ ἴσον ἔχωσι φαυλότεροι ὄντες. διὰ ταῦτα δὴ νόμῳ μὲν τοῦτο ἄδικον καὶ αἰσχρὸν λέγεται, τὸ πλέον ζητεῖν
D ἔχειν τῶν πολλῶν, καὶ ἀδικεῖν αὐτὸ καλοῦσιν· ἡ δέ γε, οἶμαι, φύσις αὐτὴ ἀποφαίνει αὐτό, ὅτι δίκαιόν ἐστι τὸν ἀμείνω τοῦ χείρονος πλέον ἔχειν καὶ τὸν δυνατώτερον τοῦ ἀδυνατωτέρου. δηλοῖ δὲ ταῦτα πολλαχοῦ ὅτι οὕτως ἔχει, καὶ ἐν τοῖς ἄλλοις ζῴοις καὶ τῶν ἀνθρώπων ἐν ὅλαις ταῖς πόλεσι καὶ τοῖς γένεσιν, ὅτι οὕτω τὸ δίκαιον κέκριται, τὸν κρείττω τοῦ ἥττονος ἄρχειν καὶ πλέον ἔχειν. ἐπεὶ ποίῳ δικαίῳ χρώμενος Ξέρξης
E ἐπὶ τὴν Ἑλλάδα ἐστράτευσεν ἢ ὁ πατὴρ αὐτοῦ ἐπὶ Σκύθας; ἢ ἄλλα μυρία ἄν τις ἔχοι τοιαῦτα λέγειν· ἀλλ', οἶμαι, οὗτοι κατὰ φύσιν τὴν τοῦ

[1] λόγον Riemann : νόμον MSS.

GORGIAS

of what is naturally so. For by nature everything is fouler that is more evil, such as suffering wrong: doing it is fouler only by convention. Indeed this endurance of wrong done is not a man's part at all, but a poor slave's, for whom it is better to be dead than alive, as it is for anybody who, when wronged or insulted, is unable to protect himself or anyone else for whom he cares. But I suppose the makers of the laws are the weaker sort of men, and the more numerous. So it is with a view to themselves and their own interest that they make their laws and distribute their praises and censures; and to terrorize the stronger sort of folk who are able to get an advantage, and to prevent them from getting one over *them*, they tell them that such aggrandizement is foul and unjust, and that wrongdoing is just this endeavour to get the advantage of one's neighbours: for I expect they are well content to see themselves on an equality, when they are so inferior. So this is why by convention it is termed unjust and foul to aim at an advantage over the majority, and why they call it wrongdoing: but nature, in my opinion, herself proclaims the fact that it is right for the better to have advantage of the worse, and the abler of the feebler. It is obvious in many cases that this is so, not only in the animal world, but in the states and races, collectively, of men—that right has been decided to consist in the sway and advantage of the stronger over the weaker. For by what manner of right did Xerxes march against Greece, or his father against Scythia? Or take the countless other cases of the sort that one might mention. Why, surely

δικαίου ταῦτα πράττουσι, καὶ ναὶ μὰ Δία κατὰ νόμον γε τὸν τῆς φύσεως, οὐ μέντοι ἴσως κατὰ τοῦτον, ὃν ἡμεῖς τιθέμεθα· πλάττοντες τοὺς βελτίστους καὶ ἐρρωμενεστάτους ἡμῶν αὐτῶν, ἐκ νέων λαμβάνοντες, ὥσπερ λέοντας, κατεπᾴδοντές τε καὶ γοητεύοντες καταδουλούμεθα λέγοντες, ὡς τὸ ἴσον χρὴ ἔχειν καὶ τοῦτό ἐστι τὸ καλὸν καὶ τὸ δίκαιον. ἐὰν δέ γε, οἶμαι, φύσιν ἱκανὴν γένηται ἔχων ἀνήρ, πάντα ταῦτα ἀποσεισάμενος καὶ διαρρήξας καὶ διαφυγών, καταπατήσας τὰ ἡμέτερα γράμματα καὶ μαγγανεύματα καὶ ἐπῳδὰς καὶ νόμους τοὺς παρὰ φύσιν ἅπαντας, ἐπαναστὰς ἀνεφάνη δεσπότης ἡμέτερος ὁ δοῦλος, καὶ ἐνταῦθα ἐξέλαμψε τὸ τῆς φύσεως δίκαιον. δοκεῖ δέ μοι καὶ Πίνδαρος ἅπερ ἐγὼ λέγω ἐνδείκνυσθαι ἐν τῷ ᾄσματι ἐν ᾧ λέγει ὅτι

νόμος ὁ πάντων βασιλεὺς
θνατῶν τε καὶ ἀθανάτων·

οὗτος δὲ δή, φησίν,—

ἄγει δικαιῶν τὸ βιαιότατον
ὑπερτάτᾳ χειρί· τεκμαίρομαι
ἔργοισιν Ἡρακλέος, ἐπεὶ ἀπριάτας—

λέγει οὕτω πως· τὸ γὰρ ᾆσμα οὐκ ἐπίσταμαι· λέγει δ᾽ ὅτι οὔτε πριάμενος οὔτε δόντος τοῦ Γηρυόνου ἠλάσατο τὰς βοῦς, ὡς τούτου ὄντος τοῦ δικαίου φύσει, καὶ βοῦς καὶ τἆλλα κτήματα εἶναι πάντα τοῦ βελτίονός τε καὶ κρείττονος τὰ τῶν χειρόνων τε καὶ ἡττόνων.

GORGIAS

these men follow nature—the nature of right—in acting thus; yes, on my soul, and follow the law[1] of nature—though not that, I dare say, which is made by us; we mould the best and strongest amongst us, taking them from their infancy like young lions, and utterly enthral them by our spells and witchcraft, telling them the while that they must have but their equal share, and that this is what is fair and just. But, I fancy, when some man arises with a nature of sufficient force, he shakes off all that we have taught him, bursts his bonds, and breaks free; he tramples underfoot our codes and juggleries, our charms and "laws," which are all against nature; our slave rises in revolt and shows himself our master, and there dawns the full light of natural justice. And it seems to me that Pindar adds his evidence to what I say, in the ode where he says—

> Law the sovereign of all,
> Mortals and immortals,

which, so he continues,—

> Carries all with highest hand,
> Justifying the utmost force: in proof I take
> The deeds of Hercules, for unpurchased [2]—

the words are something like that—I do not know the poem well—but it tells how he drove off the cows as neither a purchase nor a gift from Geryones; taking it as a natural right that cows or any other possessions of the inferior and weaker should all belong to the superior and stronger.

---

[1] Callicles boldly applies the word νόμος, which so far has been used in the sense of man-made law or convention, in its widest sense of "general rule" or "principle."

[2] Pindar, fr. 169 (Bergk).

387

PLATO

Τὸ μὲν οὖν ἀληθὲς οὕτως ἔχει, γνώσῃ δέ, ἂν ἐπὶ τὰ μείζω ἔλθῃς ἐάσας ἤδη φιλοσοφίαν. φιλοσοφία γάρ τοί ἐστιν, ὦ Σώκρατες, χαρίεν, ἄν τις αὐτοῦ μετρίως ἅψηται ἐν τῇ ἡλικίᾳ· ἐὰν δὲ περαιτέρω τοῦ δέοντος ἐνδιατρίψῃ, διαφθορὰ τῶν ἀνθρώπων. ἐὰν γὰρ καὶ πάνυ εὐφυὴς ᾖ καὶ πόρρω τῆς ἡλικίας φιλοσοφῇ, ἀνάγκη πάντων D ἄπειρον γεγονέναι ἐστίν, ὧν χρὴ ἔμπειρον εἶναι τὸν μέλλοντα καλὸν κἀγαθὸν καὶ εὐδόκιμον ἔσεσθαι ἄνδρα. καὶ γὰρ τῶν νόμων ἄπειροι γίγνονται τῶν κατὰ τὴν πόλιν, καὶ τῶν λόγων, οἷς δεῖ χρώμενον ὁμιλεῖν ἐν τοῖς συμβολαίοις τοῖς ἀνθρώποις καὶ ἰδίᾳ καὶ δημοσίᾳ, καὶ τῶν ἡδονῶν τε καὶ ἐπιθυμιῶν τῶν ἀνθρωπείων, καὶ συλλήβδην τῶν ἠθῶν παντάπασιν ἄπειροι γίγνονται. ἐπειδὰν οὖν ἔλθωσιν εἴς τινα ἰδίαν ἢ πολιτικὴν πρᾶξιν, καταγέλαστοι γίγνονται, ὥσπερ γε, οἶμαι, οἱ E πολιτικοί, ἐπειδὰν αὖ εἰς τὰς ὑμετέρας διατριβὰς ἔλθωσι καὶ τοὺς λόγους, καταγέλαστοί εἰσι. συμβαίνει γὰρ τὸ τοῦ Εὐριπίδου· λαμπρός τ' ἐστὶν ἕκαστος ἐν τούτῳ, κἀπὶ τοῦτ' ἐπείγεται,

νέμων τὸ πλεῖστον ἡμέρας τούτῳ μέρος,
ἵν' αὐτὸς αὑτοῦ τυγχάνει βέλτιστος ὤν·

485 ὅπου δ' ἂν φαῦλος ᾖ, ἐντεῦθεν φεύγει καὶ λοιδορεῖ τοῦτο, τὸ δ' ἕτερον ἐπαινεῖ, εὐνοίᾳ τῇ ἑαυτοῦ, ἡγούμενος οὕτως αὐτὸς ἑαυτὸν ἐπαινεῖν. ἀλλ', οἶμαι, τὸ ὀρθότατόν ἐστιν ἀμφοτέρων μετα-

---

[1] Eurip. fr. *Antiope*. Zethus and Amphion, twins born to Zeus by Antiope, were left by her on Mt. Cithaeron,

388

GORGIAS

Well, that is the truth of the matter; and you will grasp it if you will now put philosophy aside and pass to greater things. For philosophy, you know, Socrates, is a charming thing, if a man has to do with it moderately in his younger days; but if he continues to spend his time on it too long, it is ruin to any man. However well endowed one may be, if one philosophizes far on into life, one must needs find oneself ignorant of everything that ought to be familiar to the man who would be a thorough gentleman and make a good figure in the world. For such people are shown to be ignorant of the laws of their city, and of the terms which have to be used in negotiating agreements with their fellows in private or in public affairs, and of human pleasures and desires; and, in short, to be utterly inexperienced in men's characters. So when they enter upon any private or public business they make themselves ridiculous, just as on the other hand, I suppose, when public men engage in your studies and discussions, they are quite ridiculous. The fact is, as Euripides has it—

> Each shines in that, to that end presses on,
> Allotting there the chiefest part o' the day,
> Wherein he haply can surpass himself [1]—

whereas that in which he is weak he shuns and vilifies; but the other he praises, in kindness to himself, thinking in this way to praise himself also. But the most proper course, I consider, is to take

---

where Zethus grew up as a man of the field, and Amphion as a musician. Here probably Amphion is speaking in defence of the quieter life; further on, in the quotations given in 486 B, C, Zethus reproaches him with his effeminacy.

485

σχεῖν· φιλοσοφίας μὲν ὅσον παιδείας χάριν καλὸν
μετέχειν, καὶ οὐκ αἰσχρὸν μειρακίῳ ὄντι φιλο-
σοφεῖν· ἐπειδὰν δὲ ἤδη πρεσβύτερος ὢν ἄνθρωπος
ἔτι φιλοσοφῇ, καταγέλαστον, ὦ Σώκρατες, τὸ
χρῆμα γίγνεται, καὶ ἔγωγε ὁμοιότατον πάσχω
B πρὸς τοὺς φιλοσοφοῦντας ὥσπερ πρὸς τοὺς ψελ-
λιζομένους καὶ παίζοντας. ὅταν μὲν γὰρ παιδίον
ἴδω, ᾧ ἔτι προσήκει διαλέγεσθαι οὕτω, ψελλι-
ζόμενον καὶ παῖζον, χαίρω τε καὶ χαρίεν μοι
φαίνεται καὶ ἐλευθέριον καὶ πρέπον τῇ τοῦ παιδίου
ἡλικίᾳ, ὅταν δὲ σαφῶς διαλεγομένου παιδαρίου
ἀκούσω, πικρόν τί μοι δοκεῖ χρῆμα εἶναι καὶ
ἀνιᾷ μου τὰ ὦτα καί μοι δοκεῖ δουλοπρεπές τι
εἶναι· ὅταν δὲ ἀνδρὸς ἀκούσῃ τις ψελλιζομένου
C ἢ παίζοντα ὁρᾷ, καταγέλαστον φαίνεται καὶ
ἄνανδρον καὶ πληγῶν ἄξιον. ταὐτὸν οὖν ἔγωγε
τοῦτο πάσχω καὶ πρὸς τοὺς φιλοσοφοῦντας.
παρὰ[1] νέῳ μὲν γὰρ μειρακίῳ ὁρῶν φιλοσοφίαν
ἄγαμαι, καὶ πρέπειν μοι δοκεῖ, καὶ ἡγοῦμαι
ἐλεύθερόν τινα εἶναι τοῦτον τὸν ἄνθρωπον, τὸν δὲ
μὴ φιλοσοφοῦντα ἀνελεύθερον καὶ οὐδέποτε οὐδενὸς ἀξιώσοντα ἑαυτὸν οὔτε καλοῦ οὔτε γενναίου
D πράγματος· ὅταν δὲ δὴ πρεσβύτερον ἴδω ἔτι
φιλοσοφοῦντα καὶ μὴ ἀπαλλαττόμενον, πληγῶν
μοι δοκεῖ ἤδη δεῖσθαι, ὦ Σώκρατες, οὗτος ὁ
ἀνήρ. ὃ γὰρ νῦν δὴ ἔλεγον, ὑπάρχει τούτῳ τῷ
ἀνθρώπῳ, κἂν πάνυ εὐφυὴς ᾖ, ἀνάνδρῳ γενέσθαι
φεύγοντι τὰ μέσα τῆς πόλεως καὶ τὰς ἀγοράς,
ἐν αἷς ἔφη ὁ ποιητὴς τοὺς ἄνδρας ἀριπρεπεῖς
γίγνεσθαι, καταδεδυκότι δὲ τὸν λοιπὸν βίον βιῶναι
μετὰ μειρακίων ἐν γωνίᾳ τριῶν ἢ τεττάρων
ψιθυρίζοντα, ἐλεύθερον δὲ καὶ μέγα καὶ νεανικὸν

GORGIAS

a share of both. It is a fine thing to partake of philosophy just for the sake of education, and it is no disgrace for a lad to follow it: but when a man already advancing in years continues in its pursuit, the affair, Socrates, becomes ridiculous; and for my part I have much the same feeling towards students of philosophy as towards those who lisp or play tricks. For when I see a little child, to whom it is still natural to talk in that way, lisping or playing some trick, I enjoy it, and it strikes me as pretty and ingenuous and suitable to the infant's age; whereas if I hear a small child talk distinctly, I find it a disagreeable thing, and it offends my ears and seems to me more befitting a slave. But when one hears a grown man lisp, or sees him play tricks, it strikes one as something ridiculous and unmanly, that deserves a whipping. Just the same, then, is my feeling towards the followers of philosophy. For when I see philosophy in a young lad I approve of it; I consider it suitable, and I regard him as a person of liberal mind: whereas one who does not follow it I account illiberal and never likely to expect of himself any fine or generous action. But when I see an elderly man still going on with philosophy and not getting rid of it, that is the gentleman, Socrates, whom I think in need of a whipping. For as I said just now, this person, however well endowed he may be, is bound to become unmanly through shunning the centres and marts of the city, in which, as the poet [1] said, "men get them note and glory"; he must cower down and spend the rest of his days whispering in a corner with three or four lads, and never utter

[1] Homer, *Il.* ix. 441.

---

[1] παρὰ Stephanus: περὶ MSS.   [2] νεανικὸν Heindorf: ἱκανὸν MSS.

485

E μηδέποτε φθέγξασθαι. ἐγὼ δέ, ὦ Σώκρατες, πρὸς σὲ ἐπιεικῶς ἔχω φιλικῶς· κινδυνεύω οὖν πεπονθέναι νῦν ὅπερ ὁ Ζῆθος πρὸς τὸν Ἀμφίονα ὁ Εὐριπίδου, οὗπερ ἐμνήσθην. καὶ γὰρ ἐμοὶ τοιαῦτ' ἄττα ἐπέρχεται πρὸς σὲ λέγειν, οἷάπερ ἐκεῖνος πρὸς τὸν ἀδελφόν, ὅτι ἀμελεῖς, ὦ Σώκρατες, ὧν δεῖ σε ἐπιμελεῖσθαι, καὶ φύσιν ψυχῆς ὧδε γενναίαν μειρακιώδει τινὶ διαστρέφεις[1] μορ-
486 φώματι, καὶ οὔτ' ἂν δίκης βουλαῖσι προσθεῖ' ἂν ὀρθῶς λόγον, οὔτ' εἰκὸς ἂν καὶ πιθανὸν λάβοις, οὔθ' ὑπὲρ ἄλλου νεανικὸν βούλευμα βουλεύσαιο. καίτοι, ὦ φίλε Σώκρατες—καί μοι μηδὲν ἀχθεσθῇς· εὐνοίᾳ γὰρ ἐρῶ τῇ σῇ—οὐκ αἰσχρὸν δοκεῖ σοι εἶναι οὕτως ἔχειν, ὡς ἐγὼ σὲ οἶμαι ἔχειν καὶ τοὺς ἄλλους τοὺς πόρρω ἀεὶ φιλοσοφίας ἐλαύνοντας; νῦν γὰρ εἴ τις σοῦ λαβόμενος ἢ ἄλλου ὁτουοῦν τῶν τοιούτων εἰς τὸ δεσμωτήριον ἀπάγοι, φάσκων ἀδικεῖν μηδὲν ἀδικοῦντα, οἶσθ' ὅτι οὐκ ἂν ἔχοις ὅ τι χρήσαιο σαυτῷ, ἀλλ' ἰλιγ-
B γιῴης ἂν καὶ χασμῷο οὐκ ἔχων ὅ τι εἴποις, καὶ εἰς τὸ δικαστήριον ἀναβάς, κατηγόρου τυχὼν πάνυ φαύλου καὶ μοχθηροῦ, ἀποθάνοις ἄν, εἰ βούλοιτο θανάτου σοι τιμᾶσθαι. καίτοι πῶς σοφὸν τοῦτό ἐστιν, ὦ Σώκρατες, ἥτις εὐφυῆ λαβοῦσα τέχνη φῶτα ἔθηκε χείρονα, μήτε αὐτὸν αὑτῷ δυνάμενον βοηθεῖν μηδ' ἐκσῶσαι ἐκ τῶν μεγίστων κινδύνων μήτε ἑαυτὸν μήτε ἄλλον μηδένα,
C ὑπὸ δὲ τῶν ἐχθρῶν περισυλᾶσθαι πᾶσαν τὴν οὐσίαν, ἀτεχνῶς δὲ ἄτιμον ζῆν ἐν τῇ πόλει; τὸν δὲ τοιοῦτον, εἴ τι καὶ ἀγροικότερον εἰρῆσθαι, ἔξεστιν ἐπὶ κόρρης τύπτοντα μὴ διδόναι δίκην.

[1] διαστρέφεις Valckenaer: διατρέπεις, διαπρέπεις MSS.

GORGIAS

anything free or high or spirited. Now I, Socrates, am quite fairly friendly to you, and so I feel very much at this moment as Zethus did, whom I have mentioned, towards Amphion in Euripides. Indeed I am prompted to address you in the same sort of words as he did his brother: "You neglect, Socrates, what you ought to mind; you distort with a kind of boyish travesty a soul of such noble nature; and neither will you bring to the counsels of justice any rightly spoken word, nor will you accept any as probable or convincing, nor advise any gallant plan for your fellow." And yet, my dear Socrates—now do not be annoyed with me, for I am going to say this from goodwill to you—does it not seem to you disgraceful to be in the state I consider you are in, along with the rest of those who are ever pushing further into philosophy? For as it is, if somebody should seize hold of you or anyone else at all of your sort, and drag you off to prison, asserting that you were guilty of a wrong you had never done, you know you would be at a loss what to do with yourself, and would be all dizzy and agape without a word to say; and when you came up in court, though your accuser might be ever so paltry a rascal, you would have to die if he chose to claim death as your penalty. And yet what wisdom is there, Socrates, in "an art that found a man of goodly parts and made him worse," unable either to succour himself, or to deliver himself or anyone else from the greatest dangers, but like to be stripped by his enemies of all his substance, and to live in his city as an absolute outcast? Such a person, if one may use a rather low expression, can be given a box on the ear with

ἀλλ' ὦ 'γαθέ, ἐμοὶ πείθου, παῦσαι δ' ἐλέγχων, πραγμάτων δ' εὐμουσίαν ἄσκει, καὶ ἄσκει ὁπόθεν δόξεις φρονεῖν, ἄλλοις τὰ κομψὰ ταῦτα ἀφείς, εἴτε ληρήματα χρὴ φάναι εἶναι εἴτε φλυαρίας, ἐξ ὧν κενοῖσιν ἐγκατοικήσεις δόμοις· ζηλῶν οὐκ ἐλέγχοντας ἄνδρας τὰ μικρὰ ταῦτα, ἀλλ' οἷς ἔστι καὶ βίος καὶ δόξα καὶ ἄλλα πολλὰ ἀγαθά.

ΣΩ. Εἰ χρυσῆν ἔχων ἐτύγχανον τὴν ψυχήν, ὦ Καλλίκλεις, οὐκ ἂν οἴει με ἄσμενον εὑρεῖν τούτων τινὰ τῶν λίθων, ᾗ βασανίζουσι τὸν χρυσόν, τὴν ἀρίστην, πρὸς ἥντινα ἔμελλον προσαγαγὼν αὐτήν, εἴ μοι ὁμολογήσειεν ἐκείνη καλῶς τεθεραπεῦσθαι τὴν ψυχήν, εὖ εἴσεσθαι ὅτι ἱκανῶς ἔχω καὶ οὐδέν μοι δεῖ ἄλλης βασάνου;

ΚΑΛΛ. Πρὸς τί δὴ τοῦτ' ἐρωτᾷς, ὦ Σώκρατες;

ΣΩ. Ἐγώ σοι ἐρῶ· νῦν οἶμαι ἐγὼ σοὶ ἐντετυχηκὼς τοιούτῳ ἑρμαίῳ ἐντετυχηκέναι.

ΚΑΛΛ. Τί δή;

ΣΩ. Εὖ οἶδ' ὅτι, ἄν μοι σὺ ὁμολογήσῃς περὶ ὧν ἡ ἐμὴ ψυχὴ δοξάζει, ταῦτ' ἤδη ἐστὶν αὐτὰ τἀληθῆ. ἐννοῶ γάρ, ὅτι τὸν μέλλοντα βασανιεῖν ἱκανῶς ψυχῆς πέρι ὀρθῶς τε ζώσης καὶ μὴ τρία ἄρα δεῖ ἔχειν, ἃ σὺ πάντα ἔχεις, ἐπιστήμην τε καὶ εὔνοιαν καὶ παρρησίαν. ἐγὼ γὰρ πολλοῖς ἐντυγχάνω, οἳ ἐμὲ οὐχ οἷοί τε εἰσὶ βασανίζειν, διὰ τὸ μὴ σοφοὶ εἶναι ὥσπερ σύ· ἕτεροι δὲ σοφοὶ μέν εἰσιν, οὐκ ἐθέλουσι δέ μοι λέγειν τὴν ἀλήθειαν, διὰ τὸ μὴ κήδεσθαί μου ὥσπερ σύ· τὼ δὲ ξένω τώδε, Γοργίας τε καὶ Πῶλος, σοφὼ μὲν καὶ φίλω ἐστὸν ἐμώ, ἐνδεεστέρω δὲ παρρησίας καὶ αἰσχυν-

GORGIAS

impunity. No, take my advice, my good sir, "and cease refuting; some practical proficiency induce,"—something that will give you credit for sense: "to others leave these pretty toys,"—call them vapourings or fooleries as you will,—"which will bring you to inhabit empty halls"; and emulate, not men who probe these trifles, but who have means and repute and other good things in plenty.

soc. If my soul had happened to be made of gold, Callicles, do you not think I should have been delighted to find one of those stones with which they test gold, and the best one; which, if I applied it, and it confirmed to me that my soul had been properly tended, would give me full assurance that I am in a satisfactory state and have no need of other testing?

call. What is the point of that question, Socrates?

soc. I will tell you. I am just thinking what a lucky stroke I have had in striking up with you.

call. How so?

soc. I am certain that whenever you agree with me in any view that my soul takes, this must be the very truth. For I conceive that whoever would sufficiently test a soul as to rectitude of life or the reverse should go to work with three things which are all in your possession — knowledge, goodwill, and frankness. I meet with many people who are unable to test me, because they are not wise as you are; while others, though wise, are unwilling to tell me the truth, because they do not care for me as you do; and our two visitors here, Gorgias and Polus, though wise and friendly to me, are more lacking in frankness and inclined to bashfulness than

PLATO

τηροτέρω μᾶλλον τοῦ δέοντος· πῶς γὰρ οὔ; ᾧ γε εἰς τοσοῦτον αἰσχύνης ἐληλύθατον, ὥστε διὰ τὸ αἰσχύνεσθαι τολμᾷ ἑκάτερος αὐτῶν αὐτὸς αὑτῷ ἐναντία λέγειν ἐναντίον πολλῶν ἀνθρώπων, καὶ ταῦτα περὶ τῶν μεγίστων. σὺ δὲ ταῦτα πάντα ἔχεις, ἃ οἱ ἄλλοι οὐκ ἔχουσι· πεπαίδευσαί τε γὰρ ἱκανῶς, ὡς πολλοὶ ἂν φήσαιεν Ἀθηναίων, καὶ ἐμοὶ εἶ εὔνους. τίνι τεκμηρίῳ χρῶμαι; ἐγώ σοι C ἐρῶ. οἶδα ὑμᾶς ἐγώ, ὦ Καλλίκλεις, τέτταρας ὄντας κοινωνοὺς γεγονότας σοφίας, σέ τε καὶ Τίσανδρον τὸν Ἀφιδναῖον καὶ Ἄνδρωνα τὸν Ἀνδροτίωνος καὶ Ναυσικύδην τὸν Χολαργέα· καί ποτε ὑμῶν ἐγὼ ἐπήκουσα βουλευομένων, μέχρι ὅποι τὴν σοφίαν ἀσκητέον εἴη, καὶ οἶδα ὅτι ἐνίκα ἐν ὑμῖν τοιάδε τις δόξα, μὴ προθυμεῖσθαι εἰς τὴν ἀκρίβειαν φιλοσοφεῖν, ἀλλὰ εὐλαβεῖσθαι παρ- D εκελεύεσθε ἀλλήλοις, ὅπως μὴ πέρα τοῦ δέοντος σοφώτεροι γενόμενοι λήσετε διαφθαρέντες. ἐπειδὴ οὖν σου ἀκούω ταὐτὰ ἐμοὶ συμβουλεύοντος, ἅπερ τοῖς σεαυτοῦ ἑταιροτάτοις, ἱκανόν μοι τεκμήριόν ἐστιν, ὅτι ὡς ἀληθῶς μοι εὔνους εἶ. καὶ μὴν ὅτι γε οἷος παρρησιάζεσθαι καὶ μὴ αἰσχύνεσθαι, αὐτός τε φῂς καὶ ὁ λόγος ὃν ὀλίγον πρότερον ἔλεγες ὁμολογεῖ σοι. ἔχει δὴ οὑτωσὶ δῆλον ὅτι E τούτων πέρι νυνί. ἐάν τι σὺ ἐν τοῖς λόγοις ὁμολογήσῃς μοι, βεβασανισμένον τοῦτ᾽ ἤδη ἔσται ἱκανῶς ὑπ᾽ ἐμοῦ τε καὶ σοῦ, καὶ οὐκέτι αὐτὸ δεήσει ἐπ᾽ ἄλλην βάσανον ἀναφέρειν. οὐ γὰρ ἂν

---

[1] Andron is one of the wise men who meet in the house of Callias, *Protag.* 315; Nausicydes may be the wealthy meal-merchant mentioned in Aristoph. *Eccles.* 426, and Xen. *Mem.* ii. 7. 6. Of Tisander nothing is known.

GORGIAS

they should be: nay, it must be so, when they have carried modesty to such a point that each of them can bring himself, out of sheer modesty, to contradict himself in face of a large company, and that on questions of the greatest importance. But you have all these qualities which the rest of them lack: you have had a sound education, as many here in Athens will agree; and you are well disposed to me. You ask what proof I have? I will tell you. I know, Callicles, that four of you have formed a partnership in wisdom—you, Tisander of Aphidnae, Andron, son of Androtion, and Nausicydes of Cholarges;[1] and I once overheard you debating how far the cultivation of wisdom should be carried, and I know you were deciding in favour of some such view as this—that one should not be carried away into the minuter points of philosophy, but you exhorted one another to beware of making yourselves overwise, lest you should unwittingly work your own ruin. So when I hear you giving me the same advice as you gave your own most intimate friends, I have proof enough that you really are well disposed to me. And further, as to your aptness to speak out frankly and not be bashful, you not only claim this yourself, but you are borne out too by the speech that you made a short while ago. Well, this is clearly the position of our question at present: if you can bear me out in any point arising in our argument, that point can at once be taken as having been amply tested by both you and me, and there will be no more need of referring it to a further test; for no defect of wisdom or access

PLATO

487

ποτε αὐτὸ συνεχώρησας σὺ οὔτε σοφίας ἐνδείᾳ
οὔτ' αἰσχύνης παρουσίᾳ, οὐδ' αὖ ἀπατῶν ἐμὲ
συγχωρήσαις ἄν· φίλος γάρ μοι εἶ, ὡς καὶ αὐτὸς
φῄς. τῷ ὄντι οὖν ἡ ἐμὴ καὶ ἡ σὴ ὁμολογία τέλος
ἤδη ἕξει τῆς ἀληθείας. πάντων δὲ καλλίστη ἐστὶν
ἡ σκέψις, ὦ Καλλίκλεις, περὶ τούτων ὧν σὺ δή
μοι ἐπετίμησας, ποῖόν τινα χρὴ εἶναι τὸν ἄνδρα
488 καὶ τί ἐπιτηδεύειν καὶ μέχρι τοῦ, καὶ πρεσβύτερον
καὶ νεώτερον ὄντα. ἐγὼ γὰρ εἴ τι μὴ ὀρθῶς
πράττω κατὰ τὸν βίον τὸν ἐμαυτοῦ, εὖ ἴσθι τοῦτο
ὅτι οὐχ ἑκὼν ἐξαμαρτάνω ἀλλ' ἀμαθίᾳ τῇ ἐμῇ·
σὺ οὖν, ὥσπερ ἤρξω νουθετεῖν με, μὴ ἀποστῇς,
ἀλλ' ἱκανῶς μοι ἔνδειξαι, τί ἔστι τοῦτο ὃ ἐπιτη-
δευτέον μοι, καὶ τίνα τρόπον κτησαίμην ἂν αὐτό,
καὶ ἐάν με λάβῃς νῦν μέν σοι ὁμολογήσαντα, ἐν
δὲ τῷ ὑστέρῳ χρόνῳ μὴ ταῦτα πράττοντα ἅπερ
B ὡμολόγησα, πάνυ με ἡγοῦ βλᾶκα εἶναι καὶ μηκέτι
ποτέ με νουθετήσῃς ὕστερον, ὡς μηδενὸς ἄξιον
ὄντα. ἐξ ἀρχῆς δέ μοι ἐπανάλαβε, πῶς φῂς τὸ
δίκαιον ἔχειν καὶ σὺ καὶ Πίνδαρος τὸ κατὰ φύσιν;
ἄγειν βίᾳ τὸν κρείττω τὰ τῶν ἡττόνων καὶ ἄρχειν
τὸν βελτίω τῶν χειρόνων καὶ πλέον ἔχειν τὸν
ἀμείνω τοῦ φαυλοτέρου; μή τι ἄλλο λέγεις τὸ
δίκαιον εἶναι, ἢ ὀρθῶς μέμνημαι;

ΚΑΛΛ. Ἀλλὰ ταῦτα ἔλεγον καὶ τότε καὶ νῦν
λέγω.

ΣΩ. Πότερον δὲ τὸν αὐτὸν βελτίω καλεῖς σὺ
C καὶ κρείττω; οὐδὲ γάρ τοι τότε οἷός τ' ἦ μαθεῖν
σου τί ποτε λέγοις. πότερον τοὺς ἰσχυροτέρους
κρείττους καλεῖς καὶ δεῖ ἀκροᾶσθαι τοῦ ἰσχυ-
ροτέρου τοὺς ἀσθενεστέρους, οἷόν μοι δοκεῖς καὶ

of modesty could ever have been your motive in making this concession, nor again could you make it to deceive me: for you are my friend, as you say yourself. Hence any agreement between you and me must really have attained the perfection of truth. And on no themes could one make more honourable inquiry, Callicles, than on those which you have reproached me with—what character one should have, and what should be one's pursuits and up to what point, in later as in earlier years. For I assure you that if there is any fault of conduct to be found in my own life it is not an intentional error, but due to my ignorance: so I ask you not to break off in the middle of your task of admonishing me, but to make fully clear to me what it is that I ought to pursue and by what means I may attain it; and if you find me in agreement with you now, and afterwards failing to do what I agreed to, regard me as a regular dunce and never trouble any more to admonish me again—a mere good-for-nothing. Now, go right back and repeat to me what you and Pindar hold natural justice to consist in: is it that the superior should forcibly despoil the inferior, the better rule the worse, and the nobler have more than the meaner? Have you some other account to give of justice, or do I remember aright?

CALL. Why, that is what I said then, and I say it now also.

SOC. Is it the same person that you call "better" and "superior"? For I must say I was no more able then to understand what your meaning might be. Is it the stronger folk that you call superior, and are the weaker ones bound to hearken to the stronger one — as for instance I think you were

τότε ἐνδείκνυσθαι, ὡς αἱ μεγάλαι πόλεις ἐπὶ τὰς σμικρὰς κατὰ τὸ φύσει δίκαιον ἔρχονται, ὅτι κρείττους εἰσὶ καὶ ἰσχυρότεραι, ὡς τὸ κρεῖττον καὶ ἰσχυρότερον καὶ βέλτιον ταὐτὸν ὄν, ἢ ἔστι βελτίω μὲν εἶναι, ἥττω δὲ καὶ ἀσθενέστερον, καὶ κρείττω μὲν εἶναι, μοχθηρότερον δέ· ἢ ὁ αὐτὸς ὅρος ἐστὶ

D τοῦ βελτίονος καὶ τοῦ κρείττονος; τοῦτό μοι αὐτὸ σαφῶς διόρισον, ταὐτὸν ἢ ἕτερόν ἐστι τὸ κρεῖττον καὶ τὸ βέλτιον καὶ τὸ ἰσχυρότερον;

ΚΑΛΛ. Ἀλλ' ἐγώ σοι σαφῶς λέγω, ὅτι ταὐτόν ἐστιν.

ΣΩ. Οὐκοῦν οἱ πολλοὶ τοῦ ἑνὸς κρείττους εἰσὶ κατὰ φύσιν; οἳ δὴ καὶ τοὺς νόμους τίθενται ἐπὶ τῷ ἑνί, ὥσπερ καὶ σὺ ἄρτι ἔλεγες.

ΚΑΛΛ. Πῶς γὰρ οὔ;

ΣΩ. Τὰ τῶν πολλῶν ἄρα νόμιμα τὰ τῶν κρειττόνων ἐστίν.

ΚΑΛΛ. Πάνυ γε.

E ΣΩ. Οὐκοῦν τὰ τῶν βελτιόνων; οἱ γὰρ κρείττους βελτίους πολὺ κατὰ τὸν σὸν λόγον.

ΚΑΛΛ. Ναί.

ΣΩ. Οὐκοῦν τὰ τούτων νόμιμα κατὰ φύσιν καλά, κρειττόνων γε ὄντων;

ΚΑΛΛ. Φημί.

ΣΩ. Ἆρ' οὖν οἱ πολλοὶ νομίζουσιν οὕτως, ὡς ἄρτι αὖ σὺ ἔλεγες, δίκαιον εἶναι τὸ ἴσον ἔχειν καὶ
489 αἴσχιον τὸ ἀδικεῖν τοῦ ἀδικεῖσθαι; ἔστι ταῦτα ἢ οὔ; καὶ ὅπως μὴ ἁλώσῃ ἐνταῦθα σὺ αἰσχυνόμενος· νομίζουσιν, ἢ οὔ, οἱ πολλοὶ τὸ ἴσον ἔχειν ἀλλ' οὐ

GORGIAS

also pointing out then, that the great states attack the little ones in accordance with natural right, because they are superior and stronger, on the ground that the superior and the stronger and the better are all the same thing; or is it possible to be better and yet inferior and weaker, and to be superior and yet more wicked? Or is the definition of the better and the superior the same? This is just what I bid you declare in definite terms—whether the superior and the better and the stronger are the same or different.

CALL. Well, I tell you plainly, they are all the same.

SOC. Now, are the many superior by nature to the one? I mean those who make the laws to keep a check on the one, as you were saying yourself just now.

CALL. Of course.

SOC. Then the ordinances of the many are those of the superior.

CALL. Certainly.

SOC. And so of the better? For the superior are far better, by your account.

CALL. Yes.

SOC. And so their ordinances are by nature "fair," since they are superior who made them?

CALL. I agree.

SOC. Then is it the opinion of the many that—as you also said a moment ago—justice means having an equal share, and it is fouler to wrong than be wronged? Is that so, or not? And mind you are not caught this time in a bashful fit. Is it, or is it not, the opinion of the many that to have one's equal share, and not more than others, is just,

PLATO

τὸ πλέον δίκαιον εἶναι, καὶ αἴσχιον τὸ ἀδικεῖν τοῦ ἀδικεῖσθαι; μὴ φθόνει μοι ἀποκρίνασθαι τοῦτο, Καλλίκλεις, ἵν', ἐάν μοι ὁμολογήσῃς, βεβαιώσωμαι ἤδη παρὰ σοῦ, ἅτε ἱκανοῦ ἀνδρὸς διαγνῶναι ὡμολογηκότος.

ΚΑΛΛ. Ἀλλ' οἵ γε πολλοὶ νομίζουσιν οὕτως.

ΣΩ. Οὐ νόμῳ ἄρα μόνον ἐστὶν αἴσχιον τὸ ἀδικεῖν τοῦ ἀδικεῖσθαι, οὐδὲ δίκαιον τὸ ἴσον ἔχειν, ἀλλὰ καὶ φύσει· ὥστε κινδυνεύεις οὐκ ἀληθῆ λέγειν ἐν τοῖς πρόσθεν οὐδὲ ὀρθῶς ἐμοῦ κατηγορεῖν λέγων, ὅτι ἐναντίον ἐστὶν ὁ νόμος καὶ ἡ φύσις, ἃ δὴ καὶ ἐγὼ γνοὺς κακουργῶ ἐν τοῖς λόγοις, ἐὰν μέν τις κατὰ φύσιν λέγῃ, ἐπὶ τὸν νόμον ἄγων, ἐὰν δέ τις κατὰ τὸν νόμον, ἐπὶ τὴν φύσιν.

ΚΑΛΛ. Οὑτοσὶ ἀνὴρ οὐ παύσεται φλυαρῶν. εἰπέ μοι, ὦ Σώκρατες, οὐκ αἰσχύνῃ, τηλικοῦτος ὤν, ὀνόματα θηρεύων, καὶ ἐάν τις ῥήματι ἁμάρτῃ, ἕρμαιον τοῦτο ποιούμενος; ἐμὲ γὰρ οἴει ἄλλο τι λέγειν τὸ κρείττους εἶναι ἢ τὸ βελτίους; οὐ πάλαι σοι λέγω, ὅτι ταὐτόν φημι εἶναι τὸ βέλτιον καὶ τὸ κρεῖττον; ἢ οἴει με λέγειν, ἐὰν συρφετὸς συλλεγῇ δούλων καὶ παντοδαπῶν ἀνθρώπων μηδενὸς ἀξίων πλὴν ἴσως τῷ σώματι ἰσχυρίσασθαι, καὶ οὗτοι φῶσιν ἄττα,[1] ταῦτα εἶναι νόμιμα;

ΣΩ. Εἶεν, ὦ σοφώτατε Καλλίκλεις· οὕτω λέγεις;

ΚΑΛΛ. Πάνυ μὲν οὖν.

ΣΩ. Ἀλλ' ἐγὼ μέν, ὦ δαιμόνιε, καὶ αὐτὸς πάλαι τοπάζω τοιοῦτόν τί σε λέγειν τὸ κρεῖττον,

[1] ἄττα Heindorf : αὐτὰ MSS.

and that it is fouler to wrong than be wronged? Do not grudge me an answer to this, Callicles, so that—if I find you agree with me—I may then have the assurance that comes from the agreement of a man so competent to decide.

CALL. Well, most people do think so.

SOC. Then it is not only by convention that doing wrong is fouler than suffering it, and having one's equal share is just, but by nature also: and therefore it looks as though your previous statement was untrue, and your count against me incorrect, when you said that convention and nature are opposites and that I, forsooth, recognizing that, am an unscrupulous debater, turning to convention when the assertion refers to nature, and to nature when it refers to convention.

CALL. What an inveterate driveller the man is! Tell me, Socrates, are you not ashamed to be word-catching at your age, and if one makes a verbal slip, to take that as a great stroke of luck? Do you imagine that, when I said " being superior," I meant anything else than " better "? Have I not been telling you ever so long that I regard the better and the superior as the same thing? Or do you suppose I mean that if a pack of slaves and all sorts of fellows who are good for nothing, except perhaps in point of physical strength, gather together and say something, that is a legal ordinance?

SOC. Very well, most sapient Callicles: you mean that, do you?

CALL. Certainly I do.

SOC. Why, my wonderful friend, I have myself been guessing ever so long that you meant something of this sort by " superior," and if I repeat my

PLATO

καὶ ἀνερωτῶ γλιχόμενος σαφῶς εἰδέναι ὅ τι λέγεις. οὐ γὰρ δήπου σύ γε τοὺς δύο βελτίους ἡγῇ τοῦ ἑνός, οὐδὲ τοὺς σοὺς δούλους βελτίους σοῦ, ὅτι ἰσχυρότεροί εἰσιν ἢ σύ. ἀλλὰ πάλιν ἐξ ἀρχῆς εἰπέ, τί ποτε λέγεις τοὺς βελτίους, ἐπειδὴ οὐ τοὺς ἰσχυροτέρους; καὶ ὦ θαυμάσιε πρᾳότερόν με προδίδασκε, ἵνα μὴ ἀποφοιτήσω παρὰ σοῦ.

ΚΑΛΛ. Εἰρωνεύῃ, ὦ Σώκρατες.

ΣΩ. Μὰ τὸν Ζῆθον, ὦ Καλλίκλεις, ᾧ σὺ χρώμενος πολλὰ νῦν δὴ εἰρωνεύου πρός με· ἀλλ' ἴθι εἰπέ, τίνας λέγεις τοὺς βελτίους εἶναι;

ΚΑΛΛ. Τοὺς ἀμείνους ἔγωγε.

ΣΩ. Ὁρᾷς ἄρα, ὅτι σὺ αὐτὸς ὀνόματα λέγεις, δηλοῖς δὲ οὐδέν; οὐκ ἐρεῖς, τοὺς βελτίους καὶ κρείττους πότερον τοὺς φρονιμωτέρους λέγεις ἢ ἄλλους τινάς;

ΚΑΛΛ. Ἀλλὰ ναὶ μὰ Δία τούτους λέγω, καὶ σφόδρα γε.

ΣΩ. Πολλάκις ἄρα εἷς φρονῶν μυρίων μὴ φρονούντων κρείττων ἐστὶ κατὰ τὸν σὸν λόγον, καὶ τοῦτον ἄρχειν δεῖ, τοὺς δ' ἄρχεσθαι, καὶ πλέον ἔχειν τὸν ἄρχοντα τῶν ἀρχομένων· τοῦτο γάρ μοι δοκεῖς βούλεσθαι λέγειν—καὶ οὐ ῥήματι θηρεύω—εἰ ὁ εἷς τῶν μυρίων κρείττων.

ΚΑΛΛ. Ἀλλὰ ταῦτ' ἔστιν ἃ λέγω. τοῦτο γὰρ οἶμαι ἐγὼ τὸ δίκαιον εἶναι φύσει, τὸ βελτίω ὄντα καὶ φρονιμώτερον καὶ ἄρχειν καὶ πλέον ἔχειν τῶν φαυλοτέρων.

ΣΩ. Ἔχε δὴ αὐτοῦ. τί ποτε αὖ νῦν λέγεις;

GORGIAS

questions it is because I am so keen to know definitely what your meaning may be. For I presume you do not consider that two are better than one, or that your slaves are better than yourself, just because they are stronger than you are. Come now, tell me again from the beginning what it is you mean by the better, since you do not mean the stronger: only, admirable sir, do be more gentle with me over my first lessons, or I shall cease attending your school.

CALL. You are sarcastic, Socrates.

SOC. No, by Zethus, Callicles, whom you made use of just now[1] for aiming a good deal of sarcasm at me: but come, tell us whom you mean by the better.

CALL. I mean the more excellent.

SOC. So you see, you are uttering mere words yourself, and explaining nothing. Will you not tell us whether by the better and superior you mean the wiser, or some other sort?

CALL. Why, to be sure, I mean those, and very much so.

SOC. Then one wise man is often superior to ten thousand fools, by your account, and he ought to rule and they to be ruled, and the ruler should have more than they whom he rules. That is what you seem to me to intend by your statement—and I am not word-catching here—if the one is superior to the ten thousand.

CALL. Why, that is my meaning. For this is what I regard as naturally just—that being better and wiser he should have both rule and advantage over the baser people.

SOC. Stop there now. Once more, what is your

[1] Above, 486 A.

PLATO

ἐὰν ἐν τῷ αὐτῷ ὦμεν, ὥσπερ νῦν, πολλοὶ ἀθρόοι [ἄνθρωποι],[1] καὶ ἡμῖν ᾖ ἐν κοινῷ πολλὰ σιτία καὶ ποτά, ὦμεν δὲ παντοδαποί, οἱ μὲν ἰσχυροί, οἱ δὲ ἀσθενεῖς, εἷς δὲ ἡμῶν ᾖ φρονιμώτερος περὶ ταῦτα, ἰατρὸς ὤν, ᾖ δέ, οἷον εἰκός, τῶν μὲν ἰσχυρότερος, τῶν δὲ ἀσθενέστερος, ἄλλο τι ἢ οὗτος, φρονιμώτερος ἡμῶν ὤν, βελτίων καὶ κρείττων ἔσται εἰς ταῦτα;

ΚΑΛΛ. Πάνυ γε.

ΣΩ. Ἢ οὖν τούτων τῶν σιτίων πλέον ἡμῶν ἑκτέον αὐτῷ, ὅτι βελτίων ἐστίν, ἢ τῷ μὲν ἄρχειν πάντα ἐκεῖνον δεῖ νέμειν, ἐν δὲ τῷ ἀναλίσκειν τε αὐτὰ καὶ καταχρῆσθαι εἰς τὸ ἑαυτοῦ σῶμα οὐ πλεονεκτητέον, εἰ μὴ μέλλει ζημιοῦσθαι, ἀλλὰ τῶν μὲν πλέον, τῶν δ' ἔλαττον ἑκτέον· ἐὰν δὲ τύχῃ πάντων ἀσθενέστατος ὤν, πάντων ἐλάχιστον τῷ βελτίστῳ, ὦ Καλλίκλεις; οὐχ οὕτως, ὦ 'γαθέ;

ΚΑΛΛ. Περὶ σιτία λέγεις καὶ ποτὰ καὶ ἰατροὺς καὶ φλυαρίας· ἐγὼ δὲ οὐ ταῦτα λέγω.

ΣΩ. Πότερον οὖν τὸν φρονιμώτερον βελτίω λέγεις; φάθι ἢ μή.

ΚΑΛΛ. Ἔγωγε.

ΣΩ. Ἀλλ' οὐ τὸν βελτίω πλέον δεῖν ἔχειν;

ΚΑΛΛ. Οὐ σιτίων γε οὐδὲ ποτῶν.

ΣΩ. Μανθάνω, ἀλλ' ἴσως ἱματίων, καὶ δεῖ τὸν ὑφαντικώτατον μέγιστον ἱμάτιον ἔχειν καὶ πλεῖστα καὶ κάλλιστα ἀμπεχόμενον περιιέναι;

ΚΑΛΛ. Ποίων ἱματίων;

ΣΩ. Ἀλλ' εἰς ὑποδήματα δῆλον ὅτι δεῖ πλεονεκτεῖν τὸν φρονιμώτατον εἰς ταῦτα καὶ βέλτιστον.

[1] ἄνθρωποι om. Burnet.

GORGIAS

meaning this time? Suppose that a number of us are assembled together, as now, in the same place, and we have in common a good supply of food and drink, and we are of all sorts—some strong, some weak; and one of us, a doctor, is wiser than the rest in this matter and, as may well be, is stronger than some and weaker than others; will not he, being wiser than we are, be better and superior in this affair?

CALL. Certainly.

SOC. Then is he to have a larger ration than the rest of us because he is better, or ought he as ruler to have the distribution of the whole stock, with no advantage in spending and consuming it upon his own person, if he is to avoid retribution, but merely having more than some and less than others? Or if he chance to be the weakest of all, ought he not to get the smallest share of all though he be the best, Callicles? Is it not so, good sir?

CALL. You refer to food and drink and doctors and drivel: I mean something different.

SOC. Then tell me, do you call the wiser better? Yes or no?

CALL. Yes, I do.

SOC. But do you not think the better should have a larger share?

CALL. Yes, but not of food and drink.

SOC. I see; of clothes, perhaps; and the ablest weaver should have the largest coat, and go about arrayed in the greatest variety of the finest clothes?

CALL. What have clothes to do with it?

SOC. Well, shoes then; clearly he who is wisest in regard to these, and best, should have some advan-

PLATO

τὸν σκυτοτόμον ἴσως μέγιστα δεῖ ὑποδήματα καὶ πλεῖστα ὑποδεδεμένον περιπατεῖν.

ΚΑΛΛ. Ποῖα ὑποδήματα; φλυαρεῖς ἔχων.

ΣΩ. Ἀλλ' εἰ μὴ τὰ τοιαῦτα λέγεις, ἴσως τὰ τοιάδε· οἷον γεωργικὸν ἄνδρα περὶ γῆν φρόνιμόν τε καὶ καλὸν καὶ ἀγαθόν, τοῦτον δὴ ἴσως δεῖ πλεονεκτεῖν τῶν σπερμάτων καὶ ὡς πλείστῳ σπέρματι χρῆσθαι εἰς τὴν αὑτοῦ γῆν.

ΚΑΛΛ. Ὡς ἀεὶ ταὐτὰ λέγεις, ὦ Σώκρατες.

ΣΩ. Οὐ μόνον γε, ὦ Καλλίκλεις, ἀλλὰ καὶ περὶ τῶν αὐτῶν.

ΚΑΛΛ. Νὴ τοὺς θεούς, ἀτεχνῶς γε ἀεὶ σκυτέας τε καὶ κναφέας καὶ μαγείρους λέγων καὶ ἰατροὺς οὐδὲν παύῃ, ὡς περὶ τούτων ἡμῖν ὄντα τὸν λόγον.

ΣΩ. Οὐκοῦν σὺ ἐρεῖς περὶ τίνων ὁ κρείττων τε καὶ φρονιμώτερος πλέον ἔχων δικαίως πλεονεκτεῖ; ἢ οὔτε ἐμοῦ ὑποβάλλοντος ἀνέξῃ οὔτ' αὐτὸς ἐρεῖς;

ΚΑΛΛ. Ἀλλ' ἔγωγε καὶ πάλαι λέγω. πρῶτον μὲν τοὺς κρείττους οἵ εἰσιν οὐ σκυτοτόμους λέγω οὐδὲ μαγείρους, ἀλλ' οἳ ἂν εἰς τὰ τῆς πόλεως πράγματα φρόνιμοι ὦσιν, ὅντινα ἂν τρόπον εὖ οἰκοῖτο, καὶ μὴ μόνον φρόνιμοι, ἀλλὰ καὶ ἀνδρεῖοι, ἱκανοὶ ὄντες ἃ ἂν νοήσωσιν ἐπιτελεῖν, καὶ μὴ ἀποκάμνωσι διὰ μαλακίαν τῆς ψυχῆς.

ΣΩ. Ὁρᾷς, ὦ βέλτιστε Καλλίκλεις, ὡς οὐ ταὐτὰ σύ τ' ἐμοῦ κατηγορεῖς καὶ ἐγὼ σοῦ; σὺ μὲν γὰρ ἐμὲ φῂς ἀεὶ ταὐτὰ λέγειν, καὶ μέμφῃ

GORGIAS

tage. Perhaps the shoemaker should walk about in the biggest shoes and wear the largest number.

CALL. Shoes—what have they to do with it? You keep on drivelling.

SOC. Well, if you do not mean things of that sort, perhaps you mean something like this : a farmer, for instance, who knows all about the land and is highly accomplished in the matter, should perhaps have an advantage in sharing the seed, and have the largest possible amount of it for use on his own land.

CALL. How you keep repeating the same thing, Socrates !

SOC. Yes, and not only that, Callicles, but on the same subjects too.

CALL. I believe, on my soul, you absolutely cannot ever stop talking of cobblers and fullers, cooks and doctors, as though our discussion had to do with them.

SOC. Then will you tell me in what things the superior and wiser man has a right to the advantage of a larger share ? Or will you neither put up with a suggestion from me nor make one yourself ?

CALL. Why, I have been making mine for some time past. First of all, by " the superior " I mean, not shoemakers or cooks, but those who are wise as regards public affairs and the proper way of conducting them, and not only wise but manly, with ability to carry out their purpose to the full ; and who will not falter through softness of soul.

SOC. Do you perceive, my excellent Callicles, that your count against me is not the same as mine against you ? For you say I am ever repeating the same things, and reproach me with it, whereas I

PLATO

μοι· ἐγὼ δὲ σοῦ τοὐναντίον, ὅτι οὐδέποτε ταὐτὰ λέγεις περὶ τῶν αὐτῶν, ἀλλὰ τοτὲ μὲν τοὺς βελτίους τε καὶ κρείττους τοὺς ἰσχυροτέρους ὡρίζου, αὖθις δὲ τοὺς φρονιμωτέρους, νῦν δ' αὖ ἕτερόν τι ἥκεις ἔχων· ἀνδρειότεροί τινες ὑπὸ σοῦ λέγονται οἱ κρείττους καὶ οἱ βελτίους. ἀλλ', ὦ 'γαθέ, εἰπὼν ἀπαλλάγηθι, τίνας ποτὲ λέγεις τοὺς βελτίους τε καὶ κρείττους καὶ εἰς ὅ τι.

ΚΑΛΛ. Ἀλλ' εἴρηκά γε ἔγωγε τοὺς φρονίμους εἰς τὰ τῆς πόλεως πράγματα καὶ ἀνδρείους. τούτους γὰρ προσήκει τῶν πόλεων ἄρχειν, καὶ τὸ δίκαιον τοῦτ' ἐστί, πλέον ἔχειν τούτους τῶν ἄλλων, τοὺς ἄρχοντας τῶν ἀρχομένων.

ΣΩ. Τί δέ; αὐτῶν, ὦ ἑταῖρε; [τί ἢ τί ἄρχοντας ἢ ἀρχομένους;][1]

ΚΑΛΛ. Πῶς λέγεις;

ΣΩ. Ἕνα ἕκαστον λέγω αὐτὸν ἑαυτοῦ ἄρχοντα· ἢ τοῦτο μὲν οὐδὲν δεῖ, αὐτὸν ἑαυτοῦ ἄρχειν, τῶν δὲ ἄλλων;

ΚΑΛΛ. Πῶς ἑαυτοῦ ἄρχοντα λέγεις;

ΣΩ. Οὐδὲν ποικίλον, ἀλλ' ὥσπερ οἱ πολλοί, σώφρονα ὄντα καὶ ἐγκρατῆ αὐτὸν ἑαυτοῦ, τῶν ἡδονῶν καὶ ἐπιθυμιῶν ἄρχοντα τῶν ἐν ἑαυτῷ.

ΚΑΛΛ. Ὡς ἡδὺς εἶ· τοὺς ἠλιθίους λέγεις τοὺς σώφρονας.

ΣΩ. Πῶς γάρ [οὔ][2]; οὐδεὶς ὅστις οὐκ ἂν γνοίη, ὅτι οὐ τοῦτο λέγω.

ΚΑΛΛ. Πάνυ γε σφόδρα, ὦ Σώκρατες. ἐπεὶ πῶς ἂν εὐδαίμων γένοιτο ἄνθρωπος δουλεύων ὁτῳοῦν; ἀλλὰ τοῦτ' ἐστὶ τὸ κατὰ φύσιν καλὸν καὶ δίκαιον, ὃ ἐγώ σοι νῦν παρρησιαζόμενος λέγω,

[1] τί ... ἀρχομένους; om. Bekker.   [2] οὔ secl. Routh.

GORGIAS

charge you, on the contrary, with never saying the same thing on the same subject; but at one moment you defined the better and superior as the stronger, and at another as the wiser, and now you turn up again with something else: "the manlier" is what you now tell us is meant by the superior and better. No, my good friend, you had best say, and get it over, whom you do mean by the better and superior, and in what sphere.

CALL. But I have told you already: men of wisdom and manliness in public affairs. These are the persons who ought to rule our cities, and justice means this — that these should have more than other people, the rulers than the ruled.

SOC. How so? Than themselves, my friend?

CALL. What do you mean?

SOC. I mean that every man is his own ruler; or is there no need of one's ruling oneself, but only of ruling others?

CALL. What do you mean by one who rules himself?

SOC. Nothing recondite; merely what most people mean—one who is temperate and self-mastering, ruler of the pleasures and desires that are in himself.

CALL. You will have your pleasantry! You mean "the simpletons" by "the temperate."

SOC. How so? Nobody can fail to see that I do not mean that.

CALL. Oh, you most certainly do, Socrates. For how can a man be happy if he is a slave to anybody at all? No, natural fairness and justice, I tell you now quite frankly, is this — that he who would

ὅτι δεῖ τὸν ὀρθῶς βιωσόμενον τὰς μὲν ἐπιθυμίας τὰς ἑαυτοῦ ἐᾶν ὡς μεγίστας εἶναι καὶ μὴ κολάζειν, ταύταις δὲ ὡς μεγίσταις οὔσαις ἱκανὸν εἶναι ὑπηρετεῖν δι' ἀνδρείαν καὶ φρόνησιν, καὶ ἀποπιμπλάναι ὧν ἂν ἀεὶ ἡ ἐπιθυμία γίγνηται. ἀλλὰ τοῦτ', οἶμαι, τοῖς πολλοῖς οὐ δυνατόν· ὅθεν ψέγουσι τοὺς τοιούτους δι' αἰσχύνην, ἀποκρυπτόμενοι τὴν αὑτῶν ἀδυναμίαν, καὶ αἰσχρὸν δή φασιν εἶναι τὴν ἀκολασίαν, ὅπερ ἐν τοῖς πρόσθεν ἐγὼ ἔλεγον, δουλούμενοι τοὺς βελτίους τὴν φύσιν ἀνθρώπους, καὶ αὐτοὶ οὐ δυνάμενοι ἐκπορίζεσθαι ταῖς ἡδοναῖς πλήρωσιν ἐπαινοῦσι τὴν σωφροσύνην καὶ τὴν δικαιοσύνην διὰ τὴν αὑτῶν ἀνανδρίαν. ἐπεί γε οἷς ἐξ ἀρχῆς ὑπῆρξεν ἢ βασιλέων υἱέσιν εἶναι ἢ αὐτοὺς τῇ φύσει ἱκανοὺς ἐκπορίσασθαι ἀρχήν τινα ἢ τυραννίδα ἢ δυναστείαν ⟨τί ἂν⟩[1] τῇ ἀληθείᾳ αἴσχιον καὶ κάκιον εἴη σωφροσύνης καὶ δικαιοσύνης τούτοις τοῖς ἀνθρώποις· οἷς ἐξὸν ἀπολαύειν τῶν ἀγαθῶν καὶ μηδενὸς ἐμποδὼν ὄντος, αὐτοὶ ἑαυτοῖς δεσπότην ἐπαγάγοιντο τὸν τῶν πολλῶν ἀνθρώπων νόμον τε καὶ λόγον καὶ ψόγον; ἢ πῶς οὐκ ἂν ἄθλιοι γεγονότες εἴησαν ὑπὸ τοῦ καλοῦ τοῦ τῆς δικαιοσύνης καὶ τῆς σωφροσύνης, μηδὲν πλέον νέμοντες τοῖς φίλοις τοῖς αὑτῶν ἢ τοῖς ἐχθροῖς, καὶ ταῦτα ἄρχοντες ἐν τῇ ἑαυτῶν πόλει; ἀλλὰ τῇ ἀληθείᾳ, ὦ Σώκρατες, ἣν φῂς σὺ διώκειν, ὧδ' ἔχει· τρυφὴ καὶ ἀκολασία καὶ ἐλευθερία, ἐὰν ἐπικουρίαν ἔχῃ, τοῦτ' ἐστὶν ἀρετή τε καὶ εὐδαιμονία· τὰ δὲ ἄλλα ταῦτ' ἐστὶ τὰ καλλωπίσματα, τὰ παρὰ φύσιν συνθήματα ἀνθρώπων, φλυαρία καὶ οὐδενὸς ἄξια.

[1] τί ἂν add. Woolsey.

GORGIAS

live rightly should let his desires be as strong as possible and not chasten them, and should be able to minister to them when they are at their height by reason of his manliness and intelligence, and satisfy each appetite in turn with what it desires. But this, I suppose, is not possible for the many; whence it comes that they decry such persons out of shame, to disguise their own impotence, and are so good as to tell us that licentiousness is disgraceful, thus enslaving—as I remarked before—the better type of mankind; and being unable themselves to procure achievement of their pleasures they praise temperance and justice by reason of their own unmanliness. For to those who started with the advantage of being either kings' sons or able by their own parts to procure some authority or monarchy or absolute power, what in truth could be fouler or worse than temperance and justice in such cases? Finding themselves free to enjoy good things, with no obstacle in the way, they would be merely imposing on themselves a master in the shape of the law, the talk and the rebuke of the multitude. Or how could they fail to be sunk in wretchedness by that " fairness " of justice and temperance, if they had no larger portion to give to their own friends than to their enemies, and that too when they were rulers in their own cities? No, in good truth, Socrates—which you claim to be seeking—the fact is this: luxury and licentiousness and liberty, if they have the support of force, are virtue and happiness, and the rest of these embellishments—the unnatural covenants of mankind—are all mere stuff and nonsense.

PLATO

ΣΩ. Οὐκ ἀγεννῶς γε, ὦ Καλλίκλεις, ἐπεξέρχῃ τῷ λόγῳ παρρησιαζόμενος· σαφῶς γὰρ σὺ νῦν λέγεις, ἃ οἱ ἄλλοι διανοοῦνται μέν, λέγειν δὲ οὐκ ἐθέλουσιν. δέομαι οὖν ἐγώ σου μηδενὶ τρόπῳ ἀνεῖναι, ἵνα τῷ ὄντι κατάδηλον γένηται πῶς βιωτέον. καί μοι λέγε· τὰς μὲν ἐπιθυμίας φῂς οὐ κολαστέον, εἰ μέλλει τις οἷον δεῖ εἶναι, ἐῶντα δὲ αὐτὰς ὡς μεγίστας πλήρωσιν αὐταῖς ἁμόθεν γέ ποθεν ἑτοιμάζειν, καὶ τοῦτο εἶναι τὴν ἀρετήν;

ΚΑΛΛ. Φημὶ ταῦτα ἐγώ.

ΣΩ. Οὐκ ἄρα ὀρθῶς λέγονται οἱ μηδενὸς δεόμενοι εὐδαίμονες εἶναι.

ΚΑΛΛ. Οἱ λίθοι γὰρ ἂν οὕτω γε καὶ οἱ νεκροὶ εὐδαιμονέστατοι εἶεν.

ΣΩ. Ἀλλὰ μὲν δὴ καὶ ὥς γε σὺ λέγεις δεινὸς ὁ βίος. οὐ γάρ τοι θαυμάζοιμ' ἄν, εἰ Εὐριπίδης ἀληθῆ ἐν τοῖσδε λέγει, λέγων

τίς δ' οἶδεν, εἰ τὸ ζῆν μέν ἐστι κατθανεῖν,
τὸ κατθανεῖν δὲ ζῆν;

καὶ ἡμεῖς τῷ ὄντι ἴσως τέθναμεν· ἤδη του ἔγωγε καὶ ἤκουσα τῶν σοφῶν, ὡς νῦν ἡμεῖς τέθναμεν, καὶ τὸ μὲν σῶμά ἐστιν ἡμῖν σῆμα, τῆς δὲ ψυχῆς τοῦτο, ἐν ᾧ ἐπιθυμίαι εἰσί, τυγχάνει ὂν οἷον ἀναπείθεσθαι καὶ μεταπίπτειν ἄνω κάτω; καὶ τοῦτο ἄρα τις μυθολογῶν κομψὸς ἀνήρ, ἴσως Σικελός τις ἢ Ἰταλικός, παράγων τῷ ὀνόματι διὰ τὸ πιθανόν τε καὶ πειστικὸν ὠνόμασε πίθον, τοὺς

---

[1] Eurip. fr. (*Polyidus*).
[2] The sage was perhaps Philolaus, a Pythagorean philosopher contemporary with Socrates. The phrase σῶμα σῆμα, suggesting a mystical similarity between "body" and "tomb," was part of the Orphic doctrine.

GORGIAS

soc. Far from ignoble, at any rate, Callicles, is the frankness with which you develop your thesis: for you are now stating in clear terms what the rest of the world think indeed, but are loth to say. So I beg you not to give up on any account, that it may be made really evident how one ought to live. Now tell me: do you say the desires are not to be chastened if a man would be such as he ought to be, but he should let them be as great as possible and provide them with satisfaction from some source or other, and this is virtue?

CALL. Yes, I say that.

soc. Then it is not correct to say, as people do, that those who want nothing are happy.

CALL. No, for at that rate stones and corpses would be extremely happy.

soc. Well, but on your own view, life is strange. For I tell you I should not wonder if Euripides' words were true, when he says:

> Who knoweth if to live is to be dead,
> And to be dead, to live?[1]

and we really, it may be, are dead; in fact I once heard one of our sages say that we are now dead, and the body is our tomb,[2] and the part of the soul in which we have desires is liable to be over-persuaded and to vacillate to and fro, and so some smart fellow, a Sicilian, I daresay, or Italian,[3] made a fable in which—by a play of words[4]—he named this part, as being so impressionable and persuadable, a jar,

[3] "Sicilian" may refer to Empedocles; "Italian" to one of the Pythagoreans.
[4] The play is with πιθανόν and πίθον: πειστικόν is added to explain that πιθανόν is not used in its ordinary active sense of "impressive."

PLATO

δὲ ἀνοήτους ἀμυήτους· τῶν δ' ἀμυήτων τοῦτο τῆς
ψυχῆς, οὗ αἱ ἐπιθυμίαι εἰσί, τὸ ἀκόλαστον αὐτοῦ
καὶ οὐ στεγανόν, ὡς τετρημένος εἴη πίθος, διὰ τὴν
ἀπληστίαν ἀπεικάσας. τοὐναντίον δὴ οὗτος σοί,
ὦ Καλλίκλεις, ἐνδείκνυται ὡς τῶν ἐν Ἅιδου—τὸ
ἀιδὲς δὴ λέγων—οὗτοι ἀθλιώτατοι ἂν εἶεν, οἱ
ἀμύητοι, καὶ φοροῖεν εἰς τὸν τετρημένον πίθον
ὕδωρ ἑτέρῳ τοιούτῳ τετρημένῳ κοσκίνῳ. τὸ δὲ
κόσκινον ἄρα λέγει, ὡς ἔφη ὁ πρὸς ἐμὲ λέγων, τὴν
ψυχὴν εἶναι· τὴν δὲ ψυχὴν κοσκίνῳ ἀπῄκασε τὴν
τῶν ἀνοήτων ὡς τετρημένην, ἅτε οὐ δυναμένην στέ-
γειν δι' ἀπιστίαν τε καὶ λήθην. ταῦτ' ἐπιεικῶς μέν
ἐστιν ὑπό τι ἄτοπα, δηλοῖ μὴν ὃ ἐγὼ βούλομαί σοι
ἐνδειξάμενος, ἐάν πως οἷός τε ὦ, πεῖσαι μεταθέσθαι,
ἀντὶ τοῦ ἀπλήστως καὶ ἀκολάστως ἔχοντος βίου
τὸν κοσμίως καὶ τοῖς ἀεὶ παροῦσιν ἱκανῶς καὶ ἐξ-
αρκούντως ἔχοντα βίον ἑλέσθαι. ἀλλὰ πότερον πείθω
τί σε καὶ μετατίθεσθαι εὐδαιμονεστέρους εἶναι τοὺς
κοσμίους τῶν ἀκολάστων, ἢ οὐδ' ἂν ἄλλα[1] πολλὰ
τοιαῦτα μυθολογῶ, οὐδέν τι μᾶλλον μεταθήσῃ;

ΚΑΛΛ. Τοῦτ' ἀληθέστερον εἴρηκας, ὦ Σώκρατες.

ΣΩ. Φέρε δή, ἄλλην σοι εἰκόνα λέγω ἐκ τοῦ
αὐτοῦ γυμνασίου τῇ νῦν. σκόπει γὰρ εἰ τοιόνδε
λέγεις περὶ τοῦ βίου ἑκατέρου, τοῦ τε σώφρονος
καὶ τοῦ ἀκολάστου, οἷον εἰ δυοῖν ἀνδροῖν ἑκατέρῳ
πίθοι πολλοὶ εἶεν, καὶ τῷ μὲν ἑτέρῳ ὑγιεῖς καὶ
πλήρεις, ὁ μὲν οἴνου, ὁ δὲ μέλιτος, ὁ δὲ γάλακτος,

---

[1] οὐδ' ἂν ἄλλα Sauppe: οὐδὲν ἀλλά, οὐδὲν ἀλλ' ἄν, οὐδὲ ἀλλά, οὐδὲν ἀλλὰ κἂν MSS.

---

[1] The σοφός seems to have falsely derived ἀμυήτους from μύω (= close), with the meaning "unclosed," in order to connect it with the notion of "cracked" or "leaky."

GORGIAS

and the thoughtless he called uninitiate:[1] in these uninitiate that part of the soul where the desires are, the licentious and fissured part, he named a leaky jar in his allegory, because it is so insatiate. So you see this person, Callicles, takes the opposite view to yours, showing how of all who are in Hades—meaning of course the invisible—these uninitiate will be most wretched, and will carry water into their leaky jar with a sieve which is no less leaky. And then by the sieve, as my story-teller said, he means the soul : and the soul of the thoughtless he likened to a sieve, as being perforated, since it is unable to hold anything by reason of its unbelief and forgetfulness. All this, indeed, is bordering pretty well on the absurd ; but still it sets forth what I wish to impress upon you, if I somehow can, in order to induce you to make a change, and instead of a life of insatiate licentiousness to choose an orderly one that is set up and contented with what it happens to have got. Now, am I at all prevailing upon you to change over to the view that the orderly people are happier than the licentious ; or will no amount of similar fables that I might tell you have any effect in changing your mind ?

CALL. The latter is more like the truth, Socrates

SOC. Come now, let me tell you another parable from the same school[2] as that I have just told. Consider if each of the two lives, the temperate and the licentious, might be described by imagining that each of two men had a number of jars, and those of one man were sound and full, one of wine, another of honey, a third of milk, and various others of

[2] Probably of Pythagoras.

417

καὶ ἄλλοι πολλοὶ πολλῶν, νάματα δὲ σπάνια καὶ
χαλεπὰ ἑκάστου τούτων εἴη καὶ μετὰ πολλῶν
πόνων καὶ χαλεπῶν ἐκποριζόμενα· ὁ μὲν οὖν ἕτερος
πληρωσάμενος μήτ' ἐποχετεύοι μήτε τι φροντίζοι,
ἀλλ' ἕνεκα τούτων ἡσυχίαν ἔχοι· τῷ δ' ἑτέρῳ τὰ
μὲν νάματα, ὥσπερ καὶ ἐκείνῳ, δυνατὰ μὲν πο-
ρίζεσθαι, χαλεπὰ δέ, τὰ δ' ἀγγεῖα τετρημένα καὶ
σαθρά, ἀναγκάζοιτο δ' ἀεὶ καὶ νύκτα καὶ ἡμέραν
πιμπλάναι αὐτά, ἢ τὰς ἐσχάτας λυποῖτο λύπας·
ἆρα τοιούτου ἑκατέρου ὄντος τοῦ βίου, λέγεις τὸν
τοῦ ἀκολάστου εὐδαιμονέστερον εἶναι ἢ τὸν τοῦ κοσμίου; πείθω τί σε ταῦτα λέγων συγχωρῆσαι τὸν
κόσμιον βίον τοῦ ἀκολάστου ἀμείνω εἶναι, ἢ οὐ
πείθω;

ΚΑΛΛ. Οὐ πείθεις, ὦ Σώκρατες. τῷ μὲν γὰρ
πληρωσαμένῳ ἐκείνῳ οὐκέτ' ἔστιν ἡδονὴ οὐδεμία,
ἀλλὰ τοῦτ' ἔστιν, ὃ νῦν δὴ ἐγὼ ἔλεγον, τὸ ὥσπερ
λίθον ζῆν, ἐπειδὰν πληρώσῃ, μήτε χαίροντα ἔτι
μήτε λυπούμενον. ἀλλ' ἐν τούτῳ ἐστὶ τὸ ἡδέως
ζῆν, ἐν τῷ ὡς πλεῖστον ἐπιρρεῖν.

ΣΩ. Οὐκοῦν ἀνάγκη γ', ἂν πολὺ ἐπιρρέῃ, πολὺ
καὶ τὸ ἀπιὸν εἶναι, καὶ μεγάλ' ἄττα τὰ τρήματα
εἶναι ταῖς ἐκροαῖς;

ΚΑΛΛ. Πάνυ μὲν οὖν.

ΣΩ. Χαραδριοῦ τινὰ αὖ σὺ βίον λέγεις, ἀλλ' οὐ
νεκροῦ οὐδὲ λίθου. καί μοι λέγε· τὸ τοιόνδε λέγεις
οἷον πεινῆν καὶ πεινῶντα ἐσθίειν;

ΚΑΛΛ. Ἔγωγε.

ΣΩ. Καὶ διψῆν γε καὶ διψῶντα πίνειν;

ΚΑΛΛ. Λέγω, καὶ τὰς ἄλλας ἐπιθυμίας ἁπάσας

GORGIAS

various things, and that the sources of each of these supplies were scanty and difficult and only available through much hard toil: well, one man, when he has taken his fill, neither draws off any more nor troubles himself a jot, but remains at ease on that score; whilst the other finds, like his fellow, that the sources are possible indeed, though difficult, but his vessels are leaky and unsound, and he is compelled to fill them constantly, all night and day, or else suffer extreme distress. If such is the nature of each of the two lives, do you say that the licentious man has a happier one than the orderly? Do I, with this story of mine, induce you at all to concede that the orderly life is better than the licentious, or do I fail?

CALL. You fail, Socrates. For that man who has taken his fill can have no pleasure any more; in fact it is what I just now called living like a stone, when one has filled up and no longer feels any joy or pain. But a pleasant life consists rather in the largest possible amount of inflow.

SOC. Well then, if the inflow be large, must not that which runs away be of large amount also, and must not the holes for such outflow be of great size?

CALL. Certainly.

SOC. Then it is a plover's life [1] you are describing this time, not that of a corpse or a stone. Now tell me, is the life you mean something like feeling hunger and eating when hungry?

CALL. Yes, it is.

SOC. And feeling thirst and drinking when thirsty?

CALL. Yes, and having all the other desires, and

[1] Referring to this bird's habit of drinking water and then ejecting it.

ἔχοντα καὶ δυνάμενον πληροῦν χαίροντα εὐδαιμόνως ζῆν.

ΣΩ. Εὖγε, ὦ βέλτιστε· διατέλει γὰρ ὥσπερ ἤρξω, καὶ ὅπως μὴ ἀπαισχυνῇ. δεῖ δέ, ὡς ἔοικε, μηδ' ἐμὲ ἀπαισχυνθῆναι. καὶ πρῶτον μὲν εἰπέ, εἰ καὶ ψωρῶντα καὶ κνησιῶντα, ἀφθόνως ἔχοντα τοῦ κνῆσθαι, κνώμενον διατελοῦντα τὸν βίον εὐδαιμόνως ἔστι ζῆν.

ΚΑΛΛ. Ὡς ἄτοπος εἶ, ὦ Σώκρατες, καὶ ἀτεχνῶς δημηγόρος.

ΣΩ. Τοιγάρτοι, ὦ Καλλίκλεις, Πῶλον μὲν καὶ Γοργίαν καὶ ἐξέπληξα καὶ αἰσχύνεσθαι ἐποίησα, σὺ δὲ οὐ μὴ ἐκπλαγῇς οὐδὲ μὴ αἰσχυνθῇς· ἀνδρεῖος γὰρ εἶ. ἀλλ' ἀποκρίνου μόνον.

ΚΑΛΛ. Φημὶ τοίνυν καὶ τὸν κνώμενον ἡδέως ἂν βιῶναι.

ΣΩ. Οὐκοῦν εἴπερ ἡδέως, καὶ εὐδαιμόνως;

ΚΑΛΛ. Πάνυ γε.

ΣΩ. Πότερον εἰ τὴν κεφαλὴν μόνον κνησιῷ, ἢ ἔτι τί σε ἐρωτῶ; ὅρα, ὦ Καλλίκλεις, τί ἀποκρινῇ, ἐάν τίς σε τὰ ἐχόμενα τούτοις ἐφεξῆς ἅπαντα ἐρωτᾷ· καὶ τούτων τοιούτων ὄντων κεφάλαιον, ὁ τῶν κιναίδων βίος, οὗτος οὐ δεινὸς καὶ αἰσχρὸς καὶ ἄθλιος; ἢ τούτους τολμήσεις λέγειν εὐδαίμονας εἶναι, ἐὰν ἀφθόνως ἔχωσιν ὧν δέονται;

ΚΑΛΛ. Οὐκ αἰσχύνῃ εἰς τοιαῦτα ἄγων, ὦ Σώκρατες, τοὺς λόγους;

ΣΩ. Ἦ γὰρ ἐγὼ ἄγω ἐνταῦθα, ὦ γενναῖε, ἢ ἐκεῖνος, ὃς ἂν φῇ ἀνέδην οὕτω τοὺς χαίροντας, ὅπως ἂν χαίρωσιν, εὐδαίμονας εἶναι, καὶ μὴ διορίζηται τῶν ἡδονῶν ὁποῖαι ἀγαθαὶ καὶ κακαί;

GORGIAS

being able to satisfy them, and so with these enjoyments leading a happy life.

soc. Bravo, my fine fellow! Do go on as you have begun, and mind you show no bashfulness about it. I too, it seems, must try not to be too bashful. First of all, tell me whether a man who has an itch and wants to scratch, and may scratch in all freedom, can pass his life happily in continual scratching.

call. What an odd person you are, Socrates—a regular stump-orator!

soc. Why, of course, Callicles, that is how I upset Polus and Gorgias, and struck them with bashfulness; but you, I know, will never be upset or abashed; you are such a manly fellow. Come, just answer that.

call. Then I say that the man also who scratches himself will thus spend a pleasant life.

soc. And if a pleasant one, a happy one also?

call. Certainly.

soc. Is it so if he only wants to scratch his head? Or what more am I to ask you? See, Callicles, what your answer will be, if you are asked everything in succession that links on to that statement; and the culmination of the case, as stated—the life of catamites—is not that awful, shameful, and wretched? Or will you dare to assert that these are happy if they can freely indulge their wants?

call. Are you not ashamed, Socrates, to lead the discussion into such topics?

soc. What, is it I who am leading it there, noble sir, or the person who says outright that those who enjoy themselves, with whatever kind of enjoyment, are happy, and draws no distinction between the good and bad sorts of pleasure? But come, try

421

PLATO

ἀλλ' ἔτι καὶ νῦν λέγε, πότερον φῂς εἶναι τὸ αὐτὸ ἡδὺ καὶ ἀγαθόν, ἢ εἶναί τι τῶν ἡδέων, ὃ οὐκ ἔστιν ἀγαθόν;

ΚΑΛΛ. Ἵνα δή μοι μὴ ἀνομολογούμενος ᾖ ὁ λόγος, ἐὰν ἕτερον φήσω εἶναι, τὸ αὐτό φημι εἶναι.

ΣΩ. Διαφθείρεις, ὦ Καλλίκλεις, τοὺς πρώτους λόγους, καὶ οὐκ ἂν ἔτι μετ' ἐμοῦ ἱκανῶς τὰ ὄντα ἐξετάζοις, εἴπερ παρὰ τὰ δοκοῦντα σαυτῷ ἐρεῖς.

ΚΑΛΛ. Καὶ γὰρ σύ, ὦ Σώκρατες.

ΣΩ. Οὐ τοίνυν ὀρθῶς ποιῶ οὔτ' ἐγώ, εἴπερ ποιῶ τοῦτο, οὔτε σύ. ἀλλ', ὦ μακάριε, ἄθρει, μὴ οὐ τοῦτο ᾖ τὸ ἀγαθόν, τὸ πάντως χαίρειν· ταῦτά τε γὰρ τὰ νῦν δὴ αἰνιχθέντα πολλὰ καὶ αἰσχρὰ φαίνεται συμβαίνοντα, εἰ τοῦτο οὕτως ἔχει, καὶ ἄλλα πολλά.

ΚΑΛΛ. Ὡς σύ γε οἴει, ὦ Σώκρατες.

ΣΩ. Σὺ δὲ τῷ ὄντι, ὦ Καλλίκλεις, ταῦτα ἰσχυρίζῃ;

ΚΑΛΛ. Ἔγωγε.

ΣΩ. Ἐπιχειρῶμεν ἄρα τῷ λόγῳ ὡς σοῦ σπουδάζοντος;

ΚΑΛΛ. Πάνυ γε σφόδρα.

ΣΩ. Ἴθι δή μοι, ἐπειδὴ οὕτω δοκεῖ, διελοῦ τάδε· ἐπιστήμην πού τι καλεῖς τι;

ΚΑΛΛ. Ἔγωγε.

ΣΩ. Οὐ καὶ ἀνδρείαν νῦν δὴ ἔλεγές τινα εἶναι μετὰ ἐπιστήμης;

ΚΑΛΛ. Ἔλεγον γάρ.

ΣΩ. Ἄλλο τι οὖν ὡς ἕτερον τὴν ἀνδρείαν τῆς ἐπιστήμης δύο ταῦτα ἔλεγες;

---

[1] Cf. 482 D, where Callicles blamed Polus for not saying what he really thought.

again now and tell me whether you say that pleasant and good are the same thing, or that there is some pleasure which is not good.

CALL. Then, so that my statement may not be inconsistent through my saying they are different, I say they are the same.

SOC. You are spoiling your first statements,[1] Callicles, and you can no longer be a fit partner with me in probing the truth, if you are going to speak against your own convictions.

CALL. Why, you do the same, Socrates.

SOC. Then I am just as much in the wrong if I do, as you are. But look here, my gifted friend, perhaps the good is not mere unconditional enjoyment: for if it is, we have to face not only that string of shameful consequences I have just shadowed forth, but many more besides.

CALL. In your opinion, that is, Socrates.

SOC. And do you, Callicles, really maintain that it is?

CALL. I do.

SOC. Then are we to set about discussing it as your serious view?

CALL. Oh yes, to be sure.

SOC. Come then, since that is your opinion, resolve me this: there is something, I suppose, that you call knowledge?

CALL. Yes.

SOC. And were you not saying just now that knowledge can have a certain courage coupled with it?

CALL. Yes, I was.

SOC. And you surely meant that they were two things, courage being distinct from knowledge?

ΚΑΛΛ. Σφόδρα γε.

ΣΩ. Τί δέ; ἡδονὴν καὶ ἐπιστήμην ταὐτὸν ἢ ἕτερον;

ΚΑΛΛ. Ἕτερον δήπου, ὦ σοφώτατε σύ.

ΣΩ. Ἦ καὶ ἀνδρείαν ἑτέραν ἡδονῆς;

ΚΑΛΛ. Πῶς γὰρ οὔ;

ΣΩ. Φέρε δὴ ὅπως μεμνησόμεθα ταῦτα, ὅτι Καλλικλῆς ἔφη Ἀχαρνεὺς ἡδὺ μὲν καὶ ἀγαθὸν ταὐτὸν εἶναι, ἐπιστήμην δὲ καὶ ἀνδρείαν καὶ ἀλλήλων καὶ τοῦ ἀγαθοῦ ἕτερον.

ΚΑΛΛ. Σωκράτης δέ γε ἡμῖν ὁ Ἀλωπεκῆθεν οὐχ ὁμολογεῖ ταῦτα. ἢ ὁμολογεῖ;

ΣΩ. Οὐχ ὁμολογεῖ· οἶμαι δέ γε οὐδὲ Καλλικλῆς, ὅταν αὐτὸς αὑτὸν θεάσηται ὀρθῶς. εἰπὲ γάρ μοι, τοὺς εὖ πράττοντας τοῖς κακῶς πράττουσιν οὐ τοὐναντίον ἡγῇ πάθος πεπονθέναι;

ΚΑΛΛ. Ἔγωγε.

ΣΩ. Ἆρ' οὖν, εἴπερ ἐναντία ἐστὶ ταῦτα ἀλλήλοις, ἀνάγκη περὶ αὐτῶν ἔχειν ὥσπερ περὶ ὑγιείας ἔχει καὶ νόσου; οὐ γὰρ ἅμα δήπου ὑγιαίνει τε καὶ νοσεῖ ὁ ἄνθρωπος, οὐδὲ ἅμα ἀπαλλάττεται ὑγιείας τε καὶ νόσου.

ΚΑΛΛ. Πῶς λέγεις;

ΣΩ. Οἷον περὶ ὅτου βούλει τοῦ σώματος ἀπολαβὼν σκόπει. νοσεῖ πού ἄνθρωπος ὀφθαλμούς, ᾧ ὄνομα ὀφθαλμία;

ΚΑΛΛ. Πῶς γὰρ οὔ;

ΣΩ. Οὐ δήπου καὶ ὑγιαίνει γε ἅμα τοὺς αὐτούς;

ΚΑΛΛ. Οὐδ' ὁπωστιοῦν.

ΣΩ. Τί δὲ ὅταν τῆς ὀφθαλμίας ἀπαλλάττηται; ἆρα τότε καὶ τῆς ὑγιείας ἀπαλλάττεται τῶν

GORGIAS

CALL. Quite so.

SOC. Well now, are pleasure and knowledge the same thing, or different?

CALL. Different, I presume, O sage of sages.

SOC. And courage too, is that different from pleasure?

CALL. Of course it is.

SOC. Come now, let us be sure to remember this, that Callicles the Acharnian said pleasant and good were the same, but knowledge and courage were different both from each other and from the good.

CALL. And Socrates of Alopece refuses to grant us this; or does he grant it?

SOC. He does not; nor, I believe, will Callicles either, when he has rightly considered himself. For tell me, do you not regard people who are well off as being in the opposite condition to those who are badly off?

CALL. I do.

SOC. Then if these conditions are opposite to each other, must not the same hold of them as of health and disease? For, you know, a man is never well and ill at the same time, nor gets rid of health and disease together.

CALL. How do you mean?

SOC. Take, for instance, any part of the body you like by itself, and consider it. A man, I suppose, may have a disease of the eyes, called ophthalmia?

CALL. Certainly.

SOC. Then I presume he is not sound also at that time in those same eyes?

CALL. By no conceivable means.

SOC. And what say you, when he gets rid of his ophthalmia? Does he at that time get rid too of

425

ὀφθαλμῶν καὶ τελευτῶν ἅμα ἀμφοτέρων ἀπήλλακται;

ΚΑΛΛ. Ἥκιστά γε.

ΣΩ. Θαυμάσιον γάρ, οἶμαι, καὶ ἄλογον γίγνεται· ἢ γάρ;

ΚΑΛΛ. Σφόδρα γε.

ΣΩ. Ἀλλ' ἐν μέρει, οἶμαι, ἑκάτερον καὶ λαμβάνει καὶ ἀπολλύει;

ΚΑΛΛ. Φημί.

ΣΩ. Οὐκοῦν καὶ ἰσχὺν καὶ ἀσθένειαν ὡσαύτως;

ΚΑΛΛ. Ναί.

ΣΩ. Καὶ τάχος καὶ βραδυτῆτα;

ΚΑΛΛ. Πάνυ γε.

ΣΩ. Ἦ καὶ τἀγαθὰ καὶ τὴν εὐδαιμονίαν καὶ τἀναντία τούτων, κακά τε καὶ ἀθλιότητα, ἐν μέρει λαμβάνει καὶ ἐν μέρει ἀπαλλάττεται ἑκατέρου;

ΚΑΛΛ. Πάντως δήπου.

ΣΩ. Ἐὰν εὕρωμεν ἄρα ἄττα, ὧν ἅμα τε ἀπαλλάττεται ἄνθρωπος καὶ ἅμα ἔχει, δῆλον ὅτι ταῦτά γε οὐκ ἂν εἴη τό τε ἀγαθὸν καὶ τὸ κακόν. ὁμολογοῦμεν ταῦτα; καὶ εὖ μάλα σκεψάμενος ἀποκρίνου.

ΚΑΛΛ. Ἀλλ' ὑπερφυῶς ὡς ὁμολογῶ.

ΣΩ. Ἴθι δὴ ἐπὶ τὰ ἔμπροσθεν ὡμολογημένα. τὸ πεινῆν ἔλεγες πότερον ἡδὺ ἢ ἀνιαρὸν εἶναι; αὐτὸ λέγω τὸ πεινῆν.

ΚΑΛΛ. Ἀνιαρὸν ἔγωγε· τὸ μέντοι πεινῶντα ἐσθίειν ἡδύ λέγω.

ΣΩ. Μανθάνω.[1] ἀλλ' οὖν τό γε πεινῆν αὐτὸ ἀνιαρόν. ἢ οὐχί;

[1] λέγω. ΣΩ. Μανθάνω Stallbaum: ΣΩ. Καὶ ἐγώ· μανθάνω mss.

GORGIAS

the health of his eyes, and so at last is rid of both things together?

CALL. Far from it.

SOC. Because, I imagine, this would be an astonishing and irrational result, would it not?

CALL. Very much so.

SOC. Whereas, I take it, he gets and loses either in turn?

CALL. I agree.

SOC. And so with strength and weakness in just the same way?

CALL. Yes.

SOC. And speed and slowness?

CALL. Certainly.

SOC. And so too with good things and happiness and their opposites—bad things and wretchedness—does one take on each of these in turn, and in turn put it off?

CALL. Absolutely, I presume.

SOC. Then if we find any things that a man puts off and retains at one and the same moment, clearly these cannot be the good and the bad. Do we admit this? Now consider very carefully before you answer.

CALL. Oh, I admit it down to the ground.

SOC. So now for our former admissions: did you say that being hungry was pleasant or painful? I mean, hunger itself.

CALL. Painful, I said; though eating when one is hungry I call pleasant.

SOC. I see: but at all events hunger itself is painful, is it not?

ΚΑΛΛ. Φημί.

ΣΩ. Οὐκοῦν καὶ τὸ διψῆν;

ΚΑΛΛ. Σφόδρα γε.

ΣΩ. Πότερον οὖν ἔτι πλείω ἐρωτῶ, ἢ ὁμολογεῖς ἅπασαν ἔνδειαν καὶ ἐπιθυμίαν ἀνιαρὸν εἶναι;

ΚΑΛΛ. Ὁμολογῶ, ἀλλὰ μὴ ἐρώτα.

ΣΩ. Εἶεν· διψῶντα δὲ δὴ πίνειν ἄλλο τι ἢ ἡδὺ φῂς εἶναι;

ΚΑΛΛ. Ἔγωγε.

ΣΩ. Οὐκοῦν τούτου οὗ λέγεις τὸ μὲν διψῶντα λυπούμενον δήπου ἐστίν;

Ε ΚΑΛΛ. Ναί.

ΣΩ. Τὸ δὲ πίνειν πλήρωσίς τε τῆς ἐνδείας καὶ ἡδονή;

ΚΑΛΛ. Ναί.

ΣΩ. Οὐκοῦν κατὰ τὸ πίνειν χαίρειν λέγεις;

ΚΑΛΛ. Μάλιστα.

ΣΩ. Διψῶντά γε;

ΚΑΛΛ. Φημί.

ΣΩ. Λυπούμενον;

ΚΑΛΛ. Ναί.

ΣΩ. Αἰσθάνῃ οὖν τὸ συμβαῖνον, ὅτι λυπούμενον χαίρειν λέγεις ἅμα, ὅταν διψῶντα πίνειν λέγῃς; ἢ οὐχ ἅμα τοῦτο γίγνεται κατὰ τὸν αὐτὸν τόπον καὶ χρόνον εἴτε ψυχῆς εἴτε σώματος βούλει; οὐδὲν γάρ, οἶμαι, διαφέρει. ἔστι ταῦτα ἢ οὔ;

ΚΑΛΛ. Ἔστιν.

ΣΩ. Ἀλλὰ μὴν εὖ γε πράττοντα κακῶς πράττειν ἅμα ἀδύνατον φῂς[1] εἶναι.

---

[1] φῂς Baiter : ἔφης mss.

CALL. I agree.

SOC. And so too with thirst?

CALL. Quite so.

SOC. Then am I to ask you any further questions, or do you admit that all want and desire is painful?

CALL. I admit it; no, do not question me further.

SOC. Very good: but drinking when one is thirsty you surely say is pleasant?

CALL. I do.

SOC. Now, in this phrase of yours the words "when one is thirsty," I take it, stand for "when one is in pain"?

CALL. Yes.

SOC. But drinking is a satisfaction of the want, and a pleasure?

CALL. Yes.

SOC. So in the act of drinking, you say, one has enjoyment?

CALL. Quite so.

SOC. When one is thirsty?

CALL. I agree.

SOC. That is, in pain?

CALL. Yes.

SOC. Then do you perceive the conclusion,—that you say one enjoys oneself, though in pain at the same moment, when you say one drinks when one is thirsty? Or does this not occur at once, at the same place and time — in either soul or body, as you please? For I fancy it makes no difference. Is this so or not?

CALL. It is.

SOC. But further, you say it is impossible to be badly off, or to fare ill, at the same time as one is faring well.

ΚΑΛΛ. Φημὶ γάρ.

ΣΩ. Ἀνιώμενον δέ γε χαίρειν δυνατὸν ὡμολόγηκας.

ΚΑΛΛ. Φαίνεται.

ΣΩ. Οὐκ ἄρα τὸ χαίρειν ἐστὶν εὖ πράττειν οὐδὲ τὸ ἀνιᾶσθαι κακῶς, ὥστε ἕτερον γίγνεται τὸ ἡδὺ τοῦ ἀγαθοῦ.

ΚΑΛΛ. Οὐκ οἶδ' ἅττα σοφίζῃ, ὦ Σώκρατες.

ΣΩ. Οἶσθα, ἀλλὰ ἀκκίζῃ, ὦ Καλλίκλεις· καὶ πρόϊθι γε ἔτι εἰς τὸ ἔμπροσθεν [ὅτι ἔχων ληρεῖς],[1] ἵνα εἰδῇς, ὡς σοφὸς ὢν με νουθετεῖς. οὐχ ἅμα διψῶν τε ἕκαστος ἡμῶν πέπαυται καὶ ἅμα ἡδόμενος διὰ τοῦ πίνειν;

ΚΑΛΛ. Οὐκ οἶδα ὅ τι λέγεις·

ΓΟΡΓ. Μηδαμῶς, ὦ Καλλίκλεις, ἀλλ' ἀποκρίνου καὶ ἡμῶν ἕνεκα, ἵνα περανθῶσιν οἱ λόγοι.

ΚΑΛΛ. Ἀλλ' ἀεὶ τοιοῦτός ἐστι Σωκράτης, ὦ Γοργία· σμικρὰ καὶ ὀλίγου ἄξια ἀνερωτᾷ καὶ ἐξελέγχει.

ΓΟΡΓ. Ἀλλὰ τί σοι διαφέρει; πάντως οὐ σὴ αὕτη ἡ τιμή, ὦ Καλλίκλεις· ἀλλ' ὑπόσχες Σωκράτει ἐξελέγξαι ὅπως ἂν βούληται.

ΚΑΛΛ. Ἐρώτα δὴ σὺ τὰ σμικρά τε καὶ στενὰ ταῦτα, ἐπείπερ Γοργίᾳ δοκεῖ οὕτως.

ΣΩ. Εὐδαίμων εἶ, ὦ Καλλίκλεις, ὅτι τὰ μεγάλα μεμύησαι πρὶν τὰ σμικρά· ἐγὼ δ' οὐκ ᾤμην θεμιτὸν εἶναι. ὅθεν οὖν ἀπέλιπες, ἀποκρίνου, εἰ οὐχ ἅμα παύεται διψῶν ἕκαστος ἡμῶν καὶ ἡδόμενος.

ΚΑΛΛ. Φημί.

---

[1] ὅτι ἔχων ληρεῖς secl. Thompson.

[1] Socrates means that one cannot hope to know great things without first learning the truth about little things.

GORGIAS

CALL. Yes, I do.

SOC. But to enjoy oneself when feeling pain you have admitted to be possible.

CALL. Apparently.

SOC. Hence enjoyment is not faring well, nor is feeling pain faring ill, so that the pleasant is found to be different from the good.

CALL. I cannot follow these subtleties of yours, Socrates.

SOC. You can, but you play the innocent, Callicles. Just go on a little further, that you may realize how subtle is your way of reproving me. Does not each of us cease at the same moment from thirst and from the pleasure he gets by drinking?

CALL. I cannot tell what you mean.

GORG. No, no, Callicles, you must answer him, for our sakes also, that the arguments may be brought to a conclusion.

CALL. But Socrates is always like this, Gorgias; he keeps on asking petty, unimportant questions until he refutes one.

GORG. Why, what does that matter to you? In any case it is not your credit that is at stake, Callicles; just permit Socrates to refute you in such manner as he chooses.

CALL. Well then, proceed with those little cramped questions of yours, since Gorgias is so minded.

SOC. You are fortunate, Callicles, in having been initiated into the Great Mysteries before the Little:[1] I did not think that this was permitted. So go on answering where you left off—as to whether each of us does not cease to feel thirst and pleasure at the same time.

CALL. I grant it.

ΣΩ. Οὐκοῦν καὶ πεινῶν καὶ τῶν ἄλλων ἐπιθυμιῶν καὶ ἡδονῶν ἅμα παύεται;

ΚΑΛΛ. Ἔστι ταῦτα.

ΣΩ. Οὐκοῦν καὶ τῶν λυπῶν καὶ τῶν ἡδονῶν ἅμα παύεται;

D ΚΑΛΛ. Ναί.

ΣΩ. Ἀλλὰ μὴν τῶν ἀγαθῶν καὶ κακῶν οὐχ ἅμα παύεται, ὡς σὺ ὡμολόγεις· νῦν δὲ οὐχ ὁμολογεῖς;

ΚΑΛΛ. Ἔγωγε· τί οὖν δή;

ΣΩ. Ὅτι οὐ ταὐτὰ γίγνεται, ὦ φίλε, τἀγαθὰ τοῖς ἡδέσιν οὐδὲ τὰ κακὰ τοῖς ἀνιαροῖς. τῶν μὲν γὰρ ἅμα παύεται, τῶν δὲ οὔ, ὡς ἑτέρων ὄντων· πῶς οὖν ταὐτὰ ἂν εἴη τὰ ἡδέα τοῖς ἀγαθοῖς ἢ τὰ ἀνιαρὰ τοῖς κακοῖς; ἐὰν δὲ βούλῃ, καὶ τῇδ' ἐπίσκεψαι· οἶμαι γάρ σοι οὐδὲ ταύτῃ ὁμολογεῖσθαι. ἄθρει δέ· τοὺς ἀγαθοὺς οὐχὶ ἀγαθῶν παE ρουσίᾳ ἀγαθοὺς καλεῖς, ὥσπερ τοὺς καλοὺς οἷς ἂν κάλλος παρῇ;

ΚΑΛΛ. Ἔγωγε.

ΣΩ. Τί δέ; ἀγαθοὺς ἄνδρας καλεῖς ἄφρονας καὶ δειλούς; οὐ γὰρ ἄρτι γε, ἀλλὰ τοὺς ἀνδρείους καὶ φρονίμους ἔλεγες· ἢ οὐ τούτους ἀγαθοὺς καλεῖς;

ΚΑΛΛ. Πάνυ μὲν οὖν.

ΣΩ. Τί δέ; παῖδα ἀνόητον χαίροντα ἤδη εἶδες;

ΚΑΛΛ. Ἔγωγε.

ΣΩ. Ἄνδρα δὲ οὔπω εἶδες ἀνόητον χαίροντα;

GORGIAS

soc. And so with hunger and the rest, does he cease to feel the desires and pleasures at the same time?

CALL. That is so.

soc. And also ceases to feel the pains and pleasures at the same time?

CALL. Yes.

soc. But still he does not cease to have the good and bad at the same time, as you agreed; and now, you do not agree?

CALL. I do; and what then?

soc. Only that we get the result, my friend, that the good things are not the same as the pleasant, nor the bad as the painful. For with the one pair the cessation is of both at once, but with the other two it is not, since they are distinct. How then can pleasant things be the same as good, or painful things as bad? Or if you like, consider it another way—for I fancy that even after that you do not admit it. Just observe: do you not call good people good owing to the presence of good things, as you call beautiful those in whom beauty is present?

CALL. I do.

soc. Well now, do you give the name of good men to fools and cowards? It was not they just now but brave and wise men whom you so described. Or is it not these that you call good?

CALL. To be sure it is.

soc. And now, have you ever seen a silly child enjoying iteslf?

CALL. I have.

soc. And have you never seen a silly man enjoying himself?

433

ΚΑΛΛ. Οἶμαι ἔγωγε· ἀλλὰ τί τοῦτο;
ΣΩ. Οὐδέν· ἀλλ' ἀποκρίνου.
ΚΑΛΛ. Εἶδον.
ΣΩ. Τί δέ; νοῦν ἔχοντα λυπούμενον καὶ χαίροντα;
ΚΑΛΛ. Φημί.
ΣΩ. Πότεροι δὲ μᾶλλον χαίρουσι καὶ λυποῦνται, οἱ φρόνιμοι ἢ οἱ ἄφρονες;
ΚΑΛΛ. Οἶμαι ἔγωγε οὐ πολύ τι διαφέρειν.
ΣΩ. Ἀλλ' ἀρκεῖ καὶ τοῦτο. ἐν πολέμῳ δὲ ἤδη εἶδες ἄνδρα δειλόν;
ΚΑΛΛ. Πῶς γὰρ οὔ;
ΣΩ. Τί οὖν; ἀπιόντων τῶν πολεμίων πότεροί σοι ἐδόκουν μᾶλλον χαίρειν, οἱ δειλοὶ ἢ οἱ ἀνδρεῖοι;
Β ΚΑΛΛ. Ἀμφότεροι ἔμοιγε· εἰ δὲ μή, παραπλησίως γε.
ΣΩ. Οὐδὲν διαφέρει. χαίρουσι δ' οὖν καὶ οἱ δειλοί;
ΚΑΛΛ. Σφόδρα γε.
ΣΩ. Καὶ οἱ ἄφρονες, ὡς ἔοικεν.
ΚΑΛΛ. Ναί.
ΣΩ. Προσιόντων δὲ οἱ δειλοὶ μόνον λυποῦνται ἢ καὶ οἱ ἀνδρεῖοι;
ΚΑΛΛ. Ἀμφότεροι.
ΣΩ. Ἆρα ὁμοίως;
ΚΑΛΛ. Μᾶλλον ἴσως οἱ δειλοί.
ΣΩ. Ἀπιόντων δ' οὐ μᾶλλον χαίρουσιν;
ΚΑΛΛ. Ἴσως.
ΣΩ. Οὐκοῦν λυποῦνται μὲν καὶ χαίρουσι καὶ οἱ ἄφρονες καὶ οἱ φρόνιμοι καὶ οἱ δειλοὶ καὶ οἱ
C ἀνδρεῖοι παραπλησίως, ὡς σὺ φῄς, μᾶλλον δὲ οἱ δειλοὶ τῶν ἀνδρείων;

GORGIAS

CALL. I suppose I have; but what has that to do with it?

SOC. Nothing; only answer.

CALL. I have seen one.

SOC. And again, a man of sense in a state of pain or enjoyment?

CALL. Yes.

SOC. And which sort are more apt to feel enjoyment or pain, the wise or the foolish?

CALL. I should think there is not much difference.

SOC. Well, that will suffice. In war have you ever seen a coward?

CALL. Of course I have.

SOC. Well now, when the enemy withdrew, which seemed to you to enjoy it more, the cowards or the brave?

CALL. Both did, I thought; or if not that, about equally.

SOC. No matter. Anyhow, the cowards do enjoy it?

CALL. Very much.

SOC. And the fools, it would seem.

CALL. Yes.

SOC. And when the foe advances, do the cowards alone feel pain, or the brave as well?

CALL. Both.

SOC. Alike?

CALL. More, perhaps, the cowards.

SOC. And when the foe withdraws, do they not enjoy it more?

CALL. Perhaps.

SOC. So the foolish and the wise, and the cowardly and the brave, feel pain and enjoyment about equally, according to you, but the cowardly more than the brave?

ΚΑΛΛ. Φημί.

ΣΩ. Ἀλλὰ μὴν οἵ γε φρόνιμοι καὶ οἱ ἀνδρεῖοι ἀγαθοί, οἱ δὲ δειλοὶ καὶ ἄφρονες κακοί;

ΚΑΛΛ. Ναί.

ΣΩ. Παραπλησίως ἄρα χαίρουσι καὶ λυποῦνται οἱ ἀγαθοὶ καὶ οἱ κακοί;

ΚΑΛΛ. Φημί.

ΣΩ. Ἆρ' οὖν παραπλησίως εἰσὶν ἀγαθοὶ καὶ κακοὶ οἱ ἀγαθοί τε καὶ οἱ κακοί; ἢ καὶ ἔτι μᾶλλον ἀγαθοὶ [οἱ ἀγαθοὶ]¹ καὶ κακοί εἰσιν οἱ κακοί;

D ΚΑΛΛ. Ἀλλὰ μὰ Δί' οὐκ οἶδ' ὅ τι λέγεις.

ΣΩ. Οὐκ οἶσθ' ὅτι τοὺς ἀγαθοὺς ἀγαθῶν φῂς παρουσίᾳ εἶναι ἀγαθούς, κακοὺς δὲ κακῶν; τὰ δὲ ἀγαθὰ εἶναι τὰς ἡδονάς, κακὰ δὲ τὰς ἀνίας;

ΚΑΛΛ. Ἔγωγε.

ΣΩ. Οὐκοῦν τοῖς χαίρουσι πάρεστι τἀγαθά, αἱ ἡδοναί, εἴπερ χαίρουσιν;

ΚΑΛΛ. Πῶς γὰρ οὔ;

ΣΩ. Οὐκοῦν ἀγαθῶν παρόντων ἀγαθοί εἰσιν οἱ χαίροντες;

ΚΑΛΛ. Ναί.

ΣΩ. Τί δέ; τοῖς ἀνιωμένοις οὐ πάρεστι τὰ κακά, αἱ λῦπαι;

ΚΑΛΛ. Πάρεστιν.

E ΣΩ. Κακῶν δέ γε παρουσίᾳ φῂς σὺ εἶναι κακοὺς τοὺς κακούς. ἢ οὐκέτι φῄς;

ΚΑΛΛ. Ἔγωγε.

ΣΩ. Ἀγαθοὶ ἄρα οἳ ἂν χαίρωσι, κακοὶ δὲ οἳ ἂν ἀνιῶνται;

¹ οἱ ἀγαθοὶ secl. Routh.

GORGIAS

CALL. I agree.

SOC. But further, are the wise and brave good, and the cowards and fools bad?

CALL. Yes.

SOC. Then the good and the bad feel enjoyment and pain about equally?

CALL. I agree.

SOC. Then are the good and the bad about equally good and bad? Or are the bad in some yet greater measure good and bad?

CALL. Why, upon my word, I cannot tell what you mean.

SOC. You are aware, are you not, that you hold that the good are good by the presence of good things, and that the bad are so by the presence of bad things? And that the pleasures are the good things, and the pains bad things?

CALL. Yes, I am.

SOC. Hence in those who have enjoyment the good things—the pleasures—are present, so long as they enjoy?

CALL. Of course.

SOC. Then, good things being present, those who enjoy are good?

CALL. Yes.

SOC. Well now, in those who feel pain are not bad things present, namely pains?

CALL. They are.

SOC. And it is by the presence of bad things, you say, that the bad are bad? Or do you no longer say so?

CALL. I do say so.

SOC. Then whoever enjoys is good, and whoever is pained, bad?

ΚΑΛΛ. Πάνυ γε.

ΣΩ. Οἱ μέν γε μᾶλλον μᾶλλον, οἱ δ' ἧττον ἧττον, οἱ δὲ παραπλησίως παραπλησίως;

ΚΑΛΛ. Ναί.

ΣΩ. Οὐκοῦν φῂς παραπλησίως χαίρειν καὶ λυπεῖσθαι τοὺς φρονίμους καὶ τοὺς ἄφρονας καὶ τοὺς δειλοὺς καὶ τοὺς ἀνδρείους, ἢ καὶ μᾶλλον ἔτι τοὺς δειλούς;

ΚΑΛΛ. Ἔγωγε.

ΣΩ. Συλλόγισαι δὴ κοινῇ μετ' ἐμοῦ, τί ἡμῖν συμβαίνει ἐκ τῶν ὡμολογημένων· καὶ δὶς γάρ τοι καὶ τρίς φασι καλὸν εἶναι τὰ καλὰ λέγειν τε καὶ ἐπισκοπεῖσθαι. ἀγαθὸν μὲν εἶναι τὸν φρόνιμον καὶ ἀνδρεῖόν φαμεν. ἦ γάρ;

ΚΑΛΛ. Ναί.

ΣΩ. Κακὸν δὲ τὸν ἄφρονα καὶ δειλόν;

ΚΑΛΛ. Πάνυ γε.

ΣΩ. Ἀγαθὸν δὲ αὖ τὸν χαίροντα;

ΚΑΛΛ. Ναί.

ΣΩ. Κακὸν δὲ τὸν ἀνιώμενον;

ΚΑΛΛ. Ἀνάγκη.

ΣΩ. Ἀνιᾶσθαι δὲ καὶ χαίρειν τὸν ἀγαθὸν καὶ κακὸν ὁμοίως, ἴσως δὲ καὶ μᾶλλον τὸν κακόν;

ΚΑΛΛ. Ναί.

ΣΩ. Οὐκοῦν ὁμοίως γίγνεται κακὸς καὶ ἀγαθὸς τῷ ἀγαθῷ ἢ καὶ μᾶλλον ἀγαθὸς ὁ κακός; οὐ ταῦτα συμβαίνει καὶ τὰ πρότερα ἐκεῖνα, ἐάν τις ταὐτὰ φῇ ἡδέα τε καὶ ἀγαθὰ εἶναι; οὐ ταῦτα ἀνάγκη, ὦ Καλλίκλεις;

ΚΑΛΛ. Πάλαι τοί σου ἀκροῶμαι, ὦ Σώκρατες,

---

[1] The saying—καὶ δὶς γὰρ ὃ δεῖ καλόν ἐστιν ἐνισπεῖν—was attributed by some to Empedocles.

CALL. Certainly.

SOC. You mean, those more so who feel these things more, and those less who feel less, and those about equally who feel about equally?

CALL. Yes.

SOC. Now you say that the wise and the foolish, the cowardly and the brave, feel enjoyment and pain about equally, or the cowards even more?

CALL. I do.

SOC. Then just help me to reckon up the results we get from our admissions; for you know they say:

> That which seemeth well, 'tis well
> Twice and also thrice to tell,[1]

and to examine too. We say that the wise and brave man is good, do we not?

CALL. Yes.

SOC. And that the foolish and cowardly is bad?

CALL. Certainly.

SOC. And again, that he who enjoys is good?

CALL. Yes.

SOC. And that he who feels pain is bad?

CALL. Necessarily.

SOC. And that the good and the bad feel enjoyment and pain in a like manner, or perhaps the bad rather more?

CALL. Yes.

SOC. Then is the bad man made bad or good in a like manner to the good man, or even good in a greater measure? Does not this follow, along with those former statements, from the assumption that pleasant things and good things are the same? Must not this be so, Callicles?

CALL. Let me tell you, Socrates, all the time that

καθομολογῶν, ἐνθυμούμενος ὅτι, κἂν παίζων τίς σοι ἐνδῷ ὁτιοῦν, τούτου ἄσμενος ἔχῃ ὥσπερ τὰ μειράκια. ὡς δὴ σὺ οἴει ἐμὲ ἢ καὶ ἄλλον ὁντινοῦν ἀνθρώπων οὐχ ἡγεῖσθαι τὰς μὲν βελτίους ἡδονάς, τὰς δὲ χείρους.

ΣΩ. Ἰοῦ ἰοῦ, ὦ Καλλίκλεις, ὡς πανοῦργος εἶ, καί μοι ὥσπερ παιδὶ χρῇ, τοτὲ μὲν τὰ αὐτὰ φάσκων οὕτως ἔχειν, τοτὲ δὲ ἑτέρως, ἐξαπατῶν με. καίτοι οὐκ ᾤμην γε κατ' ἀρχὰς ὑπὸ σοῦ ἑκόντος εἶναι ἐξαπατηθήσεσθαι, ὡς ὄντος φίλου· νῦν δὲ ἐψεύσθην, καὶ ὡς ἔοικεν ἀνάγκη μοι κατὰ τὸν παλαιὸν λόγον τὸ παρὸν εὖ ποιεῖν καὶ τοῦτο δέχεσθαι τὸ διδόμενον παρὰ σοῦ. ἔστι δὲ δή, ὡς ἔοικεν, ὃ νῦν λέγεις, ὅτι ἡδοναί τινές εἰσιν αἱ μὲν ἀγαθαί, αἱ δὲ κακαί· ἢ γάρ;

ΚΑΛΛ. Ναί.

ΣΩ. Ἆρ' οὖν ἀγαθαὶ μὲν αἱ ὠφέλιμοι, κακαὶ δὲ αἱ βλαβεραί;

ΚΑΛΛ. Πάνυ γε.

ΣΩ. Ὠφέλιμοι δέ γε αἱ ἀγαθόν τι ποιοῦσαι, κακαὶ δὲ αἱ κακόν τι;

ΚΑΛΛ. Φημί.

ΣΩ. Ἆρ' οὖν τὰς τοιάσδε λέγεις, οἷον κατὰ τὸ σῶμα ἃς νῦν δὴ ἐλέγομεν ἐν τῷ ἐσθίειν καὶ πίνειν ἡδονάς; ἢ[1] ἄρα τούτων αἱ μὲν ὑγίειαν ποιοῦσαι ἐν τῷ σώματι, ἢ ἰσχὺν ἢ ἄλλην τινὰ ἀρετὴν τοῦ σώματος, αὗται μὲν ἀγαθαί, αἱ δὲ τἀναντία τούτων κακαί;

ΚΑΛΛ. Πάνυ γε.

[1] ἢ Sauppe : εἰ MSS.

GORGIAS

I have been listening to you and yielding you agreement, I have been remarking the puerile delight with which you cling to any concession one may make to you, even in jest. So you suppose that I or anybody else in the world does not regard some pleasures as better, and others worse!

soc. Oh ho, Callicles, what a rascal you are, treating me thus like a child—now asserting that the same things are one way, now another, to deceive me! And yet I started with the notion that I should not have to fear any intentional deception on your part, you being my friend; but now I find I was mistaken, and it seems I must, as the old saying goes, e'en make the best of what I have got,[1] and accept just anything you offer. Well then, what you now state, it seems, is that some particular pleasures are good, and some bad; is not that so?

call. Yes.

soc. Then are the beneficial ones good, and the harmful ones bad?

call. Certainly.

soc. And are those beneficial which do some good, and those evil which do some evil?

call. I agree.

soc. Now are these the sort you mean — for instance, in the body, the pleasures of eating and drinking that we mentioned a moment ago? Then the pleasures of this sort which produce health in the body, or strength, or any other bodily excellence, —are these good, and those which have the opposite effects, bad?

call. Certainly.

---

[1] The proverb usually has τίθεσθαι instead of ποιεῖν; cf. Lucian, Necyom. 21.

E ΣΩ. Οὐκοῦν καὶ λῦπαι ὡσαύτως αἱ μὲν χρησταί εἰσιν, αἱ δὲ πονηραί;

ΚΑΛΛ. Πῶς γὰρ οὔ;

ΣΩ. Οὐκοῦν τὰς μὲν χρηστὰς καὶ ἡδονὰς καὶ λύπας καὶ αἱρετέον ἐστὶ καὶ πρακτέον;

ΚΑΛΛ. Πάνυ γε.

ΣΩ. Τὰς δὲ πονηρὰς οὔ;

ΚΑΛΛ. Δῆλον δή.

ΣΩ. Ἕνεκα γάρ που τῶν ἀγαθῶν ἅπαντα ἡμῖν ἔδοξε πρακτέον εἶναι, εἰ μνημονεύεις, ἐμοί τε καὶ Πώλῳ. ἆρα καὶ σοὶ συνδοκεῖ οὕτω, τέλος εἶναι ἁπασῶν τῶν πράξεων τὸ ἀγαθόν, καὶ ἐκείνου ἕνεκεν δεῖν πάντα τἆλλα πράττεσθαι, ἀλλ' οὐκ 500 ἐκεῖνο τῶν ἄλλων; σύμψηφος ἡμῖν εἶ καὶ σὺ ἐκ τρίτων;

ΚΑΛΛ. Ἔγωγε.

ΣΩ. Τῶν ἀγαθῶν ἄρα ἕνεκα δεῖ καὶ τἆλλα καὶ τὰ ἡδέα πράττειν, ἀλλ' οὐ τἀγαθὰ τῶν ἡδέων.

ΚΑΛΛ. Πάνυ γε.

ΣΩ. Ἆρ' οὖν παντὸς ἀνδρός ἐστιν ἐκλέξασθαι, ποῖα ἀγαθὰ τῶν ἡδέων ἐστὶ καὶ ὁποῖα κακά, ἢ τεχνικοῦ δεῖ εἰς ἕκαστον;

ΚΑΛΛ. Τεχνικοῦ.

ΣΩ. Ἀναμνησθῶμεν δὴ ὧν αὖ ἐγὼ πρὸς Πῶλον καὶ Γοργίαν ἐτύγχανον λέγων. ἔλεγον γάρ, εἰ B μνημονεύεις, ὅτι εἶεν παρασκευαὶ αἱ μὲν μέχρι ἡδονῆς, αὐτὸ τοῦτο μόνον παρασκευάζουσαι, ἀγνοοῦσαι δὲ τὸ βέλτιον καὶ τὸ χεῖρον, αἱ δὲ γιγνώσκουσαι ὅ τί τε ἀγαθὸν καὶ ὅ τι κακόν· καὶ ἐτίθην τῶν μὲν περὶ τὰς ἡδονὰς τὴν μαγειρικὴν ἐμπειρίαν, ἀλλ' οὐ τέχνην, τῶν δὲ περὶ τὸ ἀγαθὸν τὴν ἰατρικὴν

GORGIAS

soc. And similarly in the case of pains, are some worthy and some base?

call. Of course.

soc. So it is the worthy pleasures and pains that we ought to choose in all our doings?

call. Certainly.

soc. And the base ones not?

call. Clearly so.

soc. Because, you know, Polus and I, if you recollect, decided[1] that everything we do should be for the sake of what is good. Do you agree with us in this view—that the good is the end of all our actions, and it is for its sake that all other things should be done, and not it for theirs? Do you add your vote to ours, and make a third?

call. I do.

soc. Then it is for the sake of what is good that we should do everything, including what is pleasant, not the good for the sake of the pleasant.

call. Certainly.

soc. Now is it in every man's power to pick out which sort of pleasant things are good and which bad, or is professional skill required in each case?

call. Professional skill.

soc. Then let us recall those former points I was putting to Polus and Gorgias.[2] I said, if you remember, that there were certain industries, some of which extend only to pleasure, procuring that and no more, and ignorant of better and worse; while others know what is good and what bad. And I placed among those that are concerned with pleasure the habitude, not art, of cookery, and among those concerned with good the art of medicine.

[1] *Cf.* 468 c.   [2] *Cf.* 464-5.

PLATO

τέχνην. καὶ πρὸς Φιλίου, ὦ Καλλίκλεις, μήτε αὐτὸς οἴου δεῖν πρὸς ἐμὲ παίζειν μηδ' ὅ τι ἂν τύχῃς παρὰ τὰ δοκοῦντα ἀποκρίνου, μήτ' αὖ τὰ παρ' ἐμοῦ οὕτως ἀποδέχου ὡς παίζοντος· ὁρᾷς γάρ ὅτι περὶ τούτου εἰσὶν ἡμῖν οἱ λόγοι, οὗ τί ἂν μᾶλλον σπουδάσειέ τις καὶ σμικρὸν νοῦν ἔχων ἄνθρωπος, ἢ τοῦτο, ὅντινα χρὴ τρόπον ζῆν, πότερον ἐπὶ ὃν σὺ παρακαλεῖς ἐμέ, τὰ τοῦ ἀνδρὸς δὴ ταῦτα πράττοντα, λέγοντά τε ἐν τῷ δήμῳ καὶ ῥητορικὴν ἀσκοῦντα καὶ πολιτευόμενον τοῦτον τὸν τρόπον, ὃν ὑμεῖς νῦν πολιτεύεσθε, ἢ [ἐπὶ]¹ τόνδε τὸν βίον τὸν ἐν φιλοσοφίᾳ, καὶ τί ποτ' ἐστὶν οὗτος ἐκείνου διαφέρων. ἴσως οὖν βέλτιστόν ἐστιν, ὡς ἄρτι ἐγὼ ἐπεχείρησα, διαιρεῖσθαι, διελομένους δὲ καὶ ὁμολογήσαντας ἀλλήλοις, εἰ ἔστι τούτω διττὼ τὼ βίω, σκέψασθαι, τί τε διαφέρετον ἀλλήλοιν καὶ ὁπότερον βιωτέον αὐτοῖν. ἴσως οὖν οὔπω οἶσθα τί λέγω.

ΚΑΛΛ. Οὐ δῆτα.

ΣΩ. Ἀλλ' ἐγώ σοι σαφέστερον ἐρῶ. ἐπειδὴ ὡμολογήκαμεν ἐγώ τε καὶ σὺ εἶναι μέν τι ἀγαθόν, εἶναι δέ τι ἡδύ, ἕτερον δὲ τὸ ἡδὺ τοῦ ἀγαθοῦ, ἑκατέρου δὲ αὐτοῖν μελέτην τινὰ εἶναι καὶ παρασκευὴν τῆς κτήσεως, τὴν μὲν τοῦ ἡδέος θήραν, τὴν δὲ τοῦ ἀγαθοῦ—αὐτὸ δέ μοι τοῦτο πρῶτον ἢ σύμφαθι ἢ μή· σύμφῃς;

ΚΑΛΛ. Οὕτω φημί.

ΣΩ. Ἴθι δή, ἃ καὶ πρὸς τούσδε ἐγὼ ἔλεγον, διομολόγησαί μοι, εἰ ἄρα σοι ἔδοξα τότε ἀληθῆ

¹ ἐπὶ secl. Findeisen.

GORGIAS

Now by the sanctity of friendship, Callicles, do not on your part indulge in jesting with me, or give me random answers against your conviction, or again, take what I say as though I were jesting. For you see that our debate is upon a question which has the highest conceivable claims to the serious interest even of a person who has but little intelligence—namely, what course of life is best; whether it should be that to which you invite me, with all those manly pursuits of speaking in Assembly and practising rhetoric and going in for politics after the fashion of you modern politicians, or this life of philosophy; and what makes the difference between these two. Well, perhaps it is best to do what I attempted a while ago, and distinguish them; and then, when we have distinguished them and come to an agreement with each other as to these lives being really two, we must consider what is the difference between them and which of them is the one we ought to live. Now I daresay you do not yet grasp my meaning.

CALL. No, I do not.

SOC. Well, I will put it to you more plainly. Seeing that we have agreed, you and I, that there is such a thing as " good," and such a thing as " pleasant," and that the pleasant is other than the good, and that for the acquisition of either there is a certain practice or preparation—the quest of the pleasant in the one case, and that of the good in the other—but first you must either assent or object to this statement of mine: do you assent?

CALL. I am with you entirely.

SOC. Then try and come to a definite agreement with me on what I was saying to our friends here, and see if you now find that what I then said was

λέγειν. ἔλεγον δέ που, ὅτι ἡ μὲν ὀψοποιική οὔ
μοι δοκεῖ τέχνη εἶναι ἀλλ' ἐμπειρία, ἡ δ' ἰατρική,
λέγων ὅτι ἡ μὲν τούτου οὗ θεραπεύει καὶ τὴν
φύσιν ἔσκεπται καὶ τὴν αἰτίαν ὧν πράττει, καὶ
λόγον ἔχει τούτων ἑκάστου δοῦναι, ἡ ἰατρική· ἡ
δ' ἑτέρα τῆς ἡδονῆς, πρὸς ἣν ἡ θεραπεία αὐτῆ
ἐστὶν ἅπασα, κομιδῇ ἀτέχνως ἐπ' αὐτὴν ἔρχεται,
οὔτε τι τὴν φύσιν σκεψαμένη τῆς ἡδονῆς οὔτε τὴν
αἰτίαν, ἀλόγως τε παντάπασιν, ὡς ἔπος εἰπεῖν,
οὐδὲν διαριθμησαμένη, τριβῇ καὶ ἐμπειρίᾳ μνήμην
μόνον σῳζομένη τοῦ εἰωθότος γίγνεσθαι, ᾧ δὴ καὶ
B πορίζεται τὰς ἡδονάς. ταῦτ' οὖν πρῶτον σκόπει
εἰ δοκεῖ σοι ἱκανῶς λέγεσθαι, καὶ εἶναί τινες καὶ
περὶ ψυχὴν τοιαῦται ἄλλαι πραγματεῖαι, αἱ μὲν
τεχνικαί, προμήθειάν τινα ἔχουσαι τοῦ βελτίστου
περὶ τὴν ψυχήν, αἱ δὲ τούτου μὲν ὀλιγωροῦσαι,
ἐσκεμμέναι δ' αὖ, ὥσπερ ἐκεῖ, τὴν ἡδονὴν μόνον
τῆς ψυχῆς, τίνα ἂν αὐτῇ τρόπον γίγνοιτο, ἥτις
δὲ ἢ βελτίων ἢ χείρων τῶν ἡδονῶν, οὔτε σκο-
πούμεναι οὔτε μέλον αὐταῖς ἄλλο ἢ χαρίζεσθαι
C μόνον, εἴτε βέλτιον εἴτε χεῖρον. ἐμοὶ μὲν γάρ, ὦ
Καλλίκλεις, δοκοῦσί τε εἶναι, καὶ ἔγωγέ φημι τὸ
τοιοῦτον κολακείαν εἶναι καὶ περὶ σῶμα καὶ περὶ
ψυχὴν καὶ περὶ ἄλλο ὅτου ἄν τις τὴν ἡδονὴν
θεραπεύῃ, ἀσκέπτως ἔχων τοῦ ἀμείνονός τε
καὶ τοῦ χείρονος· σὺ δὲ δὴ πότερον συγκατα-
τίθεσαι ἡμῖν περὶ τούτων τὴν αὐτὴν δόξαν ἢ
ἀντίφῃς;

ΚΑΛΛ. Οὐκ ἔγωγε, ἀλλὰ συγχωρῶ, ἵνα σοι καὶ
περανθῇ ὁ λόγος καὶ Γοργίᾳ τῷδε χαρίσωμαι.

true. I was saying, I think, that cookery seems to me not an art but a habitude, unlike medicine, which, I argued, has investigated the nature of the person whom she treats and the cause of her proceedings, and has some account to give of each of these things; so much for medicine: whereas the other, in respect of the pleasure to which her whole ministration is given, goes to work there in an utterly inartistic manner, without having investigated at all either the nature or the cause of pleasure, and altogether irrationally—with no thought, one may say, of differentiation, relying on routine and habitude for merely preserving a memory of what is wont to result; and that is how she is enabled to provide her pleasures. Now consider first whether you think that this account is satisfactory, and that there are certain other such occupations likewise, having to do with the soul; some artistic, with forethought for what is to the soul's best advantage, and others making light of this, but again, as in the former case, considering merely the soul's pleasure and how it may be contrived for her, neither inquiring which of the pleasures is a better or a worse one, nor caring for aught but mere gratification, whether for better or worse. For I, Callicles, hold that there are such, and for my part I call this sort of thing flattery, whether in relation to the body or to the soul or to anything else, whenever anyone ministers to its pleasure without regard for the better and the worse; and you now, do you support us with the same opinion on this matter, or do you gainsay us?

CALL. Not I; I agree with you, in order that your argument may reach a conclusion, and that I may gratify Gorgias here.

PLATO

ΣΩ. Πότερον δὲ περὶ μὲν μίαν ψυχὴν ἔστι τοῦτο, περὶ δὲ δύο καὶ πολλὰς οὐκ ἔστιν;

ΚΑΛΛ. Οὔκ, ἀλλὰ καὶ περὶ δύο καὶ περὶ πολλάς.

ΣΩ. Οὐκοῦν καὶ ἀθρόαις ἅμα χαρίζεσθαι ἔστι, μηδὲν σκοπούμενον τὸ βέλτιστον;

ΚΑΛΛ. Οἶμαι ἔγωγε.

ΣΩ. Ἔχεις οὖν εἰπεῖν, αἵτινές εἰσιν αἱ ἐπιτηδεύσεις αἱ τοῦτο ποιοῦσαι; μᾶλλον δέ, εἰ βούλει, ἐμοῦ ἐρωτῶντος, ἣ μὲν ἄν σοι δοκῇ τούτων εἶναι, φάθι, ἣ δ᾽ ἂν μή, μὴ φάθι. πρῶτον δὲ σκεψώμεθα τὴν αὐλητικήν. οὐ δοκεῖ σοι τοιαύτη τις εἶναι, ὦ Καλλίκλεις, τὴν ἡδονὴν ἡμῶν μόνον διώκειν, ἄλλο δ᾽ οὐδὲν φροντίζειν;

ΚΑΛΛ. Ἔμοιγε δοκεῖ.

ΣΩ. Οὐκοῦν καὶ αἱ τοιαίδε ἅπασαι, οἷον ἡ κιθαριστικὴ ἡ ἐν τοῖς ἀγῶσιν;

ΚΑΛΛ. Ναί.

ΣΩ. Τί δὲ ἡ τῶν χορῶν διδασκαλία καὶ ἡ τῶν διθυράμβων ποίησις; οὐ τοιαύτη τίς σοι καταφαίνεται; ἢ ἡγῇ τι φροντίζειν Κινησίαν τὸν Μέλητος, ὅπως ἐρεῖ τι τοιοῦτον, ὅθεν ἂν οἱ ἀκούοντες βελτίους γίγνοιντο, ἢ ὅ τι μέλλει χαριεῖσθαι τῷ ὄχλῳ τῶν θεατῶν;

ΚΑΛΛ. Δῆλον δὴ τοῦτό γε, ὦ Σώκρατες, Κινησίου γε πέρι.

ΣΩ. Τί δὲ ὁ πατὴρ αὐτοῦ Μέλης; ἦ πρὸς τὸ βέλτιστον βλέπων ἐδόκει σοι κιθαρῳδεῖν; ἢ ἐκεῖνος μὲν οὐδὲ πρὸς τὸ ἥδιστον· ἠνία γὰρ ᾄδων τοὺς θεατάς· ἀλλὰ δὴ σκόπει· οὐχὶ ἥ τε κιθαρῳ-

[1] A dithyrambic poet whose extravagant style was ridiculed by Aristophanes (*Frogs*, 153; *Clouds*, 333; *Birds*, 1379).

soc. And is this the case with only one soul, and not with two or many?

CALL. No, it is also the case with two or many.

soc. Then is it possible also to gratify them all at once, collectively, with no consideration of what is best?

CALL. I should think it is.

soc. Then can you say what are the pursuits which effect this? Or rather, if you like, when I ask you, and one of them seems to you to be of this class, say yes, and when one does not, say no. And first let us consider flute-playing. Does it not seem to you one of this sort, Callicles, aiming only at our pleasure, and caring for naught else?

CALL. It does seem so to me.

soc. And so too with all similar pursuits, such as harp-playing in the contests?

CALL. Yes.

soc. And what of choral productions and dithyrambic compositions? Are they not manifestly, in your view, of the same kind? Or do you suppose Cinesias,[1] son of Meles, cares a jot about trying to say things of a sort that might be improving to his audience, or only what is likely to gratify the crowd of spectators?

CALL. Clearly the latter is the case, Socrates, with Cinesias.

soc. And what of his father Meles? Did he ever strike you as looking to what was best in his minstrelsy? Or did he, perhaps, not even make the pleasantest his aim? For his singing used to be a pain to the audience. But consider now: do you

PLATO

δικὴ δοκεῖ σοι πᾶσα καὶ ἡ τῶν διθυράμβων ποίησις ἡδονῆς χάριν ηὑρῆσθαι;

ΚΑΛΛ. Ἔμοιγε.

ΣΩ. Τί δὲ δὴ ἡ σεμνὴ αὕτη καὶ θαυμαστή, ἡ τῆς τραγῳδίας ποίησις ἐφ᾽ ᾧ ἐσπούδακε; πότερόν ἐστιν αὐτῆς τὸ ἐπιχείρημα καὶ ἡ σπουδή, ὡς σοὶ δοκεῖ, χαρίζεσθαι τοῖς θεαταῖς μόνον, ἢ καὶ διαμάχεσθαι, ἐάν τι αὐτοῖς ἡδὺ μὲν ᾖ καὶ κεχαρισμένον, πονηρὸν δέ, ὅπως τοῦτο μὲν μὴ ἐρεῖ, εἰ δέ τι τυγχάνει ἀηδὲς καὶ ὠφέλιμον, τοῦτο δὲ καὶ λέξει καὶ ᾄσεται, ἐάν τε χαίρωσιν ἐάν τε μή; ποτέρως σοι δοκεῖ παρεσκευάσθαι ἡ τῶν τραγῳδιῶν ποίησις;

ΚΑΛΛ. Δῆλον δὴ τοῦτό γε, ὦ Σώκρατες, ὅτι πρὸς τὴν ἡδονὴν μᾶλλον ὥρμηται καὶ τὸ χαρίζεσθαι τοῖς θεαταῖς.

ΣΩ. Οὐκοῦν τὸ τοιοῦτον, ὦ Καλλίκλεις, ἔφαμεν νῦν δὴ κολακείαν εἶναι;

ΚΑΛΛ. Πάνυ γε.

ΣΩ. Φέρε δή, εἴ τις περιέλοι τῆς ποιήσεως πάσης τό τε μέλος καὶ τὸν ῥυθμὸν καὶ τὸ μέτρον, ἄλλο τι ἢ λόγοι γίγνονται τὸ λειπόμενον;

ΚΑΛΛ. Ἀνάγκη.

ΣΩ. Οὐκοῦν πρὸς πολὺν ὄχλον καὶ δῆμον οὗτοι λέγονται οἱ λόγοι;

ΚΑΛΛ. Φημί.

ΣΩ. Δημηγορία ἄρα τίς ἐστιν ἡ ποιητική.

ΚΑΛΛ. Φαίνεται.

ΣΩ. Οὐκοῦν ῥητορικὴ δημηγορία ἂν εἴη· ἢ οὐ ῥητορεύειν δοκοῦσί σοι οἱ ποιηταὶ ἐν τοῖς θεάτροις;

ΚΑΛΛ. Ἔμοιγε.

ΣΩ. Νῦν ἄρα ἡμεῖς ηὑρήκαμεν ῥητορικήν τινα

GORGIAS

not think that all minstrelsy and composing of dithyrambs have been invented for the sake of pleasure?

CALL. I do.

SOC. Then what of the purpose that has inspired our stately and wonderful tragic poetry? Are her endeavour and purpose, to your mind, merely for the gratification of the spectators, or does she strive hard, if there be anything pleasant and gratifying, but bad for them, to leave that unsaid, and if there be anything unpleasant, but beneficial, both to speak and sing that, whether they enjoy it or not? To which of these two aims, think you, is tragic poetry devoted?

CALL. It is quite obvious, in her case, Socrates, that she is bent rather upon pleasure and the gratification of the spectators.

SOC. Well now, that kind of thing, Callicles, did we say just now, is flattery?

CALL. Certainly.

SOC. Pray then, if we strip any kind of poetry of its melody, its rhythm and its metre, we get mere speeches as the residue, do we not?

CALL. That must be so.

SOC. And those speeches are spoken to a great crowd of people?

CALL. Yes.

SOC. Hence poetry is a kind of public speaking.

CALL. Apparently.

SOC. Then it must be a rhetorical public speaking; or do you not think that the poets use rhetoric in the theatres?

CALL. Yes, I do.

SOC. So now we have found a kind of rhetoric

πρὸς δῆμον τοιοῦτον οἷον παίδων τε ὁμοῦ καὶ γυναικῶν καὶ ἀνδρῶν, καὶ δούλων καὶ ἐλευθέρων, ἣν οὐ πάνυ ἀγάμεθα· κολακικὴν γὰρ αὐτήν φαμεν εἶναι.

ΚΑΛΛ. Πάνυ γε.

ΣΩ. Εἶεν· τί δὲ ἡ πρὸς τὸν Ἀθηναίων δῆμον ῥητορικὴ καὶ τοὺς ἄλλους τοὺς ἐν ταῖς πόλεσι δήμους τοὺς τῶν ἐλευθέρων ἀνδρῶν, τί ποτε ἡμῖν αὕτη ἐστί; πότερόν σοι δοκοῦσι πρὸς τὸ βέλτιστον ἀεὶ λέγειν οἱ ῥήτορες, τούτου στοχαζόμενοι, ὅπως οἱ πολῖται ὡς βέλτιστοι ἔσονται διὰ τοὺς αὐτῶν λόγους, ἢ καὶ οὗτοι πρὸς τὸ χαρίζεσθαι τοῖς πολίταις ὡρμημένοι, καὶ ἕνεκα τοῦ ἰδίου τοῦ αὐτῶν ὀλιγωροῦντες τοῦ κοινοῦ, ὥσπερ παισὶ προσομιλοῦσι τοῖς δήμοις, χαρίζεσθαι αὐτοῖς πειρώμενοι μόνον, εἰ δέ γε βελτίους ἔσονται ἢ χείρους διὰ ταῦτα, οὐδὲν φροντίζουσιν;

ΚΑΛΛ. Οὐχ ἁπλοῦν ἔτι τοῦτο ἐρωτᾷς· εἰσὶ μὲν γὰρ οἳ κηδόμενοι τῶν πολιτῶν λέγουσιν ἃ λέγουσιν, εἰσὶ δὲ καὶ οἵους σὺ λέγεις.

ΣΩ. Ἐξαρκεῖ. εἰ γὰρ καὶ τοῦτό ἐστι διπλοῦν, τὸ μὲν ἕτερόν που τούτου κολακεία ἂν εἴη καὶ αἰσχρὰ δημηγορία, τὸ δ' ἕτερον καλόν, τὸ παρασκευάζειν ὅπως ὡς βέλτισται ἔσονται τῶν πολιτῶν αἱ ψυχαί, καὶ διαμάχεσθαι λέγοντα τὰ βέλτιστα, εἴτε ἡδίω εἴτε ἀηδέστερα ἔσται τοῖς ἀκούουσιν. ἀλλ' οὐ πώποτε σὺ ταύτην εἶδες τὴν ῥητορικήν· ἢ εἴ τινα ἔχεις τῶν ῥητόρων τοιοῦτον εἰπεῖν, τί οὐχὶ καὶ ἐμοὶ αὐτὸν ἔφρασας τίς ἐστιν;

ΚΑΛΛ. Ἀλλὰ μὰ Δί' οὐκ ἔχω ἔγωγέ σοι εἰπεῖν τῶν γε νῦν ῥητόρων οὐδένα.

ΣΩ. Τί δέ; τῶν παλαιῶν ἔχεις τινὰ εἰπεῖν, δι'

GORGIAS

addressed to such a public as is compounded of children and women and men, and slaves as well as free; an art that we do not quite approve of, since we call it a flattering one.

CALL. To be sure.

SOC. Very well; but now, the rhetoric addressed to the Athenian people, or to the other assemblies of freemen in the various cities—what can we make of that? Do the orators strike you as speaking always with a view to what is best, with the single aim of making the citizens as good as possible by their speeches, or are they, like the poets, set on gratifying the citizens, and do they, sacrificing the common weal to their own personal interest, behave to these assemblies as to children, trying merely to gratify them, nor care a jot whether they will be better or worse in consequence?

CALL. This question of yours is not quite so simple; for there are some who have a regard for the citizens in the words that they utter, while there are also others of the sort that you mention.

SOC. That is enough for me. For if this thing also is twofold, one part of it, I presume, will be flattery and a base mob-oratory, while the other is noble—the endeavour, that is, to make the citizens' souls as good as possible, and the persistent effort to say what is best, whether it prove more or less pleasant to one's hearers. But this is a rhetoric you never yet saw; or if you have any orator of this kind that you can mention, without more ado let me know who he is!

CALL. No, upon my word, I cannot tell you of anyone, at least among the orators of to-day.

SOC. Well then, can you mention one among those

PLATO

ὅντινα αἰτίαν ἔχουσιν Ἀθηναῖοι βελτίους γεγονέναι, ἐπειδὴ ἐκεῖνος ἤρξατο δημηγορεῖν, ἐν τῷ πρόσθεν χρόνῳ χείρους ὄντες; ἐγὼ μὲν γὰρ οὐκ οἶδα τίς ἐστιν οὗτος.

ΚΑΛΛ. Τί δέ; Θεμιστοκλέα οὐκ ἀκούεις ἄνδρα ἀγαθὸν γεγονότα καὶ Κίμωνα καὶ Μιλτιάδην καὶ Περικλέα τουτονὶ τὸν νεωστὶ τετελευτηκότα, οὗ καὶ σὺ ἀκήκοας;

ΣΩ. Εἰ ἔστι γε, ὦ Καλλίκλεις, ἣν πρότερον σὺ ἔλεγες ἀρετήν, ἀληθής, τὸ τὰς ἐπιθυμίας ἀποπιμπλάναι καὶ τὰς αὑτοῦ καὶ τὰς τῶν ἄλλων· εἰ δὲ μὴ τοῦτο, ἀλλ᾽ ὅπερ ἐν τῷ ὑστέρῳ λόγῳ ἠναγκάσθημεν ἡμεῖς ὁμολογεῖν, ὅτι αἱ μὲν τῶν ἐπιθυμιῶν πληρούμεναι βελτίω ποιοῦσι τὸν ἄνθρωπον, ταύτας μὲν ἀποτελεῖν, αἱ δὲ χείρω, μή, τοῦτο δὲ τέχνη τις εἴη[1]· τοιοῦτον ἄνδρα τούτων τινὰ γεγονέναι οὐκ ἔχω ἔγωγε πῶς εἴπω.

ΚΑΛΛ. Ἀλλ᾽ ἐὰν ζητῇς καλῶς, εὑρήσεις.

ΣΩ. Ἴδωμεν δὴ οὑτωσὶ ἀτρέμα σκοπούμενοι, εἴ τις τούτων τοιοῦτος γέγονεν. φέρε γάρ, ὁ ἀγαθὸς ἀνὴρ καὶ ἐπὶ τὸ βέλτιστον λέγων, ἃ ἂν λέγῃ, ἄλλο τι οὐκ εἰκῇ ἐρεῖ, ἀλλ᾽ ἀποβλέπων πρός τι; ὥσπερ καὶ οἱ ἄλλοι πάντες δημιουργοὶ βλέποντες πρὸς τὸ αὑτῶν ἔργον ἕκαστος οὐκ εἰκῇ ἐκλεγόμενος προσφέρει ἃ προσφέρει πρὸς τὸ ἔργον τὸ αὑτοῦ, ἀλλ᾽ ὅπως ἂν εἶδός τι αὐτῷ σχῇ τοῦτο ὃ ἐργάζεται. οἷον εἰ βούλει ἰδεῖν τοὺς ζωγράφους, τοὺς οἰκοδόμους, τοὺς ναυπηγούς, τοὺς ἄλλους πάντας δημιουργούς, ὅντινα

[1] εἴη Burnet: εἶναι MSS.

[1] 429 B.C. We saw at 473 E that the supposed date of the discussion is 405 B.C., so that "recently" here is hardly accurate.

GORGIAS

of older times who has brought the Athenians into repute for any betterment that started at the time of his first harangues, as a change from the worse state in which he originally found them? For my part, I have no idea who the man is.

CALL. Why, do you hear no mention of Themistocles and what a good man he was, and Cimon and Miltiades and the great Pericles, who has died recently,[1] and whom you have listened to yourself?

SOC. Yes, Callicles, if that which you spoke of just now is true virtue—the satisfaction of one's own and other men's desires; but if that is not so, and the truth is—as we were compelled to admit in the subsequent discussion—that only those desires which make man better by their satisfaction should be fulfilled, but those which make him worse should not, and that this is a special art, then I for one cannot tell you of any man so skilled having appeared among them.

CALL. Ah, but if you search properly you will find one.

SOC. Then let us just consider the matter calmly, and see if any of them has appeared with that skill. Come now: the good man, who is intent on the best when he speaks, will surely not speak at random in whatever he says, but with a view to some object? He is just like any other craftsman, who having his own particular work in view selects the things he applies to that work of his, not at random, but with the purpose of giving a certain form to whatever he is working upon. You have only to look, for example, at the painters, the builders, the shipwrights, or any of the other craftsmen, whichever

455

βούλει αὐτῶν, ὡς εἰς τάξιν τινὰ ἕκαστος ἕκαστον τίθησιν ὃ ἂν τιθῇ, καὶ προσαναγκάζει τὸ ἕτερον τῷ ἑτέρῳ πρέπον τε εἶναι καὶ ἁρμόττειν, ἕως ἂν τὸ ἅπαν συστήσηται τεταγμένον τε καὶ κεκοσμημένον πρᾶγμα· καὶ οἵ τε δὴ ἄλλοι δημιουργοὶ καὶ οὓς νῦν δὴ ἐλέγομεν, οἱ περὶ τὸ σῶμα, παιδοτρίβαι τε καὶ ἰατροί, κοσμοῦσί που τὸ σῶμα καὶ συντάττουσιν. ὁμολογοῦμεν οὕτω τοῦτ' ἔχειν ἢ οὔ;

ΚΑΛΛ. Ἔστω τοῦτο οὕτως.

ΣΩ. Τάξεως ἄρα καὶ κόσμου τυχοῦσα οἰκία χρηστὴ ἂν εἴη, ἀταξίας δὲ μοχθηρά;

ΚΑΛΛ. Φημί.

ΣΩ. Οὐκοῦν καὶ πλοῖον ὡσαύτως;

ΚΑΛΛ. Ναί.

ΣΩ. Καὶ μὴν καὶ τὰ σώματά φαμεν τὰ ἡμέτερα;

ΚΑΛΛ. Πάνυ γε.

ΣΩ. Τί δ' ἡ ψυχή; ἀταξίας τυχοῦσα ἔσται χρηστή, ἢ τάξεώς τε καὶ κόσμου τινός;

ΚΑΛΛ. Ἀνάγκη ἐκ τῶν πρόσθεν καὶ τοῦτο συνομολογεῖν.

ΣΩ. Τί οὖν ὄνομά ἐστιν ἐν τῷ σώματι τῷ ἐκ τῆς τάξεώς τε καὶ τοῦ κόσμου γιγνομένῳ;

ΚΑΛΛ. Ὑγίειαν καὶ ἰσχὺν ἴσως λέγεις.

ΣΩ. Ἔγωγε. τί δὲ αὖ τῷ ἐν τῇ ψυχῇ ἐγγιγνομένῳ ἐκ τῆς τάξεως καὶ τοῦ κόσμου; πειρῶ εὑρεῖν καὶ εἰπεῖν ὥσπερ ἐκεῖνο τὸ ὄνομα.

ΚΑΛΛ. Τί δὲ οὐκ αὐτὸς λέγεις, ὦ Σώκρατες;

ΣΩ. Ἀλλ' εἴ σοι ἥδιόν ἐστιν, ἐγὼ ἐρῶ· σὺ δέ, ἂν μέν σοι δοκῶ ἐγὼ καλῶς λέγειν, φάθι· εἰ δὲ μή, ἔλεγχε καὶ μὴ ἐπίτρεπε. ἐμοὶ γὰρ δοκεῖ ταῖς μὲν τοῦ σώματος τάξεσιν ὄνομα εἶναι ὑγιεινόν,

GORGIAS

you like, to see how each of them arranges everything according to a certain order, and forces one part to suit and fit with another, until he has combined the whole into a regular and well-ordered production; and so of course with all the other craftsmen, and the people we mentioned just now, who have to do with the body—trainers and doctors; they too, I suppose, bring order and system into the body. Do we admit this to be the case, or not?

CALL. Let it be as you say.

SOC. Then if regularity and order are found in a house, it will be a good one, and if irregularity, a bad one?

CALL. I agree.

SOC. And it will be just the same with a ship?

CALL. Yes.

SOC. And further, with our bodies also, can we say?

CALL. Certainly.

SOC. And what of the soul? If it shows irregularity, will it be good, or if it has a certain regularity and order?

CALL. Our former statements oblige us to agree to this also.

SOC. Then what name do we give to the effect of regularity and order in the body?

CALL. Health and strength, I suppose you mean.

SOC. I do. And what, again, to the effect produced in the soul by regularity and order? Try to find the name here, and tell it me as before.

CALL. Why not name it yourself, Socrates?

SOC. Well, if you prefer it, I will; and do you, if I seem to you to name it rightly, say so; if not, you must refute me and not let me have my way. For it seems to me that any regularity of the body is

PLATO

ἐξ οὗ ἐν αὐτῷ ἡ ὑγίεια γίγνεται καὶ ἡ ἄλλη ἀρετὴ τοῦ σώματος. ἔστι ταῦτα ἢ οὐκ ἔστιν;

ΚΑΛΛ. Ἔστιν.

D ΣΩ. Ταῖς δὲ τῆς ψυχῆς τάξεσι καὶ κοσμήσεσι νόμιμόν τε καὶ νόμος, ὅθεν καὶ νόμιμοι γίγνονται καὶ κόσμιοι· ταῦτα δ' ἔστι δικαιοσύνη τε καὶ σωφροσύνη. φῂς ἢ οὔ;

ΚΑΛΛ. Ἔστω.

ΣΩ. Οὐκοῦν πρὸς ταῦτα βλέπων ὁ ῥήτωρ ἐκεῖνος, ὁ τεχνικός τε καὶ ἀγαθός, καὶ τοὺς λόγους προσοίσει ταῖς ψυχαῖς, οὓς ἂν λέγῃ, καὶ τὰς πράξεις ἁπάσας, καὶ δῶρον ἐάν τι διδῷ, δώσει, καὶ ἐάν τι ἀφαιρῆται, ἀφαιρήσεται, πρὸς τοῦτο
E ἀεὶ τὸν νοῦν ἔχων, ὅπως ἂν αὐτοῦ τοῖς πολίταις δικαιοσύνη μὲν ἐν ταῖς ψυχαῖς γίγνηται, ἀδικία δὲ ἀπαλλάττηται, καὶ σωφροσύνη μὲν ἐγγίγνηται, ἀκολασία δὲ ἀπαλλάττηται, καὶ ἡ ἄλλη ἀρετὴ ἐγγίγνηται, κακία δὲ ἀπίῃ. συγχωρεῖς ἢ οὔ;

ΚΑΛΛ. Συγχωρῶ.

ΣΩ. Τί γὰρ ὄφελος, ὦ Καλλίκλεις, σώματί γε κάμνοντι καὶ μοχθηρῶς διακειμένῳ σιτία πολλὰ διδόναι καὶ τὰ ἥδιστα ἢ ποτὰ ἢ ἄλλ' ὁτιοῦν, ὃ μὴ ὀνήσει αὐτὸ ἔσθ' ὅτι πλέον ἢ τοὐναντίον κατά γε τὸν δίκαιον λόγον καὶ ἔλαττον; ἔστι ταῦτα;

505 ΚΑΛΛ. Ἔστω.

ΣΩ. Οὐ γάρ, οἶμαι, λυσιτελεῖ μετὰ μοχθηρίας σώματος ζῆν ἀνθρώπῳ· ἀνάγκη γὰρ οὕτω καὶ ζῆν μοχθηρῶς· ἢ οὐχ οὕτως;

GORGIAS

called healthiness, and this leads to health being produced in it, and general bodily excellence. Is that so or not?

CALL. It is.

SOC. And the regular and orderly states of the soul are called lawfulness and law, whereby men are similarly made law-abiding and orderly; and these states are justice and temperance. Do you agree or not?

CALL. Be it so.

SOC. Then it is this that our orator, the man of art and virtue, will have in view, when he applies to our souls the words that he speaks, and also in all his actions, and in giving any gift he will give it, and in taking anything away he will take it, with this thought always before his mind—how justice may be engendered in the souls of his fellow-citizens, and how injustice may be removed; how temperance may be bred in them and licentiousness cut off; and how virtue as a whole may be produced and vice expelled. Do you agree to this or not?

CALL. I agree.

SOC. For what advantage is there, Callicles, in giving to a sick and ill-conditioned body a quantity of even the most agreeable things to eat or drink, or anything else whatever, if it is not going to profit thereby any more, let us say, than by the opposite treatment, on any fair reckoning, and may profit less? Is this so?

CALL. Be it so.

SOC. Because, I imagine, it is no gain for a man to live in a depraved state of body, since in this case his life must be a depraved one also. Or is not that the case?

ΚΑΛΛ. Ναί.

ΣΩ. Οὐκοῦν καὶ τὰς ἐπιθυμίας ἀποπιμπλάναι, οἷον πεινῶντα φαγεῖν ὅσον βούλεται ἢ διψῶντα πιεῖν, ὑγιαίνοντα μὲν ἐῶσιν οἱ ἰατροὶ ὡς τὰ πολλά, κάμνοντα δέ, ὡς ἔπος εἰπεῖν, οὐδέποτ' ἐῶσιν ἐμπίπλασθαι ὧν ἐπιθυμεῖ; συγχωρεῖς τοῦτό γε καὶ σύ;

ΚΑΛΛ. Ἔγωγε.

Β ΣΩ. Περὶ δὲ ψυχήν, ὦ ἄριστε, οὐχ ὁ αὐτὸς τρόπος; ἕως μὲν ἂν πονηρὰ ᾖ, ἀνόητός τε οὖσα καὶ ἀκόλαστος καὶ ἄδικος καὶ ἀνόσιος, εἴργειν αὐτὴν δεῖ τῶν ἐπιθυμιῶν καὶ μὴ ἐπιτρέπειν ἄλλ' ἄττα ποιεῖν ἢ ἀφ' ὧν βελτίων ἔσται· φῂς ἢ οὔ;

ΚΑΛΛ. Φημί.

ΣΩ. Οὕτω γάρ που αὐτῇ ἄμεινον τῇ ψυχῇ;

ΚΑΛΛ. Πάνυ γε.

ΣΩ. Οὐκοῦν τὸ εἴργειν ἐστὶν ἀφ' ὧν ἐπιθυμεῖ κολάζειν;

ΚΑΛΛ. Ναί.

ΣΩ. Τὸ κολάζεσθαι ἄρα τῇ ψυχῇ ἄμεινόν ἐστιν ἢ ἡ ἀκολασία, ὥσπερ σὺ νῦν δὴ ᾤου.

C ΚΑΛΛ. Οὐκ οἶδ' ἅττα λέγεις, ὦ Σώκρατες, ἀλλ' ἄλλον τινὰ ἐρώτα.

ΣΩ. Οὗτος ἀνὴρ οὐχ ὑπομένει ὠφελούμενος καὶ αὐτὸς τοῦτο πάσχων περὶ οὗ ὁ λόγος ἐστί, κολαζόμενος.

ΚΑΛΛ. Οὐδέ γέ μοι μέλει οὐδὲν ὧν σὺ λέγεις, καὶ ταῦτά σοι Γοργίου χάριν ἀπεκρινάμην.

ΣΩ. Εἶεν· τί οὖν δὴ ποιήσομεν; μεταξὺ τὸν λόγον καταλύομεν;

ΚΑΛΛ. Αὐτὸς γνώσῃ.

D ΣΩ. Ἀλλ' οὐδὲ τοὺς μύθους φασὶ μεταξὺ θέμις

GORGIAS

CALL. Yes.

SOC. And so the satisfaction of one's desires—if one is hungry, eating as much as one likes, or if thirsty, drinking—is generally allowed by doctors when one is in health; but they practically never allow one in sickness to take one's fill of things that one desires: do you agree with me in this?

CALL. I do.

SOC. And does not the same rule, my excellent friend, apply to the soul? So long as it is in a bad state — thoughtless, licentious, unjust and unholy —we must restrain its desires and not permit it to do anything except what will help it to be better: do you grant this, or not?

CALL. I do.

SOC. For thus, I take it, the soul itself is better off?

CALL. To be sure.

SOC. And is restraining a person from what he desires correcting him?

CALL. Yes.

SOC. Then correction is better for the soul than uncorrected licence, as you were thinking just now.

CALL. I have no notion what you are referring to, Socrates; do ask some one else.

SOC. Here is a fellow who cannot endure a kindness done him, or the experience in himself of what our talk is about—a correction!

CALL. Well, and not a jot do I care, either, for anything *you* say; I only gave you those answers to oblige Gorgias.

SOC. Very good. So now, what shall we do? Break off our argument midway?

CALL. You must decide that for yourself.

SOC. Why, they say one does wrong to leave off

PLATO

εἶναι καταλείπειν, ἀλλ' ἐπιθέντας κεφαλήν, ἵνα μὴ ἄνευ κεφαλῆς περιίῃ. ἀπόκριναι οὖν καὶ τὰ λοιπά, ἵνα ἡμῖν ὁ λόγος κεφαλὴν λάβῃ.

ΚΑΛΛ. Ὡς βίαιος εἶ, ὦ Σώκρατες. ἐὰν δὲ ἐμοὶ πείθῃ, ἐάσεις χαίρειν τοῦτον τὸν λόγον, ἢ καὶ ἄλλῳ τῳ διαλέξῃ.

ΣΩ. Τίς οὖν ἄλλος ἐθέλει; μὴ γάρ τοι ἀτελῆ γε τὸν λόγον καταλίπωμεν.

ΚΑΛΛ. Αὐτὸς δὲ οὐκ ἂν δύναιο διελθεῖν τὸν λόγον, ἢ λέγων κατὰ σαυτὸν ἢ ἀποκρινόμενος σαυτῷ;

ΣΩ. Ἵνα μοι τὸ τοῦ Ἐπιχάρμου γένηται, " ἃ πρὸ τοῦ δύο ἄνδρες ἔλεγον," εἷς ὢν ἱκανὸς γένωμαι. ἀτὰρ κινδυνεύει ἀναγκαιότατον εἶναι οὕτως. εἰ μέντοι ποιήσομεν, οἶμαι ἔγωγε χρῆναι πάντας ἡμᾶς φιλονίκως ἔχειν πρὸς τὸ εἰδέναι τὸ ἀληθὲς τί ἐστι περὶ ὧν λέγομεν καὶ τί ψεῦδος· κοινὸν γὰρ ἀγαθὸν ἅπασι φανερὸν γενέσθαι αὐτό. δίειμι μὲν οὖν τῷ λόγῳ ἐγὼ ὡς ἄν μοι δοκῇ ἔχειν· ἐὰν δέ τῳ ὑμῶν μὴ τὰ ὄντα δοκῶ ὁμολογεῖν ἐμαυτῷ, χρὴ ἀντιλαμβάνεσθαι καὶ ἐλέγχειν. οὐδὲ γάρ τοι ἔγωγε εἰδὼς λέγω ἃ λέγω, ἀλλὰ ζητῶ κοινῇ μεθ' ὑμῶν, ὥστε, ἄν τι φαίνηται λέγων ὁ ἀμφισβητῶν ἐμοί, ἐγὼ πρῶτος συγχωρήσομαι. λέγω μέντοι ταῦτα, εἰ δοκεῖ χρῆναι διαπερανθῆναι τὸν λόγον· εἰ δὲ μὴ βούλεσθε, ἐῶμεν δὴ χαίρειν καὶ ἀπίωμεν.

---

[1] Epicharmus of Cos produced philosophic comedies in Sicily during the first part of the fifth century. The saying is quoted in full by Athenaeus, vii. 308 τὰ πρὸ τοῦ δύ' ἄνδρες ἔλεγον εἷς ἐγὼν ἀποχρέω.

even stories in the middle; one should set a head on the thing, that it may not go about headless. So proceed with the rest of your answers, that our argument may pick up a head.

CALL. How overbearing you are, Socrates! Take my advice, and let this argument drop, or find some one else to argue with.

SOC. Then who else is willing? Surely we must not leave the argument there, unfinished?

CALL. Could you not get through it yourself, either talking on by yourself or answering your own questions?

SOC. So that, in Epicharmus's phrase,[1] " what two men spake erewhile " I may prove I can manage single-handed. And indeed it looks as though it must of sheer necessity be so. Still, if we are to do this, for my part I think we ought all to vie with each other in attempting a knowledge of what is true and what false in the matter of our argument; for it is a benefit to all alike that it be revealed. Now I am going to pursue the argument as my view of it may suggest; but if any of you think the admissions I am making to myself are not the truth, you must seize upon them and refute me. For I assure you I myself do not say what I say as knowing it, but as joining in the search with you; so that if anyone who disputes my statements is found to be on the right track, I shall be the first to agree with him. This, however, I say on the assumption that you think the argument should be carried through to a conclusion; but if you would rather it were not, let us have done with it now and go our ways.

ΓΟΡΓ. Ἀλλ' ἐμοὶ μὲν οὐ δοκεῖ, ὦ Σώκρατες, χρῆναί πω ἀπιέναι, ἀλλὰ διεξελθεῖν σε τὸν λόγον· φαίνεται δέ μοι καὶ τοῖς ἄλλοις δοκεῖν. βούλομαι γὰρ ἔγωγε καὶ αὐτὸς ἀκοῦσαί σου αὐτοῦ διιόντος τὰ ἐπίλοιπα.

ΣΩ. Ἀλλὰ μὲν δή, ὦ Γοργία, καὶ αὐτὸς ἡδέως μὲν ἂν Καλλικλεῖ τούτῳ ἔτι διελεγόμην, ἕως αὐτῷ τὴν τοῦ Ἀμφίονος ἀπέδωκα ῥῆσιν ἀντὶ τῆς τοῦ Ζήθου· ἐπειδὴ δὲ σύ, ὦ Καλλίκλεις, οὐκ ἐθέλεις συνδιαπερᾶναι τὸν λόγον, ἀλλ' οὖν ἐμοῦ γε ἀκούων ἐπιλαμβάνου, ἐάν τί σοι δοκῶ μὴ καλῶς λέγειν· καί με ἐὰν ἐξελέγχῃς, οὐκ ἀχθεσθήσομαί σοι ὥσπερ σὺ ἐμοί, ἀλλὰ μέγιστος εὐεργέτης παρ' ἐμοὶ ἀναγεγράψῃ.

ΚΑΛΛ. Λέγε, ὦ 'γαθέ, αὐτὸς καὶ πέραινε.

ΣΩ. Ἄκουε δὴ ἐξ ἀρχῆς ἐμοῦ ἀναλαβόντος τὸν λόγον. Ἆρα τὸ ἡδὺ καὶ τὸ ἀγαθὸν τὸ αὐτό ἐστιν; Οὐ ταὐτόν, ὡς ἐγὼ καὶ Καλλικλῆς ὡμολογήσαμεν. Πότερον δὲ τὸ ἡδὺ ἕνεκα τοῦ ἀγαθοῦ πρακτέον, ἢ τὸ ἀγαθὸν ἕνεκα τοῦ ἡδέος; Τὸ ἡδὺ ἕνεκα τοῦ ἀγαθοῦ. Ἡδὺ δέ ἐστι τοῦτο, οὗ παραγενομένου ἡδόμεθα, ἀγαθὸν δὲ οὗ παρόντος ἀγαθοί ἐσμεν; Πάνυ γε. Ἀλλὰ μὴν ἀγαθοί γέ ἐσμεν καὶ ἡμεῖς καὶ τἆλλα πάντα, ὅσα ἀγαθά ἐστιν, ἀρετῆς τινὸς παραγενομένης; Ἔμοιγε δοκεῖ ἀναγκαῖον εἶναι, ὦ Καλλίκλεις. Ἀλλὰ μὲν δὴ ἥ γε ἀρετὴ ἑκάστου καὶ σκεύους καὶ σώματος καὶ ψυχῆς αὖ καὶ ζῴου παντός, οὐ τῷ εἰκῇ κάλλιστα παραγίγνεται, ἀλλὰ τάξει καὶ ὀρθότητι καὶ τέχνῃ, ἥτις ἑκάστῳ ἀποδέδοται αὐτῶν· ἆρα ἔστι ταῦτα; Ἐγὼ μὲν γά

GORGIAS

GORG. Well, my opinion is, Socrates, that we ought not to go away yet, but that you should go through with the argument; and I fancy the rest of them think the same. For I myself, in fact, desire to hear you going through the remainder by yourself.

SOC. Why, to be sure, Gorgias, I myself should have liked to continue discussing with Callicles here until I had paid him an Amphion's speech in return for his of Zethus.[1] But since you, Callicles, are unwilling to join me in finishing off the argument, you must at any rate pull me up, as you listen, if it seems to you that my statements are wrong. And if you refute me, I shall not be vexed with you as you were with me; you will only be recorded in my mind as my greatest benefactor.

CALL. Proceed, good sir, by yourself, and finish it off.

SOC. Give ear, then; but first I will resume our argument from the beginning. Are the pleasant and the good the same thing? Not the same, as Callicles and I agreed. Is the pleasant thing to be done for the sake of the good, or the good for the sake of the pleasant? The pleasant for the sake of the good. And is that thing pleasant by whose advent we are pleased, and that thing good by whose presence we are good? Certainly. But further, both we and everything else that is good, are good by the advent of some virtue? In my view this must be so, Callicles. But surely the virtue of each thing, whether of an implement or of a body, or again of a soul or any live creature, does not arrive most properly by accident, but by an order or rightness or art that is apportioned to each. Is

[1] *Cf.* 485 above.

PLATO

Ε φημι. Τάξει ἄρα τεταγμένον καὶ κεκοσμημένον ἐστὶν ἡ ἀρετὴ ἑκάστου; Φαίην ἂν ἔγωγε. Κόσμος τις ἄρα ἐγγενόμενος ἐν ἑκάστῳ ὁ ἑκάστου οἰκεῖος ἀγαθὸν παρέχει ἕκαστον τῶν ὄντων; Ἔμοιγε δοκεῖ. Καὶ ψυχὴ ἄρα κόσμον ἔχουσα τὸν ἑαυτῆς ἀμείνων τῆς ἀκοσμήτου; Ἀνάγκη. Ἀλλὰ μὴν ἥ γε κόσμον ἔχουσα κοσμία; Πῶς γὰρ οὐ μέλλει;
507 Ἡ δέ γε κοσμία σώφρων; Πολλὴ ἀνάγκη. Ἡ ἄρα σώφρων ψυχὴ ἀγαθή. ἐγὼ μὲν οὐκ ἔχω παρὰ ταῦτα ἄλλα φάναι, ὦ φίλε Καλλίκλεις· σὺ δ' εἰ ἔχεις, δίδασκε.

ΚΑΛΛ. Λέγ', ὦ 'γαθέ.

ΣΩ. Λέγω δὴ ὅτι, εἰ ἡ σώφρων ἀγαθή ἐστιν, ἡ τοὐναντίον τῇ σώφρονι πεπονθυῖα κακή ἐστιν· ἦν δὲ αὕτη ἡ ἄφρων τε καὶ ἀκόλαστος. Πάνυ γε. Καὶ μὴν ὅ γε σώφρων τὰ προσήκοντα πράττοι ἂν καὶ περὶ θεοὺς καὶ περὶ ἀνθρώπους· οὐ γὰρ ἂν σωφρονοῖ τὰ μὴ προσήκοντα πράττων. Ἀνάγκη ταῦτ' εἶναι οὕτως. Καὶ μὴν περὶ μὲν ἀνθρώπους
Β τὰ προσήκοντα πράττων δίκαι' ἂν πράττοι, περὶ δὲ θεοὺς ὅσια· τὸν δὲ τὰ δίκαια καὶ ὅσια πράττοντα ἀνάγκη δίκαιον καὶ ὅσιον εἶναι. Ἔστι ταῦτα. Καὶ μὲν δὴ καὶ ἀνδρεῖόν γε ἀνάγκη· οὐ γὰρ δὴ σώφρονος ἀνδρός ἐστιν οὔτε διώκειν οὔτε φεύγειν ἃ μὴ προσήκει, ἀλλ' ἃ δεῖ[1] καὶ πράγματα καὶ ἀνθρώπους καὶ ἡδονὰς καὶ λύπας φεύγειν καὶ διώκειν, καὶ ὑπομένοντα καρτερεῖν ὅπου δεῖ· ὥστε
C πολλὴ ἀνάγκη, ὦ Καλλίκλεις, τὸν σώφρονα, ὥσπερ

[1] ἀλλ' ἃ δεῖ Heindorf: ἀλλὰ δεῖ, ἀλλὰ δὴ MSS.

GORGIAS

that so ? I certainly agree. Then the virtue of each thing is a matter of regular and orderly arrangement ? I at least should say so. Hence it is a certain order proper to each existent thing that by its advent in each makes it good ? That is my view. So then a soul which has its own proper order is better than one which is unordered ? Necessarily. But further, one that has order is orderly ? Of course it will be. And the orderly one is temperate ? Most necessarily. So the temperate soul is good. For my part, I can find nothing to say in objection to this, my dear Callicles ; but if you can, do instruct me.

CALL. Proceed, good sir.

SOC. I say, then, that if the temperate soul is good, one that is in the opposite state to this sensible [1] one is bad ; and that was the senseless and dissolute one. Certainly. And further, the sensible man will do what is fitting as regards both gods and men ; for he could not be sensible if he did what was unfitting. That must needs be so. And again, when he does what is fitting as regards men, his actions will be just, and as regards the gods, pious ; and he who does what is just and pious must needs be a just and pious man. That is so. And surely he must be brave also : for you know a sound or temperate mind is shown, not by pursuing and shunning what one ought not, but by shunning and pursuing what one ought, whether they be things or people or pleasures or pains, and by steadfastly persevering in one's duty ; so that it follows of strict necessity, Callicles, that the temperate man, as shown in our

---

[1] The argument here makes use of a more literal meaning of σώφρων—" sound-minded " (verging on " conscientious," as in what immediately follows).

PLATO

διήλθομεν, δίκαιον ὄντα καὶ ἀνδρεῖον καὶ ὅσιον ἀγαθὸν ἄνδρα εἶναι τελέως, τὸν δὲ ἀγαθὸν εὖ τε καὶ καλῶς πράττειν ἃ ἂν πράττῃ, τὸν δ' εὖ πράττοντα μακάριόν τε καὶ εὐδαίμονα εἶναι, τὸν δὲ πονηρὸν καὶ κακῶς πράττοντα ἄθλιον· οὗτος δ' ἂν εἴη ὁ ἐναντίως ἔχων τῷ σώφρονι, ὁ ἀκόλαστος, ὃν σὺ ἐπῄνεις.

Ἐγὼ μὲν οὖν ταῦτα οὕτω τίθεμαι καί φημι ταῦτα ἀληθῆ εἶναι· εἰ δὲ ἔστιν ἀληθῆ, τὸν βουλόμενον, ὡς ἔοικεν, εὐδαίμονα εἶναι σωφροσύνην μὲν διωκτέον καὶ ἀσκητέον, ἀκολασίαν δὲ φευκτέον ὡς ἔχει ποδῶν ἕκαστος ἡμῶν, καὶ παρασκευαστέον μάλιστα μὲν μηδὲν δεῖσθαι τοῦ κολάζεσθαι, ἐὰν δὲ δεηθῇ ἢ αὐτὸς ἢ ἄλλος τις τῶν οἰκείων, ἢ ἰδιώτης ἢ πόλις, ἐπιθετέον δίκην καὶ κολαστέον, εἰ μέλλει εὐδαίμων εἶναι. οὗτος ἔμοιγε δοκεῖ ὁ σκοπὸς εἶναι, πρὸς ὃν βλέποντα δεῖ ζῆν, καὶ πάντα εἰς τοῦτο καὶ τὰ αὑτοῦ συντείνοντα καὶ τὰ τῆς πόλεως, ὅπως δικαιοσύνη παρέσται καὶ σωφροσύνη τῷ μακαρίῳ μέλλοντι ἔσεσθαι, οὕτω πράττειν, οὐκ ἐπιθυμίας ἐῶντα ἀκολάστους εἶναι καὶ ταύτας ἐπιχειροῦντα πληροῦν, ἀνήνυτον κακόν, λῃστοῦ βίον ζῶντα. οὔτε γὰρ ἂν ἄλλῳ ἀνθρώπῳ προσφιλὴς ἂν εἴη ὁ τοιοῦτος οὔτε θεῷ· κοινωνεῖν γὰρ ἀδύνατος· ὅτῳ δὲ μὴ ἔνι κοινωνία, φιλία οὐκ ἂν εἴη. φασὶ δ' οἱ σοφοί, ὦ Καλλίκλεις, καὶ οὐρανὸν καὶ γῆν καὶ θεοὺς καὶ ἀνθρώπους τὴν κοινωνίαν συνέχειν καὶ φιλίαν καὶ κοσμιότητα καὶ σωφρο-

---

[1] As the various meanings of σωφροσύνη have been brought out to suggest that one side of that virtue involves the others, so here the apparent quibble of εὖ πράττειν ("act well" and

exposition, being just and brave and pious, is the perfection of a good man; and that the good man does well and fairly whatever he does; and that he who does well is blessed and happy,[1] while the wicked man or evil-doer is wretched. And this must be the man who is in an opposite case to the temperate,—the licentious man whom you were commending.

So there is my account of the matter, and I say that this is the truth; and that, if this is true, anyone, as it seems, who desires to be happy must ensue and practise temperance, and flee from licentiousness, each of us as fast as his feet will carry him, and must contrive, if possible, to need no correction; but if he have need of it, either himself or anyone belonging to him, either an individual or a city, then right must be applied and they must be corrected, if they are to be happy. This, in my opinion, is the mark on which a man should fix his eyes throughout life; he should concentrate all his own and his city's efforts on this one business of providing a man who would be blessed with the needful justice and temperance; not letting one's desires go unrestrained and in one's attempts to satisfy them—an interminable trouble—leading the life of a robber. For neither to any of his fellow-men can such an one be dear, nor to God; since he cannot commune with any, and where there is no communion, there can be no friendship. And wise men tell us, Callicles, that heaven and earth and gods and men are held together by communion and friendship, by orderliness, temperance, and

"fare well") is intended to suggest a real dependence of happiness upon virtue.

συνην καὶ δικαιότητα, καὶ τὸ ὅλον τοῦτο διὰ ταῦτα κόσμον καλοῦσιν, ὦ ἑταῖρε, οὐκ ἀκοσμίαν οὐδὲ ἀκολασίαν. σὺ δέ μοι δοκεῖς οὐ προσέχειν τὸν νοῦν τούτοις, καὶ ταῦτα σοφὸς ὤν, ἀλλὰ λέληθέ σε ὅτι ἡ ἰσότης ἡ γεωμετρικὴ καὶ ἐν θεοῖς καὶ ἐν ἀνθρώποις μέγα δύναται· σὺ δὲ πλεονεξίαν οἴει δεῖν ἀσκεῖν· γεωμετρίας γὰρ ἀμελεῖς. εἶεν· ἢ ἐξελεγκτέος δὴ οὗτος ὁ λόγος ἡμῖν ἐστίν, ὡς οὐ
B δικαιοσύνης καὶ σωφροσύνης κτήσει εὐδαίμονές οἱ εὐδαίμονες, κακίας δὲ οἱ ἄθλιοι ἄθλιοι,[1] ἢ εἰ οὗτος ἀληθής ἐστι, σκεπτέον τί τὰ συμβαίνοντα. τὰ πρόσθεν ἐκεῖνα, ὦ Καλλίκλεις, συμβαίνει πάντα, ἐφ' οἷς σύ με ἤρου, εἰ σπουδάζων λέγοιμι, λέγοντα ὅτι κατηγορητέον εἴη καὶ αὑτοῦ καὶ υἱέος καὶ ἑταίρου, ἐάν τι ἀδικῇ, καὶ τῇ ῥητορικῇ ἐπὶ τοῦτο χρηστέον· καὶ ἃ Πῶλον αἰσχύνῃ ᾤου συγχωρεῖν,
C ἀληθῆ ἄρα ἦν, τὸ εἶναι τὸ ἀδικεῖν τοῦ ἀδικεῖσθαι, ὅσῳπερ αἴσχιον, τοσούτῳ κάκιον· καὶ τὸν μέλλοντα ὀρθῶς ῥητορικὸν ἔσεσθαι δίκαιον ἄρα δεῖ εἶναι καὶ ἐπιστήμονα τῶν δικαίων, ὃ αὖ Γοργίαν ἔφη Πῶλος δι' αἰσχύνην ὁμολογῆσαι.

Τούτων δὲ οὕτως ἐχόντων σκεψώμεθα, τί ποτ' ἐστὶν ἃ σὺ ἐμοὶ ὀνειδίζεις, ἆρα καλῶς λέγεται ἢ οὔ, ὡς ἄρα ἐγὼ οὐχ οἷός τ' εἰμὶ βοηθῆσαι οὔτε ἐμαυτῷ οὔτε τῶν φίλων οὐδενὶ οὐδὲ τῶν οἰκείων, οὐδ' ἐκσῶσαι ἐκ τῶν μεγίστων κινδύνων, εἰμὶ δὲ ἐπὶ τῷ βουλομένῳ ὥσπερ οἱ ἄτιμοι τοῦ ἐθέ-
D λοντος, ἄν τε τύπτειν βούληται, τὸ νεανικὸν δὴ

[1] ἄθλιοι add. Heindorf.

---

[1] Κόσμος ("order") was the name first given to the universe by the Pythagoreans.

GORGIAS

justice; and that is the reason, my friend, why they call the whole of this world by the name of order,[1] not of disorder or dissoluteness. Now you, as it seems to me, do not give proper attention to this, for all your cleverness, but have failed to observe the great power of geometrical equality amongst both gods and men: you hold that self-advantage is what one ought to practise, because you neglect geometry. Very well: either we must refute this statement, that it is by the possession of justice and temperance that the happy are happy and by that of vice the wretched are wretched; or if this is true, we must investigate its consequences. Those former results, Callicles, must all follow, on which you asked me if I was speaking in earnest when I said that a man must accuse himself or his son or his comrade if he do any wrong, and that this is what rhetoric must be used for; and what you supposed Polus to be conceding from shame is after all true—that to do wrong is worse, in the same degree as it is fouler, than to suffer it, and that whoever means to be the right sort of rhetorician must really be just and well-informed of the ways of justice, which again Polus said that Gorgias was only shamed into admitting.

If this is the case, let us consider what weight, if any, there is in the reproaches you cast upon me:[2] is it fairly alleged or not that I am unable to stand up for myself or any of my friends and relations, or to deliver them from the sorest perils, but am exposed like an outcast to the whim of anyone who chooses to give me—the dashing phrase is yours—a box

[2] Socrates proceeds to recall the reproaches of Callicles, above, 486.

PLATO

τοῦτο τοῦ σοῦ λόγου, ἐπὶ κόρρης, ἐάν τε χρήματα ἀφαιρεῖσθαι, ἐάν τε ἐκβάλλειν ἐκ τῆς πόλεως, ἐάν τε, τὸ ἔσχατον, ἀποκτεῖναι· καὶ οὕτω διακεῖσθαι πάντων δὴ αἴσχιστόν ἐστιν, ὡς ὁ σὸς λόγος. ὁ δὲ δὴ ἐμὸς ὅστις, πολλάκις μὲν ἤδη εἴρηται, οὐδὲν δὲ κωλύει καὶ ἔτι λέγεσθαι· οὔ φημι, ὦ Καλλίκλεις, τὸ τύπτεσθαι ἐπὶ κόρρης ἀδίκως αἴσχιστον εἶναι, οὐδέ γε τὸ τέμνεσθαι οὔτε τὸ σῶμα τὸ ἐμὸν οὔτε τὸ βαλάντιον, ἀλλὰ τὸ τύπτειν καὶ ἐμὲ καὶ τὰ ἐμὰ ἀδίκως καὶ τέμνειν καὶ αἴσχιον καὶ κάκιον, καὶ κλέπτειν γε ἅμα καὶ ἀνδραποδίζεσθαι καὶ τοιχωρυχεῖν καὶ συλλήβδην ὁτιοῦν ἀδικεῖν καὶ ἐμὲ καὶ τὰ ἐμὰ τῷ ἀδικοῦντι καὶ κάκιον καὶ αἴσχιον εἶναι ἢ ἐμοὶ τῷ ἀδικουμένῳ. ταῦτα ἡμῖν ἄνω ἐκεῖ ἐν τοῖς πρόσθε λόγοις οὕτω φανέντα, ὡς ἐγὼ λέγω, κατέχεται καὶ δέδεται, καὶ εἰ ἀγροικότερόν τι εἰπεῖν ἔστι, σιδηροῖς καὶ ἀδαμαντίνοις λόγοις, ὡς γοῦν ἂν δόξειεν οὑτωσί, οὓς σὺ εἰ μὴ λύσεις ἢ σοῦ τις νεανικώτερος, οὐχ οἷόν τε ἄλλως λέγοντα ἢ ὡς ἐγὼ νῦν λέγω καλῶς λέγειν· ἐπεὶ ἔμοιγε ὁ αὐτὸς λόγος ἐστὶν ἀεί, ὅτι ἐγὼ ταῦτα οὐκ οἶδα ὅπως ἔχει, ὅτι μέντοι ὧν ἐγὼ ἐντετύχηκα, ὥσπερ νῦν, οὐδεὶς οἷός τ᾽ ἐστὶν ἄλλως λέγων μὴ οὐ καταγέλαστος εἶναι. ἐγὼ μὲν οὖν αὖ τίθημι ταῦτα οὕτως ἔχειν· εἰ δὲ οὕτως ἔχει καὶ μέγιστον τῶν κακῶν ἐστιν ἡ ἀδικία τῷ ἀδικοῦντι καὶ ἔτι τούτου μεῖζον μεγίστου ὄντος, εἰ οἷόν τε, τὸ ἀδικοῦντα μὴ διδόναι δίκην, τίνα ἂν βοήθειαν μὴ δυνάμενος ἄνθρωπος βοηθεῖν ἑαυτῷ καταγέλαστος ἂν τῇ ἀληθείᾳ εἴη; ἆρ᾽ οὐ ταύτην, ἥτις ἀποτρέψει τὴν μεγίστην ἡμῶν βλάβην; ἀλλὰ πολλὴ ἀνάγκη

GORGIAS

on the ear; or strip me of my substance or expel me from the city; or, worst of all, put me to death; and that to be in such a case is the lowest depth of shame, as your account has it? But mine—though it has been frequently stated already, there can be no objection to my stating it once again—is this: I deny, Callicles, that to be wrongfully boxed on the ear is the deepest disgrace, or to have either my person cut or my purse; I hold that to strike or cut me or mine wrongfully is yet more of a disgrace and an evil, and likewise stealing and kidnapping and housebreaking, and in short any wrong whatsoever done to me or mine, are both worse and more shameful to the wrongdoer than to me the wronged. All this, which has been made evident on the lines I have stated some way back in our foregoing discussion, is held firm and fastened—if I may put it rather bluntly—with reasons of steel and adamant (so it would seem, at least, on the face of it) which you or somebody more gallant than yourself must undo, or else find you cannot make a right statement in terms other than I now use. For my story is ever the same, that I cannot tell how the matter stands, and yet of all whom I have encountered, before as now, no one has been able to state it otherwise without making himself ridiculous. Well now, once more I assume it to be so; but if it is so, and injustice is the greatest of evils to the wrongdoer, and still greater than this greatest, if such can be, when the wrongdoer pays no penalty, what rescue is it that a man must be able to effect for himself if he is not to be ridiculous in very truth? Is it not one which will avert from us the greatest harm? Nay, rescue

ταύτην εἶναι τὴν αἰσχίστην βοήθειαν, μὴ δύνασθαι βοηθεῖν μήτε αὑτῷ μήτε τοῖς αὑτοῦ φίλοις τε καὶ οἰκείοις, δευτέραν δὲ τὴν τοῦ δευτέρου κακοῦ καὶ τρίτην τὴν τοῦ τρίτου καὶ τἆλλα οὕτως· ὡς ἑκάστου κακοῦ μέγεθος πέφυκεν, οὕτω καὶ κάλλος τοῦ δυνατὸν εἶναι ἐφ' ἕκαστα βοηθεῖν καὶ αἰσχύνη τοῦ μή. ἆρα ἄλλως ἢ οὕτως ἔχει, ὦ Καλλίκλεις;

ΚΑΛΛ. Οὐκ ἄλλως.

ΣΩ. Δυοῖν οὖν ὄντοιν, τοῦ ἀδικεῖν τε καὶ ἀδικεῖσθαι, μεῖζον μέν φαμεν κακὸν τὸ ἀδικεῖν, ἔλαττον δὲ τὸ ἀδικεῖσθαι. τί οὖν ἂν παρασκευασάμενος ἄνθρωπος βοηθήσειεν αὑτῷ ὥστε ἀμφοτέρας τὰς ὠφελείας ταύτας ἔχειν, τήν τε ἀπὸ τοῦ μὴ ἀδικεῖν καὶ τὴν ἀπὸ τοῦ μὴ ἀδικεῖσθαι; πότερα δύναμιν ἢ βούλησιν; ὧδε δὲ λέγω· πότερον ἐὰν μὴ βούληται ἀδικεῖσθαι, οὐκ ἀδικήσεται, ἢ ἐὰν δύναμιν παρασκευάσηται τοῦ μὴ ἀδικεῖσθαι, οὐκ ἀδικήσεται;

ΚΑΛΛ. Δῆλον δὴ τοῦτό γε, ὅτι ἐὰν δύναμιν.

ΣΩ. Τί δὲ δὴ τοῦ ἀδικεῖν; πότερον ἐὰν μὴ βούληται ἀδικεῖν, ἱκανὸν τοῦτ' ἐστίν—οὐ γὰρ ἀδικήσει—ἢ καὶ ἐπὶ τοῦτο δεῖ δύναμίν τινα καὶ τέχνην παρασκευάσασθαι, ὡς, ἐὰν μὴ μάθῃ αὐτὰ καὶ ἀσκήσῃ, ἀδικήσει; τί οὐκ αὐτό γέ μοι τοῦτο ἀπεκρίνω, ὦ Καλλίκλεις, πότερόν σοι δοκοῦμεν ὀρθῶς ἀναγκασθῆναι ὁμολογεῖν ἐν τοῖς ἔμπροσθεν λόγοις ἐγώ τε καὶ Πῶλος ἢ οὔ, ἡνίκα ὡμολογήσαμεν μηδένα βουλόμενον ἀδικεῖν, ἀλλ' ἄκοντας τοὺς ἀδικοῦντας πάντας ἀδικεῖν;

ΚΑΛΛ. Ἔστω σοι τοῦτο, ὦ Σώκρατες, οὕτως, ἵνα διαπεράνῃς τὸν λόγον.

GORGIAS

must needs be at its shamefullest, if one is unable to rescue either oneself or one's own friends and relations, and second to it is inability in face of the second sort of evil, and third in face of the third, and so on with the rest; according to the gravity attaching to each evil is either the glory of being able to effect a rescue from each sort, or the shame of being unable. Is it so or otherwise, Callicles?

CALL. Not otherwise.

SOC. Then of these two, doing and suffering wrong, we declare doing wrong to be the greater evil, and suffering it the less. Now with what should a man provide himself in order to come to his own rescue, and so have both of the benefits that arise from doing no wrong on the one hand, and suffering none on the other? Is it power or will? What I mean is, will a man avoid being wronged by merely wishing not to be wronged, or will he avoid it by providing himself with power to avert it?

CALL. The answer to that is obvious: by means of power.

SOC. But what about doing wrong? Will the mere not wishing to do it suffice—since, in that case, he will not do it—or does it require that he also provide himself with some power or art, since unless he has got such learning or training he will do wrong? I really must have your answer on this particular point, Callicles—whether you think that Polus and I were correct or not in finding ourselves forced to admit, as we did in the preceding argument, that no one does wrong of his own wish, but that all who do wrong do it against their will.

CALL. Let it be as you would have it, Socrates, in order that you may come to a conclusion of your argument.

PLATO

ΣΩ. Καὶ ἐπὶ τοῦτο ἄρα, ὡς ἔοικε, παρασκευαστέον ἐστὶ δύναμίν τινα καὶ τέχνην, ὅπως μὴ ἀδικήσομεν.

ΚΑΛΛ. Πάνυ γε.

ΣΩ. Τίς οὖν ποτ' ἐστὶ τέχνη τῆς παρασκευῆς τοῦ μηδὲν ἀδικεῖσθαι ἢ ὡς ὀλίγιστα; σκέψαι εἰ σοὶ δοκεῖ ἥπερ ἐμοί. ἐμοὶ μὲν γὰρ δοκεῖ ἥδε· ἢ αὐτὸν ἄρχειν δεῖν ἐν τῇ πόλει ἢ καὶ τυραννεῖν, ἢ τῆς ὑπαρχούσης πολιτείας ἑταῖρον εἶναι.

ΚΑΛΛ. Ὁρᾷς, ὦ Σώκρατες, ὡς ἐγὼ ἕτοιμός εἰμι ἐπαινεῖν, ἄν τι καλῶς λέγῃς; τοῦτό μοι δοκεῖς πάνυ καλῶς εἰρηκέναι.

ΣΩ. Σκόπει δὴ καὶ τόδε ἐάν σοι δοκῶ εὖ λέγειν. φίλος μοι δοκεῖ ἕκαστος ἑκάστῳ εἶναι ὡς οἷόν τε μάλιστα, ὅνπερ οἱ παλαιοί τε καὶ σοφοὶ λέγουσιν, ὁ ὅμοιος τῷ ὁμοίῳ. οὐ καὶ σοί;

ΚΑΛΛ. Ἔμοιγε.

ΣΩ. Οὐκοῦν ὅπου τύραννός ἐστιν ἄρχων ἄγριος καὶ ἀπαίδευτος, εἴ τις τούτου ἐν τῇ πόλει πολὺ βελτίων εἴη, φοβοῖτο δήπου ἂν αὐτὸν ὁ τύραννος καὶ τούτῳ ἐξ ἅπαντος τοῦ νοῦ οὐκ ἄν ποτε δύναιτο φίλος γενέσθαι;

ΚΑΛΛ. Ἔστι ταῦτα.

ΣΩ. Οὐδέ γε εἴ τις πολὺ φαυλότερος εἴη, οὐδ' ἂν οὗτος· καταφρονοῖ γὰρ ἂν αὐτοῦ ὁ τύραννος καὶ οὐκ ἄν ποτε ὡς πρὸς φίλον σπουδάσειεν.

ΚΑΛΛ. Καὶ ταῦτ' ἀληθῆ.

ΣΩ. Λείπεται δὴ ἐκεῖνος μόνος ἄξιος λόγου φίλος τῷ τοιούτῳ, ὃς ἂν ὁμοήθης ὤν, ταὐτὰ ψέγων καὶ ἐπαινῶν, ἐθέλῃ ἄρχεσθαι καὶ ὑποκεῖσθαι τῷ ἄρχοντι. οὗτος μέγα ἐν ταύτῃ τῇ

GORGIAS

soc. Then for this purpose also, of not doing wrong, it seems we must provide ourselves with a certain power or art.

CALL. To be sure.

soc. Now what can be the art of providing so that we suffer no wrong, or as little as possible? Consider if you take the same view of it as I do. For in my view it is this: one must either be a ruler, or even a despot, in one's city, or else an associate of the existing government.

CALL. Do you note, Socrates, how ready I am to praise, when you say a good thing? This seems to me excellently spoken.

soc. Then see if this next statement of mine strikes you as a good one too. It seems to me that the closest possible friendship between man and man is that mentioned by the sages of old time as "like to like." Do you not agree?

CALL. I do.

soc. So where you have a savage, uneducated ruler as despot, if there were some one in the city far better than he, I suppose the despot would be afraid of him and could never become a friend to him with all his heart?

CALL. That is so.

soc. Nor a friend to anyone who was much inferior to him either; for the despot would despise him and never show him the attention due to a friend.

CALL. That is true also.

soc. Then the only friend of any account that remains for such a person is a man of his own temper, who blames and praises the same things, and is thus willing to be governed by him and to be subject to his rule. He is a man who will have great power

477

πόλει δυνήσεται, τοῦτον οὐδεὶς χαίρων ἀδικήσει. οὐχ οὕτως ἔχει;

ΚΑΛΛ. Ναί.

ΣΩ. Εἰ ἄρα τις ἐννοήσειεν ἐν ταύτῃ τῇ πόλει τῶν νέων, "Τίνα ἂν τρόπον ἐγὼ μέγα δυναίμην καὶ μηδείς με ἀδικοῖ;" αὕτη, ὡς ἔοικεν, αὐτῷ ὁδός ἐστιν, εὐθὺς ἐκ νέου ἐθίζειν αὑτὸν τοῖς αὐτοῖς χαίρειν καὶ ἄχθεσθαι τῷ δεσπότῃ, καὶ παρασκευάζειν ὅπως ὅτι μάλιστα ὅμοιος ἔσται ἐκείνῳ. οὐχ οὕτως;

ΚΑΛΛ. Ναί.

ΣΩ. Οὐκοῦν τούτῳ τὸ μὲν μὴ ἀδικεῖσθαι καὶ μέγα δύνασθαι, ὡς ὁ ὑμέτερος λόγος, ἐν τῇ πόλει διαπεπράξεται.

ΚΑΛΛ. Πάνυ γε.

ΣΩ. Ἆρ' οὖν καὶ τὸ μὴ ἀδικεῖν; ἢ πολλοῦ δεῖ, εἴπερ ὅμοιος ἔσται τῷ ἄρχοντι ὄντι ἀδίκῳ καὶ παρὰ τούτῳ μέγα δυνήσεται; ἀλλ' οἶμαι ἔγωγε, πᾶν τοὐναντίον οὑτωσὶ ἡ παρασκευὴ ἔσται αὐτῷ ἐπὶ τὸ οἵῳ τε εἶναι ὡς πλεῖστα ἀδικεῖν καὶ ἀδικοῦντα μὴ διδόναι δίκην· ἦ γάρ;

ΚΑΛΛ. Φαίνεται.

ΣΩ. Οὐκοῦν τὸ μέγιστον αὐτῷ κακὸν ὑπάρξει μοχθηρῷ ὄντι τὴν ψυχὴν καὶ λελωβημένῳ διὰ τὴν μίμησιν τοῦ δεσπότου καὶ δύναμιν.

ΚΑΛΛ. Οὐκ οἶδ' ὅπῃ στρέφεις ἑκάστοτε τοὺς λόγους ἄνω καὶ κάτω, ὦ Σώκρατες· ἢ οὐκ οἶσθα ὅτι οὗτος ὁ μιμούμενος τὸν μὴ μιμούμενον ἐκεῖνον ἀποκτενεῖ, ἐὰν βούληται, καὶ ἀφαιρήσεται τὰ ὄντα;

ΣΩ. Οἶδα, ὦ 'γαθὲ Καλλίκλεις, εἰ μὴ κωφός γ' εἰμί, καὶ σοῦ ἀκούων καὶ Πώλου ἄρτι πολλάκις

in that state; him none will wrong with impunity. Is it not so?

CALL. Yes.

SOC. Hence if one of the young men in that city should reflect: In what way can I have great power, and no one may do me wrong?—this, it would seem, is the path he must take, to accustom himself from his earliest youth to be delighted and annoyed by the same things as his master, and contrive to be as like the other as possible. Is it not so?

CALL. Yes.

SOC. And so this man will have attained to a condition of suffering no wrong and having great power—as your party maintain—in the city.

CALL. Certainly.

SOC. And of doing no wrong likewise? Or is it quite the contrary, if he is to be like his unjust ruler, and have great influence with him? Well, for my part, I think his efforts will be all the opposite way, that is, towards enabling himself to do as much wrong as possible and to pay no penalty for the wrong he does; will they not?

CALL. Apparently.

SOC. And thus he will find himself possessed of the greatest evil, that of having his soul depraved and maimed as a result of his imitation of his master and the power he has got.

CALL. You have a strange way of twisting your arguments, at each point, this way or that, Socrates! Surely you know that this imitator will put to death anyone who does not imitate his master, if he pleases, and will strip him of his property.

SOC. I know that, my good Callicles, if I am not deaf, as I have heard it so often of late from you and

PLATO

καὶ τῶν ἄλλων ὀλίγου πάντων τῶν ἐν τῇ πόλει·
ἀλλὰ καὶ σὺ ἐμοῦ ἄκουε, ὅτι ἀποκτενεῖ μέν, ἂν
βούληται, ἀλλὰ πονηρὸς ὢν καλὸν κἀγαθὸν ὄντα.

ΚΑΛΛ. Οὐκοῦν τοῦτο δὴ καὶ τὸ ἀγανακτητόν;

ΣΩ. Οὐ νοῦν γε ἔχοντι, ὡς ὁ λόγος σημαίνει.
ἢ οἴει δεῖν τοῦτο παρασκευάζεσθαι ἄνθρωπον,
ὡς πλεῖστον χρόνον ζῆν, καὶ μελετᾶν τὰς τέχνας
ταύτας, αἳ ἡμᾶς ἀεὶ ἐκ τῶν κινδύνων σώζουσιν,
ὥσπερ καὶ ἣν σὺ κελεύεις ἐμὲ μελετᾶν τὴν ῥητορικὴν τὴν ἐν τοῖς δικαστηρίοις διασώζουσαν;

ΚΑΛΛ. Ναὶ μὰ Δί᾽ ὀρθῶς γέ σοι συμβουλεύων.

ΣΩ. Τί δέ, ὦ βέλτιστε; ἦ καὶ ἡ τοῦ νεῖν ἐπιστήμη σεμνή τίς σοι δοκεῖ εἶναι;

ΚΑΛΛ. Μὰ Δί᾽ οὐκ ἔμοιγε.

ΣΩ. Καὶ μὴν σώζει γε καὶ αὕτη ἐκ θανάτου
τοὺς ἀνθρώπους, ὅταν εἰς τοιοῦτον ἐμπέσωσιν,
οὗ δεῖ ταύτης τῆς ἐπιστήμης. εἰ δ᾽ αὕτη σοι
δοκεῖ σμικρὰ εἶναι, ἐγώ σοι μείζονα ταύτης
ἐρῶ, τὴν κυβερνητικήν, ἣ οὐ μόνον τὰς ψυχὰς
σώζει, ἀλλὰ καὶ τὰ σώματα καὶ τὰ χρήματα, ἐκ
τῶν ἐσχάτων κινδύνων, ὥσπερ ἡ ῥητορική· καὶ
αὕτη μὲν προσεσταλμένη ἐστὶ καὶ κοσμία, καὶ
οὐ σεμνύνεται ἐσχηματισμένη ὡς ὑπερήφανόν τι
διαπραττομένη, ἀλλὰ ταὐτὰ διαπραξαμένη τῇ
δικανικῇ, ἐὰν μὲν ἐξ Αἰγίνης δεῦρο σώσῃ, οἶμαι
δύ᾽ ὀβολοὺς ἐπράξατο, ἐὰν δὲ ἐξ Αἰγύπτου ἢ ἐκ
τοῦ Πόντου, ἐὰν πάμπολυ, ταύτης τῆς μεγάλης
εὐεργεσίας, σώσασ᾽ ἃ νῦν δὴ ἔλεγον, καὶ αὐτὸν

---

[1] *Cf.* Callicles' warning (486 B) against the danger of being put to death on the false accusation of some paltry rascal.

[2] About fourpence.

GORGIAS

Polus, and from almost every one else in the town; but you in return must hear what I say—that he will put a man to death if he pleases, but it will be a villain slaying a good man and true.

CALL. And is not this the very thing that makes one indignant?[1]

SOC. Not if one is a man of sense, as our argument indicates. Or do you suppose that the object of a man's efforts should be to live as long a time as possible, and to cultivate those arts which preserve us from every danger; such as that which you bid me cultivate—rhetoric, the art that preserves us in the law courts?

CALL. Yes, on my word I do, and sound advice it is that I give you.

SOC. But now, my excellent friend, do you think there is anything grand in the accomplishment of swimming?

CALL. No, in truth, not I.

SOC. Yet, you know, that too saves men from death, when they have got into a plight of the kind in which that accomplishment is needed. But if this seems to you too small a thing, I will tell you of a more important one, the art of piloting, which saves not only our lives but also our bodies and our goods from extreme perils, as rhetoric does. And at the same time it is plain-fashioned and orderly, not giving itself grand airs in a pretence of performing some transcendent feat; but in return for performing the same as the forensic art—bringing one safely over, it may be, from Aegina—it charges a fee, I believe, of two obols[2]; or if it be from Egypt or the Pontus, at the very most—for this great service of bringing safe home, as I said just now, oneself

PLATO

καὶ παῖδας καὶ χρήματα καὶ γυναῖκας, ἀποβιβάσασ᾽ εἰς τὸν λιμένα δύο δραχμὰς ἐπράξατο, καὶ αὐτὸς ὁ ἔχων τὴν τέχνην καὶ ταῦτα διαπραξάμενος ἐκβὰς παρὰ τὴν θάλατταν καὶ τὴν ναῦν περιπατεῖ ἐν μετρίῳ σχήματι. λογίζεσθαι γάρ, οἶμαι, ἐπίσταται, ὅτι ἄδηλόν ἐστιν, οὕστινάς τε ὠφέληκε τῶν συμπλεόντων οὐκ ἐάσας καταποντωθῆναι καὶ οὕστινας ἔβλαψεν, εἰδὼς ὅτι οὐδὲν αὐτοὺς βελτίους ἐξεβίβασεν ἢ οἷοι ἐνέβησαν, οὔτε τὰ σώματα οὔτε τὰς ψυχάς. λογίζεται οὖν, ὅτι οὐκ, εἰ μέν τις μεγάλοις καὶ ἀνιάτοις νοσήμασι κατὰ τὸ σῶμα συνεχόμενος μὴ ἀπεπνίγη, οὗτος μὲν ἄθλιός ἐστιν ὅτι οὐκ ἀπέθανε, καὶ οὐδὲν ὑπ᾽ αὐτοῦ ὠφέληται· εἰ δέ τις ἄρα ἐν τῷ τοῦ σώματος τιμιωτέρῳ, τῇ ψυχῇ, πολλὰ νοσήματα ἔχει καὶ ἀνίατα, τούτῳ δὲ βιωτέον ἐστὶ καὶ τοῦτον ὀνήσει,[1] ἄν τε ἐκ θαλάττης ἄν τε ἐκ δικαστηρίου ἄν τε ἄλλοθεν ὁποθενοῦν σώσῃ, ἀλλ᾽ οἶδεν, ὅτι οὐκ ἄμεινόν ἐστι ζῆν τῷ μοχθηρῷ ἀνθρώπῳ· κακῶς γὰρ ἀνάγκη ἐστὶ ζῆν.

Διὰ ταῦτα οὐ νόμος ἐστὶ σεμνύνεσθαι τὸν κυβερνήτην, καίπερ σώζοντα ἡμᾶς· οὐδέ γε, ὦ θαυμάσιε, τὸν μηχανοποιόν, ὃς οὔτε στρατηγοῦ, μὴ ὅτι κυβερνήτου, οὔτε ἄλλου οὐδενὸς ἐλάττω ἐνίοτε δύναται σώζειν· πόλεις γὰρ ἔστιν ὅτε ὅλας σώζει. μή σοι δοκεῖ κατὰ τὸν δικανικὸν εἶναι; καίτοι εἰ βούλοιτο λέγειν, ὦ Καλλίκλεις, ἅπερ ὑμεῖς, σεμνύνων τὸ πρᾶγμα, καταχώσειεν ἂν ὑμᾶς τοῖς λόγοις, λέγων καὶ παρακαλῶν ἐπὶ τὸ δεῖν γίγνεσθαι μη-

---

[1] ὀνήσει Deuschle : ὀνήσειεν MSS.

---

[1] A few shillings.

GORGIAS

and children and goods and womenfolk—on landing us in harbour it charges a couple of drachmae[1]; and the actual possessor of the art, after performing all this, goes ashore and strolls on the quay by his vessel's side, with an unobtrusive demeanour. For he knows, I expect, how to estimate the uncertainty as to which of his passengers he has benefited by not letting them be lost at sea, and which he has injured, being aware that he has put them ashore not a whit better than when they came aboard, either in body or in soul. And so he reckons out how wrong it is that, whereas a victim of severe and incurable diseases of the body who has escaped drowning is miserable in not having died, and has got no benefit at his hands, yet, if a man has many incurable diseases in that part of him so much more precious than the body, his soul, such a person is to live, and he will be doing him the service of saving him either from the sea or from a law-court or from any other peril whatsoever: no, he knows it cannot be better for a man who is vicious to live, since he must needs live ill.

This is why it is not the custom for the pilot to give himself grand airs, though he does save our lives; nor for the engineer either, my admirable friend, who sometimes has the power of saving lives in no less degree than a general—to say nothing of a pilot—or anyone else: for at times he saves whole cities. Can you regard him as comparable with the lawyer? And yet, if he chose to speak as you people do, Callicles, magnifying his business, he would bury you in a heap of words, pleading and urging the duty of becoming engineers, as the only

483

PLATO

χανοποιούς, ὡς οὐδὲν τἆλλά ἐστιν· ἱκανὸς γὰρ αὐτῷ ὁ λόγος. ἀλλὰ σὺ οὐδὲν ἧττον αὐτοῦ καταφρονεῖς καὶ τῆς τέχνης τῆς ἐκείνου, καὶ ὡς ἐν ὀνείδει ἀποκαλέσαις ἂν μηχανοποιόν, καὶ τῷ υἱεῖ αὐτοῦ οὔτ᾽ ἂν δοῦναι θυγατέρα ἐθέλοις, οὔτ᾽ ἂν αὐτὸς λαβεῖν τὴν ἐκείνου. καίτοι ἐξ ὧν τὰ σαυτοῦ ἐπαινεῖς, τίνι δικαίῳ λόγῳ τοῦ μηχανοποιοῦ καταφρονεῖς καὶ τῶν ἄλλων ὧν νῦν δὴ ἔλεγον; οἶδ᾽ ὅτι φαίης ἂν βελτίων εἶναι καὶ ἐκ βελτιόνων. τὸ δὲ βέλτιον εἰ μὴ ἔστιν ὃ ἐγὼ λέγω, ἀλλ᾽ αὐτὸ τοῦτ᾽ ἐστὶν ἀρετή, τὸ σώζειν αὑτὸν καὶ τὰ ἑαυτοῦ ὄντα ὁποῖός τις ἔτυχε, καταγέλαστός σοι ὁ ψόγος γίγνεται καὶ μηχανοποιοῦ καὶ ἰατροῦ καὶ τῶν ἄλλων τεχνῶν, ὅσαι τοῦ σώζειν ἕνεκα πεποίηνται. ἀλλ᾽, ὦ μακάριε, ὅρα μὴ ἄλλο τι τὸ γενναῖον καὶ τὸ ἀγαθὸν ᾖ τοῦ σώζειν τε καὶ σώζεσθαι. μὴ γὰρ τοῦτο μέν, τὸ ζῆν ὁποσονδὴ χρόνον, τόν γε ὡς ἀληθῶς ἄνδρα ἐατέον ἐστὶ καὶ οὐ φιλοψυχητέον, ἀλλὰ ἐπιτρέψαντα περὶ τούτων τῷ θεῷ καὶ πιστεύσαντα ταῖς γυναιξίν, ὅτι τὴν εἱμαρμένην οὐδ᾽ ἂν εἷς ἐκφύγοι, τὸ ἐπὶ τούτῳ σκεπτέον, τίν᾽ ἂν τρόπον τοῦτον ὃν μέλλοι χρόνον βιῶναι ὡς ἄριστα βιῴη, ἆρα ἐξομοιῶν αὑτὸν τῇ πολιτείᾳ ταύτῃ ἐν ᾗ ἂν οἰκῇ, καὶ νῦν δὲ ἆρα δεῖ σὲ ὡς ὁμοιότατον γίγνεσθαι τῷ δήμῳ τῷ Ἀθηναίων, εἰ μέλλεις τούτῳ προσφιλὴς εἶναι καὶ μέγα δύνασθαι ἐν τῇ πόλει· τοῦθ᾽ ὅρα εἰ σοὶ λυσιτελεῖ καὶ ἐμοί, ὅπως μή, ὦ δαιμόνιε, πεισόμεθα ὅπερ φασὶ τὰς τὴν σελήνην καθαιρούσας, τὰς Θετταλίδας· σὺν τοῖς

---

[1] Socrates alludes to the popular theory that the practice of witchcraft is a serious danger or utter destruction to the practiser.

thing; for he would find reasons in plenty. But you none the less despise him and his special art, and you would call him "engineer" in a taunting sense, and would refuse either to bestow your daughter on his son or let your own son marry his daughter. And yet after the praises you sing of your own pursuits what fair ground have you for despising the engineer and the others whom I was mentioning just now? I know you would claim to be a better man and of better birth. But if "better" has not the meaning I give it, but virtue means just saving oneself and one's belongings, whatever one's character may be, you are merely ridiculous in cavilling at the engineer and the doctor and every other art that has been produced for our safety. No, my gifted friend, you may find that the noble and the good are something different from saving and being saved. For as to living any particular length of time, this is surely a thing that any true man should ignore, and not set his heart on mere life; but having resigned all this to Heaven and believing what the women say—that not one of us can escape his destiny—he should then proceed to consider in what way he will best live out his allotted span of life; whether in assimilating himself to the constitution of the state in which he may be dwelling—and so therefore now, whether it is your duty to make yourself as like as possible to the Athenian people, if you intend to win its affection and have great influence in the city : see if this is to your advantage and mine, so that we may not suffer, my distinguished friend, the fate that they say befalls the creatures who would draw down the moon—the hags of Thessaly;[1] that our

485

PLATO

513

φιλτάτοις ἡ αἵρεσις ἡμῖν ἔσται ταύτης τῆς δυνάμεως τῆς ἐν τῇ πόλει. εἰ δέ σοι οἴει ὁντινοῦν ἀνθρώπων παραδώσειν τέχνην τινὰ τοιαύτην, ἥτις σε ποιήσει μέγα δύνασθαι ἐν τῇ πόλει τῇδε ἀνόμοιον ὄντα τῇ πολιτείᾳ εἴτ᾽ ἐπὶ τὸ βέλτιον εἴτ᾽ ἐπὶ τὸ χεῖρον, ὡς ἐμοὶ δοκεῖ, οὐκ ὀρθῶς βουλεύῃ, ὦ Καλλίκλεις· οὐ γὰρ μιμητὴν δεῖ εἶναι ἀλλ᾽ αὐτοφυῶς ὅμοιον τούτοις, εἰ μέλλεις τι γνήσιον ἀπεργάζεσθαι εἰς φιλίαν τῷ Ἀθηναίων δήμῳ καὶ ναὶ μὰ Δία τῷ Πυριλάμπους γε πρός. ὅστις οὖν σε τούτοις ὁμοιότατον ἀπεργάσεται, οὗτός σε ποιήσει, ὡς ἐπιθυμεῖς πολιτικὸς εἶναι, πολιτικὸν καὶ ῥητορικόν. τῷ αὑτῶν γὰρ ἤθει λεγομένων τῶν λόγων ἕκαστοι χαίρουσι, τῷ δὲ ἀλλοτρίῳ ἄχθονται, εἰ μή τι σὺ ἄλλο λέγεις, ὦ φίλη κεφαλή. λέγομέν τι πρὸς ταῦτα, ὦ Καλλίκλεις;

ΚΑΛΛ. Οὐκ οἶδ᾽ ὅντινά μοι τρόπον δοκεῖς εὖ λέγειν, ὦ Σώκρατες, πέπονθα δὲ τὸ τῶν πολλῶν πάθος· οὐ πάνυ σοι πείθομαι.

ΣΩ. Ὁ δήμου γὰρ ἔρως, ὦ Καλλίκλεις, ἐνὼν ἐν τῇ ψυχῇ τῇ σῇ ἀντιστατεῖ μοι· ἀλλ᾽ ἐὰν πολλάκις ἴσως καὶ βέλτιον ταὐτὰ ταῦτα διασκοπώμεθα πεισθήσῃ. ἀναμνήσθητι δ᾽ οὖν, ὅτι δύο ἔφαμεν εἶναι τὰς παρασκευὰς ἐπὶ τὸ ἕκαστον θεραπεύειν καὶ σῶμα καὶ ψυχήν, μίαν μὲν πρὸς ἡδονὴν ὁμιλεῖν, τὴν ἑτέραν δὲ πρὸς τὸ βέλτιστον, μὴ καταχαριζόμενον ἀλλὰ διαμαχόμενον. οὐ ταῦτα ἦν ἃ τότε ὡριζόμεθα;

ΚΑΛΛ. Πάνυ γε.

---

[1] *Cf.* above, 481 D.

486

GORGIAS

choice of this power in the city may not cost us all that we hold most dear. But if you suppose that anyone in the world can transmit to you such an art as will cause you to have great power in this state without conforming to its government either for better or for worse, in my opinion you are ill-advised, Callicles; for you must be no mere imitator, but essentially like them, if you mean to achieve any genuine sort of friendship with Demus the Athenian people, ay, and I dare swear, with Demus son of Pyrilampes[1] as well. So whoever can render you most like them is the person to make you a statesman in the way that you desire to be a statesman, and a rhetorician; for everybody is delighted with words that are designed for his special temper, but is annoyed by what is spoken to suit aliens—unless you have some other view, dear creature. Have we any objection to this, Callicles?

CALL. It seems to me, I cannot tell how, that your statement is right, Socrates, but I share the common feeling; I do not quite believe you.

SOC. Because the love of Demus, Callicles, is there in your soul to resist me: but if haply we come to examine these same questions more than once, and better, you will believe. But now, remember that we said there were two treatments that might be used in the tendance of any particular thing, whether body or soul: one, making pleasure the aim in our dealings with it; the other, working for what is best, not indulging it but striving with it as hard as we can. Was not this the distinction we were making at that point?

CALL. Certainly.

PLATO

ΣΩ. Οὐκοῦν ἡ μὲν ἑτέρα, ἡ πρὸς ἡδονήν, ἀγεννὴς καὶ οὐδὲν ἄλλο ἢ κολακεία τυγχάνει οὖσα· ἢ γάρ;

ΚΑΛΛ. Ἔστω, εἰ βούλει, σοὶ οὕτως.

ΣΩ. Ἡ δέ γε ἑτέρα, ὅπως ὡς βέλτιστον ἔσται τοῦτο, εἴτε σῶμα τυγχάνει ὂν εἴτε ψυχή, ὃ θεραπεύομεν;

ΚΑΛΛ. Πάνυ γε.

ΣΩ. Ἆρ' οὖν οὕτως ἐπιχειρητέον ἡμῖν ἐστι τῇ πόλει καὶ τοῖς πολίταις θεραπεύειν, ὡς βελτίστους αὐτοὺς τοὺς πολίτας ποιοῦντας; ἄνευ γὰρ δὴ τούτου, ὡς ἐν τοῖς ἔμπροσθεν ηὑρίσκομεν, οὐδὲν ὄφελος ἄλλην εὐεργεσίαν οὐδεμίαν προσφέρειν, ἐὰν μὴ καλὴ κἀγαθὴ ἡ διάνοια ᾖ τῶν μελλόντων ἢ χρήματα πολλὰ λαμβάνειν ἢ ἀρχήν τινων ἢ ἄλλην δύναμιν ἡντινοῦν. φῶμεν οὕτως ἔχειν;

ΚΑΛΛ. Πάνυ γε, εἴ σοι ἥδιον.

ΣΩ. Εἰ οὖν παρεκαλοῦμεν ἀλλήλους, ὦ Καλλίκλεις, δημοσίᾳ πράξοντες τῶν πολιτικῶν πραγμάτων ἐπὶ τὰ οἰκοδομικά, ἢ τειχῶν ἢ νεωρίων ἢ ἱερῶν ἐπὶ τὰ μέγιστα οἰκοδομήματα, πότερον ἔδει ἂν ἡμᾶς σκέψασθαι ἡμᾶς αὐτοὺς καὶ ἐξετάσαι, πρῶτον μὲν εἰ ἐπιστάμεθα τὴν τέχνην ἢ οὐκ ἐπιστάμεθα, τὴν οἰκοδομικήν, καὶ παρὰ τοῦ ἐμάθομεν; ἔδει ἂν ἢ οὔ;

ΚΑΛΛ. Πάνυ γε.

ΣΩ. Οὐκοῦν δεύτερον αὖ τόδε, εἴ τι πώποτε οἰκοδόμημα ᾠκοδομήκαμεν ἰδίᾳ ἢ τῶν φίλων τινὶ ἢ ἡμέτερον αὐτῶν, καὶ τοῦτο τὸ οἰκοδόμημα καλὸν ἢ αἰσχρόν ἐστι· καὶ εἰ μὲν ηὑρίσκομεν σκοπούμενοι διδασκάλους τε ἡμῶν ἀγαθοὺς καὶ ἐλλογίμους γεγονότας καὶ οἰκοδομήματα πολλὰ μὲν καὶ καλὰ

GORGIAS

soc. Then the one, aiming at pleasure, is ignoble and really nothing but flattery, is it not?

CALL. Be it so, if you like.

soc. And the aim of the other is to make that which we are tending, whether it be body or soul, as good as may be.

CALL. To be sure.

soc. Then ought we not to make it our endeavour, in tending our city and its citizens, to make those citizens as good as possible? For without this, you see, as we found in our former argument, there is no use in offering any other service, unless the intentions of those who are going to acquire either great wealth or special authority or any other sort of power be fair and honourable. Are we to grant that?

CALL. Certainly, if you so prefer.

soc. Then if you and I, Callicles, in setting about some piece of public business for the state, were to invite one another to see to the building part of it, say the most important erections either of walls or arsenals or temples, would it be our duty to consider and examine ourselves, first as to whether we understood the art of building or not, and from whom we had learnt it? Would we have to do this, or not?

CALL. Certainly.

soc. And so again, in the second place, whether we had ever erected any building privately for one of our friends or for ourselves, and whether such building was handsome or ugly? And if we found on consideration that we had been under good and reputable masters, and that there were many handsome buildings that had been erected by us with our

μετὰ τῶν διδασκάλων ᾠκοδομημένα ἡμῖν, πολλὰ δὲ καὶ ἴδια ἡμῶν, ἐπειδὴ τῶν διδασκάλων ἀπηλλάγημεν, οὕτω μὲν διακειμένων νοῦν ἐχόντων ἦν ἂν ἰέναι ἐπὶ τὰ δημόσια ἔργα· εἰ δὲ μήτε διδάσκαλον εἴχομεν ἡμῶν αὐτῶν ἐπιδεῖξαι οἰκοδομήματά τε ἢ μηδὲν ἢ πολλὰ καὶ μηδενὸς ἄξια, οὕτω δὴ ἀνόητον ἦν δήπου ἐπιχειρεῖν τοῖς δημοσίοις ἔργοις καὶ παρακαλεῖν ἀλλήλους ἐπ᾽ αὐτά. φῶμεν ταῦτα D ὀρθῶς λέγεσθαι ἢ οὔ;

ΚΑΛΛ. Πάνυ γε.

ΣΩ. Οὐκοῦν οὕτω πάντα, τά τε ἄλλα, κἂν εἰ ἐπιχειρήσαντες δημοσιεύειν παρεκαλοῦμεν ἀλλήλους ὡς ἱκανοὶ ἰατροὶ ὄντες, ἐπεσκεψάμεθα δήπου ἂν ἐγώ τε σὲ καὶ σὺ ἐμέ, Φέρε πρὸς θεῶν, αὐτὸς δὲ ὁ Σωκράτης πῶς ἔχει τὸ σῶμα πρὸς ὑγίειαν; ἢ ἤδη τις ἄλλος διὰ Σωκράτην ἀπηλλάγη νόσου, ἢ δοῦλος ἢ ἐλεύθερος; κἂν ἐγώ, οἶμαι, περὶ σοῦ ἕτερα τοιαῦτα ἐσκόπουν· καὶ εἰ μὴ ηὑρίσκομεν δι᾽ E ἡμᾶς μηδένα βελτίω γεγονότα τὸ σῶμα, μήτε τῶν ξένων μήτε τῶν ἀστῶν, μήτε ἄνδρα μήτε γυναῖκα, πρὸς Διός, ὦ Καλλίκλεις, οὐ καταγέλαστον ἂν ἦν τῇ ἀληθείᾳ, εἰς τοσοῦτον ἀνοίας ἐλθεῖν ἀνθρώπους, ὥστε, πρὶν ἰδιωτεύοντας πολλὰ μὲν ὅπως ἐτύχομεν ποιῆσαι, πολλὰ δὲ κατορθῶσαι καὶ γυμνάσασθαι ἱκανῶς τὴν τέχνην, τὸ λεγόμενον δὴ τοῦτο ἐν τῷ πίθῳ τὴν κεραμείαν ἐπιχειρεῖν μανθάνειν, καὶ αὐτούς τε δημοσιεύειν ἐπιχειρεῖν καὶ ἄλλους τοιούτους παρακαλεῖν; οὐκ ἀνόητόν σοι δοκεῖ ἂν εἶναι οὕτω πράττειν;

ΚΑΛΛ. Ἔμοιγε.

---

[1] That is, instead of a small pot involving little waste in case of failure.

GORGIAS

masters' guidance, and many also by ourselves alone, after we had dispensed with our masters, it might, in those circumstances, be open to men of sense to enter upon public works: but if we had neither a master of ourselves to point to, nor any buildings at all, or only a number of worthless ones, in that case surely it would be senseless to attempt public works or invite one another to take them in hand. Shall we agree to the correctness of this statement or not?

CALL. Yes, to be sure.

SOC. And so too with all the rest: suppose, for instance, we had undertaken the duties of state-physicians, and were to invite one another to the work as qualified doctors, we should, I presume, have first inquired of each other, I of you and you of me: Let us see now, in Heaven's name; how does Socrates himself stand as regards his body's health? Or has anyone else, slave or free, ever had Socrates to thank for ridding him of a disease? And I also, I fancy, should make the same sort of inquiry about you; and then, if we found we had never been the cause of an improvement in the bodily condition of anyone, stranger or citizen, man or woman,—by Heaven, Callicles, would it not in truth be ridiculous that men should descend to such folly that, before having plenty of private practice, sometimes with indifferent results, sometimes with success, and so getting adequate training in the art, they should, as the saying is, try to learn pottery by starting on a wine-jar,[1] and start public practice themselves and invite others of their like to do so? Do you not think it would be mere folly to act thus?

CALL. I do.

PLATO

515 ΣΩ. Νῦν δέ, ὦ βέλτιστε ἀνδρῶν, ἐπειδὴ σὺ μὲν αὐτὸς ἄρτι ἄρχῃ πράττειν τὰ τῆς πόλεως πράγματα, ἐμὲ δὲ παρακαλεῖς καὶ ὀνειδίζεις ὅτι οὐ πράττω, οὐκ ἐπισκεψόμεθα ἀλλήλους, Φέρε, Καλλικλῆς ἤδη τινὰ βελτίω πεποίηκε τῶν πολιτῶν; ἔστιν ὅστις πρότερον πονηρὸς ὤν, ἄδικός τε καὶ ἀκόλαστος καὶ ἄφρων, διὰ Καλλικλέα καλός τε κἀγαθὸς γέγονεν, ἢ ξένος ἢ ἀστός, ἢ δοῦλος ἢ ἐλεύθερος; λέγε μοι, B ἐάν τίς σε ταῦτα ἐξετάζῃ, ὦ Καλλίκλεις, τί ἐρεῖς; τίνα φήσεις βελτίω πεποιηκέναι ἄνθρωπον τῇ συνουσίᾳ τῇ σῇ; ὀκνεῖς ἀποκρίνασθαι, εἴπερ ἔστι τι ἔργον σὸν ἔτι ἰδιωτεύοντος, πρὶν δημοσιεύειν ἐπιχειρεῖν;

ΚΑΛΛ. Φιλόνικος εἶ, ὦ Σώκρατες.

ΣΩ. Ἀλλ' οὐ φιλονικίᾳ γε ἐρωτῶ, ἀλλ' ὡς ἀληθῶς βουλόμενος εἰδέναι, ὅντινά ποτε τρόπον οἴει δεῖν πολιτεύεσθαι ἐν ἡμῖν. ἢ ἄλλου του ἄρα C ἐπιμελήσῃ ἡμῖν ἐλθὼν ἐπὶ τὰ τῆς πόλεως πράγματα, ἢ ὅπως ὅτι βέλτιστοι οἱ πολῖται ὦμεν; ἢ οὐ πολλάκις ἤδη ὡμολογήκαμεν τοῦτο δεῖν πράττειν τὸν πολιτικὸν ἄνδρα; ὡμολογήκαμεν ἢ οὔ; ἀποκρίνου. ὡμολογήκαμεν· ἐγὼ ὑπὲρ σοῦ ἀποκρινοῦμαι. εἰ τοίνυν τοῦτο δεῖ τὸν ἀγαθὸν ἄνδρα παρασκευάζειν τῇ ἑαυτοῦ πόλει, νῦν μοι ἀναμνησθεὶς εἰπὲ περὶ ἐκείνων τῶν ἀνδρῶν ὧν ὀλίγῳ πρότερον ἔλεγες, εἰ ἔτι σοι δοκοῦσιν ἀγαθοὶ πολῖται D γεγονέναι, Περικλῆς καὶ Κίμων καὶ Μιλτιάδης καὶ Θεμιστοκλῆς.

ΚΑΛΛ. Ἔμοιγε.

ΣΩ. Οὐκοῦν εἴπερ ἀγαθοί, δῆλον ὅτι ἕκαστος

GORGIAS

soc. And now, most excellent sir, since you are yourself just entering upon a public career, and are inviting me to do the same, and reproaching me for not doing it, shall we not inquire of one another : Let us see, has Callicles ever made any of the citizens better ? Is there one who was previously wicked, unjust, licentious, and senseless, and has to thank Callicles for making him an upright, honourable man, whether stranger or citizen, bond or free ? Tell me, if anyone examines you in these terms, Callicles, what will you say ? What human being will you claim to have made better by your intercourse ? Do you shrink from answering, if there really is some work of yours in private life that can serve as a step to your public practice ?

CALL. You are contentious, Socrates !

soc. No, it is not from contentiousness that I ask you this, but from a real wish to know in what manner you can imagine you ought to conduct yourself as one of our public men. Or can it be, then, that you will let us see you concerning yourself with anything else in your management of the city's affairs than making us, the citizens, as good as possible ? Have we not more than once already admitted that this is what the statesman ought to do ? Have we admitted it or not ? Answer. We have : I will answer for you. Then if this is what the good man ought to accomplish for his country, recall now those men whom you mentioned a little while ago, and tell me if you still consider that they showed themselves good citizens—Pericles and Cimon and Miltiades and Themistocles.

CALL. Yes, I do.

soc. Then if they were good, clearly each of them

PLATO

αὐτῶν βελτίους ἐποίει τοὺς πολίτας ἀντὶ χειρόνων. ἐποίει ἢ οὔ;

ΚΑΛΛ. Ναί.

ΣΩ. Οὐκοῦν ὅτε Περικλῆς ἤρχετο λέγειν ἐν τῷ δήμῳ, χείρους ἦσαν οἱ Ἀθηναῖοι ἢ ὅτε τὰ τελευταῖα ἔλεγεν;

ΚΑΛΛ. Ἴσως.

ΣΩ. Οὐκ ἴσως δή, ὦ βέλτιστε, ἀλλ' ἀνάγκη ἐκ τῶν ὡμολογημένων, εἴπερ ἀγαθός γ' ἦν ἐκεῖνος πολίτης.

ΚΑΛΛ. Τί οὖν δή;

ΣΩ. Οὐδέν· ἀλλὰ τόδε μοι εἰπὲ ἐπὶ τούτῳ, εἰ λέγονται Ἀθηναῖοι διὰ Περικλέα βελτίους γεγονέναι, ἢ πᾶν τοὐναντίον διαφθαρῆναι ὑπ' ἐκείνου. ταυτὶ γὰρ ἔγωγε ἀκούω, Περικλέα πεποιηκέναι Ἀθηναίους ἀργοὺς καὶ δειλοὺς καὶ λάλους καὶ φιλαργύρους, εἰς μισθοφορίαν πρῶτον καταστήσαντα.

ΚΑΛΛ. Τῶν τὰ ὦτα κατεαγότων ἀκούεις ταῦτα, ὦ Σώκρατες.

ΣΩ. Ἀλλὰ τάδε οὐκέτι ἀκούω, ἀλλὰ οἶδα σαφῶς καὶ ἐγὼ καὶ σύ, ὅτι τὸ μὲν πρῶτον ηὐδοκίμει Περικλῆς καὶ οὐδεμίαν αἰσχρὰν δίκην κατεψηφίσαντο αὐτοῦ Ἀθηναῖοι, ἡνίκα χείρους ἦσαν· ἐπειδὴ δὲ καλοὶ κἀγαθοὶ ἐγεγόνεσαν ὑπ' αὐτοῦ, ἐπὶ τελευτῇ τοῦ βίου τοῦ Περικλέους, κλοπὴν αὐτοῦ κατεψηφίσαντο, ὀλίγου δὲ καὶ θανάτου ἐτίμησαν, δῆλον ὅτι ὡς πονηροῦ ὄντος.

ΚΑΛΛ. Τί οὖν; τούτου ἕνεκα κακὸς ἦν Περικλῆς;

---

[1] This refers especially to the payment of dicasts or jurors, introduced by Pericles in 462–1 B.C.

GORGIAS

was changing the citizens from worse to better. Was this so, or not?

CALL. Yes.

SOC. So when Pericles began to speak before the people, the Athenians were worse than when he made his last speeches?

CALL. Perhaps.

SOC. Not "perhaps," as you say, excellent sir; it follows of necessity from what we have admitted, on the assumption that he was a good citizen.

CALL. Well, what then?

SOC. Nothing: but tell me one thing in addition,—whether the Athenians are said to have become better because of Pericles, or quite the contrary, to have been corrupted by him. What I, for my part, hear is that Pericles has made the Athenians idle, cowardly, talkative, and avaricious, by starting the system of public fees.[1]

CALL. You hear that from the folk with battered ears,[2] Socrates.

SOC. Ah, but what is no longer a matter of hearsay, but rather of certain knowledge, for you as well as for me, is that Pericles was popular at first, and the Athenians passed no degrading sentence upon him so long as they were "worse"; but as soon as they had been made upright and honourable by him, at the end of our Pericles' life they convicted him of embezzlement, and all but condemned him to death, clearly because they thought him a rogue.

CALL. What then? Was Pericles a bad man on that account?

[2] *i.e.* people who show their Spartan sympathies by an addiction to boxing; *cf. Protag.* 342 B.

PLATO

ΣΩ. Ὄνων γοῦν ἂν ἐπιμελητὴς καὶ ἵππων καὶ βοῶν τοιοῦτος ὢν κακὸς ἂν ἐδόκει εἶναι, εἰ παραλαβὼν μὴ λακτίζοντας ἑαυτὸν μηδὲ κυρίττοντας μηδὲ δάκνοντας ἀπέδειξε ταῦτα ἅπαντα ποιοῦντας δι' ἀγριότητα. ἢ οὐ δοκεῖ σοι κακὸς εἶναι ἐπιμελητὴς ὁστισοῦν ὁτουοῦν ζῴου, ὃς ἂν παραλαβὼν ἡμερώτερα ἀποδείξῃ ἀγριώτερα ἢ παρέλαβε; δοκεῖ ἢ οὔ;

ΚΑΛΛ. Πάνυ γε, ἵνα σοι χαρίσωμαι.

ΣΩ. Καὶ τόδε τοίνυν μοι χάρισαι ἀποκρινάμενος· πότερον καὶ ὁ ἄνθρωπος ἓν τῶν ζῴων ἐστὶν ἢ οὔ;

ΚΑΛΛ. Πῶς γὰρ οὔ;

ΣΩ. Οὐκοῦν ἀνθρώπων Περικλῆς ἐπεμέλετο;

ΚΑΛΛ. Ναί.

ΣΩ. Τί οὖν; οὐκ ἔδει αὐτούς, ὡς ἄρτι ὡμολογοῦμεν, δικαιοτέρους γεγονέναι ἀντὶ ἀδικωτέρων ὑπ' ἐκείνου, εἴπερ ἐκεῖνος ἐπεμελεῖτο αὐτῶν ἀγαθὸς ὢν τὰ πολιτικά;

ΚΑΛΛ. Πάνυ γε.

ΣΩ. Οὐκοῦν οἵ γε δίκαιοι ἥμεροι, ὡς ἔφη Ὅμηρος· σὺ δὲ τί φῄς; οὐχ οὕτως;

ΚΑΛΛ. Ναί.

ΣΩ. Ἀλλὰ μὴν ἀγριωτέρους γε αὐτοὺς ἀπέφηνεν ἢ οἵους παρέλαβε, καὶ ταῦτ' εἰς αὐτόν, ὃν ἥκιστ' ἂν ἐβούλετο.

ΚΑΛΛ. Βούλει σοι ὁμολογήσω;

ΣΩ. Εἰ δοκῶ γέ σοι ἀληθῆ λέγειν.

ΚΑΛΛ. Ἔστω δὴ ταῦτα.

ΣΩ. Οὐκοῦν εἴπερ ἀγριωτέρους, ἀδικωτέρους τε καὶ χείρους;

GORGIAS

soc. Well, at any rate a herdsman in charge of asses or horses or oxen would be considered a bad one for being like that—if he took over animals that did not kick him or butt or bite, and in the result they were found to be doing all these things out of sheer wildness. Or do you not consider any keeper of any animal whatever a bad one, if he turns out the creature he received tame so much wilder than he found it? Do you, or do you not?

CALL. Certainly I do, to oblige you.

soc. Then oblige me still further by answering this: is man also one of the animals, or not?

CALL. Of course he is.

soc. And Pericles had charge of men?

CALL. Yes.

soc. Well now, ought they not, as we admitted this moment, to have been made by him more just instead of more unjust, if he was a good statesman while he had charge of them?

CALL. Certainly.

soc. And the just are gentle, as Homer said.[1] But what say you? Is it not so?

CALL. Yes.

soc. But, however, he turned them out wilder than when he took them in hand, and that against himself, the last person he would have wished them to attack.

CALL. You wish me to agree with you?

soc. Yes, if you consider I am speaking the truth.

CALL. Then be it so.

soc. And if wilder, more unjust and worse?

---

[1] Our text of Homer contains no such saying. The nearest is that in *Od.* vi. 120, and ix. 175—ἤ ῥ' οἵγ' ὑβρισταί τε καὶ ἄγριοι, οὐδὲ δίκαιοι, "Wanton and wild are they, not just."

497

ΚΑΛΛ. Ἔστω.

ΣΩ. Οὐκ ἄρ' ἀγαθὸς τὰ πολιτικὰ Περικλῆς ἦν ἐκ τούτου τοῦ λόγου.

ΚΑΛΛ. Οὐ σύ γε φῄς.

ΣΩ. Μὰ Δί' οὐδέ γε σὺ ἐξ ὧν ὡμολόγεις. πάλιν δὲ λέγε μοι περὶ Κίμωνος· οὐκ ἐξωστράκισαν αὐτὸν οὗτοι οὓς ἐθεράπευεν, ἵνα αὐτοῦ δέκα ἐτῶν μὴ ἀκούσειαν τῆς φωνῆς; καὶ Θεμιστοκλέα ταὐτὰ ταῦτα ἐποίησαν καὶ φυγῇ προσεζημίωσαν; Μιλτιάδην δὲ τὸν Μαραθῶνι εἰς τὸ βάραθρον ἐμβαλεῖν ἐψηφίσαντο, καὶ εἰ μὴ διὰ τὸν πρύτανιν, ἐνέπεσεν ἄν; καίτοι οὗτοι, εἰ ἦσαν ἄνδρες ἀγαθοί, ὡς σὺ φῄς, οὐκ ἄν ποτε ταῦτα ἔπασχον. οὔκουν οἵ γε ἀγαθοὶ ἡνίοχοι κατ' ἀρχὰς μὲν οὐκ ἐκπίπτουσιν ἐκ τῶν ζευγῶν, ἐπειδὰν δὲ θεραπεύσωσι τοὺς ἵππους καὶ αὐτοὶ ἀμείνους γένωνται ἡνίοχοι, τότ' ἐκπίπτουσιν· οὐκ ἔστι ταῦτ' οὔτ' ἐν ἡνιοχείᾳ οὔτ' ἐν ἄλλῳ ἔργῳ οὐδενί· ἢ δοκεῖ σοι;

ΚΑΛΛ. Οὐκ ἔμοιγε.

ΣΩ. Ἀληθεῖς ἄρα, ὡς ἔοικεν, οἱ ἔμπροσθεν λόγοι ἦσαν, ὅτι οὐδένα ἡμεῖς ἴσμεν ἄνδρα ἀγαθὸν γεγονότα τὰ πολιτικὰ ἐν τῇδε τῇ πόλει. σὺ δὲ ὡμολόγεις τῶν γε νῦν οὐδένα, τῶν μέντοι ἔμπροσθεν, καὶ προείλου τούτους τοὺς ἄνδρας· οὗτοι δὲ ἀνεφάνησαν ἐξ ἴσου τοῖς νῦν ὄντες, ὥστε, εἰ οὗτοι ῥήτορες ἦσαν, οὔτε τῇ ἀληθινῇ ῥητορικῇ ἐχρῶντο—οὐ γὰρ ἂν ἐξέπεσον—οὔτε τῇ κολακικῇ.

ΚΑΛΛ. Ἀλλὰ μέντοι πολλοῦ γε δεῖ, ὦ Σώ-

GORGIAS

CALL. Be it so.

SOC. Then Pericles was not a good statesman, by this argument.

CALL. You at least say not.

SOC. And you too, I declare, by what you admitted. And now about Cimon once more, tell me, did not the people whom he tended ostracize him in order that they might not hear his voice for ten years? And Themistocles, did they not treat him in just the same way, and add the punishment of exile? And Miltiades, the hero of Marathon, they sentenced to be flung into the pit, and had it not been for the president, in he would have gone. And yet these men, had they been good in the way that you describe them, would never have met with such a fate. Good drivers, at any rate, do not keep their seat in the chariot at their first race to be thrown out later on, when they have trained their teams and acquired more skill in driving! This never occurs either in charioteering or in any other business; or do you think it does?

CALL. No, I do not.

SOC. So what we said before, it seems, was true, that we know of nobody who has shown himself a good statesman in this city of ours. You admitted there was nobody among those of the present day, but thought there were some amongst those of former times, and you gave these men the preference. But these we have found to be on a par with ours of the present day; and so, if they were orators, they employed neither the genuine art of rhetoric—else they would not have been thrown out—nor the flattering form of it.

CALL. But still there can be no suggestion, Socrates,

κρατες, μή ποτέ τις τῶν νῦν ἔργα τοιαῦτα ἐργά-
B σηται, οἷα τούτων ὃς βούλει εἴργασται.

ΣΩ. Ὦ δαιμόνιε, οὐδ' ἐγὼ ψέγω τούτους ὥς
γε διακόνους εἶναι πόλεως, ἀλλά μοι δοκοῦσι
τῶν γε νῦν διακονικώτεροι γεγονέναι καὶ μᾶλλον
οἷοί τε ἐκπορίζειν τῇ πόλει ὧν ἐπεθύμει· ἀλλὰ
γὰρ μεταβιβάζειν τὰς ἐπιθυμίας καὶ μὴ ἐπιτρέπειν, πείθοντες καὶ βιαζόμενοι ἐπὶ τοῦτο, ὅθεν
ἔμελλον ἀμείνους ἔσεσθαι οἱ πολῖται, ὡς ἔπος
C εἰπεῖν, οὐδὲν τούτων διέφερον ἐκεῖνοι· ὅπερ μόνον
ἔργον ἐστὶν ἀγαθοῦ πολίτου. ναῦς δὲ καὶ τείχη
καὶ νεώρια καὶ ἄλλα πολλὰ τοιαῦτα καὶ ἐγώ σοι
ὁμολογῶ δεινοτέρους εἶναι ἐκείνους τούτων ἐκπορίζειν. πρᾶγμα οὖν γελοῖον ποιοῦμεν ἐγώ τε
καὶ σὺ ἐν τοῖς λόγοις· ἐν παντὶ γὰρ τῷ χρόνῳ,
ὃν διαλεγόμεθα, οὐδὲν παυόμεθα εἰς τὸ αὐτὸ ἀεὶ
περιφερόμενοι καὶ ἀγνοοῦντες ἀλλήλων ὅ τι λέγομεν. ἐγὼ γοῦν σε πολλάκις οἶμαι ὡμολογη-
κέναι καὶ ἐγνωκέναι, ὡς ἄρα διττὴ αὕτη τις ἡ
D πραγματεία ἔστι καὶ περὶ τὸ σῶμα καὶ περὶ τὴν
ψυχήν, καὶ ἡ μὲν ἑτέρα διακονική ἐστιν, ᾗ δυνατὸν
εἶναι ἐκπορίζειν, ἐὰν μὲν πεινῇ τὰ σώματα ἡμῶν,
σιτία, ἐὰν δὲ διψῇ, ποτά, ἐὰν δὲ ῥιγῷ, ἱμάτια,
στρώματα, ὑποδήματα, ἄλλ' ὧν ἔρχεται σώματα
εἰς ἐπιθυμίαν· καὶ ἐξεπίτηδές σοι διὰ τῶν αὐτῶν
εἰκόνων λέγω, ἵνα ῥᾷον καταμάθῃς. τούτων γὰρ
ποριστικὸν εἶναι ἢ κάπηλον ὄντα ἢ ἔμπορον ἢ
δημιουργόν του αὐτῶν τούτων, σιτοποιὸν ἢ ὀψο-
E ποιὸν ἢ ὑφάντην ἢ σκυτοτόμον ἢ σκυτοδεψόν,
οὐδὲν θαυμαστόν ἐστιν ὄντα τοιοῦτον δόξαι καὶ

GORGIAS

that any of the present-day men has ever achieved anything like the deeds of anyone you may choose amongst those others.

soc. My admirable friend, neither do I blame the latter, at least as servants of the state; indeed, I consider they have shown themselves more serviceable than those of our time, and more able to procure for the city the things she desired. But in diverting her desires another way instead of complying with them—in persuading or compelling her people to what would help them to be better—they were scarcely, if at all, superior to their successors; and that is the only business of a good citizen. But in providing ships and walls and arsenals, and various other things of the sort, I do grant you that they were cleverer than our leaders. Thus you and I are doing an absurd thing in this discussion: for during all the time that we have been debating we have never ceased circling round to the same point and misunderstanding each other. I at all events believe you have more than once admitted and decided that this management of either body or soul is a twofold affair, and that on one side it is a menial service, whereby it is possible to provide meat for our bodies when they are hungry, drink when thirsty, and when they are cold, clothing, bedding, shoes, or anything else that bodies are apt to desire: I purposely give you the same illustrations, in order that you may the more easily comprehend. For as to being able to supply these things, either as a tradesman or a merchant or a manufacturer of any such actual things—baker or cook or weaver or shoemaker or tanner— it is no wonder that a man in such capacity should appear

501

αὐτῷ καὶ τοῖς ἄλλοις θεραπευτὴν εἶναι σώματος,
παντὶ τῷ μὴ εἰδότι, ὅτι ἔστι τις παρὰ ταύτας
ἁπάσας τέχνη γυμναστική τε καὶ ἰατρική, ἣ δὴ
τῷ ὄντι ἐστὶ σώματος θεραπεία, ᾗπερ καὶ προσήκει τούτων ἄρχειν πασῶν τῶν τεχνῶν καὶ
χρῆσθαι τοῖς τούτων ἔργοις διὰ τὸ εἰδέναι, ὅ
τι χρηστὸν καὶ πονηρὸν τῶν σιτίων ἢ ποτῶν
ἐστὶν εἰς ἀρετὴν σώματος, τὰς δ᾽ ἄλλας πάσας
ταύτας ἀγνοεῖν· διὸ δὴ καὶ ταύτας μὲν δουλο-
πρεπεῖς τε καὶ διακονικὰς καὶ ἀνελευθέρους εἶναι
περὶ σώματος πραγματείαν, τὰς ἄλλας τέχνας,
τὴν δὲ γυμναστικὴν καὶ ἰατρικὴν κατὰ τὸ δίκαιον
δεσποίνας εἶναι τούτων. ταὐτὰ οὖν ταῦτα ὅτι
ἔστι καὶ περὶ ψυχήν, τοτὲ μέν μοι δοκεῖς μανθάνειν
ὅτι λέγω, καὶ ὁμολογεῖς ὡς εἰδὼς ὅ τι ἐγὼ λέγω·
ἥκεις δὲ ὀλίγον ὕστερον λέγων, ὅτι ἄνθρωποι
καλοὶ κἀγαθοὶ γεγόνασι πολῖται ἐν τῇ πόλει, καὶ
ἐπειδὰν ἐγὼ ἐρωτῶ οἵτινες, δοκεῖς μοι ὁμοιο-
τάτους προτείνεσθαι ἀνθρώπους περὶ τὰ πολιτικά, ὥσπερ ἂν εἰ περὶ τὰ γυμναστικὰ ἐμοῦ
ἐρωτῶντος, οἵτινες ἀγαθοὶ γεγόνασιν ἢ εἰσὶ σωμάτων θεραπευταί, ἔλεγές μοι πάνυ σπουδάζων,
Θεαρίων ὁ ἀρτοκόπος καὶ Μίθαικος ὁ τὴν ὀψο-
ποιίαν συγγεγραφὼς τὴν Σικελικὴν καὶ Σάραμβος
ὁ κάπηλος, ὅτι οὗτοι θαυμάσιοι γεγόνασι σωμάτων θεραπευταί, ὁ μὲν ἄρτους θαυμαστοὺς
παρασκευάζων, ὁ δὲ ὄψον, ὁ δὲ οἶνον. ἴσως ἂν
οὖν ἠγανάκτεις, εἴ σοι ἔλεγον ἐγὼ ὅτι ἄνθρωπε,
ἐπαΐεις οὐδὲν περὶ γυμναστικῆς· διακόνους μοι
λέγεις καὶ ἐπιθυμιῶν παρασκευαστὰς ἀνθρώπων,
οὐκ ἐπαΐοντας καλὸν κἀγαθὸν οὐδὲν περὶ αὐτῶν,
οἵ, ἂν οὕτω τύχωσιν, ἐμπλήσαντες καὶ παχύ-

GORGIAS

to himself and his neighbours to be a minister of the body; to every one, in fact, who is not aware that there is besides all these an art of gymnastics and medicine which really is, of course, ministration to the body, and which actually has a proper claim to rule over all those arts and to make use of their works, because it knows what is wholesome or harmful in meat and drink to bodily excellence, whereas all those others know it not; and hence it is that, while those other arts are slavish and menial and illiberal in dealing with the body, gymnastics and medicine can fairly claim to be their mistresses. Now, that the very same is the case as regards the soul you appear to me at one time to understand to be my meaning, and you admit it as though you knew what I meant; but a little later you come and tell me that men have shown themselves upright and honourable citizens in our city, and when I ask you who, you seem to me to be putting forward men of exactly the same sort in public affairs; as if, on my asking you who in gymnastics have ever been or now are good trainers of the body, you were to tell me, in all seriousness, " Thearion, the baker, Mithaecus, the author of the book on Sicilian cookery, Sarambus, the vintner—these have shown themselves wonderful ministers of the body; the first providing admirable loaves, the second tasty dishes, and the third wine." Now perhaps you would be indignant should I then say to you: " Sir, you know nothing about gymnastics; servants you tell me of, and caterers to appetites, fellows who have no proper and respectable knowledge of them, and who peradventure will first stuff and fatten men's

503

νάντες τὰ σώματα τῶν ἀνθρώπων, ἐπαινούμενοι
ὑπ' αὐτῶν, προσαπολοῦσιν αὐτῶν καὶ τὰς ἀρχαίας
D σάρκας· οἱ δ' αὖ δι' ἀπειρίαν οὐ τοὺς ἑστιῶντας
αἰτιάσονται τῶν νόσων αἰτίους εἶναι καὶ τῆς
ἀποβολῆς τῶν ἀρχαίων σαρκῶν, ἀλλ' οἳ ἂν αὐτοῖς
τύχωσι τότε παρόντες καὶ συμβουλεύοντές τι,
ὅταν δὴ αὐτοῖς ἥκῃ ἡ τότε πλησμονὴ νόσον φέ-
ρουσα συχνῷ ὕστερον χρόνῳ, ἄτε ἄνευ τοῦ ὑγιεινοῦ
γεγονυῖα, τούτους αἰτιάσονται καὶ ψέξουσι καὶ
κακόν τι ποιήσουσιν, ἂν οἷοί ·' ὦσι, τοὺς δὲ
προτέρους ἐκείνους καὶ αἰτίους τῶν κακῶν ἐγκω-
E μιάσουσι. καὶ σὺ νῦν, ὦ Καλλίκλεις, ὁμοιότατον
τούτῳ ἐργάζῃ· ἐγκωμιάζεις ἀνθρώπους, οἳ τούτους
εἰστιάκασιν εὐωχοῦντες ὧν ἐπεθύμουν. καί φασι
μεγάλην τὴν πόλιν πεποιηκέναι αὐτούς· ὅτι δὲ
οἰδεῖ καὶ ὕπουλός ἐστι δι' ἐκείνους τοὺς παλαιούς,
519 οὐκ αἰσθάνονται. ἄνευ γὰρ σωφροσύνης καὶ δικαιοσύνης λιμένων καὶ νεωρίων καὶ τειχῶν καὶ
φόρων καὶ τοιούτων φλυαριῶν ἐμπεπλήκασι τὴν
πόλιν· ὅταν οὖν ἔλθῃ ἡ καταβολὴ αὕτη τῆς ἀσθε-
νείας, τοὺς τότε παρόντας αἰτιάσονται συμβού-
λους, Θεμιστοκλέα δὲ καὶ Κίμωνα καὶ Περικλέα
ἐγκωμιάσουσι, τοὺς αἰτίους τῶν κακῶν· σοῦ
δὲ ἴσως ἐπιλήψονται, ἐὰν μὴ εὐλαβῇ, καὶ τοῦ
ἐμοῦ ἑταίρου Ἀλκιβιάδου, ὅταν καὶ τὰ ἀρχαῖα
B προσαπολλύωσι πρὸς οἷς ἐκτήσαντο, οὐκ αἰτίων
ὄντων τῶν κακῶν ἀλλ' ἴσως συναιτίων. καίτοι
ἔγωγε ἀνόητον πρᾶγμα καὶ νῦν ὁρῶ γιγνόμενον
καὶ ἀκούω τῶν παλαιῶν ἀνδρῶν πέρι. αἰσθάνομαι γάρ, ὅταν ἡ πόλις τινὰ τῶν πολιτικῶν

GORGIAS

bodies to the tune of their praises, and then cause them to lose even the flesh they had to start with; and these in their turn will be too ignorant to cast the blame of their maladies and of their loss of original weight upon their regalers, but any people who chance to be by at the time and offer them some advice—just when the previous stuffing has brought, after the lapse of some time, its train of disease, since it was done without regard to what is wholesome — these are the people they will accuse and chide and harm as far as they can, while they will sing the praises of that former crew who caused the mischief. And you now, Callicles, are doing something very similar to this: you belaud men who have regaled the citizens with all the good cheer they desired. People do say they have made the city great; but that it is with the swelling of an imposthume, due to those men of the former time, this they do not perceive. For with no regard for temperance and justice they have stuffed the city with harbours and arsenals and walls and tribute and suchlike trash; and so whenever that access of debility comes they will lay the blame on the advisers who are with them at the time, and belaud Themistocles and Cimon and Pericles, who caused all the trouble; and belike they will lay hold of you, if you are not on your guard, and my good friend Alcibiades, when they are losing what they had originally as well as what they have acquired, though you are not the authors, except perhaps part-authors, of the mischief. And indeed there is a senseless thing which I see happening now, and hear of, in connexion with the men of former times. For I observe that whenever the state proceeds against one of her

PLATO

ἀνδρῶν μεταχειρίζηται ὡς ἀδικοῦντα, ἀγανακτούντων καὶ σχετλιαζόντων ὡς δεινὰ πάσχουσι· πολλὰ καὶ ἀγαθὰ τὴν πόλιν πεποιηκότες ἄρα ἀδίκως ὑπ' αὐτῆς ἀπόλλυνται, ὡς ὁ τούτων λόγος. τὸ δὲ ὅλον ψεῦδός ἐστι· προστάτης γὰρ πόλεως οὐδ' ἂν εἷς ποτὲ ἀδίκως ἀπόλοιτο ὑπ' αὐτῆς τῆς πόλεως ἧς προστατεῖ· κινδυνεύει γὰρ ταὐτὸν εἶναι, ὅσοι τε πολιτικοὶ προσποιοῦνται εἶναι καὶ ὅσοι σοφισταί. καὶ γὰρ οἱ σοφισταί, τἆλλα σοφοὶ ὄντες, τοῦτο ἄτοπον ἐργάζονται πρᾶγμα· φάσκοντες γὰρ ἀρετῆς διδάσκαλοι εἶναι πολλάκις κατηγοροῦσι τῶν μαθητῶν, ὡς ἀδικοῦσι σφᾶς αὐτούς, τούς τε μισθοὺς ἀποστεροῦντες καὶ ἄλλην χάριν οὐκ ἀποδιδόντες, εὖ παθόντες ὑπ' αὐτῶν· καὶ τούτου τοῦ λόγου τί ἂν ἀλογώτερον εἴη πρᾶγμα, ἀνθρώπους ἀγαθοὺς καὶ δικαίους γενομένους, ἐξαιρεθέντας μὲν ἀδικίαν ὑπὸ τοῦ διδασκάλου, σχόντας δὲ δικαιοσύνην, ἀδικεῖν τούτῳ ὃ οὐκ ἔχουσιν; οὐ δοκεῖ σοι τοῦτο ἄτοπον εἶναι, ὦ ἑταῖρε; ὡς ἀληθῶς δημηγορεῖν με ἠνάγκασας, ὦ Καλλίκλεις, οὐκ ἐθέλων ἀποκρίνεσθαι.

ΚΑΛΛ. Σὺ δ' οὐκ ἂν οἷός τ' εἴης λέγειν, εἰ μή τίς σοι ἀποκρίνοιτο;

ΣΩ. Ἔοικά γε· νῦν γοῦν συχνοὺς τείνω τῶν λόγων, ἐπειδή μοι οὐκ ἐθέλεις ἀποκρίνεσθαι· ἀλλ', ὦ 'γαθέ, εἰπὲ πρὸς Φιλίου, οὐ δοκεῖ σοι ἄλογον εἶναι ἀγαθὸν φάσκοντα πεποιηκέναι τινὰ μέμφεσθαι τούτῳ, ὅτι ὑφ' ἑαυτοῦ ἀγαθὸς γεγονώς τε καὶ ὢν ἔπειτα πονηρός ἐστιν;

ΚΑΛΛ. Ἔμοιγε δοκεῖ.

statesmen as a wrongdoer, they are indignant and protest loudly against such monstrous treatment: after all their long and valuable services to the state they are unjustly ruined at her hands, so they protest. But the whole thing is a lie; since there is not a single case in which a ruler of a city could ever be unjustly ruined by the very city that he rules. For it is very much the same with pretenders to statesmanship as with professors of sophistry. The sophists, in fact, with all their other accomplishments, act absurdly in one point: claiming to be teachers of virtue, they often accuse their pupils of doing them an injury by cheating them of their fees and otherwise showing no recognition of the good they have done them. Now what can be more unreasonable than this plea? That men, after they have been made good and just, after all their injustice has been rooted out by their teacher and replaced by justice, should be unjust through something that they have not! Does not this seem to you absurd, my dear friend? In truth you have forced me to make quite a harangue, Callicles, by refusing to answer.

CALL. And you are the man who could not speak unless somebody answered you?

SOC. Apparently I can. Just now, at any rate, I am rather extending my speeches, since you will not answer me. But in the name of friendship, my good fellow, tell me if you do not think it unreasonable for a man, while professing to have made another good, to blame him for being wicked in spite of having been made good by him and still being so?

CALL. Yes, I do.

PLATO

ΣΩ. Οὐκοῦν ἀκούεις τοιαῦτα λεγόντων τῶν φασκόντων παιδεύειν ἀνθρώπους εἰς ἀρετήν;

ΚΑΛΛ. Ἔγωγε· ἀλλὰ τί ἂν λέγοις ἀνθρώπων πέρι οὐδενὸς ἀξίων;

ΣΩ. Τί δ᾽ ἂν περὶ ἐκείνων λέγοις, οἳ φάσκοντες προεστάναι τῆς πόλεως καὶ ἐπιμελεῖσθαι, ὅπως ὡς βελτίστη ἔσται, πάλιν αὐτῆς κατηγοροῦσιν, ὅταν τύχωσιν, ὡς πονηροτάτης; οἴει τι διαφέρειν τούτους ἐκείνων; ταὐτόν, ὦ μακάρι᾽, ἐστὶ σοφιστὴς καὶ ῥήτωρ, ἢ ἐγγύς τι καὶ παραπλήσιον, ὥσπερ ἐγὼ ἔλεγον πρὸς Πῶλον· σὺ δὲ δι᾽ ἄγνοιαν τὸ μὲν πάγκαλόν τι οἴει εἶναι, τὴν ῥητορικήν, τοῦ δὲ καταφρονεῖς. τῇ δὲ ἀληθείᾳ κάλλιόν ἐστι σοφιστικὴ ῥητορικῆς ὅσῳπερ νομοθετικὴ δικαστικῆς καὶ γυμναστικὴ ἰατρικῆς· μόνοις δ᾽ ἔγωγε καὶ ᾤμην τοῖς δημηγόροις τε καὶ σοφισταῖς οὐκ ἐγχωρεῖν μέμφεσθαι τούτῳ τῷ πράγματι, ὃ αὐτοὶ παιδεύουσιν, ὡς πονηρόν ἐστιν εἰς σφᾶς, ἢ τῷ αὐτῷ λόγῳ τούτῳ ἅμα καὶ ἑαυτῶν κατηγορεῖν, ὅτι οὐδὲν ὠφελήκασιν οὕς φασιν ὠφελεῖν. οὐχ οὕτως ἔχει;

ΚΑΛΛ. Πάνυ γε.

ΣΩ. Καὶ προέσθαι γε δήπου τὴν εὐεργεσίαν ἄνευ μισθοῦ, ὡς τὸ εἰκός, μόνοις τούτοις ἐνεχώρει, εἴπερ ἀληθῆ ἔλεγον. ἄλλην μὲν γὰρ εὐεργεσίαν τις εὐεργετηθείς, οἷον ταχὺς γενόμενος διὰ παιδοτρίβην, ἴσως ἂν ἀποστερήσειε τὴν χάριν, εἰ προοῖτο αὐτῷ ὁ παιδοτρίβης καὶ μὴ συνθέμενος αὐτῷ μισθὸν ὅτι μάλιστα ἅμα μεταδιδοὺς τοῦ τάχους λαμβάνοι τὸ ἀργύριον· οὐ γὰρ τῇ βραδυτῆτι,

GORGIAS

soc. Well, and you hear such things said by those who profess to give men education in virtue?

CALL. I do; but what is one to say of such worthless people?

soc. And what is one to say of those who, professing to govern the state and take every care that she be as good as possible, turn upon her and accuse her, any time it suits them, of being utterly wicked? Do you see any difference between these men and the others? Sophist and orator, my estimable friend, are the same thing, or very much of a piece, as I was telling Polus; but you in your ignorance think the one thing, rhetoric, a very fine affair, and despise the other. Yet in reality sophistic is a finer thing than rhetoric by so much as legislation is finer than judicature, and gymnastic than medicine: in fact, for my own part, I always regarded public speakers and sophists as the only people who have no call to complain of the thing that they themselves educate, for its wickedness towards them; as otherwise they must in the same words be also charging themselves with having been of no use to those whom they say they benefit. Is it not so?

CALL. Certainly.

soc. And they alone, I presume, could most likely afford to give away their services without fee, if their words were true. For when a man has received any other service, for example, if he has acquired a fast pace from a trainer's lessons, he might possibly cheat him of his due if the trainer freely offered himself and did not stipulate for a fee to be paid down by the other as nearly as possible at the moment when he imparted to him the fast pace he required; for it is not through a slow pace,

PLATO

οἶμαι, ἀδικοῦσιν οἱ ἄνθρωποι, ἀλλ' ἀδικίᾳ· ἢ γάρ;

ΚΑΛΛ. Ναί.

ΣΩ. Οὐκοῦν εἴ τις αὐτὸ τοῦτο ἀφαιρεῖ, τὴν ἀδικίαν, οὐδὲν δεινὸν αὐτῷ μήποτε ἀδικηθῇ, ἀλλὰ μόνῳ ἀσφαλὲς ταύτην τὴν εὐεργεσίαν προέσθαι, εἴπερ τῷ ὄντι δύναιτό τις ἀγαθοὺς ποιεῖν. οὐχ οὕτως;

ΚΑΛΛ. Φημί.

ΣΩ. Διὰ ταῦτ' ἄρα, ὡς ἔοικε, τὰς μὲν ἄλλας συμβουλὰς συμβουλεύειν λαμβάνοντα ἀργύριον, οἷον οἰκοδομίας πέρι ἢ τῶν ἄλλων τεχνῶν, οὐδὲν αἰσχρόν.

ΚΑΛΛ. Ἔοικέ γε.

ΣΩ. Περὶ δέ γε ταύτης τῆς πράξεως, ὄντιν' ἂν τις τρόπον ὡς βέλτιστος εἴη καὶ ἄριστα τὴν αὑτοῦ οἰκίαν διοικοῖ ἢ πόλιν, αἰσχρὸν νενόμισται μὴ φάναι συμβουλεύειν, ἐὰν μή τις αὐτῷ ἀργύριον διδῷ. ἦ γάρ;

ΚΑΛΛ. Ναί.

ΣΩ. Δῆλον γὰρ ὅτι τοῦτο αἴτιόν ἐστιν, ὅτι μόνη αὕτη τῶν εὐεργεσιῶν τὸν εὖ παθόντα ἐπιθυμεῖν ποιεῖ ἀντ' εὖ ποιεῖν, ὥστε καλὸν δοκεῖ τὸ σημεῖον εἶναι, εἰ εὖ ποιήσας ταύτην τὴν εὐεργεσίαν ἀντ' εὖ πείσεται· εἰ δὲ μή, οὔ. ἔστι ταῦτα οὕτως ἔχοντα;

ΚΑΛΛ. Ἔστιν.

ΣΩ. Ἐπὶ ποτέραν οὖν με παρακαλεῖς τὴν θεραπείαν τῆς πόλεως, διόρισόν μοι· τὴν τοῦ διαμάχεσθαι Ἀθηναίοις, ὅπως ὡς βέλτιστοι ἔσονται, ὡς ἰατρόν, ἢ ὡς διακονήσοντα καὶ πρὸς χάριν ὁμιλήσοντα; τἀληθῆ μοι εἰπέ, ὦ Καλλίκλεις·

GORGIAS

I conceive, that men act unjustly, but through injustice; is it not?

CALL. Yes.

SOC. And so whoever removes this particular thing, injustice, need never have a fear of being unjustly treated; this benefit alone may be freely bestowed without risk, granted that one really had the power of making people good. Is it not so?

CALL. I agree.

SOC. Then this, it seems, is the reason why there is no disgrace in taking money for giving every other kind of advice, as about building or the rest of the arts.

CALL. It does seem so.

SOC. But about this business of finding the way to be as good as possible, and of managing one's own household or city for the best, it is recognized to be a disgrace for one to decline to give advice except for a payment in cash, is it not?

CALL. Yes.

SOC. The reason evidently being that this is the only sort of service that makes the person so served desire to do one in return; and hence it is felt to be a good sign when this service that one has done is repaid to one in kind; but when this is not so, the contrary is felt. Is the case as I say?

CALL. It is.

SOC. Then please specify to which of these two ministrations to the state you are inviting me—that of struggling hard, like a doctor, with the Athenians to make them as good as possible, or that of seeking to serve their wants and humour them at every turn? Tell me the truth, Callicles;

PLATO

521

δίκαιος γὰρ εἶ, ὥσπερ ἤρξω παρρησιάζεσθαι πρὸς
ἐμέ, διατελεῖν ἃ νοεῖς λέγων· καὶ νῦν εὖ καὶ γενναίως εἰπέ.

ΚΑΛΛ. Λέγω τοίνυν ὅτι ὡς διακονήσοντα.

Β ΣΩ. Κολακεύσοντα ἄρα με, ὦ γενναιότατε,
παρακαλεῖς.

ΚΑΛΛ. Εἴ σοι Μυσόν γε ἥδιον καλεῖν, ὦ Σώ-
κρατες· ὡς εἰ μὴ ταῦτά γε ποιήσεις—

ΣΩ. Μὴ εἴπῃς ὃ πολλάκις εἴρηκας, ὅτι ἀποκτενεῖ
με ὁ βουλόμενος, ἵνα μὴ αὖ καὶ ἐγὼ εἴπω, ὅτι
πονηρός γε ὢν ἀγαθὸν ὄντα· μηδ' ὅτι ἀφαιρήσεται
C ἐάν τι ἔχω, ἵνα μὴ αὖ ἐγὼ εἴπω ὅτι ἀλλ' ἀφελό-
μενος οὐχ ἕξει ὅ τι χρήσεται αὐτοῖς, ἀλλ' ὥσπερ
με ἀδίκως ἀφείλετο, οὕτω καὶ λαβὼν ἀδίκως
χρήσεται, εἰ δὲ ἀδίκως, αἰσχρῶς, εἰ δὲ αἰσχρῶς,
κακῶς.

ΚΑΛΛ. Ὥς μοι δοκεῖς, ὦ Σώκρατες, πιστεύειν
μηδ' ἂν ἓν τούτων παθεῖν, ὡς οἰκῶν ἐκποδὼν καὶ
οὐκ ἂν εἰσαχθεὶς εἰς δικαστήριον ὑπὸ πάνυ ἴσως
μοχθηροῦ ἀνθρώπου καὶ φαύλου.

ΣΩ. Ἀνόητος ἄρα εἰμί, ὦ Καλλίκλεις, ὡς
ἀληθῶς, εἰ μὴ οἴομαι ἐν τῇδε τῇ πόλει ὁντινοῦν
ἄν, ὅ τι τύχοι, τοῦτο παθεῖν. τόδε μέντοι εὖ οἶδ'
ὅτι, ἐάνπερ εἰσίω εἰς δικαστήριον περὶ τούτων
τινὸς κινδυνεύων ὃ σὺ λέγεις, πονηρός τίς με ἔσται
D ὁ εἰσάγων· οὐδεὶς γὰρ ἂν χρηστὸς μὴ ἀδικοῦντ'
ἄνθρωπον εἰσαγάγοι· καὶ οὐδέν γε ἄτοπον εἰ ἀπο-

---

[1] The Mysians, like the Carians (*cf. Euthyd.* 285 c), were regarded as the lowest of the low. Callicles heatedly taunts Socrates with putting the matter in its worst light.

GORGIAS

for it is only right that, as you began by speaking to me frankly, you should continue to tell me what you think. So now speak out like a good, generous man.

CALL. I say then, the way of seeking to serve them.

SOC. So it is to a flatterer's work, most noble sir, that you invite me?

CALL. Work for a mean Mysian,[1] if you prefer the name, Socrates; for unless you do as I say——

SOC. Do not tell me, what you have so often repeated, that anyone who pleases will put me to death, lest I on my side should have to tell you that it will be a villain killing a good man; nor that anyone may strip me of whatever I have, lest I should have to say in my turn: Well, but when he has stripped me, he will not know what use to make of his spoil, but as he stripped me unjustly so will he use his spoil unjustly, and if unjustly, foully, and if foully, ill.

CALL. It quite strikes me, Socrates, that you believe not one of these troubles could befall you, as though you dwelt out of the way, and could never be dragged into a law court by some perhaps utterly paltry rascal.

SOC. Then I am a fool, Callicles, in truth, if I do not suppose that in this city anyone, whoever he was, might find himself, as luck should have it, in any sort of plight. Of one thing, however, I am sure—that if ever I am brought before the court and stand in any such danger as you mention, it will be some villain who brings me there, for no honest man would prosecute a person who had done no wrong; and it would be no marvel if I were put

513

PLATO

θάνοιμι βούλει σοι εἴπω δι' ὅ τι ταῦτα προσδοκῶ;

ΚΑΛΛ. Πάνυ γε.

ΣΩ. Οἶμαι μετ' ὀλίγων Ἀθηναίων, ἵνα μὴ εἴπω μόνος, ἐπιχειρεῖν τῇ ὡς ἀληθῶς πολιτικῇ τέχνῃ καὶ πράττειν τὰ πολιτικὰ μόνος τῶν νῦν· ἅτε οὖν οὐ πρὸς χάριν λέγων τοὺς λόγους οὓς λέγω ἑκάστοτε, ἀλλὰ πρὸς τὸ βέλτιστον, οὐ πρὸς τὸ ἥδιστον, καὶ οὐκ ἐθέλων ποιεῖν ἃ σὺ παραινεῖς, τὰ κομψὰ ταῦτα, οὐχ ἕξω ὅ τι λέγω ἐν τῷ δικαστηρίῳ. ὁ αὐτὸς δέ μοι ἥκει λόγος, ὅνπερ πρὸς Πῶλον ἔλεγον· κρινοῦμαι γὰρ ὡς ἐν παιδίοις ἰατρὸς ἂν κρίνοιτο κατηγοροῦντος ὀψοποιοῦ. σκόπει γάρ, τί ἂν ἀπολογοῖτο ὁ τοιοῦτος ἄνθρωπος ἐν τούτοις ληφθείς, εἰ αὐτοῦ κατηγοροῖ τις λέγων ὅτι ὦ παῖδες, πολλὰ ὑμᾶς καὶ κακὰ ὅδε εἴργασται ἀνὴρ καὶ αὐτούς, καὶ τοὺς νεωτάτους ὑμῶν διαφθείρει τέμνων τε καὶ κάων, καὶ ἰσχναίνων καὶ πνίγων ἀπορεῖν ποιεῖ, πικρότατα πώματα διδοὺς καὶ πεινῆν καὶ διψῆν ἀναγκάζων, οὐχ ὥσπερ ἐγὼ πολλὰ καὶ ἡδέα καὶ παντοδαπὰ ηὐώχουν ὑμᾶς· τί ἂν οἴει ἐν τούτῳ τῷ κακῷ ἀποληφθέντα ἰατρὸν ἔχειν εἰπεῖν; ἢ εἰ εἴποι τὴν ἀλήθειαν, ὅτι ταῦτα πάντα ἐγὼ ἐποίουν, ὦ παῖδες, ὑγιεινῶς, ὁπόσον οἴει ἂν ἀναβοῆσαι τοὺς τοιούτους δικαστάς; οὐ μέγα;

ΚΑΛΛ. Ἴσως· οἴεσθαί γε χρή.

ΣΩ. Οὐκοῦν οἴει ἐν πάσῃ ἀπορίᾳ ἂν αὐτὸν ἔχεσθαι, ὅ τι χρὴ εἰπεῖν;

ΚΑΛΛ. Πάνυ γε.

---

[1] Socrates retorts the phrase of Euripides, which Callicles applied (above, 486 c) to philosophic debate, upon the practical pursuits which Callicles recommended.

GORGIAS

to death. Would you like me to tell you my reason for expecting this ?

CALL. Do, by all means.

SOC. I think I am one of few, not to say the only one, in Athens who attempts the true art of statesmanship, and the only man of the present time who manages affairs of state: hence, as the speeches that I make from time to time are not aimed at gratification, but at what is best instead of what is most pleasant, and as I do not care to deal in " these pretty toys "[1] that you recommend, I shall have not a word to say at the bar. The same case that I made out to Polus will apply to me; for I shall be like a doctor tried by a bench of children on a charge brought by a cook.[2] Just consider what defence a person like that would make at such a pass, if the prosecutor should speak against him thus : " Children, this fellow has done you all a great deal of personal mischief, and he destroys even the youngest of you by cutting and burning, and starves and chokes you to distraction, giving you nasty bitter draughts and forcing you to fast and thirst; not like me, who used to gorge you with abundance of nice things of every sort." What do you suppose a doctor brought to this sad pass could say for himself ? Or if he spoke the truth—" All this I did, my boys, for your health "—how great, think you, would be the outcry from such a bench as that ? A loud one, would it not ?

CALL. I daresay : one must suppose so.

SOC. Then you suppose he would be utterly at a loss what to say ?

CALL. Quite so.

[2] *Cf.* 464 D.

PLATO

ΣΩ. Τοιοῦτον μέντοι καὶ ἐγὼ οἶδα ὅτι πάθος πάθοιμι ἂν εἰσελθὼν εἰς δικαστήριον. οὔτε γὰρ ἡδονὰς ἃς ἐκπεπόρικα ἕξω αὐτοῖς λέγειν, ἃς οὗτοι εὐεργεσίας καὶ ὠφελείας νομίζουσιν, ἐγὼ δὲ οὔτε τοὺς πορίζοντας ζηλῶ οὔτε οἷς πορίζεται· ἐάν τέ τίς με ἢ νεωτέρους φῇ διαφθείρειν ἀπορεῖν ποιοῦντα, ἢ τοὺς πρεσβυτέρους κακηγορεῖν λέγοντα πικροὺς λόγους ἢ ἰδίᾳ ἢ δημοσίᾳ, οὔτε τὸ ἀληθὲς ἕξω εἰπεῖν, ὅτι δικαίως πάντα ταῦτα ἐγὼ λέγω, καὶ πράττω τὸ ὑμέτερον δὴ τοῦτο, ὦ ἄνδρες δικασταί, οὔτε ἄλλο οὐδέν· ὥστε ἴσως, ὅ τι ἂν τύχω, τοῦτο πείσομαι.

ΚΑΛΛ. Δοκεῖ οὖν σοι, ὦ Σώκρατες, καλῶς ἔχειν ἄνθρωπος ἐν πόλει οὕτω διακείμενος καὶ ἀδύνατος ὢν ἑαυτῷ βοηθεῖν;

ΣΩ. Εἰ ἐκεῖνό γε ἐν αὐτῷ ὑπάρχοι, ὦ Καλλίκλεις, ὃ σὺ πολλάκις ὡμολόγησας· εἰ βεβοηθηκὼς εἴη αὑτῷ, μήτε περὶ ἀνθρώπους μήτε περὶ θεοὺς ἄδικον μηδὲν μήτε εἰρηκὼς μήτε εἰργασμένος. αὕτη γάρ τις βοήθεια ἑαυτῷ πολλάκις ἡμῖν ὡμολόγηται κρατίστη εἶναι. εἰ μὲν οὖν ἐμέ τις ἐξελέγχοι ταύτην τὴν βοήθειαν ἀδύνατον ὄντα ἐμαυτῷ καὶ ἄλλῳ βοηθεῖν, αἰσχυνοίμην ἂν καὶ ἐν πολλοῖς καὶ ἐν ὀλίγοις ἐξελεγχόμενος καὶ μόνος ὑπὸ μόνου, καὶ εἰ διὰ ταύτην τὴν ἀδυναμίαν ἀποθνῄσκοιμι, ἀγανακτοίην ἄν· εἰ δὲ κολακικῆς ῥητορικῆς ἐνδείᾳ τελευτῴην ἔγωγε, εὖ οἶδα ὅτι ῥᾳδίως ἴδοις ἄν με φέροντα τὸν θάνατον. αὐτὸ μὲν γὰρ τὸ ἀποθνῄσκειν οὐδεὶς φοβεῖται, ὅστις μὴ παντάπασιν ἀλόγιστός τε καὶ ἄνανδρός ἐστι, τὸ δὲ ἀδικεῖν φοβεῖται·

GORGIAS

soc. Such, however, I am sure would be my own fate if I were brought before the court. For not only shall I have no pleasures to plead as having been provided by me—which they regard as services and benefits, whereas I envy neither those who provide them nor those for whom they are provided—but if anyone alleges that I either corrupt the younger men by reducing them to perplexity, or revile the older with bitter expressions whether in private or in public, I shall be unable either to tell the truth and say—" It is on just grounds that I say all this, and it is your interest that I serve thereby, gentlemen of the jury "—or to say anything else; and so I daresay any sort of thing, as luck may have it, will befall me.

CALL. Then do you think, Socrates, that a man in such a case and with no power of standing up for himself makes a fine figure in a city?

soc. Yes, if he had that one resource, Callicles, which you have repeatedly admitted; if he had stood up for himself by avoiding any unjust word or deed in regard either to men or to gods. For this has been repeatedly admitted by us to be the most valuable kind of self-protection. Now if I were convicted of inability to extend this sort of protection to either myself or another, I should be ashamed, whether my conviction took place before many or few, or as between man and man; and if that inability should bring about my death, I should be sorely vexed: but if I came to my end through a lack of flattering rhetoric, I am quite sure you would see me take my death easily. For no man fears the mere act of dying, except he be utterly irrational and unmanly; doing wrong is what one

PLATO

πολλῶι γὰρ ἀδικημάτων γέμοντα τὴν ψυχὴν εἰς
Ἅιδου ἀφικέσθαι πάντων ἔσχατον κακῶν ἐστίν.
εἰ δὲ βούλει, σοὶ ἐγώ, ὡς τοῦτο οὕτως ἔχει, ἐθέλω
λόγον λέξαι.

ΚΑΛΛ. Ἀλλ' ἐπείπερ γε καὶ τἆλλα ἐπέρανας,
καὶ τοῦτο πέρανον.

ΣΩ. Ἄκουε δή, φασί, μάλα καλοῦ λόγου, ὃν
σὺ μὲν ἡγήσῃ μῦθον, ὡς ἐγὼ οἶμαι, ἐγὼ δὲ λόγον·
ὡς ἀληθῆ γὰρ ὄντα σοι λέξω ἃ μέλλω λέγειν.
ὥσπερ γὰρ Ὅμηρος λέγει, διενείμαντο τὴν ἀρχὴν
ὁ Ζεὺς καὶ ὁ Ποσειδῶν καὶ ὁ Πλούτων, ἐπειδὴ
παρὰ τοῦ πατρὸς παρέλαβον. ἦν οὖν νόμος ὅδε
περὶ ἀνθρώπων ἐπὶ Κρόνου, καὶ ἀεὶ καὶ νῦν ἔτι
ἔστιν ἐν θεοῖς, τῶν ἀνθρώπων τὸν μὲν δικαίως
τὸν βίον διελθόντα καὶ ὁσίως, ἐπειδὰν τελευτήσῃ,
εἰς μακάρων νήσους ἀπιόντα οἰκεῖν ἐν πάσῃ εὐ-
δαιμονίᾳ ἐκτὸς κακῶν, τὸν δὲ ἀδίκως καὶ ἀθέως
εἰς τὸ τῆς τίσεώς τε καὶ δίκης δεσμωτήριον, ὃ
δὴ Τάρταρον καλοῦσιν, ἰέναι. τούτων δὲ δικασταὶ ἐπὶ Κρόνου καὶ ἔτι νεωστὶ τοῦ Διὸς τὴν
ἀρχὴν ἔχοντος ζῶντες ἦσαν ζώντων, ἐκείνῃ τῇ
ἡμέρᾳ δικάζοντες ᾗ μέλλοιεν τελευτᾶν. κακῶς
οὖν αἱ δίκαι ἐκρίνοντο· ὅ τε οὖν Πλούτων καὶ οἱ
ἐπιμεληταὶ οἱ ἐκ μακάρων νήσων ἰόντες ἔλεγον
πρὸς τὸν Δία, ὅτι φοιτῷέν σφιν ἄνθρωποι ἑκα-
τέρωσε ἀνάξιοι. εἶπεν οὖν ὁ Ζεύς· Ἀλλ' ἐγώ,
ἔφη, παύσω τοῦτο γιγνόμενον. νῦν μὲν γὰρ
κακῶς αἱ δίκαι δικάζονται. ἀμπεχόμενοι γάρ,
ἔφη, οἱ κρινόμενοι κρίνονται· ζῶντες γὰρ κρί-
νονται. πολλοὶ οὖν, ἦ δ' ὅς, ψυχὰς πονηρὰς
ἔχοντες ἠμφιεσμένοι εἰσὶ σώματά τε καλὰ καὶ

[1] *Il.* xv. 187 foll.

GORGIAS

fears : for to arrive in the nether world having one's soul full fraught with a heap of misdeeds is the uttermost of all evils. And now, if you do not mind, I would like to tell you a tale to show you that the case is so.

CALL. Well, as you have completed the rest of the business, go on and complete this also.

SOC. Give ear then, as they say, to a right fine story, which you will regard as a fable, I fancy, but I as an actual account; for what I am about to tell you I mean to offer as the truth. By Homer's account,[1] Zeus, Poseidon, and Pluto divided the sovereignty amongst them when they took it over from their father. Now in the time of Cronos there was a law concerning mankind, and it holds to this very day amongst the gods, that every man who has passed a just and holy life departs after his decease to the Isles of the Blest, and dwells in all happiness apart from ill; but whoever has lived unjustly and impiously goes to the dungeon of requital and penance which, you know, they call Tartarus. Of these men there were judges in Cronos' time, and when Zeus had but newly begun his reign—living men to judge the living upon the day when each was to breathe his last; and thus the cases were being decided amiss. So Pluto and the overseers from the Isles of the Blest came before Zeus with the report that they found men passing over to either abode undeserving. Then spake Zeus : " Nay," said he, " I will put a stop to these proceedings. The cases are now indeed judged ill; and it is because they who are on trial are tried in their clothing, for they are tried alive. Now many," said he, " who have wicked souls are clad in fair bodies and ancestry and wealth,

PLATO

γένη καὶ πλούτους, καί, ἐπειδὰν ἡ κρίσις ᾖ, ἔρχονται αὐτοῖς πολλοὶ μάρτυρες, μαρτυρήσοντες ὡς δικαίως βεβιώκασιν· οἱ οὖν δικασταὶ ὑπό τε τούτων ἐκπλήττονται, καὶ ἅμα καὶ αὐτοὶ ἀμπεχόμενοι δικάζουσι, πρὸ τῆς ψυχῆς τῆς αὑτῶν ὀφθαλμοὺς καὶ ὦτα καὶ ὅλον τὸ σῶμα προκεκαλυμμένοι. ταῦτα δὴ αὐτοῖς πάντα ἐπίπροσθεν γίγνεται, καὶ τὰ αὑτῶν ἀμφιέσματα καὶ τὰ τῶν κρινομένων. πρῶτον μὲν οὖν, ἔφη, παυστέον ἐστὶ προειδότας αὐτοὺς τὸν θάνατον· νῦν γὰρ προΐσασι. τοῦτο μὲν οὖν καὶ δὴ εἴρηται τῷ Προμηθεῖ ὅπως ἂν παύσῃ αὐτῶν. ἔπειτα γυμνοὺς κριτέον ἁπάντων τούτων· τεθνεῶτας γὰρ δεῖ κρίνεσθαι. καὶ τὸν κριτὴν δεῖ γυμνὸν εἶναι, τεθνεῶτα, αὐτῇ τῇ ψυχῇ αὐτὴν τὴν ψυχὴν θεωροῦντα ἐξαίφνης ἀποθανόντος ἑκάστου, ἔρημον πάντων τῶν συγγενῶν καὶ καταλιπόντα ἐπὶ τῆς γῆς πάντα ἐκεῖνον τὸν κόσμον, ἵνα δικαία ἡ κρίσις ᾖ. ἐγὼ μὲν οὖν ταῦτα ἐγνωκὼς πρότερος ἢ ὑμεῖς ἐποιησάμην δικαστὰς υἱεῖς ἐμαυτοῦ, δύο μὲν ἐκ τῆς Ἀσίας, Μίνω τε καὶ Ῥαδάμανθυν, ἕνα δὲ ἐκ τῆς Εὐρώπης, Αἰακόν· οὗτοι οὖν ἐπειδὰν τελευτήσωσι, δικάσουσιν ἐν τῷ λειμῶνι, ἐν τῇ τριόδῳ, ἐξ ἧς φέρετον τὼ ὁδώ, ἡ μὲν εἰς μακάρων νήσους, ἡ δ' εἰς Τάρταρον. καὶ τοὺς μὲν ἐκ τῆς Ἀσίας Ῥαδάμανθυς κρινεῖ, τοὺς δὲ ἐκ τῆς Εὐρώπης Αἰακός· Μίνῳ δὲ πρεσβεῖα δώσω ἐπιδιακρίνειν, ἐὰν ἀπορῆτόν τι τὼ ἑτέρω, ἵνα ὡς δικαιοτάτη ἡ κρίσις ᾖ περὶ τῆς πορείας τοῖς ἀνθρώποις.

Ταῦτ' ἔστιν, ὦ Καλλίκλεις, ἃ ἐγὼ ἀκηκοὼς πιστεύω ἀληθῆ εἶναι· καὶ ἐκ τούτων τῶν λόγων τοιόνδε τι λογίζομαι συμβαίνειν. ὁ θάνατος τυγ-

GORGIAS

and at their judgement appear many witnesses to testify that their lives have been just. Now, the judges are confounded not only by their evidence but at the same time by being clothed themselves while they sit in judgement, having their own soul muffled in the veil of eyes and ears and the whole body. Thus all these are a hindrance to them, their own habiliments no less than those of the judged. Well, first of all," he said, " we must put a stop to their foreknowledge of their death; for this they at present foreknow. However, Prometheus has already been given the word to stop this in them. Next they must be stripped bare of all those things before they are tried; for they must stand their trial dead. Their judge also must be naked, dead, beholding with very soul the very soul of each immediately upon his death, bereft of all his kin and having left behind on earth all that fine array, to the end that the judgement may be just. Now I, knowing all this before you, have appointed sons of my own to be judges; two from Asia, Minos and Rhadamanthus, and one from Europe, Aeacus. These, when their life is ended, shall give judgement in the meadow at the dividing of the road, whence are the two ways leading, one to the Isles of the Blest, and the other to Tartarus. And those who come from Asia shall Rhadamanthus try, and those from Europe, Aeacus; and to Minos I will give the privilege of the final decision, if the other two be in any doubt; that the judgement upon this journey of mankind may be supremely just."

This, Callicles, is what I have heard and believe to be true; and from these stories, on my reckoning, we must draw some such moral as this: death, as

PLATO

χάνει ὤν, ὡς ἐμοὶ δοκεῖ, οὐδὲν ἄλλο ἢ δυοῖν πραγμάτοιν διάλυσις, τῆς ψυχῆς καὶ τοῦ σώματος, ἀπ' ἀλλήλοιν· ἐπειδὰν δὲ διαλυθῆτον ἄρα ἀπ' ἀλλήλοιν, οὐ πολὺ ἧττον ἑκάτερον αὐτοῖν ἔχει τὴν ἕξιν τὴν αὑτοῦ, ἥνπερ καὶ ὅτε ἔζη ὁ ἄνθρωπος, τό τε σῶμα τὴν φύσιν τὴν αὑτοῦ καὶ τὰ θεραπεύματα καὶ τὰ παθήματα ἔνδηλα πάντα. οἷον
C εἴ τινος μέγα ἦν τὸ σῶμα φύσει ἢ τροφῇ ἢ ἀμφότερα ζῶντος, τούτου καὶ ἐπειδὰν ἀποθάνῃ ὁ νεκρὸς μέγας, καὶ εἰ παχύς, παχὺς καὶ ἀποθανόντος, καὶ τἆλλα οὕτως· καὶ εἰ αὖ ἐπετήδευε κομᾶν, κομήτης τούτου καὶ ὁ νεκρός. μαστιγίας αὖ εἴ τις ἦν καὶ ἴχνη εἶχε τῶν πληγῶν οὐλὰς ἐν τῷ σώματι ἢ ὑπὸ μαστίγων ἢ ἄλλων τραυμάτων ζῶν, καὶ τεθνεῶτος τὸ σῶμα ἔστιν ἰδεῖν ταῦτα ἔχον· κατεαγότα τε εἴ του ἦν μέλη ἢ διεστραμμένα ζῶντος, καὶ τεθνεῶτος ταὐτὰ ταῦτα ἔνδηλα.
D ἑνὶ δὲ λόγῳ, οἷος εἶναι παρεσκεύαστο τὸ σῶμα ζῶν, ἔνδηλα ταῦτα καὶ τελευτήσαντος ἢ πάντα ἢ τὰ πολλὰ ἐπί τινα χρόνον. ταὐτὸν δή μοι δοκεῖ τοῦτ' ἄρα καὶ περὶ τὴν ψυχὴν εἶναι, ὦ Καλλίκλεις· ἔνδηλα πάντα ἐστὶν ἐν τῇ ψυχῇ, ἐπειδὰν γυμνωθῇ τοῦ σώματος, τά τε τῆς φύσεως καὶ τὰ παθήματα, ἃ διὰ τὴν ἐπιτήδευσιν ἑκάστου πράγματος ἔσχεν ἐν τῇ ψυχῇ ὁ ἄνθρωπος. ἐπει-
E δὰν οὖν ἀφίκωνται παρὰ τὸν δικαστήν, οἱ μὲν ἐκ τῆς Ἀσίας παρὰ τὸν Ῥαδάμανθυν, ὁ Ῥαδάμανθυς ἐκείνους ἐπιστήσας θεᾶται ἑκάστου τὴν ψυχήν, οὐκ εἰδὼς ὅτου ἐστίν, ἀλλὰ πολλάκις τοῦ μεγάλου βασιλέως ἐπιλαβόμενος ἢ ἄλλου ὁτουοῦν βασιλέως ἢ δυνάστου κατεῖδεν οὐδὲν ὑγιὲς ὂν τῆς ψυχῆς, ἀλλὰ διαμεμαστιγωμένην

522

GORGIAS

It seems to me, is actually nothing but the disconnexion of two things, the soul and the body, from each other. And so when they are disconnected from one another, each of them keeps its own condition very much as it was when the man was alive, the body having its own nature, with its treatments and experiences all manifest upon it. For instance, if anyone's body was large by nature or by feeding or by both when he was alive, his corpse will be large also when he is dead; and if he was fat, it will be fat too after his death, and so on for the rest; or again, if he used to follow the fashion of long hair, long-haired also will be his corpse. Again, if anyone had been a sturdy rogue, and bore traces of his stripes in scars on his body, either from the whip or from other wounds, while yet alive, then after death too his body has these marks visible upon it; or if anyone's limbs were broken or distorted in life, these same effects are manifest in death. In a word, whatever sort of bodily appearance a man had acquired in life, that is manifest also after his death either wholly or in the main for some time. And so it seems to me that the same is the case with the soul too, Callicles: when a man's soul is stripped bare of the body, all its natural gifts, and the experiences added to that soul as the result of his various pursuits, are manifest in it. So when they have arrived in presence of their judge, they of Asia before Rhadamanthus, these Rhadamanthus sets before him and surveys the soul of each, not knowing whose it is; nay, often when he has laid hold of the Great King or some other prince or potentate, he perceives the utter unhealthiness of his soul, striped all over with the

καὶ οὐλῶν μεστὴν ὑπὸ ἐπιορκιῶν καὶ ἀδικίας, ἃ
525 ἑκάστῃ ἡ πρᾶξις αὐτοῦ ἐξωμόρξατο εἰς τὴν ψυχήν,
καὶ πάντα σκολιὰ ὑπὸ ψεύδους καὶ ἀλαζονείας
καὶ οὐδὲν εὐθὺ διὰ τὸ ἄνευ ἀληθείας τεθράφθαι·
καὶ ὑπὸ ἐξουσίας καὶ τρυφῆς καὶ ὕβρεως καὶ
ἀκρατίας τῶν πράξεων ἀσυμμετρίας τε καὶ αἰ-
σχρότητος γέμουσαν τὴν ψυχὴν εἶδεν· ἰδὼν δὲ
ἀτίμως ταύτην ἀπέπεμψεν εὐθὺ τῆς φρουρᾶς,
οἷ μέλλει ἐλθοῦσα ἀνατλῆναι τὰ προσήκοντα
B πάθη. προσήκει δὲ παντὶ τῷ ἐν τιμωρίᾳ ὄντι,
ὑπ᾽ ἄλλου ὀρθῶς τιμωρουμένῳ, ἢ βελτίονι γίγνεσθαι καὶ ὀνίνασθαι ἢ παραδείγματι τοῖς ἄλλοις
γίγνεσθαι, ἵνα ἄλλοι ὁρῶντες πάσχοντα ἃ ἂν
πάσχῃ φοβούμενοι βελτίους γίγνωνται. εἰσὶ δὲ
οἱ μὲν ὠφελούμενοί τε καὶ δίκην διδόντες ὑπὸ
θεῶν τε καὶ ἀνθρώπων οὗτοι, οἳ ἂν ἰάσιμα ἁμαρτήματα ἁμάρτωσιν· ὅμως δὲ δι᾽ ἀλγηδόνων καὶ
ὀδυνῶν γίγνεται αὐτοῖς ἡ ὠφελία καὶ ἐνθάδε καὶ
C ἐν Ἅιδου· οὐ γὰρ οἷόν τε ἄλλως ἀδικίας ἀπαλλάττεσθαι. οἳ δ᾽ ἂν τὰ ἔσχατα ἀδικήσωσι καὶ
διὰ τὰ τοιαῦτα ἀδικήματα ἀνίατοι γένωνται, ἐκ
τούτων τὰ παραδείγματα γίγνεται, καὶ οὗτοι
αὐτοὶ μὲν οὐκέτι ὀνίνανται οὐδέν, ἅτε ἀνίατοι
ὄντες, ἄλλοι δὲ ὀνίνανται οἱ τούτους ὁρῶντες διὰ
τὰς ἁμαρτίας τὰ μέγιστα καὶ ὀδυνηρότατα καὶ
φοβερώτατα πάθη πάσχοντας τὸν ἀεὶ χρόνον,
ἀτεχνῶς παραδείγματα ἀνηρτημένους ἐκεῖ ἐν Ἅιδου ἐν τῷ δεσμωτηρίῳ, τοῖς ἀεὶ τῶν ἀδίκων
D ἀφικνουμένοις θεάματα καὶ νουθετήματα. ὧν ἐγώ
φημι ἕνα καὶ Ἀρχέλαον ἔσεσθαι, εἰ ἀληθῆ λέγει
Πῶλος, καὶ ἄλλον ὅστις ἂν τοιοῦτος τύραννος
ᾖ· οἶμαι δὲ καὶ τοὺς πολλοὺς εἶναι τούτων τῶν

GORGIAS

scourge, and a mass of wounds, the work of perjuries and injustice; where every act has left its smirch upon his soul, where all is awry through falsehood and imposture, and nothing straight because of a nurture that knew not truth: or, as the result of a course of license, luxury, insolence, and incontinence, he finds the soul full fraught with disproportion and ugliness. Beholding this he sends it away in dishonour straight to the place of custody, where on its arrival it is to endure the sufferings that are fitting. And it is fitting that every one under punishment rightly inflicted on him by another should either be made better and profit thereby, or serve as an example to the rest, that others seeing the sufferings he endures may in fear amend themselves. Those who are benefited by the punishment they get from gods and men are they who have committed remediable offences; but still it is through bitter throes of pain that they receive their benefit both here and in the nether world; for in no other way can there be riddance of iniquity. But of those who have done extreme wrong and, as a result of such crimes, have become incurable, of those are the examples made; no longer are they profited at all themselves, since they are incurable, but others are profited who behold them undergoing for their transgressions the greatest, sharpest, and most fearful sufferings evermore, actually hung up as examples there in the infernal dungeon, a spectacle and a lesson to such of the wrongdoers as arrive from time to time. Among them I say Archelaus also will be found, if what Polus tells us is true, and every other despot of his sort. And I think, moreover, that most of these examples have

παραδειγμάτων ἐκ τυράννων καὶ βασιλέων καὶ
δυναστῶν καὶ τὰ τῶν πόλεων πραξάντων γε-
γονότας· οὗτοι γὰρ διὰ τὴν ἐξουσίαν μέγιστα
καὶ ἀνοσιώτατα ἁμαρτήματα ἁμαρτάνουσι. μαρ-
τυρεῖ δὲ τούτοις καὶ Ὅμηρος· βασιλέας γὰρ καὶ
δυνάστας ἐκεῖνος πεποίηκε τοὺς ἐν Ἅιδου τὸν
ἀεὶ χρόνον τιμωρουμένους, Τάνταλον καὶ Σίσυφον
καὶ Τιτυόν· Θερσίτην δέ, καὶ εἴ τις ἄλλος πονηρὸς
ἦν ἰδιώτης, οὐδεὶς πεποίηκε μεγάλαις τιμωρίαις
συνεχόμενον ὡς ἀνίατον· οὐ γάρ, οἶμαι, ἐξῆν
αὐτῷ· διὸ καὶ εὐδαιμονέστερος ἦν ἢ οἷς ἐξῆν.
ἀλλὰ γάρ, ὦ Καλλίκλεις, ἐκ τῶν δυναμένων εἰσὶ
καὶ οἱ σφόδρα πονηροὶ γιγνόμενοι ἄνθρωποι·
οὐδὲν μὴν κωλύει καὶ ἐν τούτοις ἀγαθοὺς ἄνδρας
ἐγγίγνεσθαι, καὶ σφόδρα γε ἄξιον ἄγασθαι τῶν
γιγνομένων· χαλεπὸν γάρ, ὦ Καλλίκλεις, καὶ
πολλοῦ ἐπαίνου ἄξιον ἐν μεγάλῃ ἐξουσίᾳ τοῦ
ἀδικεῖν γενόμενον δικαίως διαβιῶναι. ὀλίγοι δὲ
γίγνονται οἱ τοιοῦτοι· ἐπεὶ καὶ ἐνθάδε καὶ ἄλλοθι
γεγόνασιν, οἶμαι δὲ καὶ ἔσονται καλοὶ κἀγαθοὶ
ταύτην τὴν ἀρετὴν τὴν τοῦ δικαίως διαχειρίζειν
ἃ ἄν τις ἐπιτρέπῃ· εἷς δὲ καὶ πάνυ ἐλλόγιμος
γέγονε καὶ εἰς τοὺς ἄλλους Ἕλληνας, Ἀριστείδης
ὁ Λυσιμάχου· οἱ δὲ πολλοί, ὦ ἄριστε, κακοὶ
γίγνονται τῶν δυναστῶν. ὅπερ οὖν ἔλεγον, ἐπειδὰν ὁ Ῥαδάμανθυς ἐκεῖνος τοιοῦτόν τινα λάβῃ,
ἄλλο μὲν περὶ αὐτοῦ οὐκ οἶδεν οὐδέν, οὔθ' ὅστις
οὔθ' ὧντινων, ὅτι δὲ πονηρός τις· καὶ τοῦτο
κατιδὼν ἀπέπεμψεν εἰς Τάρταρον, ἐπισημηνά-
μενος, ἐάν τε ἰάσιμος ἐάν τε ἀνίατος δοκῇ εἶναι.

GORGIAS

come from despots and kings and potentates and public administrators; for these, since they have a free hand, commit the greatest and most impious offences. Homer also testifies to this; for he has represented kings and potentates as those who are punished everlastingly in the nether world—Tantalus and Sisyphus and Tityus; but Thersites, or any other private person who was wicked, has been portrayed by none as incurable and therefore subjected to heavy punishment; no doubt because he had not a free hand, and therefore was in fact happier than those who had. For in fact, Callicles, it is among the powerful that we find the specially wicked men. Still there is nothing to prevent good men being found even among these, and it deserves our special admiration when they are; for it is hard, Callicles, and deserving of no slight praise, when a man with a perfectly free hand for injustice lives always a just life. The men of this sort are but few,—for indeed there have been, and I expect there yet will be, both here and elsewhere, men of honour and excellence in this virtue of administering justly what is committed to their charge: one in fact there has been whose fame stands high among us and throughout the rest of Greece, Aristeides, son of Lysimachus. But most of those in power, my excellent friend, prove to be bad. So, as I was saying, whenever the judge Rhadamanthus has to deal with such an one, he knows nothing else of him at all, neither who he is nor of what descent, but only that he is a wicked person; and on perceiving this he sends him away to Tartarus, first setting a mark on him to show whether he deems it a curable or an incurable case;

PLATO

C ὁ δὲ ἐκεῖσε ἀφικόμενος τὰ προσήκοντα πάσχει. ἐνίοτε δ' ἄλλην εἰσιδὼν ὁσίως βεβιωκυῖαν καὶ μετ' ἀληθείας, ἀνδρὸς ἰδιώτου ἢ ἄλλου τινός, μάλιστα μέν, ἔγωγέ φημι, ὦ Καλλίκλεις, φιλοσόφου τὰ αὑτοῦ πράξαντος καὶ οὐ πολυπραγμονήσαντος ἐν τῷ βίῳ, ἠγάσθη τε καὶ ἐς μακάρων νήσους ἀπέπεμψε. ταὐτὰ δὲ ταῦτα καὶ ὁ Αἰακός· ἑκάτερος τούτων ῥάβδον ἔχων δικάζει· ὁ δὲ Μίνως ἐπισκοπῶν κάθηται, μόνος ἔχων χρυσοῦν
D σκῆπτρον, ὥς φησιν Ὀδυσσεὺς ὁ Ὁμήρου ἰδεῖν αὐτὸν

χρύσεον σκῆπτρον ἔχοντα, θεμιστεύοντα νέκυσσιν.

ἐγὼ μὲν οὖν, ὦ Καλλίκλεις, ὑπὸ τούτων τῶν λόγων πέπεισμαι, καὶ σκοπῶ ὅπως ἀποφανοῦμαι τῷ κριτῇ ὡς ὑγιεστάτην τὴν ψυχήν· χαίρειν οὖν ἐάσας τὰς τιμὰς τὰς τῶν πολλῶν ἀνθρώπων, τὴν ἀλήθειαν σκοπῶν πειράσομαι τῷ ὄντι ὡς ἂν δύνωμαι βέλτιστος ὢν καὶ ζῆν καὶ ἐπειδὰν ἀπο-
E θνῄσκω ἀποθνῄσκειν. παρακαλῶ δὲ καὶ τοὺς ἄλλους πάντας ἀνθρώπους, καθ' ὅσον δύναμαι, καὶ δὴ καὶ σὲ ἀντιπαρακαλῶ ἐπὶ τοῦτον τὸν βίον καὶ τὸν ἀγῶνα τοῦτον, ὃν ἐγώ φημι ἀντὶ πάντων τῶν ἐνθάδε ἀγώνων εἶναι, καὶ ὀνειδίζω σοι, ὅτι οὐχ οἷός τ' ἔσῃ σαυτῷ βοηθῆσαι, ὅταν ἡ δίκη σοι ᾖ καὶ ἡ κρίσις ἣν νῦν δὴ ἐγὼ ἔλεγον, ἀλλὰ ἐλθὼν παρὰ τὸν δικαστὴν τὸν τῆς Αἰγίνης υἱόν,
527 ἐπειδάν σου ἐπιλαβόμενος ἄγῃ, χασμήσῃ καὶ ἰλιγγιάσεις οὐδὲν ἧττον ἢ ἐγὼ ἐνθάδε σὺ ἐκεῖ,

---

[1] *Od.* xi. 569.
[2] *i.e.* in return for Callicles' invitation to him to pursue the life of rhetoric and politics, 521 A.

GORGIAS

and when the man arrives there he suffers what is fitting. Sometimes, when he discerns another soul that has lived a holy life in company with truth, a private man's or any other's—especially, as I claim, Callicles, a philosopher's who has minded his own business and not been a busybody in his lifetime—he is struck with admiration and sends it off to the Isles of the Blest. And exactly the same is the procedure of Aeacus: each of these two holds a rod in his hand as he gives judgement; but Minos sits as supervisor, distinguished by the golden sceptre that he holds, as Odysseus in Homer tells how he saw him—

Holding a golden sceptre, speaking dooms to the dead.[1]

Now for my part, Callicles, I am convinced by these accounts, and I consider how I may be able to show my judge that my soul is in the best of health. So giving the go-by to the honours that most men seek I shall try, by inquiry into the truth, to be really good in as high a degree as I am able, both in my life and, when I come to die, in my death. And I invite all other men likewise, to the best of my power, and you particularly I invite in return,[2] to this life and this contest, which I say is worth all other contests on this earth; and I make it a reproach to *you*, that you will not be able to deliver yourself when your trial comes and the judgement of which I told you just now; but when you go before your judge, the son of Aegina,[3] and he grips you and drags you up, you will gape and feel dizzy there no less than I do here, and some one perhaps

[3] Aegina, daughter of the river-god Asopus, was the mother of Aeacus by Zeus.

PLATO

καί σε ἴσως τυπτήσει τις καὶ ἐπὶ κόρρης ἀτίμως καὶ πάντως προπηλακιεῖ.

Τάχα δ' οὖν ταῦτα μῦθός σοι δοκεῖ λέγεσθαι ὥσπερ γραὸς καὶ καταφρονεῖς αὐτῶν, καὶ οὐδέν γ' ἂν ἦν θαυμαστὸν καταφρονεῖν τούτων, εἴ πη ζητοῦντες εἴχομεν αὐτῶν βελτίω καὶ ἀληθέστερα εὑρεῖν· νῦν δὲ ὁρᾷς, ὅτι τρεῖς ὄντες ὑμεῖς, οἵπερ σοφώτατοί ἐστε τῶν νῦν Ἑλλήνων, σύ τε καὶ Πῶλος καὶ Γοργίας, οὐκ ἔχετε ἀποδεῖξαι, ὡς δεῖ ἄλλον τινὰ βίον ζῆν ἢ τοῦτον, ὅσπερ καὶ ἐκεῖσε φαίνεται συμφέρων. ἀλλ' ἐν τοσούτοις λόγοις τῶν ἄλλων ἐλεγχομένων μόνος οὗτος ἠρεμεῖ ὁ λόγος, ὡς εὐλαβητέον ἐστὶ τὸ ἀδικεῖν μᾶλλον ἢ τὸ ἀδικεῖσθαι, καὶ παντὸς μᾶλλον ἀνδρὶ μελετητέον οὐ τὸ δοκεῖν εἶναι ἀγαθὸν ἀλλὰ τὸ εἶναι, καὶ ἰδίᾳ καὶ δημοσίᾳ· ἐὰν δέ τις κατά τι κακὸς γίγνηται, κολαστέος ἐστί, καὶ τοῦτο δεύτερον ἀγαθὸν μετὰ τὸ εἶναι δίκαιον, τὸ γίγνεσθαι καὶ κολαζόμενον διδόναι δίκην· καὶ πᾶσαν κολακείαν καὶ τὴν περὶ ἑαυτὸν καὶ τὴν περὶ τοὺς ἄλλους, καὶ περὶ ὀλίγους καὶ περὶ πολλούς, φευκτέον· καὶ τῇ ῥητορικῇ οὕτω χρηστέον ἐπὶ τὸ δίκαιον ἀεί, καὶ τῇ ἄλλῃ πάσῃ πράξει. ἐμοὶ οὖν πειθόμενος ἀκολούθησον ἐνταῦθα, οἷ ἀφικόμενος εὐδαιμονήσεις καὶ ζῶν καὶ τελευτήσας, ὡς ὁ λόγος σημαίνει. καὶ ἔασόν τινά σου καταφρονῆσαι ὡς ἀνοήτου καὶ προπηλακίσαι, ἐὰν βούληται, καὶ ναὶ μὰ Δία σύ γε θαρρῶν πατάξαι τὴν ἄτιμον ταύτην πληγήν· οὐδὲν γὰρ δεινὸν πείσῃ, ἐὰν τῷ ὄντι ᾖς καλὸς κἀγαθός, ἀσκῶν ἀρετήν. κἄπειτα οὕτω κοινῇ ἀσκήσαντες, τότε ἤδη, ἐὰν δοκῇ

will give you, yes, a degrading box on the ear, and will treat you with every kind of contumely.

Possibly, however, you regard this as an old wife's tale, and despise it; and there would be no wonder in our despising it if with all our searching we could somewhere find anything better and truer than this: but as it is, you observe that you three, who are the wisest of the Greeks in our day—you and Polus and Gorgias—are unable to prove that we ought to live any other life than this, which is evidently advantageous also in the other world. But among the many statements we have made, while all the rest are refuted this one alone is unshaken—that doing wrong is to be more carefully shunned than suffering it; that above all things a man should study not to seem but to be good both in private and in public; that if one becomes bad in any respect one must be corrected; that this is good in the second place,—next to being just, to become so and to be corrected by paying the penalty; and that every kind of flattery, with regard either to oneself or to others, to few or to many, must be avoided; and that rhetoric is to be used for this one purpose always, of pointing to what is just, and so is every other activity. Take my advice, therefore, and follow me where, if you once arrive, you will be happy both in life and after life's end, as this account declares. And allow anyone to contemn you as a fool and foully maltreat you if he chooses; yes, by Heaven, and suffer undaunted the shock of that ignominious cuff; for you will come to no harm if you be really a good and upright man, practising virtue. And afterwards, having practised it together, we shall in due course, if we

χρῆναι, ἐπιθησόμεθα τοῖς πολιτικοῖς, ἢ ὁποῖον ἄν τι ἡμῖν δοκῇ, τότε βουλευσόμεθα, βελτίους ὄντες βουλεύεσθαι ἢ νῦν. αἰσχρὸν γὰρ ἔχοντάς γε ὡς νῦν φαινόμεθα ἔχειν, ἔπειτα νεανιεύεσθαι ὡς τὶ ὄντας, οἷς οὐδέποτε ταὐτὰ δοκεῖ περὶ τῶν αὐτῶν, καὶ ταῦτα περὶ τῶν μεγίστων· εἰς τοσοῦτον ἥκομεν ἀπαιδευσίας· ὥσπερ οὖν ἡγεμόνι τῷ λόγῳ χρησώμεθα τῷ νῦν παραφανέντι, ὃς ἡμῖν σημαίνει, ὅτι οὗτος ὁ τρόπος ἄριστος τοῦ βίου, καὶ τὴν δικαιοσύνην καὶ τὴν ἄλλην ἀρετὴν ἀσκοῦντας καὶ ζῆν καὶ τεθνάναι. τούτῳ οὖν ἑπώμεθα, καὶ τοὺς ἄλλους παρακαλῶμεν, μὴ ἐκείνῳ, ᾧ σὺ πιστεύων ἐμὲ παρακαλεῖς· ἔστι γὰρ οὐδενὸς ἄξιος, ὦ Καλλίκλεις.

GORGIAS

deem it right, embark on politics, or proceed to consult on whatever we may think fit, being then better equipped for such counsel than we are now. For it is disgraceful that men in such a condition as we now appear to be in should put on a swaggering, important air when we never continue to be of the same mind upon the same questions, and those the greatest of all—we are so sadly uneducated. Let us therefore take as our guide the doctrine now disclosed, which indicates to us that this way of life is best—to live and die in the practice alike of justice and of all other virtue. This then let us follow, and to this invite every one else; not that to which you trust yourself and invite me, for it is nothing worth, Callicles.

INDEX OF NAMES

Academy, gymnasium, 7
Achilles, son of Thetis, 105–7, 197, 239
Acumenus, father of Eryximachus, physician, 78
Acusilaus, Argive genealogist,101 n.
Admetus, husband of Alcestis, 197
Aeacus, 521, 529 n.
Aegina, island, 481
Aegina, mother of Aeacus, 529 n.
Aeschylus, Athenian dramatist (c. 525–456 B.C.), 107 n.
Aexone, Attic deme, 11
Agamemnon, 87, 116 n.
Agathon, Athenian dramatist (c. 447–400 B.C.), 78 ff., 339 n.
Aglaophon, father of Polygnotus and Aristophon, 263
Ajax, 233
Alcestis, daughter of Pelias, and wife of Admetus, 103, 107, 197
Alcetas, brother of Perdiccas, 341
Alcibiades (c. 450–404 B.C.), 75, 77, 78, 209 ff., 379, 505
Alcidamas, sophist, 156 n.
Alexander, son of Alcetas, 341
Amphion, son of Zeus, 388 n., 393, 465
Anaxagoras of Clazomenae, Ionian philosopher in Athens (c. 500–430 B.C.), 321
Andron, son of Androtion, 396 n.
Antenor, 239
Anubis, Egyptian god, 306 n.
Aphrodite, goddess of love, 99, 109, 179 ff.
Apollo, 139, 159
Apollodorus, disciple of Socrates, 78 ff.
Arcadians, 145
Archelaus, king of Macedonia (413–399 B.C.), 252, 339 n., 341, 345, 373, 525
Arginusae (battle, 406 B.C.), 350 n.
Aristeides, son of Lysimachus, 527
Aristocrates, son of Scellias, Athenian general (d. 406 B.C.), 345
Aristodemus, disciple of Socrates, 78 ff.
Aristogeiton, Athenian tyrannicide (514 B.C.), 113
Aristophanes, Athenian comic poet (c. 444–380 B.C.), 78 ff., 237 n., 396 n., 448 n.
Aristophon, brother of Polygnotus, painter, 263
Aristotle, 4, 101 n., 156 n., 339 n.
Asclepiadae, medical guild, 78
Asclepius, legendary founder of medicine, 127
Asopus, river-god, father of Aegina, 529 n.
Athenaeus, 462 n.
Athene, 159

Birth, 101
Boeotia, 113
Brasidas, Spartan general (d. 422 B.C.), 239

Callias, patron of sophists, 396 n.
Callicles, of Acharnae (Attica), 250 ff.
Carians, 512 n.
Chaerephon, disciple of Socrates, 250, 259 ff.
Chaos, 101
Charmides, son of Glaucon and maternal uncle of Plato, 241
Cimon, son of Miltiades (d. 449 B.C.), 455, 493, 499, 505

INDEX

Cinesias, son of Meles, dithyrambic poet, 448 n.
Cleinias, father of Alcibiades, 379
Cleopatra, wife of Perdiccas, 341
Codrus, legendary king of Athens, 197 n.
Corinth, 13 n.
Cronos, Titan, 153 n., 519
Ctesippus, 7 ff.
Cunning, mother of Resource, 179
Cydathenaeum, Attic deme, 83

Darius, king of Persia, 27, 35
Delium, in Boeotia, 237 n.
Delphi, 13 n., 345
Democrates, father of Lysis, 11, 13
Demophon, father of Menexenus, 19
Demus, son of Pyrilampes, 379 n., 487
Diocles, father of Euthydemus, 241
Diomedes, 231 n.
Dione, female Titan, 109
Dionysium (temple of Dionysus), 344 n.
Dionysus, god of wine and drama, 99
Diotima, of Mantinea, 78, 173 ff.

Earth, 101
Egypt, 381, 481
Elis, 113
Empedocles, of Acragas, Sicily philosopher (c. 475-415 B.C.), 43 n., 125 n., 415 n., 438 n.
Ephialtes, giant, 137
Epicharmus, of Cos, comic poet, 462 n.
Eryximachus, son of Acumenus, physician, 78 ff.
Euclid, of Alexandria, geometrician (c. 370-290 B.C.), 319 n.
Euripides, Athenian dramatist (480-406 B.C.), 97 n., 157 n., 165 n., 339 n., 388 n., 393, 414 n., 514 n.
Euthydemus, son of Diocles, 241

Geryones, a monstrous giant, 387
Glaucon, father of Charmides, 82 n., 241
Glaucus, 231 n.
Gorgias, of Leontini, Sicily, sophist (c. 490-395 B.C.), 78, 163 n., 250 ff.
Gorgon, 163 n.

Hades, 417
Harmodius, Athenian tyrannicide (514 B.C.), 113
Hector, 105
Hephaestus, 143, 159
Heracleitus of Ephesus, philosopher (c. 500 B.C.), 127 n.
Hercules, 13, 97
Hermaea (festival), 17
Herodicus, brother of Gorgias, physician, 263
Herodotus, 109 n.
Hesiod, 47, 101 n., 153 n., 201
Hieronymus, father of Hippothales, 7
Hippias, of Elis, sophist, 78
Hippothales, son of Hieronymus, 7 ff.
Homer, 41 n., 87, 89, 103 n., 105 n., 107 n., 116 n., 137 n., 143, 153 n., 155 n., 158-9, 163 n., 201, 215 n., 231 n., 235 n., 241 n., 265 n., 391 n., 497 n., 518 n., 527, 528 n.

Iapetus, 153 n.
Ionia, 113
Ionians, 235
Isthmian Games, 12 n.

Lacedaemonians, 145, 201
Laches, Athenian general (d. 418 B.C.), 237
Leuctra, Boeotia, 103 n.
Lucian, 441 n.
Lucretius, 135 n.
Lyceum, gymnasium, 7, 245
Lycurgus, legendary Spartan lawmaker, 201 n.
Lysimachus, father of Aristeides, 527
Lysis, 3 ff.

Macrobius, 137 n.
Mantinea, 145 n.
Marsyas, satyr, 219
Meles, father of Cinesias, minstrel, 449
Menelaus, 87
Menexenus, son of Demophon, 3 ff.
Miccus, wrestling-master, 9
Miltiades, Athenian general (d. 488 B.C.), 455, 493, 499
Minos, 521, 529
Mithaecus, writer on cookery, 503

535

INDEX

Myrrhinus, Attic deme, 95
Mysians, 512 n.
Mysteries, Great and Little, 430 n.

Nausicydes, of Cholarges, 396 n.
Necessity, 159
Nemean Games, 13 n.
Nestor, 116 n., 239
Nicias, son of Niceratus, Athenian general (*d.* in Sicily, 413 B.C.), 344 n.

Odysseus, 529
Oeagrus, father of Orpheus, 105
Olympus, Phrygian flute-player, 219
Orpheus, son of Oeagrus, legendary bard, 105
Otus, giant, 137

Paeania, Attic deme, 7
Panops (Hermes), 7
Parmenides, 101 n., 153, 159 n.
Patroclus, 105-7, 197
Pausanias, friend of Agathon, 78 ff.
Pausanias, traveller and writer (2nd cent. A.D.), 109 n.
Pelias, father of Alcestis, 103
Perdiccas, king of Macedonia (*d. c.* 414 B.C.) 341
Pericles (*c.* 490-429 B.C.), 221, 239, 254, 256, 289, 345, 455, 493 ff., 505
Persian king, 27, 35, 339, 523
Phaedrus of Myrrhinus, 78 ff.
Phalerum, Athenian sea-port, 81, 288 n.
Philip, father of Phoenix, 81
Philolaus, Pythagorean, 414 n.
Phoenix, son of Philip, 81
Pindar, of Boeotia, lyric poet (*c.* 520-440 B.C.), 105 n., 233 n., 387 n.
Piraeus, Athenian sea-port, 288 n.
Pluto, 519
Polus, disciple of Gorgias, 250 ff.
Polygnotus of Thasos, painter in Athens (*c.* 495-430 B.C.)
Pontus (Black Sea), 481
Poseidon, 519
Potidaea, in Chalcidice, 233
Poverty, 179 ff.

Prodicus of Ceos, sophist, 78, 97 n.
Prometheus, 521
Pyrilampes, father of Demus, 379, 487
Pythagoreans, 255, 414 n., 415 n., 417 n., 470 n.
Pythian Games, 12 n.
Pythium, 345

Quintilian, Roman rhetorician (*c.* 35-95 A.D.), 315 n.

Resource, son of Cunning, 179 ff.
Rhadamanthus, 521 ff.

Sarambus, vintner, 503
Scellias, father of Aristocrates, 345
Scythia, 385
Shakespeare, 259 n.
Silenus, 219, 223, 239, 241
Sirens, 221
Sisyphus, 527
Solon, Athenian law-giver and poet (*c.* 638-555 B.C.), 37 n., 201
Sophocles, Athenian dramatist (495-406 B.C.), 115 n., 157 n., 233 n.

Tantalus, 527
Tartarus, 519 ff.
Thearion, baker, 503
Thebes, Boeotia, 103 n.
Themistius (*c.* 320-390 A.D.), 250
Themistocles (*c.* 514-449 B.C.), 256, 289, 455, 493, 499, 505
Thersites, 527
Thessalian witches, 485
Thetis, mother of Achilles, 105
Thucydides, Athenian historian, 237 n.
Tisander, of Aphidnae, 396 n.
Tityus, 527

Xenophon, 145 n., 396 n.
Xerxes, 385

Zethus, son of Zeus, 388 n., 393, 405, 465
Zeus, 13, 109, 137 ff., 159, 388 n., 519, 529 n.
Zeuxis, of Heraclea (S. Italy), painter (*c.* 450-370 B.C.), 281